SYSTEM
administration
Preparing for Network+ Certification

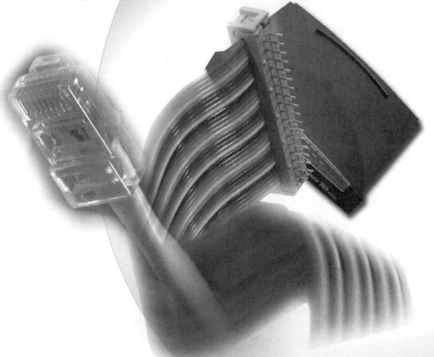

Jerry K. Ainsworth
Shawnee Community College

Kristine A. Kriegel
Technology Trainer and Independent Consultant

EMCParadigm
PUBLISHING

Developmental Editor	Michael Sander
Cover Designer	Leslie Anderson
Text Designer	Jennifer Wreisner
Desktop Production	Leslie Anderson
Illustrator	Colin Hayes
Copyeditor	Gretchen A. Bratvold
Proofreader	Sharon O'Donnell
Indexer	Nancy Fulton

Publishing Team: George Provol, Publisher; Janice Johnson, Director of Product Development; Tony Galvin, Acquisitions Editor; Lori Landwer, Marketing Manager; Shelley Clubb, Electronic Design and Production Manager.

Acknowledgment: The authors and publisher wish to thank Mark Brown, Program Manager, Network Engineering Technology, Polk Community College, Winter Haven, FL, and Steve Henderson, Ozarks Technical Community College, Springfield, MO, for their academic and technical contributions.

Library of Congress Cataloging-in-Publication Data

Ainsworth, Jerry K.
System Administration: Preparing for Network+ Certification/Jerry K. Ainsworth, Kristine A. Kriegel.
     p. cm.—(Netability series)
Includes index.
ISBN 0-7638-1972-7

© 2004 by Paradigm Publishing Inc.
     Published by **EMC**Paradigm
     875 Montreal Way
     St. Paul, MN 55102

     (800) 535-6865
     E-mail: educate@emcp.com
     Web Site: www.emcp.com

Trademarks: Microsoft and Windows are registered trademarks of the Microsoft Corporation in the United States and other countries. Network+ is a registered trademark of CompTIA. Some of the product names and company names included in this book have been used for identification purposes only and may be trademarks or registered trademarks of their respective manufacturers and sellers. The authors, editor, and publisher disclaim any affiliation, association, or connection with, or sponsorship or endorsement by, such owners.

Care has been taken to provide accurate and useful information about the Internet. However, the author, editor, and publisher cannot accept any responsibility for Web, e-mail, newsgroup, or chat room subject matter or content, or for consequences from any application of the information in this book, and make no warranty, expressed or implied, with respect to the book's content.

Printed in the United States of America
10 9 8 7 6 5 4 3 2 1

BRIEF CONTENTS

Photo Acknowledgments

pp. 94, 100, 122, 125, 140, 142, 143, 144, 489, 491, 519, 626: Courtesy of Faithe Wempen

pp. 126, 134, 139: Courtesy of Enterasys Networks

pp. 130, 146: Courtesy of Linksys

p. 141: Courtesy of ZyXEL

p. 145: Courtesy of Intel

p. 618: Image: www.freeimages.co.uk

p. 619, top: Copyright 2002 Eclipse Enterprises, Inc.

p. 619, bottom: Courtesy of Verkkokauppa

p. 622: Copyright 2001 Wilcom, Inc.

p. 623: © Royalty-Free/CORBIS

p. 624: Courtesy of Test-Um, Inc.

DETAILED CONTENTS

INTRODUCTION

Are you considering the benefits of CompTIA Network+ Certification for your career? You are in good company. To date, over 70,000 people have become Network+ Certified, demonstrating that they have the skills and knowledge to function competently as a network administration and support technician. The CompTIA Network+ certification is the worldwide standard of competency for professionals with nine months of experience in network support or administration.

WHAT IS NETWORK+ CERTIFICATION?

The Network+ Certification validates technical competency in networking administration and support. Those holding Network+ Certification demonstrate critical knowledge in all areas of network administration and support, to include media and topologies, protocols and standards, network implementation, and network support.

The exam is administered by CompTIA, a company that also offers many other certification programs, including A+, i-Net+, Server+, and Linux+.

The logo of the CompTIA Authorized Quality Curriculum Program and the status of this or other training material as "Authorized" under the CompTIA Authorized Curriculum Program signifies that, in CompTIA's opinion, such training material covers the content of CompTIA's related certification exam. CompTIA has not reviewed or approved the accuracy of the contents of this training material and specifically disclaims any warranties of merchantability or fitness for a particular purpose. CompTIA makes no guarantee concerning the success of persons using any such "Authorized" or other training material in order to prepare for any CompTIA certification exam.

The contents of this training material were created for the CompTIA Network+ exam covering CompTIA certification exam objectives that were current as of July 2003.

HOW TO BECOME NETWORK+ CERTIFIED

This training material can help you prepare for and pass a related CompTIA certification exam or exams. In order to achieve CompTIA certification, you must register for and pass a CompTIA certification exam or exams.

In order to become CompTIA certified, you must:
1. Select a certification exam provider. For more information please visit http://www.comptia.org/certification/test_locations.htm.
2. Register for and schedule a time to take the CompTIA certification exam(s) at a convenient location.
3. Read and sign the Candidate Agreement, which will be presented at the time of the exam(s). The text of the Candidate Agreement can be found at www.comptia.org/certification.
4. Take and pass the CompTIA certification exam(s).

For more information about CompTIA's certifications, such as their industry acceptance, benefits, or program news, please visit www.comptia.org/certification.

CompTIA is a non-profit information technology (IT) trade association. CompTIA's certifications are designed by subject-matter experts from across the IT industry. Each CompTIA certification is vendor-neutral, covers multiple technologies, and requires demonstration of skills and knowledge widely sought after by the IT industry.

To contact Comp TIA with any questions or comments:
Please call + 1 630 268 1818
questions@comptia.org

EXAM CONTENT

Network+ Certification is attained by passing one examination. The main topic areas, or domains, in the exam cover specific percentages of the total score.

1.0	Media and Topologies	20%
2.0	Protocols and Standards	25%
3.0	Network Implementation	23%
4.0	Network Support	32%

Within each of those domains are several individual objectives. For example, Domain 3 has 11 objectives:

Objective 3.1: Identify the basic capabilities (i.e., client support, interoperability, authentication, file and print services, application support, and security) of the following server operating systems: UNIX/Linux; NetWare; Windows; Macintosh.
Objective 3.2: Identify the basic capabilities of client workstations (i.e., client connectivity, local security mechanisms, and authentication).
Objective 3.3: Identify the main characteristics of VLANs.
Objective 3.4: Identify the main characteristics of network attached storage.
Objective 3.5: Identify the purpose and characteristics of fault tolerance.
Objective 3.6: Identify the purpose and characteristics of disaster recovery.
Objective 3.7: Given a remote connectivity scenario (e.g., IP, IPX, dial-up, PPPoE, authentication, physical connectivity, etc.), configure the connection.
Objective 3.8: Identify the purpose, benefits, and characteristics of using a firewall.
Objective 3.9: Identify the purpose, benefits, and characteristics of using a proxy.
Objective 3.10: Given a scenario, predict the impact of a particular security implementation on network functionality (e.g., blocking port numbers, encryption, etc.).
Objective 3.11: Given a network configuration, select the appropriate NIC and network configuration settings (DHCP, DNS, WINS, protocols, NetBIOS/host name, etc.).

At the CompTIA Web site, a detailed document listing these objectives and what they cover is available in PDF (Adobe Acrobat) format. These individual objectives are mapped to the pages of this book in the "Guide to Examination Objectives" on page xv, following this Introduction, and on the inside front cover of the book.

OTHER EXAM DETAILS

The Network+ exam consists of 72 questions to be completed in 90 minutes. The exam is graded on a scale of 100–900. The minimum passing score is 646.

Each exam costs $139 to take (undiscounted price). Some courses include exam vouchers in their prices, and some companies may be eligible for preferred pricing and/or volume discounts. See http:/ /www.comptia.org/certification/ new _pricing.htm for pricing information for countries other than the United States.

What Are the Special Features of this Book?

By opening this book, you have taken the first step toward achieving two important goals: (1) preparing to pass the Network+ exam, and (2) preparing to be a network administration and support technician. Many Network+ textbooks focus solely on passing the exam, teaching you only what you need to know to pass. But simply passing the exam will not necessarily help you succeed in a real job. By focusing equally on both goals, this book will prepare you not only for exam success, but also for a successful career as a professional network technician.

This book provides information in a variety of ways, with something to suit every learning style. Here is an overview of the major features of the text:

- **On the Test.** Each chapter begins by stating the CompTIA Network+ exam objectives covered in that chapter. More information about these objectives is available at CompTIA's Web site at http:/ /www.comptia.com.
- **On the Job.** At the beginning of each chapter is a quick review of the real-life job skills that correspond to the chapter content, so you can better understand how reading the chapter will translate into practical benefits in your career.
- **In Real Life.** These side notes provide extra items of practical wisdom for applying chapter concepts on the job, or introduce useful options and features not covered specifically on the exam.
- **Test Tips.** These boxes are important for those who plan to take the certification exam. They point out items that are highly testable and provide information that will help with your test preparation.
- **Try It!** Sometimes it is more interesting and useful to try a hands-on skill right away rather than waiting for the review at the end. These Try It! notes offer suggestions for quick activities using the equipment and features discussed in the chapter.
- **Vocabulary words.** New terms are defined in the margins, and also collected in a master Glossary at the back of the book.
- **Study Guide.** At the end of each chapter is a bulleted outline of the major concepts presented, for point-by-point study and review.
- **Practice Test.** Each chapter has a selection of multiple-choice questions similar to those you might encounter on the Network+ exam. There are also over 1,000 additional questions on the accompanying Encore! Companion CD (see the next section).
- **Troubleshooting.** Build your critical thinking skills with these problem-and-solution scenarios, useful for group discussion or individual study.

- **Customer Service.** Being a good technician means listening to a client and deciphering what is really going on, even when the client does not know the correct terms for what is happening. These critical-thinking scenarios test your ability to do just that.
- **Project Labs.** At the end of each major section of the book you will find a number of hands-on exercises you can perform in a computer lab or on an individual PC to build your confidence with handling hardware and installing, troubleshooting, and running software.
- **Internet Resource Center.** The IRC, at www.emcp.com, provides enriching material that reinforces the text, including links to numerous related Web sites.

Students in a formal classroom or lab environment will find that this book makes an excellent basis for group discussions and exercises, especially the Troubleshooting and Customer Service questions at the end of each chapter and the Project Labs at the end of each part.

What Is on the Encore! CD?

This book includes an Encore! Companion CD that amplifies and enriches the content of the text. Chapter by chapter, this multimedia tool serves as a study guide and adds action to the images displayed in the book. The Flash animations and videos in Tech Tutor offer visual demonstrations of concepts that are presented in the text, while the Tech Demos provide graphic demonstration of common network support and administration tasks.

The Encore! CD also includes a Test Bank that provides guided preparation for taking the Network+ exam. There are two levels of tests: book and chapter, and each level functions in two different modes. In the Practice mode you receive immediate feedback on each test item and a report of your total score. In the Test mode your results are e-mailed both to you and your instructor, highlighting the correct answers given in each of the domains contained in the exams.

In addition, the Encore! CD contains an Image Bank, with numerous colorful illustrations and photographs of selected objects and concepts discussed in the book, and a Glossary that includes graphic depictions as well as verbal definitions. Finally, the Encore! CD provides a link to the EMC/Paradigm Internet Resource Center, at www.emcp.com.

What Is in the Workbook?

The Workbook that accompanies this book provides an opportunity to practice and demonstrate your mastery of the skills presented in the text. A series of projects for each chapter calls for hands-on demonstration of the practical tasks required of the network technician. Written answers to pertinent questions about network operations and systems, identification of parts, and your own drawings of various systems will reinforce your knowledge of the application of these skills. These activities, which can be performed by an individual or in varied group sizes, will add practical experience to your preparation for a career as a network technician, and improve and deepen your understanding of the concepts to be mastered for the Network+ Certification exam.

Guide to Examination Objectives

PART 1

Media and Topologies

TEST OBJECTIVES IN PART 1

NETWORK+ EXAMINATION

- **Objective 1.1:** Recognize the following logical or physical network topologies given a schematic diagram or description: star/hierarchical; bus; mesh; ring; wireless.

- **Objective 1.2:** Specify the main features of 802.2 (LLC), 802.3 (Ethernet), 802.5 (token ring), 802.11b (wireless), and FDDI network technologies, including: speed; access; method; topology; media.

- **Objective 1.3:** Specify the characteristics (e.g., speed, length, topology, cable type, etc.) of the following: 802.3 (Ethernet) standards; 10BASE-T; 100BASE-TX; 10BASE-2; 10BASE- 5; 100BASE-FX; Gigabit Ethernet.

- **Objective 1.4:** Recognize the following media connectors and/or describe their uses: RJ-11; RJ-45; AUI; BNC; ST; SC.

- **Objective 1.5:** Choose the appropriate media type and connectors to add a client to an existing network.

- **Objective 1.6:** Identify the purpose, features, and functions of the following network components: Hubs; Switches; Bridges; Routers; Gateways; CSU/DSU; Network Interface Cards/ISDN adapters/system area network cards; Wireless access points; Modems.

- **Objective 2.1:** Given an example, identify a MAC address.

- **Objective 2.2:** Identify the seven layers of the OSI Model and their functions.

- **Objective 2.4:** Identify the OSI layers at which the following network components operate: hubs; switches; bridges; routers; network interface cards.

- **Objective 3.3:** Identify the main characteristics of VLANs.

- **Objective 4.10:** Given a troubleshooting scenario involving a network with a particular physical topology (i.e., bus, star/hierarchical, mesh, ring, and wireless) and including a network diagram, identify the network area affected and the cause of the problem.

- **Objective 4.12:** Given a network troubleshooting scenario involving a wiring/infrastructure problem, identify the cause of the problem (e.g., bad media, interference, network hardware).

Logical and Physical Network Topologies

Network+ Examination
- **Objective 1.1:** Recognize the following logical or physical network topologies given a schematic diagram or description: star/hierarchical; bus; mesh; ring; wireless.
- **Objective 4.10:** Given a troubleshooting scenario involving a network with a particular physical topology (i.e., bus, star/hierarchical, mesh, ring, and wireless) and including a network diagram, identify the network area affected and the cause of the problem.

ON THE JOB

It is important to understand why we network computers and the common configurations used on those networks. Networking allows computer users to work more efficiently. For example, many companies use Microsoft Excel spreadsheets to maintain financial information. Assume that five copies are made of a spreadsheet that reflects sales totals for one month. Each department manager is given a copy of the spreadsheet on a monthly basis, although the administrative assistant who maintains the spreadsheet makes changes on a daily basis. To ensure all department managers have an up-to-date copy of the spreadsheet, the administrative assistant would have to make and distribute copies of the spreadsheet every time it changed. A better solution would be to maintain a single copy of the spreadsheet that is stored in a shared folder on the network. Each manager could then open, review, and make changes to a single, up-to-date spreadsheet whenever it was wanted. Figure 1.1 shows a typical network.

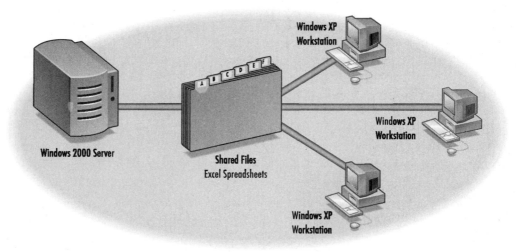

FIGURE 1.1
A Typical Network

This chapter will help you, as a network technician or administrator, understand the importance of networks as well as their basic structures and use.

Understanding Computer Networking

Networking is the process of connecting together two or more devices, such as two computers, so they can share resources. The key term here is *sharing*.

When computers are networked together, they can share their data files, hardware, and software with other users on the network. Networks allow users within the network to access the same data files, hardware, and software. Almost any type of data file or application can be made available for general use on a network. Printers, CD-ROMs, and modems are examples of hardware that you will commonly see being shared. This ability to share resources has several advantages:

- It results in reduced costs. For example, consider a customer service office with ten employees who take orders by phone and then print copies of those orders. Assuming the ten workers each use a stand-alone computer (not connected to a network), each of those stand-alone computers would need its own printer. When the workstations are networked, all ten workers can share one or two printers.

- Networks also increase productivity. In a stand-alone environment, workers must resort to "sneaker-netting." *Sneaker-netting* is the process of copying files onto external or removable media, such as a floppy or Zip disk, and passing the disk from one computer to another. For example,

Networking

Connecting two computers to communicate, or share information, with each other.

Sharing

Making a resource on one computer available to users on other computers.

Sneaker-netting

Copying files onto external or removable media, such as a floppy or Zip disk, and passing the disk from one computer to another.

assume that a customer service representative takes orders by phone and is then required to print a hard copy of that order. If that customer service representative does not have a printer physically attached to his computer, he must copy the order to a floppy disk or some other removable type of media, and then take that disk to a computer that has access to a printer. Each step of this process—producing, distributing, and keeping track of the copies—requires additional time. Also, whenever multiple copies of a single document are distributed, rarely are all the copies maintained with up-to-date information.

- Networking increases the efficiency and usefulness of the computers. When computers are networked, centrally stored and managed applications, such as e-mail or database management systems, are available to the users. For example, most ordering, manufacturing, and accounting systems are based on database management systems. Specialized database management software such as Microsoft SQL Server allows a company to have a centralized business system that all network users can access.

Understanding Network Structure

The structure of a network is typically defined by the size of the area it covers and the type of security that is implemented. The two most common terms used in describing network structures are local area network and wide area network.

LOCAL AREA NETWORK (LAN)

A *local area network (LAN)* can range from two computers being connected by a single cable, to a very complex, mesh network that involves many *nodes or hosts*. LANs may be confined to one building or several buildings in a small geographical area. If they encompass more than one building, LANs will not use *public carriers* to maintain connectivity. LANs are categorized as either peer-to-peer or client-server.

Peer-to-Peer Networks

In a *peer-to-peer network*, all computers are peers, or equal members, participating in the network (see Figure 1.2). Each computer on a peer-to-peer network acts as both a *client* and a *server*. As a client, the computer is able to access resources that other users have made available on the network. As a server, the computer provides shared resources to other users of the

Local area network (LAN)

A physical data communications infrastructure that is usually contained in a small geographic area such as an office, a floor of a building, or a whole building.

Node or host

Any device that is connected to communicate on a computer network. The device can be a computer, printer, server, switch, hub, etc.

Public carrier

A telephone line leased from a telephone company.

Peer-to-peer network

A network in which each computer is an equal member.

Client

A computer that has the necessary hardware and software installed to enable it to connect to a network.

Server

A computer that serves, or provides a service or resource for, the other clients on a network.

network. Peer-to-peer LANs do not have any centralized security, and user names and passwords may or may not be required to gain access to the resources on the network.

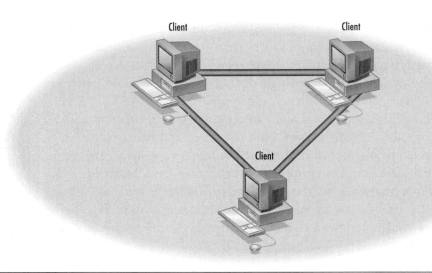

FIGURE 1.2
Typical Peer-to-Peer
Network

A small company or single office would be an ideal situation for a peer-to-peer LAN. For example, the ABC Company does medical transcription for a number of doctors in the local area. The work involves taking notes created by doctors and typing the data into a form. That form is then printed and placed in the patient's medical file. Assuming ABC employs ten people, each person could have a computer running the Windows 98 operating system. Two of those computers could have printers attached, which are then made available (shared) to the other eight users on the network. In this situation, the only hardware required is ten network cards, ten network cables, and a small hub or switch, so for a minimal investment, the company has a fully functional, peer-to-peer data network.

IN REAL LIFE

An object, such as a folder or printer, that is shared on a network is commonly referred to as a resource.

Peer-to-peer networks use *share-level security*. In share-level security, one or more passwords are assigned to a shared resource. In order for another user to gain access to that shared resource, he or she must know the password for it. In addition, the individual password(s) will also determine the level of access the user has to the shared object. For example, to access a shared folder on the network, one password would be assigned for read-only access and a different password would be assigned for full access (see Figure 1.3).

Share-level security

A security system in which one or more passwords are assigned to a shared resource.

Downloads Properties

General | Sharing |

○ Not Shared
● Shared As:
   Share Name: Spreadsheets
   Comment: Shared folder containing spreadsheets
   Access Type:
   ○ Read-Only
   ○ Full
   ● Depends on Password
   Passwords:
   Read-Only Password:
   Full Access Password:

OK | Cancel | Apply

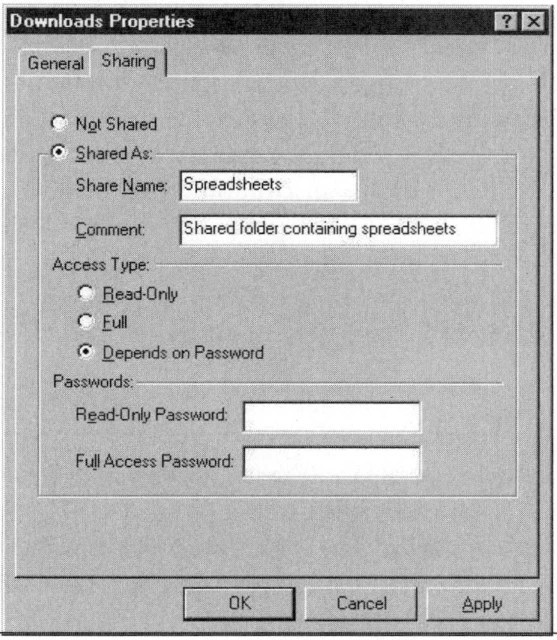

FIGURE 1.3
Assigning Passwords to a Shared Folder in Windows 98, Using Share-Level Security

To share a folder using share-level security in Windows 98, follow these steps:

1. Open Windows Explorer or My Computer.
2. Locate the drive containing the folder you want to share. Using the left button on your mouse, double-click on the drive to open it.
3. Locate the folder you want to share. Using the right button on your mouse, click once on the folder.
4. A menu will appear. On the menu, select the *Sharing* option.
5. The Downloads Properties dialog box appears, similar to that in Figure 1.3.
6. On the Sharing tab, using the left button on your mouse, click once on the *Shared As* option.
7. Assign a share name, an optional comment, and the level of security.

8. Assign passwords to each level of security, either Read-Only, Full, or Depends on Password.
9. Assign a password appropriate to the selections you made.
10. Provide the appropriate passwords to network users who require access to the shared folder.
11. Click the OK button at the bottom of the Downloads Properties dialog box.

Peer-to-peer networks are generally small, limited to around ten nodes. They are easy and inexpensive to implement, but they may require more administration than client-server networks because they lack centralized control. In a peer-to-peer network, the computer owning the resource has control of it. That is, the computer that has the shared folder on its hard drive or that has the printer physically attached to it owns and controls that shared resource. In the medical transcription office example given earlier in this section, the person sitting at the computer that has a printer attached to it controls which users on the network have access to the printer and which level of access they have. If each of the ten computers has a shared resource, then in effect you have ten administrators controlling access to those resources.

— TRY IT!

On a computer running the Windows 95 or 98 operating system, share a folder following the instructions provided in the preceding section.
1. Open the My Computer utility and share a folder that contains several files.
2. From a second computer, use the Network Neighborhood utility to view the shared folder.
3. Access the folder and test the permissions assignment.

Client-Server Networks

In a *client-server configuration,* one or more computers are designated as servers to centrally control network security for all other computers, called clients, on the network (see Figure 1.4). Servers run a network operating system (NOS) such as Microsoft Windows 2000 Server, Microsoft Windows NT Server, Novell NetWare, or UNIX. Network operating systems contain additional *network services,* or functions, above and beyond those provided by desktop operating systems, such as Microsoft Windows 98, Windows ME, and Windows XP Home Edition. For example, the *Dynamic Host Configuration Protocol (DHCP)* service (see Chapter 9) can be installed and configured on a server. Once installed and configured, that

Logical and Physical Network Topologies

service will automatically assign Internet Protocol (IP) addresses to host, or client, computers.

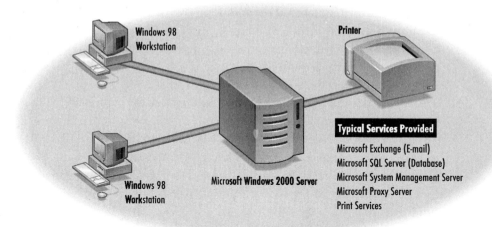

Microsoft Windows 2000 Server

Typical Services Provided

Microsoft Exchange (E-mail)
Microsoft SQL Server (Database)
Microsoft System Management Server
Microsoft Proxy Server
Print Services

FIGURE 1.4
Typical Client-Server Network

In a client-server network, one or more network administrators are responsible for creating user and group accounts, assigning passwords, and controlling the type of access required by the user. To log in to a client-server network, users commonly enter a set of credentials, such as a user name and password. The server that is providing the security service for the network verifies the validity of the credentials. If the correct credentials are entered, the user gains access to the network.

Client-server networks have *user-level security*. With user-level security, access to network resources is assigned to the individual user or group, not to the object being accessed. For example, access to shared network objects such as printers or folders is normally granted to groups. Groups are containers that hold user accounts. When a user requires access to a shared network object, she is placed in a group that has access to that object (see Figure 1.5).

User-level security

A security system in which access to network resources is assigned to the individual user or group, not to the object being accessed.

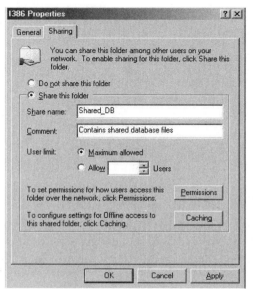

FIGURE 1.5
Assigning Access to a Shared Folder in Windows 2000 Professional, with User-Level Security

To share a folder with user-level security in Windows 2000, follow these steps:

1. Open Windows Explorer or My Computer.
2. Locate the drive containing the folder you want to share. Using the left button on your mouse, double-click on the drive to open it.
3. Locate the folder you want to share. Using the right button on your mouse, click once on the folder.
4. A menu will appear. On the menu, select the *Sharing* option.
5. The Properties dialog box appears, similar to that in Figure 1.5.
6. On the Sharing tab, using the left button on your mouse, click once on the *Share this folder* option.
7. Assign a share name and an optional comment.
8. Establish an optional user limit. This limit will determine how many users may connect to the shared folder concurrently, or at the same time.
9. With your left mouse button, click the Permissions button and you will see a dialog box similar to that in Figure 1.6.

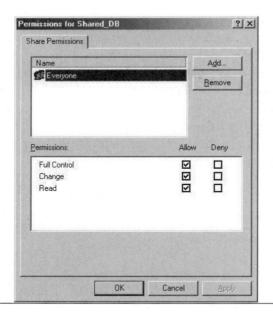

FIGURE 1.6
Permissions to a Shared Folder

10. The Permissions dialog box will show you the users and groups who currently have permission to access the folder and the level of access they have. By default, the Everyone group will have full access to the shared folder. You can choose to remove these permissions.

11. With your left mouse button, click the Add button. A dialog box similar to that in Figure 1.7 will appear displaying all of the users and groups that are available.

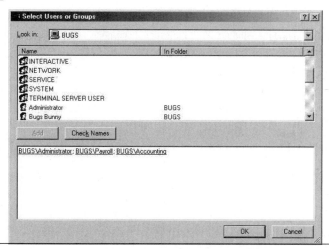

FIGURE 1.7
Selecting Users and Groups

12. Select users and groups in the top window by clicking on them and then clicking the Add button, to add them to the bottom window. When you are finished, click the OK button.

13. You will see a dialog box similar to that in Figure 1.8. To assign permissions, use your left mouse button to click on the user name or group in the *Name* list box and then place a check mark in the appropriate box in the *Permissions* list box. In Figure 1.8, the Payroll group has been given *Change* and *Read* permissions.

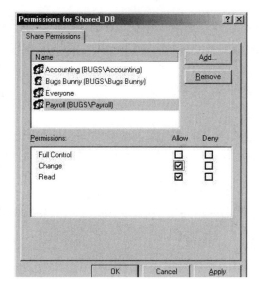

FIGURE 1.8
Assigning Permissions to a
Shared Folder

14. Once you have assigned or denied permissions to each user and group, click the OK button.

TRY IT!

On a computer running the Windows 2000 Professional operating system, share a folder following the instructions provided in the preceding section.
1. Share a folder that contains several files.
2. Assign permissions to the shared folder.
3. From a second computer, use My Network Places to view the shared folder.
4. Access the folder and test the permissions assignment.

After the user has been placed in the appropriate group, he can log in to the network and have access to that object. With user-level security, unlike share-level security, users do not need a separate password for each object they access.

Client-server networks may be any size; however, they are usually larger than peer-to-peer networks and may include separate servers to run different specialty applications, such as controlling files and printers, database management systems, and e-mail services.

 TEST TIP

To keep track of which security level is used on a given network, think of the level where security is assigned. In a network using share-level security, access is granted at the level of the shared object. In a network using user-level security, access is granted at the level where the user or group enters the system.

WIDE AREA NETWORK (WAN)

Wide area network (WAN)

A data communications network that spans a large geographic area and usually makes use of third-party transmission facilities or infrastructures, discretely integrating remote LANs into the structure.

A *wide area network* is unlimited in size and may span several states or countries. WANs are almost always client-server based. More complex than LANs, WANs typically use a public carrier and one or more routers to facilitate network communications. WAN links are commonly used to connect two or more LANs together. For example, consider a company based in Boston with manufacturing facilities in St. Louis and Phoenix (see Figure 1.9). Each facility would have a LAN designed to service employees at that specific location. However, the company may want to share data files and a single e-mail service among all of the locations. The LAN at each facility could be connected through a public carrier to the other networks at the geographically separate locations. Since each LAN could then "talk" to the others, all of the users in the company could exchange data files and share the corporate e-mail system.

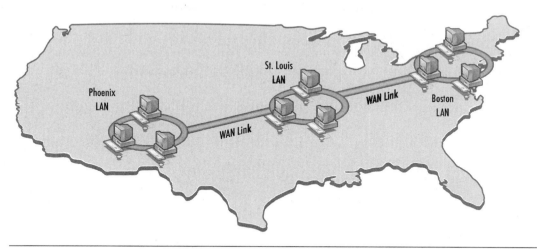

FIGURE 1.9
Wide Area Network
Configuration

The speed with which data travels over a WAN link is usually slower than the speeds found on a LAN. While LAN speeds run in the range of 10 to 100Mbps (megabits per second), WAN speeds average between 256Kbps (kilobits per second) and 1.544 Mbps. Data speeds become very important when planning where to place shared resources and servers that service log-in requests. The largest WAN in use today is the Internet.

IN REAL LIFE

Do not confuse Mbps, megabits per second, with MBps, megabytes per second. Also notice that Kbps, or kilobits per second, is different from KBps, or kilobytes per second. Mbps and Kbps are used to measure bandwidth, while MBps and KBps are commonly used as a measurement associated with storage.

Topologies

Topology is the description of the layout of the network. Two types of topologies are used to describe the two main aspects of laying out a network: the logical and the physical arrangement

- The *logical topology* is the way data travels across the network from node to node. It will determine critical communications requirements such as

Topology

From a Greek word that means "locality" or "layout"; the physical layout of a computer network.

Logical topology

The method or path data uses to travel across a network from node to node.

media, or cable, access methods. Media access methods determine how multiple nodes communicate when sharing a single cable. Two examples of logical topologies are Carrier Sense Multiple Access with Collision Detection (CSMA/CD), a media access method commonly found in Ethernet networks, and token passing, a media access method commonly found in Token Ring networks. (Chapter 2 explains media access methods in detail.)

- The *physical topology* of a network includes the location and arrangement of all of the nodes and how they are interconnected. It also includes the network hardware, such as hubs and switches, that is required to connect network devices, including computers and printers.

The following example might sound confusing at first, but consider this: Many Token Ring networks are actually wired as a physical star. If you look at this statement, the term "Token Ring" might lead you to believe that the network is wired in a physical ring topology, which would be untrue. Physically, the wiring configuration is a star. However, Token Ring networks use a token passing media access method, where the data travels from one node to the next, resulting in a logical ring topology.

The most common physical topologies in use today are star, bus, mesh, ring, and wireless.

TESTTIP

Given a scenario, or set of requirements, identify the correct network topology to use. Also, be sure you can identify a physical topology by looking at a drawing.

STAR

The most common physical topology in use today, the *star topology* is most often used in new network installations. In the star topology, each node uses its own cable—a twisted pair cable, either shielded or unshielded—to connect to a central device, typically a switch or a hub (see Figure 1.10). When communicating, each node sends a signal directly to the central device, which then forwards that signal to other computers or devices connected to the network.

The star is considered *fault tolerant*, since the failure of a single node or piece of cable does not affect any other nodes on the network. The weakness, however, is in the hub or switch, because a failure of this device will affect the entire network.

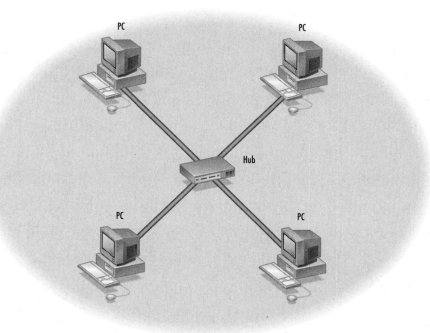

FIGURE 1.10
Typical Star Topology

Several variations of the star design are possible. The most common is the star bus or star-wired bus configuration. Figure 1.10 demonstrates a simplified star network. In a typical star topology, each workstation is connected to a jack that is mounted on the wall. The wire connected to the rear of the wall jack runs to either a punch-down block or a patch panel (see Figure 1.11). Both of these devices are commonly located in a wiring closet along with other networking hardware. At the patch panel or punch-down block, another length of wire runs to the switch or hub. If a router is being used on the network, it will also be connected to the switch or hub (see Figure 1.12).

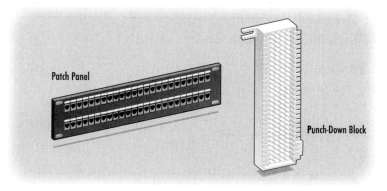

FIGURE 1.11
Typical Patch Panel and
Punch-Down Block

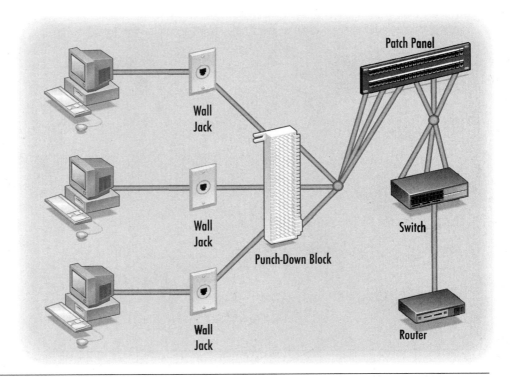

FIGURE 1.12
Advanced Star Topology

Advantages of the star topology:
- Easy to install.
- The failure of a single node or cable segment affects only that node.
- Network faults are easier to troubleshoot and repair.
- Components are common and supported by many manufacturers.

Disadvantages of the star topology:
- The switch or hub constitutes a potential single point of failure.
- The star requires more wiring than other topologies.

— TRY IT! —

Set up a star network. You will need the following:

1. A hub or switch.
2. Two or more computers.
3. Twisted pair cables for each computer.

Logical and Physical Network Topologies

BUS

The *bus topology* is linear and consists of several lengths of cable that are used to connect the nodes together (see Figure 1.13). Coaxial cable is commonly used in a bus configuration. Each length of cable connects to a bayonet nut connector (BNC). The BNC connector is plugged in to a barrel connector on the network interface card at each computer or printer. Since a cable is attached to each end of the barrel connector, it appears as if a single cable is used. As a result, people often report that a single piece of cable is used over the length of the network.

Bus topology

A physical arrangement of nodes on a network in which several lengths of cable connect the nodes directly to each other.

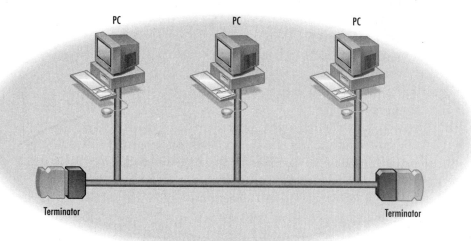

FIGURE 1.13
Typical Bus Topology

Trunk, or backbone

The main wire that connects all of the nodes on the network.

These pieces of cable are commonly referred to as a *trunk* or *backbone* cable because they run the length of the network. The backbone cable is then terminated at each end. This termination is done by placing a cap terminator, or resistor, on the end of the cable. The terminator connects the inner and outer conductors together, completing an electrical circuit. Once the electrical circuit is completed, electrical signals can flow through the cable. Since the data is *broadcast* to all nodes on the network, it travels the entire length of the trunk cable. If a piece of coaxial cable that is used for data transfer loses a terminator, network traffic would continue to move from end to end on the wire, causing a phenomenon known as *signal bounce,* which interrupts the communications taking place on the wire.

Broadcast

A message sent to all nodes on a network segment. Broadcasts are not transmitted by routers; therefore, their usefulness is limited to the local segment.

Signal bounce

A phenomenon that occurs when a piece of coaxial cable loses a terminator, causing network traffic to move from end to end on the wire and interrupting the communications taking place on the wire.

Since little cable or networking hardware is required, the bus is the simplest way to create a network. Although most new networks are installed in a star topology, you will encounter many existing networks that are still using the bus configuration.

When a node communicates in the bus topology, it addresses its data to a specific node, but the data is sent to all of the nodes on the network. When the nodes see the information, only the node with the correct address accepts the transmitted data, while the other nodes reject it.

The bus topology is normally used for small networks. Since it requires little wire and networking hardware, this topology is less expensive to implement than some other topologies, such as the star. By extending the trunk line, additional nodes can be added.

Advantages of the bus topology:

- Uses less cable and hardware than other topologies, which makes it
  - less expensive.
  - easier to manage and keep track of wiring.
- It is simple to install.

Disadvantages of the bus topology:

- Less fault tolerant due to the use of a trunk cable; a single break in the trunk can bring down a segment or the entire network.
- Adding nodes may affect network performance.
- Can be tough to troubleshoot connection problems.
- Coaxial cable and network adapter cards that support it are becoming more difficult to find and more expensive to purchase.

── TRY IT! ──────────

Set up a bus network. You will need the following:

1. Two or more computers.
2. Thinnet coaxial cable.

MESH

In a *mesh topology,* every node has a path, or connection, with every other node on the network (see Figure 1.14). This redundancy allows for a high level of fault tolerance on a network. That is, these multiple paths allow for communications to continue between nodes even if one pathway or connection fails. Due to the cost and complexity, mesh topologies are generally used only by businesses that require a high level of network availability. An example of a business that might require a mesh network is a bank or a company that relies on online orders from customers.

Mesh topology

A physical arrangement of nodes on a network in which every node has a path, or connection, with every other node on the network.

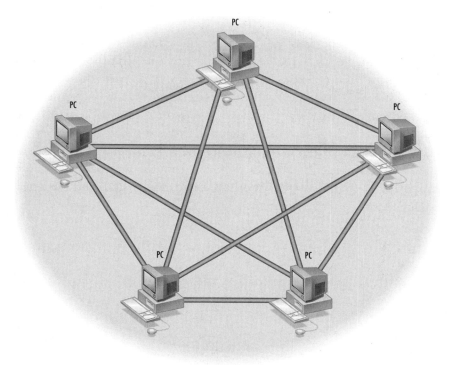

FIGURE 1.14
Typical Mesh Topology

Mesh topologies can be quite complex to install and manage. For every node on the network *(n),* there are *n(n-1)/2* connections. For example, if a network contains 20 computers, there will be 190 connections (20 * 19 / 2 = 190).

The Internet uses a hybrid mesh topology, which allows for multiple pathways between networks. The Internet is not considered to be a true mesh because it does not provide a dedicated pathway between every computer that has access. Instead, routers and alternate data links work together to reroute users, allowing access to the Internet even when one router or data link fails. The hybrid mesh is established primarily to allow for redundant routes between computer networks.

Advantages of the mesh topology:
- Provides a high level of fault tolerance.
- Network problems are generally easy to isolate.

Disadvantages of the mesh topology:
- Complexity makes installation and management difficult.
- Redundancy makes it expensive.
- Reconfiguration of the network or the addition of another node affects all of the other nodes.

RING

A physical arrangement of nodes on a network in which the cable connects each computer to the next, so that the cable forms a continuous loop, or ring.

In a *ring topology*, lengths of cable connect one computer to another in a ring fashion (see Figure 1.15). Data packets travel around the ring, in one direction only, from one computer to the next. As the packet travels to the next workstation, that node checks the destination address and either accepts or rejects the packet. If the data is rejected, that workstation regenerates the electrical signal of the packet and drops it back onto the network, causing it to pass to the next computer in the ring. When the data arrives at the receiving computer, the data is removed from the network. Since each computer is wired directly to two others, there are no "ends" on the ring topology requiring termination.

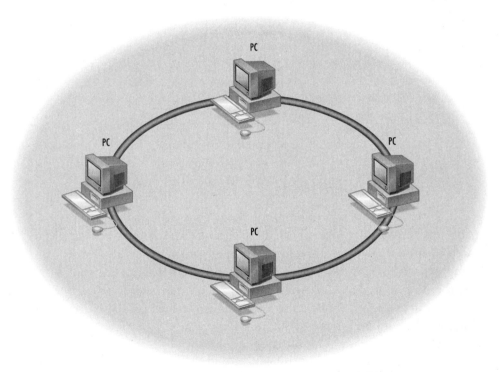

FIGURE 1.15
Typical Ring Topology

Logical and Physical Network Topologies

Token passing is one common method used to transmit data on a ring network. In token passing, a packet, or token, is placed on the network and passed around the ring from node to node.

To send a message on the network, a node picks up the token from the network, attaches the data and the address of the destination node, and drops the token back into the ring. Once the packet reaches the destination node, the receiving computer removes the token from the ring and detaches the data. The destination node will then send an acknowledgement to the sender stating that it has received the data. Once the sending node receives the acknowledgement, it will drop a new token back into the ring. Using this method, only one node at a time can communicate on the network. Since each node is involved in the passing process and maintains the ability to regenerate the token, the token passing topology is considered an *active topology.*

Like bus networks, ring networks have a low fault tolerance. A break in the ring or a malfunctioning node can disable a segment or an entire network. Also, ring networks tend to get slower as more nodes are added.

Ring networks do not generally use a pure ring topology. Ring and token passing networks are typically wired in a star configuration.

Advantages of the ring topology:
- Requires less wire than a star network.
- Each workstation can regenerate a signal.
Disadvantages of the ring topology:
- Lack of fault tolerance.
- Most rings are physically wired as a star.

WIRELESS

Wireless technology is rapidly emerging in the network communications market. A *wireless topology* relies on either radio frequency (RF) or infrared (IR) frequencies, or channels, to connect directly to each other or to access points (APs). Wireless communication devices connect, or network, using one of the following methods:
- *Ad hoc mode,* in which devices such as portable computers or portable digital assistants (PDAs) connect directly to each other without using an AP. Devices send out radio waves that can be intercepted by other wireless devices whenever they move within a certain distance range of each other (see Figure 1.16). When the devices detect radio waves from another device, they can begin to communicate with each other and share data across their newly formed frequency network. The network is

Token passing

A method used on a ring network to transmit data from node to node in a packet, called a token.

Active topology

A topology in which each node is involved in the passing process and maintains the ability to regenerate the token.

Wireless topology

A physical arrangement of nodes within a certain distance that will allow them to communicate with other nodes or access points on the network using either radio frequency (RF) or infrared (IR) frequencies, or channels.

Ad hoc mode

A form of wireless communication in which wireless clients communicate directly with each other via radio waves, without going through a wireless access point (AP).

created as needed and nodes can be moved from this network to another simply by changing their location and proximity to another wireless device.

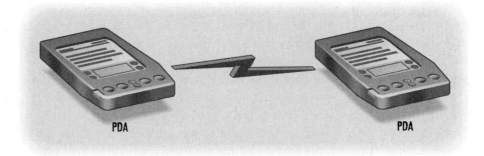

FIGURE 1.16
Two PDAs Using Infrared Communications

Infrastructure, or multipoint networking

A method used by wireless devices to connect to a fixed network through a wireless bridge that serves as an AP.

- *Infrastructure,* or *multipoint networking,* is used when wireless nodes connect to a fixed network using a wireless bridge that functions as an AP. The AP is generally wired to the network backbone and serves essentially the same purpose as a switch or hub on a wired network. Devices must be within the operating range of the wireless AP in order to access the network (see Figure 1.17).

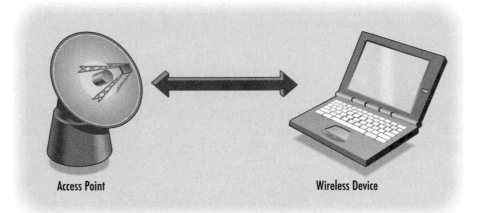

Access Point   Wireless Device

FIGURE 1.17
Communicating with an Access Point

Although wireless networks have shown great promise and a plethora of networking components are available, development and implementation has been slow due to a lack of standards. Recently, the Institute of Electrical and Electronics Engineers (IEEE) 802.11b working group has established wireless networking standards to help address those problems.

Troubleshooting Problems with Shared Resources

Since networks are established for the purpose of sharing resources, it is particularly troublesome when network users cannot access those resources. These types of failures are generally easy to troubleshoot and repair. Begin by browsing to the resource with Network Neighborhood or My Network Places. If you can see the resource but it does not allow you access, check the permissions on the share.

If, however, you cannot see the shared resource on the network, try these steps:

- Check that the computer that hosts the resource is turned on. For example, if another user is sharing a folder of Microsoft Excel spreadsheets and the folder is physically located on the hard drive of that user's computer, you will not be able to see or access the shared folder unless that computer is turned on.
- If the host computer is on, check the resource on that computer to ensure it is still shared. It is very easy to disable the sharing of a resource.
- If both of these things check out and you are still unable to access the resource, determine if you can see other computers on the network. Since a physical connection problem may be causing the difficulty, you must determine if the problem is at your computer, the computer with the shared object, or the entire network. If you can see other computers on the network and access their resources, check the physical connections at the computer hosting the share.
- If you cannot see any other computer on the network, check the physical connection of the computer from which you are trying to access the shared resource.

STUDY GUIDE

In this chapter, we discussed the purpose for networking computers and the differences between local area and wide area networks. We also examined the various topologies encountered in network environments. Here are some key points to remember.

UNDERSTANDING NETWORK STRUCTURE

- Networking is the process of connecting together two or more devices, such as two computers or a computer and a printer, so that they can share resources.
- The structure of a network is typically defined by the size of the area it covers.
- The two most common terms used in describing network structures are local area network (LAN) and wide area network (WAN).
  - A local area network is generally limited to a specific geographical area.
  - A wide area network ties together local area networks.
- LANs are categorized as peer-to-peer or client-server based.
  - In a peer-to-peer network, all computers are considered to be equal.
  - In a client-server network, security and user access is controlled at the server level.

TOPOLOGIES

Star

- A star topology is commonly used for new network installations.
- Nodes in a star network connect to a multistation access unit (MAU), generally a switch or a hub.
- Star networks typically use twisted pair cable.
- Star networks are considered fault tolerant, because the failure of a single piece of cable or a workstation will not affect the rest of the network.
- The switch or hub can be a single point of failure.

Bus

- A bus network uses coaxial cable.
- A single length of cable connects the nodes together in a daisy-chain fashion.
- A bus network requires termination to eliminate signal bounce.
- Bus networks are not fault tolerant; a single break can bring down the entire network.

Mesh

- Each computer is connected directly to every other computer.
- A mesh network is used when critical information must be available without interruption.
- This topology is highly fault tolerant.
- Mesh topologies can be quite complex to install and manage.
- For every node on the network *(n)*, you will have *n(n-1)/2* connections.

Ring

- A cable connects each computer to the next in a continuous loop, or ring.
- Data travels around the ring, in one direction only, from one computer to the next.
- Since each computer is wired directly to two others, there are no "ends" on the ring topology requiring termination.
- Token passing is one common method used to transmit data on a ring network.
- With a ring topology, only one node at a time may communicate on the network.
- Since each node is involved in the passing process and maintains the ability to regenerate the token, token passing makes the ring configuration an active topology.
- A break in the ring or a malfunctioning node can disable a segment or an entire network.
- Ring networks tend to get slower as more nodes are added.
- Ring networks do not generally use a pure ring topology. Instead, they are typically wired in a physical star configuration.

Wireless

- Wireless technology is rapidly emerging in the network communications market.
- Wireless systems rely on either radio frequency (RF) or infrared (IR) frequencies, or channels, to connect directly to each other or to access points (APs).
- Wireless communication devices connect, or network, using either ad hoc mode or infrastructure (multipoint networking).
- Devices such as portable computers or portable digital assistants (PDAs) use ad hoc mode by connecting directly to each other without using an AP.

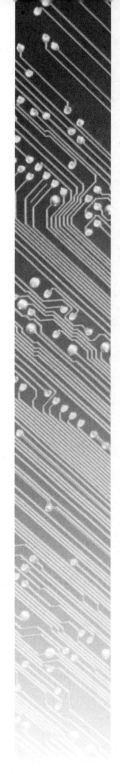

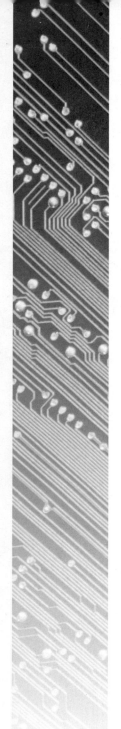

- In ad hoc mode, devices send out radio waves that can be intercepted by other wireless devices whenever they move within a certain distance range of each other.
  - The network is created as needed and nodes can be moved from this network to another simply by changing their location and proximity to another wireless device.
- Nodes use infrastructure, or multipoint networking, when connecting to a fixed network.
- The wireless nodes connect to a wireless bridge functioning as an AP.
- The AP is generally wired to the network backbone and serves essentially the same purpose as a switch or hub on a wired network.
- Devices must be within the operating range of the wireless AP in order to access the network.

TROUBLESHOOTING PROBLEMS WITH SHARED RESOURCES

- Begin by browsing to the resource with Network Neighborhood or My Network Places. If you can see the resource but it does not allow you access, check the permissions on the share.
- If you cannot see the shared resource on the network, try these steps:
  - Check that the computer that hosts the resource is turned on.
  - Check the resource on the host computer to ensure it is still shared.
  - If both of these things check out, determine if you can see other computers on the network. Since a physical connection may be causing the problem, you must determine if the problem is at your computer, the computer with the share, or the entire network.
  - If you can see other computers on the network and access their resources, check the connectivity at the computer hosting the share.
  - If you cannot see any other computer on the network, check the connection on the computer from which you are trying to access the shared resource.

PRACTICE TEST

Try this test to check your mastery of the concepts in this chapter.

1. The purpose of a network is to allow for
   a. security.
   b. sharing.
   c. remote access.
   d. telephone service.

Logical and Physical Network Topologies

2. The _____ is generally limited to a specific geographical area.
   a. topology
   b. local area network
   c. client-server network
   d. wide area network

3. In a stand-alone environment, workers must often resort to _____ in order to pass data from one computer to another.
   a. the telephone
   b. the fax machine
   c. sneaker-netting
   d. subnetting

4. _____ run a network operating system.
   a. Workstations
   b. Hosts
   c. Routers
   d. Servers

5. Which of the following network topologies uses coaxial cable?
   a. bus
   b. star
   c. wireless
   d. DSL

6. Which topology is most commonly used in new network installations?
   a. bus
   b. wireless
   c. star
   d. ring

7. In a _____ network, all computers are considered to be equal members.
   a. local area
   b. bus
   c. client-server
   d. peer-to-peer

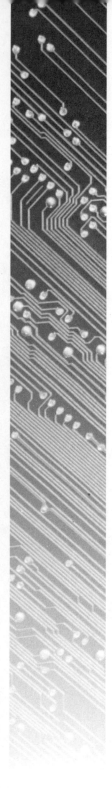

8. How many tokens travel around a Token Ring network at any given time?
   a. one
   b. three
   c. five
   d. ten

9. Access to your company network requires the use of a user name and password that is assigned by a network administrator and changed at a central computer. What type of network structure is most likely being used?
   a. LAN
   b. peer-to-peer
   c. client-server
   d. wireless

10. Your company has offices in five states. Each location is connected to the other, which allows them to send and receive e-mail and to share financial data that is stored on a corporate server. What type of network is represented in this example?
    a. WAN
    b. peer-to-peer
    c. ad hoc
    d. bus

11. You have been asked to install a mesh network consisting of eight computers. How many connections will be required on this network?
    a. 16
    b. 24
    c. 28
    d. 32

$$n \cdot (n-1)/2$$
$$8 \cdot (8-1)/2$$
$$56/2$$
$$28$$

12. What is the largest WAN in use today?
    a. IEEE network
    b. Microsoft's network
    c. Internet
    d. mesh network

13. A network hub or switch is an example of a
    a. central connectivity device.
    b. multistation protocol unit.
    c. many station wireless unit.
    d. many station protocol unit.

14. Portable digital assistants (PDAs) connect to each other using which of the following modes?
    a. peer-to-peer mode
    b. ad hoc mode
    c. infrastructure
    d. multipoint

15. Which of the following topologies is considered an active topology?
    a. ring
    b. star
    c. bus
    d. token passing

16. A public carrier is properly defined as
    a. radio waves.
    b. a switch.
    c. television signals.
    d. telephone lines.

17. The wire connected to the rear of the wall jack runs to a
    a. switch.
    b. router.
    c. patch panel.
    d. computer.

18. Which of the following network topologies use packets seen by all of the nodes on the network?
    a. ring
    b. star
    c. mesh
    d. wireless

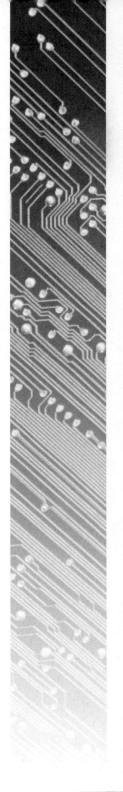

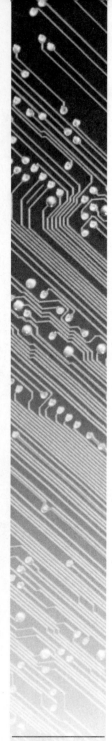

19. Which network topology provides the highest level of fault tolerance?
    a. star
    b. ring
    c. bus
    d. mesh

20. Which of the following terms best describes the client-server security model?
    a. The individual users determine the level of security.
    b. A workstation can be both a client and a server.
    c. A network administrator creates user and group accounts.
    d. They are very small and easy to implement.

TROUBLESHOOTING

1. You are the administrator for a small bus network consisting of seven personal computers and one printer. Several of the users just complained that the network is "down." What assumptions can you make and what are some of the steps you should take to troubleshoot the problem?

2. You are the network administrator for a mid-sized company located in the northeastern United States. Your client-server network is configured in the star topology outlined in Figure 1.18.

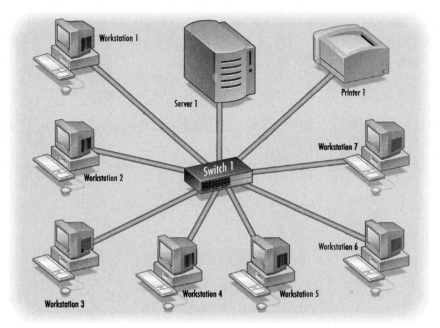

FIGURE 1.18
Star Network

Logical and Physical Network Topologies

The user at workstation 3 calls the help desk to report that he cannot log in to the network. While troubleshooting the problem, you ask the user to attempt to log in to the network from a different workstation. A short time later, the user phones back to report that he logged in to the network successfully at workstations 6 and 7. He also reports that other network users are logging in successfully at their workstations. What assumptions can you make from this conversation about the problems at workstation 3?

CUSTOMER SERVICE

1. Your company is located in New York. The company's sales force is having its annual meeting in Las Vegas. You have recently purchased some new wireless networking equipment and would like to set up a small network in a conference room at the meeting site using laptop computers. Which wireless networking components would you need to set up the network as requested?

2. Your company has recently decided to connect the corporate local area network to the Internet. In preparation, you obtain a leased line and router from a national telecommunications company. To which networking device on the corporate LAN would you connect the router?

3. A small financial consulting business has contracted with you to set up a local area network with connections to the Internet. The network will have approximately 25 users and the owners of the business have stated that they do not want to buy a server or any extra computing equipment. What type of network structure would you advise the company to use?

FOR MORE INFORMATION

For links to Web sites that provide further information about the topics covered in this chapter, go to the EMC/Paradigm Internet Resource Center at www.emcp.com/College Division/Internet Resource Centers/Networking/System Administration/Web Resources: For More Information.

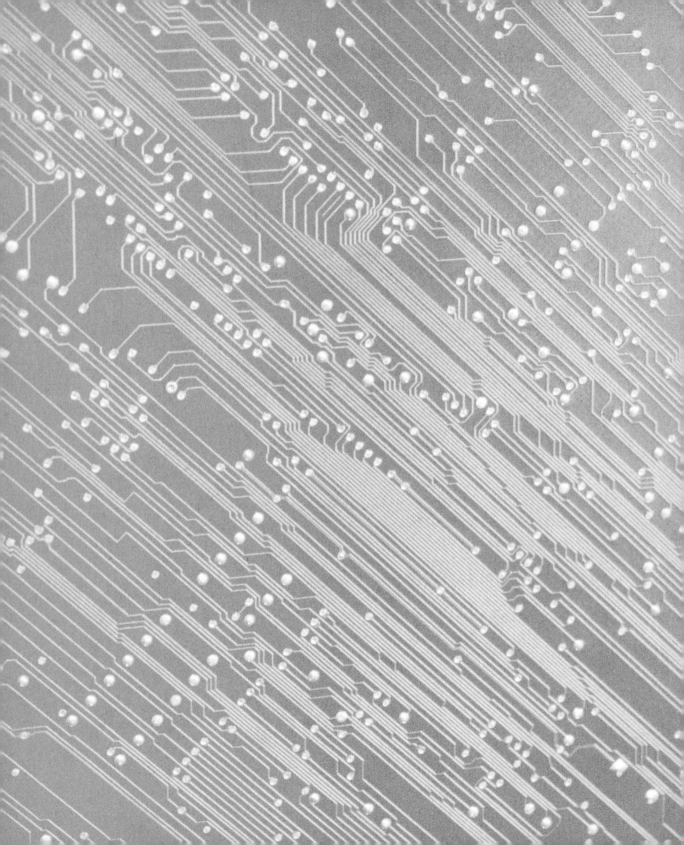

The OSI Model

ON THE TEST

Network+ Examination
- **Objective 2.1:** Given an example, identify a MAC address.
- **Objective 2.2:** Identify the seven layers of the OSI Model and their functions.
- **Objective 2.4:** Identify the OSI layers at which the following network components operate: hubs; switches; bridges; routers; network interface cards.

ON THE JOB

Understanding the OSI Model, and how data communications take place, can help you troubleshoot communication problems, talk with vendors in the industry, and make decisions concerning which *protocols* to run and which devices to use in your network.

The OSI Model

The *Open Systems Interconnection (OSI) Model* was designed to provide a standardized framework of rules for data communications. When we build a network of computers, the basis of the network is to share information. That information is broken down into sections for transmission over the physical cables and devices that allow the computers to talk to each other. Prior to the OSI Model, different vendors transmitted data in their own way, using their own special set of rules. That was fine for a limited network (within a building, for example). But as companies grew, so did their networks. As networks grew, the need to share information between networks also grew, and here is where the problems began. Because the various vendors who built all those networks used *proprietary* rules for data communications, networks could not talk to each other.

Protocol

A set of rules used by computers to communicate with other devices.

Open Systems Interconnection (OSI) Model

A standardized, layered framework for data communications that allows devices and protocols from different vendors to be used harmoniously on a network or *internetwork*.

Internetwork

Two or more networks connected by a device, usually a router, capable of recognizing multiple network segments.

Proprietary

Relating to or characteristic of a product or methodology that is owned exclusively by a single company, which takes a special interest in safeguarding internal knowledge and information about that product or methodology from others, especially competitors.

International Organization for Standardization (ISO)

A global organization formed to create unified, worldwide standards for the transmission of data communications on computer networks.

The *International Organization for Standardization (ISO)* looked at data communications and identified common elements that allowed data to be transmitted. Based on these common elements, as well as on an attempt to predict future network needs, the ISO built the OSI Model in beta format during the late 1970s. When this model was published in the early 1980s, it became the guide for the development of modern data communications and networking technologies. The OSI Model allowed network operators to choose any vendor—not necessarily the same one that built the network—to design and produce devices and protocols. Now, when you buy a computer from one company, your routers from another company, and your cable from a third company, you can be assured that all the components will work together and support data transmissions across your network because they all conform to the same set of basic rules for data communications.

The rules that we are talking about start with the application that creates the data and end with the actual data being placed on the network cabling attached to the sending device.

Header

A section of a datagram, or packet, that precedes the payload, or data unit, of the packet. The header contains vital information—such as the source address, destination address, and port number—that allows the packet to travel from the source to the destination.

As data moves through the different layers of the OSI Model, each layer adds a *header*. The header contains specific information about how the corresponding layer at the receiving device should handle the data. Once the data reaches the Physical layer and is ready to be transmitted to one or more receivers, it is considered a data frame, or simply a frame. Figure 2.1 shows how headers are added at each layer.

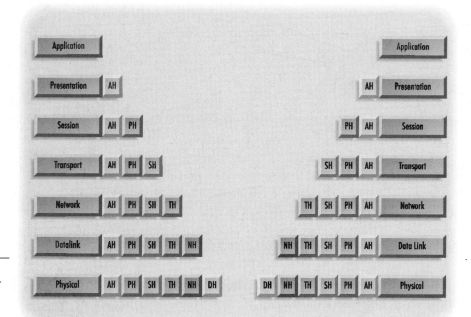

FIGURE 2.1
Headers Added at Each Layer of the OSI Model

One of the rules within this framework says that the relationship of any layer to any other layer is "plus one"/"minus one." That means that data cannot skip around in its transit of the OSI Model. Another rule is that peer-layer communication can take place. Thus, the Network layer of one node can communicate with the Network layer of another node. As you can see from Figure 2.2, a data transmission will progress from the Application layer on one machine to the Application layer on another machine following a prescribed method.

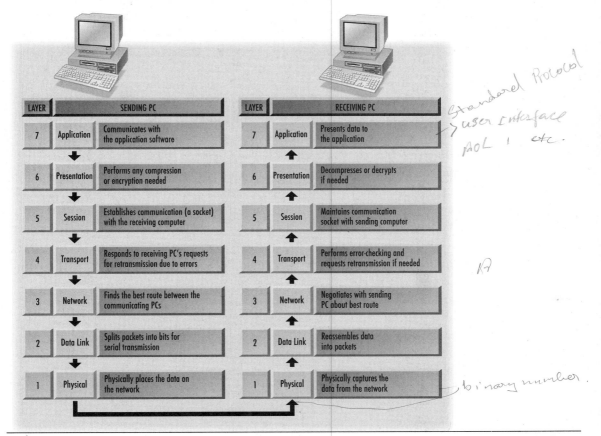

FIGURE 2.2
Data Flow through the OSI Model

For example, suppose you create an e-mail to send to a friend. After the e-mail is created, you will press the Send button to transmit it. The OSI Model contains the guidelines that the protocol must follow to ensure that the message leaves your computer, travels to the destination, and arrives complete and in readable form at your friend's computer.

The Seven Layers

The seven layers of the OSI Model and their primary functions are shown in Table 2.1.

Layer	Purpose
Application	Services applications that run over a network.
Presentation	Formats data for exchange; handles encryption and compression.
Session	Establishes and maintains sessions between network devices.
Transport	Manages the data flow between network devices.
Network	Handles the logical addressing of network devices and packet routing.
Data Link	Turns data from upper layers into bits for transmission.
Physical	Defines the network's physical aspects: interface cards, cable, and connectors.

TABLE 2.1
Seven Layers of the OSI Model

Each of these layers participates in getting the information you enter into an application on your computer transmitted across the network to your colleague's computer. We use a layered model to separate the major task of data transmission into a series of steps, each with a less complex function. Using this layered approach has several benefits. First, it prevents changes to one aspect of communications from impacting all functions of data transmission. For example, suppose a vendor wants to build a new network device. Prior to the OSI Model, the vendor would need not only to build the device but also to define new protocols. That device and the protocols it recognized would have been proprietary, because existing devices and protocols would not know how to interact with the new elements. Second, the OSI Model supports *Plug and Play compatibility* and multi-vendor participation in the development of new hardware and protocols.

Plug and Play compatibility

A function first developed by Microsoft for the Windows 95 platform that enables an operating system to recognize a new device placed in a computer.

Keep in mind that the OSI Model specifies a framework for data transmission. It does not define the specific criteria for protocols or devices. Although vendors are not bound to adhere to the characteristics of each of the layers of the model, it is in their best interest to use these guidelines if they wish to provide *interoperability* to their customers.

Interoperability

The ability of an operating system to talk to operating systems from other vendors.

You are probably asking yourself how to remember all these layers. Here is a mnemonic that can help: "**A**ll **P**eople **S**eem **T**o **N**eed **D**ata **P**rocessing." If you prefer to remember from the Physical to the Application layer, try this one: "**P**lease **D**o **N**ot **T**hrow **S**ausage **P**izza **A**way."

Finally, as data makes its way from the Application layer down to the Physical layer, the data changes its name. Four of the layers—Application, Presentation, Session, and Transport—call their version of the data a *Protocol Data Unit (PDU)*. The PDU specifies the layer of interaction by appending the first letter of the layer to the beginning of the term *PDU*. In Figure 2.3, you can see that the data unit at the Application layer is known as the APDU. Although the lower layers of data units are really also PDUs, these lower layers have their own names for data. At the Network layer, data is called a packet. At the Data Link layer, it is a frame. At the Physical layer, the data is broken into the smallest unit for transmission, the *bit*.

The term "bit" is used to describe a unit of data, the capability of a computer, or, in some cases, the classification and color state for graphic images. For example, a computer's processor can be classified as a 32-bit, meaning that the computer uses 32 bits to identify each memory address. For graphics classification, a 1-bit image is monochrome; an 8-bit image has 256 colors; and a 24- or 32-bit image is true color.

PDU — All — Application
PDU — People — Presentation
PDU — Seen — Session
PDU — To — Transportation
PDU — Need — Network
PDU — Data — Data Link → Frame
PDU — Processing — Physical

PDU Protocol Data Unit

Called Packet

Broken into the smallest unit for Transmission

Application Layer	→	Application PDU (APDU)
Presentation Layer	→	Presentation PDU (PPDU)
Session Layer	→	Session PDU (SPDU)
Transport Layer	→	Transport PDU (TPDU)
Network Layer	→	Network PDU (NPDU)
Data Link Layer	→	Data Link PDU (DPDU)
Physical Layer	→	Physical PDU (PPDU)

Protocol Data Units for
each layer of the OSI Model

cable

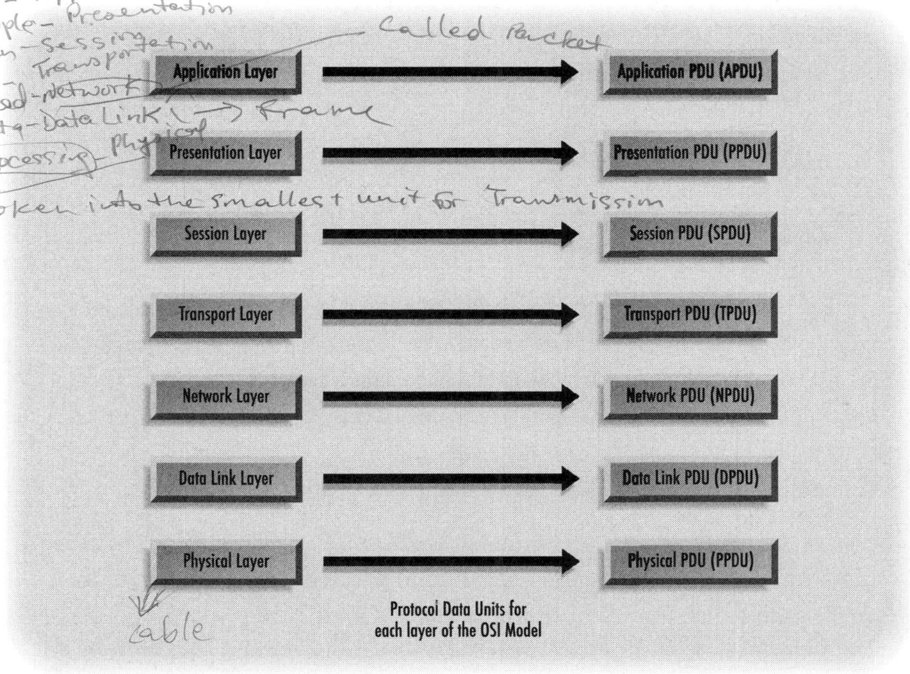

FIGURE 2.3
The OSI Model and the Protocol Data Units for Each Layer

Now we will take a closer look at the specific functions of each of the seven layers of the OSI Model.

PDU Please — Physical
PDU Do — Data
PDU not — Network
PDU Throw — Transportation
PDU Sausage — Session
PDU Pizza — Presentation
PDU Away — Application

The Physical Layer

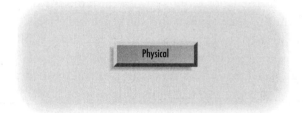

Physical

The *Physical layer* of the OSI Model (Figure 2.4) defines and standardizes the way in which the data is transmitted over the physical connections of the network. Here, we are concerned with the smallest unit, the bit. The bit is the piece of data sent over the physical media, such as cable. Other transmission components that are identified at the Physical layer include the physical topology, or layout of the network; the connection types; the state of the signal (analog or digital); the bandwidth used (baseband or broadband; defined later in this chapter); and the bit synchronization.

In Real Life

The Physical layer of the OSI Model is responsible for the way in which data is transmitted over the physical connections of the network. This layer handles the physical media and devices such as network interface cards and repeaters.

Physical Topology

include hubs & switches, network devices, printer, computer

The physical topology of a network includes the location and arrangement of all of the nodes and how they are interconnected. It also includes the network hardware, such as hubs and switches, that is required to connect network devices, including computers and printers. There are five major topologies: bus, star, ring, mesh, and wireless. The choice will depend on a number of factors, as discussed in Chapter 1, where we talk more specifically about each network layout. Sometimes cost is the determining element; sometimes permanence of the network determines which layout to use.

You will see many more pieces of the physical topology of a network in coming chapters. The following descriptions review the basic terminology of physical networks that is presented in Chapter 1.

The Star

[handwritten: require hub or switch widely used because its easy trouble shoot and one node failure does not cripple the whole system]

The star topology is the most common physical setup for networks today. It requires a central switch, or hub, and drop cables from the hub to each node on the segment. It is widely used because it is easy to troubleshoot and a node failure does not bring down the entire segment.

The Bus

[handwritten: to quickly build or tear down a network]

A bus topology allows all computers to connect to the same piece of cable, which is commonly known as a backbone. We use the bus topology when we want to be able to quickly build or tear down a network.

The Mesh

[handwritten: used today in a modify way called a hybrid mesh]

Mesh topology networks are characterized by redundant links between all nodes, or devices, on the network. If computer 1 talks to computer 2, computer 3, and computer 4, then there would be a link from computer 1 to each of these other computers. This configuration is usually used today in a modified way called a hybrid mesh, in which some, but not all, nodes function with redundant links.

The Ring

[handwritten: data travel in a single direction only]

The ring topology connects nodes in a continuous loop in which any single node can talk directly only to the node on either side of it. Data is transmitted in a single direction only. Each node on the ring can accept and respond to packets addressed to it and passes other packets to the next node on the ring.

Wireless

A wireless topology relies on either radio frequency (RF) or infrared (IR) frequencies, or channels, to connect directly to each other or to access points (APs). Wireless communication devices connect, or network, using either ad hoc or infrastructure networking.

CONNECTION TYPES

[handwritten: 2 types of communication - point-to-point - multi point]

Two types of connections exist in data communications: point-to-point and multipoint.

- A point-to-point connection occurs when two computers are connected and exchange information. Two computers connected by a modem on each system is an example of a point-to-point connection.

*[handwritten margin note: Five major Topologies
* Star - easy to troubleshoot
Bus - easy to build or tear down
Ring - data travel in single direction
mesh - multiple
Wireless -
- Radio frequency
- Infrared Frequency]*

- With multipoint connections, many devices are connected to the network or transmission media. A typical corporate network in which many computers are attached to cables and hubs is an example of a multipoint connection. This also means that all of the computers must share the available bandwidth

SIGNAL TYPES

When data is processed by the seven layers of the OSI Model, each layer takes steps to ready the data for transmission, with the ultimate goal being to convert that data to an energy unit for transmission. Bits must be represented in some manner so that the sending node can create a message and the receiving node can recreate that message. This is known as converting the data to *signals.*

The two types of signaling that are used in data communications are analog and digital.

- Analog signaling uses a continually varying *voltage,* or signal. If you think of an old-fashioned clock, you can understand how analog transmissions work. The second hand continually sweeps around the clock face, always changing the time. The clock is never in a static state. Most home telephone systems use analog transmission to carry the telephone signal across the wire.

- The digital format uses an electrical pulse. Digital data transmission looks different. The signal will always exist in one of two states: on or off. If we go back to the example of the clock, think about a modern clock this time. A digital clock will present the time as 5:00 or 5:01, with no variation in between. The two states are reached by applying either positive voltage or negative voltage to the bit. Positive voltage equals the on (1) state, while negative voltage equals the off (0) state.

All signal transmissions are subject to stress on the transmitted signal, causing degradation of the signal. This is known as attenuation. Periodically the signal must be amplified, or regenerated, to continue. This is where additional problems can occur. If the signal becomes distorted, amplification will enhance that distortion. It is always a race to get the signal to its destination before the signal becomes uselessly distorted.

As engineers looked at signal transmission, they discovered that analog and digital signaling, even in their purest form, were not the most efficient transmitters of bits. So the engineers devised a variety of *encoding schemes* to make the data transmission more efficient. It is not necessary to understand all of the details of these encoding schemes, but you should be able to recognize the names.

Signal

An electric current that carries data from one place to another; often used generically to indicate anything that is sent or received across a cable plant.

Voltage

The potential difference in charge between two entities in an electrical field. The greater the voltage, the greater the electrical current.

Encoding scheme

A means of building a signal for transmission, developed to take advantage of the available bandwidth and efficiently move data aross a network or internetwork.

The OSI Model

Analog encoding schemes are based on three characteristics of a continually varying voltage:

- Amplitude: The magnitude of the voltage; that is, strength of the signal.
- Frequency: The time it takes a voltage, or wave, to go from high to low to high again.
- Phase: The state of a wave measured by its relationship to another wave.

Three encoding schemes have been devised to improve the efficiency of transmission of analog signals, each using one of the characteristics of analog signals. They are shown in Figure 2.5.

- **Amplitude Shift Keying (ASK):** The magnitude of the voltage determines the on or off state of the bit.
- **Frequency Shift Keying (FSK):** How often the voltage changes from its high point to low point determines the on or off state of the bit.
- **Phase Shift Keying (PSK):** The presence or absence of a change in the wave determines the on or off state of the bit.

FIGURE 2.5
Analog Encoding Schemes

The two categories of digital encoding schemes are shown in Figure 2.6.

- **Current-State Encoding:** Data is encoded by the presence or absence of a characteristic of the signal.
- **State-Transition Encoding:** Transition in a signal state represents the data being transmitted.

FIGURE 2.6
Digital Encoding Schemes

The choice between digital and analog signal communication is made based on network type and the equipment used.

BASEBAND VERSUS BROADBAND

Baseband and broadband refer to the way in which signals are passed across the cable media. In *baseband transmissions,* one signal uses the entire capacity of the media (or the entire bandwidth). Baseband transmission is frequently used for LANs using twisted pair cable. When transmitting over a *broadband* network, many signals share the same channel, or available bandwidth. Your cable television service is a broadband service. The cable media must be capable of large bandwidth, such as fiber-optic cable or gigabit channels.

Baseband transmission

A digital communications signal in which only one signal may be present on the wire at a time. Data networks generally use base band communications.

Broadband transmission

A digital communications signal in which multiple signals can be transmitted on the cable at the same time. An example is cable TV.

Baseband transmission can best be compared to a very narrow bridge over a creek out in the country. The bridge was probably built for horse and wagon traffic. It is old and rickety, but it is still useful for cars. Because of its age, the bridge has been designated for crossing by only one car at a time. This is how baseband transmission works.

Now consider the interstate highway. Four lanes of cars continually speed by. Each lane is marked off with white dashed lines, letting drivers know where they need to stay on the road. Traffic can branch off from that interstate by using exit lanes to access other roadways. This is broadband traffic—many cars sharing the available interstate road space.

Broadband traffic is more efficient because many signals are carried over the cable media. Broadband transmission is also less susceptible to signal degradation than baseband networks.

BIT SYNCHRONIZATION

The previous discussions have introduced you to topologies, encoding, use of media, and a wealth of other characteristics of data transmission. But the bottom line is still the action of creating units of energy to represent the bits that will pass over the cable. Many types of devices are needed to support all of this activity, and those devices are not intelligent entities. They understand what a bit is and the format for the signal, but they have no way of knowing how to determine the beginning and the end of a distinct signal. That is where bit synchronization comes in.

Bit synchronization is a timing function that enables devices (computers, routers, bridges, switches, and so forth) to understand when a signal starts and when it stops. The two types of bit synchronization are *asynchronous* and *synchronous*.

Asynchronous

Signals between a sender and a receiver occur based on different clocks without a reference to unify them.

Synchronous

When two entities are in a synchronous state, they are coordinated in a time field.

- When using asynchronous communication, a marker called a start bit must be sent to alert the receiving device that the message is beginning, and a stop bit must be sent when the message is complete.
- When using synchronous communication, a clocking signal enables the sending and receiving nodes to synchronize with each other and identify the beginning and end of a transmitted message.

In Real Life

When two entities are in a synchronous state, they are coordinated in a time field. In technology, synchronization occurs when signals occur by the same clock rates and when all clocks are based on a single reference clock. Synchronous communication can also occur when two programs are communicating, each in their own turn, without starting a new session each time.

In Real Life

Asynchronous communication takes place when signaling between the sender and the receiver occurs based on different clocks without a reference to unify them. A sender may transmit using one signal clock, and the receiver may respond using a completely different clock (where "clock" refers to a special signal sent to keep track of time). Each end of the communication operates independently from the other. In this case, the communication will be opened for sending and then closed immediately, requiring the receiver to open a new communication in order to respond.

Synchronous devices use the clocking methods cited in Figure 2.7.

- **Guaranteed State Change:** Clocking data is embedded in the data signal itself.
- **Separate Clock Signals:** Clocking data has its own channel, or section of the bandwidth, for the clocking signal.
- **Oversampling:** Clocking functions are managed by the receiving station, which samples signals at a very fast rate to allow the receiver to determine the data flow.

FIGURE 2.7
Clocking Methods Used by Synchronous Devices

The Data Link Layer

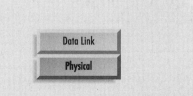

FIGURE 2.8
Building the OSI Model:
The Data Link Layer

Data Link layer

The layer of the OSI Model that is responsible for media access and physical addresses on the network.

Data frames

Units into which the Data Link layer breaks down data into bits for transmission across a physical medium, such as copper wire.

Media Access Control (MAC) layer

A sublayer of the Data Link layer of the OSI Model; responsible for physical addresses on the network.

Logical Link Control (LLC) layer

A sublayer of the Data Link layer of the OSI Model; defines the way network communications take place.

The *Data Link layer* of the OSI Model handles all of the data coming into a computer (receiving) from the network and all of the data leaving the computer (sending) destined for another device on the network.

The Data Link layer begins by setting up a logical connection between the devices that wish to communicate. If a networked device is transmitting information, the Data Link layer takes the data that will be transmitted and packages it into *data frames.* Those data frames are then sent to the Physical layer, which places them on the network cable so they can travel to their destination. The Data Link layer will then listen for an acknowledgement from the receiving station. This acknowledgement means that the destination device has received the transmitted data frames. If the transmitter does not receive this acknowledgement, it will wait a predetermined period and retransmit the data frames.

If a networked device is receiving data, the Data Link layer checks the data frames to ensure that the incoming data has been received successfully. It does this by analyzing bit patterns that are included in the data frames. Once it is satisfied that all of the data was received, the receiving device sends an acknowledgement to the sender.

The Data Link layer is divided into two separate sublayers: the *Media Access Control (MAC) layer* and the *Logical Link Control (LLC) layer* (see Figure 2.9).

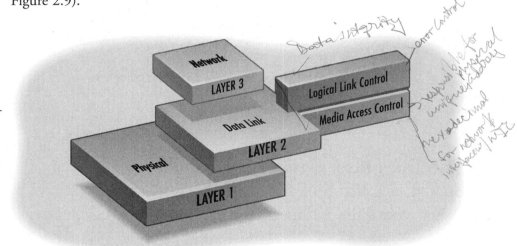

FIGURE 2.9
Sublayers of the Data Link Layer

These two sublayers are discussed in much greater depth in Chapter 3, so a brief explanation will suffice for now.

THE LLC SUBLAYER

The LLC sublayer addresses a set of standards that govern how network communications should take place, allowing vendors to provide consistent network access methods.

Many devices may share the same physical cable. If all of these devices attempt to talk at the same time, transmission problems will occur. The frames will bump into one another, become corrupt, and perhaps never reach their destination. The LLC sublayer ensures that data will be delivered successfully by identifying the methods by which many devices can communicate simultaneously.

The LLC sublayer also determines the standards for two logical topologies used in networking: the logical bus and the logical star. The logical bus follows the same structure as the physical bus: a single cable is used to connect all devices on the segment. Earlier we talked about the star and the ring physical topologies. Chapter 1 noted that the physical ring is often wired in a logical star. This means that although each machine functions with a drop cable from a central device, there is a receiving and a transmitting channel, which together form the physical ring.

The LLC sublayer manages LLC-level error control and LLC-level flow control. Error control management ensures that the data *will* arrive, and in good condition. Flow control manages the amount of data sent in a given period. When two machines are communicating, each machine has a maximum receiving capacity and a maximum transmitting capacity. These limits are identified at the start of a conversation, and the LLC sublayer makes sure that the limits are imposed during the transmission.

THE MAC SUBLAYER

The MAC sublayer is responsible for the unique physical address of a device that participates in a network. The MAC address is built as a hexadecimal number. The MAC address for a *network interface card (NIC)* in your computer might look like this:

02:45:FD:1C:E6:31

Each vendor must guarantee that every network interface card carries a unique address. All vendors keep close track of the MAC addresses they assign to the cards to prevent duplication. Part of each MAC address is a vendor code to identify the manufacturer of the card.

Network interface card (NIC)

Hardware in the form of an expansion card that is installed inside the computer to allow the computer to connect to the network.

The MAC sublayer is where the true media access control takes place. Think of the MAC sublayer as a street stoplight. When the light is red, you must stop your vehicle and allow cross traffic to pass. When the stoplight turns green, you may continue down the street. The MAC layer functions much the same way, permitting or prohibiting data transmission.

The Network Layer

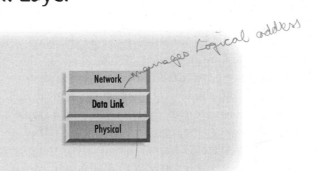

manages Logical addess

The *Network layer* of the OSI Model (Figure 2.10) is where all the action that is important to networking happens. At this layer, we use logical addressing so that machines can identify a unique location, or host, on the network. With all of those machines talking to each other on the local network, and maybe even talking to machines on the public network, the packets being sent with Internet Protocol (IP) addresses in the header or front portion of the PDU must have a systematic way to get from the source machine to the destination machine. This systematic process of getting PDUs or packets from the source machine to the destination machine is called routing. You will hear more about routing. In the case of the Internet, none of this could happen without the TCP/IP suite of protocols to provide all of the transport and services necessary for communication. At this layer we find logical addressing, routing, and the network layer protocols.

Internet Protocol

LOGICAL ADDRESSING AND NETWORK LAYER PROTOCOLS

IP addressing is a special way to provide a unique identifier for each and every device attached to each and every network and internetwork in the world. That is a lot of logical addresses. This addressing scheme is based on binary mathematics—a system of calculations using just 0 and 1.
In Chapter 8, we discuss exactly how this addressing scheme works and how to manipulate it to provide addresses for your network.

Another commonly used network protocol is IPX/SPX, Novell's Internet Packet Exchange/Sequenced Packet Exchange protocol. Like IP, IPX provides a logical address to all nodes on the network that will uniquely identify them and allow them to advertise services to the network.

ROUTING

Routing functions provide the systematic method for moving a packet from the source machine to the destination machine across multiple networks. Special devices called routers handle these packets in a "store and forward" method. The router receives the packet, stores it while it figures out the best path to send the packet on its way to the destination, and then forwards it down that path. Routers learn about the path to destination addresses from other routers on the network. These devices are often a chatty bunch, exchanging information about routes every 30 seconds or so. This keeps all routers on the network up to date on the best path to take. The information learned from other routers is stored in the routing table on each router. Routers that exchange information with each other are known as dynamic routers.

When we want routers to talk to each other about the network, we use a routing protocol. Two of the most common routing protocols are Routing Information Protocol (RIP) and Open Shortest Path First (OSPF).

Sometimes we do not want those routers chatting on the network because it increases traffic and can slow down data communications. We can build our own routing tables by typing in the destination network address and other information. This is known as static routing.

The Transport Layer

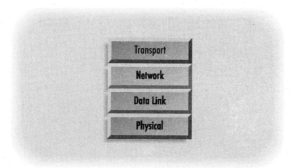

FIGURE 2.11
Building the OSI Model:
The Transport Layer

Transport layer

The layer of the OSI Model that provides reliable and guaranteed delivery of data packets through the network or internetwork.

The *Transport layer* (Figure 2.11) takes charge of making sure the data is transmitted reliably between nodes. Several important functions provide this reliability.

The Transport layer breaks long packets into segments that conform to the maximum size tolerated by the type of network you happen to be running. For example, Ethernet networks have a maximum packet size of 1,500 bytes. Any packet exceeding this size would be broken down into multiple segments, and each of those segments would be sequentially numbered. When the packets arrive at the destination, the sequence numbers allow the data to be reassembled into the proper sequence and read by upper layers.

Transport layer protocols also manage the rate of transmission between sending and receiving nodes, known as flow control. The sending node must understand how fast to transmit the data. The receiving node will inform the sending node of its capacity. To understand why this is important, think about a friend who speaks very quickly. When holding a conversation with that friend, you can process the conversation only at a certain rate. But if your friend speaks so fast that you find yourself losing parts of the conversation, you have to stop and ask your friend to repeat what she said. This could be avoided if, at the beginning of the conversation, you had asked your friend to speak more slowly.

Another important function of the Transport layer is to acknowledge when a packet has been received. This is known as the ACK. If the transmission contained errors, the receiving node would then request a retransmission of the bad packet, providing error-free transmission of data.

The Session Layer

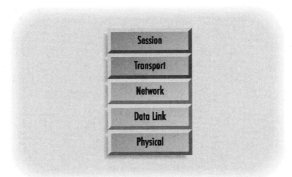

FIGURE 2.12
Building the OSI Model: The Session Layer

The *Session layer* of the OSI Model (Figure 2.12) structures the session, or conversation, between two nodes. This layer sets up the conversation, discussing the ground rules, maintaining the exchange, and closing the session. You can think of the Session layer as the police officer in charge of traffic.

To understand the functions of the Session layer, think about the process that takes place when you make a telephone call. The sender picks up the phone and dials the number of a friend (receiver). The phone rings and is answered by the friend. The sender says, "Hello, this is Joe," to establish the conversation. The two friends carry on the conversation. When the sending friend speaks too fast, the receiving friend can ask, "Would you please repeat that. I didn't understand." The sender can then repeat the words to make sure the receiver gets the message clearly. When the sender has completed the conversation, the two parties can agree to terminate the conversation (or session). In this example, each of the control elements—establishing the session, discussing topics, repeating parts of the conversation due to errors, and terminating the call—are functions of the Session layer.

The Presentation Layer

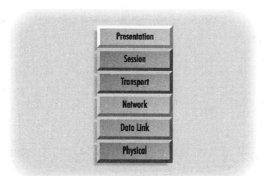

Session layer

The layer of the OSI Model that defines the session between two nodes, including the setup, maintenance, and closure of the conversation. This layer also manages "friendly" names for nodes on the network using NetBIOS.

FIGURE 2.13
Building the OSI Model:
The Presentation Layer

Presentation layer

The layer of the OSI Model that makes sure that the data format can be understood between the sending and receiving nodes. This layer also manages encryption and compression.

Presentation layer (Figure 2.13) functions are best described as translators. This layer makes sure that the data format, or presentation, is appropriate for the computer system. Most computer systems use the American Standard Code for Information Interchange (ASCII) format for character generation. Several other formats also are possible, including Extended Binary Coded Decimal Interchange Code (EBCDIC), which is used by mainframe computers and some IBM systems. In order to exchange information between systems using different character formats, a translation from one to the other must occur. This is one of the responsibilities of the Presentation layer.

This layer also manages encryption and decryption of data. When you purchase goods over the Internet and you provide your personal information such as name, address, telephone number, and credit card information, that data must be encrypted to protect it from theft during transmission. The Presentation layer takes care of the details. Should you enable compression (or compaction) of data for storage on a hard drive, this layer will take care of those functions as well.

IN REAL LIFE

One special term we have not defined yet is "gateway." A gateway is a translator between two different network environments. Gateways can be software or hardware. A common use for a gateway is with e-mail services. Different e-mail applications cannot directly communicate with each other, so an e-mail gateway is installed with the software, allowing LAN-based e-mail messages to be translated into SMTP (the Internet e-mail service) messages.

The Application Layer

FIGURE 2.14
Building the OSI Model: The Application Layer

Application layer

The layer of the OSI Model that provides services to applications running on computers on the network.

The *Application layer* (Figure 2.14) is often erroneously called the user interface layer of the OSI Model. Rather, this layer provides the services that applications need to do the work we ask them to do. Those services reflect a set of standards that allow any application to use them if needed. Some of those services include file transfer, print access, e-mail transmission, and file management.

Without the Application layer services, someone using Microsoft Exchange Server and Outlook to read his e-mail could not send to or receive messages from a friend using Novell GroupWise as her e-mail application.

In the following section you will see a table listing some of the protocols that function at this layer, and you will recognize them as service providers to applications you run every day.

Putting It All Together

Before we leave our discussion of the OSI Model, it will be helpful to you to understand how all of these functions fit together in an integrated model. In Table 2.2 you see a representation of the OSI Model, its function, devices commonly associated with that model, and protocols that function at a specific point in the model. Do not worry about topics we have not discussed yet. In upcoming chapters you will find answers to many questions you might have now. Also keep in mind that this is not a comprehensive table. Rather, it serves as an example and will be extremely valuable as a study aid.

TEST TIP

Be sure to know each of the layers of the OSI Model and their function and associated devices.

OSI MODEL	FUNCTION	PROTOCOLS	DEVICES	DATA UNITS
Application layer	Services to applications	FTP, DNS, NDS, SMTP, HTTP, TFTP, TELNET, NCP, SMB, MIME, SNMP, BOOTP	Gateways	APDU
Presentation layer	Data format		Gateway, Redirector	PPDU
Session layer	Connection maintenance	RPC, Named Pipes, NetBIOS	Gateway	SPDU
Transport layer	Reliable delivery of data, segmentation, sequencing	TCP, UDP, SPX, NetBEUI/NetBIOS, ATP	Gateway, Router	TPDU
Network layer	Logical addressing, routing	IP, ARP, RARP, RIP, OSPF, IGMP, ICMP, IPX, NWLink, NetBEUI,	Routers, layer 3 Switches, Router	Packet
Data Link layer	Logical connections, media access	IEEE 802.2 LLC, MAC 802.3 CSMA/CD, 802.4 token bus, 802.5 Token Ring	Bridge, layer 2 Switches, ISDN Router	Frame
Physical layer	Physical topology, bit synchronization, physical media, signal type	IEEE 802, IEEE 802.2, ISDN	Hub, MAU, Repeater, Transceiver, Multiplexer (MUX), NIC	Bit

TABLE 2.2
The Seven Layers of the OSI Model and Their Key Characteristics

STUDY GUIDE

Through the course of this chapter, we learned about the Open Systems Interconnection Model (OSI Model) that forms the framework for data communications and its importance in the field of networking. We also looked at the specific characteristics of each layer.

THE OSI MODEL

- The OSI Model was designed by the International Organization for Standardization (ISO) as a structural framework for the rules of data communications.
- This model allows any vendor who adheres to the framework to design a component for data communications with the assurance that it can be used with products from any other vendor and provide seamless interoperability.

THE PHYSICAL LAYER

The Physical layer defines the way data is transmitted over the physical connections of the network. Other component characteristics of this layer include physical topology, connection types, signal type, baseband and broadband, and bit synchronization.

PHYSICAL TOPOLOGY

Star

- The star topology is the most commonly used physical layout for networks today.
- When building a star topology, a hub or switch will be the central device connecting all nodes on the segment.
- When a node fails, there are three places where the failure can occur: the port on the hub, the cable connecting the node to the hub, or the network interface on the node itself.
- A star topology is relatively easy to set up, and it can be expanded as long as the physical limitations are not exceeded.

Bus

- The bus topology is the easiest to install and the most difficult to troubleshoot.

- Cables must be terminated.
- The bus topology has strict physical limitations to cable length and distance from other nodes.
- Connector types include vampire clamps for Thicknet and t-connectors for Thin Ethernet.

Mesh

- Mesh networks provide redundant links between all nodes on the network, thus creating a fault-tolerant data communications topology.
- The mesh network is time-consuming and somewhat expensive to install because of the multiple connections between nodes.
- Troubleshooting mesh networks is relatively easy because the failure points are easily identified.

Ring

- The ring topology connects nodes in a circle, allowing only nodes directly connected to talk to each other.
- Data is transmitted in a single direction only.
- A node can accept and respond to packets addressed to it, then pass the packets on to the next node on the ring.

Wireless

- A wireless topology relies on either radio frequency (RF) or infrared (IR) frequencies, or channels, to connect directly to each other or to access points (APs).
- Wireless communication devices connect, or network, using either ad hoc or infrastructure networking.

CONNECTION TYPES

- Point-to-point connections occur when two computers are connected and exchange information. An example is a modem connection.
- Multipoint connections use many devices connected to transmission media, sharing the available bandwidth. The corporate network is an example.

SIGNAL TYPES

- There are two broad categories of signal types: digital and analog.
- Analog signals use constantly varying voltages, or waves.

- Digital signals use electrical pulses.
- All signals are subject to deterioration of the signal over distance or attenuation.
- Each category of signal has a set of specific encoding schemes that allow for the efficient transmission of the data.

Baseband versus Broadband

- Baseband and broadband refer to the way the signals are passed across the media.
- Baseband transmission requires a single transmission to use the entire bandwidth.
- Broadband transmission allows many signals to share the same bandwidth.
- Broadband traffic is more efficient for data transmission.

Bit Synchronization

- Bit synchronization is the timing function that allows devices to understand the beginning and end of a transmission.
- Asynchronous transmissions require that a start bit begin the transmission and a stop bit close the transmission.
- Synchronous transmissions use a clocking signal to identify the beginning and end of a transmission.

The Data Link Layer

- The Data Link layer is subdivided into two sublayers known as the Logical Link Control layer (LLC) and the Media Access Control layer (MAC).
- The LLC is responsible for the standards that govern how network communication will take place.
- The MAC maintains the physical addressing scheme used by nodes connected on a network, allowing each node to be uniquely identified as a participant on the network.

The Network Layer

- The Network layer is responsible for two important functions: logical addressing of nodes on the network or internetwork and routing of packets from source to destination.

- The logical addressing scheme used most frequently is Internet Protocol (IP) addressing, a binary method for building large numbers of unique addresses.
- Routing is a "store and forward" action that allows the best path to be chosen when sending a packet from a source node to a destination node.

THE TRANSPORT LAYER

- The Transport layer makes sure that data is transmitted reliably between nodes.
- This layer also segments large packets based on the type of network.
- Each segment is given a sequence number so that the receiving node can recreate the message correctly.
- Transport layer functions also include flow control, or the management of the rate of data transmission.
- To maintain reliable delivery of segments, this layer will issue either an ACK (acknowledgement) or a request for retransmission if errors are detected.

THE SESSION LAYER

- Session layer functions include the management of sessions, or conversations, between nodes.

THE PRESENTATION LAYER

- The Presentation layer makes sure that both nodes understand in what format the data will arrive.
- It functions as a translator when two different data formats are present.
- Encryption and decryption are managed at this layer.
- Compression and decompression of data are managed at this layer.

THE APPLICATION LAYER

- The Application layer provides services to software applications.
- Some of these functions include file access services, printing services, e-mail services, file transfer services, and file management services.

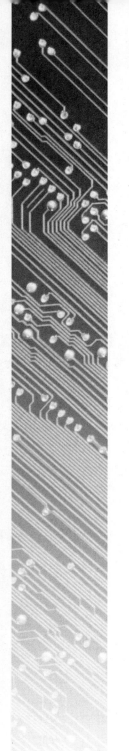

PRACTICE TEST

Try this test to check your mastery of the concepts in this chapter.

1. The OSI Model for networking and data communications provides
   a. a set of standard configurations.
   b. a framework for standards.
   c. structural rules for data communications.
   d. a list of vendor devices that work together.

2. The layer of the OSI Model that is responsible for error-free delivery is the
   a. Physical layer.
   b. Network layer.
   c. Transport layer.
   d. Application layer.

3. A _____ topology connects many computers across multiple paths.
   a. ring
   b. star
   c. mesh
   d. bus

4. _____ communication employs the bit synchronization method that uses stop bits and start bits.
   a. Polysynchronous
   b. Synchronous
   c. Multisynchronous
   d. Asynchronous

5. Which of the following is a MAC address?
   a. 127.0.0.1
   b. 06:G1:45:72:B0:47:D3:4C
   c. BB:BB:BB:BB:BB:BB
   d. 197.45.43.231

6. The _____ network topology is easiest to reconfigure.
   a. ring
   b. star
   c. mesh
   d. bus

7. Messages are broken into appropriate-sized packages by the _____ layer of the OSI Model.
   a. Presentation
   b. Session
   c. Transport Data Link
   d. Network

8. Digital signaling converts the bits to a(n) _____ format for transmission.
   a. electrical
   b. mechanical
   c. light
   d. electromagnetic

9. _____ causes signals to degrade over distance.
   a. Multiplication
   b. Attenuation
   c. Diminution
   d. Channeling

10. Synchronous communication requires that a _____ be sent with the transmission to make sure the receiving node understands where the message starts and stops.
    a. stop and start bit
    b. marker
    c. clocking signal
    d. designator

11. Two functions of the Network layer of the OSI Model are
    a. bridging.
    b. routing.
    c. logical transmissions.
    d. logical addressing.

12. To provide reliable data delivery, protocols functioning at the Transport layer of the OSI Model send a(n) _____ to let the sending node know that the packet has been delivered.
    a. DACK
    b. RACK
    c. NACK
    d. ACK

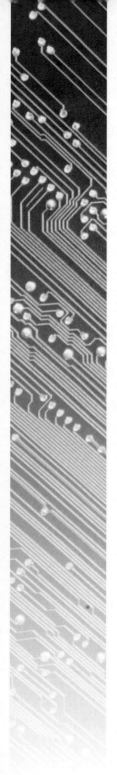

13. The purpose of a _____ is to translate between two different network environments.
    a. doorway
    b. gateway
    c. connector
    d. by-pass

14. Beyond data format translation, the Presentation layer is responsible for
    a. encryption and decryption.
    b. logical addressing and physical addressing.
    c. language translation and language usage.
    d. compression and decompression.

15. A network interface card operates at the _____ and _____ layers of the OSI Model.
    a. Network
    b. Data Link
    c. Transport
    d. Physical

TROUBLESHOOTING

You are working the help desk for your company. A user calls to say that she cannot get access to the network. You go to the user's desk, check for lights on the network interface card, and find none. This problem represents a failure at what layer of the OSI Model?

FOR MORE INFORMATION

For links to Web sites that provide further information about the topics covered in this chapter, go to the EMC/Paradigm Internet Resource Center at www.emcp.com/College Division/Internet Resource Centers/Networking/System Administration/Web Resources: For More Information.

(handwritten note at top of page): http://www.comtia.org/certification/Network
✓ click Prepare for Exam

IEEE Specifications and Their Characteristics

3

Network+ Examination
- **Objective 1.2:** Specify the main features of 802.2 (LLC), 802.3 (Ethernet), 802.5 (token ring), 802.11b (wireless), and FDDI network technologies, including
  - Speed
  - Access
  - Method
  - Topology
  - Media

ON THE JOB

In the early days of networking, which really were not that long ago, many companies were working to develop new computing and networking technologies. In their rush to get these new products to market, several things happened. First, some of these new products were not very good and did not work very well. Second, many times they were proprietary products. That is, these products were particular to one company and would not work well or at all with another company's products.

As computers and networking began to get really popular, some people in the industry saw a need to establish *standards* for these new technologies. Standards typically ensure that products function at the level promised by the manufacturer and also that they will work with other vendors' products.

Standards

Specifications that ensure that products will function at the level promised by the manufacturer and will work with other vendors' products.

Last, standards serve to narrow the focus of companies working on a specific technology. For example, the 802.11 standard provides guidelines for companies that want to make products for the wireless communications market. The 802.11 standard sets the guidelines, or rules, that manufacturers should follow if they intend to make these products. Although manufacturers are not legally required to follow these standards, failure to do so may result in a product that is not compatible with anyone else's, leading to failure in the market.

Understanding Project 802 Standards

In February 1980, the Institute of Electrical and Electronics Engineers (IEEE) began working to establish standards for local area networks (LANs) and metropolitan area networks (MANs). The results of this effort became known as *Project 802* (80 for the year 1980 and 2 for the month of February). The IEEE 802 standards address hardware that interacts with the Physical and Data Link layers of the Open Systems Interconnection (OSI) Model. Specifically, the 802 standards establish requirements for components such as network interface cards, wide area networking components, and the components used to make twisted pair and coaxial cable networks.

Project 802 has been expanded over the years to include many different facets of networking technology. Whenever a new technology, such as wireless communication, is introduced, a committee is formed to investigate and make recommendations on that technology. The committee results are often published as standards. These standards are written to address how networking should occur between devices that are using that particular technology.

Each committee is assigned an 802.*X* number, with the *X* indicating the actual committee number. For example, the 802.11 committee developed and issued the wireless networking standards; therefore, the standards are known as 802.11 standards. In some cases the number will also be assigned a letter designation, such as 802.11b. The letter denotes a specific technology under the broader category. For example, while the 802.11 committee addresses wireless networking, 802.11b addresses coding techniques that are particular to wireless networking. Table 3.1 identifies the current 802 standards.

Project 802

A set of standards created by the Institute of Electrical and Electronics Engineers (IEEE) that establishes requirements for hardware that interacts with the Physical and Data Link layers of the Open Systems Interconnection (OSI) Model.

Standard	Defines
802.1	Network management.
802.2	General standards for the Logical Link Control sublayer of the Data Link layer.
802.3	Networks using Carrier Sense Multiple Access with Collision Detection (CSMA/CD). This is the Ethernet standard. The 802.3u standard addresses fast Ethernet.
802.4	MAC sublayer standards for bus networks using token-passing (token bus) networks.
802.5	MAC sublayer standards for Token Ring networks.
802.6	Metropolitan area networks (MANs).
802.7	Broadband local area network (LAN) standards.
802.9	Integrated voice-data networks.
802.10	Network security on LANs and MANs.
802.11	Wireless network standards.
802.12	Demand Priority Access LAN, 100BaseVG-AnyLAN.
802.15	Personal area networks.
802.16	Broadband wireless standards.
802.17	Resilient Packet Ring Access Protocol.

TABLE 3.1.
Current 802 Standards

TEST TIP

If presented with an 802 committee number, know which technology that committee addresses.

IN REAL LIFE

In many publications, you may find the 802.8 standard linked to fiber-optic standards. The 802.8 committee has been disbanded, so that standard is now referred to as Fiber Distributed Data Interface (FDDI).

Although Project 802 has addressed many technologies, this chapter will focus on only those standards required for the examination:

- 802.2
- 802.3
- 802.5
- FDDI
- 0802.11

Project 802 standards are primarily concerned with the Data Link layer of the OSI Model. Before discussing these standards, a brief review of the Data Link layer and its sublayers will be helpful.

The Data Link Layer

You will remember from Chapter 2 that the Data Link layer of the OSI Model handles all of the data a computer receives from the network and all of the data a computer sends to other devices on the network.

The Data Link layer begins by setting up a logical connection for communication between devices. If a networked device is transmitting information, the Data Link layer takes the data that will be transmitted and packages it into data frames. Those data frames are then sent to the Physical layer, which places them on the network cable so they can travel to their destination. The Data Link layer will then listen for an acknowledgement from the receiving station. This acknowledgement means that the destination device has received the transmitted data frames. If the transmitter does not receive this acknowledgement, it will wait a predetermined period of time and retransmit the data frames.

If a networked device is receiving data, the Data Link layer checks the data frames to ensure that the incoming data has been received successfully. It does this by analyzing bit patterns that are included in the data frames. Once it is satisfied that all of the data was received, the receiving device sends an acknowledgement to the sender.

You will recall that the Data Link layer is divided into two separate sublayers: the Media Access Control (MAC) layer and the Logical Link Control (LLC) layer. (As a reminder, Figure 2.9 in Chapter 2 is repeated here as Figure 3.1.)

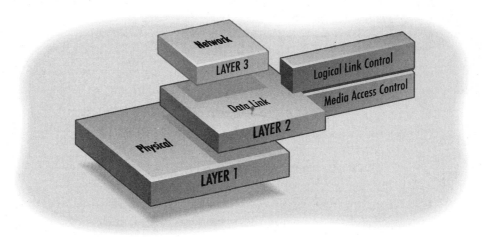

FIGURE 3.1
Sublayers of the Data Link Layer

802.2: Logical Link Control (LLC)

The 802.2 standard defines how network communications should take place within the Logical Link Control (LLC) sublayer. The LLC acts as an interface between the MAC sublayer and the *Network layer* of the OSI Model by managing data frames that it sends and receives through the Physical layer components (network interface card, cable, connectors, etc).

The Data Link layer controls access to the network cable and dictates how data that comes from upper layers of the OSI Model, in the form of either packets or datagrams, is placed into data frames for delivery to a destination device on the network. When the LLC receives information from the Network layer, it formats the data so that the appropriate *port,* or *service access point,* on the destination device can read it.

The data is then passed down through the Media Access Control (MAC) sublayer. The MAC adds the *physical address* of the destination computer to the data frame. The physical address (commonly called the MAC address) is obtained from the network interface card (NIC) of the destination device. The MAC sublayer passes the data frames to the networking components that operate at the Physical layer. These components then transmit the data frames across the network cable to the destination.

Port, or service access point

The software process, or service, on a destination device through which data is received.

Physical (MAC) address

The 48-bit address on the NIC that serves as the network address for the device. When displayed, it appears as 12 digits, grouped into pairs, separated by dashes; for example: 00-04-5A-6C-98-06.

TRY IT!

View the MAC address of a Windows computer with an installed network interface card.

1. On a computer running Windows NT, 2000, or XP, at a command prompt, type the following command: IPCONFIG/ALL
2. On a computer running Windows 95, 98, or ME, at a command prompt, type the following command: WINIPCFG

When the LLC communicates upward to the Network layer, it uses either connectionless or connection-oriented mode.

- **Connectionless mode:** When using *connectionless mode*, the LLC simply sends out packets of information. It does not check to determine whether the intended station actually receives the information, and it has no error-checking device or control in place to monitor this flow of information. As a result, connectionless communication tends to be fast. Connectionless mode is also known as a Type 1 operation.

  Think of connectionless communication as mailing a letter through the postal system. After you write your letter (data), you place it in an envelope that contains a sending address, a destination address, and the desired postage (frame). To send the letter, you drop it into a post office box. Although the postal system is usually reliable, there is always a chance the letter will get dropped, lost, or sent to the wrong destination. If you want to verify delivery, another mechanism is required. For example, you could call the recipient and ask if she received the letter, or you could use some other service that the post office has to offer. An example of a connectionless protocol is IP (Internet Protocol), which is part of the TCP/IP protocol suite.

- **Connection-oriented mode:** In *connection-oriented mode*, the receiving node sends a message to the sending node, acknowledging when it received the information. As a result, this mode has the ability to error check, or to make sure all of the data frames sent from the sending device actually reach the destination. A side effect of this error checking is that connection-oriented mode is slower than connectionless mode; however, it is a more reliable method of communication. Connection-oriented mode is also known as a Type 2 operation.

  Think of connection-oriented communications as a phone call. When you wish to call someone, you pick up the phone, dial a number, and wait for someone to answer. Once they answer, you have established a connection between the two parties. As long as that connection remains in place, you are able to send and receive information. Since you get immediate feedback from the other party, you can be assured that the desired information is delivered. An example of a connection-oriented protocol is TCP (Transmission Control Protocol), which is also a part of the TCP/IP protocol suite.

IEEE Specifications and Their Characteristics

When using connection-oriented mode, the LLC monitors the flow of data between nodes and checks the data for errors through a process called *cyclical redundancy checking (CRC)*. CRC begins prior to transmitting a packet, when the sending device executes a mathematical formula using the data. The results of that computation, known as a *checksum*, are included with the transmitted data. Once the data is received, the receiver runs the same formula and compares the results (checksums) to ensure data integrity. If the checksums do not match, the receiving computer will destroy the frame and ask the sender to transmit it again.

Network communications within the LLC sublayer work exactly the same on all network topologies. In general, the LLC sublayer provides an interface between the protocols (IPX/SPX, TCP/IP) being used on the network and the type of *network access method* being used (Ethernet, Token Ring). Network access methods provide rules concerning how stations communicate while sharing a common cabling system. That is, since computer networks contain many devices and the devices all need to communicate, they must find a way to share the network media to ensure that transmitted data does not become corrupted.

802.3: Carrier Sense Multiple Access with Collision Detection (CSMA/CD)

The IEEE standards covered in *802.3* relate to *Ethernet* networking. Specifically, 802.3 defines how the *Carrier Sense Multiple Access with Collision Detection (CSMA/CD)* network access method operates over different types of media, such as coaxial, twisted pair, and fiber-optic cabling. The term "Ethernet" originally referred to network standards developed jointly by Digital, Intel, and Xerox; therefore, it is occasionally called the DIX standard.

Ethernet uses the CSMA/CD access method, which provides rules concerning how stations communicate while sharing a common cabling system. When CSMA/CD stations want to broadcast on the network, they must first exercise "carrier sense"; that is, they must listen for other transmissions. If there is no traffic, then "multiple access" is possible; any station can transmit data. If two stations begin to transmit simultaneously, then collisions can occur, and "collision detection" is needed. If a collision occurs, the stations will adjust their transmitting algorithm, wait a period of time, and try to transmit again (see Figure 3.2).

Cyclical redundancy checking (CRC)

A process used with connection-oriented mode in which the LLC checks network data for errors between sending and receiving nodes and retransmits data when it loses integrity.

Checksum

A count of the number of bits in a transmission that can be compared with the Checksum field in the packet. If the numbers agree, the packet has arrived safely. If the numbers disagree, the packet must be retransmitted.

Network access method

A set of communication rules that allows multiple devices on a network to share cabling without corrupting data during transmission.

Ethernet, or 802.3

The IEEE standard for the CSMA/CD network access method, which enables multiple nodes to share a common cabling system. Developed jointly by Digital, Intel, and Xerox, Ethernet is sometimes called DIX.

Carrier Sense Multiple Access with Collision Detection (CSMA/CD)

A network access method with rules concerning how Ethernet stations communicate while sharing a common cabling system. When a collision is detected, transmission is halted and the data is resent later.

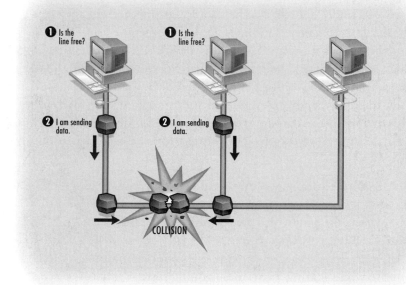

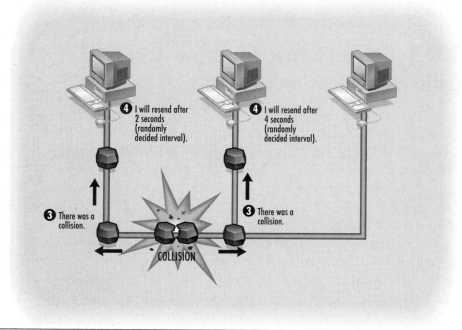

FIGURE 3.2
Carrier Sense Multiple Access
with Collision Detection

IEEE Specifications and Their Characteristics

TestTip

Ethernet uses the Carrier Sense Multiple Access with Collision Detection (CSMA/CD) network access method.

TestTip

Collisions in an Ethernet network are common and require no corrective action, unless they begin to occur at a rapid rate and slow network traffic significantly.

A variant of CSMA/CD is *Carrier Sense Multiple Access with Collision Avoidance (CSMA/CA).* Instead of detecting collisions and resending later, CSMA/CA attempts to avoid the collisions completely. When devices want to communicate on the cable, they listen to ensure no other devices are transmitting. If the channel is clear, the device will transmit its signal. If the device detects traffic on the network, it will choose a "back off factor," which is a random amount of time the node will wait before attempting to transmit again. Once that period of time expires, the device will begin transmitting. AppleTalk networks use the CSMA/CA access method.

Carrier Sense Multiple Access with Collision Avoidance (CSMA/CA)

A media access method with rules concerning how nodes communicate while sharing a common cabling system. In this case, transmission collisions are avoided completely rather than being detected and later resending the data.

In Real Life

The industry typically uses the name Ethernet to refer to any network that uses the CSMA/CD network access method. The correct name is IEEE 802.3; however, almost all vendors and publications refer to it as simply Ethernet.

A network that meets 802.3 standards has the following characteristics:
- Uses a star or bus topology.
  - Although the physical topologies differ, in both cases a single Ethernet signal is carried simultaneously to all stations on the segment. In other words, the entire cable segment operates as a single communication channel, and transmissions made at one computer are broadcast to all other computers on the cable segment.
- Uses the following media:
  - Thinnet (10Base-2): Thinnet coaxial cable can support data transfer speeds of 10Mbps. Thinnet segments are limited to 185 meters (approximately 607 feet). If additional length is needed, a repeater is required.

- Thicknet (10Base-5): Thicknet coaxial cable can support data transfer speeds of 10Mbps. Thicknet segments can extend 500 meters (approximately 1,640 feet). If additional length is needed, a repeater is required.
- Twisted pair wiring (10Base-T): Shielded or unshielded twisted pair cable (STP or UTP) supports a data transfer rate up to 10Mbps. The segment between network devices (when wired as a star) can extend 100 meters (approximately 328 feet).
- Fiber-optic cabling (10Base-FX): Uses fiber-optic cable with a segment length up to 4 kilometers with transmission at 100Mbps.
- Fast Ethernet (100Base-TX): Uses Category 5 UTP or Category 1 STP cable to attain speeds of 100Mbps.
- Fast Ethernet (100Base-T4): Uses four pairs of Category 3, 4, or 5 UTP wiring to achieve speeds of 100Mbps.

- Uses the CSMA/CD access method.
- A repeater can be used to extend an Ethernet LAN by amplifying and retiming the data signals.

802.5: Token Ring

802.5

The IEEE standard that identifies the access protocols, cabling, and interfaces for Token Ring LANs.

Token Ring

A network that is set up with a ring topology and that uses packets called tokens to transmit data from node to node.

Deterministic

Used to describe a topology in which stations access the network in a predetermined sequence.

The *802.5* standard identifies the access protocols, cabling, and interfaces for Token Ring LANs. Token Ring is an IBM standard that came to prominence in the mid-1980s.

Token Ring, or token passing, networks use a special type of data packet known as a token. A Token Ring network is said to be *deterministic,* because the sequence in which stations access the network is predetermined. A single token travels around the ring, from computer to computer (see Figure 3.3). If a computer has data to transmit, it removes the token from the ring, attaches its data to the token, and places the token back into the ring. As the token travels around the ring, each device will read the destination address to determine if it is for them. If not, the computer will send the token to the next station in the ring. If the destination address matches that of the device, it will remove the data and modify the token to show that it was properly received. It then places the token back on the network, addressed to the original sender. When the sender receives the modified token indicating the information was received, it can either attach more data to it and repeat the process or clear the token and place it back in the ring for other devices to use. Since there is only one token on the network at a time, there are no collisions to contend with.

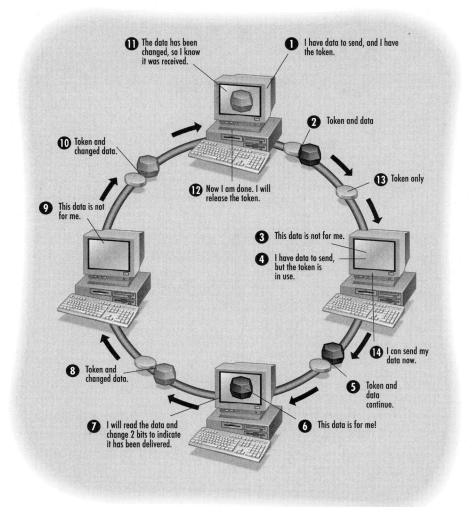

Figure content labels:
- 11 The data has been changed, so I know it was received.
- 1 I have data to send, and I have the token.
- 2 Token and data
- 10 Token and changed data.
- 13 Token only
- 9 This data is not for me.
- 12 Now I am done. I will release the token.
- 3 This data is not for me.
- 4 I have data to send, but the token is in use.
- 8 Token and changed data.
- 14 I can send my data now.
- 5 Token and data continue.
- 7 I will read the data and change 2 bits to indicate it has been delivered.
- 6 This data is for me!

FIGURE 3.3
Token Passing

Token Ring networks use several different methods of detecting and compensating for network faults. For example, one station on the Token Ring network is selected to be the *active monitor*. This station monitors network activities such as the timing of the circulating token. It will also remove frames that continue to circle around the ring, which is commonly caused when a sending device experiences a failure. A token that continues to circle the ring prevents other stations from transmitting and can eventually cause the network to stop working. The active monitor attempts to detect these frames and remove them from the ring; then the monitor generates a new token.

Active monitor

A station on a ring network that monitors network activities, such as the timing of a circulating token, to prevent network failures.

In the token, a field exists in which workstations can request a higher than normal priority for their transmission. A regulation mechanism is built that prevents one station from keeping a token for too long a period of time. The purpose of priority is to grant a station a longer period of time to transmit before releasing the token. Other stations on the network compare the workstation's request with their own priority levels. If the workstation's priority is higher than theirs, the workstation is granted access to the token for longer periods of time. Workstations can override these priority requests when necessary.

A network that meets 802.5 standards has the following characteristics:

- Uses a ring topology.
- Supports a data transfer rate up to 16Mbps.
- Commonly uses UTP or STP, two pairs per station. Fiber-optic cable may also be used.
- Supports up to 250 stations per ring.

Although Token Ring networks use a ring topology, it physically appears as a star. Internally, signals travel around the network from one station to the next in a ring. Each station is directly connected to a central hub, called a multistation access unit (MAU) (see Figure 3.4). The MAU uses a ring-in/ring-out configuration to move data around the network.

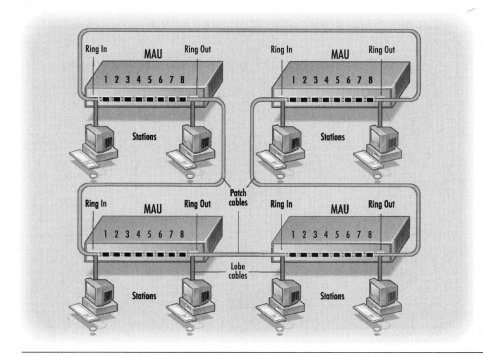

FIGURE 3.4
Token Ring Network with
MAU

When a token passing network experiences a hardware error, such as a break in a cable, a process known as *beaconing* takes place. Beaconing establishes a *fault domain* (see Figure 3.5), which isolates the area of the network where the error occurred in an attempt to recover from the error. A fault domain consists of

- the station reporting the failure (the beaconing station);
- the next station upstream from the beaconing station (also known as the nearest active upstream neighbor (NAUN); and
- the section of cable that connects the two stations.

Beaconing

The process of establishing a fault domain when a hardware error occurs on a token passing network.

Fault domain

An area on a token passing network that has been isolated in an attempt to recover from a hardware error.

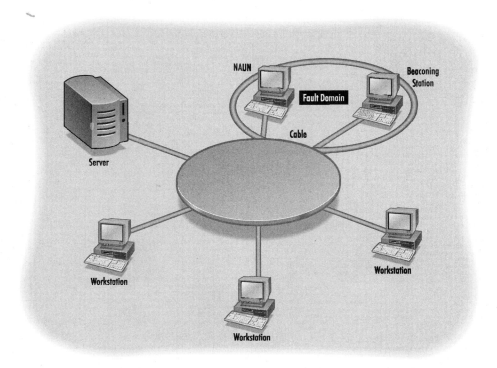

FIGURE 3.5
Establishing a Fault Domain

When the beaconing process begins, all stations on the ring are notified that communications have been suspended. Called ring poll/neighbor notification, this notification process also informs each station of the address of its nearest upstream neighbor and identifies the members within the failure domain.

Beaconing then initiates a process called *auto reconfiguration.* In auto reconfiguration, devices located within the failure domain automatically perform diagnostics in an attempt to reconfigure the network around the failed area. If the stations involved are not able to resolve the problem, user intervention is required.

Fiber Distributed Data Interface (FDDI) LANS and MANS

Fiber Distributed Data Interface (FDDI, pronounced "fiddy") is a high-speed networking standard originally designed for fiber-optic cable.

Auto reconfiguration

A part of the beaconing process in which devices located within the failure domain automatically perform diagnostics in an attempt to reconfigure the network around the failed area.

Fiber Distributed Data Interface (FDDI)

A high-speed networking standard originally designed for fiber-optic cable.

FDDI-based networks are another type of token passing technology. In a FDDI network layout, a pair of fiber-optic rings connects all of the devices (see Figure 3.6). Each ring contains a single token, and the two tokens travel in opposite directions between the devices. If a break or other problem occurs in the primary ring, the secondary ring acts as a backup, ensuring that data continues to move on the network.

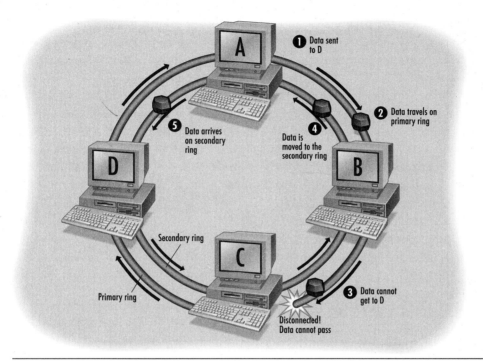

FIGURE 3.6
FDDI Network with Dual Rings

Most devices that are connected to the network are dual-attached, which means that the device is attached to both rings. The dual-attached station has two ports:
• A port, on which the primary ring comes in and the secondary ring goes out.
• B port, on which the secondary ring comes in and the primary goes out.
Some devices use one or more M ports. An M port is used for stations that are attached to only one ring. Stations that utilize an M port are called *concentrators*.

The sequence in which stations communicate on the network is predetermined. When a station wants to transmit data, it captures the token that is circling around the network from one device to the next. Possession of the token gives a station the right-of-way to transmit data.

Concentrator

A device that functions like a hub to combine transmissions from a cluster of nodes. Concentrators are used in fiber-optic networks.

This station appends its data to the token and then releases the token back onto the network. The header of the token includes the address of the destination device. As the token circulates around the network, all of the devices will stop the token and read the destination address to see if the data is intended for them. If the data is not intended for a particular station, that station will drop the token back into the ring. If the station is the intended recipient, the station removes the data from the token and then places the token back onto the network to return to the sending station. The sending station then strips the header, or control, information from the token and drops it back into the ring so other stations may transmit.

Since FDDI networks are fault tolerant and support high data transmission speeds, they are commonly used for network backbones. Because these networks are more expensive to implement than wire ones, in many cases they are being replaced by less expensive 100Base-TX Ethernet.

A network that meets FDDI standards has the following characteristics:

- Uses single-mode or multimode fiber-optic cabling.
- Supports speed up to 100Mbps.
- Can extend to distances up to 60 miles.
- Commonly used for network backbones.
- Much more expensive to implement than wire (UTP/STP/coaxial) based networks.

802.11: Wireless LANS

802.11

The IEEE standard that addresses the actions that must take place at the Physical layer and Media Access Control sublayer for communications to occur on a wireless LAN.

In 1997 the IEEE ratified the specification for *802.11*. This standard addresses the actions that must take place at the Physical layer and the Media Access Control (MAC) sublayer for communications to occur on a wireless local area network (LAN).

The 802.11 standard is designed to provide network access for computing devices regardless of where they are located physically. To obtain this physical independence, devices use radio waves rather than network cabling. Wireless networks use the Ethernet low-level protocol, which behaves the same on a wireless network as it does on an Ethernet network that uses wire. The 802.11 standard addresses transmission requirements at both the Physical and Media Access Control layers of the OSI Model. The Physical layer handles the actual data transmission duties between devices. The transmission medium can be frequency-hopping spread spectrum, direct-sequence spread spectrum, or infrared-pulse position modulation.

The Media Access Control sublayer determines the network access method. Wireless LANs use the CSMA/CA access method. When a station wants to communicate, it will sense the air for other traffic. If it doesn't detect any, the station will wait a random period of time and then begin transmitting if the air is still free. If the receiving station receives the information, it will send an acknowledgement that the data was received intact. If the sending station does not receive an acknowledgement, it assumes a collision has occurred and retransmits the data after waiting another random period of time.

The network speed of wireless LANs depends on the products that are used on the network as well as on their configuration. The speed of the network is further determined by the number of wireless users, the physical distance between the network components, the type of wireless LAN system that is installed, and the quality of the wireless network components. Most commercial wireless LAN components perform at speeds ranging from 11Mbps to 54Mbps.

There are currently four separate specifications within the 802.11 family: 802.11, 802.11a, 802.11b, and 802.11g. All rely on the Ethernet protocol and the CSMA/CA network access method.

- The 802.11a standard applies to wireless hubs on wireless ATM systems and is aimed at wireless hubs. Devices meeting the 802.11a standard operate at radio wave frequencies of 5 and 6 gigahertz (GHz).
- Ratified in 1999, the 802.11b standard (also referred to as "Wi-Fi") addresses wireless communications operating on radio frequencies of 2.45GHz, with network speeds up to 11Mbps.
- The newest standard, 802.11g, raises transmission rates to 54Mbps provided short distances are used.

The wireless components on the LAN must be set up to connect to other devices using one of two modes: infrastructure or ad hoc.

INFRASTRUCTURE MODE

In a typical wireless LAN configuration, a device that both transmits and receives, commonly referred to as an *access point (AP)*, connects to the wired network from a fixed location using a standard Ethernet cable (see Figure 3.7). The access point receives, buffers, and transmits data between wireless components, such as a laptop computer with a wireless network adapter installed on the wired network. An access point can support a small group of users and generally has a range up to several hundred feet. The access point can be installed anywhere provided there is good radio coverage. This type of wireless network operates in *infrastructure mode.*

Access point (AP)

A device on a wireless LAN that receives, buffers, and transmits data between wireless components.

Infrastructure mode

A form of wireless communication that enables the wireless components on a LAN to connect via an access point to the wired network.

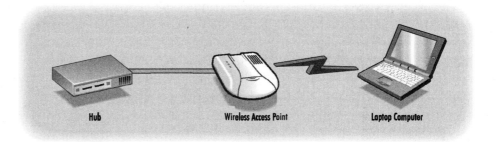

FIGURE 3.7
Laptop Computer Using a
Wireless Access Point

When a wireless device operating in infrastructure mode is turned on, it scans the wireless frequencies for a wireless access point. Once the device has selected an AP and established a connection, the wireless device switches to the channel assigned by the AP and negotiates the use of a port. This is known as establishing an association.

If a wireless device encounters difficulties in connecting with an AP (perhaps due to low signal strength), the device continues scanning for other wireless APs. When another AP is located, the wireless device switches to the channel of that AP and negotiates the use of a port. This process is called reassociation.

AD HOC MODE

Another form of wireless communication is known as ad hoc mode, or peer-to-peer mode. In ad hoc mode, wireless clients communicate directly with each other, without the use of a wireless AP. An example would be two personal digital assistants (PDAs) that transfer information directly from one to the other (see Figure 3.8).

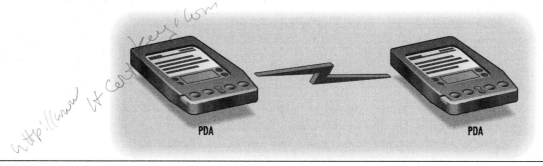

FIGURE 3.8
Personal Digital Assistants
Using Ad Hoc Mode

TRY IT!

Use two personal digital assistants to create an ad hoc wireless network. Using the PDAs, transfer files between the two.

STUDY GUIDE

In this chapter, we discussed the purpose of the 802 series of networking standards developed by the IEEE. Here are some key points to remember.

UNDERSTANDING PROJECT 802 STANDARDS

- Project 802 addresses aspects of networking technology.
- Whenever a new technology, such as wireless communications, is introduced, a committee is formed to investigate and make recommendations on that technology.
- Their results are often published as standards.
- These standards are written to address how networking should occur between devices that are using that particular technology.

802.2: LOGICAL LINK CONTROL

- The Data Link layer of the OSI Model is divided into two separate sublayers:
  - Media Access Control (MAC).
  - Logical Link Control (LLC). The LLC acts as an interface between the MAC sublayer and the Network layer by managing the data frames.
- The 802.2 standard defines how network communications should take place within the LLC sublayer.
- The LLC communicates upward to the Network layer using either connectionless or connection-oriented mode:
  - Connectionless mode: The LLC simply sends out packets of information, with no ability to check for errors. Communication tends to be fast. This mode is also known as a Type 1 operation.
  - Connection-oriented mode: The receiving node sends a message to the sending node, acknowledging receipt of the information. This mode is slower but more reliable. It is also known a Type 2 Operation.
- The LLC also monitors the flow of data between nodes and watches for errors using cyclical redundancy checking (CRC).

802.3: CARRIER SENSE MULTIPLE ACCESS WITH COLLISION DETECTION (CSMA/CD)

- Defines Ethernet networking standards.
- Also called the DIX standard.

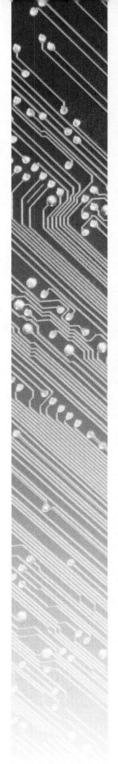

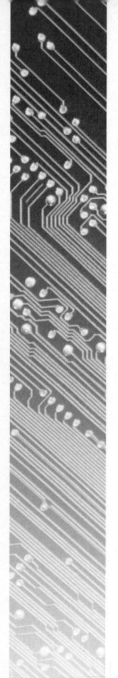

- Provides rules concerning how stations communicate while sharing a common cabling system.
- Uses a bus topology.
- Uses the following media:
    ○ Thinnet (10Base-2): Thinnet coaxial cable can support data transfer speeds of 10Mbps. Thinnet segments are limited to 185 meters (approximately 607 feet). If additional length is needed, a repeater is required.
    ○ Thicknet (10Base-5): Thicknet coaxial cable can support data transfer speeds of 10Mbps. Thicknet segments can extend 500 meters (approximately 1,640 feet). If additional length is needed, a repeater is required.
    ○ Twisted pair wiring (10Base-T): Shielded or unshielded twisted pair cable (STP or UTP) supports a data transfer rate up to 100Mbps. The segment between network devices (when wired as a star) can extend 100 meters (approximately 328 feet).

802.5: TOKEN RING

- Token Ring, or token passing, networks use a token that travels around the ring, from computer to computer.
- Since there is only one token, there are no collisions.
- Uses a ring topology.
- Supports a data transfer rate up to 16Mbps
- Commonly uses UTP, STP, or fiber-optic cable

FIBER DISTRIBUTED DATA INTERFACE (FDDI) LANS AND MANS

- A type of token passing technology.
- A pair of fiber-optic rings connects each device. Each ring contains a single token and the tokens travel in opposite directions between the devices.
- If a break or other problem occurs in the primary ring, the secondary ring acts as a backup, ensuring that data continues to move on the network.
- FDDI networks are fault tolerant and support high data transmission speeds.
- Commonly used as network backbones.
- Use single-mode or multimode fiber-optic cabling.
- Support speeds up to 100Mbps.

IEEE Specifications and Their Characteristics

- Can extend to distances up to 60 miles.
- Much more expensive to implement than wire (UTP/STP/coaxial) based networks.
- Development of 100Base-TX Ethernet is replacing FDDI.

802.11: WIRELESS LANS

- Provide network access for computing devices regardless of where they are located physically.
- Devices use radio waves rather than network cabling.
- The 802.11 standard addresses transmission requirements at both the Physical layer and the Media Access Control sublayer of the OSI Model.
- The Physical layer handles the actual data transmission duties between devices.
- The Media Access Control layer controls the network access method.
- Access method is Carrier Sense Multiple Access with Collision Avoidance (CSMA/CA).
- The 802.11b standard boosts wireless network speeds to 11Mbps.
- 802.11g raises transmission rates to 54Mbps provided short distances are used.

PRACTICE TEST

Try this test to check your mastery of the concepts in this chapter.

1. Match the following standards to the technologies they represent:
   - a. 802.2
   - b. 802.3
   - c. 802.5
   - d. FDDI
   - e. 802.11

   1. Wireless e
   2. Ethernet
   3. Fiber-optic networks d
   4. Logical Link Control
   5. Token Ring c

2. Which of the following are sublayers of the Data Link layer? (Select two)
   - a. Media Access Control
   - b. Physical
   - c. Application
   - d. Logical Link Control

3. Which of the following sublayers interacts directly with the Network layer?
   a. Transport
   b. Application
   c. Logical Link Control
   d. Media Access Control

4. Which of the following communication methods is considered the fastest?
   a. connection-oriented
   b. Ethernet
   c. Token Ring
   d. connectionless

5. What is the benefit of the connection-oriented communication method?
   a. It is faster.
   b. It is more secure.
   c. It is more reliable.
   d. It is easier to configure.

6. Which media access method does Ethernet rely on?
   a. CSMA/CD
   b. CSMA/CA
   c. tokens
   d. contention

7. Which of the following terms is also referred to as the DIX standard?
   a. Token Ring
   b. CSMA/CD
   c. Ethernet
   d. wireless

8. What is the primary difference between the CSMA/CD and CSMA/CA media access methods?
   a. CSMA/CA is implemented on Token Ring networks.
   b. CSMA/CD is implemented on Token Ring networks.
   c. CSMA/CA seeks to avoid collisions.
   d. CSMA/CD seeks to avoid collisions.

9. How many tokens travel around a Token Ring network at any given time?
   a. one
   b. two
   c. three
   d. four

10. Token Ring networks are physically wired in a _____ configuration.
    a. ring
    b. wireless
    c. bus
    d. star

11. What is the maximum speed commonly found on a Token Ring network?
    a. 4Mbps
    b. 10Mbps
    c. 16Mbps
    d. 100Mbps

12. Which of the following networks is considered fault tolerant due to the double ring of network media?
    a. Ethernet
    b. FDDI => supports up 100   goes to 60 miles
       another Token Ring Technology
    c. Token Ring
    d. wireless

13. Which of the following network configurations is commonly used as a network backbone?
    a. FDDI
    b. Ethernet
    c. Token Ring
    d. wireless

14. The development of _____ Ethernet is taking the place of FDDI.
    a. 100Base-T
    b. 100Base-TX
    c. 100Base-CA
    d. 100Base-TR

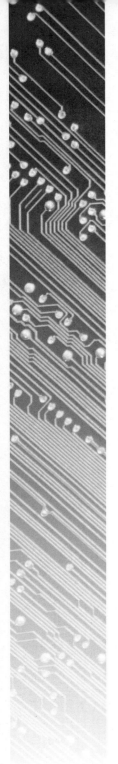

15. Which of the following layers handles the actual data transmission duties between devices on a wireless network?
    a. Transport
    b. Session
    c. Network
    d. Physical

16. Wireless LANs use which of the following media access methods?
    a. CSMA/CD
    b. CSMA/CA
    c. Ethernet
    d. Token Ring

17. Which of the following 802.11 standards boosted wireless network speeds to 11Mbps?
    a. 802.11
    b. 802.11b
    c. 802.11
    d. 802.11g

18. Which of the following 802 standards can extend networks to distances up to 60 miles?
    a. 802.3
    b. 802.5
    c. FDDI
    d. 802.11

19. In network communications, the LLC sublayer provides an interface between the protocols (IPX/SPX, TCP/IP) being used on the network and the
    a. device.
    b. application.
    c. method of contention.
    d. type of network.

20. The 802.2 standard defines how network communications should take place within the
    a. LLC sublayer.
    b. MAC sublayer.
    c. Network layer.
    d. Physical layer.

TROUBLESHOOTING

1. While working the help desk, a user on a newly installed network segment calls to report intermittent network problems. Specifically, the customer states that users on his end of the network routinely lose their connection to the network and their connection and transfer speeds are extremely slow. Prior to dispatching a technician, you review the wiring plan for the network and find the following information:
   a. Cat5 unshielded twisted pair cable was used.
   b. Each computer connects to a wall jack using a 25-foot cable
   c. The wall jack connects to a patch panel using a 500-foot cable.
   d. The patch panel is connected to a series of switches running at 100Mbps.

   Wireless ethernet [handwritten annotation]

   Given this information, what is the probable cause of the network problems?
2. While running a network sniffing utility, you discover that collisions occur on an occasional basis between data packets. Describe what action you should take to correct this problem.

   FDDI because of the double cable and more fault tolerant! — used as a backbone [handwritten annotation]

CUSTOMER SERVICE

1. You are the network administrator for a small company. You have been directed to install a small network in a group of offices where several computers are moved on a regular basis. Since the existing network wiring is permanently mounted in the walls, an assortment of network cabling has been required in the past to support the many relocations of computer equipment. What type of new network configuration would work well in this situation?
2. You have been given the task of installing a new backbone cable to connect network segments located in adjacent buildings. This backbone should allow for the network to continue operating, even if one piece of the cabling becomes damaged. What type of network should you select?

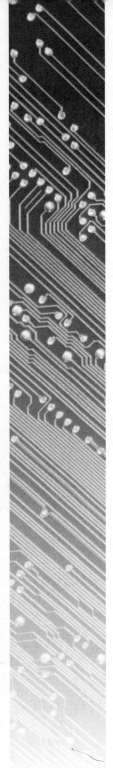

FOR MORE INFORMATION

For links to Web sites that provide further information about the topics covered in this chapter, go to the EMC/Paradigm Internet Resource Center at www.emcp.com/College Division/Internet Resource Centers/Networking/System Administration/Web Resources: For More Information.

Network Media, Connectors, and Their Characteristics

Network+ Examination
- **Objective 1.3:** Specify the characteristics (e.g., speed, length, topology, cable type, etc.) of the following:
  - 802.3 (Ethernet) standards
  - 10BASE-T
  - 100BASE-TX
  - 10BASE-2
  - 10BASE-5
  - 100BASE-FX
  - Gigabit Ethernet

- **Objective 1.4:** Recognize the following media connectors and/or describe their uses:
  - RJ-11
  - RJ-45
  - AUI
  - BNC
  - ST
  - SC

- **Objective 1.5:** Choose the appropriate media type and connectors to add a client to an existing network.
- **Objective 4.12:** Given a network troubleshooting scenario involving a wiring/infrastructure problem, identify the cause of the problem (e.g., bad media, interference, network hardware).

ON THE JOB

When working with computer networks, either new or existing, you will often be asked to select and install networking components. To complete this task successfully, you must consider many factors. For example, what type of cable will be used? The cable is the communications media that works to tie all of your networking devices, such as computers and printers, together. In many cases, the required cable length will dictate the type of cable you can use. In other cases, environmental conditions, such as cable that will be located in close proximity to heavy machinery, will dictate the type of cable you should use. Once you have selected the type of cable (twisted pair, coaxial, fiber-optic, etc.), you will need to select a category, or grade, for that particular cable to achieve the desired data transfer speeds.

The type of cable you choose will also determine which connectors and networking hardware are appropriate. The cable connectors—along with motherboard bus types and media access methods (CSMA/CD, CSMA/CA, and Token Ring)—will determine which network interface cards are compatible. Here are some additional items to consider when choosing media for a network implementation:

- Type and grade of existing cable.
- The network topology you plan to use.
- The cost of the cable and cable components.
- Additional network equipment that may be required.
- Ease of installation.
- Upgrade options.

As you can see, you cannot simply create a new network or add to an existing network arbitrarily. There is no substitute for thorough planning prior to beginning work on a network. Detailed planning establishes a solid foundation for your network and identifies the nuts and bolts that are necessary to make it work. Proper planning will result in a stable network with good throughput, minimal downtime, and the ability to expand to meet the needs of a growing client base. This chapter focuses on the common physical and mechanical characteristics of the Ethernet network. In doing so, it will help you make the correct choices when working with your network.

Understanding Ethernet Standards

In Chapter 3 we discussed the Institute of Electrical and Electronics Engineers (IEEE) 802 standards and how these standards address local area networks (LANs) and *metropolitan area networks (MANs)*. Remember that the IEEE 802 standard addresses hardware that interacts with the Physical and Data Link layers of the OSI Model. Specifically, it establishes standards for components such as network interface cards, wide area networking components, and the components used to make twisted pair, coaxial cable, and fiber-optic networks.

Since Ethernet network designations are based around the type of cable used, the following sections will begin with a description of each of the three major types of cabling: twisted pair, coaxial, and fiber-optic. Under the

Metropolitan area network (MAN)

A physical data communications infrastructure that involves one or more networks that work together to provide access and services in a geographic area.

appropriate cable types, the specific Ethernet technology will be discussed. We will begin our discussion with description of signaling methods. We will then take a detailed look at twisted pair cable. Coaxial cable and fiber-optic cabling will be discussed later in the chapter.

Understanding Baseband and Broadband Communications

Computers use signaling methods to communicate with each other. The signaling method is the way in which one device located on a computer network sends its data to another device located on the network. The terms "baseband" and "broadband" are examples of signaling methods.

BASEBAND

Computers communicate with each other using digital signals. In baseband communications, the digital signals from networked devices are sent through the network cable using *direct current (DC)* electrical pulses. Since every device on a baseband network must use a common wiring scheme, or channel, to communicate, only one networked device can communicate at a time, or only one signal may be present on the wire at one time. Another device must wait for the first device to finish before they can start transmitting. The electrical pulses use the entire capacity, or bandwidth, of the network wire. Ethernet is an example of a baseband network.

Direct current (DC)

An electric current that flows in one direction only.

BROADBAND

Broadband signaling uses radio frequency (RF) analog pulses to divide the bandwidth of the cable into different frequencies. This allows multiple signals to be transmitted on the cable at the same time, which means that the speed of the data transfer is much faster than with baseband. An example of broadband signaling is the cable television service that is installed in many homes.

IN REAL LIFE

The "xBase-x" designation is an IEEE identifier. For example, when referring to 10Base-T, the "10" refers to the transmission speed of 10Mbps. "Base" refers to baseband signals. The "T" designates twisted-pair cable. If there is an "F" at the end, for example, 100Base-FX, it refers to fiber-optic cable. If there is a numeric identifier at the end, as in 10Base-2, the number refers to the coaxial cable segment length.

Understanding Duplexing

The term *duplexing* refers to the transmission of data on a network. You will encounter two types of duplexing when working with data networks: half duplexing and full duplexing.

TEST TIP

Given a scenario, demonstrate that you understand the difference between baseband and broadband communications.

HALF DUPLEXING

Half duplex Ethernet refers to how two-way traffic is transferred on a network: traffic can move in only one direction at a time. That is, a computer can either send traffic or receive traffic, but it cannot do both at the same time. Think of half duplexing as a conversation that takes place on a pair of walkie-talkies. When you want to communicate, you press a button and begin talking. While the transmit button is pressed, you can only transmit; you cannot receive any information. When someone else is transmitting, however, you can only listen. When one person stops transmitting, another person can then transmit. In an Ethernet network, this method of communication can take place at 10Mbps or 100Mbps.

FULL DUPLEXING

In a *full duplex* Ethernet network, devices can transmit and receive at the same time. Think of full duplex communication as a telephone conversation. If several parties are having a conversation, they can both talk at the same time, both listen, or one can talk and one can listen. The benefit is faster speeds, since networked devices can both send and receive at the same time. From a performance point of view, devices such as file and print servers benefit because they can respond to numerous requests for service at the same time.

Twisted Pair Cable

Twisted pair cable—the same type of wire that is used to connect telephones—is also used to connect network devices together. It is called twisted pair because the actual cable includes at least two pairs of insulated copper wires that are twisted together and housed in a plastic sheath.

Different grades of twisted pair cable have different numbers of wires. For example, the twisted pair cable used for telephones has either four or six wires (see Figure 4.1). Twisted pair cable used in computer networks has eight wires.

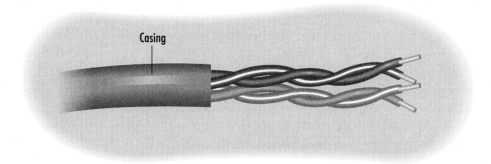

Casing

FIGURE 4.1
Twisted Pair Cable

There are several different categories of twisted pair wire. Higher categories have more twists per foot, which provides for faster data transfer speed and less chance of *crosstalk* or outside *electromagnetic interference (EMI)*. Crosstalk can happen when using cable that contains several wires running within the same sheath. For example, with a lower category of twisted pair cable, the electrical signal from one wire can bleed over to an adjacent wire. To help reduce this crosstalk between wires, the wires are twisted more tightly together to produce a higher category of twisted pair cable.

Crosstalk is one type of electromagnetic interference. Other types of EMI emanate from another electrical device outside of the twisted pair cable, such as a motor, an electrical appliance, or another cable that carries electricity. All types of cable are subject to a certain amount of EMI, but some cable types are more susceptible than others. For this reason, data cable should not be contained in a raceway, or conduit, that also contains electrical cable. Also, data cable should not be laid over fluorescent ceiling fixtures or any other device that uses or produces electricity.

As electrical signals travel down a length of wire, they begin to lose their strength. This process is known as *attenuation*. To avoid attenuation, all types of cable have a maximum run length that specifies how long a single piece of cable should be. The maximum length varies from cable type to cable type. For cable types that attenuate quickly, the signal fades very fast and the run length, therefore, must be short.

Crosstalk

A type of electromagnetic interference caused by the bleeding of an electrical signal from one wire to another housed within the same sheath.

Electromagnetic interference (EMI)

Interference on one electrical device that emanates from another electrical device, either between wires within the same plastic sheath (crosstalk) or between two completely separate devices.

Attenuation

The degradation, or fading, of an electrical signal that occurs as the signal travels down a length of cable.

TEST TIP

Ensure that you understand the terms attenuation, crosstalk, and electromagnetic interference, as well as how they relate to networking.

Using a higher category of twisted pair cable can also help avoid EMI from outside sources. For example, Cat5 cable has more twists per foot than Cat3, enabling it to transfer data at faster rates than Cat3 and, therefore, having less chance of exposing the data to EMI. In order to use twisted pair in a *10Base-T* network, the twisted pair cabling must be rated at a minimum of Cat3. Table 4.1 lists the most common categories of twisted pair cable and their suggested uses and data speed ratings.

10Base-T

The most common form of Ethernet networking, in which networks are wired in a star configuration using twisted pair cable.

Cable Category (CAT)	Cable Use	Data Speed
Cat1	Voice communications	20Kbps
Cat2	Data	4Mbps
Cat3	Data	10Mbps (16MHz signal rate)
Cat4	Data	10Mbps (Ethernet) 16Mbps (Token Ring) (20MHz signal rate)
Cat5	Data	100Mbps (100MHz signal rate)
Enhanced Cat5	Data	1,000Mbps (350MHz signal rate)
Cat6	Data	3.2 Gbps (400MHz signal rate)
NOTE: Signal rate as listed in this table refers to bandwidth measurement.		

use for networking

TABLE 4.1
Twisted Pair Cable Categories

Networks using twisted pair cabling are typically wired in a star topology. The connections that are required to establish this topology are shown in Figure 4.2.

Twisted pair wire used in data networks can be either unshielded (UTP) or shielded (STP). Also, the sheath, or exterior covering, of the cable can be either plenum grade or non-plenum grade. Resistant to fire, *plenum-grade cable* does not emit poisonous gasses when burned. Some local building codes require you to use plenum-grade cable in network installations.

Plenum-grade cable

Cable that is resistant to fire and does not emit poisonous gasses when burned.

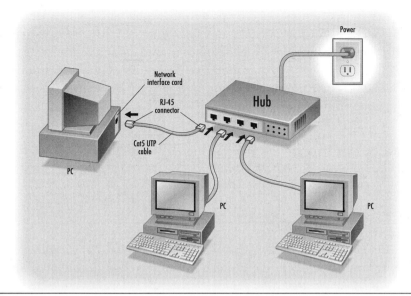

FIGURE 4.2
Typical Network Using Twisted
Pair Cable

UNSHIELDED TWISTED PAIR CABLE (UTP)

Unshielded twisted pair (UTP) cable used in voice communications commonly has two pairs of wires. One pair uses red and green wires and the other pair uses yellow and black wires. A single phone line uses one pair of wires; therefore, a two-pair voice cable can support two separate phone lines. When only one phone line is being used, the cable is terminated with RJ-11 connectors. When both wire pairs are used in support of two phone lines, RJ-14 connectors are used.

UTP used in data communications contains four wire pairs (eight wires total). Each individual wire is insulated by a color-coded protective cover and then housed in a plastic sheath (see Figure 4.3). The pairs of wires in UTP cable are color-coded so that a single wire can be identified at each end of the cable. This makes it much simpler to attach connectors correctly at both ends.

Unshielded twisted pair (UTP) cable

A cable with two or four pairs of insulated copper wires twisted together and housed in a plastic sheath, each individual wire insulated by a color-coded protective cover. Does not contain additional shielding for the twisted pairs, so it is more susceptible than STP to electromagnetic interference.

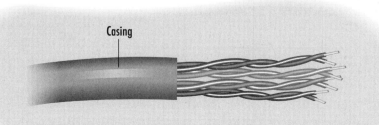

Casing

FIGURE 4.3
Unshielded Twisted Pair Cable

The wires are also color-coded by pair so that each pair can be identified. A typical Cat5 unshielded twisted pair cable contains four wire pairs (eight individual wires). A wire pair is made up of a solid color and the same solid color striped onto a white background (see Table 4.2). The most common color scheme is the Electronic Industry Association/Telecommunications Industry Association's Standard 568B.

Wire Pairs	First Wire	Second Wire
Wire Pair 1	White and blue	Blue
Wire Pair 2	White and orange	Orange
Wire Pair 3	White and green	Green
Wire Pair 4	White and brown	Brown

TABLE 4.2
Twisted Pair Cabling Wire Pairs

Following are some characteristics of unshielded twisted pair cabling:

- The maximum length a cable can run is 100 meters. This includes both the patch cable and the cable run. For example, if a patch cable (the cable between the computer and the wall jack) is 10 meters, then the horizontal run (to the patch panel) can be only 90 meters.
- Data transfer rates can be as high as 100Mbps, provided the appropriate category of cable is used. (Note: Cat6 cable can support data speeds up to 1000Mbps.)
- UTP is used in Ethernet and Token Ring networks.
- UTP is relatively inexpensive and easy to install and support. Purchased in bulk, expect to pay around $.08 per foot.
- It uses RJ-45 connectors.
- Networks using UTP are typically wired in a star configuration.
- UTP attenuates quickly.

— TRY IT! —————

Examine an unshielded twisted pair cable.

1. Strip part of the outer sheathing from the cable.
2. Notice how the wire pairs are twisted together.
3. Record the color scheme of the wires that are twisted together.

Shielded twisted pair (STP) cable

A twisted pair cable with a foil or braided-metal shield encasing the pairs of wires to draw electromagnetic interference away from the inside of the wire pairs.

SHIELDED TWISTED PAIR CABLE (STP)

Shielded twisted pair (STP) cable attempts to alleviate some of the EMI issues that are experienced with UTP by adding either a foil shield or braided metal shielding around the pairs of wire (see Figure 4.4). This shielding acts as an antenna to draw the interference away from the inside wire pairs. That interference, which generally presents itself as noise, is then converted, or sent to a ground. The individual wires used in STP have a thicker diameter than in UTP.

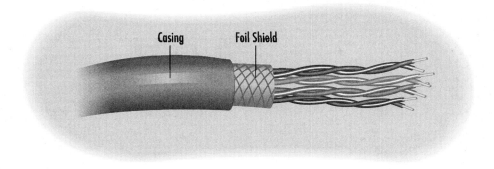

FIGURE 4.4
Shielded Twisted Pair Cable

Following are some characteristics of shielded twisted pair cabling:
- STP is more expensive than UTP cable. Purchased in bulk, expect to pay around $.53 per foot.
- Distance limitations are the same for both STP and UTP cable. Distance is limited to 100 meters.
- Shielding reduces outside electromagnetic interference.
- Cabling must be grounded, making installation more difficult than for UTP.
- STP uses RJ-45 connectors.

TRY IT!

Examine a shielded twisted pair cable.

1. Strip part of the outer sheathing from the cable.
2. Notice how the wire pairs are twisted together.
3. Note the type of shielding used to protect the wire pairs.

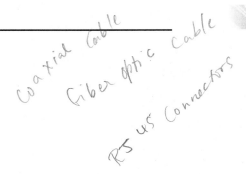

RJ-45 CONNECTORS

Twisted pair 10Base-T, 100Base-T, and 1000Base-T networks use *RJ-45 connectors*. The RJ-45 connector is an eight-pin modular plug that connects into ports on network interface cards, patch panels, switches, etc. (see Figure 4.5).

When using twisted pair cable with RJ-45 connectors in a 10Base-T network configuration, only pins 1, 2, 3, and 6 are used. Wire pair 2 (white and orange stripe, and solid orange) and pair 3 (white and green stripe, and solid green) are the only two pairs used (see Table 4.3). The remaining two wire pairs (pairs 1 and 4) are connected as shown in Table 4.4.

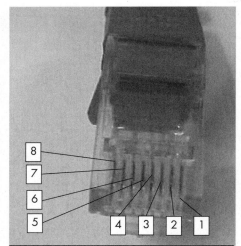

FIGURE 4.5
RJ-45 Connector

RJ-45 connector

An eight-pin modular plug that connects into ports on network interface cards, patch panels, switches, etc.

TABLE 4.3
Wire Pairs Used in a 10Base-T Network

Pins	Wires
Pin #1	White and orange striped wire
Pin #2	Orange wire
Pin #3	White and green striped wire
Pin #6	Green wire

Pins	Wires
Pin #4	Blue wire
Pin #5	White and blue striped wire
Pin #7	White and brown striped wire
Pin #8	Brown wire

TABLE 4.4
Unused Wire Pairs in a 10Base-T Network

Crossover cable

A cable in which the pin-out connections have been changed on one end of the cable. Typically used when connecting network hardware, such as hubs, together.

When connecting two network devices directly together, such as two hubs or two computers containing network interface cards, a *crossover cable* configuration must be used. To make a crossover cable, you must change the pin-out connections on one end of the cable. Note that this change is made on only one end; otherwise you have essentially made a regular data cable that has a nonstandard pin connection. Your crossover configuration is made as shown in Table 4.5.

Pins	Wires
Pin #1	White and green striped wire
Pin #2	Green wire
Pin #3	White and orange striped wire
Pin #6	Orange wire

TABLE 4.5
Wire Pairs Used in Crossover Cable

TRY IT!

Attach an RJ-45 connector to twisted pair cable.
1. Strip part of the outer sheathing from the cable.
2. Strip the plastic coating from the wires.
3. Insert the wires into the connector.
4. Crimp the connector.

10Base-T

The most common form of Ethernet networking is referred to as 10Base-T. 10Base-T networks are wired in a star configuration and use either shielded or unshielded twisted pair cable. A common 10Base-T network configuration is depicted in Figure 4.6.

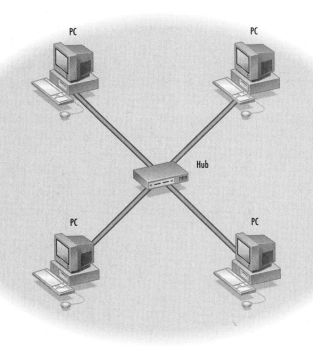

FIGURE 4.6
Ethernet Network Wired in a Star Configuration

10Base-T networks have the following characteristics:

- RJ-45 connectors are used to terminate one or more ends of the twisted pair cable. One end of the cable may also be terminated at a punch-down block or in the back of a patch panel.
- Each station has its own network cable and that cable is not shared with any other stations.
- Network speeds are 10Mbps.
- A maximum of 1,024 stations are allowed per network.
- The maximum distance of a cable run is 100 meters (328 feet).
- Networking components are plentiful and supported by many manufacturers.

100Base-T

Increasing demands for greater network speeds led to the development and introduction of the 100Base-T standard. 100Base-T is described by IEEE 802.3u and is commonly referred to as *Fast Ethernet.* Essentially, Fast Ethernet is just an upgraded Ethernet standard for computers that are connected to a local area network. 100Base-T Ethernet works just like regular Ethernet except that it can obtain data transfer speeds up to 100Mbps. 100Base-T technology is well suited for use in network backbones.

One of the primary benefits of the 100Base-T standard is that it is based on the existing Ethernet technology. Since it uses the same transmission protocol as 10Base-T (CSMA/CD) and functions with the same types of cable, it costs less money to convert an existing Ethernet 10Base-T network to Fast Ethernet than to some other forms of high-speed networking, such as fiber-optic cabling. Also, since 100Base-T is based on the old Ethernet standards, most of your existing network analysis tools and applications will continue to function with both types of networks.

Fast Ethernet can be divided into two categories: 100Base-TX and 100Base-T4. Both 100Base-TX and 100Base-T4 work with twisted pair cable. 100Base-FX, which uses fiber-optic cabling, will be discussed later in the chapter.

Fast Ethernet

A form of Ethernet networking that can obtain data transfer speeds up to 100Mbps; also referred to as 100Base-T.

100Base-T4

100Base-T4 can attain data transfer speeds up to 100Mbps over Cat3 cable. 100Base-T4 uses four pairs of wiring (all eight wires):
- One pair is used for transmission.
- One pair is used for reception.
- The two remaining pairs can either transmit or receive data.

Since 100Base-T4 has use of three wire pairs for transmitting or receiving data, it reduces the average frequency of signals on the cable, allowing lower-quality cable to adequately handle the electrical signal.

In Real Life

Although 100Base-T4 will function over Cat3 cables, this is not recommended since Cat3 cables were not intended to transfer data at that speed. Also, this standard assumes you are using perfect cables, which is rarely the case. Most industry professionals recommend that only Cat5 cables be used in networks designed to run at 100Mbps.

100Base-TX

100Base-TX requires Cat5 UTP cable. All associated networking hardware, such as patch panels and connectors, must comply with Cat5 standards (see Table 4.1). In any 100Mbps network implementation, all intermediate devices, such as hubs and switches, must be capable of supporting network speeds of 100Mbps.

Finally, the network interface cards installed in your computers must support 100Mbps transmission speeds. This can be accomplished by purchasing adapters designed specifically for transmitting and receiving data at 100Mbps or by using adapters that support *auto-sensing*. Adapters that support *auto-sensing* have the ability to automatically sense, or detect, 10Mbps or 100Mbps data transmission speeds. When an auto-sensing device is powered on, it will send a broadcast message across the network informing other devices that it is capable of 100Mbps speeds. If the receiving station, usually a switch or hub, is also capable of transferring data at 100Mbps, it will reply with a message that places both stations in 100Mbps mode. If the receiving station is not capable of 100Mbps speeds, it will not reply to the station's broadcast. This lack of reply will cause the sender and receiver to communicate with each other at 10Mbps.

100Base-T4

A category of Fast Ethernet that can attain data transfer speeds up to 100Mbps over Cat3 cable. 100Base-T4 uses four pairs of wiring.

100Base-TX

A category of Fast Ethernet that requires Cat5 UTP cable.

Auto-sensing

The ability of an adapter to automatically detect 10Mbps or 100Mbps data transmission speeds.

Coaxial Cable

Although *coaxial cable* is rarely used in new network installations, numerous existing installations that have coaxial cable require ongoing maintenance and support. Therefore, a thorough understanding of the standards, makeup, and use of this cable type is important.

Coaxial cable used to transfer data is similar in appearance to that used to connect the television in your home to a cable television provider. Coaxial cable has two conductors, a center copper core that is shrouded by insulating Teflon or plastic foam, and a foil wrap or a braided metal shield that covers the insulating plastic foam (see Figure 4.7). The inner core carries the electrical signals while the outer foil wrap shields against noise. All of these components are then enclosed in a plastic casing material.

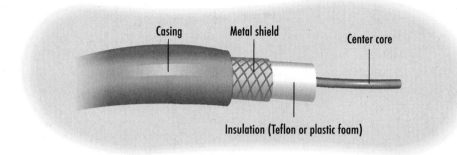

FIGURE 4.7
Section of Coaxial Cable

Coaxial cable is commonly used in a bus configuration, with many lengths of cable connecting one computer to the next in a daisy chain until either the final computer is connected or the maximum cable length has been reached. At the end of a segment, or section, the cable must be terminated with a cap terminator, or resistor. The terminator connects the inner and outer conductors together, completing a circuit. As with electricity, once the circuit is completed, electrical signals can flow through the cable. Each type of coaxial cable requires a different type of terminator, whose size is measured in *ohms*. Ohms are the measurement of resistance to electrical current. One ohm is equal to the current of one ampere, which will flow when the voltage of one volt is applied.

If a piece of coaxial cable that is used for data transfer loses a terminator, a phenomenon known as *signal bounce* occurs. When a signal reaches the end of the unterminated wire, the physics of electronics causes that signal to bounce back the way it came. This bouncing continues until the signal fades out, or attenuates. Since only one computer at a time can transmit on a baseband network, every other computer on the network is prohibited from communicating until the signal completely dies out.

The most common types of coaxial cables, along with their uses and impedance and termination requirements, are listed in Table 4.6.

Signal bounce

A phenomenon that occurs when a piece of coaxial cable loses a terminator, causing network traffic to move from end to end on the wire and interrupting the communications taking place on the wire.

Cable Type	Usage	Impedance and Termination
RG-8	Thick Ethernet (10Base-5)	50 ohms
RG-11	Thick Ethernet (10Base-5)	50 ohms
RG-58	Thin Ethernet (10Base-2)	50 ohms
RG-59	Television	75 ohms
RG-62	ARCnet	93 ohms

TABLE 4.6
Coaxial Cable Standards

Coaxial cable has the following characteristics:

- Data speeds up to 100Mbps are possible, with 10Mbps the most common.
- Coaxial cable tends to be stiff and can be difficult to work with.
- The metal shielding provides good resistance to outside interference.
- Attenuation is moderate or low. Maximum lengths can be extended through the use of repeaters.

— TRY IT! —

Examine a thin coaxial cable.

1. Strip part of the outer sheathing from the cable.
2. Fold back the wire mesh material.
3. Strip some of the insulating material from the center conductor.

BNC CONNECTOR

Thinnet coaxial cable uses a *bayonet nut connector*, or *BNC connector*. Like the actual wire, the BNC connector is a two-pin connector that slips over the end of the wire and is then clamped on. The center copper wire (pin 1), which carries the data signal, protrudes through the center of the connector. The metal braiding (pin 2) is folded back and acts as a ground (see Figure 4.8).

Bayonet nut connector, or BNC connector

A two-pin connector commonly used on Thinnet coaxial cable.

You may also choose to provide a thin coaxial segment with a grounding point for electrical safety. To avoid disrupting the Ethernet signals carried by the cable, there must be only one grounding point. All of the other metal parts on the cable should be insulated. When running new pieces of cable, be sure to route it carefully, making sure that any metal component attached to the cable does not become inadvertently grounded or exposed to an electrical source. Consider using plastic cable ties at various spots along the length of the cable to ensure it does not move around once it is in place.

FIGURE 4.8
Bayonet Nut Connector

TRY IT!

Attach a BNC connector.

1. Strip part of the outer sheathing from the cable.
2. Fold back the wire mesh material.
3. Strip some of the insulating material from the center conductor.
4. Attach the BNC connector.
5. Crimp the connector.

AUI/DIX CONNECTOR

Attachment Unit Interface (AUI)

A 15-pin connector that is used as an interface between a computer's network interface card and an Ethernet cable.

DEC-Intel-Xerox (DIX)

A 15-pin connector that uses a pin-out configuration slightly different from the AUI connector.

Thicknet uses an *Attachment Unit Interface (AUI)* or *DEC-Intel-Xerox (DIX)* connector to connect RG-8 and RG-11 cable to another device. The AUI is a 15-pin connector that is used as an interface between a computer's network interface card and an Ethernet cable (see Figure 4.9). In a 10Base-5 network, a short cable is used to connect the AUI connector on the computer with a transceiver-vampire tap that has been connected to the cable used on the segment.

Network Media, Connectors, and Their Characteristics

FIGURE 4.9
AUI/DIX Connector

The pin configuration for an AUI connector is depicted in Table 4.7. The AUI and DIX are generally considered to be the same; however, the DIX cable actually uses a slightly different pin-out configuration. Under the DIX design, pin 1 is connected to a chassis ground.

Pin Number	Signal
1	Control in circuit shield
2	Control in circuit A
3	Data out circuit A
4	Data in circuit shield
5	Data in circuit A
6	Voltage common
7	Control out circuit A (not used)
8	Control out circuit shield (not used)
9	Control in circuit B
10	Data out circuit B
11	Data out circuit shield
12	Data in circuit B
13	Voltage plus
14	Voltage shield
15	Control out circuit B (not used)

TABLE 4.7
AUI Pin Definitions

10BASE-2 AND THIN COAXIAL CABLE

10Base-2 networks use thin coaxial cable (RG-58), also known as Thinnet, and BNC connectors (see Figure 4.10). 10Base-2 networks are typically wired in a bus configuration, like the example shown in Figure 4.11.

10Base-2

A network that uses thin coaxial cable (Thinnet) and BNC connectors.

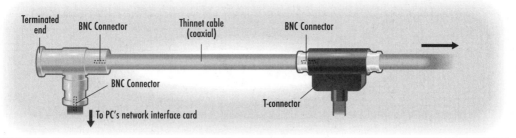

FIGURE 4.10
10Base-2 Network Technology

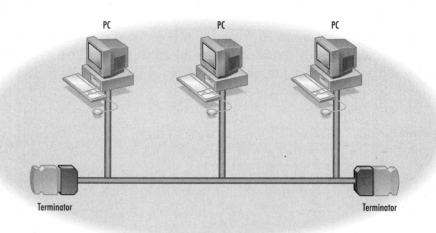

FIGURE 4.11
Typical Bus Network Using Thinnet Coaxial Cable

10Base-2 networks have the following characteristics:

- They use RG-58 cable (Thinnet). Cable types RG-58 A/U or RG-58 C/U are commonly used.
- RG-58 is fairly inexpensive, about the same price or slightly higher than twisted pair cabling. When purchased in bulk, expect to pay around $.10 per foot.
- Each end of the segment must be equipped with a 50-ohm terminating resistor.
- Pieces of coaxial cable may be no shorter than 0.5 meter (1.64 feet) in length. This means that the minimum spacing between network connections must be at least 0.5 meter.
- Thinnet segments may be a maximum of 185 meters (607 feet) long. (Note: Following the *xBase-x* guidelines, 10Base-2 would lead you to believe that a segment could extend for 200 meters; however, that is not the case. Instead, the quantity of 185 meters was rounded up to 200 meters.) A total of five segments may be used, but only three segments may have devices attached to them.

Network Media, Connectors, and Their Characteristics

- Repeaters can be used to extend the length of the segment. Up to four repeaters can be used on a network.
- Up to 30 stations are allowed on each segment. If a repeater has been used, it counts toward the 30-station total.

10BASE-5 AND THICK COAXIAL CABLE

Thick coaxial cable (RG-8/RG-11), also known as Thicknet, is commonly used in *10Base-5* networks (see Figure 4.12). Thicknet is well suited for network backbones or for connecting hubs together.

10Base-5

A network that uses thick coaxial cable (Thicknet).

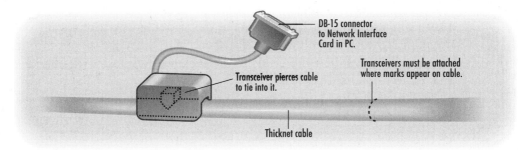

DB-15 connector to Network Interface Card in PC.

Transceivers must be attached where marks appear on cable.

Transceiver pierces cable to tie into it.

Thicknet cable

Here are some characteristics of the 10Base-5 networks:
- They use RG-8 or RG-11 cable, which has a solid center conductor.
- They use a thick (0.4-inch diameter) and inflexible coaxial cable (Thicknet). The outer casing of the cable may be polyvinyl chloride (PVC), which will be yellow, or Teflon, which will be orange or brown.
- Thicknet is hard to find and fairly expensive when located. Purchased in bulk, expect to pay around $.65 per foot.
- Plenum cable may be used to meet fire regulations.
- The cable must be terminated at each end with 50-ohm terminators and should be grounded at one end for electrical safety.
- A maximum of 100 devices may be attached to a segment.

FIGURE 4.12
10Base-5 Network Technology

- Pieces of Thicknet may be no shorter than 2.5 meters. This means that the minimum spacing between network connections must be at least 2.5 meters.
- Each segment has a maximum length of 500 meters, which may be extended with repeaters. A maximum of five segments may be used.
- Transceivers are used to attach nodes or devices to the cable.

Fiber-Optic Cabling

Instead of using copper wire to transmit electrical signals, *fiber-optic cabling* uses light-conducting glass fibers as its core. Data is then transmitted either through pulses of light that are sent by a laser or through light-emitting diodes (LED). When using lasers, a laser at one end of the cable turns on and off to send each bit. Modern fiber systems equipped with a single laser can transmit billions of bits per second, since the laser can switch on and off several billions of times per second. Newer systems use multiple lasers, with each laser generating a different color. This allows multiple signals to use the same piece of fiber.

The actual cable contains one or more glass fibers that are surrounded by a layer of glass *cladding*. The purpose of the cladding is to act as a mirror, reflecting light back into the glass fiber core. This reflection allows the pulses of light to follow the bends in the cable without losing any signal quality.

Outside of the cladding are two more layers of material: a layer of plastic and, on top of that, a layer of Kevlar. These two layers work together to keep the inner core from being damaged. A plastic sleeve or jacket then covers all of the components (see Figure 4.13).

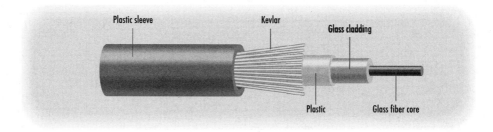

FIGURE 4.13
Fiber-Optic Cable

Since fiber-optic cable transmits light rather than electronic signals, it does not experience problems with electromagnetic interference. This makes it ideal for use in environments that contain a large amount of electrical interference, such as a manufacturing area or any area that uses large machinery. It is also considered very secure, since it would be difficult to capture and decode data that is being transmitted by light waves. There are several different types of fiber-optic cabling, as shown in Figure 4.14.

- **Single-mode fiber:** Single-mode fiber contains a single, tiny strand of fiber-optic glass, usually 7.1 or 8.5 microns in diameter. Single-mode fiber is typically used in telephone applications, cable television, or as a backbone. It allows only a single ray of light to pass through the fiber at a time; however, it can be used for very long runs.
- **Multimode fiber:** In multimode fiber, the core is usually 62.5 microns in diameter, much larger than that used by single-mode. Multimode can handle many rays of light at once, making it ideal for voice and data applications. Telephone companies typically use this type of fiber because it can accommodate hundreds of phone conversations along one fiber. Multimode cable is the type most commonly used in computer networks.
- **Simplex fiber:** Simplex is a cable containing a single strand of fiber.
- **Duplex fiber:** Duplex is a cable with two strands of fiber bound together in separate jackets.

FIGURE 4.14
Types of Fiber-Optic Cabling

Single-mode fiber

A type of fiber-optic cabling that contains a single, tiny strand of fiber-optic glass, usually 7.1 or 8.5 microns in diameter. Typically used in telephone applications, cable television, or as a backbone.

Multimode fiber

A type of fiber-optic cabling with a relatively large core, usually 62.5 microns in diameter, that can handle many rays of light at once, making it ideal for voice and data applications.

Simplex fiber

A type of fiber-optic cable containing a single strand of fiber.

Duplex fiber

A type of fiber-optic cable with two strands of fiber bound together in separate jackets.

Here are some characteristics of fiber-optic cable:
- It must follow the prescribed bend radius during installation; if the cable is bent too sharply, it will break.
- It is difficult to terminate; several types of connectors can be used. You must ensure that you purchase the correct connectors, especially when working in an area where fiber has already been installed.
- Fiber-optic cable is expensive. When buying in bulk, expect to pay about $1.00 per foot.
- Fiber-optic capable devices, such as network cards and media converters, must also be used.
- For proper installation, fiber-optic cable should be laid in a metal raceway or conduit for protection.
- Transmitted data is very secure, since data is transmitted using pulses of light rather than electrical signals.

- Fiber-optic cable is resistant to EMI since it does not transmit electrical signals.
- Maximum length is measured in miles, approximately 2.4 (or 4 kilometers).
- Fiber-optic cable does not attenuate very quickly.

— TRY IT! —

Examine fiber-optic cable.

1. Remove some of the outer sheathing from the cable.
2. Strip some of the insulating material from the fiber conductors.

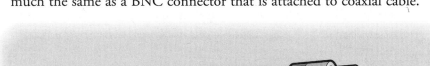

CONNECTORS

The most common connectors used for fiber-optic cabling are either ST or SC connectors.

- The *straight tip (ST) connector* is probably the most widely used (see Figure 4.15). The ST is a round, keyed, bayonet-style connector that functions much the same as a BNC connector that is attached to coaxial cable.

Straight tip (ST) connector

A round, keyed, bayonet-style connector that functions much the same as a BNC connector that is attached to coaxial cable.

FIGURE 4.15
Straight Tip Connector

The *square (SC) connector* is crimped or latched onto the fiber-optic cabling. The SC is square and uses a locking mechanism, usually with a button type release, to ensure a secure connection (see Figure 4.16). The SC has an advantage in that it can be used with both single-mode and multimode fibers.

Square (SC) connector

A square-shaped connector with a locking mechanism that is crimped or latched onto fiber-optic cabling.

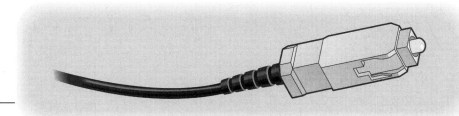

FIGURE 4.16
Square Connector

Network Media, Connectors, and Their Characteristics

100Base-FX

100Base-FX uses fiber-optic cabling to transfer data at 100Mbps, while maintaining the existing Ethernet standards. 100Base-FX has the following advantages and disadvantages.

- Advantages:
  - It provides a fast, reliable, and secure connection.
  - It is highly resistant to EMI.
  - Can transmit up to approximately 2 kilometers (approximately 1.2 miles).
- Disadvantages:
  - It is very expensive, especially when compared to 100Base-T using copper wiring.
  - It is more difficult than copper to install and terminate.
  - You must also purchase networking hardware with fiber connections or else purchase media converters.

100Base-FX

A type of network that uses fiber-optic cabling to transfer data at 100Mbps, while maintaining the existing Ethernet standards.

Gigabit Ethernet

Gigabit Ethernet is a transmission technology that is based on Ethernet standards. It provides a data transfer rate of 1 billion bits per second (one gigabit) and is frequently used as the backbone in large-enterprise networks. Fiber-optic cable is the primary medium used on Gigabit Ethernet networks, although copper cable may be used for very short distances.

The 1000Base-T technology is a member of the Gigabit Ethernet family of standards. Here are some of the key points of 1000Base-T:

- It uses the CSMA/CD media access method.
- It handles full-duplex data transfer at 1000Mbps.
- It can be used with Cat5 or above unshielded twisted pair (UTP) cable at distances up to 100 meters.

Gigabit Ethernet

A transmission technology that is based on Ethernet standards, providing a data transfer rate of 1 billion bits per second.

An alternative technology that competes with Gigabit Ethernet is ATM. A newer standard, 10 Gigabit Ethernet, is also becoming available.

TestTip

Use Table 4.8 as a study tool for the test.

Network Type	Wire	Distance Limits	Connectors	Speed
10Base-2	Thin coaxial	185 meters	BNC	10Mbps
10Base-5	Thick coaxial	500 meters	AUI/DIX	100Mbps
10Base-T	UTP, Cat2-5	100 meters	RJ-45	10-100Mbps
100Base-TX	UTP, Cat5	100 meters	RJ-45	100Mbps
Fiber-optic	Fiber-optic	2000 meters (2 km)	SC or ST	100+Mbps

TABLE 4.8
Review for Network+
Examination

Troubleshooting Network Cabling Problems

This section outlines some common problems that you can expect to experience with network cabling and some ideas on how to troubleshoot and repair them.

Although each cable type has its unique features, they also all share some common features. The steps listed below can be used with all cable types.

- Ensure the connectors are secure. Pull lightly on each connector to ensure it is firmly attached.
- Check to make sure the connector is installed correctly.
- Check the cable for severe kinks or damage. For example, a twisted pair cable that has been sucked into a vacuum cleaner and then yanked back out tends to stop working. Replace damaged cables.
- Measure the cable to ensure it does not exceed maximum distance limitations.
- Make use of cable testers if the wire is suspect.
- When using copper cable, ensure that it does not cross fluorescent lights or other sources of electromagnetic interference.

Twisted Pair Cable

- Look at the wire colors in the connector. Are the wire pairs inserted correctly? Check both ends.
- Ensure that you are not using a crossover cable instead of a straight-through cable, or vice versa, depending on the intended purpose of that wire.

Network Media, Connectors, and Their Characteristics

- Check the length of all cables involved in the run. For example, the maximum length of twisted pair cable is 100 meters. This means that if the patch cable (running from the computer to the wall jack) is 10 meters long, the cable run (from the back of the wall jack to the hub or switch) cannot exceed 90 meters.

Coaxial Cable

- Termination is one of the most common problems in a network using coaxial cable. When more than one computer has trouble communicating, always check that the connector is attached. If you suspect a bad connector, try another one.
- Ensure that you are using the right type of wire. Do not use cable intended for television installations on a computer network.
- When working with Thicknet, ensure the vampire taps are secure.
- Remember the 5-4-3 rule:
  - 5 total segments.
  - 4 repeaters.
  - 3 segments with devices.

Fiber-Optic Cable

- Observe the bend radius. The glass fibers will break when bent too severely.
- Fiber-optic cable should be laid in a metal raceway or conduit for protection.
- Check the connectors. Adding connectors to fiber-optic cable is tedious, exacting work and requires practice.

STUDY GUIDE

In this chapter, we discussed the characteristics of Ethernet networks, including the types of cabling systems, the benefits and drawbacks of each, and the types of connectors that each cable type uses. Here are some key points to remember.

UNDERSTANDING ETHERNET STANDARDS

- The IEEE 802 standard addresses hardware that interacts with the Physical and Data Link layers of the OSI Model.
- Specifically, IEEE 802 establishes standards for components such as network interface cards, wide area networking components, and the components used to make twisted pair and coaxial cable networks.
- The two most common cables are twisted pair and coaxial.

TWISTED PAIR CABLE

- Twisted pair wire, the same type used to connect telephones, is used to connect network devices together. UTP contains four wire pairs (eight wires total).
- Each type includes at least two pairs of insulated copper wires that are twisted together and housed in a plastic sheath.
- Higher categories have more twists per foot, which provides for better throughput and less chance of crosstalk or outside electromagnetic interference (EMI).
- For 10Base-T networks, the twisted pair cabling must be rated a minimum of Cat3.
- Twisted pair wire used in data networks can be either unshielded (UTP) or shielded (STP).
- The sheath, or exterior covering, of the cable pairs can be either plenum grade or non-plenum grade.
- Twisted pair cabling uses RJ-45 connectors.

10BASE-T

- Shielded or unshielded twisted pair cable is used.
- RJ-45 connectors are used to terminate one or more ends of the cable. The cable may also be terminated at a punch-down block or in the back of a patch panel.

- Each station has its own network cable; it is not shared with any other station.
- Network speeds are 10Mbps.
- A maximum of 1,024 stations are allowed per network.
- The maximum distance of a cable run is 100 meters (328 feet).

100BASE-T

- 100Base-T Ethernet works just like regular Ethernet except that it can obtain data transfer speeds up to 100Mbps.
- Fast Ethernet can be divided into two categories: 100Base-TX and 100Base-T4. Both 100Base-TX and 100Base-T4 work with twisted pair cable.

100Base-T4

- 100Base-T4 can attain data transfer speeds up to 100Mbps over Cat3 cable.
- 100Base-T4 uses four pairs of wiring (all eight wires).

100Base-TX

- 100Base-TX requires Cat5 unshielded twisted pair cable.
- All associated networking hardware, such as patch panels and connectors, must comply with Cat5 standards.

10BASE-2 AND THIN COAXIAL CABLE

- Coaxial cable has two conductors: a center copper core that is shrouded by insulating Teflon or plastic foam, and a foil wrap or a braided metal shield that covers the insulating plastic foam. The inner core carries the electrical signals, while the outer foil wrap shields against noise.
- Coaxial cable is commonly used in a bus configuration.
- 10Base-2 networks use RG-58 cable (Thinnet). Cable types RG-58 A/U or RG-58 C/U are commonly used.
- Each end of the segment must be equipped with a 50-ohm terminating resistor.
- Pieces of coaxial cable may be no shorter than 0.5 meter (1.64 feet). This means that the minimum spacing between network connections must be at least 0.5 meter.
- Thinnet segments may be a maximum of 185 meters (607 feet).

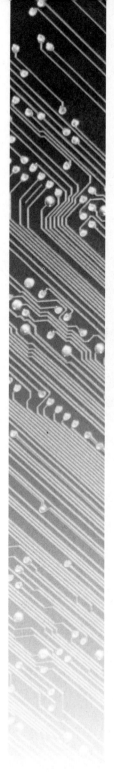

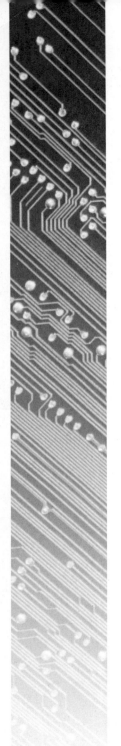

10BASE-5 AND THICK COAXIAL CABLE

- Thick coaxial cable, also known as Thicknet (RG-8/RG-11) is commonly used in 10Base-5 networks.
- Thicknet is well suited for network backbones or for connecting hubs.
- Uses RG-8 or RG-11 cable, which has a solid center conductor.
- Uses a thick (0.4-inch diameter) and inflexible coaxial cable. The outer casing of the cable may be polyvinyl chloride (PVC), which will be yellow, or Teflon, which will be orange or brown.
- Plenum cable may be required to meet fire regulations.
- Must be terminated at each end with 50-ohm terminators and should be grounded at one end for electrical safety reasons.
- A maximum of 100 devices may be attached to a segment.
- Pieces of Thicknet may be no shorter 2.5 meters. This means that the minimum spacing between network connections must be at least 2.5 meters.
- Each segment has a maximum length of 500 meters, which may be extended with repeaters. A maximum of five segments may be used.
- Transceivers are used to attach nodes to the cable.

FIBER-OPTIC CABLING

- Instead of using copper wire to transmit electrical signals, fiber-optic cabling uses light-conducting glass fibers as its core.
- Data is then transmitted either through pulses of light that are sent by a laser or through light-emitting diodes (LED).
- There are several different types of fiber-optic cabling:
  - Single-mode fiber: Contains a single, tiny strand of fiber-optic glass, usually 7.1 or 8.5 microns in diameter. Single-mode fiber is typically used in telephone applications, cable television, or as a backbone.
  - Multimode fiber: In multimode fiber, the core is usually 62.5microns in diameter, much larger than that used by single-mode. Multimode can handle many rays at once, making it ideal for voice and data applications. Multimode cable is the most commonly used in computer networks.
  - Simplex fiber: Simplex is a cable containing a single strand of fiber.
  - Duplex fiber: Duplex is a cable with two strands of fiber bound together in separate jackets.
- Must follow the prescribed bend radius during installation; if the cable is bent too sharply, it will break.

- Difficult to terminate; several types of connectors can be used. Must ensure you purchase the correct connectors, especially when working in an area where fiber has already been installed.
- Fiber-optic cable is expensive. When buying in bulk, expect to pay about $1.00 per foot.
- Fiber-optic devices, such as network cards and media converters, must also be used.
- Very secure, since data is transmitted using pulses of light rather than electrical signals.
- Resistant to EMI, since it does not transmit electrical signals.
- Maximum length is measured in miles, approximately 2.4 (or 4 kilometers).
- Does not attenuate very quickly.
- The most common connectors are either ST or SC connectors.

100Base-FX

- 100Base-FX uses fiber-optic cabling to transfer data at 100Mbps, while maintaining Ethernet standards.
- Advantages:
  - It provides a fast, reliable, and secure connection.
  - It is highly resistant to EMI.
  - It can transmit up to approximately 4 kilometers (approximately 2.4 miles).
- Disadvantages:
  - Very expensive, especially when compared to 100Base-T using copper wiring.
  - More difficult than copper to install and terminate.
  - Must also purchase networking hardware with fiber connections, or purchase media converters.

Gigabit Ethernet

- Gigabit Ethernet is a transmission technology that is based on Ethernet standards.
- Provides a data transfer rate of 1 billion bits per second (one gigabit).
- Frequently used as the backbone in large enterprise networks.
- Fiber-optic cable is the primary medium used on Gigabit Ethernet networks, although copper cable may be used for very short distances.

PRACTICE TEST

Try this test to check your mastery of the concepts in this chapter.

1. What does the "T" in 10Base-T stand for?
   a. timing
   b. transfer
   c. twisted pair
   d. telephone cable

2. For 10Base-T networks, the cabling must be rated at a minimum of Cat
   a. 1.
   b. 2.
   c. 3.
   d. 4.
   e. 5.

3. In a twisted pair network, which of the following devices is located between the punch-down block and the switch or hub?
   a. wall jack
   b. patch panel
   c. computer
   d. router

4. Which is the correct term to describe what happens when the electrical signal from one wire bleeds over to an adjacent wire?
   a. crosstalk
   b. EMI
   c. EMR
   d. attenuation

5. Which of the following cable types will not emit poisonous gasses when burned?
   a. plenum
   b. non-plenum
   c. Cat5 enhanced
   d. shielded twisted pair

6. Unshielded twisted pair cable contains how many total wires?
   a. 4
   b. 6
   c. 8
   d. 10

7. Which of the following is a characteristic of unshielded twisted pair wire? (Select two)
   a. used in both Ethernet and Token Ring networks
   b. uses BNC connectors
   c. is immune to EMI
   d. distance is limited to 100 meters

8. A 10Base-T network is physically wired using which topology?
   a. bus
   b. ring
   c. Ethernet
   d. star

9. What is the shortest length of cable that can be used in a 10Base-T network?
   a. 1 foot
   b. 1 meter
   c. 2 feet
   d. 2 meters

10. Which of the following 100Mbps technologies can use Cat3 twisted pair cable as the transmission medium?
    a. 100Base-T
    b. 100Base-T4
    c. 100Base-TX
    d. 100Base-FX

11. What is one of the primary benefits of using 100Base-T technology instead of 100Base-FX?
    a. It is faster.
    b. It is newer.
    c. It uses less wire.
    d. It is cheaper.

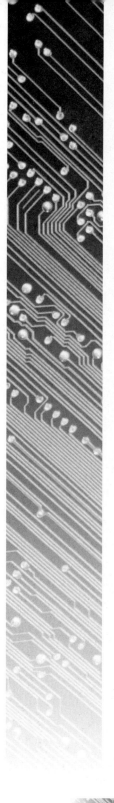

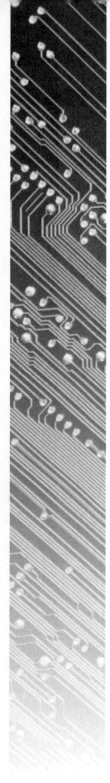

12. You recently purchased a new computer for use on your network. The new computer uses an auto-sensing network card. During boot-up, the computer issues a broadcast to other network devices. The other network devices do not respond. Which of the following statements correctly describes what will happen?
    a. All devices on the network will transmit data at 10Mbps.
    b. All devices on the network will transmit data at 100Mbps.
    c. The computer will transmit data at 100Mbps; all other devices will transmit at 10Mbps.
    d. The computer will transmit data at 10Mbps; all other devices will transmit at 100Mbps.

13. Which of the following topologies is typically used with coaxial cable?
    a. star
    b. ring
    c. mesh
    d. bus

14. What type of terminator is used with RG-11 coaxial cable?
    a. 50 ohm
    b. 67 ohm
    c. 75 ohm
    d. 93 ohm

15. Which of the following statements describe coaxial cable? (Select two)
    a. The most common data transfer rate is 100Mbps.
    b. The metal shielding provides good resistance to EMI.
    c. The maximum distance is 2 kilometers.
    d. Attenuation is moderate or low

16. What type of connector does RG-8 cable use to connect to another device?
    a. BNC
    b. RG-11
    c. AUI
    d. RJ-45

17. What is the maximum length that RG-58 cable can run?
    a. 100 meters
    b. 185 meters
    c. 200 meters
    d. 2 kilometers

18. Which of the following types of cable is well suited for use as a backbone cable
    a. shielded twisted pair
    b. unshielded twisted pair
    c. Thicknet
    d. Thinnet

19. Which of the following types of cable would be well suited for use in a manufacturing environment where large machinery is in use?
    a. Thicknet
    b. shielded twisted pair
    c. Thinnet
    d. fiber-optic cable

20. Which of the following types of fiber-optic cabling is most commonly used in computer networks?
    a. single-mode fiber
    b. multimode fiber
    c. simplex fiber
    d. duplex fiber

21. What types of connectors are most commonly used on fiber-optic cables? (Select two)
    a. straight tip
    b. round tip
    c. square connector
    d. locking connector

22. What is the maximum length that a piece of fiber-optic cabling can run?
    a. 500 meters
    b. 1,000 meters
    c. 2 kilometers
    d. 4 kilometers

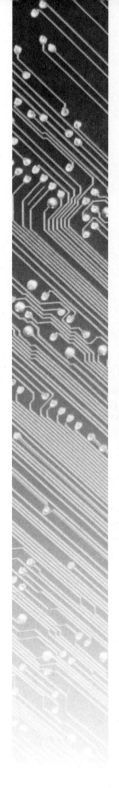

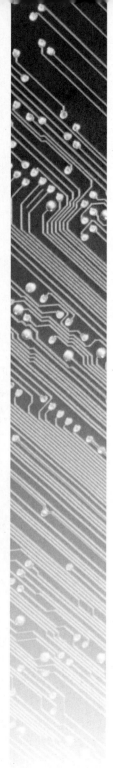

23. What cable type is primarily used in Gigabit Ethernet?
    a. Thicknet
    b. Cat5e UTP
    c. Cat6 UTP
    d. fiber-optic cable

24. What is an alternative technology that competes directly with Gigabit Ethernet?
    a. packet switching
    b. ATM
    c. X.25
    d. Token Ring

25. If Cat5 unshielded twisted pair cable is used in a Gigabit Ethernet network, what distance limit will be imposed?
    a. 100 meters
    b. 1,000 meters
    c. 1 kilometer
    d. 2 kilometers

TROUBLESHOOTING

1. Recently, you hired a wiring contractor to run unshielded twisted pair cable from your wiring closet to 10 computers that are located in a newly remodeled office. The same day the computers were hooked up to the network, users began complaining about intermittent problems connecting to the network. For example, one user reported that she was able to log in to the network, but she later lost her connection. While troubleshooting these reported problems, you inspected the new wiring and found that several of the wires were running across fluorescent light fixtures in the ceiling. Given this information, what is the most likely cause of the problem?

2. You work for a small manufacturing company that is housed in two buildings. The buildings are located across the street from each other and wired in the configuration shown in Figure 4.17.

Network Media, Connectors, and Their Characteristics

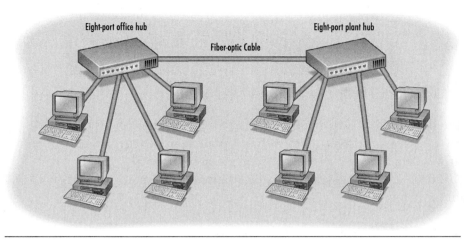

FIGURE 4.17
A power supply from
Current Network Setup

Currently, the plant has four computers; however, you are in the process of adding eight more. In preparation for adding the additional computers, you purchased another eight-port hub and, using a patch cable, plugged one end into the existing hub and one end into the new hub. When the new hub was powered on, you plugged one of the new computers into the new hub but were unable to log in to the network. When troubleshooting, you discovered there were no link or data lights glowing on the new hub. What is the most likely cause of this failure?

CUSTOMER SERVICE

1. Your company has recently purchased a building located next door to your current administration building. You have been asked to develop a plan to add a data line that will allow the new inhabitants of that building access to your corporate network. This line will run underground in a piece of conduit pipe. The building is located approximately 740 meters from your administration building. What type of cable would you use to make this connection?

2. The manager of the Management Information Systems (MIS) department would like to upgrade your network speed from 10Mbps to 100Mbps. You have been asked to identify the steps that are necessary to make this conversion. While developing your plan, you

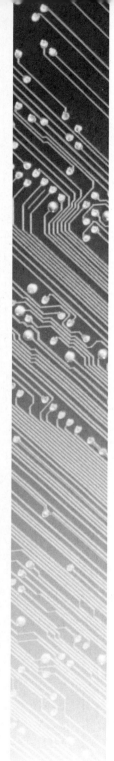

discovered that much of your current network infrastructure is Cat3 unshielded twisted pair cable. What can be done with this cable to meet your goals, if anything?

FOR MORE INFORMATION

For links to Web sites that provide further information about the topics covered in this chapter, go to the EMC/Paradigm Internet Resource Center at www.emcp.com/College Division/Internet Resource Centers/Networking/System Administration/Web Resources: For More Information.

Networking Components

Network+ Examination
- **Objective 1.6:** Identify the purpose, features, and functions of the following network components:
  - Hubs
  - Switches
  - Bridges
  - Routers
  - Gateways
  - CSU/DSU
  - Network interface cards/ISDN adapters/system area network cards
  - Wireless access points
  - Modems

- **Objective 3.3:** Identify the main characteristics of VLANs.

ON THE JOB

Whether you are involved with large-enterprise networks or merely setting up a small network in your home or office, the proper selection of networking components is critical to the success and performance of that network. This chapter helps you select the proper networking components for any given situation. It also provides you with information on how various devices interact with each other and some general rules for their use.

Hubs

Hub

A piece of networking hardware used to connect computers and printers to each other in a star topology.

Hubs are the most basic form of multistation access unit. They are used to connect devices, such as computers and printers, on a network. A hub joins multiple network devices together to form a network segment. On this network segment, all computers can communicate directly with each other. Each hub contains multiple ports; generally 4, 8, 16, or 32 (see Figure 5.1). One device will be connected to each port with a dedicated line, normally twisted pair cable (see Figure 5.2).

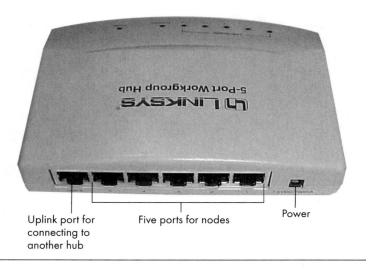

Uplink port for connecting to another hub

Five ports for nodes

Power

FIGURE 5.1
A Typical Small Hub

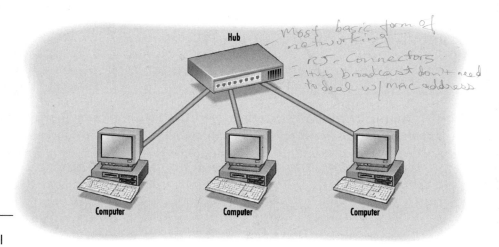

FIGURE 5.2
Using a Hub to Build a Small Network

Networking Components

When a networked device transmits data, it is sent through the dedicated line to the hub. When the data arrives at a port on the hub, the data is copied and sent to all of the ports on the hub. The data is then sent back out of the hub to all of the other devices on the network. Although all of the devices connected to the hub receive the data, only the destination device will remove the data from the wire and read it.

Hubs typically have a number of lights on the front, which indicate link connectivity and data activity. The link connectivity light indicates that a good connection has been made between the networked device and the hub. The data activity light indicates that data is being passed through the hub. Each port on the hub will have both a link light and a data light. These lights are very useful when troubleshooting a network connection problem. For example, if a user complains that they cannot get access to the network, you could check the link connectivity light for the port that the device is plugged into. If the light is on, you will know there is a good connection between the workstation and the hub and the problem must rest elsewhere. If the light is not on, it could indicate a bad cable, a bad connector, a bad port on the hub, or a malfunctioning network interface card in the computer.

Hubs may also be used to connect different network segments together (see Figure 5.3). In this example, the accounts payable and accounts receivable departments each had a small network consisting of several workstations connected by an eight-port hub. The accounts payable department did not have access to a printer, so whenever they needed to print a document, they were forced to copy that document to a floppy disk and carry it to the accounts receivable department where it could be printed. A better solution is to link the two hubs together with a piece of twisted pair cable that has been wired in a crossover configuration (refer to Chapter 4). Once this connection is made, the two small networks become one larger network and both departments have access to a printer.

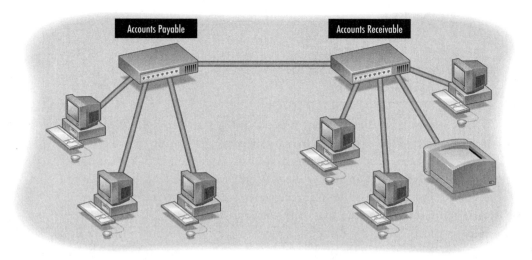

FIGURE 5.3
Linking Network Segments

Hubs are generally classified based on their level of sophistication, or, more accurately, on how many functions they contain. Common classifications include passive, active, and intelligent. Intelligent hubs are also known as managed hubs.

PASSIVE HUBS

Passive hub

A hub that does not amplify, clean up, or change the data signal.

A *passive hub* is essentially the one described above. It takes the signal (data) that it receives from a device, copies it, and sends it out the other ports in the hub to all of the other networked devices. It does not manipulate or view the data and it does nothing to amplify, clean up, or change the data signal. Passive hubs extend only as far as the length of the cable that is being used on the network. Passive hubs may or may not require a power source.

Networking Components

ACTIVE HUBS

Active hubs add functionality to the original design. Active hubs have the ability to repair weak signals. They do this by regenerating or amplifying the data signal. This regeneration consists of intercepting a weak signal and raising it back up to the original voltage. Once the signal is regenerated, it is sent back out of the hub to all of the other devices. Active hubs require a power source.

Some active hubs also have the ability to resynchronize electrical signals if they are not timed correctly. An active hub can be used to add additional computers to a network or to allow for increased distances between workstations and servers. An active hub is commonly called a repeater, or, more accurately, a multiport repeater (see Figure 5.4).

Active hub

A hub that is able to amplify or regenerate a data signal.

FIGURE 5.4
Active Hub

MANAGED OR INTELLIGENT HUBS

A *managed,* or *intelligent, hub* allows you to configure and monitor each individual port. Further, ports can be enabled or disabled through a hub management utility that is normally provided by the manufacturer. Hub management will also allow you to gather network parameters such as the number or types of packets that have been transmitted, the number of errors that have occurred, and the number of collisions taking place on the network.

When selecting hubs, here are some of the factors that should be considered:
• Throughput or speed required (normally 10Mbps or 100Mbps).

Managed, or intelligent, hub

A hub that is able to configure and monitor individual ports.

- Number of ports required.
- Need for manageability.
- Ease of installation and use.
- Quality of the product.

TEST TIP

Hubs operate at the Physical layer of the OSI Model, since they are concerned only with electrical signal processing.

— TRY IT! —

Explore the available options on a managed hub.

1. Depending on the hub you have available, follow the instructions for loading the software on a PC.
2. Connect the PC to the managed hub.
3. Connect to the hub and explore the options available for managing the device.

Switches

Switch

A networking device that learns the physical address of connected devices and routes traffic accordingly.

A *switch,* or switching hub, adds additional features to the active hub configuration (see Figure 5.5). Instead of just copying and sending data out to every device on the network, a switch has the ability to learn the physical addresses of all of the devices on the network. When one device sends data through its network cable to the switch, the switch will open the data packet and look for the physical address of the destination device. Once it has that address, it will send the data to the port to which the destination device is connected. By sending data only to its intended recipient, network traffic is dramatically reduced, providing more available bandwidth and cutting down on the number of data collisions that take place on Ethernet networks.

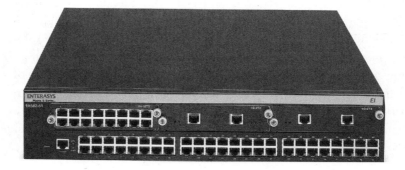

FIGURE 5.5
A Typical Switch

Networking Components

Most switches have the ability to auto-sense network transmission speeds. For example, if you have several devices on a network that transmit at 10Mbps and other devices that transmit at 100Mbps, the switch can automatically sense those transmission speeds and make adjustments to ensure the data gets delivered reliably. It does this by using a buffering process. The switch will intercept the data, place it in memory, and then transmit it at either a faster or slower speed.

— TRY IT! —

Explore the available options for configuring a switch.

1. Depending on the switch you have available, follow the instructions for loading the software on a PC.
2. Connect the PC to the switch.
3. Connect to the switch and explore the options available for managing the device.

LAYER 3 SWITCHES

Most switches operate at the Data Link layer of the OSI Model; however, a newer technology is the layer 3, or Network layer, switch. *Layer 3 switches* incorporate features of both routers and switches.

Like a layer 2 switch, a layer 3 switch passes data, but it also has the ability to make some decisions on how the network traffic gets to its destination. So which should you use? If working in a local area network environment, a switch passes network traffic faster than a router. When working with a wide area network, a router is the best choice due to the sheer number of routing decisions that must be made.

All switches allow you to isolate each individual port or a group of ports. This isolation process allows you to divide your segment into smaller, logical segments. These smaller segments are commonly referred to as virtual local area networks (VLANs).

VIRTUAL LOCAL AREA NETWORK (VLAN)

A *virtual local area network (VLAN)* is a collection of network devices (workstations, servers, printers, etc.) that can be grouped into a logical network, without regard to physical location. All of the devices act as though they are connected to a single network segment, even though they may be physically located in different buildings or even different states (see Figure 5.6).

Layer 3 switch

A switch that operates at the Network layer (layer 3) of the OSI Model rather than at the Data Link layer; incorporates features of both switches and routers.

Virtual local area network (VLAN)

A collection of network devices that are grouped into a logical network, without regard to physical location.

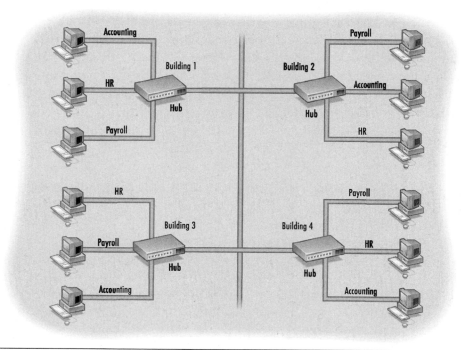

FIGURE 5.6
Virtual Local Area Network
(VLAN)

For example, the accounting department personnel are spread throughout a building or campus. Each workstation is connected to a switch, and these switches are connected to a common backbone. A network administrator would first identify the ports on each switch that are connected to computers being used by accounting personnel. These ports would then be isolated and grouped together into a VLAN. The accounting folks would then all occupy a single LAN space. Although human resource (HR) and payroll department personnel may also have computers plugged into ports on these switches, they are isolated from the accounting personnel, and cannot even see each other on the network.

Figure 5.7 describes the three basic VLAN models, which are identified by how the VLAN is established.

Networking Components

- **Port-based:** A network administrator assigns each port of a switch to a VLAN. For example, ports 1 through 5 might be assigned to the accounting department, while ports 5 through 16 are assigned to the human resources department. The switch determines how to route data packets by making note of which port the data arrives on. If a user is moved to a different computer that is a part of another VLAN, the administrator can reassign the new computers port to the user's original VLAN.
- **MAC address-based:** Membership on the VLAN is based on the source and destination MAC addresses of the devices that are attached to the switch. The switch maintains a table of MAC addresses and their corresponding VLAN membership. An advantage of this method is that the switch does not need to be reconfigured if a user's computer is moved to a different port. One drawback of this method is that a single MAC address cannot easily be a member of more than one VLAN. This method can also cause serious problems when working in a network that also contains bridges and routers.
- **Protocol-based:** Protocol-based VLANs, also known as layer 3 VLANs, are based on the protocols being used (IP, IPX, etc.) and their respective layer 3 (Network layer) addresses. VLAN assignments can be based on IP subnets, when using the TCP/IP protocol, or on network number, when using the IPX/SPX protocol. Protocol-based VLANS are the most flexible and provide for a very logical grouping of users.

FIGURE 5.7
Basic VLAN Models

When selecting switches, here are some of the things that should be considered:
- Whether provisions are available for VLANS.
- What network data transfer speeds are available.
- The need for switches to communicate with each other (trunking).
- Quality of the product.
- Number of ports required.

TestTip

Switches operate at the Data Link layer of the OSI Model. Switches understand and process physical addresses.

Bridges ✓

Before switches were widely adopted, bridges were used to connect similar network segments together or to divide a single network into multiple segments (see Figure 5.8). The primary purpose of a bridge is to allow devices that are attached to separate LANs or LAN segments to communicate as if they are all located on the same LAN.

FIGURE 5.8
A Typical Bridge

Bridges are also able to contain, or limit, network traffic to the section of the network to which it belongs. This is accomplished by filtering the network traffic. The bridge can be configured to deny traffic on one segment from being transmitted to another segment. For example, if a network has a lot of traffic that is being generated by only a few machines, those machines could be placed on their own segment, or on one side of the bridge. The remaining users could be placed on another segment, or the other side of the bridge. By doing this, the traffic from the busy machines will be confined to its own segment and not cause the entire network to slow down. However, if a computer on one segment needs to communicate with a computer on the other segment, the bridge will still allow that traffic to pass from segment to segment.

Bridges decide which packets to pass between networks through the use of a routing table. To do this, the bridge checks the source and destination addresses of each packet that it sees and then adds this information to its routing table. As a packet is presented to the bridge, it checks to see if the destination device is listed in its routing table. If the bridge cannot find the address, it forwards the packet to all of the network segments. If the destination is listed in its routing table, the bridge forwards the packet to the appropriate segment.

Bridges can also be used in the following situations:

- To increase the physical length of a network segment.
- To allow for more devices on the network.
- To link different types of physical media, such as twisted pair and coaxial cable.
- To link different network segments, such as Ethernet and Token Ring. Once linked, the bridge has the ability to forward network traffic between these segments.

Bridges work at the Data Link layer of the OSI Model and are not able to distinguish between one protocol and another. As a result, bridges simply pass all transmitted data along the network. Since bridges pass all protocols along, the individual network devices must select only the protocols they can recognize.

Bridges are typically classified as either local or remote.

- *Local bridges* exist when there is a direct connection between several LAN segments. That is, when a LAN segment has a cable attached directly to the bridge, it is considered local.
- *Remote bridges* use WAN connections, generally leased telephone lines, to connect LAN segments.

Bridges got their name from their ability to "bridge," or connect networks together. The ability to move traffic between network segments is based on bridging algorithms. There are four basic types of bridging algorithms: transparent, source-route, translational, and source-route transparent.

TRANSPARENT

Commonly found on Ethernet networks, *transparent bridges* are also called learning bridges. The transparent bridge has the capability of automatically identifying all of the devices that are connected to each segment of the network. The transparent bridge listens to the traffic traveling on the network and learns the addresses of devices that are located on the segments. This information is then stored in a table within the bridge. Whenever the bridge receives a packet, it can check its internal table to determine exactly where the destination device is located. Once it finds the location, it directs the packet to that device.

Local bridge

A networking device used when there is a direct connection between LAN segments.

Remote bridge

A networking device that is used over WAN connections.

Transparent bridge

A bridge that can automatically identify all of the devices connected to the network segment.

SOURCE-ROUTE

A *source-route bridge* is commonly found on Token Ring networks. To communicate on a source-route network, a device first sends a broadcast across the network. The broadcast includes the address of the destination device. The purpose of the broadcast is to locate all of the routes that are available to the destination device. When the destination device hears the broadcast, it replies back to sender. This reply includes the route that the broadcast packet took to get to the destination device. The sender then uses that route to communicate with the destination device.

TRANSLATIONAL

Translational bridges are used to connect dissimilar networks together. For example, a bridge could be used to connect an Ethernet network segment to a Token Ring network segment. Translational bridges contain ports for each of the two different network types. The Ethernet network plugs into one port and the Token Ring network plugs into the second. The bridge can then forward traffic back and forth between the two networks (see Figure 5.9).

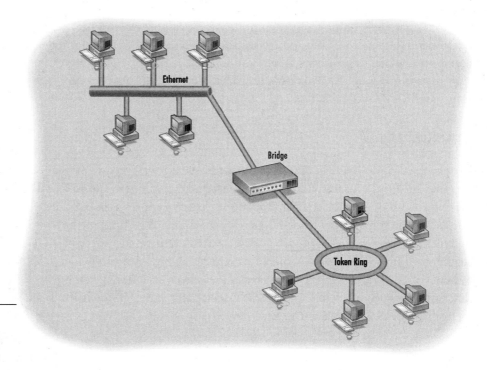

FIGURE 5.9
Translational Bridge Connecting Token Ring and Ethernet Networks Together

The process that translational bridges use to pass data depends on the type of networks they are connecting. The conversion of the data frames from one type to another is typically done through encapsulation. That is, the data format of one network is packaged into the data format of the other network.

SOURCE-ROUTE TRANSPARENT ✓ *will not be on test* ~~*will not be on test*~~

Source-route transparent bridges combine aspects of both source-route and translational bridges in order to enable network communications on networks with a mix of Ethernet and Token Ring technologies. Since bridges are transparent to higher-level protocols, all network segments remain a part of the same logical network.

Routers ✓ *will be on Exam*

A *router* is a device that either connects multiple network segments together to form a larger network, or connects large networks together to form an internetwork. Routers are the devices used to connect local area networks (LANs), making a wide area network (WAN). Routers join networks together by ensuring that traffic generated by a host on one network finds its way to a host on another network. In addition, routers have the ability to use redundant paths. Essentially, that means that routers know more than one way to get data traffic to its destination (see Figure 5.10).

Source-route transparent bridge

A bridge that combines aspects of both source-route and translational bridges. Enables communications on mixed Ethernet and Token Ring networks.

Router

A device used to connect either multiple LAN segments together to form a WAN, or large networks together to form an internetwork.

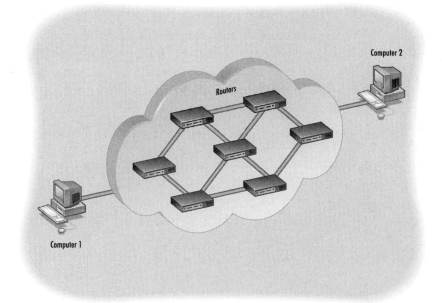

FIGURE 5.10
Typical Routed Network

Routers also have the ability to regulate traffic using many routes. For example, while forwarding data, routers can detect whether a particular route is congested and, if it is, find an alternate route to help the data arrive at is destination faster. They also have the ability to filter traffic, ensuring that unauthorized users do not send data into or out of a specific network.

Initially, it seems that routers perform the same functions as a bridge; however, routers function at the Network layer of the OSI Model, while bridges are at the Data Link layer. This means that routers perform different functions than bridges. Routers can also handle many protocols at once and can translate between those protocols.

Essentially, routers are small microcomputers containing their own processors, memory, and operating system (see Figure 5.11). All of these elements work together to decide how to route or reroute network traffic.

FIGURE 5.11
Router

Routing table

A file used by the router to make routing decisions.

Routing is the technique used to help data find its way from one computer to another, or from one network to another. Routers are able to handle this direction of traffic through routing tables. A *routing table* (see Figure 5.12) contains an assortment of information, including:

- Which router connection or port to use to forward traffic to a particular network.
- How to prioritize network traffic.
- How to handle data that flows through the router.

```
C:\>route print
========================================================================
Interface List
0x1 .......................... MS TCP Loopback interface
0x10003 ...00 04 5a 6b 97 09 ...... Linksys LNE100TX Fast Ethernet Adapter(LNE10
0TX v4)
0x10004 ...00 03 47 2b a3 4a ...... Intel(R) PRO/100 Network Connection
========================================================================
========================================================================
Active Routes:
Network Destination        Netmask          Gateway        Interface  Metric
        0.0.0.0          0.0.0.0     66.189.236.1   66.189.237.135      20
   66.189.236.0    255.255.252.0   66.189.237.135   66.189.237.135      20
 66.189.237.135  255.255.255.255      127.0.0.1        127.0.0.1        20
 66.255.255.255  255.255.255.255   66.189.237.135   66.189.237.135      20
      127.0.0.0        255.0.0.0      127.0.0.1        127.0.0.1         1
      224.0.0.0        240.0.0.0   66.189.237.135   66.189.237.135      20
255.255.255.255  255.255.255.255   66.189.237.135          10004        1
255.255.255.255  255.255.255.255   66.189.237.135   66.189.237.135      1
Default Gateway:       66.189.236.1
========================================================================
Persistent Routes: None
```

FIGURE 5.12
Routing Table

Routing tables may be either static or dynamic.

- *Static tables* are built manually by an administrator. When changes to the routing table are required, the administrator connects to the router and adds, edits, or deletes entries from the routing table. This process is time consuming and can cause network problems if entries are not accurate.

- *Dynamic tables* are built automatically by the router. When powered on, the router listens for broadcasts from other routers. As it hears these broadcasts, it notes the location of each router and the contents of their routing tables. This information is automatically entered into the listening router's dynamic routing table. Dynamic routing is more efficient than static routing and is the preferred method of building routing tables, especially for a large network.

Static table

A routing table that is built manually by an administrator. *More chances of errors.*

Dynamic table

A routing table that is built automatically by the router. *It's also safer*

─ TRY IT! ─

Explore the routing table of a router.

1. Depending on the router you have available, follow the instructions for connecting the PC to the router.
2. Log in to the router.
3. Using the appropriate command, at the console, display the routing table.
4. For example, when using most Cisco-brand routers, type the following command at the console: **show ip route**

In order for routers to build a routing table dynamically, routers must have the ability to talk with each other and exchange information. To do this, they use one of two types of algorithms, distance vector or link state.

DISTANCE VECTOR ALGORITHM

Distance vector

An algorithm used by routers to periodically broadcast the entire contents of their routing tables.

Routers using *distance vector* protocols periodically broadcast the entire contents of their routing tables to other routers. As a router receives an update from a direct neighboring router, it adds the contents to its own routing table. Additionally, it adds a metric, or hop count, to the update. The purpose of the hop count is to determine how far away the neighboring router is. It then broadcasts its routing table again, complete with the updates from neighboring routers. For example, using Figure 5.13, Router 1 will broadcast the contents of its routing table to Router 2. When Router 2 receives the update, it will add the information to its own routing table. It also adds a metric, or count of one, and passes its updated routing table to Router 3. When Router 3 receives the update from Router 2, Router 3 understands that Router 1 is two hops away, and not a directly connected neighbor.

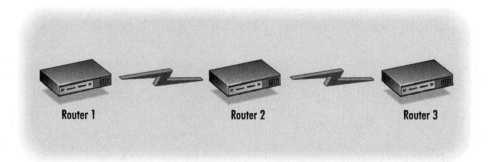

FIGURE 5.13
Updating Routing Tables Using a Distance Vector Algorithm

Routers using distance vector protocols do not know the physical or logical topology of the network. They only know their distance from other routers. The primary disadvantage to using distance vector protocols is the amount of network traffic they create. Each router typically broadcasts the entire contents of its routing tables across the network every 30 seconds. The most common distance vector protocol is Routing Information Protocol (RIP).

Routing Information Protocol (RIP) *Limited to 15 hops*

Routers that use the *Routing Information Protocol (RIP)* broadcast their entire routing table to neighboring routers every 30 seconds. During the broadcast, every device on the network sees the information. This is a severe waste of bandwidth, when the information needs to be seen only by other routers. RIP is limited to 15 hops; therefore, any routers that are more than 15 hops away are unreachable.

Routers using RIP have problems with slow *convergence.* Convergence means that all routers have matching routing tables that are complete and up-to-date. With slow convergence, if a link between routers fails, it will take some time before the other routers converge, or are aware of the failure.

LINK STATE ALGORITHM

Routers using a *link state* protocol are more efficient than routers using distance vector protocols. Routers using link state protocols *multicast* their updates to other routers. Multicast routers send only one copy of the routing table. It addresses the packets containing the routing table information to the routers that should receive it. Also, instead of sending the entire contents of the routing table, only the updated information is sent. Finally, the updates are sent about every 5 minutes, instead of at 30-second intervals. A commonly used link state protocol is Open Shortest Path First (OSPF).

Open Shortest Path First (OSPF) — *Know*

Open Shortest Path First (OSPF) was designed to address some of the limitations imposed by RIP. Some of the issues addressed include the hop count limitation. In OSPF, there is no limit on the number of hops between routers. Also, OSPF uses multicast to send routing table updates. This means an end to broadcasts; only routers running OSPF will receive updates. Furthermore, the updates are sent only when a routing table change actually occurs, instead of at predetermined intervals. This not only avoids unnecessary network traffic but also enables convergence to happen faster, since routing changes are sent as soon as they occur.

Routing Information Protocol (RIP)

A distance vector protocol with a specific set of rules and behaviors employed by a router for the purpose of moving datagrams from the source node to the destination node across an internetwork. The two most commonly used forms of RIP are employed by IP networks (RIP for IP) and IPX networks (RIP for IPX).

Convergence

The time it takes for all routers to update their routing tables.

Link state

An algorithm that uses multicast instead of broadcasts to send updates. *only send out the changes*

Multicast

Sending updates to a specific group of routers.

Open Shortest Path First (OSPF)

A link state protocol used by routers, designed to address some of the limitations imposed by Routing Information Protocol.

Gateways

Gateway

Hardware or software, or both, that is used to translate data or protocols from one network to another.

A *gateway* is used to connect dissimilar networks. For example, a gateway could be used to connect a local area network to a mainframe network. The gateway, which is generally a combination of hardware and software, converts or translates data or protocols from one network to the other.

Another example is mail gateways, which allow mail services designed to run on local area networks to communicate with other mail servers on the Internet. These mail gateways translate the e-mail messages into formats that other mail servers can understand.

Over the years, computer experts have debated how a gateway matches up with the OSI Model. Since a gateway is a combination of both hardware and software, many people believe that gateways work at all levels of the OSI Model. More recent schools of thought, however, believe that gateways use the top four layers (4 through 7: Application, Presentation, Session, and Transport) of the OSI Model. For the purposes of this book and the test, we will assume gateways work with the top four layers of the OSI Model (see Figure 5.14).

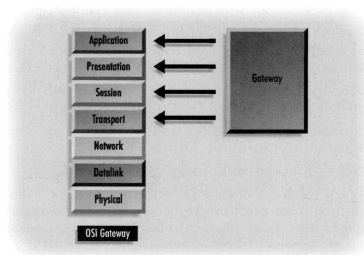

FIGURE 5.14
Gateway versus OSI Model

Channel Service Unit (CSU) and Data Service Unit (DSU)

The *Channel Service Unit (CSU)* is a piece of equipment containing an interface that is used to terminate a data line, such as a T1 or T3 line. Each

Networking Components

CSU communicates with another CSU that is located at the other end of the data line. The CSU has the ability to monitor the data line and provides some error correction for the data line.

A *Data Service Unit (DSU)* provides a terminal connection to a digital line. It operates essentially as a digital modem, converting the digital data frame that is used on the LAN into a frame that can be transmitted over a WAN, and vice versa.

CSUs and DSUs are often contained within a single piece of hardware (see Figure 5.15) or are integrated into a router. When connecting two networks, for example when creating a wide area network, you will use a digital line, such as a T1 or T3, and the line will terminate at both ends with a CSU/DSU (see Figure 5.16). On the LAN end, the CSU/DSU unit will connect to either a multiplexer or a router.

Channel Service Unit (CSU)

A piece of equipment containing an interface that is used to terminate a data line.

Data Service Unit (DSU)

A piece of networking hardware that converts a LAN digital data frame for use on a WAN, and vice versa.

FIGURE 5.15
Channel Service Unit/Data Service Unit (CSU/DSU)

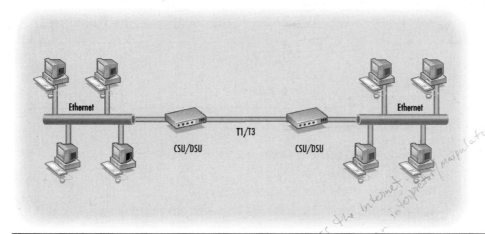

FIGURE 5.16
CSU/DSU Making a WAN Connection

Network Interface Cards

The network interface card (NIC) is the piece of hardware installed inside a computer that allows the computer to be connected to the network (see Figure 5.17). The NIC is plugged into an expansion slot on the computer's motherboard. Once the NIC is physically installed, a network cable can be plugged into a port on the back of the NIC. A piece of software known as a driver is then installed to allow the computer's operating system to interact with the NIC. The NIC and the driver work together to support the Data Link layer protocol (Ethernet or Token Ring), network access method (CSMA/CD or token passing), and other features. In addition, some newer model NICs include an encryption chip that supports data encryption at the Physical (NIC) layer.

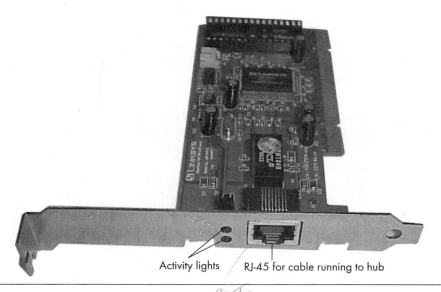

Activity lights   RJ-45 for cable running to hub

FIGURE 5.17
Network Interface Card

— TRY IT! —

Install a network interface card.

1. Open the cover of a computer and insert a NIC into an open slot.
2. Replace the cover and start the computer.
3. When prompted, specify the path to the driver files.
4. Open the Network Properties page and view the installed network components.

Networking Components

Integrated Services Digital Network (ISDN) Adapters

Integrated Services Digital Network (ISDN) is a communications technology that allows digital signals to pass through normal telephone lines, also referred to as "plain old telephone service" *(POTS)* or "public switched telephone networks" *(PSTN)*. ISDN allows you to combine one or more communications channels to provide high data transfer speeds, generally in the area of 128Kbps.

An ISDN *terminal adapter* is used as the interface between the ISDN line and your computer. The adapter can be internal (installed inside a computer like a network interface card), or external (plugged into a serial port on the back of the computer). (See Figure 5.18.)

Integrated Services Digital Network (ISDN)

A communications standard that allows digital signals to pass through existing PSTN lines.

POTS

An acronym for "plain old telephone service."

PSTN

An acronym for "public switched telephone network."

Terminal adapter

The interface between the ISDN line and the computer.

FIGURE 5.18
A Terminal Adapter

The ISDN adapter will support one of two interfaces, U interface or S/T interface:

- The *U interface* is used when transmitting the data signal over long distances, such as from your home to a telephone switching station or the central telephone office.
- The *S/T interface* is used when transmitting the data signal over short distances, such as from a wall jack to your ISDN adapter. If your adapter has an S/T interface, you will need to purchase a network termination, commonly referred to as an NT-1. Most ISDN adapters include both an NT-1 and the terminal adapter.

U interface

The interface used by an ISDN adapter when transmitting data signals over long distances.

S/T interface

The interface used by an ISDN adapter when transmitting data over short distances.

Although people routinely refer to the ISDN adapter as a modem, this is incorrect. A modem is used to convert digital signals to analog and vice versa. Since the ISDN line is digital, conversion is not necessary.

You can also purchase ISDN bridges and routers.

Wireless Access Points (AP) ✓

A wireless access point (AP) (Figure 5.19) is the unit a wireless network card (Figure 5.20) communicates with in order to connect to the network. A wireless access point acts like a hub in a wired network. The access point receives, buffers, and transmits data between wireless components, such as a laptop computer with a wireless network adapter installed and the wired network. An access point can support a small group of users and generally has a range up to several hundred feet.

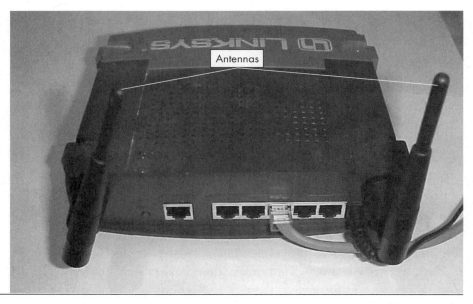

FIGURE 5.19
Wireless Router/Access Point

When a device with a wireless adapter is turned on, it scans the wireless frequencies for a wireless access point. If the device is operating in infrastructure mode, the device selects the access point with which to connect. Once the connection is made, the wireless device switches to the channel assigned by the access point and negotiates the use of a port. This is known as establishing an association.

Networking Components

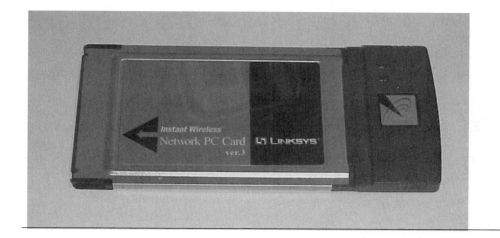

FIGURE 5.20
Wireless PC Card NIC

TRY IT!

Connect to a wireless access point.

1. Using a laptop computer or PC, connect to a wireless access point.
2. Log in to the network.
3. Explore the network through Network Neighborhood or My Network Places (depending on operating system).

If you have a problem connecting with an access point, such as low signal strength, the wireless device continues its scan for another one. If another access point is located, the wireless device switches to the channel of that access point and negotiates the use of a port. This process is called reassociation.

Modems ~ is on the physical layer. send by 0 1
or binary.

A *modem* is a piece of hardware that converts data from inside the computer into a form that can be transmitted over some type of cable media. The modem can be connected to a computer in a variety of ways. Once the modem is physically installed, a piece of software known as a driver must be installed to allow the computer's operating system to interact with the modem.

Modem

Hardware that converts computer data into a form that can be transmitted and received over cable media.

The word "modem" is actually a combination of two words, "**mo**dulation" and "**dem**odulation." When using a modem for data communications, the modem "modulates," which means it takes the digital signal from your computer and changes it into an analog signal that can be transmitted over the cable media. When the modem receives data, it "demodulates," meaning it takes the analog signal from the cable and changes it into a digital signal that can be understood by the computer.

There are three basic categories of modems: traditional, Digital Subscriber Line (DSL), and cable.

TRADITIONAL

Traditional modem

A device that allows a computer to connect to a network over a dial-up telephone line.

The *traditional modem* allows your computer to connect to a network using a dial-up telephone line The modem can be installed in an expansion slot inside a computer (see Figure 5.21) or connected externally to a serial port on the outside of the computer case. After the software is installed, one end of a telephone cable is connected into a port on the modem and the other end is connected to a POTS or PSTN jack. You can then use the modem to dial into another computer containing a modem that is acting as a server. The traditional modem is the most common type; however, it is quickly being replaced with higher speed network connections.

FIGURE 5.21
Installing an Internal Modem

Networking Components

[handwritten: Regular Phone Jack]
[handwritten: RJ11 & RJ45 → DSL]
[handwritten: max speed on modem 56K]

DIGITAL SUBSCRIBER LINE (DSL)

Digital Subscriber Line (DSL) modems also support data transfer over POTS or PSTN networks; however, DSL uses higher frequencies than traditional modems. Using these higher frequencies allows for faster data transfer speeds, up to 9Mbps.

To use DSL, you must install an Ethernet NIC inside your computer. A network cable, normally twisted pair, runs from the NIC into an external DSL modem (see Figure 5.22), also called an endpoint. The DSL modem is then plugged into a POTS or PSTN outlet.

Digital Subscriber Line (DSL) modem

A modulation technique that allows data transmission over higher POTS frequencies for faster transfer speeds.

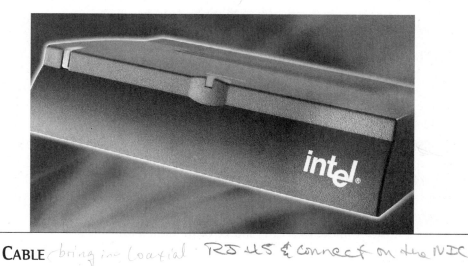

FIGURE 5.22
DSL Modem

CABLE *[handwritten: bring in coaxial RJ45 & connect on the NIC]*

Cable modem service is another high-speed networking technology that uses the same coaxial cable that powers cable television in most homes. When the coaxial cable enters the home, it will terminate in a splitter. A cable

Cable modem

A high-speed networking technology that uses the same coaxial cable that powers cable television.

runs from one branch of the splitter to an external cable modem (see Figure 5.23). A standard Ethernet network cable, normally twisted pair, then runs from the cable modem to an Ethernet network interface card installed inside the computer. Newer cable modems also support Universal Serial Bus (USB) connections. Cable modems can also feed entire networks when they are plugged into a network hub or switch.

FIGURE 5.23
Cable Modem

One benefit of cable is that it provides a continuous connection that doesn't require dialing into a network before it can be used. The data transfer speed of cable modem service is quoted as 3Mbps to 50Mbps; however, in practice it is more like 2Mbps to 3Mbps.

Troubleshooting Network Devices

Network connectivity problems are extremely common and can range from problems with a single device to an entire network failure. While these problems are common, network hardware such as switches, hubs, and bridges tend to be very reliable. Although these devices do fail from time to time, it is far more likely that a cable or host is the culprit.

A simple test is to determine the scope of the problem. If only a single workstation is affected, most likely the problem does not exist at the network device. If a network segment or the entire network is affected, the network device is more likely the source of the problem.

If you suspect a network hardware device to be faulty, here are some troubleshooting procedures you can follow to verify or disprove your theory.

TROUBLESHOOTING HUBS AND SWITCHES

- Check the lights over each port to see if they are glowing or flashing, depending on the lighting configuration on the device. If the light on the port where the device is plugged in is not glowing or flashing, there is a connectivity problem.
  - Plug the cable into another port and see if that light comes on. If it does, a bad port on the device is indicated.
  - If the light does not come on, check the cable.
- If all of the port lights are glowing instead of flashing, recycle the power on the device.
- If you are using a switch in a VLAN configuration, recheck the configuration of the ports on the switch.
- Always check for recent configuration changes that may affect the performance of the device, especially with managed hubs and switches.

TROUBLESHOOTING BRIDGES AND ROUTERS

Many of the same procedures outlined for hubs and switches apply to bridges as well. If you can determine through the procedures outlined above that the problem is not a physical issue (i.e., a bad cable, port, or connection), then suspect a configuration problem.

TROUBLESHOOTING GATEWAYS

Gateways present unique problems because they are a combination of hardware and software. For example, with a mail gateway, you typically install a network operating system and associated service packs (software) on a server (hardware). Once the network operating system is installed and functioning correctly, you install an e-mail system and its required service packs (more software). This server must be connected by cable to the rest of the network (hardware and software) and typically sits behind a firewall (more hardware and software).

Troubleshooting gateway problems involves working at all layers, requiring a thorough understanding of each component involved. The first step in the process is to determine where in the chain the problem lies.

- Use standard troubleshooting tools such as error messages or event logs to narrow down the problem.
- Work on one concern at a time. That is, if you suspect a hardware problem, do not start substituting new hardware while someone else makes software configuration changes.

- If you determine that the problem is hardware related, repair or replace the hardware. This includes the associated cables.
- If the problem is software related, follow the manufacturer's recommendations for making repairs.

TROUBLESHOOTING NICS AND OTHER ADAPTERS

- Check the Device Manager utility to ensure the adapter is installed and functioning correctly.
- Check all cable connections to make sure they are secure and plugged into the correct ports.
- Is the data line functioning? Try to make a phone call or turn on your cable television to see if you have a signal.
- Use some of the TCP/IP utilities to check possible problem areas, such as the default gateway and DNS servers.

TROUBLESHOOTING WIRELESS ACCESS POINTS

- Check the signal strength in the area around the access point.
- Check the wireless network device to see if it can associate with another access point.
- Check the configuration of the access point to see if only certain devices are allowed to connect to it.
- Check the channel settings of both the access point and the wireless device.

STUDY GUIDE

In this chapter, we discussed the selection and use of networking hardware. Here are some key points to remember.

HUBS

- Hubs are the most basic form of multistation access unit.
- They are used to connect devices, such as computers and printers, in a network.
- Hubs may also be used to connect different network segments together.

Passive Hubs

- A passive hub takes the signal (data) that it receives from a device, copies it, and sends it out the other ports in the hub to all of the other networked devices.
- It does not manipulate or view the data and it does nothing to amplify, clean up, or change the data signal.
- Passive hubs extend only the length of the cable that is being used on the network.

Active Hubs

- Active hubs have the ability to repair weak signals.
- They do this by regenerating or amplifying the data signal. This regeneration consists of intercepting a weak signal and raising it back up to the original voltage.
- Once the signal is regenerated, it is sent back out of the hub to all of the other devices.
- An active hub can be used to add computers to a network or to allow for increased distances between workstations and servers.
- An active hub is commonly called a repeater.

Managed, or Intelligent, Hubs

- A managed, or intelligent, hub allows you to configure and monitor each individual port.
- Ports can be enabled or disabled through a hub management utility that is normally provided by the manufacturer.
- Hub management will also allow you to gather network parameters such as the number or types of packets that have been transmitted, the number of errors that have occurred, and the number of collisions taking place on the network.

SWITCHES

- Instead of just copying and sending data out to every device on the network, a switch has the ability to learn the physical addresses of all of the devices on the network.
- Once it has learned the addresses of each device, the switch will send data only to the port to which the destination device is connected.
- By sending data only to its intended recipient, network traffic is dramatically reduced, providing more available bandwidth.

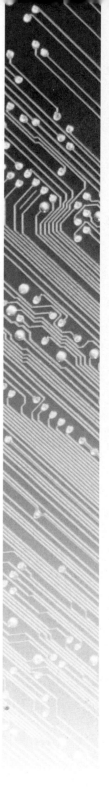

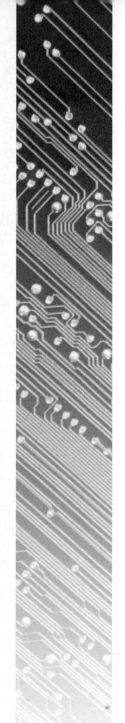

- Reducing network traffic also helps cut down on the number of data collisions that take place on Ethernet networks.
- Most switches have the ability to auto-sense network transmission speeds.
- Layer 3 switches incorporate features of both routers and switches.

VIRTUAL LOCAL AREA NETWORK (VLAN)

- A VLAN is a group of network devices (workstations, servers, printers, etc.) that can be grouped into a logical network, without regard for physical location.
- All of the devices act as though they are connected to a single network segment, even though they may be physically located in different buildings or even different states.
- The three basic VLAN models are identified by how the VLAN is established.
    o Port-based: A network administrator assigns each port a switch to a VLAN.
    o MAC address-based: Membership on the VLAN is based on source and destination MAC addresses of the devices that are attached to the switch.
    o Protocol-based: Protocol-based VLANs, also known as Layer 3 VLANs, are based on the protocols being used (IP, IPX, etc.) and their respective Layer 3 (OSI Model Network layer) addresses.

BRIDGES

- The primary purpose of a bridge is to allow devices that are attached to separate LANs or LAN segments to communicate as if they were all located on the same LAN.
- Bridges are also able to contain network traffic to the section of the network to which it belongs.
- The bridge can be configured to deny or reject traffic on one segment from being transmitted to another segment.
- Bridges decide which packets to pass between networks through the use of a routing table.
- Bridges are typically classified as either local or remote.
    o Local bridges exist when there is a direct connection between several LAN segments.
    o Remote bridges use WAN connections, generally leased telephone lines, to connect LAN segments.

- The four basic types of bridging algorithms are transparent, source-route, translational, and source-route transparent.

Transparent

- The transparent bridge has the capability of automatically identifying all of the devices that are connected to each segment of the network.
- The transparent bridge listens to the traffic traveling on the network and learns the addresses of devices that are located on the segments.
- This information is then stored in a table within the bridge.
- Whenever the bridge receives a packet, it can check its internal table to determine exactly where the destination device is located.

Source-Route

- Source-route bridging is commonly found on Token Ring networks.
- To communicate on a source-route network, a device first sends a broadcast across the network.
- When the destination device hears the broadcast, it replies back to sender. This reply includes the route that the broadcast packet took to get to the destination device.
- The sender then uses that route to communicate with the destination device.

Translational

- Translational bridges are used to connect dissimilar networks together.
- For example, a bridge could be used to connect an Ethernet network segment to a Token Ring network segment.
- The conversion of the frames from one type to another is typically done through encapsulation.

Source-Route Transparent

- Source-route transparent bridges combine aspects of both source-route and translational bridges in order to enable communications on networks with a mix of Ethernet and Token Ring technologies.

ROUTERS

- A router is a device that connects multiple network segments together to form a larger network, or large networks together to form an internetwork.

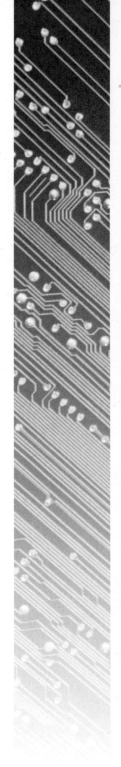

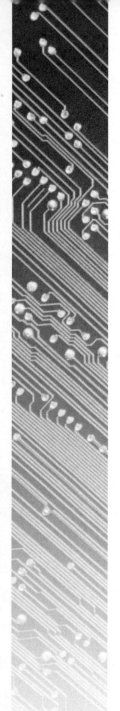

- Routers are the devices used to connect local area networks (LANs), making a wide area network (WAN).
- Routers join networks together by ensuring that traffic generated by a host on one network finds its way to a host on another network.
- Routers have the ability to use redundant paths.
- Routers are small microcomputers containing their own processors, memory, and operating system.
- Routing is the technique used to help data find its way from one computer to another, or one network to another.
- Routing tables may be either static or dynamic.
  - Static tables are built manually by an administrator.
  - Dynamic tables are built automatically by the router.
- In order for routers to build a routing table dynamically, routers must have the ability to talk with each other and exchange information. To do this, they use one of two types of algorithms, distance vector or link state.

Distance Vector Algorithm

- Routers using distance vector protocols periodically broadcast the entire contents of their routing tables to other routers.
- The primary disadvantage to using distance vector protocols is the amount of network traffic they create.
- Each router typically broadcasts the entire contents of its routing tables across the network every 30 seconds.
- The most common distance vector protocol is Routing Information Protocol (RIP).

Routing Information Protocol (RIP)

- Routers that use the Routing Information Protocol (RIP) broadcast their entire routing table to neighboring routers every 30 seconds.
- When broadcasts are used, the broadcasted data is sent to every device on the network, which creates a lot of traffic and wastes bandwidth, since only routers need to see the data.
- RIP is limited to 15 hops; therefore, any routers that are more than 15 hops away are unreachable.
- Routers using RIP have problems with slow convergence.
- Convergence means that all routers have matching routing tables that are complete and up-to-date.

Link State Algorithm

- Routers using a link state protocol are more efficient than routers using distance vector protocols.
- Routers using link state protocols multicast their updates to other routers.
- Multicast routers send only one copy of the routing table.
- The sending router addresses the packets containing the routing table information to the routers that should receive it.
- Instead of sending the entire contents of the routing table, only updates are sent.
- Updates are sent about every 5 minutes, instead of at 30-second intervals.
- A commonly used link state protocol is Open Shortest Path First (OSPF).

Open Shortest Path First (OSPF)

- Open Shortest Path First (OSPF) was designed to address some of the limitations imposed by RIP. (Routing Information Protocol)
- In OSPF, there is no limit on the number of hops between routers.
- OSPF uses multicast to send routing table updates. This means an end to broadcasts; only routers running OSPF will receive updates.
- Updates are sent only when a routing table change actually occurs, instead of at predetermined intervals.
- OSPF converges faster, since routing changes are sent as soon as they occur.

GATEWAYS

- A gateway is used to connect dissimilar networks.
- For example, a gateway could be used to connect a local area network to a mainframe network.
- The gateway, which is generally a combination of hardware and software, converts data or protocols from one network to the other.
- Gateways work at the top four layers (4 through 7: Application, Presentation, Session, and Transport) of the OSI Model.

CHANNEL SERVICE UNIT (CSU) AND DATA SERVICE UNIT (DSU)

- The CSU is a piece of equipment containing an interface that is used to terminate a data line, such as a T1 or T3 line.

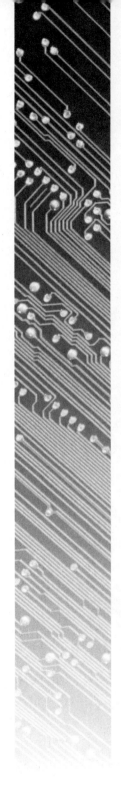

- Each CSU communicates with another CSU that is located at the other end of the data line.
- The CSU has the ability to monitor the data line and provides some error correction for the data line.
- A DSU provides a terminal connection to a digital line.
- A DSU operates essentially as a digital modem, converting the digital data frame that is used on the LAN into a frame that can be transmitted over a WAN and vice versa.

Network Interface Cards

- The network interface card (NIC) is the piece of hardware installed inside a computer that allows the computer to be connected to the network.
- The NIC is plugged into an expansion slot on the computer's motherboard.
- Once the NIC is physically installed, a network cable can be plugged into a port on the back of the NIC.
- A piece of software known as a driver is then installed to allow the computer's operating system to interact with the NIC.
- The NIC and the driver work together to support the Data Link layer protocol (Ethernet or Token Ring), the network access method (CSMA/CD or token passing), and other features.

Integrated Services Digital Network (ISDN) Adapters

- Integrated Services Digital Network (ISDN) is a communications technology that allows digital signals to pass through normal telephone lines, also referred to as plain old telephone service (POTS) or public switched telephone networks (PSTN).
- ISDN allows you to combine one or more communications channels to provide high data transfer speeds, generally in the area of 128Kbps.
- An ISDN terminal adapter is used as the interface between the ISDN line and your computer.
- The ISDN adapter will support one of two interfaces, U interface or S/T interface:
  - The U interface is used when transmitting the data signal over long distances, such as from your home to a telephone switching station or the central telephone office.
  - The S/T interface is used when transmitting the data signal over short distances, such as from a wall jack to your ISDN adapter.

○ If your adapter has an S/T interface, you will need to purchase a network termination, commonly referred to as an NT-1.

Wireless Access Points (APs)

- A wireless access point (AP) is the place a wireless network interface card communicates with to connect to the network.
- A wireless network card acts like a hub on a wired network.
- An access point can support a small group of users and generally has a range up to several hundred feet.

Modems

- A modem is a piece of hardware that transforms data from inside the computer into a form that can be transmitted over some type of cable media.
- When using a modem for data communication, the modem "modulates," which means it takes the digital signal from your computer and changes it into an analog signal that can be transmitted over the cable media.
- When it receives data, the modem "demodulates," meaning it takes the analog signal from the cable and changes it into a digital signal that can be understood by the computer.
- There are three basic categories of modems: traditional, Digital Subscriber Line (DSL), and cable.

Traditional

- The traditional modem allows a computer to connect to a network using a dial-up telephone line.

Digital Subscriber Line (DSL)

- DSL modems also support data transfer over POTS or PSTN networks; however, DSL uses higher frequencies than traditional modems.

Cable

- Cable modem service is another high-speed networking technology that uses the same coaxial cable that powers cable television in most homes.

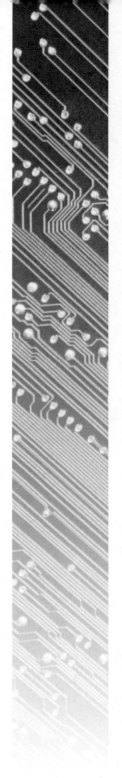

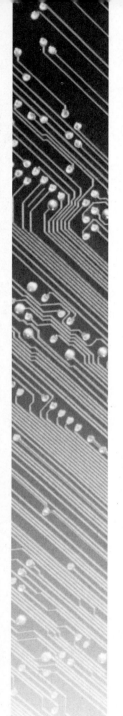

TROUBLESHOOTING NETWORK DEVICES

- Network connectivity problems are extremely common and can range from problems with a single device to an entire network failure.
- Determine the scope of the problem.
  - If only a single workstation is affected, most likely the problem does not exist at the network level.
  - If a network segment or the entire network is affected, the network device is more likely the source of the problem.

TROUBLESHOOTING HUBS AND SWITCHES

- Check the lights over each port to see if they are glowing or flashing, depending on the lighting configuration on the device. If the light on the port where the device is plugged in is not glowing or flashing, there is a connectivity problem.
  - Plug the cable into another port and see if that light comes on. If it does, a bad port on the device is indicated.
  - If the light does not come on, check the cable.
- If all of the port lights are glowing instead of flashing, recycle the power on the device.
- If you are using a switch in a VLAN configuration, recheck the configuration of the ports on the switch.
- Always check for recent configuration changes that may affect the performance of the device, especially with managed hubs and switches.

TROUBLESHOOTING BRIDGES AND ROUTERS

- Many of the same procedures outlined for hubs and switches apply to bridges as well.

TROUBLESHOOTING GATEWAYS

- Gateways present unique problems because they are a combination of hardware and software.
- Troubleshooting gateway problems involves working at all layers, requiring a thorough understanding of each component involved. The first step in the process is to determine where in the chain the problem lies.
- Use standard troubleshooting tools such as error messages or event logs to narrow down where the problem is.

- Work on one concern at a time. For example, if you suspect a hardware problem, do not start substituting new hardware while someone else makes software configuration changes.
- If you determine that the problem is hardware related, repair or replace the hardware. This includes the associated cables.
- If the problem is software related, follow the manufacturer's recommendations for repairing the problem.

TROUBLESHOOTING NETWORK INTERFACE CARDS AND OTHER ADAPTERS

- Check the Device Manager utility to ensure the adapter is installed and functioning correctly.
- Check all cable connections to make sure they are secure and plugged into the correct ports.
- Is the data line functioning? Try to make a phone call or turn on your cable television to see if you have a signal.
- Use some of the TCP/IP utilities to check for problem areas, such as the default gateway and DNS servers.

TROUBLESHOOTING WIRELESS ACCESS POINTS

- Check the signal strength in the area around the access point.
- Check the wireless network device to see if it can associate with another access point.
- Check the configuration of the access point to see if only certain devices are allowed to connect to it.
- Check the channel settings of both the access point and the wireless device.

PRACTICE TEST

Try this test to check your mastery of the concepts in this chapter.

1. _____ are the most basic form of multistation access unit.
   a. Routers
   b. Computers
   c. Hubs
   d. Switches

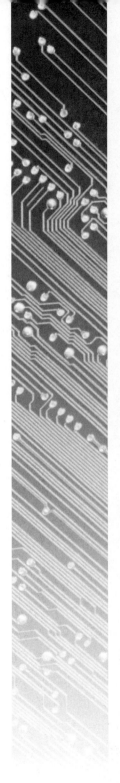

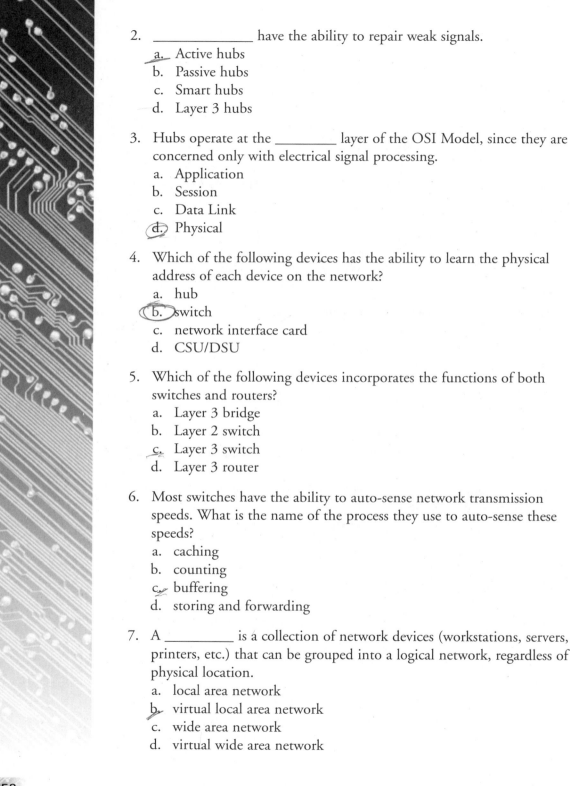

2. _____ have the ability to repair weak signals.
   a. Active hubs
   b. Passive hubs
   c. Smart hubs
   d. Layer 3 hubs

3. Hubs operate at the _____ layer of the OSI Model, since they are concerned only with electrical signal processing.
   a. Application
   b. Session
   c. Data Link
   d. Physical

4. Which of the following devices has the ability to learn the physical address of each device on the network?
   a. hub
   b. switch
   c. network interface card
   d. CSU/DSU

5. Which of the following devices incorporates the functions of both switches and routers?
   a. Layer 3 bridge
   b. Layer 2 switch
   c. Layer 3 switch
   d. Layer 3 router

6. Most switches have the ability to auto-sense network transmission speeds. What is the name of the process they use to auto-sense these speeds?
   a. caching
   b. counting
   c. buffering
   d. storing and forwarding

7. A _____ is a collection of network devices (workstations, servers, printers, etc.) that can be grouped into a logical network, regardless of physical location.
   a. local area network
   b. virtual local area network
   c. wide area network
   d. virtual wide area network

Networking Components

8. Bridges decide which packets to pass between networks through the use of a
   a. protocol.
   b. TCP/IP address.
   c. routing table.
   d. physical address.

9. What type of bridging would you find in a Token Ring network?
   a. source-route
   b. transparent
   c. translational
   d. source-route transparent

10. What will a bridge do with a packet it receives if it cannot find the address of the destination computer?
   a. It destroys the packet.
   b. It forwards the packet to the next bridge in the chain.
   c. It keeps the packet.
   d. It forwards the packet to all of the network segments.

11. Bridges work at the _____ layer of the OSI Model.
   a. Application
   b. Session
   c. Network
   d. Data Link

12. The _____ bridge has the capability of automatically identifying all of the devices that are connected to each segment of the network.
   a. source-route
   b. transparent
   c. translational
   d. source-route transparent

13. _____ are the devices used to connect local area networks (LANs) together, making a wide area network (WAN).
   a. Routers
   b. Bridges
   c. Layer 3 switches
   d. CSUs and DSUs

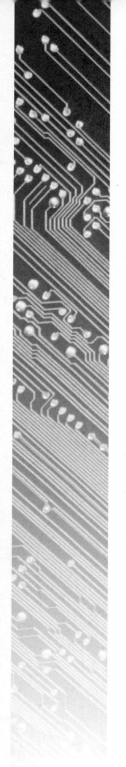

14. At which layer of the OSI Model do you find routers?
    a. Physical
    b. Data Link
    c. Network
    d. Transport

15. The router on your network requires a network administrator to connect to the router and manually make changes whenever a new network is needed. What type of routing table is being used?
    a. manual
    b. static
    c. dynamic
    d. physical

16. What are the drawbacks of using the Routing Information Protocol (RIP) with a router? (Select two)
    a. RIP is limited to 15 router hops.
    b. RIP requires manual updates of the routing table.
    c. RIP suffers from slow convergence.
    d. RIP suffers from fast convergence.

17. Which of the following devices function at the top four layers of the OSI Model?
    a. switches
    b. CSUs and DSUs
    c. network interface cards
    d. gateways

18. A _____ provides a terminal connection to a digital line.
    a. DSU
    b. modem
    c. CSU
    d. multiplexer

19. The _____ interface is used when transmitting a data signal over long-distance ISDN lines, such as from your home to a telephone switching station or the central telephone office.
    a. S/T
    b. NT-1
    c. POTS
    d. U

20. What is the correct definition of the term *demodulation?*
    a. changes the analog signal into a digital signal
    b. changes the digital signal into an analog signal
    c. changes the POTS or PSTN signal into an analog signal
    d. changes the cable signal into an analog signal

TROUBLESHOOTING

1. A user has phoned the help desk to report that he cannot log on to the network. You began the troubleshooting process by verifying that the user has typed his user name and password correctly. A visit to the user's computer disclosed that the network cable is plugged into the network interface card. After tracing the network cable to the wiring closet, you notice that the link and data lights on the hub port that the cable is plugged into are not lit. List at least three items that could cause this condition.

2. A user telephoned the help desk to report a problem using a newly installed network interface card. The user outlined these steps:
    a. After removing the cover from the computer, he installed the network interface card in an available slot.
    b. The cover was replaced and a network card was plugged into the back of the computer.
    c. The other end of the network cable was plugged into a hub.
    d. The user verified that the hub was working correctly for other users.
    e. The computer was turned on, but there was no network connection.

Given these details, what is the most likely problem?

CUSTOMER SERVICE

1. The shipping and warehouse departments each have a small network consisting of several workstations connected by an eight-port hub. These networks are located in adjacent rooms within the same building. The shipping department does not have access to a printer, so whenever they need to print a document, they copy that document to a floppy disk and carry it to the warehouse to be printed. Since this printing procedure wastes a lot of time and effort, the shipping department has asked you to implement a method that will allow them to print from their computers. This department is on a tight

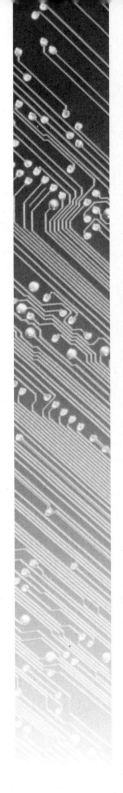

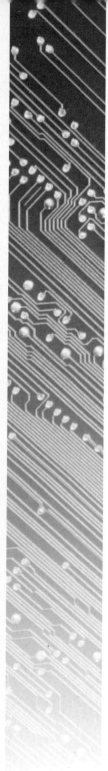

budget and has asked for a cheap solution. What method would you suggest? Is there more than one solution?

2. Your company network has 30 people working on a single network. Ten of these people are power users; that is, the majority of their work is done on client computers that communicate with a database server. The traffic between these clients and the server uses considerable network bandwidth. The remaining 20 users also use computers; however, they are average users, relying on the network for e-mail and small file transfer. Recently, several of the users have begun complaining about the network being slow and have asked you to fix the problem. What would be a good solution to this problem?

FOR MORE INFORMATION

For links to Web sites that provide further information about the topics covered in this chapter, go to the EMC/Paradigm Internet Resource Center at www.emcp.com/College Division/Internet Resource Centers/Networking/System Administration/Web Resources: For More Information.

Project Lab, Part
Media and Topologies

CHAPTER 1

PROJECT #1: CREATING A PEER–TO–PEER NETWORK

1. Create a checklist of hardware and software items necessary to connect two personal computers in a star topology using a peer-to-peer network environment.
2. Assemble the hardware and software required.
3. Install the hardware and software.
4. Test the connectivity between the two computers.

PROJECT #2: SHARING FILES USING SHARE–LEVEL SECURITY

1. Install file and print services on the computers in the peer-to-peer network.
2. On one of the computers, share a folder containing several files.
3. Establish security on the shared folder and files contained within by assigning the appropriate passwords.
4. On the client computer, access the shared folder.

PROJECT #3: CREATING A CLIENT–SERVER NETWORK

1. Create a checklist of hardware and software items necessary to connect one personal computer and one server in a client-server network environment.
2. Assemble the hardware and software required.
3. Install the hardware and software.
4. Test the connectivity between the client and the server.

PROJECT #4: CREATING A NETWORK USER

1. On the server, create a user and assign a password.
2. At the client workstation, launch the network client and log on to the server using the new user name and password.

PROJECT #5: SHARING FILES USING USER-LEVEL SECURITY

1. On the server, share a folder containing several files.
2. Create a group and add the user account you created above to the new group.
3. Assign read-only permissions to the group.
4. At the client workstation, using the user account created above, log on to the network.
5. Locate the shared folder and attempt to modify the files.

CHAPTER 2

PROJECT #1: IDENTIFYING THE MAC ADDRESS

For each listed operating system, use the appropriate utility to identify the MAC address for the machine. Record your findings.

    a. Windows 95/98.
    b. Windows 2000.
    c. Windows XP.

PROJECT #2: CHARTING FUNCTIONS AND HARDWARE DEVICES IN THE OSI MODEL

1. Build a chart listing the seven layers of the OSI Model.
2. Add the function of each level in data communications and add any hardware devices that you have learned about up to this point.
3. Keep this chart, as it will be used in another Project Lab.

PROJECT #3: RESEARCHING THE HISTORY OF THE OSI MODEL

1. Using the Internet search resources, research the history of the OSI Model and telecommunications.
2. Write a one-page summary of the history and its effect on the development of telecommunications in the twenty-first century.

PROJECT #4: USING THE OSCILLOSCOPE

1. Using an oscilloscope, measure the voltage of various types of signals.
2. Record the patterns of the various signals in a drawing.
3. For each type of signal measured, determine its encoding scheme. Mark that on your drawings.

CHAPTER 3

PROJECT #1: CREATING A CHART OF 802 STANDARDS

1. Create a chart containing 802 standards.
2. Match each standard to its appropriate technology.

PROJECT #2: WORKING WITH THE MAC ADDRESS

1. Examine a network interface card (NIC) and identify the following items:
   - Brand.
   - MNnetwork speeds supported.
   - Media access protocol supported.
   - Cable types and connectors supported.
   - MAC address (if available).
2. Install the NIC and appropriate drivers in a computer.
3. Using the appropriate utility, display the MAC address of your installed NIC.
4. Record the MAC address of each computer in your network.

PROJECT #3: IDENTIFYING NETWORK TYPES

1. Examine a network in use at your facility.
2. Identify and document the following items:
   - Physical topology.
   - Logical topology.
   - Media access method.

PROJECT #4: DOCUMENTING YOUR NETWORK

Using the information obtained in Project 3, document the characteristics of your network. The documentation should include:
- a drawing of the physical layout;
- locations of all networking hardware; and
- locations of all clients and servers.

CHAPTER 4

PROJECT #1: IDENTIFYING NETWORK MEDIA

1. Examine a network in use at your facility.
2. Identify and document the following items:
   - Types of cable media in use.
   - Grades of existing cable.
   - Types of connectors in use.
   - Roles of specific pieces of cable:
     a. Network backbone.
     b. Patch cables.
     c. Workstation cable runs.
     d. Crossover cables.
   - Number and locations of punch-down blocks.
   - Number and locations of patch panels.

PROJECT #2: COMPARING YOUR NETWORK WITH ESTABLISHED STANDARDS

1. Using the information obtained in Project 1, compare the characteristics of your network with the specifications listed in the book. Identify the following characteristics of media used in your network:
   - Distance limitations of cabling used.
   - Types of connectors.
   - Maximum number of stations allowed per network.
   - Shortest length of cable that can be used.
2. Document each of these standards.

Project #3: Making and Testing Twisted Pair Cables

1. Obtain several sections of twisted pair cable and the appropriate connectors.
2. Using a wire crimper, create several network cables.
3. Plug the wires into an existing network and verify that they function correctly.

Project #4: Making and Testing Thin Coaxial Cables

1. Obtain several sections of thin coaxial cable and the appropriate connectors.
2. Using a wire crimper, create several network cables.
3. Plug the wires into an existing network or create a small network.
4. Correctly terminate each cable run.
5. Verify that the cables work correctly.

Project #5: Making and Testing Thick Coaxial Cables

1. Obtain several sections of thick coaxial cable and the appropriate connectors.
2. Identify by marking on the cable where the connectors should be attached.
3. Attach the appropriate connectors by vampire clamp.
4. Verify that the cables work correctly.

Project #6: Making and Testing Fiber-Optic Cables

1. Obtain several sections of fiber optic cable and the appropriate connectors.
2. Attach the connectors to the cable. Use the appropriate installation method for the type of connector that you are using.
3. Plug the wires into an existing network.
4. Verify that the cables work correctly.

CHAPTER 5

Project #1: Examining a Hub or Switch

1. Examine the device externally. Notice the ports and associated lights available for each port.

2. Examine the pin placement in each port. Insert an RJ-45 connector into a port to verify pin alignment.
3. Identify the hub type: passive or active.
4. Carefully remove the cover.
5. Examine the wiring inside the device.
6. Notice how each port is linked to each other port.
7. On a white board or piece of paper, document how the connections are made inside the hub.

PROJECT #2: CREATING A STAR TOPOLOGY NETWORK

1. Using the hub or switch, create a small network using a star topology.
2. Use the link and data lights to monitor connectivity and data traffic.

PROJECT #3: EXAMINING A BRIDGE

1. Examine the device externally. Notice the ports and associated lights available for each port.
2. Identify the role of the bridge: local or remote.
3. Identify the bridging algorithm being used: transparent, source-route, translational, or source-route transparent.
4. Carefully remove the cover from the bridge.
5. Examine the wiring inside the device.
6. On a white board or piece of paper, document the layout of the wiring.

PROJECT #4: INSTALLING A ROUTER

1. Examine the external features of a router. Identify the:
   a. make;
   b. model; and
   c. number and types of ports.

2. Identify and document the purpose of each port.

PROJECT #5: EXAMINING A ROUTING TABLE

1. Connect a computer to the router using the appropriate ports and cable.
2. Using HyperTerminal or another terminal utility, establish a session with the router.

3. Log into the router.
4. Using the appropriate command (varies with manufacturer) identify the routing protocols being used.
5. Using the appropriate command (varies with manufacturer) identify the protocols that are being routed.
6. Using the appropriate command (varies with manufacturer) view the contents of the routing table.
7. Download the routing table to a disk or the attached computer and print the routing table.
8. Examine the contents of the routing table.

PROJECT #6: EXAMINING A CHANNEL SERVICE UNIT (CSU)/DATA SERVICE UNIT (DSU)

1. Examine the external features of a CSU/DSU. Identify the:
   a. make;
   b. model;
   c. type of data line being supported; and
   d. any error correction being used.

2. Document your findings.

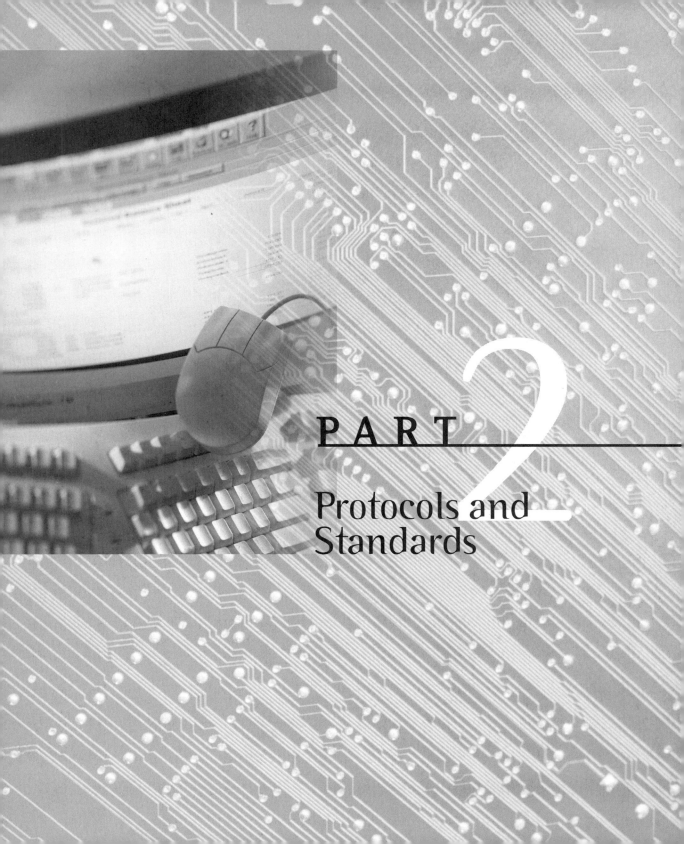

PART 2

Protocols and Standards

TEST OBJECTIVES IN PART 2

NETWORK+ EXAMINATION

- **Objective 2.3:** Differentiate between the following network protocols in terms of routing, addressing schemes, interoperability, and naming conventions: TCP/IP; IPX/SPX; NetBEUI; AppleTalk.
- **Objective 2.5:** Define the purpose, function, and/or use of the following protocols within TCP/IP: IP; TCP; UDP; FTP; TFTP; SMTP; HTTP; HTTPS; POP3/IMAP4; Telnet; ICMP; ARP; NTP.]
- **Objective 2.6:** Define the function of TCP/UDP ports. Identify well-known ports.
- **Objective 2.7:** Identify the purpose of the following network services (e.g., DHCP/BOOTP, DNS, NAT/ICS, WINS, and SNMP).
- **Objective 2.8:** Identify IP addresses (IPv4, IPv6) and their default subnet masks.
- **Objective 2.9:** Identify the purpose of subnetting and default gateways.
- **Objective 2.10:** Identify the differences between public vs. private networks.
- **Objective 2.11:** Identify the basic characteristics (e.g., speed, capacity, media) of the following WAN technologies: Packet switching vs. circuit switching; ISDN; FDDI; ATM; Frame Relay; SONet/SDH; T1/E1; T3/E3; OCx.
- **Objective 2.12:** Define the function of the following remote access protocols and services: RAS; PPP; PPTP; ICA.
- **Objective 2.13:** Identify the following security protocols and describe their purpose and function: IPSec; L2TP; SSL; Kerberos.
- **Objective 3.7:** Given a remote connectivity scenario (e.g., IP, IPX, dial-up, PPPoE, authentication, physical connectivity, etc.), configure the connection.
- **Objective 3.8:** Identify the purpose, benefits, and characteristics of using a firewall.
- **Objective 3.9:** Identify the purpose, benefits, and characteristics of using a proxy.
- **Objective 3.10:** Given a scenario, predict the impact of a particular security implementation on network functionality (e.g., blocking port numbers, encryption, etc.).
- **Objective 4.3.** Given a troubleshooting scenario involving a remote connectivity problem (e.g., authentication failure, protocol config-uration, physical connectivity) identify the cause of the problem.

Networking Protocols

Network+ Examination
- **Objective 2.3:** Differentiate between the following network protocols in terms of routing, addressing schemes, interoperability, and naming conventions:
  - TCP/IP
  - IPX/SPX
  - NetBEUI
  - AppleTalk

ON THE JOB

As a technician or a consultant, you will need to understand the positive and negative features of each of the major protocols used today. You may be asked to assess networks, including their operating systems and connectivity needs, with consideration for which of the protocols will meet the requirements for a particular network. By knowing which protocols function with what operating systems, and the characteristics of each protocol, you will be able to make astute judgments about the use of these protocols.

TRY IT!

Before you get started on this chapter, check what protocols you are running on your computer. On a Windows 2000 Professional machine, try the following:

1. Right-click My Network Places.
2. Click Properties.
3. Right-click Local Area Connection.
4. Click Properties.
5. Observe the protocols installed on this computer.
6. Compare your results with those listed in Figure 6.1.
7. Click Cancel to return to your screen without making any changes.

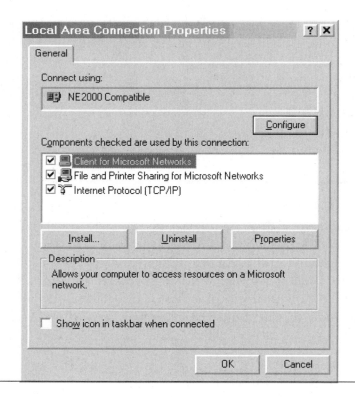

FIGURE 6.1
Local Area Connection Property
Sheet with Installed Protocols
Listed

Transmission Control Protocol/Internet Protocol (TCP/IP)

TCP/IP (Transmission Control Protocol/Internet Protocol), the most commonly run protocol on networks today, is actually a suite of protocols that allows communication to take place between nodes without concern for the operating system platform that the nodes are running. For example, Node 1 could be running Windows 2000 Professional as its operating system, and Node 2 may be running Linux. Those two machines can still transfer files, exchange e-mail, and locate printing services because they share the same protocol (see Figure 6.2).

TCP/IP (Transmission Control Protocol/Internet Protocol)

A set of protocols, or rules, that enables the transmission of datagrams across a network and that provides additional services to those datagrams, such as guaranteed delivery, node addressing, and application services.

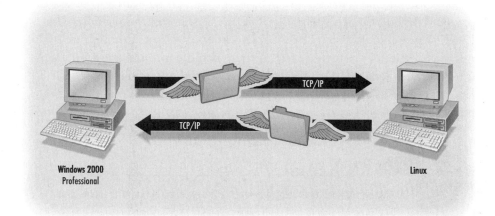

Windows 2000 Professional

Linux

FIGURE 6.2
TCP/IP allows communication between nodes of different operating systems.

This protocol is based on the services of the two core protocols, TCP and IP. Each manages services in layers that correspond to layers of the OSI Model.

- *Transmission Control Protocol (TCP)* is a Transport layer connection-oriented protocol that manages reliable delivery of data between nodes. If a packet is lost during transmission, for example, TCP will continue attempting to retransmit until the data is complete and received in a noncorrupt state.
- *Internet Protocol (IP)* is a Network layer protocol that manages transmission of data between nodes. IP uses the destination node address

Transmission Control Protocol (TCP)

A connection-oriented protocol, or set of rules, that is responsible for the guaranteed delivery of datagrams across a network.

Internet Protocol (IP)

A connectionless protocol, or set of rules, that is responsible for the transport of datagrams across a network.

Packet

One segment of a message that has been prepared for network transmission and that contains the address of both sender and receiver. Also contains a sequence number used for reassembling all segments of the message once the message has been received.

Defense Advanced Research Projects Agency (DARPA)

A Department of Defense (DOD) research group that originated the TCP/IP suite of protocols.

(a logical address) to forward the *packet* from the sending node's router to the receiving router and on to the destination node. IP is a connectionless protocol that concerns itself only with the transmission of the packet, not the reliable delivery of the data.

HISTORY

TCP/IP has an interesting history. Its development began in 1969, when the Cold War was raging. The U.S. Department of Defense (DOD) realized that its communications network would surely sustain damage should the Cold War become warmer. The DOD needed a way to ensure that communications would not be brought to a halt if any one node or phone line broke down or was damaged. So a DOD research group called the *Defense Advanced Research Projects Agency (DARPA)* built and tested the protocol. In addition to preventing breakdowns in communications, the DARPA program also sought to solve another problem: Although many networks existed at that time, few of them could communicate with each other because each vendor used proprietary communications protocols. Data could be exchanged only if the destination machine used the same proprietary protocol as the source machine, and this often was not the case.

IN REAL LIFE

DARPA was formed to develop a means for independent networks to communicate with each other and to provide a means whereby node-to-node communications could use multiple paths to get from a source to a destination.

While DARPA was working on the program, it also built a model for communications. This model looks a little different from the OSI Model. It has only four layers, as you can see from Figure 6.3. Some of the layers from the OSI Model are grouped together in the DOD Model.

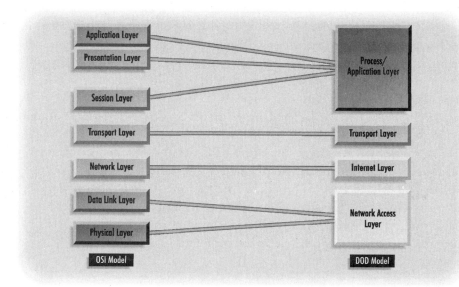

Figure diagram labels:

OSI Model: Application Layer, Presentation Layer, Session Layer, Transport Layer, Network Layer, Data Link Layer, Physical Layer

DOD Model: Process/Application Layer, Transport Layer, Internet Layer, Network Access Layer

FIGURE 6.3
The DOD Model and the OSI Model Compared

The DARPA program became the pet project of the military and academic researchers who were funded by the military. As the 1970s rolled on, DARPA continued to evolve new standards that would remove vendor-specific needs from communications and that would also provide recovery features. By 1980, TCP/IP had been developed and tested and was ready for adoption. The DARPA program name was changed to *ARPANET (Advanced Research Projects Agency Network),* and the groundwork had been laid for what we now know as the Internet.

In 1983, ARPANET declared that all connected hosts (562 were registered at the time) would adopt TCP/IP. At the same time, the University of California at Berkeley was modifying AT&T's UNIX operating system. This version of UNIX became BSD UNIX, which would become the most common of all the platforms used on the Internet.

The combined results of DARPA'S ARPANET and UC/Berkeley's BSD UNIX led to a robust set of protocols (eventually called Transmission Control Protocol/Internet Protocol) that manage the basic network communications needs identified by DARPA and a large set of services developed at Berkeley (BSD UNIX). Today, not only can we transfer files, log in to servers remotely, and print to nonlocal printers, but we can also resolve friendly names to a unique node identifier, check the network for errors, transfer e-mail, and route messages from one network to another. All this came to be because of a set of rules called TCP/IP.

beginning of the internet

ARPANET (Advanced Research Projects Agency Network)

The name given to the finished program developed by DARPA. ARPANET became the basis of the Internet as we know it today.

TCP/IP has one other unique characteristic. It is a *public domain* protocol. This means that anyone can use the protocol, and no one owns it. It is like a song that has been released from copyright and becomes part of the public domain; anyone can use the song without needing to notify an owner or pay usage fees. TCP/IP is managed, modified, and governed by a set of agencies under the Internet Society (ISOC). The Internet Engineering Task Force (IETF) manages modifications to the suite through Request for Comment (RFC) documents. The Internet Engineering Steering Group (IESG) takes submitted RFCs, tests them, and determines an adoption status for the proposed change. Two other agencies help maintain other facets of this protocol. The Internet Assigned Numbers Authority (IANA) is responsible for keeping track of all IP addresses and distributing them fairly. Another agency is the InterNIC. The InterNIC keeps the registry of all domain names and manages domain name resolvability.

LOGICAL ADDRESSING

Earlier we noted that TCP/IP is not just one or two protocols, but a whole suite of protocols that can provide services and functions on the network. This protocol requires a special addressing scheme that is logical in nature; hence, it is called *logical addressing*. Where a MAC (Media Access Control) address represents the physical location on the network, an IP address represents a logical location on the network or *internetwork*.

IN REAL LIFE

The addressing schemes used for logical addressing usually contain a segment identifier and a unique node identifier that are combined to form the entire logical address. When the node is shut down, or is removed from the network, the identifier may be assigned to another node.

All nodes participating on a TCP/IP network must acquire a unique IP address to access services and communicate with other nodes. Later in this book, you will learn about the methods for acquiring an address, as well as the supporting services for TCP/IP.

Two versions of IP exist today, each with its own addressing format. The most commonly used version is IPv4 (Internet Protocol version 4). A newer version of the protocol stack, IPv6, waits in the wings for adoption across many types of networks. Because IPv6 is a much longer address space (128 bits in the IPv6 address as opposed to 32 bits in the IPv4 address), internetwork devices require reconfiguration to adopt this new version.

IP AS A TRANSPORT VEHICLE

IP (Internet Protocol) is the most basic component of this suite. It is datagram-oriented in that it treats each packet independently. The result of this treatment is that every packet that is part of a full message must have complete addressing information: the *source address* (sending node) and the *destination address* (receiving node). This allows any single packet that may get lost on its journey to be redirected to the destination node and arrive safely. IP does not guarantee reliable delivery, but protocols from upper layers can make that guarantee.

A number of IP services go beyond addressing and transport facilities. Some of them are described in Figure 6.4.

Source address

An address that identifies the sender of the message in the header of the datagram.

Destination address

An address that identifies the receiver of the message in the header of the datagram.

- **Fragmentation:** Large IP packets may be split into smaller packets if an intermediary network is able to process only smaller packets. IP will transparently reassemble the smaller packets into the original large one.
- **Packet Timeout:** Every IP packet includes a special section called the Time tso Live field (TTL). Anytime a packet crosses a router, the TTL is lowered by a count of one. If the TTL reaches zero, the packet is discarded (sent to the bit bucket), and in most cases an error message is sent back to the source node (another service provided by one of the upper layer protocols).
- **Type of Service:** Some devices allow IP packets to be prioritized for delivery.
- **Options:** Some of the options include the ability to set a requirement on the path from source to destination node, the ability to trace the route a packet may take, and adding security features to an IP packet.

FIGURE 6.4
Some Services Provided by IP

All TCP/IP transmissions use IP as the transport protocol. If you think about a large trailer rig traveling down the interstate, you will understand the meaning of transport protocol. All tractor-trailers have two components: the cab where the driver sits and where the engine resides, and the trailer attached to the cab with special fittings. Without the cab, the trailer is useless. It has no power of its own to move goods between the source and destination. When the trailer is attached to the cab, the cargo can be transported anywhere. That is much like this suite of protocols. IP is the cab, responsible for transporting the services from the upper layers of the OSI Model. Figure 6.5 displays the transport method for the TCP/IP suite of protocols.

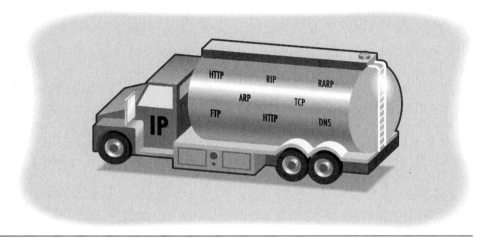

FIGURE 6.5
IP Transport for the TCP/IP
Suite of Protocols

IP PACKET STRUCTURE

IP functions at the Internet layer of the DOD Model and at the Network layer of the OSI Model. Remember from Chapter 2 that every layer adds specific information to the packet. The portion of information that IP adds to a packet is called the IP Datagram. This information allows a packet to traverse multiple internetworks to locate its destination. The IP Datagram and the data it carries, expressed in its most minute form in *bits,* cannot exceed 65,535 *bytes* in size. If it is larger, it will be split to accommodate this limitation.

The information carried in the IP header is displayed in Figure 6.6. Each section of the header has a particular responsibility with the end goal of getting this data to the destination node. The contents of each section are described in Figure 6.7.

Bit

The smallest unit of data on a computer. Bits can be one of two states: on (1) or off (0).

Byte

A unit of data that is 8 bits in length. Bytes are used to refer to units of data because they express the size of the data unit more efficiently than bits.

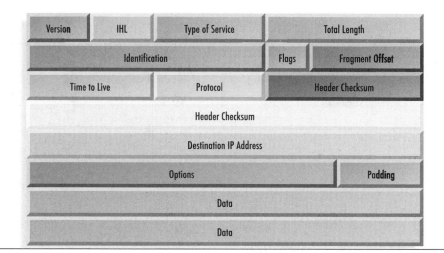

Version	IHL	Type of Service	Total Length
Identification		Flags	Fragment Offset
Time to Live	Protocol	Header Checksum
Header Checksum
Destination IP Address
Options	Padding
Data
Data

FIGURE 6.6
IP Header in an IP Datagram

- **Version:** Identifies the IP version number, either IPv4 or IPv6.
- **Internet Header Length:** Describes the length of the header information in bits. The most common header length is five 32-bit words. This field is important because it tells the destination node where the data begins.
- **Type of Service:** Indicates the priority of the service provided.
- **Total Length:** This part of the header defines the total length of the datagram, including header and data. The minimum size is 576 bytes, with a maximum size of 65,535 bytes.
- **Identification:** To reassemble a segmented or fragmented datagram at the destination node, the node must know to what message the datagram belongs. This section provides that information.
- **Flags: Two flag types are used in an IP header:** "don't fragment" and "more fragments." The first flag tells intervening routers that a packet can be sent only across subnetworks that can handle its original size. The second flag is used for the last datagram in a fragmented packet.
- **Fragment Offset:** This indicator identifies the original location of this part of the data in the full packet and allows reassembly of the packet.
- **Time to Live:** TTL can indicate the number of seconds the packet may remain on the network before being discarded. Or more commonly, this portion of the datagram is used to indicate the number of hops, or routers, the packet has encountered in its path. The TTL is decremented by one each time it crosses a router until it hits the zero count. At that time, the packet will be discarded.
- **Protocol:** This field identifies the upper (Transport) layer protocol type. The choices will be either TCP or User Datagram Protocol (UDP).
- **Header Checksum:** To detect corruption in the packet, a checksum is run against the packet.
- **Source IP Address:** This indicates the IP address of the source node.

FIGURE 6.7
Sections of the IP Header

continued

- **Destination IP Address:** This indicates the IP address of the destination node.
- **Options:** This field contains information that may be needed for routing and timing as well as any security enforced for the data stream.
- **Padding:** If a header does not contain information that works out to a multiple of 32 bits, additional filler information will be added.
- **Data:** This is where the original data created by the source node will be stored, plus any TCP information needed for the packet.

FIGURE 6.7
Continued

ROUTING OF IP PACKETS

In Chapter 5, you learned about the various networking components that can be used to connect segments, LANs, and WANs. The router provides connectivity for TCP/IP networks. Routers use the "store and forward" action to move packets from the source node to the destination node in the most efficient manner (see Figure 6.8).

IN REAL LIFE

A router is a device that moves packets from one network to another. A router can be used to connect multiple LAN segments together to form a WAN, or large networks together to form an internetwork. Routers read the destination address in the packet header, check the entries in the routing table, and forward the packet toward the destination node.

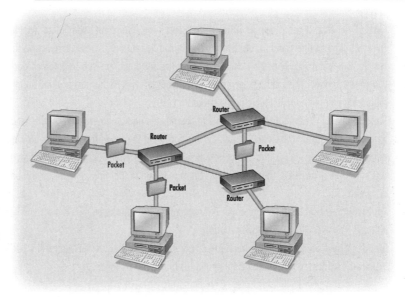

FIGURE 6.8
Routers provide connectivity as packets travel through the network.

Two routing protocols support the movement of packets: RIP (Routing Information Protocol) and OSPF (Open Shortest Path First). Each protocol uses a standard method to identify the best path for the packet and was discussed in Chapter 5.

All of this packet movement is based on one core characteristic of the TCP/IP protocol: logical addressing. Recall from Figure 6.6 that the IP header contains fields that identify the source IP address and the destination IP address. These two addresses are compared at the source node to determine if the packet is destined for a node on its own network segment or for a node on a remote network segment (a segment with a different network identifier). The network identifier portion of the IP addresses for the source and destination go through a mathematical computation to see if they are the same. If the network identifiers are the same, an attempt is made to deliver the packet to the correct node on this segment. If the network identifiers are different, the packet is forwarded to the nearest router interface indicated as the default gateway setting in the IP properties for the node. Figure 6.9 displays the IP address properties for a Windows 2000 Professional machine with the default gateway address in place.

FIGURE 6.9
Internet Protocol Properties
for a Windows 2000
Professional Computer

Ultimately, the delivery of a packet to the destination node relies not on the logical IP address, but on the MAC address for the node. When a packet reaches a router where the destination node may be located, the router interface uses a special IP protocol to find the exact location of that node. The router interface sends an *Address Resolution Protocol (ARP)* request across the segment. The ARP request asks if there is a node with X.X.X.X IP address; if there is such a node, the node is asked to send back its MAC address. The node will respond if it is attached to the network and listening for broadcasts. The router keeps track of which nodes are located on the segment and their MAC addresses in an ARP table so that ARP requests do not have to interrupt network traffic every time a packet needs to be delivered. You will find more discussion of this in Chapter 7.

NAMING CONVENTIONS

Imagine that we are administering a network of 25 segments, 2,000 nodes, 52 printers, and 18 servers. Our users have resources available to them on several servers. And of course, we are using TCP/IP as our network protocol. All of those nodes—the client machines, printers, and servers—are identified on the network by a unique IP address, which is how we can locate the servers we need or the printer we want to print our documents.

Wait a minute! You mean we have to distinguish among the 52 printers by remembering the IP address for all those printers? No, we do not have to remember all those printer addresses. The designers of the TCP/IP protocol suite anticipated that human beings would not be able to remember all of those numbers. A service protocol called *Domain Name System (DNS)* allows users to distinguish among printers, servers, services, and workstations by using a name that makes sense to them: a friendly name.

When you surf the Internet, you use the DNS protocol every time you enter a location in the locator bar of your browser. For instance, to search for information, you might enter **www.google.com** in your locator bar. The name you entered is the friendly name for a machine that is hosting Web services. In order to reach that machine and its services, the friendly name must be translated into an IP address that routers along the path can understand. DNS is the service that allows the friendly names to be translated into IP addresses. There will be much more discussion on the characteristics and operations of DNS in coming chapters.

Address Resolution Protocol (ARP)

A service protocol, part of the TCP/IP suite of protocols, that queries the network segment by broadcasting an IP address. The response is the MAC address of the node holding the destination IP address.

Domain Name System (DNS)

A service protocol that translates the node's "friendly" name to an IP address that can be used by nodes and devices to identify an exact location for the machine or service.

(handwritten margin notes: "will not be on test", "Proprietary - made & used for the company only")

Internetwork Packet Exchange/Sequenced Packet Exchange (IPX/SPX)

IPX/SPX (Internetwork Packet Exchange/Sequenced Packet Exchange) is a Novell proprietary protocol originally developed by Xerox and known as XNS (Xerox Network Systems). Novell modified XNS in the 1980s for the NetWare Operating System, and IPX/SPX became the required protocol used by Novell up through version 4.11 servers. Later versions of NetWare can use either IPX/SPX or Pure IP, or both. Microsoft created its own version of IPX/SPX called NWLink to provide Microsoft/NetWare interoperability. Other network operating systems, such as Windows 9.x peer-to-peer networks and Windows NT networks, can also communicate using NWLink.

IPX/SPX supports a client-server architecture that allows the client, or workstation, to request services from the network. This might include file services and print services, among others. This client-server architecture supports remote access to resources through *remote procedure calls*.

Like TCP/IP, IPX/SPX is a suite of protocols, but it is not quite as extensive as the former. All communications and services rely on the core protocols:

- *Internetwork Packet Exchange (IPX)* is an OSI Network layer protocol. It is a connectionless, datagram-oriented protocol like IP. It is responsible for the routing of packets and is efficient in its delivery methods, but it does not guarantee delivery of the data. Upper layer protocols handle reliable delivery. All other protocols in the IPX/SPX suite rely on IPX for transport services. In order to create an SPX session, IPX must be available to transport those packets.
- *Sequenced Packet Exchange (SPX)* is an OSI Transport layer protocol. It is connection-oriented; therefore, it must create a session, manage that session, and provide error control and retransmission functions to guarantee delivery of intact data.
- Service Advertising Protocol (SAP) announces which services are available to the network and where they are located. All NetWare servers send out SAP packets for the different services hosted on the servers. For instance, a server hosting file services might say to the network "I'm Server02, and I have file services available to any client on the network." This information will be sent out as a broadcast and, by default, will be rebroadcast every 60 seconds.

IPX/SPX (Internetwork Packet Exchange/Sequenced Packet Exchange)

A Novell proprietary protocol suite that uses the Network and Transport layers of the OSI Model to transport and deliver data across a network or internetwork.

Remote procedure call

A request (or call) made by a local machine, or an application running on that machine, for a procedure from a remote server. The remote server then sends the requested information to the local machine.

Internetwork Packet Exchange (IPX)

A connectionless, Network layer protocol that is responsible for the transport of datagrams across a network or internetwork.

Sequenced Packet Exchange (SPX)

A connection-oriented protocol that provides services such as error-checking to the IPX protocol.

Eventually, the SAP servers and the routers build tables listing the services that have been announced on the network. A client (workstation) can contact a SAP server to locate services or request service from a specific device. SAP frees the user from knowing the IPX address of all services they might need.

SAP announcements, because of their frequency, can congest bandwidth, especially over WAN connections. Administrators often create SAP filters on routers to prevent SAP announcements from flowing over network segments where those services are meaningless. This helps conserve use of both bandwidth and WAN connections.

On a network using Novell Directory Services (NDS), an administrator may be able to turn off SAP. NDS maintains a list of services, and the client can query NDS for the information. For example, when a client needs to print, the client can ask NDS for the printer information and be pointed directly to the printer.

NetWare Core Protocol (NCP) handles requests for services between the workstation and the server. NCP functions as the intermediary between the client and the server. When the client needs a service, it sends an NCP request. NCP notifies the server that a request is pending. When that request receives an answer from the server, it is called an NCP response. Only then can the client transmit data. NCP provides high reliability within the network, but it also creates large amounts of traffic.

To see how the IPX/SPX protocol maps to the OSI Model, see Table 6.1. (NLSP is discussed under "IPX Routing," below.) Notice that like the TCP/IP protocol suite, several additional protocols support the internetwork communication functions of IPX.

OSI Model	IPX/SPX
Application	NCP, SAP, (RIP, NLSP)
Presentation	
Session	NetBIOS
Transport	SPX
Network	IPX, RIP, NLSP
Data Link	Transmission media and protocols such as Ethernet
Physical	

TABLE 6.1
The IPX/SPX Protocol and the OSI Model Compared

LOGICAL ADDRESSING

IPX uses a logical addressing format that is based on the machine's MAC address. Chapter 2 noted that the MAC address is a 12-digit *hexadecimal number* that is unique to the network interface to which it is assigned. The MAC address is a Data Link layer address.

IPX makes logical addressing, or Network layer addressing, easier to maintain than IP addressing. An IPX address contains two parts: the network address and the node address. The network address is determined by the network administrator and is set on the server. The node portion of the address is the MAC address for the machine. These two are combined to form a unique logical address for each node on the network.

For example, when adding a new segment to an IPX network, the administrator sets a network ID on the server NIC attached to this new segment. It must be an 8-bit hexadecimal number. An example of a network address is 00003452. Or if you are creative and find that you remember words better than numbers, you might use 0000BEAD. Remember with hexadecimal notation, we use the numbers 0–9 and the letters A–F.

Now for the node address: just add the network address to the node address, and you have the logical IPX address for a particular machine on your network. If the node MAC address is 00F6AB430012, and the network address is 0000BEAD, the unique logical address for the machine would be 0000BEAD:00F6AB4300012.

But we are not done yet with this addressing format. It also uses an *IPX socket* number to identify processes that are running. Sockets add another section to the logical address. Some commonly used IPX socket numbers are listed in Table 6.2.

Socket	Process/Function
451h	NetWare Core Protocol
452h	Service Advertising Protocol
453h	Routing Information Protocol
455h	NetBIOS
456h	NetWare Diagnostics

Now if we look at the address example from above, with the addition of the socket number to the address, here is what we have: 0000BEAD:00F6AB4300012:455h.

Certain IPX addresses are reserved for special functions. 00000000 is a null value and cannot be used for any assigned device. FFFFFFFF is the broadcast address, and likewise, cannot be assigned.

Hexadecimal number

A number that relies on a base-16 numbering system, which uses 16 base units including 0. The 16 corresponds to 10 in the decimal system. Hexadecimal numbers are expressed using a combination of the characters A–F and the numbers 0–9.

IPX socket

A network-addressable service access point that binds an application process to a unique identifier for that process. Sockets are created using function calls or APIs (Application Programming Interfaces) in the software. A socket is considered an endpoint in a connection. Servers use sockets to distinguish one request for service from another.

TABLE 6.2
IPX Socket Numbers and Their Processes

IPX/SPX PACKET STRUCTURE

Like TCP/IP, IPX/SPX designates a specific layout for the IPX header portion of the packet. When the packet encounters other devices during transmission, each of the fields in the header tells those devices where to find important information about the packet and where that packet is going. Figure 6.10 shows what an IPX packet header looks like. The number in parentheses indicates the length of that field in bytes (B). Figure 6.11 provides an explanation of each field.

FIGURE 6.10
IPX Socket Numbers and Their Processes

- **Field A, Checksum:** The checksum provides proof of integrity for the IPX packet.
- **Field B, Packet Length:** This field indicates the length of the entire packet in bytes.
- **Field C, Transport Protocol:** Every router hop must be accounted for with IPX packets because they are discarded at the sixteenth router. This field functions in much the same way as the TTL parameter in IP by keeping track of each router hop the packet takes.
- **Field D, Packet Type:** Packet Type identifies the service provided by or required by the packet.
- **Field E, Destination Network:** When packets are routed over an internetwork, the routers are most concerned with the network identifier. This field provides the destination information to routers.
- **Field F, Destination Node Address:** Eventually the packet will have to be delivered to a specific device. This field allows the packet to be delivered to the correct device in the internetwork. This is actually the MAC address for the destination node.
- **Field G, Destination Socket:** Each process identifies itself with a socket address. The packet may be a request or response to a process and therefore must indicate which process it is part of. This field makes sure that those requests and responses stay in order and work with the correct processes.
- **Field H, Source Network:** This field identifies the origination network of the packet.
- **Field I, Source Node Address:** This is the MAC address of the source machine for the packet.
- **Field H, Source Socket:** The Source Socket field identifies the socket number for the process running on the source device.
- **Field K, Data:** This is the "payload" portion of the packet that contains the data originally sent by the source.

FIGURE 6.11
Fields in the IPX Packet Header

Networking Protocols

SPX adds information into the packet. In the data section of the packet, SPX slips in 12 bytes of additional information to provide the OSI Transport layer services for the packet. Those fields are discussed in Figure 6.12.

- **Connection Control:** This identifies whether the packet is a system or application datagram.
- **Data Stream Type:** This field indicates what position in the full message this packet occupies. It would mark the packet as part of the beginning of the data stream or end of the data stream.
- **Source Connection ID:** This field holds information about the source node.
- **Destination Connection ID:** This field holds information about the destination node.
- **Sequence Number:** When data is segmented into transmittable pieces, each piece receives a Transport layer sequence number so the data may be reassembled into the original message. The sequence number allows reassembly.
- **Acknowledgement Number:** In order to fully guarantee that data will be delivered reliably, the receiving node sends an ACK, or acknowledgement that the packet has been received in good condition. The format for the ACK is the sequence number of the next packet in the stream.
- **Allocation Number:** This indicator is used to manage the flow control processes between applications in the communication process.

FIGURE 6.12
Additional Information in
the Data Section

IPX ENCAPSULATION

IPX uses special *encapsulation* schemes to work with the various versions of NetWare. This encapsulation takes place at the Data Link layer of the OSI Model. There are four frame types supported by IPX. The version of NetWare you are running, and the additional protocols implemented on the network will determine which frame types must be enabled. All frame types are IEEE defined, as noted in Figure 6.13.

Encapsulation

A process in which upper-layer protocol information is packaged into a frame.

- **802.3:** This frame type is often referred to as 802.3 RAW. It is the default frame type setting for NetWare 3.11 and earlier versions.
- **802.2:** Later versions of NetWare (3.12 and later) use this frame type. It is a fully IEEE-compliant encapsulation method.
- **ETHERNET_II:** When providing interoperability with NetWare networks and TCP/IP, it is necessary to encapsulate the packets in an IPX-compatible format. This frame type was also used by DEC networks and AppleTalk Phase I (the original AppleTalk protocol) networks.
- **ETHERNET_SNAP:** AppleTalk Phase II requires this frame type. It is a standard IEEE802.2 frame with SNAP extensions.

FIGURE 6.13
IEEE Definition of Frame
Types

IPX/SPX is implemented in the Windows family of products as NWLink Protocol. Figure 6.14 displays the property sheet for NWLink installed on a Windows 2000 Professional machine. Note that Windows sets the frame type to "Auto." To determine which frame type to use, Windows will *auto-detect* the frame type. This setting in the registry reflects the first frame type encountered by the network interface card.

Auto-detect

A function whereby the computer will find a setting (or piece of hardware) without intervention from a user or administrator.

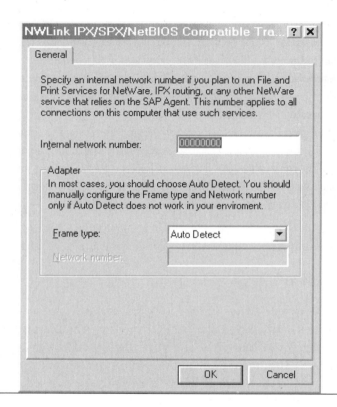

FIGURE 6.14
The NWLink Property Sheet for Windows 2000 Professional

IPX ROUTING

IPX can provide support for network communications on a single LAN segment or within a large internetwork. Two *routing protocols* manage IPX routing on internetworks.

Routing Information Protocol (RIP) works much the same way as it does with IP. Routers learn about remote network segments through the exchange of routing tables. Tables are exchanged every 60 seconds by default. Every route that comes to a router is incremented by 1 hop to account for the addition of a router into the path to the destination network. The decision about the best path for a packet is based on the

Routing protocol

A set of rules that allows a router to make decisions about how a datagram will move from the source node to the destination node. The routing protocol often provides services such as exchanging network information with its neighbors.

number of hops to the destination network. This is known as a distance vector protocol. Like RIP for IP, RIP for IPX limits the path a packet can take to 15 hops. At the sixteenth router, the packet will be discarded, and an error (nondelivery) message is sent back to the source node.

Although it is a very common routing protocol, RIP has fallen out of favor for large networks because of the excess traffic generated by the exchange of routing tables. In an internetwork with five or six routers, the tables remain small, and the traffic generated by table exchange also remains small. Once the internetwork reaches 50 or more routers, the tables are quite large and will be sent to neighboring routers every 60 seconds by default. When there is a failure in a subnetwork or at a router interface and the routes are no longer valid, the router waits a period of time (3 minutes by default) to remove the route from the table. This means that in a large internetwork, routers will have inaccurate tables for long periods of time before converging after the failure.

For IPX networks and internetworks, a newer, more efficient protocol has become popular. *NetWare Link State Protocol (NLSP)* uses a link state algorithm to decide how to get a packet to a destination address. It is more efficient because NLSP routers learn the network or internetwork. Through link state packets, all routers have full knowledge of their environment. When there is a failure on a section of the network, a link state announcement will flood the environment with a notification that a certain path is out of commission. All routers listen for link state announcements. After the failure, convergence occurs very quickly, so the bandwidth remains unimpeded by routers on the network talking to each other.

Additionally, the link state algorithm builds the best path to a remote network using a number of parameters, including the speed of the path, congestion on the network, and hop count, all neatly combined into a mathematical computation to determine the most efficient path for the packet. If we could have a similar system when we are driving home in rush hour traffic, we would be able to know how all the possible routes home looked and choose the one with the least traffic and the fastest speed limit, so we could get home on time and far less anxious than usual.

IPX NAMING CONVENTIONS

Unlike the TCP/IP protocol suite, the Novell IPX/SPX protocol does not employ naming conventions. The only nodes that require a name are those that run one of the NetWare network operating systems. Servers must be identified with a friendly name, and the administrator must enter that

NetWare Link State Protocol (NLSP)

A routing protocol that provides the efficient exchange of routing table information between routers on an IPX network; addresses the limitations of RIP for IPX, which was designed for small independent networks.

name during installation. NetWare server names cannot exceed 64 alphanumeric characters in length (47 for really old versions of NetWare), and they cannot include any of the "illegal" characters, such as a period (.), a comma (,), or a backslash (\).

Of course, other operating systems, such as the Microsoft Windows family of operating systems, also require a friendly name during installation. So all of the machines on the network will have a name that is easy for human beings to remember. The difference comes in how those friendly names are used. IPX does not propagate service availability using those friendly names on any system but the server.

If the workstations are sharing resources to the network, they will use another method to notify other nodes of the availability of the resources. This is commonly done through the use of *NetBIOS (Network Basic Input/Output System)* and the browser function of Microsoft Windows systems. The browser function allows a node to broadcast its attachment to the network and the resources it serves. One machine on each network segment takes on the role of "browse list keeper" for the segment. Now, when a service or resource is needed, a broadcast request is placed on the segment and the browse list keeper responds with the location of the node that is hosting that resource. This causes additional use of bandwidth, especially on segments where large numbers of nodes are attached.

AppleTalk

The Macintosh computer and *AppleTalk* protocol were introduced to the world in 1984. Both the computers and the protocol (actually a suite of protocols) were designed for peer-to-peer networks. The Macintosh was quickly adopted by users and organizations involved in art and education. Many schools, graphic designers, printing companies, and the like still stand by the Macintosh as the perfect solution for their industries.

Today, Macintosh computers and AppleTalk can be routed through internetworks and enhanced through additional client software to participate in Microsoft and NetWare networks. Although many improvements have been made allowing this integration and expansion from single-segment networks, AppleTalk remains best suited to small LANs rather than large internetworks or WANs.

AppleTalk networks separate computers into logical groupings called zones. Zones enable users to share resources with other Macintosh users. Each zone is given a name, but these names are not subject to severe restrictions. The names are typically descriptive of the grouping. A zone

NetBIOS (Network Basic Input/Output System)

A protocol dating back to the early IBM PC networks that allows applications on different computers to communicate with each other.

AppleTalk

A protocol that services Macintosh computers. The protocol was designed for peer-to-peer networks (small networks without a server), but it has been enhanced over time and is now capable of routing between networks.

Networking Protocols

name for the top brass of a company, for example, might be simply "Management Team." Multiple zones may exist on the same network, but a computer can belong to only one zone.

Like the other protocols we have already discussed, AppleTalk is really a protocol suite. Figure 6.15 displays how AppleTalk compares to the OSI Model, and Figure 6.16 provides an explanation of the various protocols.

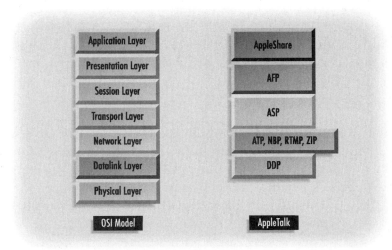

FIGURE 6.15
The AppleTalk Protocol and the OSI Model Compared

- **AppleShare:** This is one of the core protocols for AppleTalk, allowing file-sharing services, print queuing services, user accounting data, and remote password-controlled access to files and folders.
- **AppleTalk Filing Protocol (AFP):** This protocol controls transparent local and remote access to files.
- **AppleTalk Session Protocol (ASP):** ASP manages and maintains connections between nodes on an AppleTalk network.
- **AppleTalk Transaction Protocol (ATP):** To provide reliable delivery of data, ATP performs checks against the connections between nodes, packet sequencing, and retransmission of any lost or corrupt data.
- **Name Binding Protocol (NBP):** NBP provides friendly name-to-machine address resolution.
- **Routing Table Maintenance Protocol (RTMP):** This protocol maintains the routing table for zones and uses ZIP to update the data in the table.
- **Zone Information Protocol (ZIP):** ZIP keeps track of all zone information and maps that information to the zones' networks to support routing.
- **Datagram Delivery Protocol (DDP):** At startup, DDP handles all addressing for AppleTalk nodes.

FIGURE 6.16
AppleTalk Protocols

LOGICAL ADDRESSING

Like most routable protocols, AppleTalk employs logical addressing for nodes and networks. The address assigned to a specific machine is known as an AppleTalk node ID. AppleTalk assigns the node ID when the node attaches to the network. It is a randomly chosen, 8-bit or 16-bit number from a group of available addresses. Once a node has an address, it stores and recalls that address so it can be used at a later time.

AppleTalk network numbers identify the network segment to which a node attaches. When the AppleTalk network is routed, the router uses these network numbers to determine where to send the packets.

ROUTING AND APPLETALK

Remember from our previous discussion that when AppleTalk was first designed, its purpose was to provide peer-to-peer network services for small networks. Only later did the need arise to broaden the capability of this protocol. AppleTalk version 2 included routing capability through the Routing Table Maintenance Protocol (RTMP). RTMP follows the RIP protocols, as it is a distance vector routing protocol.

NAMING CONVENTIONS

Name Binding Protocol (NBP)

An AppleTalk protocol that provides friendly names and name resolution for nodes on an AppleTalk network.

In order to use friendly names for computers, AppleTalk uses the *Name Binding Protocol (NBP)*. A broadcast-based protocol, NBP broadcasts the name of a node when it attaches to the network. The AppleTalk router caches this name and the address for the node. It will also respond to an NBP request from any node on its network by providing the requesting node with information from the cached table. NBP also allows a node to delete an entry in the cached table when it is no longer useful or the node is removing itself from the network.

NetBIOS and NetBEUI

NetBEUI (NetBIOS Enhanced User Interface)

A fast, efficient, nonconfigurable, nonroutable protocol used by single-segment networks, usually peer-to-peer.

NetBIOS and its partner in crime, *NetBEUI (NetBIOS Enhanced User Interface),* are remnants from the IBM LAN Manager operating system that eventually became the foundation for the Microsoft Windows NT network operating system.

NetBEUI is a very efficient, fast, and nonconfigurable network protocol. That makes NetBEUI ideal for small, single-segment networks where users need to share resources. With NetBEUI, the administrator, or at least the person in the office who knows the most about computers, does not have to worry about addressing, configuring special settings, or bandwidth usage. On the flip side, NetBEUI lacks a Network layer addressing convention, and therefore is nonroutable and limited to 254 nodes on a network. It was used in the early days of Microsoft Windows for small groups of computers.

Due to NetBEUI's limitations, both NetBEUI and NetBIOS are paired with TCP/IP or IPX/SPX to provided services. Figure 6.17 shows how these two protocols compare to the OSI model. You will also see the Network and Transport layer protocols from the two suites mentioned above.

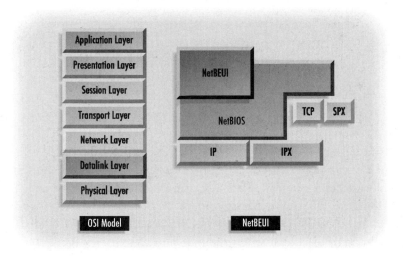

FIGURE 6.17
NetBEUI, NetBIOS, and the
OSI Model Compared

NetBEUI, when installed on a Microsoft Windows system, cannot be configured in any way. A small network running NetBEUI as its networking protocol is easy to maintain for the service technician or the local computer expert. Figure 6.18 shows the Windows 2000 property sheet for NetBEUI. Notice on the network property sheet that NetBEUI property options are unavailable.

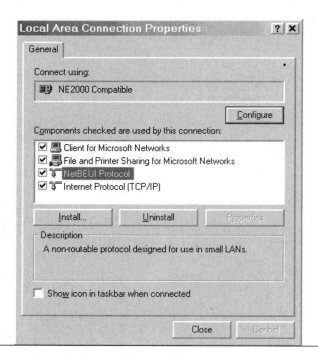

FIGURE 6.18
NetBEUI Property Sheet
Showing NetBEUI Protocol

NETBIOS ADDRESSING AND NAMING CONVENTIONS

With no innate Network layer services in the NetBEUI or NetBIOS
protocol environment, addressing is not of concern. However, names take
on more importance here. Every node using NetBEUI must be assigned a
NetBIOS name. That name must contain 16 or fewer characters, and may
be letters or numbers. Once the NetBIOS name has been discovered
(usually through broadcast when the machine attaches to the network), the
MAC address is also discovered, and the information is cached and used
when looking for resources.

Interoperability

Now that you have learned the basics about each of the "big four" network
protocols, it is time to look at when each of these protocols can and should
be used, and when more than one protocol may have to be deployed on the
network.

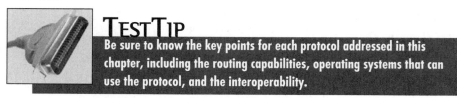

TESTTIP

Be sure to know the key points for each protocol addressed in this
chapter, including the routing capabilities, operating systems that can
use the protocol, and the interoperability.

Networking Protocols

TCP/IP is the most versatile of the four. All operating systems released in the last three to four years encourage the use of this protocol. Microsoft Windows, Novell NetWare version 5 and version 6, Macintosh, Linux, and UNIX operating systems implement all standard services using TCP/IP, as well as the proprietary services such as Novell Directory Services. These operating systems also support a native TCP/IP stack. In other words, the operating system comes with TCP/IP. Whenever an organization provides Internet connectivity for the employee users, TCP/IP must be installed to access Web-based resources.

IPX/SPX is also a strong protocol, but without all the flexibility of TCP/IP. This stack does not give access to Web resources naturally. It does provide communication services for many operating systems, including Microsoft Windows, all Novell NetWare versions, OS/2, and some versions of Linux. Microsoft's version of IPX/SPX is known as NWLink. IPX/SPX is a great option for either routed or nonrouted networks, and it can be used successfully in client-server or peer-to-peer networks.

AppleTalk has far more limited use. The only operating system and machine that comes with AppleTalk natively installed is the Macintosh. Other operating systems provide an AppleTalk-compatible stack, as an optional installation, to integrate Macintosh systems into an existing network. AppleTalk does not support Internet connectivity.

NetBEUI is the least widely used network protocol. Because of the limitations of NetBEUI, most notably its inability to route, this protocol is suitable only for a very small peer network that does not need Internet connectivity. The Microsoft Windows operating systems, as well as OS/2 and LAN Manager (both from IBM), do support NetBEUI, but Macintosh has no provision for installing this protocol.

Table 6.3 summarizes which operating systems can use which network protocols for communication. This table is a handy reference and a good study guide.

Protocol	Microsoft Windows	Macintosh	Novell NetWare	Linux	UNIX	Native Internet Access
TCP/IP	X	X	X	X	X	X
IPX/SPX	X	X	X			
AppleTalk	X	X	X			
NetBEUI	X					

TABLE 6.3
Network Operating Systems and Network Protocols

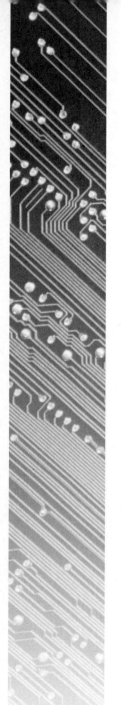

STUDY GUIDE

In this chapter, we discussed the positive and negative features of the major protocols used today, including which protocols function with what operating systems. Here are some key points to remember.

TCP/IP

- TCP/IP is a suite of protocols that allows nodes to communicate with each other in a network environment without regard to the type of machine or operating system on that machine.
- The TCP/IP suite contains two core protocols, IP and TCP.
- IP is a connectionless protocol used for transport at the Network layer of the OSI Model. IP manages logical addressing and routing functions for packet delivery.
- TCP is a connection-oriented Transport layer protocol that manages reliable delivery of packets. Error checking, sequencing, and retransmission of lost or corrupt packets are functions of TCP.
- The original developers of TCP/IP were the military and academic institutions.
- Logical addressing in TCP/IP is necessary to route packets between networks or internetworks.
- IP provides fragmentation services, packet timeout services, and many options for transporting packets.
- The two most important fields in the IP header are the source and destination address fields.
- An IP packet header and the data cannot exceed 65,535 bytes.
- When a node sends an IP packet, it compares the destination address to its own address, determines the network identifier, and either forwards the packet to the router interface or attempts to deliver it on its own segment.
- Two protocols are used to support routing services: RIP and OSPF.
- RIP is a distance vector routing protocol, meaning that routing decisions are based only on the number of hops in the path.
- OSPF is a link state protocol, meaning that routing decisions are made on a number of criteria, including hop count, congestion, speed of network, and other criteria.
- Friendly names are supported for nodes running TCP/IP. DNS supports friendly names to IP address resolution services on the network.

IPX/SPX

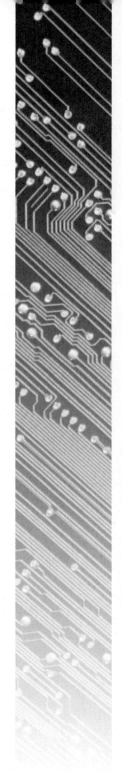

- IPX/SPX is a Novell proprietary protocol used with all versions of Novell's NetWare products.
- IPX/SPX was designed to support a client-server architecture, using remote procedure calls to request service and respond with service. It can also be used as a peer-to-peer network protocol.
- Like TCP/IP, IPX/SPX supports two core protocols: IPX and SPX.
- IPX is a connectionless protocol responsible for the routing of packets, efficient delivery of datagrams, and logical addressing.
- SPX is a connection-oriented protocol that manages a session between nodes, including error control and retransmission of missing or corrupt packets, providing reliable delivery of data.
- SAP notifies the network when a service is available. Done via a broadcast, this notification can congest bandwidth when the network is busy. It may be necessary to filter SAP announcements at routers.
- NCP handles requests for services between the client (workstation) and the server. This service protocol is very reliable, but it can create large amounts of traffic.
- To form a logical address when using IPX/SPX, the administrator must add a network identifier in hexadecimal format. The network identifier is 8 bits long.
- Once the network identifier is available, the node will combine the network identifier and its own MAC address to form a unique node address.
- IPX/SPX uses socket numbers to uniquely identify APIs and client requests to those APIs. Often sockets are assigned on the fly, but some socket numbers are reserved by the NetWare operating system.
- Like TCP/IP, the two most important fields in the IPX header are the source and destination node addresses. IPX also includes individual fields for source and destination network, and source and destination socket.
- An IPX header will contain approximately 28 bytes of information plus the payload.
- IPX routing employs two protocols: RIP for IPX and NLSP.
- RIP is a distance vector protocol, making routing decisions solely on the number of hops to the destination network.
- NLSP is a link state protocol, more efficient, and capable of making routing decisions on hop count combined with bandwidth utilization, speed of network, and other criteria.

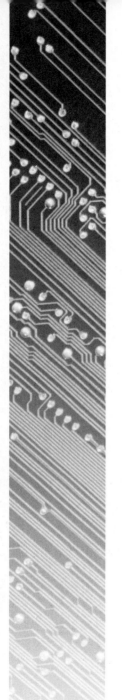

- IPX/SPX does not require any specific naming conventions for workstations (clients), but requires that server names use alphanumeric characters and do not exceed 64 characters in length (old NetWare versions are limited to 47 characters).

AppleTalk

- AppleTalk is the protocol of Macintosh computers, originally designed for peer-to-peer networks.
- Although a later version of AppleTalk supports internetworks and routing, it remains best suited for smaller networks.
- Logical addresses in AppleTalk are formed when the node attaches to the network. The address is an 8-bit or 16-bit number that will be stored and used again.
- AppleTalk also uses network numbers to identify segments.
- AppleTalk zones divide the network into logical groupings for file sharing, printing, and other services.
- RTMP supports routing services.
- Nodes using AppleTalk will broadcast their friendly name when attaching to the network. NBP will cache the name and supply it to any node requesting a service.

NetBEUI

- NetBEUI is an efficient, nonroutable protocol that is useful for small networks where Internet connectivity is not needed.
- No configuration is needed for NetBEUI.
- All nodes using NetBEUI must have a name.
- NetBIOS supports friendly names for NetBEUI.
- No Network layer services are available with NetBEUI and NetBIOS, so these protocols are usually paired with other routable protocols such as TCP/IP or IPX/SPX.

Interoperability

- TCP/IP is a versatile protocol that supports global connectivity without regard to operating system.
- All major operating systems contain a TCP/IP protocol stack, including Microsoft operating systems, NetWare server versions 5.X and 6.X, Linux, and UNIX.

- If an organization allows Internet connectivity for users, the TCP/IP protocol must be implemented.
- IPX/SPX does not support access to Internet resources, but it is a robust network protocol.
- Many operating systems include support for IPX/SPX.
- AppleTalk is native only to the Macintosh computer; Microsoft includes AppleTalk compatible services with many of its operating systems.
- NetBEUI is native to the IBM LAN Manager and Microsoft Windows products.
- Because NetBEUI is nonroutable, it is suitable only for very small peer networks.
- Macintosh has no provision for NetBEUI.

PRACTICE TEST

Try this test to check your mastery of the concepts in this chapter.

1. Which of the following network protocols is suitable only for single-segment, small networks?
   a. TCP/IP
   b. IPX/SPX
   c. NetBEUI
   d. AppleTalk

2. Which of the following protocols use a connection-oriented transmission method?
   a. SPX
   b. NetBEUI
   c. IP
   d. IPX

3. What protocol uses names as addresses?
   a. AppleTalk
   b. IPX/SPX
   c. TCP/IP
   d. NetBEUI

4. Which of the following addresses represents the node's MAC address?
   a. 197.46.54.1
   b. 00:4D:6A:BC:51:02
   c. 465h
   d. 1015 Parkway

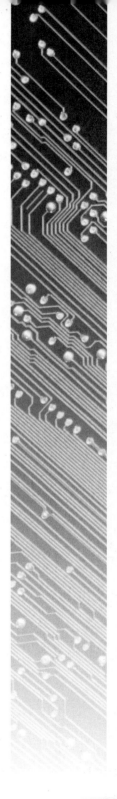

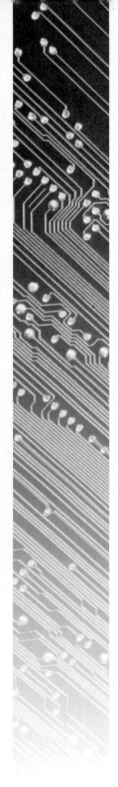

5. IPX/SPX uses a combination of addresses to uniquely identify a node. Which combination of addresses represents an IPX logical address?
   a. node address, network address, station number
   b. MAC address, socket number, machine name
   c. network address, MAC address, socket number
   d. station name, MAC address, network number

6. In an IP network, delivery of the packet to the destination node relies on the _____ address.
   a. MAC
   b. NetBEUI
   c. IP
   d. TCP

7. _____ is a nonroutable network protocol.
   a. TCP
   b. IPX/SPX
   c. Banyan Vines
   d. NetBEUI

8. Which of the following protocols resolves names to physical addresses in AppleTalk?
   a. RTMP
   b. NBP
   c. AARP
   d. AFP

9. Transport layer services are rendered by the _____ protocol from the IPX/SPX suite of protocols.
   a. IPX
   b. SPX   error checking
   c. NCP
   d. RIP

10. When using the TCP/IP suite for the network, which of the following will guarantee delivery of the data in good condition?
    a. TCP
    b. UDP
    c. IP
    d. DNS

11. Which of the following TCP/IP routing protocols provides the most conservative usage of bandwidth while still efficiently routing packets to their destination?
    a. OSPF
    b. NLSP
    c. EIGRP
    d. BGP

12. What TCP/IP protocol resolves friendly names to IP addresses?
    a. HTTP
    b. ARP
    c. FTP
    d. DNS

13. The only machines that run AppleTalk natively are
    a. IBM PCs.
    b. Gateway laptops.
    c. Macintosh systems.
    d. Dell desktops.

14. Your IP packets are not getting from the source node to the destination node. At which layer of the OSI Model does the problem lie?
    a. Physical layer
    b. Data Link layer
    c. Network layer
    d. Transport layer

15. Which protocol will recover from lost packets during a data transmission?
    a. IPX
    b. NCP
    c. RIP
    d. SPX

16. Which of the following protocols would you implement if you wanted your users to have Internet connectivity?
    a. IPX/SPX
    b. NetBEUI
    c. TCP/IP
    d. AppleTalk

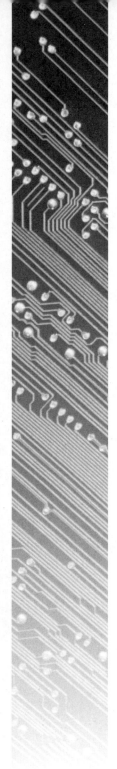

17. What frame type would you configure on the server if you were running the NetWare 5.1 network operating system using IPX/SPX?
    a. 802.3
    b. ETHERNET_SNAP
    c. ETHERNET_II
    d. 802.2

18. Which of the following agencies is responsible for the distribution and management of IP addresses?
    a. ISOC
    b. IEEE
    c. IANA
    d. ARIN

19. Which of the following IPX logical addresses represents a unique node with no services pending?
    a. 0C020041:B473AC680001
    b. 0C020041:B473AC680001:455h
    c. 198.56.12.89
    d. 198.56.12.0

20. A(n) _____ consists of two or more LANS connected by routers.
    a. network
    b. WAN
    c. bridge
    d. internetwork

TROUBLESHOOTING

1. The three Macintosh computers in the Advertising department on your network cannot print to a network print device called PTR3. These computers can connect to other printers on the network. You reset the print device, but the computers still cannot print. Windows users are not complaining of any printing problems. Where should you begin to resolve this problem for the Macintosh users?

2. You have installed a Windows 98 workstation and connected it to the network. This workstation must have access to the NetWare 4.11 server, the Windows NT server, and the Internet. When the user attempts to connect to the Windows NT server and the Internet, no connection is made. Which of the following could be the reason for the connection problems?

CUSTOMER SERVICE

1. You have been hired as a consultant for a small business. The business is revamping its network and needs some guidance. Currently, the network uses both a NetWare 4.1 server and a Windows NT 4.0 server to provide file and print services to the network. The president of the company wants to make the network run more efficiently but also wants to keep both the NetWare server and the NT server. Recently, users have been complaining that things are slow on the network. What suggestions would you make to the president of the company to speed up the network?

2. You have been sent to a customer site where the office has four computers. All computers are running Microsoft Windows 98. The owner of the business wants to share files and printers among all of the users, but does not require a server. The owner does not want to spend a lot of money, but is willing to purchase cabling to connect the computers and one or two devices. This new network must be self-contained, easy to manage, and efficient. No access to the Internet is required. After cabling the network and installing a small hub, you must decide what protocol to add. Which one will you choose and why?

FOR MORE INFORMATION

For links to Web sites that provide further information about the topics covered in this chapter, go to the EMC/Paradigm Internet Resource Center at www.emcp.com/College Division/Internet Resource Centers/Networking/System Administration/Web Resources: For More Information.

7

TCP/IP

Network+ Examination
- **Objective 2.5:** Define the purpose, function, and/or use of the following protocols within TCP/IP:
  - IP
  - TCP
  - UDP
  - FTP
  - TFTP
  - SMTP
  - HTTP
  - HTTPS
  - POP3/IMAP4
  - Telnet
  - ICMP
  - ARP
  - NTP
- **Objective 2.6:** Define the function of TCP/UDP ports. Identify well-known ports.

ON THE JOB

The theory that has been presented thus far is important to the Network+ certified technician because, in order to service clients on the LAN, you must understand those pieces of networking technology that allow data to traverse the network. Understanding the varied TCP/IP protocols and the services and utilities they bring to networking will help you troubleshoot client problems and take on larger tasks as your experience grows.

OSI Model Review

In Chapter 2, we learned about the OSI Model for data communications. Each of the seven layers of the OSI Model manages certain functions of the communication process. The layers work together to provide a consistent method for converting the original message into bits that can travel across the cable media or wireless media that connect computers together, thereby allowing those computers to share information. It is important as we begin the exploration of the protocols that make up the TCP/IP suite to keep in mind what each of the layers does and where the protocols fit into this layered model. If you can remember which layer provides what services, the protocols fall into place easily. Table 7.1 identifies the layers of the OSI Model, the layers of the original TCP/IP DOD Model, the functions for each layer, and the protocols associated with each layer.

TRY IT!

Let's see what IP address is assigned to your machine. On a computer equipped with Windows 2000 Professional, open a command prompt by going to Start/Programs/Accessories/Command Prompt (a shorter way to get there is to click Start/Run and type in **cmd**). Once the command prompt window is open, type in the following: **IPCONFIG/ALL**. IPCONFIG is the utility that allows the user or administrator to view the IP configuration for this machine. Pay close attention to the way in which your machine is receiving its IP address. In the second list of information, look for the line "DHCP Enabled." If the line says "Yes," your machine is getting its address automatically. If it says "No," your machine is manually configured for its IP address. See the example in Figure 7.1. You will learn more about these options later in the chapter.

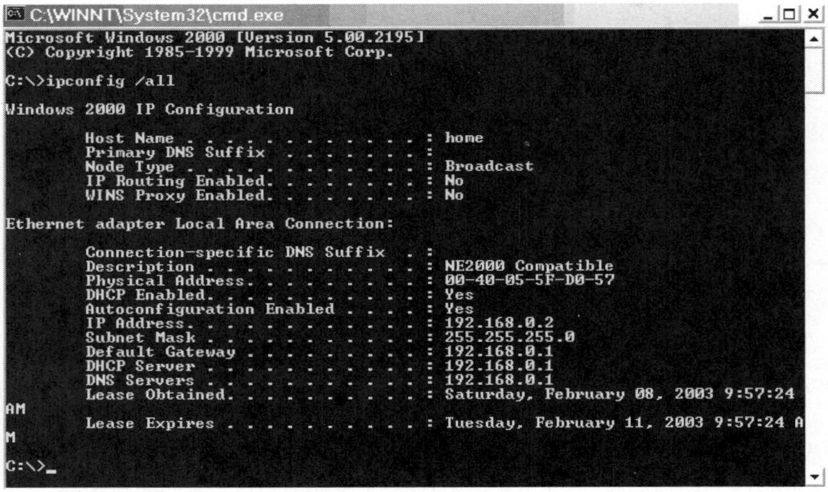

FIGURE 7.1
IP Configuration for a Windows 2000 Professional Machine Displayed using IPCONFIG/ALL

OSI Layer	DOD Layer	Function	Protocols
Application	Process/Application	• Services applications • Handles network access, flow control, and error recovery for applications designed to run over the network	DNS, FTP, TFTP, BOOTP, SNMP, MIME, NFS, Telnet, SMTP
Presentation		• Provides character conversion, encryption, decryption, compression, decompression	
Session		• Opens, maintains, and ends sessions • Provides name recognition services to limit participation in sessions • Originates synchronization services to provide reliable data delivery	
Transport	Host-to-Host	• Establishes flow control between parties over the network • Divides data streams into packets and provides the sequencing and reassembly services for the data • Engages in error-checking for reliable data delivery • Sends acknowledgements (ACKs) and negative ACKs (NACKs) • Requests retransmission for lost or corrupt packets	TCP, UDP (ARP/RARP)
Network	Internet	• Provides logical addressing and routing	IP, UDP, ARP, RARP, ICMP
Data Link	Network Access	• Converts packets into bits • Manages physical addressing • Identifies the ways to transmit and receive data by providing the access standards to the physical media	
Physical		• Transmits data across physical media • Sets standards for physical components such as cable, NIC, repeater	

TABLE 7.1
The TCP/IP Protocol Suite Compared to the OSI and DOD Models

Keep in mind that some of the protocols we will discuss are service protocols, and some of the protocols are utility protocols. Those distinctions may not seem clear at first, but consider this example: Think about the Application protocols—Domain Name Service (DNS), File Transfer Protocol (FTP), Simple Mail Transport Protocol (SMTP), and so forth. Each of those offers a service to an application. For instance, SMTP allows e-mail applications to exchange messages without regard to the actual application being used on either side. Other protocols, such as Address Resolution Protocol (ARP), work as a utility to the protocol suite by requesting the physical address when the logical address is known. No distinction is made within this book concerning the two types of subprotocols, but some resources do differentiate between the two.

In Chapter 6, Transmission Control Protocol (TCP) and Internet Protocol (IP) were discussed at length and will be reviewed briefly in this chapter. Then we will look at several other TCP/IP protocols.

Transmission Control Protocol (TCP)

Transmission Control Protocol (TCP) is a connection-oriented, reliable protocol that provides many necessary services for the delivery of packets through the internetwork. For instance, TCP will break a data stream into a series of segments known as packets. Those packets are numbered (sequenced). No matter what path (route) a packet takes from the source to destination, the packets can be reassembled into the original data stream (message), and any missing or corrupt packets can be retransmitted. TCP guarantees safe delivery of the packets.

Another check against the integrity of the packet (or datagram, as it is sometimes called) is the checksum. A checksum is calculated by totaling the contents of the packet; the resulting number is placed in the Checksum field in the TCP header. The destination node can then recalculate the contents of the packet, compare it to the checksum number in the header, and determine whether the packet has arrived intact or could be corrupt and requires retransmission.

Port number

A number that designates the identity of a process to which packets, or a message, will be forwarded. The port number is part of both the TCP and UDP header formats.

TCP also uses a source *port number* and destination port number to make sure that data sent between nodes is forwarded to the correct process or processes running on each node. During the discussion of IPX/SPX in Chapter 6, we talked about sockets, and their use with IPX. Sockets are very similar to ports. We will discuss ports in more detail later in this chapter.

Internet Protocol (IP)

Internet Protocol (IP) is the most basic of all the protocols in the TCP/IP suite of protocols. IP transports data for the TCP/IP stack. All other protocols in the suite rely on IP to move packets from the source node to the destination node. IP allows decisions to be made regarding which path to take to the destination or how to route the packets. This protocol can be compared to the interstate highway system in the United States. Throughout the states, there is a system of interconnected highways that allow motorists to go from New York City to Los Angeles without worrying about stoplights, stop signs, or other conditions that might impede the motorist. The interstates do not dictate what kind of vehicle you can use to ride on the roadways; they only specify speed limits and expect motorists to abide by general etiquette for driving (laws of the road).

IP is a connectionless protocol. It does not guarantee safe delivery of the packets to the destination. Other protocols higher up in the model can offer these services. Normally, guaranteed delivery is the responsibility of Transmission Control Protocol (TCP).

User Datagram Protocol (UDP)

User Datagram Protocol (UDP) is an interesting protocol. If you look back at Table 7.1, you will notice that UDP is listed in both the Network layer and the Transport layer of the OSI Model. The reason we often see UDP listed in two layers, or bridged between the Network and Transport layers, is simply because it services data transmission with characteristics from both layers. UDP is a connectionless protocol (very IP-like and therefore a Network layer characteristic). But, UDP does some error-checking on the data being transmitted (very TCP-like and therefore a Transport layer characteristic). This protocol seems to have an identity crisis going on, but it has become a favorite protocol for process management and port assignment without the session overhead of TCP. In other words, it is much more efficient than TCP (lower overhead), but it is safer than IP (some error checking on the transmission).

UDP is especially important for the application developer. As mentioned above, this is a connectionless protocol and therefore is not subject to the delay of setting up the connection when two nodes must communicate. It gets points for speed. Second, UDP does not maintain a connection-state parameter. This means that less information is tracked on the network resource, and more clients can access an application built for network access. More points for UDP. Last, TCP adds overhead with its flow control parameter and can choke a network-based application using real-time information. Most applications of this type tolerate some packet loss, but they also require a maintained minimum send rate. Because UDP can send at speeds constrained by only the bandwidth, congestion, and port speed, it is more efficient and gets even more points.

Many applications or application services now use UDP as their primary protocol. DNS usually makes use of UDP for all the reasons listed in the previous paragraph. It originally used TCP. When using TCP, the request-response mechanisms serviced by DNS become very slow.

User Datagram Protocol (UDP)

A communications protocol that closely resembles IP in its transport abilities; however, like TCP, it provides two services to make delivery more reliable than IP: a checksum and port numbering. UDP does not guarantee delivery.

File Transfer Protocol (FTP) — will be on Test

upload & download

File Transfer Protocol (FTP) was one of the first add-on protocols for the TCP/IP suite. In the early days of TCP/IP, the designers were interested in allowing computers to communicate and to share information, regardless of platform (RISC, Macintosh, PC), or operating system (Windows 9x, Windows NT, Windows 2000, UNIX, System 10). To that end, programmers developed the file transfer capabilities of FTP. It was based on the UNIX operating system commands, but it functions on most other non-UNIX systems, as well.

With FTP, a local node sends a request to a remote node configured to listen for FTP requests. The remote machine acts as an interpreter, taking the requests and responding with actions that allow files to be manipulated, retrieved, and placed on the remote node. FTP is the primary method for file transfer over the Internet simply because it functions outside any one operating system or platform. The FTP request-response mechanism is managed by TCP connections. This is often added as a special service to the operating system.

The administrator configures FTP services to work with two types of access to the files available: traditional user account login or anonymous login. With traditional user account login, access to files managed under FTP is controlled by a user account with a password. The operating system allows certain access rights or permissions to be set on the files. The user gains access to download those files only if the user account has at least minimal rights. This controls who has privileges on the FTP host.

The other configuration option is the anonymous login. Using the Anonymous account, any user may access those files where Anonymous has been given the appropriate rights or permissions. When using the Anonymous account, it is traditional to use your e-mail address when asked for a password. This allows the administrator of the FTP host to view the logs and identify the types of users who access the FTP files. (It is also a great market research tool, if you assume everyone who comes to your FTP site is using his real e-mail address. In reality, FTP service is only looking for the "@" (at) sign, so you can enter a partial e-mail address, or on some systems just the "@" sign. Figure 7.2 shows the initial login and request for password.

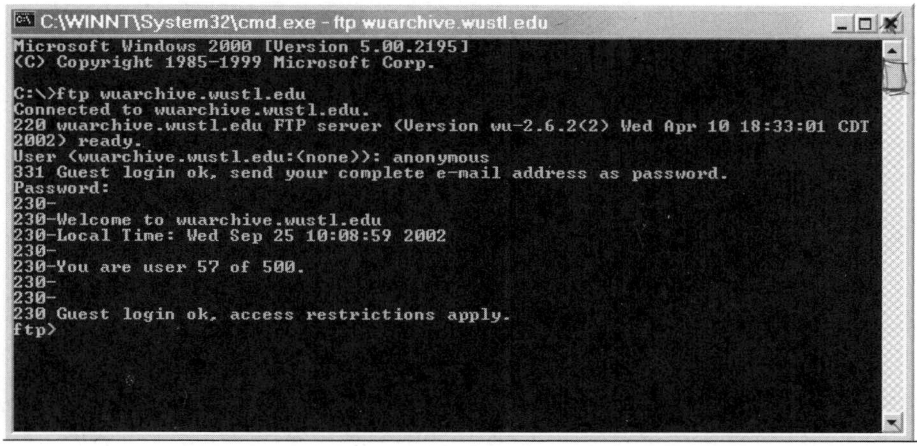

FIGURE 7.2
Initial Login Window to Open
an FTP Session

Many vendors maintain FTP services for the purpose of posting software updates, new drivers, and documentation for their products. The vendor need not worry about what type of machine or operating system their clients are using when resources are handled this way.

As efficient as FTP is, the speed of the FTP transfer will be affected by the speed of the user's connection as well as the speed of the site that is hosting FTP. In addition, the number of users connected to an FTP site will also have an impact on how quickly (or slowly) you can download (or upload) files.

This raises an additional use for FTP. The most typical usage is to store files for download by remote clients. FTP can also be used as a repository for files created at remote locations. One example is a publisher. Many books are in progress at any given moment. Authors may be scattered across the globe, each working on a specific project. As chapters of books are completed, the author can upload those chapters to the publisher's FTP site, where they can be integrated into the publishing process.

FTP uses a set of commands that are considered "standard," that everyone knows and can use. These commands can be used when initiating an FTP session from a command prompt. A few of the most commonly used commands are described in Figure 7.3.

- **ftp:** Opens an FTP session with a remote node. Following this command, the user enters either the domain name for the site or the site's IP address:

    ftp *wuarchive.wustl.com*

    or

    ftp xxx.xxx.xxx.xxx

- **dir:** At the ftp> prompt, you can enter the *dir* command to see what files are available to you. The listing looks a little different from a DOS *dir* command because the file name is at the far right side of the listing. Figure 7.4 shows the results of a *dir* command.

- **cd:** When you begin an FTP session, the session always starts you at the top of the available directory structure. To move down through the directory structure, use the *cd* command followed by the directory name you are looking for. You could type **cd pub** to move into the "pub," or public directory. (FTP is full of hints about what you might find in a directory, or where to look for something specific, like "pub" being a public area on the site.)

    ftp> *cd* pub

    To move up from a lower-level directory, type in **cd ..** That moves you up one level. Continue to enter this same command until you have reached the directory level you want.

    ftp> *cd* ..

- **Get** and **put:** This is where the UNIX history becomes very evident with FTP. *Get* and *put* are classic UNIX commands that mean exactly what they say: get a file or put a file in the directory structure. You can either *get* or *put* a file and rename it by adding the new file name at the end of the command. Below are examples of these commands.

    ftp> g*et* newthisweek.z

    ftp> *get* newthisweek.z archive-new

    When you transfer files from a remote node to the local node, the files will land in the directory where you began the FTP session. If you know you will be downloading files, make sure you are located in the correct directory before opening the FTP session.

- **mget** and **mput:** These two commands allow you to move multiple files or a whole set of files at one time. Are you getting the hang of FTP commands? Hidden in the commands is a logic that at first seems difficult, but after a bit of time, you come to recognize that these are short forms for the actions the commands provide. You can use these two commands with a shortened form for the files, as well. The example below says retrieve all the files in this directory that start with the letter "s."

    m*get* s*

    To avoid getting a command prompt for every file you have requested, you can turn off the prompt by typing **prompt**.

    ftp> *prompt*

FIGURE 7.3
Commonly Used FTP
Commands.

214

```
C:\WINNT\System32\cmd.exe - ftp wuarchive.wustl.edu                    _ □ ×
ftp> dir
200 PORT command successful.
150 Opening ASCII mode data connection for /bin/ls.
total 50
lrwxrwxrwx   1 0        other          17 Jun 29 07:03 archive2 -> /export1/arch
ive2
lrwxrwxrwx   1 0        other           9 Apr 26  2000 bin -> ./usr/bin
drwxr-xr-x  10 0        other         512 Apr 26  2000 decus
drwxr-xr-x   2 0        other         512 Apr 27  2000 dev
drwxr-xr-x  22 0        other         512 Apr 26  2000 doc
drwxr-xr-x   4 0        other         512 Mar 23  2002 edu
drwxr-xr-x   3 0        other         512 Apr 26  2000 etc
-rw-rw-r--   1 1001     archive      6481 Sep 15 02:03 index.html
-rw-r--r--   1 0        other        4506 Jan 19  2000 index.html.1
-rw-------   1 0        other        4108 Sep 28  2000 index.html.2
-rw-rw-r--   1 0        root         4101 Mar 13  2002 index.html.veryold
drwxr-xr-x   7 0        archive       512 Mar 29  2002 info
drwxr-xr-x  13 0        other         512 Mar 19  2002 languages
drwx------   3 0        root         1024 Aug  6  2001 lost+found
drwxrwxrwx   9 1001     1001          512 Aug 28 09:13 mirrors
-rw-rw-r--   1 1001     archive      9455 Jun 26 07:47 news.html
drwxr-xr-x   2 0        other        1024 Jun 21 02:19 packages
drwxr-xr-x   2 1001     1002          512 Mar 23  2002 projects
drwxr-xr-x   2 20025    other         512 Mar 23  2002 pub
drwxr-xr-x   4 0        other         512 Jun 26 09:41 systems
drwxr-xr-x   5 1001     users         512 Mar 23  2002 users
drwxr-xr-x   5 0        other         512 Apr 26  2000 usr
drwxrwxr-x   4 1001     1004          512 Apr  7 12:33 web
226 Transfer complete.
ftp: 1511 bytes received in 0.05Seconds 30.22Kbytes/sec.
ftp>
```

FIGURE 7.4
Dir Command Results
When Used with FTP

ASCII (American Standard Code for Information Interchange)

A code that represents alphanumeric characters as numbers (which will eventually be resolved into a series of bits in the on/off state). The code also contains representations for certain functions that were necessary when it was first developed.

Sometimes files will not transfer correctly. This occurs because of differences in systems. By default, all file transfers will use the *ASCII* code, which, for some systems, may incorrectly translate some characters. Because computers understand only numbers, and those numbers must eventually be resolved into bits in the on/off state, ASCII uses numbers to represent alphanumeric characters. As an example, the capital letter "W" corresponds to the number 87, while the lowercase "w" corresponds to the number 119. ASCII code also contains representations for certain functions that were necessary when the coding was developed. (See "For More Information" for this chapter on the Internet Resource Center for a resource for the ASCII code conversion.)

To avoid the translation problems sometimes associated with ASCII, switch to binary, which does not translate codes. Switching between the two codes is easy. Just follow the FTP prompt with either the word "ascii" or the word "binary."

One more thing before we leave FTP: if you are not pleased with accessing an FTP site through a command prompt, or if you have forgotten how to use a command prompt, many utilities exist that can make life with FTP much easier. You can also avoid the problem of "where did my files go" when downloading. Remember: you must start your FTP session in the directory where you want the downloaded files to be stored. With many of the utilities available, you can choose the directory for storage from within the utility, just prior to the download with FTP. Many of these utilities are free or very low priced for home or educational use. Some of those utilities are:

- WS FTP
- CUTEFTP
- FTP Explorer
- SmartFTP

Trivial File Transfer Protocol (TFTP)

Trivial File Transfer Protocol (TFTP) is very similar to FTP with one exception. Where FTP manages the connections using TCP, TFTP employs UDP for the connections, thus resulting in more efficient file transfer, but without guaranteed delivery. It is called "trivial" because several functions in FTP have been eliminated, enhancing the efficiency. For instance, user login is not supported with TFTP.

TFTP runs on a machine as a server: it hosts services for remote nodes. Common usage includes storing router configuration files for quick and easy retrieval, and storing operating system files for easy access. Several server applications have been written for TFTP, providing a friendly user interface for the service. A quick search on the Internet will yield many choices. Any node running TCP/IP can act as a client to the TFTP server using the familiar syntax "tftp *server name*" or "*TFTP ip address*."

Simple Mail Transfer Protocol (SMTP)

Simple Mail Transfer Protocol (SMTP) is the glue that binds together all of the various applications used to support electronic mail services. Many different implementations for the exchange of e-mail have been introduced over the years. Three of the top runners are Microsoft Exchange, Lotus Notes, and Novell GroupWise. Each application handles incoming and outgoing messages in a slightly different manner. How can all these differences in the way the applications handle e-mail be smoothed over to permit the unobstructed exchange of messages? SMTP, of course.

SMTP is a specialized service protocol that uses TCP to guarantee safe delivery of packets that make up the e-mail messages. When an application like Microsoft Exchange is installed on a server node, SMTP listens to the packets being sent across the media to the node. When a packet's destination is that server node, with a port number of 25 designated in the packet, the server node allows SMTP to open a session with the sending node (usually also an e-mail server). The sending node identifies itself and waits for the receiving node to acknowledge its readiness to receive mail. If the receiving node is prepared, the sending node announces from whom the e-mail is coming, and to whom the e-mail is going. If this is a matching recipient on the receiving e-mail server, the message is passed through. If there is no match on the receiving e-mail server, an error message is generated, the sender is notified of nondelivery, and the packet is discarded. TCP's guaranteed delivery allows notification of nondelivery.

E-mail services need more than just SMTP to manage the exchange of messages. The designated e-mail server uses either Post Office Protocol (POP) or Internet Mail Access Protocol (IMAP) to manage the storage and retrieval of all of those e-mail messages. We will discuss these two protocols in the next two sections.

Post Office Protocol v.3 (POP3)

Post Office Protocol v.3 (POP3) allows e-mail messages to be stored for clients that are not connected to the Internet. Your POP3 e-mail server will require that you identify yourself by entering a valid user name and password before access is allowed to the stored messages. Once an account has been validated, the message store (or mailbox, as it is more commonly called) will dynamically transmit the messages to the client machine.

POP3 holds "conversations" with clients when e-mail is requested. These conversations have three states, or stages (see Figure 7.5).

Post Office Protocol v.3 (POP3)

A client-server e-mail protocol that allows mail messages to be stored until the account holder chooses to read those messages.

- **Authorization State:** In the authorization state, the POP3 server is announcing its readiness to service clients. The client in turn passes the user name and password to the POP3 server for verification. If the user name and password are known, the process moves to the next state.
- **Transaction State:** During the transaction state, the POP3 server is sending messages to the client, deleting indicated messages, retrieving messages from the client that need to be forwarded to other e-mail servers, and completing any other e-mail housekeeping chores as needed.
- **Update State:** The update state closes the conversation between the client and the POP3 server. The client sends a "quit" notice, and the server says "OK."

FIGURE 7.5
States in POP3 Conversations

Keep in mind that POP3 assumes that the client will access the message store from the same node at all times. Therefore, POP3 will store messages until the client authenticates, downloads the messages to the client node, and removes the messages from the message store on the POP3 server.

Internet Message Access Protocol v.4 (IMAP4)

Internet Message Access Protocol (IMAP) provides access to messages from multiple computers. It does not require that messages be downloaded to the client node when a request for access to the messages is made. This makes IMAP the solution for the global business world. Users (e-mail clients) can read mail and delete, answer, or send messages, but they cannot download those messages to the local node.

Many e-mail applications provide this type of access to e-mail messages through a browser interface. This is known as Web-access e-mail. In addition to reading messages, through the services provided by IMAP, a client can create, delete, and check for new messages, as well as set and clear flags. Full functionality to e-mail manipulation is provided while maintaining the messages on the IMAP server.

Hypertext Transfer Protocol (HTTP)

Hypertext Transfer Protocol (HTTP) is a generic, stateless protocol (meaning that it does not care what operating system or platform the computer is running) that allows access to Internet resources regardless of the platform of either the requesting node (client) or the servicing node (usually a server). HTTP acts as the go-between from your browser to the service. It forms the set of rules governing the transfer of files such as text, graphic images, sound, and video across the Internet.

The terms "generic" and "stateless" indicate that usage and function of HTTP is not tied to any one or two operating systems. Nor is there any tie to machine platform (PC, RISC, PowerPC). Instead, HTTP provides the framework for requesting a resource (a Web page, for example) from the browser window, and transferring that page to the requesting node's browser. In that page, there may be many links. When a client clicks on one of those links, HTTP requests that new resource and displays it on the local client.

The major concept behind HTTP is that files can contain links to other files, which, when selected, will create additional transfer requests from other resources to the client browser. Like other TCP/IP protocols, these actions are managed because the resource node runs a *daemon* that listens for specific requests.

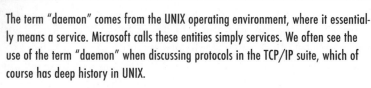

HTTP works in conjunction with Hypertext Markup Language (HTML). HTML is the code embedded in a Web resource that is accessible because the client and the server nodes are using TCP/IP and the appropriate services are running on the resource (server) node.

Hypertext Transfer Protocol over Secure Sockets Layer (HTTPS)

Hypertext Transfer Protocol over Secure Sockets Layer (HTTPS) is an extension of the HTTP protocol used to protect the transfer of sensitive or confidential data from a browser to a Web resource or vice versa. HTTPS was first developed by Netscape. The process involves encrypting data or page requests and then decrypting that data or page request at the destination.

HTTPS is frequently used by Web sites that provide E-commerce opportunities. A client visits a Web site and chooses to make a purchase. Cash cannot be exchanged, a check cannot be sent, but the client can use a credit card to make the purchase. Now, that credit card number is a very personal piece of information, and the Internet is a very public place. Through HTTPS, the confidential information is encrypted using one of several algorithms before transmission. Only the true destination node will be able to decrypt those packets containing that credit card number (and name, address, and telephone number). HTTPS does require the services of a certificate provider, such as VeriSign or Microsoft Certificate Server, to validate the security of the transmission.

To determine that you are connected to an E-commerce site in a secure manner, check the locator bar in your browser. Where you would normally see "http://website," you will see "https://website." The "s" following the "http" indicates that there is a secure channel between your node and the server node.

Hypertext Transfer Protocol over Secure Sockets Layer (HTTPS)

An extension of HTTP that is used to protect the transfer of sensitive or confidential data from a browser to a Web resource or vice versa. The authenticity of users and computers is validated with certificates, or keys, to ensure security.

Telnet ~~Terminal emulation~~

Telnet

An upper-layer TCP/IP protocol that allows access to a remote device (typically routers and computers).

The *Telnet* utility protocol of the TCP/IP suite was designed for one purpose: to give access to remote nodes. That may seem very simplistic today, when much of what we do involves remote nodes. But in the early days of computing and TCP/IP usage, remote access to other nodes was a very new and impressive capability for both the nodes and the users. Telnet gave anyone who was connected to the global internetwork (first ARPANET and then the Internet) the ability to discover information that previously was exchanged using only snail mail or books. The academic world made quick use of this capability because now professors and researchers half a globe away could immediately share information and data on projects they had in common.

"Telnet" is short for terminal emulation. Its method is to mimic the remote node so that it appears as if the user is sitting in front of the remote node. Virtually all operating systems have Telnet capability providing the node has the TCP/IP protocol installed. When running one of the Microsoft Windows family of operating systems, the user actually has two choices for terminal emulation: use of the Telnet utility from the command prompt or HyperTerminal, a more user-friendly Telnet format.

Starting Telnet in a command prompt environment appears a bit archaic for those who have grown up using the graphical Windows operating systems. To open a Telnet session, go to the Start/Run utility in a Windows operating system and type in **telnet** followed by the name or IP address of the resource you wish to use (see Figure 7.6). Telnet also requires users to remember all commands and switches or use the "help" facility by typing **/help** at the command prompt. Figure 7.7 shows the initial Telnet session just after the user has entered a correct user name and password.

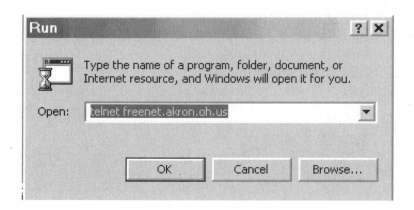

FIGURE 7.6
Opening a Telnet Session Using the Run Utility in a Windows Operating System

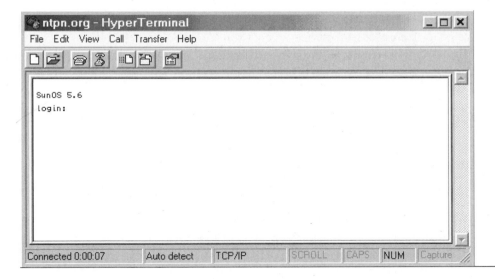

```
C:\WINNT\System32\telnet.exe

                   Unregistered visitors to the
           Akron Community Online Resource Network
                   may log in as "visitor".
           Use the <Enter/Return> key as a password.

login: visitor
Password:
Last login: Sun Sep 29 12:36:42 from 200.43.252.135

     ** You have 30 minutes for this session. **

     SCRI-Net, version 2.2beta * Free-Net User Interface
     Copyright 1994, Supercomputer Computations Research Institute

***Type 'help' at the 'Your Choice:' prompt for instructions***

Enter terminal type (default = vt100):
```

FIGURE 7.7
Initial Login Window for a
Telnet Session

You can also use the Telnet utility while still enjoying the user-friendly interface by opening a HyperTerminal session. HyperTerminal offers the familiar window, Menu bar, icons, and folder and file functions of all Windows environments (see Figure 7.8).

```
ntpn.org - HyperTerminal

File  Edit  View  Call  Transfer  Help



SunOS 5.6
login:




Connected 0:00:07    Auto detect    TCP/IP    SCROLL  CAPS  NUM  Capture
```

FIGURE 7.8
HyperTerminal Session

Today's administrators use many other utilities to connect to remote nodes. One situation where they often make use of Telnet concerns router management. All routers allow remote sessions through Telnet. By opening a Telnet session, the administrator has access to the entire configuration for the router and can make changes and adjustments quickly and efficiently.

Internet Control Message Protocol (ICMP)

Internet Control Message Protocol (ICMP)

A TCP/IP protocol that is used for message control and error reporting.

PING

A utility that tests whether TCP/IP is functioning correctly on a host computer and that checks connectivity between devices.

Tracert (traceroute)

A TCP/IP command-line diagnostic utility that is used to determine the route a packet uses to get to a destination.

Internet Control Message Protocol (ICMP) notifies the sending node of an error in the delivery of packets to the destination node. When a packet fails to reach a destination, ICMP generates the notification packet that will be sent to the source address in the header of the packet. ICMP is used by other utility protocols. *PING* and *tracert* are two examples (you will learn more about those utilities in Chapter 19).

ICMP creates several distinct types of notification, depending on the type of error that has been detected (see Figure 7.9).

- **Destination Unreachable:** A router sends this type of message when the router is unable to send the packet to its destination address. Once the error message is sent, the packet is discarded. Two situations will precipitate this type of message: first, the destination address is nonexistent; second, the router does not have a route to the destination. There are four types of destination unreachable messages:
  - Network-unreachable: This indicates a routing problem.
  - Host-unreachable: This type of message is produced when there is a delivery failure, usually due to a bad subnet mask.
  - Protocol-unreachable: Here the upper-level protocol is not supported on the network.
  - Port-unreachable: The TCP or UDP port is unavailable (ports are commonly turned off for security reasons and therefore unavailable).
- **Echo-Request Message:** The PING command uses the echo-request message to test node access across an internetwork. An echo-reply packet is sent from the destination node to indicate that the path to the node is complete. Figure 7.10 displays the result of a PING request.

  The tracert utility also uses ICMP. Tracert is used to trace the path from a source to a destination node. Each node or device in the path of the packet will be asked to return an echo-reply packet to identify itself as a step in the path. Tracert is commonly used to determine where a breakdown occurs in transmission between nodes. Figure 7.11 displays the result of a tracert command, and the echo-request message returned to the source node.
- **ICMP Redirect:** A router sends this type of message to the source node to encourage more efficient routing.
- **ICMP Time-Exceeded:** When the TTL (Time-to-Live) indicator in a packet runs out, the packet cannot be forwarded any further toward the destination node. ICMP notifies the sender that the TTL has expired and the router can then discard the packet.

FIGURE 7.9
Types of ICMP Notification

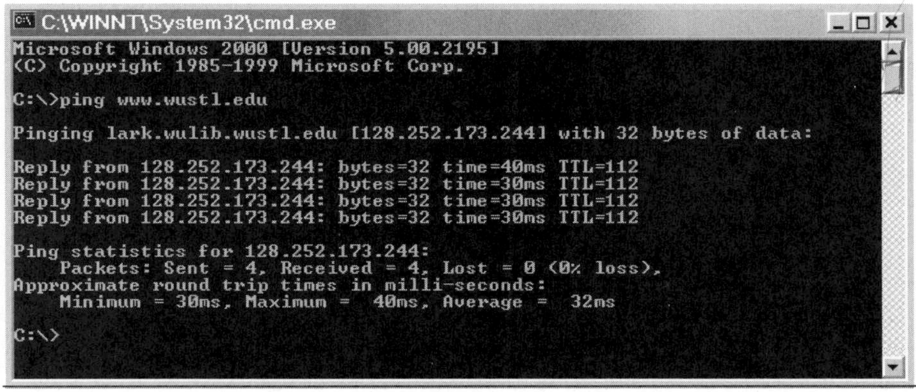

```
C:\WINNT\System32\cmd.exe                                        _ □ X
Microsoft Windows 2000 [Version 5.00.2195]
(C) Copyright 1985-1999 Microsoft Corp.

C:\>ping www.wustl.edu

Pinging lark.wulib.wustl.edu [128.252.173.244] with 32 bytes of data:

Reply from 128.252.173.244: bytes=32 time=40ms TTL=112
Reply from 128.252.173.244: bytes=32 time=30ms TTL=112
Reply from 128.252.173.244: bytes=32 time=30ms TTL=112
Reply from 128.252.173.244: bytes=32 time=30ms TTL=112

Ping statistics for 128.252.173.244:
    Packets: Sent = 4, Received = 4, Lost = 0 (0% loss),
Approximate round trip times in milli-seconds:
    Minimum = 30ms, Maximum = 40ms, Average = 32ms

C:\>
```

FIGURE 7.10
PING Request Response with ICMP-Generated Information

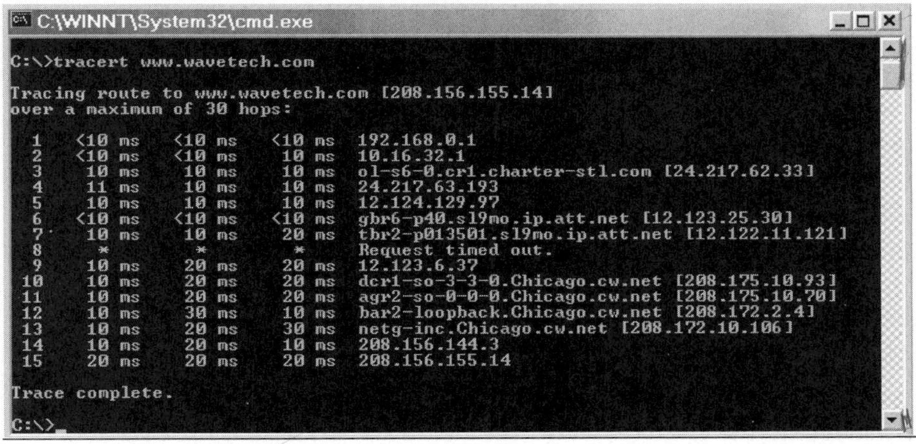

```
C:\WINNT\System32\cmd.exe                                        _ □ X
C:\>tracert www.wavetech.com

Tracing route to www.wavetech.com [208.156.155.14]
over a maximum of 30 hops:

  1    <10 ms    <10 ms    <10 ms   192.168.0.1
  2    <10 ms    <10 ms     10 ms   10.16.32.1
  3     10 ms     10 ms     10 ms   ol-s6-0.cr1.charter-stl.com [24.217.62.33]
  4     11 ms     10 ms     10 ms   24.217.63.193
  5     10 ms     10 ms     10 ms   12.124.129.97
  6    <10 ms    <10 ms    <10 ms   gbr6-p40.sl9mo.ip.att.net [12.123.25.30]
  7     10 ms     10 ms     20 ms   tbr2-p013501.sl9mo.ip.att.net [12.122.11.121]
  8      *         *         *      Request timed out.
  9     10 ms     10 ms     20 ms   12.123.6.37
 10     10 ms     20 ms     20 ms   dcr1-so-3-3-0.Chicago.cw.net [208.175.10.93]
 11     10 ms     20 ms     20 ms   agr2-so-0-0-0.Chicago.cw.net [208.175.10.70]
 12     10 ms     30 ms     10 ms   bar2-loopback.Chicago.cw.net [208.172.2.4]
 13     10 ms     20 ms     30 ms   netg-inc.Chicago.cw.net [208.172.10.106]
 14     10 ms     20 ms     10 ms   208.156.144.3
 15     20 ms     20 ms     20 ms   208.156.155.14

Trace complete.

C:\>
```

FIGURE 7.11
TRACERT Results Using the ICMP Echo-Request Message

Address Resolution Protocol/Reverse Address Resolution Protocol (ARP/RARP) (Know)

Address Resolution Protocol (ARP) provides the information necessary to deliver the packet to the destination node by associating a Network layer address (logical) to a Data Link layer address (physical). Logical addressing, usually IP addresses, allows the packet to traverse the internetwork router to router.

Looking at this in more depth, we can see specifically how ARP works across an internetwork. When your computer is ready to send a message to a node on a remote network, it packages that message with the source IP address and the destination IP address. These are Network layer addresses. As this message, in packets, is readied for the network and specifically for

Know

Address Resolution Protocol (ARP)

A utility protocol that allows the mapping of an IP address (Network layer logical address) to a MAC address (Data Link layer physical address).

the Data Link layer, it is wrapped in a Data Link layer header and becomes a frame. Remember that the Data Link layer uses MAC (physical) addresses for delivery.

Your computer will take that Network layer packet and provide the Data Link layer header with the nearest router interface (or designated gateway) MAC address as the destination address for the frame. When the router (gateway) gets this frame, it will strip the Data Link header and check the IP (Network layer) destination address. After consulting the routing table, the router will add a Data Link layer header with the MAC address of the next hop router interface. This process continues until the packet reaches the router that is attached to the destination network.

When the packet gets to the router closest to the actual destination node, the router must ask the local segment to identify specifically which node is using a particular IP address. The ARP request is sent over the local segment as a broadcast. The node holding the IP address in the broadcast replies to the broadcast and sends its MAC address to the router interface. Then the router can put the MAC address in the header of the packet and send the packet on its way to the destination.

Look at the diagram in Figure 7.12. Our source machine address is 200.10.1.1. In order to send a message to the computer at 200.10.3.2, the packet must cross two routers. If we apply what we learned just above, when the source machine gets ready to send the packet and adds a Data Link header, the destination address will be the MAC address of the router interface at 200.10.1.2. Then the router takes charge of the frame by stripping the Data Link layer header, discovering that the packet is going to network 200.10.3.0. It will add a Data Link header with the destination address being the MAC address of the router interface 200.10.2.1. Once again, the packet (frame) is sent to the next router. This router strips off the Data Link header and discovers that the packet is destined for a node on one of its own networks. It will send out an ARP broadcast asking for the MAC address of the node with IP address 200.10.3.2. When that machine replies with its MAC address, the new Data Link layer header is placed on the packet (now frame) and the frame is delivered to the destination node.

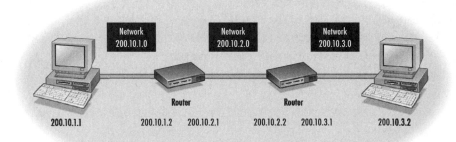

FIGURE 7.12
ARP Process over a TCP/IP
Internetwork

To get an idea of how you might add an entry to the ARP cache, here is an example:

C:>arp -s   177.22.1.6   05-BB-00-F1-32-16

Most operating systems allow the local node to cache ARP responses for a period of time. Figure 7.13 displays the content of the local ARP cache.

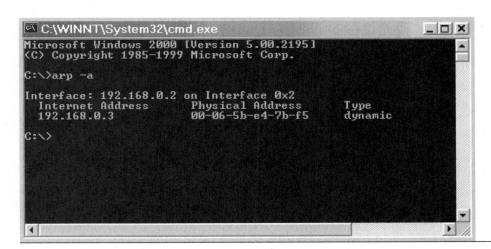

FIGURE 7.13
Contents of ARP Cache on
the Local Node

A few switches for the ARP utility are very helpful in troubleshooting connectivity problems. The most commonly used switches and their functions are listed in Figure 7.14. This information is readily available by typing **arp/help** at a command prompt.

- **-a:** Displays the current ARP entries in cache.
- **inet_addr:** Indicates an IP address will follow.
- **eth_addr:** Indicates a physical or MAC address will follow.
- **-d:** Will delete a host when a specific IP address is indicated.
- **-s:** Adds a permanent host entry when followed by an IP address and MAC address.

FIGURE 7.14
Commonly Used ARP Switches

Reverse Address Resolution Protocol (RARP) ✓

A utility protocol that allows the mapping of a MAC address (Data Link layer physical address) to an IP address (Network layer logical address).

Network Time Protocol (NTP) ✓

A protocol that provides network computers with the ability to synchronize their clocks with each other.

Reverse Address Resolution Protocol (RARP) does just the opposite. When a node's MAC address is known but its IP address is not, a RARP broadcast will be issued to the local segment requesting the IP address from the node owning the MAC address in the header. Some operating systems do not recognize the RARP utility when a generic installation process is used. The utility may be available as an add-on from the original installation media.

Network Time Protocol (NTP)

Network Time Protocol (NTP) allows computers throughout the Internet to achieve time synchronization. Time synchronization remains important for some applications as well as for timely delivery of e-mail and for access to resources.

NTP comes in two versions that are used by many operating systems: NTP v.3 and NTP v.4. Microsoft Windows NT and Windows 2000 both use NTP v.4; UNIX can use either version; Novell NetWare uses both versions; and Microsoft Windows 9x cannot use either one because it lacks kernel functions that are needed for this protocol.

NTP runs as a service or daemon on a node. The nodes function in one of three roles, as shown in Figure 7.15.

- **Client:** Requests the time from one or more time servers.
- **Server:** Makes the time setting on itself available to other nodes.
- **Peer:** Compares its time setting to that of other equal (peer) nodes until all peers agree on what is the correct time.

FIGURE 7.15
Roles of NTP Nodes

NTP gets the time from external sources designed just for the purpose of keeping time and disseminating the time to Internet resources. Two

agencies in the United States maintain time: the National Institute for
Standards and Technology (NIST) and the United States Naval
Observatory (USNO). These two agencies measure time and distribute true
time readings. They maintain time to within 0.0000001 of a second.

Know

TestTip

**Be sure to understand the functions of each of the protocols in the
TCP/IP suite for the test.**

TCP/UDP Ports

In Chapter 6, we discussed the use of the IPX socket. We said that an IPX
socket is a network-addressable service access point that allows the binding
of an application process to a unique identifier for that process. TCP/IP
uses the port in much the same way.

A port is a way to identify a specific process. You can think of a port as
the endpoint in a logical connection (between the client and the server, for
example). Data may be forwarded by way of a network message or Internet
message. To make sure that the service provider will know exactly where to
deliver the data or message, both the sending and receiving nodes are
assigned port numbers.

Both TCP and UDP add a 16-bit field to the header of the message.
There are 65,535 port values available for assignment. Port numbers are
divided into three categories, as shown in Figure 7.16.

- **Well-Known Ports:** The well-known port values are those from 0 through 1023 (or 1,024 available ports). Most network technicians and administrators are very familiar with many of these port values. These ports are used by system processes, and are not available for assignment to application processes. Some of the most familiar ports are listed in Table 7.2.
- **Registered Ports:** Registered ports run from 1024 through 49151. This group of ports is managed by IANA (as are all port listings), specifically for assignment to particular application processes. For instance, Iberiagames has registered ports 1726/TCP and 1726/UDP with IANA. Those two ports may not be used by any other vendor for any other purpose. Iberiagames must be confident that when a user loads its software, ports 1726 TCP/UDP will be available for use by the application and its processes.
- **Dynamic and Private Ports:** The balance of the available ports, from 49152 through 65534, are unassigned and may be dynamically or randomly used by operating systems, processes, and programmers.

FIGURE 7.16
Categories of TCP/UDP
Ports

Port Number	Protocol
UDP port 15	NETSTAT
TCP port 21	FTP
TCP port 23	Telnet
TCP port 25	SMTP
UDP port 53	DNS
TCP/UDP port 69	TFTP
TCP/UDP port 80	HTTP
TCP port 110	POP3
UDP port 111	RPC
TCP port 123	NTP
UDP port 161	SNMP
TCP/UDP port 443	HTTPS

(handwritten: ✓ Know)

TABLE 7.2
Well-Known Port Numbers and the Protocol Associated with the Port

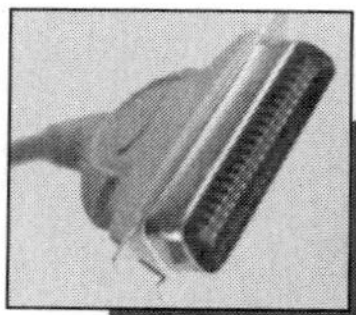

TEST TIP

For the test, you should be very familiar with all the port numbers and associated protocols listed in Table 7.2.

Keep in mind that ports give administrators a means to control access to certain services. For example, an administrator may disable port 80 on certain router interfaces to prevent any type of HTTP traffic from being passed on by the router interface. If the administrator wished to prohibit any outbound FTP traffic, port 21 could be disabled on the public router interface for outbound traffic. This is considered a low-level security feature. Several other products on the market do much the same thing but are more sophisticated. One of those products is Microsoft's Proxy Server, which we will explore in a coming chapter.

STUDY GUIDE

In this chapter, we discussed many of the utilities and services available for use under the TCP/IP protocol. We also provided instructions for configuring and using those components. Here are some key points to remember.

OSI Model Review

- The OSI Model is a layered framework that provides structure for data communications.
- The Application layer services applications. Protocols such as DNS, FTP, TFTP, Telnet, SNMP, and SMTP function at this layer.
- The Presentation layer is responsible for character conversion, encryption/decryption, and compression/decompression. No TCP/IP protocols function at this layer.
- The Session layer opens, maintains, and ends sessions. It also provides name-recognition services and aids in reliable data delivery. No TCP/IP protocols function at this layer.
- The Transport layer guarantees delivery of packets to the destination, divides messages into packets, provides the sequencing services necessary to reassemble messages upon delivery, requests retransmission when nondelivery errors occur, and manages flow control between the source and destination nodes. TCP and UDP function at this layer.
- The Network layer is responsible for logical addressing and the routing of packets through the internetwork. IP, UDP, ARP, RARP, and ICMP are part of this layer.
- Data Link layer responsibilities include converting packets into bits and defining the access methods used to allow data to be transmitted and received. No TCP/IP protocols function at this layer.
- The Physical layer transmits data across the physical media and sets standards for the physical components of a network, such as cable, NICs, and repeaters. No TCP/IP protocols function at this layer.

TCP

- Transmission Control Protocol is a connection-oriented, reliable protocol that uses IP for transport.
- TCP guarantees delivery of packets through use of the checksum.
- TCP uses port identities to provide a logical connection between the source and destination nodes.

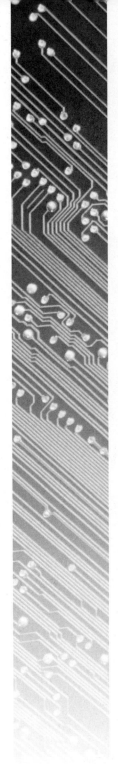

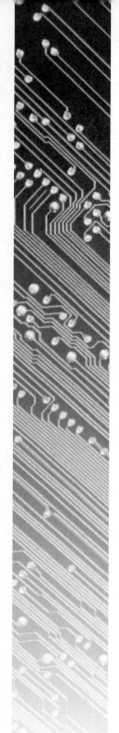

IP

- IP is the most basic of all the protocols in the TCP/IP suite because it is the transport protocol all other protocols rely on.
- IP delivers packets; however, it does not guarantee delivery.
- IP is a connectionless protocol.

UDP

- UDP is a connectionless protocol used to transport data.
- UDP uses some very basic error-checking methods to validate the delivery of the packets.
- UDP is commonly used for service protocols (and therefore, applications) because of its efficiency and lower overhead.

FTP

- FTP allows remote nodes to share files by providing the method to retrieve those files to a local machine.
- FTP uses TCP for transport.
- FTP has two components: the client (requestor) component, and the server (service provider) component. These two components can be configured on any type of machine because FTP does not look at the machine or the operating system. It is concerned only with the service availability.
- Access to files is controlled in one of two ways: using a user account and password for access; or using the anonymous account. Both require that the appropriate permissions or rights be configured on the files.
- The anonymous account requires a password that is an e-mail address.
- The bandwidth speed, congestion on the media, and speed of the computer hosting FTP determine the speed of an FTP session.
- FTP uses many commands that allow the user to download files, upload files, change directories, and request a multiple file download or upload.
- Other utilities are available to make FTP a more user-friendly process.

TFTP

- TFTP does many of the same things FTP does but without the overhead of a TCP connection.
- TFTP uses UDP for efficient transport of files.

- TFTP is commonly used to access router configuration files and operating system files stored on a remote computer.
- Any node running the TCP/IP protocol can act either as a service provider or as a client.

SMTP

- SMTP is the protocol used to support the transfer of e-mail messages from one e-mail system to another over a TCP/IP connection.
- SMTP uses TCP to provide guaranteed delivery of the packets that form an e-mail message.
- Use of TCP connections allows an error message to be sent to the source node if delivery of the message cannot be completed.

POP3

- POP3 is a protocol that runs on an e-mail server and allows e-mail messages to be stored on the e-mail server.
- POP3 assumes that the client will always use the same machine when requesting e-mail messages from the server.
- POP3 requires a client to authenticate with a valid user name and password. It will then dynamically transmit all stored messages to the client machine.
- POP3 holds conversations with the client and takes those conversations through three states:
  - Authorization—readiness to service the client by validating the user name and password.
  - Transaction—sends the waiting messages to the client machine and takes care of deleting, sending, and forwarding any marked messages.
  - Update—closes the conversation with the client.

IMAP

- IMAP allows administrators to provide their users with the ability to access e-mail through a Web browser such as Internet Explorer or Netscape.
- IMAP does not require that the messages stored for a user account be downloaded to the client machine; rather, IMAP stores all messages on the e-mail server, carries out commands against those messages (delete, modify, reply), and continues to store messages for a client.

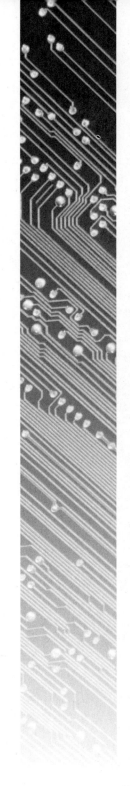

HTTP

- HTTP is a generic, stateless protocol that gives access to Internet resources regardless of the platform or operating system of the requesting node.
- HTTP forms the set of rules governing the transfer of files in text format, graphic image format, audio format, and video format.
- HTTP can access links to other files, which create additional requests for file transfer.
- Hypertext Markup Language (HTML) is the coding embedded within the HTTP request.

HTTPS

- HTTPS is an extension of the HTTP protocol.
- HTTPS uses Secure Sockets Layer to encrypt data and protect that data during transmission over public media.
- Multiple algorithms are available to encrypt data. The algorithm chosen is dependent on the security need.
- HTTPS requires the presence of a certificate provider such as VeriSign or Microsoft Certificate Server.

TELNET

- Telnet is a terminal emulation protocol.
- Telnet allows a user to access a remote node as if the user were sitting at that node.
- A Telnet session is initialized by typing **telnet *resource-name*** at a command prompt, or opening a HyperTerminal session if you are using a Microsoft Windows operating system.
- Telnet is frequently used to access router configurations and to make changes to those router configurations.

ICMP

- ICMP generates an error message when delivery of a packet cannot be completed.
- A destination-unreachable error indicates that the router is unable to complete the delivery. Routers issue four types of destination-unreachable messages:
  - Network-unreachable

- Host-unreachable
- Protocol-unreachable
- Port-unreachable
- The PING utility issues an echo-request message, which ICMP then takes to the destination address or next router. When that destination is reached, an echo reply is issued to acknowledge that the path for the packet is good.
- To encourage more efficient routing, a router issues an ICMP redirect message.
- When the packet's route exceeds the TTL on the packet and the packet has not been delivered, the packet is discarded and an ICMP time-exceeded message is issued to the sending node.

ARP/RARP

- ARP allows a router to discover the MAC address of the destination node *(Physical)* and deliver the packet to that node.
- ARP requests are sent as broadcasts over the destination segment (based *(logical)* on the destination IP address in the header of the packet).
- The node holding the IP address will respond to the broadcast with its MAC address, thus allowing delivery of the packet.
- Most operating systems allow ARP caching.
- RARP is used when the MAC address is known but the IP address has not been identified.
- Some operating systems do not allow RARP requests with default installations of the TCP/IP protocol.

NTP

- NTP allows synchronization of computer clocks on a network, internetwork, or the Internet.
- Time synchronization is important to some applications, as well as to some operating systems that log events with a time marker.
- NTP servers have three functions:
    - Client—requests time.
    - Server—provides time.
    - Peer—argues with other peers to come up with an agreed-upon time.
- NTP typically uses one of two resources for the true time setting: the United States Naval Observatory (USNO) or the National Institute for Standards and Technology (NIST).

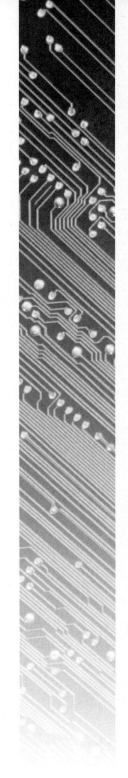

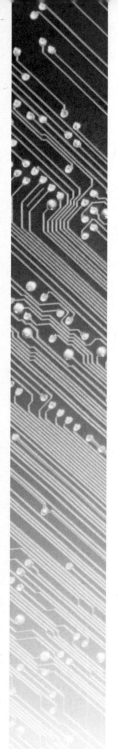

TCP/UDP PORTS

- A port is a logical entity that identifies a specific process on both a source and destination node: it is the endpoint in a logical connection.
- There are 65,535 ports, and those ports are grouped into three categories:
  - Well-known ports—0–1023; assigned to common services.
  - Registered ports—1024–49151; registered to vendors.
  - Dynamic and private ports—unassigned for dynamic use.

PRACTICE TEST

Try this test to check your mastery of the concepts in this chapter.

1. Your users routinely need to copy files from a UNIX server to their desktop computers. The network uses TCP/IP as its transport protocol. Which of the following utilities should your users employ?
   a. SMTP
   b. FTP
   c. DHCP
   d. HTTP

2. Which of the following protocols supports e-mail services?
   a. SMTP
   b. FTP
   c. TFTP
   d. Telnet

3. Which of the following ports does the HTTP protocol use?
   a. 110
   b. 23
   c. 443
   d. 80

4. Which of the following utility protocols allows you to view the IP address to MAC address resolutions?
   a. ARP
   b. RARP
   c. Telnet
   d. FTP

5. Telnet uses the _____ OSI layer 4 protocol.
   a. IP
   b. UDP
   c. TCP
   d. UTP

6. What port number does the NTP protocol use?
   a. 122
   b. 123
   c. 124
   d. 125

7. A remote procedure call will attempt to set up a logical connection on port
   a. 80.
   b. 25.
   c. 443.
   d. 111.

8. When a packet cannot be delivered to the destination address, which protocol generates an error message and sends it to the source address in the header?
   a. IGRP
   b. ARP
   c. ICMP
   d. SNMP

9. To change directories during an FTP session, which command would you use?
   a. dir
   b. cd
   c. cd ..
   d. get

10. Which of the following protocols allows Internet mail to be sent between mail servers?
   a. SNMP
   b. SMTP
   c. FTP
   d. ARP

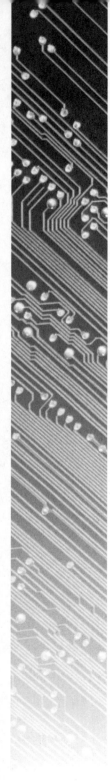

11. The administrator has disabled port 23 at the proxy server. What service is unavailable?
    a. SMTP
    b. ICMP
    c. PING
    d. Telnet

12. Your network uses an e-mail software package that assumes the user will always check for new mail from the same computer. Which of the following protocols does your e-mail system employ?
    a. SMTP
    b. POP3
    c. SNMP
    d. IMAP

13. The router admin group within your network must have access to the router configuration files on the router. All members are running a Windows operating system. Which two utilities might the members of the router admin group use to manage the routers' configurations?
    a. Telnet
    b. SNMP
    c. ICMP
    d. HyperTerminal

14. Confidential information stored on the Web server is available to the users in the Human Resources department. To protect the confidentiality of that data when accessed by a Human Resources employee, what additional feature would you add to your network?
    a. HTTP
    b. FTP
    c. HTTP over SSL (HTTPS)
    d. FTP over SSL (FTPS)

15. You wish to view the MAC addresses known to your computer. You open a command prompt and type which of the following commands?
    a. ARP -a
    b. RARP -a
    c. ARP
    d. RARP

16. To download a set of files that begin with the letter "z" from the FTP server, which of the following commands might you use?
    a. FTP *z
    b. MGET *z
    c. GET *z
    d. PUT *z

17. Which OSI layer 3 protocol is responsible for transporting packets without guaranteed delivery?
    a. UDP
    b. TCP
    c. UTP
    d. IP

18. The router admin group needs to store the configuration files for 12 routers in such a way as to make those files easily accessible to all members of the group. The network uses TCP/IP as its standard protocol. Which of the following solutions best meets this need?
    a. Load TFTP on a computer and give the IP address for this node to all members of the group.
    b. Tell the router administrators to store the configuration files on their workstation.
    c. Create a special Web site for the router administrators and allow hyperlinks to the configuration files.
    d. Allow anonymous access on the FTP server and tell the router administrators what folder you have stored the files in.

19. Which of the following is another word for a service?
    a. delegate
    b. daemon
    c. distractor
    d. doorway

20. What function does the TCP/IP protocol SNMP serve on the network?
    a. manages e-mail application services
    b. manages name resolution
    c. manages agents that monitor the network
    d. manages print services

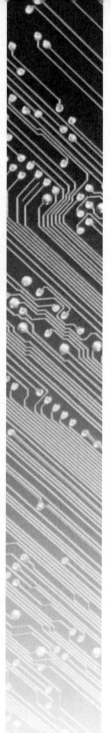

TROUBLESHOOTING

1. Your corporate LAN has a permanent connection to the Internet, and users are allowed access during business hours. The administrator has recently become concerned about hackers getting into the internal network services. He has disabled ports 90 through 190. Which service might this impede?
2. One of your users calls to say that he has been trying to access documentation at a vendor's Web location using FTP, but he cannot get to the files. He can get to the FTP site. He is using the anonymous login. What might be the problem?

CUSTOMER SERVICE

1. Many users within your company frequently access e-mail from many different computers. The users complain because their e-mail messages are spread among all of the computers used for mail access. Your supervisor asks you to research an alternative to this method of e-mail access. You begin exploring different e-mail applications. What one key factor will help you in your search?
2. A user complains that he cannot access the intranet Web server. He can access the file server and print services as well as the FTP server. The intranet Web server is located in the building across the street, as are the other two servers. What could cause this problem?

FOR MORE INFORMATION

For links to Web sites that provide further information about the topics covered in this chapter, go to the EMC/Paradigm Internet Resource Center at www.emcp.com/College Division/Internet Resource Centers/Networking/System Administration/Web Resources: For More Information.

Internet Protocol (IP) Addressing

8

Network+ Examination
- **Objective 2.8:** Identify IP addresses (IPv4, IPv6) and their default subnet masks.
- **Objective 2.9:** Identify the purpose of subnetting and default gateways.

ON THE JOB

Understanding the format to build an IP address will aid you in troubleshooting network connectivity problems. Using preconfigured charts to assign addresses makes some tasks easier, but this does not build the skills that will serve you as you move up the job ladder. As your understanding of IP addressing grows, you will become more aware of the options you have in assigning addresses. These options allow you to be quite creative with the addresses available to you, supplying all of your clients with an address appropriate to the network.

IP is the protocol of choice for most networks today. It is supported by all major client operating systems and network operating systems. IP is also the protocol of the Internet. Many networks are actually a part of the global set of internetworks that form the Internet. Every IP address for every host that will access this global internetwork must be unique.

Internet Protocol Version 4 (IPv4)

Internet Protocol version 4 (IPv4) addressing was standardized in 1981. This logical addressing scheme uses a 32-bit address space to form a unique identifier for each node that connects to the network or the internetwork. Each address contains two significant parts: the *network number* (or network prefix) and the *host number*. These two parts are combined to form the whole 32-bit address. This structure is known as a two-level address:

Network Number or Prefix . Host Number

Managing these addresses and distributing them fairly and equitably is a large task. IANA (Internet Assigned Numbers Authority) distributes address blocks to regional registries. Three such registries exist in the world. The servicing agency for the United States is the American Registry for Internet Numbers (ARIN), which also services the remainder of North America, South America, and Sub-Saharan Africa. These regional registries distribute address blocks to Internet Service Providers (ISPs). This creates a hierarchy that controls how IP addresses are used globally. This hierarchy is relatively new. When IP logical addressing made its way to the public after standardization in 1981, it was assumed that a 32-bit address space would provide enough addresses to last indefinitely. With the explosion of the Internet during the 1990s and the creativity of engineers and scientists, the available addresses were quickly becoming scarce. Many organizations claimed IP address blocks but did not make use of all of the addresses in the block. The various agencies that manage the TCP/IP protocol issued Request for Comment (RFC) 1917, an appeal to organizations to return unused address blocks. As a result, IP addresses are now distributed more fairly.

IPv4 ADDRESS STRUCTURE

As mentioned above, every IP address contains 32 bits. These bits are grouped in sets of 8 bits, called an *octet,* with each octet separated by a dot and represented in decimal format. This is known as dotted decimal notation. Each octet represents 1 byte within the address space. Figure 8.1 represents the 4 octets.

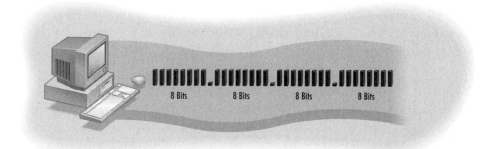

FIGURE 8.1
Bit Representation for the
32-Bit IP Address Format

Each bit within the octet carries a binary weight that can be represented by a decimal value. Figure 8.2 displays the decimal equivalent value for each bit in an octet.

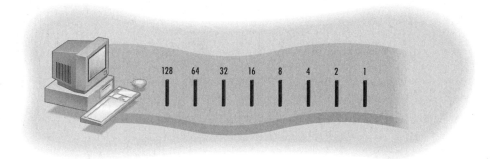

FIGURE 8.2
Decimal Value for Bits in
an Octet

Keep in mind that bits exist in one of two states: 1 (on); 0 (off). Because computers are electrical machines, they recognize only these two states—the presence or absence of an electrical charge. Consequently, IP addresses must be written as a series of 1s and 0s—a format that follows a *binary (base-two) number system*. Realizing what all those 1s and 0s mean will help you understand how machines move packets from a source to a destination, as well as where decisions are made about the path a packet will take.

Binary (base-two) number system

A numbering scheme that has only two numbers: 0 and 1.

IN REAL LIFE

The digits in a binary number increase from right to left by a power of 2. That means that the value of the digit farthest to the right is 1. The second digit from the right is 2 to a power of 1 (2^1), or 2. The value of the third digit from the right is 2 to a power of 2 (2^2), or 4. Another numbering scheme that may be more familiar is the decimal, or base-ten, system.

To represent an IP address as a series of bits, you must convert the decimal number to the binary equivalent. For example, look at the address 173.71.22.59. This is a valid host device address. Figure 8.3 shows the binary (or bit) representation of this IP address.

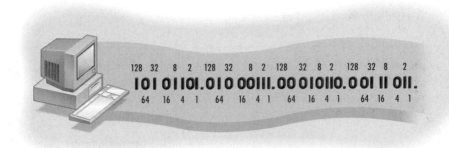

FIGURE 8.3
Binary Representation for the IP Address 173.71.22.59

Most significant bit

The leftmost bit in an IP address when represented in binary format. The bit's placement may be leftmost in the entire address, or leftmost in the octet to which it belongs. The most significant bit is sometimes referred to as the "high order bit."

The calculation for the binary representation is relatively simple. The first octet is 173. Beginning with the *most significant bit* (the leftmost number) and its decimal value, subtract 128 from 173. The result is 45. Because 128 is a portion of 173, the bit is turned on (see Figure 8.4).

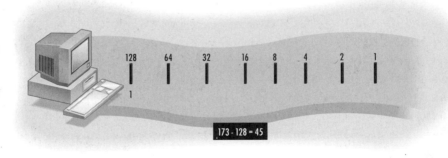

FIGURE 8.4
First Step in the Binary Notation: 173 - 128 = 45

Now try to subtract 64 from 45. Of course, this will not work because the remainder from the first step is only 45. The second most significant bit gets a value of 0, or off. Our next bit has a decimal value of 32. Subtract 32 from 45 and the result is 13. That bit gets turned on (see Figure 8.5).

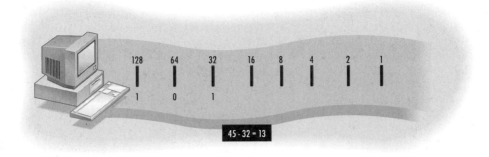

FIGURE 8.5
Second Step in the Binary
Notation: 45 - 32 = 13

The fourth most significant bit is valued at 16. Because 16 is larger than 13, we set the bit to the off (or 0) state. Bit 5 is valued at 8. Subtract 8 from our earlier remainder of 13, getting 5. The fifth bit is turned on (see Figure 8.6).

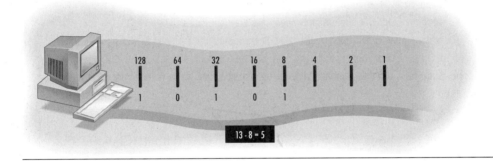

FIGURE 8.6
Third Step in the Binary
Notation: 13 - 8 = 5

Least significant bit

The rightmost bit in an IP address when represented in binary format. The least significant bit is sometimes referred to as the "low order bit."

Take the remainder, 5, and subtract the next bit value, 4. This time the remainder is 1. We can turn on the bit. Can we subtract 2 from our remainder? This will not work, so we turn off the bit. Our last remainder is included but turning on the *least significant* (rightmost, or low order) *bit*. The binary equivalent of the value of our first octet—173—is 10101101. See Figure 8.7 for the last calculation.

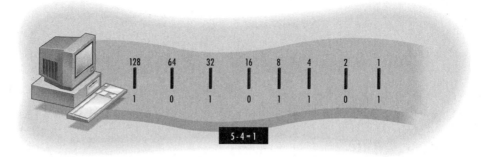

FIGURE 8.7
Final Step in the Binary
Calculation of 173

TRY IT!

To convert decimal numbers into their binary equivalent, you do not have to rely on your binary mathematics skills. The Microsoft Windows family of operating systems provides a full-feature calculator that will do the conversions for you. To use the Windows Calculator, follow these steps:

1. Click the Start button.
2. Choose Programs/Accessories.
3. Under Accessories, locate the *Calculator* option.
4. Once the Calculator application is open, click View on the Menu bar. Choose the *Scientific* option in the listing. The default setting in the radio buttons should be Dec (for "decimal").
5. Enter your decimal number.
6. Click the Bin radio button and view the binary equivalent of the number you entered.

Figure 8.8 shows the binary equivalent of the decimal number 215.

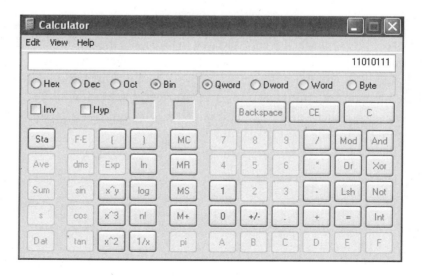

FIGURE 8.8
Binary Result for the Decimal
Number 215

IP Address Classes

IP addresses are broken down into five classes, or groupings: A, B, C, D, and E. The first three classes—A, B, and C—are available for consumer use. Each class can be identified by the state of the high order bit or bits in the first octet of the address. It may be 1, 2, 3, or 4 bits that indicate the class of the address (i.e., class A: first bit is always 0; class B: first bit is always 1, second is always 0; class C: first bit is always 1, second is always 1, third is always 0).

In total, there are 4,294,967,296 (or 2^{32}) IP addresses available for use on host devices. Of those addresses, Class A addresses represent 50 percent of the total address space, Class B addresses represent 25 percent, and Class C addresses represent 12.5 percent. Figure 8.9 displays the bit allocation for the five TCP/IP address classes.

Class	Bit Allocation		
A	**7 bits** Network	**24 bits** Host	
B	**14 bits** Network	**16 bits** Network	
C	**21 bits** Network	**8 bits** Host	
D	**28 bits** Multicast Addresses		
E	**28 bits** Experimental		

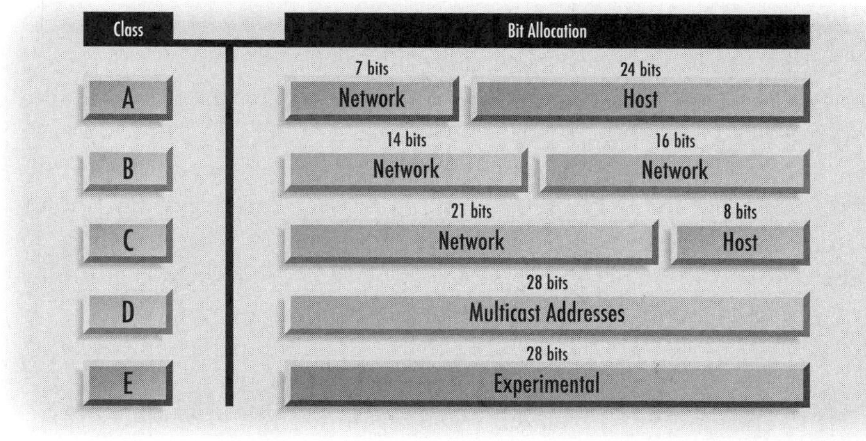

FIGURE 8.9
Bit Allocation for the TCP/IP Address Classes

Table 8.1 shows the five address classes, the state of their high order bits, which bits represent the network identifier, the number of networks available, and the maximum number of host addresses for each available network. In Table 8.1, you will note that for the maximum number of hosts available on each network, two addresses are subtracted from the total $(2^n - 2)$. These two addresses are removed because they have a special use on each network. One address is reserved for broadcast, and the other represents the network identifier.

Handwritten margin notes (top): 1   126   255.255.255   224   2^16   NA?   128-191   192-223   224-239

Handwritten margin notes (left): 1st 2octet determin how many network and next 2octet host.

Address Class	Address Range	High Order Bit State	Maximum Number of Networks	Maximum Number of Hosts
A	1.0.0.0 to 126.255.255.255	0	126	16,777,214 (2^{24} - 2)
B	128.0.0.0 to 191.255.255.255	1 0	16,384	65.534 (2^{16} - 2)
C	192.0.0.0 to 223.255.255.255	1 1 0	2,097,152	254 2^8 - 2)
D	224.0.0.0 to 239.255.255.255	1 1 1 0	Multicast (not for commercial use)	N/A
E	240.0.0.0 to 254.255.255.255	1 1 1 1	Experimental (not for commercial use)	N/A

TABLE 8.1
Everything You Ever Wanted to Know about IP Address Classes

Earlier in the chapter, the term "network number" was used to describe the portion of an IP address that all hosts on an IP network segment share. The network number is significant for several reasons:

- It identifies the network segment shared by multiple host devices.
- It helps the source node decide whether to send the packet to the network or to the gateway (router) for that segment.
- It determines how routers on the way to the destination address handle a packet.

The network number is to the network much like a street name to the post office. Using the street name alone, the postal carrier has no clue to determine which house to deliver the letter to. Here is where the host number comes into play. The second part of every IP address is a unique host number that is much like the residence number in a mailing address. The host number guarantees that packets are delivered to the correct node.

With IP addresses, we can make some assumptions about addresses. If the address is a Class A address, with the numbers of the first octet falling between 1 and 126, we can assume that the first 8 bits (or the first octet) represent the network number. With a Class B address, we use the first 16 bits to represent the network number, and with Class C addresses, the first 24 bits. When addressing schemes follow this convention, we call it *classful addressing*. Figure 8.10 shows each of the three consumer address classes, their opening bits, and what parts of the address space are reserved for the network identifier and what parts are reserved for the host number.

Classful addressing

The conventional pattern used in IP addressing in which the address class determines how many of the opening bits in the address represent the network number.

Internet Protocol (IP) Addressing

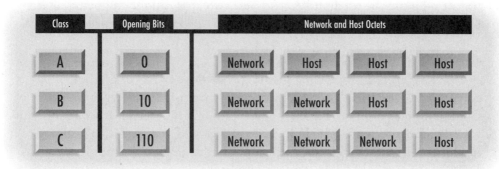

Class	Opening Bits	Network and Host Octets			
A	0	Network	Host	Host	Host
B	10	Network	Network	Host	Host
C	110	Network	Network	Network	Host

FIGURE 8.10
Address Classes, Opening Bits, and Classful Address Representation

TEST TIP

Be sure to know the address classes and their associated default subnet masks for classful addressing.

In addition to the five main address classes, technicians need to be aware of some very specialized address classes.

Private Addresses

Three address ranges or sections of address spaces are reserved for use on private networks. The term "private network" means that the hosts on the LAN will never directly communicate with Internet-based hosts. The addresses set aside have one other characteristic: their network identifiers are not included in any public (Internet) routing tables, and therefore, any packets with one of the following network numbers will be silently discarded if it reaches the public area. The private addresses in IP addressing are:

- 10.x.x.x through 10.255.255.255
- 172.16.x.x through 172.31.255.255
- 192.168.x.x through 192.168.255.255

The purpose for the private addresses becomes obvious when we think back about the state of IP addresses just a few short years ago. IP addresses were becoming scarce. The agencies controlling IP and the address spaces restructured the distribution of addresses. In an effort to conserve as many IP addresses as possible while still providing public addresses to everyone who needed them, the IETF (Internet Engineering Task Force) recommended that an application gateway such as *proxy service* or *network address translation (NAT)* be used at the public interface, and that

Proxy service

Specialized software that allows network address translation to take place, plus caching of Internet resources, blocking certain public IP addresses, and granting access permissions to access the Internet. As the term "proxy" implies, proxy service acts on behalf of an internal client machine.

Network address translation (NAT)

A service that allows a network to use the private addresses on the local LAN while still maintaining a connection for users to the Internet. The process is a routing function that occurs on the machine running the NAT service.

Automatic Private IP Addressing (APIPA)

A function that self-assigns an IP address when a DHCP client cannot obtain an IP address any other way.

private addresses be used on LANs. These two applications will be discussed further in Chapters 9 and 10 respectively.

Automatic Private IP Addressing (APIPA)

Automatic Private IP Addressing (APIPA) is used when a host machine is configured to get an IP address automatically from DHCP (Dynamic Host Configuration Protocol), but cannot reach the DHCP server. After trying multiple times to reach a DHCP server to receive an address, the local machine, if it supports APIPA, will allocate itself an address from the 169.254.0.X network. This network number is not routed; therefore, if a router receives a packet with a destination address from the range 169.254.0.X network, the packet is silently discarded. Hosts that have self-configured can communicate only with other hosts that have also self-configured on the local segment.

TEST TIP

For the test, be able to recognize the APIPA address space and the three address spaces reserved for private network use.

The Loopback Address

If you look back to Table 8.1, you will see that the Class A address space is missing a network address: 127.x.x.x. This address, with a host bit of 1, is the *loopback address*, used to test the TCP/IP protocol stack on the local machine. When you enter the PING command (see Chapter 7) followed by the address 127.0.0.1, an echo-request message is sent through the machine, and when an echo-reply packet is returned, a successful test of the stack has been completed.

Loopback address ✓

A special IP address used to test a computer's installation of the TCP/IP protocol.

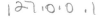

Subnet mask ✓

A series of bits in an IP address that identifies for host machines which bits in the address are network number bits and which are host number bits.

— TRY IT! —

To see what IP address a Windows 2000 Professional or Windows XP Professional machine is using, follow these steps:

1. Click the Start button.
2. Click Programs/Accessories.
3. Click the Command Prompt listing.
4. At the command prompt, type the following: **IPCONFIG**. This will display the three most important configuration settings for the machine: the IP address, the *subnet mask,* and the default gateway. You can use a switch with IPCONFIG that will allow you to see additional configuration information. Enter **IPCONFIG/ALL**. Now you can see other settings, as well as the MAC address and the machine name.

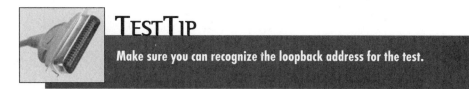

TestTip

Make sure you can recognize the loopback address for the test.

Assigning IP Addresses

With the knowledge that no two nodes, or host machines, can use the same IP address, whether on a private network or the Internet, how can a technician or administrator go about assigning addresses to host devices? Two methods can be used to assign addresses: manual configuration and Dynamic Host Configuration Protocol (DHCP). When assigning addresses manually, great care must be given to documenting which hosts have what addresses. Accidentally duplicating addresses is a very easy mistake to make with manual assignment. When this happens, the second machine with the duplicate address will not be able to connect to the network using the TCP/IP protocol. Instead, it will receive an error message that a duplicate address exists. The first machine to be configured with the address will also receive an error message, but it will stay connected to the network. The solution for the user of the second machine is to wait until the first machine shuts down so it can connect, or call the technician or administrator for an address reconfiguration.

If manual addressing sounds too difficult, DHCP can be used to automatically allocate addresses to all machines on the network. This takes the burden of documentation away from any human and turns it over to the server providing the service. Once the addresses are set up on the DHCP server and the clients are configured as DHCP clients (see Figure 8.11), no further concerns will crop up for host addressing. DHCP will be discussed at length in Chapter 9.

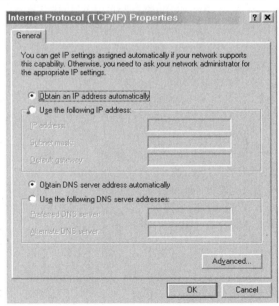

FIGURE 8.11
Internet Protocol Properties
Dialog Box

IP Address Subnet Masks

One of the required configuration settings for any client machine is the subnet mask for the IP address. A subnet mask is a series of bits that identifies for host machines which bits are network number bits and which are host number bits.

To designate which bits are used for the network number, all network bits are set to 1 (on). For example, if the machine's address is 204.2.76.12, we know that this is a Class C address and the first three octets are used for the network number. Therefore, the subnet mask for this address would be 255.255.255.0. The network number is comprised of 24 bits, and the host address has 8 bits. For the Class B address 157.28.0.48, the subnet mask is 255.255.0.0, identifying the first 16 bits as network bits. No doubt you can figure out what the mask is for a Class A address. If the host were configured with an address of 4.0.0.35, the mask would be 255.0.0.0.

Another way to write the subnet mask for an IP address is known as *slash notation*. Instead of writing out a Class C mask as 255.255.255.0, the IP address can simply be followed by /24. This says that 24 bits are used for the network portion of the address, leaving 8 bits for the host portion. Administrators commonly use this format to configure routers or to simplify the documentation of the network.

The subnet mask plays a large role in determining where the packet is sent as it leaves the source machine and travels to the destination. Before sending the packet out on the wire, the source machine applies an interesting mathematical computation, called ANDING, to the destination address in the packet. The ANDING process is used to determine the network identifier of the destination address. Once the network identifier is determined the machine can decide whether to send an ARP request, if the network number matches the source machine's, or, if the network number does not match, to send the packet to the default gateway (router interface).

The ANDING process is different from a regular addition problem. Remember, we are dealing with bits, either 1s or 0s, here. When ANDING is used, the results can only be:

- 1 AND 1 equals 1
- 1 AND 0 equals 0
- 0 AND 1 equals 0
- 0 AND 0 equals 0

Slash notation

A shorthand way of indicating the subnet mask for an IP address. In slash notation, the IP address 200.20.1.1 with subnet mask 255.255.255.0 would instead be written 200.20.1.0/24, indicating that 24 bits are used in the network portion of the IP address.

ANDING ✓

A logical function that looks for the presence or absence of a match between two numbers that have been converted into binary notation. The results can be either 0 or 1, but the sum is 1 only when both of the numbers are 1.

When the binary result is converted back to decimal, you can see if the network numbers are the same or different. Let's take a source and destination address and put them through the ANDING process (see Table 8.2). As shown in the table, the networks are different, so the packet goes to the default gateway (router interface).

Source	Destination
194.34.55.204, mask 255.255.255.0	196.34.55.204, mask 255.255.255.0
11000010.00100010.00110111.11001100 11111111. 11111111. 11111111.00000000	110000100.00100010.00110111.11001100 11111111. 11111111. 11111111.00000000
11000010.00100010.00110111.——— 194 . 34 . 55 . 0	110000100.00100010.00110111.——— 196 . 34 . 55 . 0
Source network: 194.34.55.0	Destination network: 196.34.55.0

Subnet mask (handwritten annotation at left)

TABLE 8.2
The ANDING Process

This was an easy example to acquaint you with the ANDING process. In the next section, we talk about IP address subnetting, which is where ANDING gets really important.

128 64 32 16 8 4 2 1 (handwritten annotation)

IP ADDRESS SUBNETTING

When the IP address scheme was standardized in the early 1980s, it had some interesting, but unforeseen, consequences. No one at that time could begin to predict what the IP protocol would mean to data communications in just less than 15 years. The designers certainly could not have predicted the explosion of the Internet over that same time period. Here are some of the situations that led to unforeseen consequences:

- **Allocation of addresses:** In the early days of the Internet, IP addresses were allocated—often in an entire block—to any organization that requested them. For instance, Digital Equipment Company (DEC) received an entire Class A block of addresses. Remember that a single Class A network has addresses for 16,777,214 host devices. DEC could never hope to use all of those addresses. Besides, 16 million hosts could never communicate on a single network. The traffic would stop all data transmission. At the time, however, the agency that issued numbers was not concerned about the requests that DEC and many other organizations were making for large blocks of numbers. No one was assessing what an organization's needs were for IP addresses.
- **32-bit address space:** The design decision to build a 32-bit address space meant that there were 2^{32} or 4,294,967,296 available addresses. Although seemingly a large number, it seems inadequate when viewed globally.

Had the decision been made to expand by even two octets, IPv6 would not have been developed because we would not have a shortage of IP addresses today.

- **Classful addresses:** Classful addresses are easy to recognize and understand, but they do not make efficient use of all of the addresses within the Class A, B, and C boundaries. When organizations were given blocks of addresses, a large number went idle. This contributed to the depletion of addresses, first experienced within Class A and B. Soon, all that was left for medium-sized organizations were Class C addresses, which, in turn, negatively affected the Internet routers' routing tables by increasing the number of entries in those tables.

All of these difficulties led to the callback of unused addresses during the 1990s. Further, an RFC was issued that defined a set of steps that would allow Class A, B, and C network numbers to be subdivided into what are now called subnets. *Subnetting* would also help to solve two other dilemmas created by classful addressing: ever-expanding Internet router tables and the need to request an additional network number when a company's network size increased.

Subnetting adds another level to the IP address. Earlier, we defined two parts to an address: the network number and the host number. Now we add a third level—the subnet address. The original network number is retained, while the subnet number uses bits from the host number of the IP address to create the subnet number. The host number is built from the remaining host bits. As an example, consider the address 179.66.35.27, subnet mask 255.255.255.0. Note the location of the subnet number within the address:

Network Number or Prefix . Subnet Number . Host Number

IIIIIIII . IIIIIIII . IIIIIIII . IIIIIIII

Subnetting requires planning. The network administrator must address four key issues before getting down to the mathematics of subnetting:
- The number of subnets that will accommodate the network today.
- The planned growth in the number of subnets for the network in the future.
- The number of hosts on the largest subnet today.
- The planned growth in the number of hosts on the largest subnet of the future.

Once an assessment of these issues is complete, the network administrator can get down to the business of building the subnetworks for the

---

Subnetting ✓

The action of using available host bits in an IP address to create additional network identifiers, or subnets. This is often done to segment an IP network, or it is used because the segments are small and cannot use an entire class network address efficiently.

Internet Protocol (IP) Addressing

- organization. There are five basic steps in the process of building a series of subnetworks.

1. Determine the number of subnetworks needed and the maximum number of hosts on any subnetwork.
2. Determine the number of bits to "steal" from the host bit portion of the IP address that will accommodate the needed number of networks. Use the formula $2^N - 2 =$ the maximum number of networks available. N will be the number of bits to "steal."
3. Build a new custom subnet mask to reflect the number of bits now used for the network portion of the address.
4. Build the new network numbers.
5. Build the range of IP host addresses for each new network by combining the new network numbers with the identified range of host bits.

This process may sound very complex to you now, but as we work through the process, you will see that these five steps cover everything you need to know to build custom subnetwork numbers and host addresses.

For our example, let's start up a new small business. Our business is called Susie's Software. Susie is starting out small, but wants to do things right from the start. She has rented office space and had an IT contracting company come in to install the network cabling and a router. She also requested a Class C network address and was given 200.1.10.0, subnet mask 255.255.255.0 Susie will have four departments (albeit small ones) at the start: Marketing, Sales, Admin, and Developers. She wants to keep the network traffic localized for each department while still allowing the departments to communicate with each other. That is why she had the IT contracting company install a router. Figure 8.12 shows Susie's planned network and the largest number of hosts she foresees on each subnetwork.

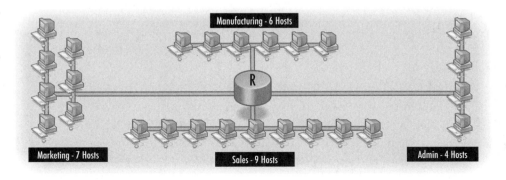

FIGURE 8.12
Susie's Software
Subnetworks and Hosts

The largest subnet at Susie's Software is the Sales Department subnet with nine host devices. Always make sure you take into consideration not only the number of user workstations, but also the number of network printers, servers, and router interfaces on any given subnetwork. All of these will need an IP address. We know we need a minimum of four subnetworks with at least nine host addresses on each subnetwork. The first step is complete.

It is time to determine how many host bits to "steal" and move over into the network portion of the address. Remember that Class C networks use 24 bits for the network number, leaving 8 bits for the host addresses. That means there are 8 bits to use. If we apply the formula in step 2, we can identify how many bits we will need to solve the network issue. The formula, $2^N - 2$ = maximum number of networks, can be applied. If we try the power of 2, then $2^2 - 2 = 2$ available subnets. This will not work. If we try the power of 3, then $2^3 - 2 = 6$ available subnets. In this case, 6 is larger than the 4 networks currently needed. Susie will have room to add more departments. If N or the power of 2 equals the number of bits to steal, the three most significant bits will be moved into the network number and become the subnetwork identifier for Susie's host addresses.

Figure 8.13 shows the 8 host bits with a line drawn to designate the bits that will become the subnetwork portion of the IP address. Three bits will move and step 2 is complete.

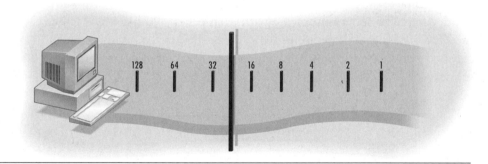

FIGURE 8.13
Of the 8 host bits shown in this Class C address, 3 will move to the subnetwork portion of the address.

There must be a means to tell host devices that 3 bits have moved from the host portion of the address into the subnetwork portion. This is accomplished by creating a custom subnet mask. Earlier in the chapter, you learned that the mask identifies network bits to host devices and is used to determine where a packet will be sent—onto the local segment for delivery or to the default gateway (router interface) for delivery on a remote network. You also learned the mask is built by turning on all the bits in the network portion of the address.

A Class C address has a default mask of 255.255.255.0, indicating that the first 24 bits are used as network bits. That cannot be changed. Now we have to build a new mask to show the 3 bits that have been stolen. We determine the mask by adding the decimal value of the stolen bits: 128 + 64 + 32 = 224. Then we add that number into the mask: 255.255.255.224. Step 3 is done.

Step 4, building the new network numbers, is accomplished by turning the 3 stolen bits on and off and converting those binary numbers to decimal numbers. Figure 8.14 shows all the bit configurations possible with the 3 stolen bits (six possible network numbers).

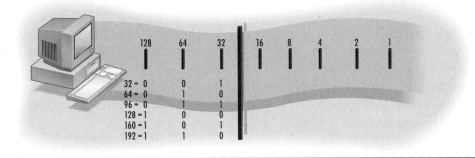

FIGURE 8.14
All Possible Bit Configurations and Decimal Network Numbers for Subnet Mask 255.255.255.224

Our network numbers, or network identifiers, now look like the following:

> 200.1.10.32
> 200.1.10.64
> 200.1.10.96
> 200.1.10.128
> 200.1.10.160
> 200.1.10.192

Although step 4 is now complete, we still do not have any assignable host addresses for our subnetworks.

To build the host addresses, a range value of the remaining host bits is calculated and added to the subnetwork numbers. All possible bit configurations could be calculated as they were for the network numbers, but this would take a great deal of time and be prone to error. Instead, turning off all the host bits except for the least significant bit identifies the low end of the range, and turning on all the bits except for the least significant bit identifies the top end of the range. Then the binary values are converted to decimal. Figure 8.15 shows how the host range is calculated, and that means only one more step in the process.

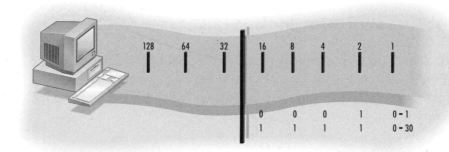

FIGURE 8.15
Decimal Value of Host Bit
Range

Broadcast

A message sent to all nodes on a network segment. Broadcasts are not transmitted by routers; therefore, their usefulness is limited to the local segment.

Take a minute to notice in Figure 8.15 that for neither the low end of the range nor the top end of the range are all the bits turned off or on. When all the bits are turned on in the host portion, the resulting address is known as the *broadcast* address. The broadcast address is used to notify all hosts on this network. If all the bits are turned off in the host portion, the resulting address is actually the network number for that segment.

Using the example from above, if we have a network address of 200.1.10.32 and all the bits in the host portion of the address are turned on, the broadcast address for this network is 200.1.10.63. Likewise, for the next network number, 200.1.10.64, the broadcast address is 200.1.10.95. Remember from our steps above, particularly step 2, we use the calculation $2^N - 2$ to determine how many subnets we can build from a particular mask. The −2 accounts for the network number and the broadcast address.

The last step in building custom subnetworks is to build the assignable host address ranges using the new network identifiers and the host range shown in Figure 8.15. This is a simple addition problem. Take the network number created in step 4 and add the range of host bits to the network number. Remember to keep the placeholders so that numbers are added to the correct octet, in this case, the fourth octet.

The first network number was 200.1.10.32. The host bit range in decimal notation is 1 to 30, and those host bits are part of the fourth octet. So here is how the math problem will look:

200.1.10.32		200.1.10.32	
+ .1		+ .30	
200.1.10.33	to	200.1.10.62	This is the range of host addresses.

Each subnetwork is treated the same way: the host bit range is added to the network number and a set of assignable addresses is created for each subnetwork. Step 5 is complete.

All of these subnet directions can be very confusing, and when time is critical, sitting down to figure out subnets and masks manually will be frustrating. Table 8.3 displays the subnet masks for Class B and C networks. Use this as a reference guide once you have mastered the process of subnetting.

Bits to Steal	Network Bits	Subnet Mask	Number of Subnets	Number of Subnet Hosts
		Class B		
0	/16	255.255.0.0	0	65534
1	/17	255.255.128.0	2 {0}	32776
2	/18	255.255.192.0	4 {2}	16382
3	/19	255.255.224.0	8 {6}	8190
4	/20	255.255.240.0	16 {14}	4094
5	/21	255.255.248.0	32 {30}	2046
6	/22	255.255.252.0	64 {62}	1022
7	/23	255.255.254.0	128 {126}	510
8	/24	255.255.255.0	256 {254}	254
9	/25	255.255.255.128	512 {510}	126
10	/26	255.255.255.192	1024 {1022}	62
11	/27	255.255.255.224	2048 {2046}	30
12	/28	255.255.255.240	4096 {4094}	14
13	/29	255.255.255.248	8192 {8190}	6
14	/30	255.255.255.252	16384 {16382}	2
		Class C		
0	/24	255.255.255.0	0	254
1	/25	255.255.255.128	2 {0}	126
2	/26	255.255.255.192	4 {2}	62
3	/27	255.255.255.224	8 {6}	30
4	/28	255.255.255.240	16 {14}	14
5	/29	255.255.255.248	32 {30}	6
6	/30	255.255.255.252	64 {62}	2

TABLE 8.3
Subnet Mask Chart for Class B and Class C Addresses

This last section has taken you through the process of manually subnetting a network address. However, the network address may deal with hundreds of subnetworks and hundreds or even thousands of host addresses. A far simpler way to subnet your IP network address is to use a subnet calculator. Many free calculators are available on the Internet for both PCs and PDAs. These will save time and energy when you need to quickly calculate subnetworks. But it is important to understand the concepts behind those calculators, as well. See "For More Information" for this chapter on the Internet Resource Center to find a subnet calculator.

Internet Protocol Version 6 (IPv6)

Earlier in this chapter, we discussed IPv4's limitations and the consequences of limited address space. While the experts thought 4 billion IP addresses would certainly be enough to service every device that needed an address, it was soon apparent that IPv4 addresses would either become scarce or be used up entirely. Steps were taken between 1992 and 1996 to conserve as many addresses as possible and to control the distribution of those addresses. It was during this time that work started on IP next generation (IPng). In 1995, IPv6 was chosen as the next generation of IP addressing.

IPv6 promises to fix some of the major problems encountered with IPv4. It provides three key features:

- **A much larger address space:** The address space of IPv6 is four times larger than that of IPv4. IPv6 uses 128 bits in each address. The format is also different. Where IPv4 uses binary notation to represent the address, IPv6 uses a hexadecimal number to represent the address. (Hexadecimal digits are more efficient than binary digits. One hexadecimal digit can represent four binary digits.) This larger address space will eliminate the need for application gateways like Proxy Server and NAT. All devices can be continuously connected to the Internet.

- **Built-in support for secure transmission, such as IPSec:** IPv6 supports the security requirement set by IETF (Internet Engineering Task Force) and other agencies. *Internet Protocol Security (IPSec)* is built in to this new version. IPSec supports authentication, encryption, and compression of IP traffic. The machines and the IPv6 protocol stack will handle secure transmission without the need for application gateways or translators. The policies governing the behavior of IPSec can be set at the machine or be imposed at the network level.

- **Support for mobile devices:** IPv6 supports a subprotocol called Mobile IP, making this version of the stack compatible with mobile devices such as PDAs and mobile telephones. This also allows mobile devices to move among networks without having to completely reconfigure these devices.

Internet Protocol Security (IPSec) ✓

A security protocol that supports authentication, encryption of data, and compression of data during transmission. It is expected to become the standard for communication over networks and internetworks to protect the privacy and security of message transmission.

IPv6 Address Structure

IPv6 uses 128 bits in the address space, allowing up to 2^{128} addresses, or 340 undecillion addresses. This large quantity of available addresses should meet the needs of all the machines needing IP addresses, plus all the cell phones, PDAs, and even home-controlled devices of the future.

An IPv6 address is written as eight groups of 16 bits, displayed in hexadecimal format. Remember that the hexadecimal system uses numbers 0–9 and alpha characters A–F to represent the bits. An address might look like the following:

be04:0021:65f7:dae4:0000:0000:91ed:66c2

You can shorten these addresses under certain circumstances. For example, a series of consecutive zeros may be shortened to a single "::" one time per v6 address. Leading zeros can be omitted as well. If the original address were rewritten using these shortcuts, it would look like this:

be04:21:65f7:dae4::91ed:66c2

Each address consists of two parts: the bits that identify the network where the machine is currently connected, or netbits, and the bits that uniquely identify the machine, or host bits. This is similar to an IPv4 address. The number of netbits used for an address is shown by slash notation. If we take the above example, we would write it as follows:

be04:21:65f7:dae4::91ed:66c2/64

IPv6 addresses may be subnetted just like IPv4 addresses. Again, ISPs are distributing these addresses and will normally assign a /48 mask. The host bit portion of the address is always a fixed 64-bit field, leaving 16 bits for self-assigned subnets. While the fields for the netbits and the subnets seem adequate, the fixed 64-bit host bit section of the address may seem excessive. That number of host bits could result in several billion hosts on any given subnet. The reason the host bit section of the address remains as a fixed 64-bit field is that it is not assigned manually or through DHCP. Rather, a recommendation has been made that host addresses be built from the Extended Unique Identifier 64 address (EUI64 address) of the device. This address is commonly known as the MAC address. A MAC address is 48 bits in length. When using the EUI64 address, the system will fill in the remaining 16 bits with "fffe" in the middle as a sort of padding. That means that a MAC address

08:32:ed:42:71:ab

will result in an EUI64 address of

08:32:ed:ff:fe:42:71:ab,

which creates the following host bits for an IPv6 address:

::0832:edff:fe42:71ab

The major significance here is that any device always carries its host address with it, making reconfiguration of the device very simple. The only piece that needs configuration is the network portion of the address when the device moves from network to network.

IPv6 employs more than one address per host. Every interface on the device has a globally unique address. In addition, two other types of addresses can also be assigned to a device. All three types are described in Figure 8.16.

- **Globally unique addresses:** Globally unique addresses are the network identifiers generally distributed by ISPs. These network numbers, along with the host bit portion of the address, allow any device to communicate globally—both on its own network and on the Internet—without concern that the address may be duplicated.
- **Link-local addresses:** Link-local addresses have a prefix of fe80::/64. The host bits are built from the EUI64 address. Link-local addresses are used for communication with hosts and router interfaces on the local subnet. These addresses are not visible from any other subnet.
- **Site-local addresses:** Site-local addresses use the network address fec0::/10. They are not visible to outside hosts. This is similar to the private address spaces of IPv4.

FIGURE 8.16
Address Types Assigned by IPv6

The most common practice is to assign a globally unique address and to use a link-local address as well. Site-local addresses are seldom used.

IPv6 is the solution to many of today's problems with IPv4. However, it will be some time before a complete transition can be made to this newer version. Many machines—both business and home devices—use operating systems that do not understand IPv6. They must be patched to accept the longer address and to recognize the hexadecimal format. IPv6 is used for some addressing needs at the highest levels of Internet connectivity, but as yet it has not filtered down to the desktop.

Troubleshooting TCP/IP

When a client node cannot access resources as expected on the network, check the IP configuration on the machine (using WINIPCFG for Windows 9X machines and the command prompt utility IPCONFIG for Windows 2000 and for Windows XP). Look carefully at the IP address assigned to the machine to determine if it falls within the range for the subnet. If the address displayed is from the subnet 169.254.0.X, it has assumed an APIPA address. That means the client node could not contact the DHCP server. Check to make sure the DHCP server is functional and that it has addresses available for distribution in the correct range.

If a client node cannot connect to the network, begin troubleshooting the node by PINGing the loopback address 127.0.0.1. This will tell you if the TCP/IP protocol stack is working. Then try PINGing the machine by its displayed address. Continue to troubleshoot by PINGing the default gateway address, and finally by PINGing an address on the far side of the router. The point at which the PING fails is where the problem has occurred.

STUDY GUIDE

In this chapter, we learned about the structure of an IPv4 host address, the consumer classes of IP addresses, and how to subnet an address space to accommodate individual networks. We also discussed IPv6, the newest version of IP, including the benefits of the new version and the structure of the address space. Here are some key points to remember.

IP VERSION 4 (IPV4)

- IPv4 uses a 32-bit address space expressed in either binary format or decimal format.
- Every IP address is composed of two parts: the network number and the host number.
- Every IP host address must be unique. Duplicate addresses result in host devices that cannot communicate.
- Distribution of addresses is managed by IANA, which distributes addresses to regional agencies. The regional agency covering the United States is ARIN.
- ARIN allocates IP address blocks to ISPs for distribution to customers.

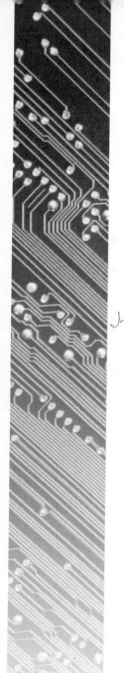

IPv4 Address Structure

- The 32 bits of an IPv4 address are broken into four 8-bit groups called octets.
- Each octet is 1 byte of information.
- When an address is written in decimal format, the four octets are separated by a dot. This is known as dotted decimal notation.
- In each octet, all 8 bits are assigned a binary value that is often expressed in decimal format. The decimal values, beginning with the most significant bit, are 128, 64, 32, 16, 8, 4, 2, and 1 respectively.
- In binary format, bits are turned on or off to build the unique address for a node. Bits have a value of either 1 (on) or 0 (off).
- Conversion of binary to decimal notation and vice versa can be done manually or by using the Windows Calculator set in Scientific mode.

IP Address Classes

$2^n - 2 = 2^{24} - 2 =$

- IPv4 addresses belong to one of five classes of addresses.
- Class A addresses use the first octet (or 8 bits) to express the network number, leaving the last three octets (or 24 bits) for host numbers. This allows 126 networks with 16,777,214 hosts on each network. The opening bit value is 0.
- Class B addresses use the first two octets (or 16 bits) for the network number and the last two octets (or 16 bits) for the host number. This gives us 16,384 network numbers with 65,534 hosts on each network. The opening bit values are 10.
- Class C addresses use the first three octets (or 24 bits) to indicate the network number and the last octet (or 8 bits) for host numbers. There are 2,097,152 network numbers available, with 254 hosts on each of those networks. The opening bit value for Class C addresses is 110.
- Class D addresses are used for multicast transmission and are not manageable by the public. The opening bit value for a Class D address is 1110.
- Class E addresses are used for experimental purposes. The opening bit value for a Class E address is 1111.
- Two addresses from every network range of addresses are reserved for special use. One is the network number; the other is the broadcast address, used to send out notices to all hosts on a network.
- Classful addressing uses the default values in each class for all IP addressing.

Private Addresses

- Some addresses have been set aside for use on private networks. Those address spaces are as follows:
  - 10.0.0.0–10.255.255.255
  - 172.16.0.0–172.31.255.255
  - 192.168.0.0–192.168.255.255
- Private addresses are not routed publicly. Therefore, if a router gets a packet with a private destination address in the header, the packet will not be routed and will be silently discarded.

Automatic Private IP Addressing (APIPA)

- Automatic Private IP Addressing (APIPA) provides a means for a DHCP client to self-configure when it cannot reach a DHCP server. APIPA uses the address space 169.254.0.X.

The Loopback Address

- Another special address encompasses an entire network number: 127.0.0.0 is set aside for the loopback test. The loopback test sends a packet through the IP stack on the local host. If a response is received, the stack is installed and functioning.
- To assign addresses to host devices, the network administrator may configure every device manually, or the administrator may choose to use DHCP to allocate addresses to host devices.

IP ADDRESS SUBNET MASKS

- A subnet mask identifies the bits that make up the network number of an IP address.
- The mask number is built by turning on (setting to 1) all bits used for the network number.
- The default subnet masks for the three consumer classes of addresses are as follows:
  - Class A — 255.0.0.0
  - Class B — 255.255.0.0
  - Class C — 255.255.255.0
- A shorter way to write the mask for an IP address is to use slash notation. Calculate the number of bits in the mask and follow the IP address with a slash and the number of bits: 202.16.22.45/24.
- The subnet mask also tells the local machine what to do with an outgoing packet. The destination address is compared to the source

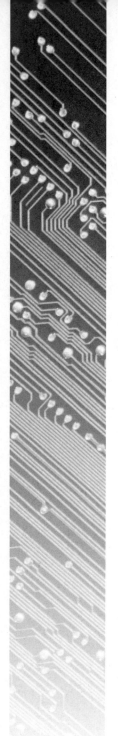

address, the two network numbers are compared, and the decision is made based on the result of the comparison. If the network numbers are the same, the packet is going to a host on the local subnet, and an ARP request is sent. If the network numbers are different, the packet is going to a remote network, and it will be forwarded to the default gateway (router interface) for processing.

- ANDING is the process by which the network number is resolved from an IP address by ANDING the mask against the host address.

IP ADDRESS SUBNETTING

- Subnetting is the process whereby a classful network address may be broken down into several smaller subnets.
- Subnetted addresses add an additional level to the address space in the form of the subnet number.
- When designing a network that will include subnets, some important points must be considered: the current needs of the network and host addresses, as well as the future needs of the network and host addresses.
- Subnetting has five steps:
  1. Determine the number of subnets needed and the maximum number of hosts on each subnet.
  2. Determine the number of bits to "steal" from the host bit portion of the IP address. Use the formula $2^N - 2$ = the maximum number of subnets available, where N = the number of bits to steal.
  3. Build a new custom subnet mask to reflect the number of bits taken from the host section of the address and moved to the network section of the address.
  4. Build the new network numbers.
  5. Build the range of IP host addresses for each new subnet by combining the new network numbers with the identified range of host bits.

IP VERSION 6 (IPv6)

- IPv6 is the newest version of Internet Protocol. Three key changes make IPv6 the solution for the future:
  - A much larger address space using 128 bits as opposed to 32 bits in IPv4.
  - Built-in support for secure transmission through the inclusion of IPSec in the protocol stack.

o Support for mobile devices, allowing users to move readily and rely on their devices to function without reconfiguration.

IPv6 Address Structure

- IPv6 addresses are expressed as eight 16-bit fields written in hexadecimal notation.
- The address space is divided into a network number and a host number, and it may include a subnet identifier as well.
- The host portion of the IPv6 address is always a fixed 64 bits in length.
- The host portion is usually derived from the MAC address of the device with filler bits in the center. This is known as the EUI64 address.
- A series of zeros in contiguous fields of an address may be abbreviated as a double colon (::), but this may occur only one time in the address. Leading zeros may be dropped.
- Three types of IPv6 addresses are used:
  o Globally unique addresses are the common addresses of devices. They use the MAC address and the current network number to form the address. These addresses can be seen locally and globally (outside the subnet).
  o Link-local addresses are used to identify devices on the local subnet. These addresses are not visible outside the local subnet.
  o Site-local addresses are used within a site and always read fec0::/10. They are similar to the private addresses of IPv4.

PRACTICE TEST

Try this test to check your mastery of the concepts in this chapter.

1. How many bits make up an IPv4 address?
   a. 28
   b. 32
   c. 64
   d. 128

2. The regional agency for IP address distribution is known as
   a. IANA.
   b. INTERNIC.
   c. IETF.
   d. ARIN.

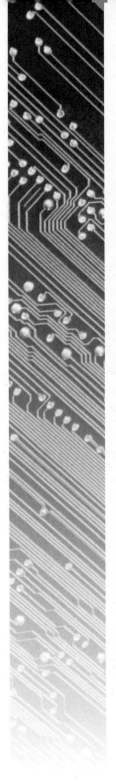

3. Which of the following is a Class B address?
   a. 127.0.0.1
   b. 193.1.6.4
   c. 155.155.155.154
   d. 255.255.255.254

4. IPv6 addresses are comprised of _____ bits.
   a. 128
   b. 224
   c. 64
   d. 192

5. Which of the following IP addresses belong to the subnetwork address 197.89.78.128, subnet mask 255.255.255.224? (Choose two)
   a. 197.89.78.203
   b. 197.89.78.120
   c. 197.89.78.158
   d. 197.89.78.132

6. Which of the following binary expressions equates to the decimal expression of the IP address 101.143.66.13?
   a. 11010010.00111111.01011010.11100010
   b. 01100101.10001111.01000010.00001101
   c. 11110010.10110010.01110001.11001010
   d. 01010110.11001111.01011110.00001100

7. The high order bit is located in which position in an octet?
   a. rightmost
   b. fourth from left
   c. leftmost
   d. third from right

8. _____ and _____ are the two basic component parts of every IPv4 host address.
   a. Network number, subnet number
   b. Subnet number, host number
   c. Local link number, network number
   d. Network number, host number

9. Identify the classful subnet mask for the IP address 197.88.43.158.
   a. 255.255.0.0
   b. 255.255.255.0
   c. 255.0.0.0
   d. 255.255.240.0

10. How many octets does a Class B address have available for host addresses?
    a. 1
    b. 2
    c. 3
    d. 0

11. Private addresses can be used on a network for both local and Internet communications with no concern for address duplication or additional gateway software.
    a. True
    b. False

12. Which of the following is an example of an IPv6 host address?
    a. fc06::1001:2012:8da4
    b. 197.42.43.44
    c. 241.224.224.212
    d. xy06:::0001.maf5

13. Which of the following is an example of a Class A address?
    a. 127.0.0.1
    b. 255.205.205.0
    c. 124.6.5.254
    d. 169.254.0.0

14. Which of the following IPv6 address types will a client machine need to communicate across the Internet?
    a. link-local address
    b. globally unique address
    c. site-local address
    d. EUI64 address

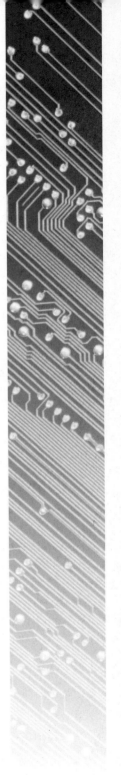

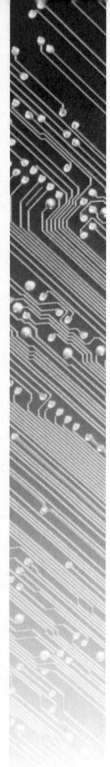

15. You are given a network number 210.27.36.0, mask 255.255.255.0, allowing a single network configuration. You need a minimum of 10 subnetworks. Which of the following subnet masks will allow at least 10 subnets? (Choose two)
    a. 255.255.255.224
    b. 255.255.255.240
    c. 255.255.255.128
    d. 255.255.255.248

16. Which of the following is a valid IP address with a default subnet mask of 255.0.0.0?
    a. 137.2.1.2
    b. 193.2.1.2
    c. 202.2.1.2
    d. 101.2.1.2

17. Which portion of an IPv6 address space uniquely identifies the host device and stays with that host device no matter where the device connects?
    a. network number
    b. EUI64 number
    c. subnet number
    d. subnet mask

18. Network Y is an IP subnet with network number 202.17.45.0/24. What is the default gateway address for a computer connected to network Y?
    a. 202.17.45.1
    b. 202.17.45.0
    c. 202.17.48.1
    d. 202.48.17.0

19. Using the default subnet mask, what is the network number for the address 138.15.22.31?
    a. 138
    b. 138.15
    c. 138.15.22
    d. 138.15.22.0

20. Which of the following IP addresses represents the broadcast address for all nodes on the same network segment?
    a. 0.0.0.0
    b. 0:0:0:0
    c. 255:255:255:255
    d. 255.255.255.255

21. An IPv6 address uses the last _____ bits to uniquely identify the host on the network.
    a. 16
    b. 32
    c. 64
    d. 96

22. Which of the following IP addresses represents the broadcast address for network 153.20.0.0?
    a. 153.20.0.1
    b. 153.20.255.255
    c. 153.20.0.255
    d. 255.255.255.255

23. What is the name given to the rightmost bit in each octet in an IPv4 address?
    a. least noticeable bit
    b. most righteous bit
    c. least significant bit
    d. lowest bit of all

TROUBLESHOOTING

1. A user calls the help desk because she cannot access resources on the network. In particular, she cannot talk to the server that usually authenticates her identity. You ask the user to open a command prompt and type **IPCONFIG.** Here is what the user reports from this command:

    IP address..........................147.23.22.156
    Subnet mask.......................255.255.255.0
    Default gateway...................149.23.22.156

    What is wrong with this user's machine?

2. While looking at your to-do list for the day, the phone rings, and it is a user complaining that he cannot access network resources. Other users on the same subnet are complaining of the same problem. You ask the user to open a command prompt and type **IPCONFIG.** Here is what the user says he sees:

IP address.........................169.254.0.13
Subnet mask......................255.255.0.0
Default Gateway..................

What could be causing the access problem reported by the user?

CUSTOMER SERVICE

1. You are a contract technician working at your client's site. Your client has requested an IP network address from the ISP and was given 199.1.7.0. Your client needs at least three networks, but the ISP will not give your client any more network numbers unless the client is willing to pay steep fees every year. You need to make the client happy by using the assigned network number while also allowing three networks. The largest segment has 10 hosts. How will you resolve this problem?
2. The administrator for your network is trying to determine a new IP address scheme for the enterprise. She plans to use one of the private address spaces in conjunction with Microsoft Proxy Server for Internet connectivity. The enterprise supports 1,200 users, 20 servers, 40 printers, and 12 routers. The largest segment supports 321 users. What class of address should be used for this enterprise and why?

FOR MORE INFORMATION

For links to Web sites that provide further information about the topics covered in this chapter, go to the EMC/Paradigm Internet Resource Center at www.emcp.com/College Division/Internet Resource Centers/Networking/System Administration/Web Resources: For More Information.

Network Services

Network+ Examination
- **Objective 2.7:** Identify the purpose of the following network services:
  - DHCP/BOOTP
  - DNS
  - NAT/ICS
  - WINS
  - SNMP

ON THE JOB

Network services complete the configuration of the network for use by employees or general users. The technician must have a good grasp of what each service provides to the network. Users may be unable to access the network because one of these services has been improperly configured. If the technician understands the functions of the services it is much easier to troubleshoot problems. *Every time you go on line you get a new one*

Dynamic Host Configuration Protocol/Bootstrap Protocol (DHCP/BOOTP)

The Dynamic Host Configuration Protocol (DHCP) and the Bootstrap Protocol (BOOTP) were developed to make the allocation of IP addresses an easier task for administrators. Both of these protocols provide host nodes with a unique IP address and at least the basic information needed to communicate with other host nodes on the network or internetwork. Although similar in their intent, each protocol displays a particular set of characteristics.

Bootstrap Protocol (BOOTP)

When using the TCP/IP protocol to provide transport services on your LAN or across the internetwork, each host node on the network must have a unique IP address. This applies not only to workstations, but also to devices like printers, servers, and any other network-connected element. In the early days of TCP/IP, the network administrator would write a configuration file for each workstation that included the information the host node needed—the IP address, the subnet mask, and the default gateway—to be a viable entity on the network. When the network was small, the administrator's task was reasonable. But as networks grew, the technical staff might have had to manage the configuration files for thousands of workstations, making sure that none of them had duplicate addresses. At this point, the task became unreasonable unless the administrator had a very large technical staff. Along came the *BOOTP (Bootstrap Protocol)*, which was designed to provide IP addresses to client workstations and was frequently used by *diskless workstations*.

BOOTP (Bootstrap Protocol)

An addressing protocol that assigns IP addresses to workstations and that initiates the operating system in that process.

Diskless workstation

A desktop computer that does not contain a disk or hard drive.

In Real Life

In the diskless workstation, all files are stored on the network server, including those files that are needed to boot the system. Diskless workstations usually contain programmable read-only memory (PROM) that can be used to connect the workstation to the network and get the attention of the server so the boot process can proceed.

When BOOTP is enabled on the network, a workstation can boot up, attach itself to the network, broadcast its MAC address on the local segment, and receive its IP address, subnet mask, default gateway, and host name of the server that provided the information. If the host node is a diskless workstation, it stores just enough information in read-only memory to attach itself to the network and send out the BOOTP broadcast packet to acquire the IP address.

The BOOTP server holds a table of all the IP addresses and the associated MAC addresses of the host nodes. Although the BOOTP table, known as the BOOTPTAB file, can become quite large if the network is large, the table allows all address information to be managed easily. BOOTP also eliminates the need to visit every host node to enable the configuration file. When a host node moves from one IP segment to another, only the entry in the BOOTPTAB file needs adjusting, and this can be accomplished quite quickly.

Once an IP address has been assigned to a host node's MAC address, that host node keeps that IP address forever, unless a change is made (the IP address is changed or the host node is removed from the network and will not be reattached).

Should the host node and BOOTP server reside on different networks, routers can be enabled to pass this broadcast packet to another remote network (segment). The router packages the broadcast as an IP packet, using the source address of the router interface and the destination address of the BOOTP server. Now that newly repackaged packet can safely make its way to the BOOTP server, acquire all of the host node's information, and send the packet back the way it came. The repackaging service that is performed by the router is a function of enabling BOOTP on the router interface and configuring the protocol with the BOOTP server's IP address.

This method of distributing IP addresses to host nodes is used very little today. Most host nodes need local processing power. You may encounter BOOTP during the configuration of router interfaces, depending on the architecture of the LAN.

DYNAMIC HOST CONFIGURATION PROTOCOL (DHCP)

Dynamic Host Configuration Protocol (DHCP) gives the administrator of a LAN or WAN the ability to distribute IP addresses automatically to the host nodes on the network. Other configuration parameters, such as the default gateway, the IP address of the DNS server, and the domain name for the host, can also be sent to the host node with the IP address, saving the administrator and technical staff many hours of adding all of this information to each and every host node on the network or internetwork. DHCP is both a *server service* and a *client-side process*.

> ### ─ TRY IT! ─────────────────
>
> On a Windows 2000 Professional machine, check to see if your IP address is DHCP assigned or manually assigned. To find out, complete the following steps:
>
> 1. Click the Start button.
> 2. Click the *Run* option.
> 3. In the *Open* text box, type **cmd** (a shortcut to the command prompt).
> 4. Once the command prompt window has opened, type **IPCONFIG/ALL**.
> 5. Read the display, noting the line "DHCP enabled." If this line reads "yes," then your machine is getting its IP address through DHCP. If it is blank, then your machine is manually configured.
> 6. When you are done, type **exit** at the command prompt. This will close the command prompt window.

Dynamic Host Configuration Protocol (DHCP)

A TCP/IP protocol that allows administrators to distribute IP addresses to nodes on the network automatically and to manage that distribution process centrally.

Server service

A special piece of software that runs on a network server to add some kind of capability to the server or to the network. Examples of server services that can be added to server operating systems include Remote Access Service (RAS) and Domain Name System (DNS).

Client-side process

A software function that a workstation uses to accomplish a task. Examples include using the operating system capabilities to share documents with other network users, or acquiring an IP address through a number of conversations with the DHCP server.

Most major network operating systems include the DHCP service. To add this service in a Microsoft Windows 2000 server operating system, follow these steps:

1. Go to Start/Settings/Control Panel/Add/Remove Programs/Add/Remove Windows Components.
2. Click Add/Remove Windows Components.
3. Scroll down the list of available services to Networking Services, and choose Details.
4. In the Details dialog box, choose DHCP by checking the box.
5. Click OK.
6. Click Next. The installation will begin and ask you for your source files (the I386 directory). Once the source files are found, the installation will be complete. When complete, choose Finish. The DHCP management tool is added to Administrative Tools.

DHCP Scopes

DHCP scope

A range of IP addresses that can be assigned to a specific segment of nodes on the network. Any DHCP-configured node on a given segment will receive an IP address that allows it to talk with other nodes on that segment.

Scope options

Optional settings that may be sent to a node on a segment when the node requests an IP address. Examples of scope options include the default gateway setting, the DNS server address, and the domain name for the node.

Once the service has been added, it will need to be configured. Figure 9.1 shows the DHCP management utility. The administrator will create *DHCP scopes,* or sets of IP addresses for each network or subnetwork. See Figure 9.2 to view a scope. Each scope has a set of configuration options, usually referred to as *scope options,* that will include important information, such as default gateway address and domain name. Figure 9.3 shows the scope options for a newly created scope.

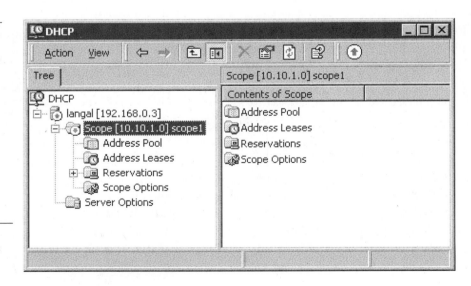

FIGURE 9.1
The DHCP manager provides access to all scope configurations.

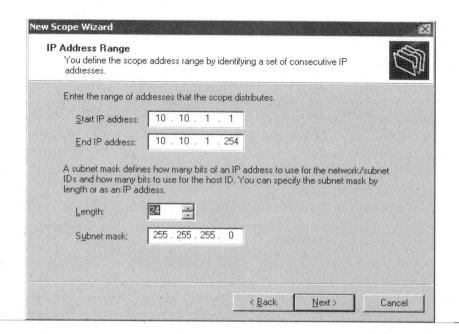

FIGURE 9.2
Setting Up the DHCP Scope

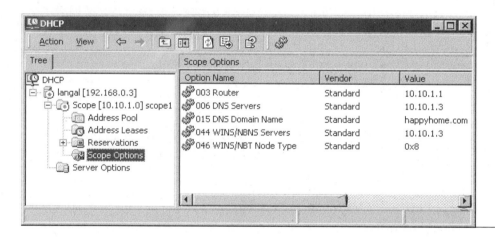

FIGURE 9.3
The administrator has access to all scope options for each scope created.

DHCP lease ✓

A designated length of time that the client node may use an IP address.

One particularly important scope parameter is the *DHCP lease*. The lease is the amount of time the IP address remains associated with the client node. The duration of the lease is dependent on the characteristics of the LAN, as well as on the number of IP addresses available versus the number of host nodes needing IP addresses. If many of the computers that make up the LAN are mobile units attached to the network for relatively brief time periods, the lease time for the IP addresses should be kept short—one day or less. If the LAN consists of mostly desktop workstations and those workstations are not moved frequently, the lease time can be longer—a week or more—or even indefinite if there are plenty of addresses to go around.

In some situations, public IP addresses are used for client workstations. There may not be enough addresses to cover all workstations if the organization is running multiple shifts per day. In this case, the administrator can set lease times to reflect the length of a shift and, where supported by the operating system, force a "release address on shutdown" action. This will return the workstation's IP address to the pool of assignable addresses, making it available for another machine.

Once the scope is created and all the scope options are added, the administrator can activate the scope. Clients can then begin requesting an IP address from this DHCP server.

DHCP generally includes some other features in the server component. For example, when a host device needs a constant IP address but the administrator or technician does not want to hard code the address, the administrator can create a *DHCP reservation* in the scope. A reservation assigns one of the IP addresses on the network segment to the MAC address of the host device. When the host device connects to the network and requests an IP address, the server will always assign the same address. Another feature of the DHCP service allows certain sets of IP addresses to be excluded from the assignable addresses in the scope. These are called *exclusions*. Often, you will have certain devices on a segment that must have manually configured addresses, such as servers and network printers. These addresses may belong to a range of IP addresses that become a scope, but they should not be allocated dynamically. By excluding the addresses from the scope, they will not be distributed to other hosts on the network.

Acquiring an IP Address with DHCP

As mentioned above, there is also a client-side function to DHCP. After all, the whole reason for DHCP is to assign IP addresses to host nodes. When a host node that is configured as a DHCP client attaches itself to the network on boot-up, the client begins a process to acquire an IP address (see Figure 9.4).

DHCP reservation

An address assignment to a client node that will remain constant for that node instead of changing each time the node boots up to the network. Servers, printers, and other devices must remain at a constant address so that users and services can reach them. The reservation eliminates the need to manually add addresses to the configuration for each machine.

DHCP exclusion

An option that allows an administrator to remove one or more addresses within a scope from the pool of automatically assignable addresses.

Internet Protocol (TCP/IP) Properties

General

You can get IP settings assigned automatically if your network supports this capability. Otherwise, you need to ask your network administrator for the appropriate IP settings.

○ Obtain an IP address automatically

○ Use the following IP address:

IP address:

Subnet mask:

Default gateway:

○ Obtain DNS server address automatically

○ Use the following DNS server addresses:

Preferred DNS server:

Alternate DNS server:

Advanced...

OK   Cancel

FIGURE 9.4
The Client Configuration for DHCP Addressing

DORA process ✓

The conversation between a client node and the DHCP server in which the node receives an IP address dynamically.

The client exchanges a series of broadcast packets with the DHCP server. This exchange is known as the *DORA process*. The name comes from the type of packet being exchanged with the DHCP server. Figure 9.5 shows how the client node and the DHCP server communicate to get an address to the client node. Figure 9.6 describes the steps in the process.

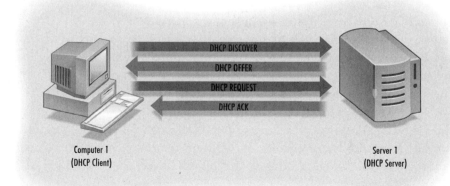

DHCP DISCOVER
DHCP OFFER
DHCP REQUEST
DHCP ACK

Computer 1
(DHCP Client)

Server 1
(DHCP Server)

FIGURE 9.5
The DORA Process

1. **DHCPDISCOVER packet:** The client node sends a DHCPDISCOVER packet to locate a DCHP server. Every DHCP server on the local network will pick up this packet.
2. **DHCPOFFER packet:** All DHCP servers that receive the discover packet will respond with an IP address appropriate for that local network (the network number in the address must match the network number for that segment). This response goes to the client machine.
3. **DHCPREQUEST packet:** The client responds with a request to keep the IP address. Clients will request the "most attractive offer," which is the first offer from a DHCP server.
4. **DHCPACK packet:** Once the client node has requested an IP address offer, the DHCP server acknowledges (the ACK part of the name of this packet) that the IP address will be assigned to the client node, and sends the rest of the configuration information to the client, such as the lease duration, gateway address, DNS server address, and perhaps domain name as well.

FIGURE 9.6
Steps in the DORA Process

T1 time ✓

The time at which a client node will attempt to renew its IP address lease. This occurs when 50 percent of the lease time has been used.

T2 time ✓

The time at which a client node will begin the DORA process to request a new IP address. This happens if the lease has not been renewed by the point at which 87.5 percent of the lease time has been used.

Broadcast-based process

A process in which all requests are created in a broadcast format. This works well for single-segment networks, but because broadcast messages do not go through routers, LANs need additional services to be able to distribute IP addresses dynamically through broadcasts.

Now the client node has an IP address and can communicate with other servers and nodes on the network and internetwork. But keep in mind that leases must be renewed periodically, depending on the duration of the lease assignment. The lease has two important milestone times associated with it: T1 time and T2 time.

- *T1 time* marks the halfway point in the lease time. When 50 percent of the lease time has been used, the client node will attempt to contact the DHCP server that originally leased the address to request a lease renewal. If the DHCP server is available, it will generally renew the lease. If the DHCP server is not available, the client node will continue to attempt contact with the server until T2 time is reached.
- *T2 time* marks when 87.5 percent of the lease time has been used. If the DHCP server has not renewed the lease by this point, the client will initiate the DORA process to locate a new address.

Earlier we noted that the DORA process uses broadcast packets. With a *broadcast-based process,* the packets do not cross routers. What happens if the client node and the DHCP server are on two different network segments? How will the client acquire an address?

The solution comes from a protocol we learned about at the start of this chapter—BOOTP. When providing addresses through DHCP on a routed network, the administrator enables BOOTP on the router interface. When the protocol is added, the IP address of the DHCP server is also added to the BOOTP configuration. The router interface will listen for DHCPDISCOVER packets, capture them, repackage them as IP packets, and send them on their way to the DHCP server. Part of the information included in this newly formed IP packet is the source address, which is the router interface IP address. That is how the DHCP server knows what scope to choose for an address. The DHCPOFFER packet is sent back to the router interface, which in turn sends it to the client node. The client node sends out the DHCPREQUEST and it is picked up by the router interface, which of course sends it to the DHCP server. Finally, the DHCPACK is sent back, again to the router interface, and back to the client node—little more complex, but the client gets the address.

Now that our client node has an IP address and all of the needed configuration parameters, it can make use of the services on the network. Following are some of those services needed by the client nodes to access resources on the network or internetwork.

Domain Name System (DNS)

The Domain Name System (DNS) converts friendly host names into their numeric IP addresses. DNS servers are located worldwide so that users can reach resources such as www.microsoft.com or www.google.com. But to access those resources, computers use numbers rather than names. People, on the other hand, remember names much more easily than they remember numeric addresses (just ask someone her own phone number…). So this global system of servers was established to allow human beings to use friendly names, while the servers perform the numeric resolution so that computers can recognize the addresses.

Originally, a file called the *host table* (also referred to as a hosts file) was used to list all the resources and their IP addresses (see Figure 9.7 for an example of a host table). That worked until the Web began to grow. The tables became unwieldy and the time it took to parse the tables began to impact the internetwork of computers. Added to this size issue was the fact that updates to the table were difficult to get out to all the servers needing the information, so large parts of the Web could be outdated or inaccessible.

Host table ✔

An ASCII file that contains a listing of network resources (client nodes, servers, printers) by host name (friendly name) and associated IP address. Host tables are used to locate resources on the network.

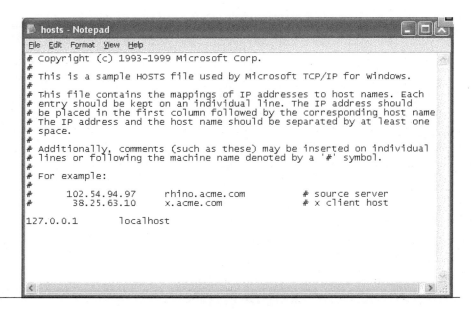

FIGURE 9.7
Sample Hosts File from a
Windows 2000 Server
Installation

THE DOMAIN NAME SPACE

To solve the problems associated with host tables, a man by the name of
Paul Mockapetris designed DNS in 1984. DNS is often described as a
distributed, hierarchical database of host names and their associated IP
addresses. To understand, you need to be familiar with the *domain name
space,* which uses an inverted tree structure that allows many servers to host
parts of the DNS database. Each server maintains information about where
the next DNS server resides (a pointer, if you will). Look at Figure 9.8.
Here we see the "root" of the upside-down tree structure, with a series of
top-level domains directly under the root. From there, each top-level
domain may have pointers to thousands of second-level domains, and so on
down the inverted tree.

Figure 9.8 represents the domain name space, with the ".{root}" at the
top of the inverted tree structure. The "." designates the endpoint of the
name space, and when writing out a host name this dot is usually dropped
(them.com). The next layer is known as the *top-level domains.* Six of these
domains are listed in the figure, but many more exist. Each of those top-
level domains represents a type of organization (see Table 9.1).

Domain name space

The inverted, hierarchical tree
structure of the Domain
Name System. Domain name
space can also be used in
reference to a specific part of
the name space.

Top-level domain

A domain that falls
immediately under the {root}
domain in the domain name
space hierarchy.

Network Services

Domain	Type of Organization
ORG	Noncommercial organizations (nonprofit agencies)
MIL	U.S. military entities
COM	Commercial organizations, typically businesses
EDU	Educational institutions
GOV	Governmental agencies
NET	Network entities, such as ISPs

TABLE 9.1
Top-Level Domains in DNS Hierarchy

One domain not listed in Figure 9.8 is the *ARPA domain.* This domain is the reverse lookup domain, which is a special function entity well beyond the scope of this course. It resolves IP addresses to host names in the DNS structure.

ARPA (Advanced Research Projects Agency) domain

The DNS domain that provides the reverse lookup capabilities of DNS by listing key domains by their IP address first and friendly name second.

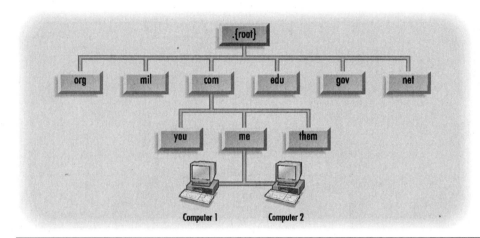

FIGURE 9.8
The DNS Hierarchy

In the last few years, top-level domains have been added to represent every country worldwide (us, uk, ca).

The third layer shown in Figure 9.8 represents three subdomains within the .com domain. Within one of these subdomains—the "me" domain—we see two computers. If we look at the host name for the first computer, computer1.me.com, we can identify the exact location within the DNS hierarchy. This complete name is known as the *fully qualified domain name (FQDN).*

Fully qualified domain name (FQDN)

The complete name of a node that defines its exact location within the DNS hierarchy.

What does all this mean to a user? When the user opens up a browser and types in the name of a resource she would like to use (www.google.com), the client machine will query the DNS server listed in the client node's IP configuration. If the local DNS server has a record of the resource, the IP address for www.google.com is sent back to the client node. If the local DNS server does not have a record, then a set of queries will be performed. The queries start at the .{root} domain and work their way out. So the first DNS server to receive a query would be the .{root} server. The request would be, "Where is the .com DNS server?" Once an answer is received, the local DNS server can query the .com DNS server to ask, "Where is the google.com domain DNS server?" When the query gets to the google.com DNS server, the local DNS server will ask, "Where is the www.google.com server?" Because the google.com server is an *authoritative DNS server* for that resource, the server has the IP address that matched the friendly name in its part of the DNS database. That information is forwarded back to the local DNS server, and finally back to the client node (see Figure 9.9).

Authoritative DNS server

The DNS server that has the original record in its table for a requested resource. A DNS server is authoritative for all resources contained within its part of the domain name space. Other DNS servers may have a cached listing for the resource, but those servers are not the authority for the resource.

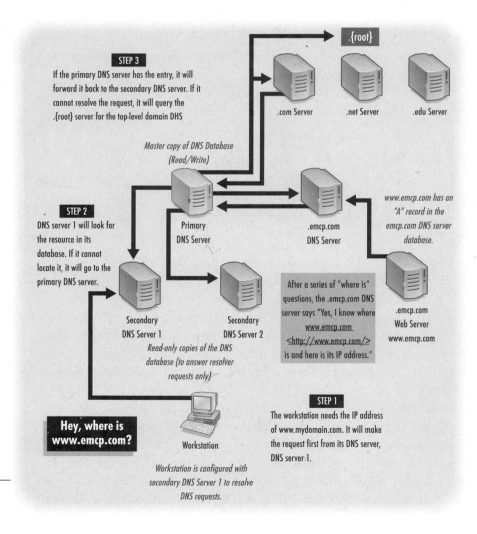

STEP 3
If the primary DNS server has the entry, it will forward it back to the secondary DNS server. If it cannot resolve the request, it will query the .{root} server for the top-level domain DHS

.{root}

.com Server   .net Server   .edu Server

Master copy of DNS Database (Read/Write)

Primary DNS Server

.emcp.com DNS Server

www.emcp.com has an "A" record in the emcp.com DNS server database.

STEP 2
DNS server 1 will look for the resource in its database. If it cannot locate it, it will go to the primary DNS server.

Secondary DNS Server 1

Secondary DNS Server 2

Read-only copies of the DNS database (to answer resolver requests only)

After a series of "where is" questions, the .emcp.com DNS server says "Yes, I know where www.emcp.com <http://www.emcp.com/> is and here is its IP address."

.emcp.com Web Server www.emcp.com

Hey, where is www.emcp.com?

Workstation

Workstation is configured with secondary DNS Server 1 to resolve DNS requests.

STEP 1
The workstation needs the IP address of www.mydomain.com. It will make the request first from its DNS server, DNS server 1.

FIGURE 9.9
The DNS Process

DNS services are divided into two key functions: name servers and *resolvers*. The DNS name server holds the database of host names and their IP addresses for which that server is authoritative. In other words, it holds a piece of the global DNS database. A resolver is a host on the Internet or intranet that needs to locate an IP address for a resource when all it knows is the friendly name. The resolver capability is built into the TCP/IP applications that use it: HTTP, FTP, and Telnet. When a resource is needed and the IP address is unknown, the application in use will start a host name resolution process to convert the user-friendly name to the numeric IP address.

Resolver

A node that has requested that a DNS server resolve, or convert, a resource's user-friendly name into its IP address.

 TEST TIP

DNS is a generic TCP/IP service that all nodes running TCP/IP can use for name resolution.

As you can see from the two functions noted above, DNS runs as a service on a server as well as a configuration parameter at the client node. Figure 9.10 shows how to configure the client node for DNS capability.

Advanced TCP/IP Settings

IP Settings | DNS | WINS | Options

DNS server addresses, in order of use:
10.10.1.3

Add... | Edit... | Remove

The following three settings are applied to all connections with TCP/IP enabled. For resolution of unqualified names:

○ Append primary and connection specific DNS suffixes
  ☑ Append parent suffixes of the primary DNS suffix
○ Append these DNS suffixes (in order):

Add | Edit | Remove

DNS suffix for this connection:

☑ Register this connection's addresses in DNS
☐ Use this connection's DNS suffix in DNS registration

OK | Cancel

FIGURE 9.10
Client Configuration for a Windows 2000 Operating System

DNS Record Types

DNS implementations vary, depending on the network operating system in place on the server where DNS will be added. Some operating systems add other functions to DNS. But generally, DNS databases are manually built. An administrator or DNS technician enters each record in the database, and each record is marked with a record type. Some of the *DNS record types* are shown in Figure 9.11. These are the most commonly used entries in a DNS database. There are many other record types, as well.

DNS record type

A designation attached to an entry in the DNS database that identifies its use. For example, an MX record identifies a node as an e-mail server (or mail exchanger).

- **A records:** These records represent entries that have a unique host name and IP address.
- **MX records:** MX records are mail exchangers, also known as e-mail servers.
- **C-name records:** In the old UNIX days, case made a difference. C-name records allow the administrator to enter several iterations of a name, telling the system that these are all one in the same entities. For example, if we have a host name "computer1," it can be written in several ways: computer1, Computer1, COMPUTER1, or even ComputerOne. Each of these names identifies the same resource. So the host file would have C-name entries for each spelling or case of the name of the resource.
- **NS records:** NS records designate the name and IP address of a name server (another DNS server, or this DNS server).
- **SOA records:** Earlier in this section, we talked about authoritative DNS servers. These are DNS servers that hold the record for a resource, and therefore can answer a query from another machine. These authoritative servers get a special record type—the SOA record—in addition to a normal A record.

FIGURE 9.11
Record Types in DNS Databases

DNS Server Roles

Primary DNS server

The DNS server that owns the records for that part of the DNS name space. Records can be changed on a primary DNS server.

Zone

A section of the domain name space.

DNS servers take on different roles. Some servers are *primary DNS servers,* which "own" the records in their databases. This is the site of the original entry or registration of the DNS record. They are typically known as the authoritative DNS server for a section of the domain name space. Those sections are known as *zones*. Some servers are *secondary DNS servers*. A secondary DNS server does not "own" any records. It merely holds a copy of the DNS database that has been sent to it by way of a zone transfer, or exchange of database information. The secondary copy of the DNS database is a read-only copy from the database on the primary DNS server. Secondary servers are used for fault tolerance or for load-balancing on the network.

Windows Internet Name Service (WINS)

Windows Internet Name Service (WINS) is a Microsoft proprietary service that allows client nodes to resolve NetBIOS names to IP addresses. It is based on a generic TCP/IP service called *NetBIOS Name Service (NBNS)*.

— TRY IT! —

On a Windows 2000 Professional machine, check to see if your IP address is DHCP assigned or manually assigned. To find out, complete the following steps:

1. Click the Start button.
2. Click the *Run* option.
3. In the *Open* text box, type **cmd.**
4. Once the command prompt window has opened, type **IPCONFIG/ALL**.
5. Read the display, noting the settings. Look for your DNS server address. Look for a WINS server address (not all nodes will use this option).
6. When you are done, type **exit** to close the command prompt window.

WINS is similar to DNS in some respects. It is a database of entries. Each entry includes the host's NetBIOS name and the IP address assigned to that host. Client nodes may query the WINS database to locate resources. And NetBIOS name resolution also started out with a text file that contains the table of NetBIOS host names and IP addresses. This file is known as the *LMHosts file.* Figure 9.12 shows a sample LMHosts file.

Secondary DNS server

A server that holds a read-only copy of the DNS database owned by a primary DNS server. The secondary server can respond to local requests for DNS resolution, but it cannot change records.

Windows Internet Name Service (WINS)

A Microsoft proprietary service that allows client nodes to resolve NetBIOS names to IP addresses.

NetBIOS Name Service (NBNS)

The generic TCP/IP implementation of the Windows Internet Name Service; allows location of resources by associating a NetBIOS name to an IP address. NBNS functions in a very similar way to DNS.

LMHosts file

A method of resolving NetBIOS names to their IP addresses. This implementation preceded the dynamic WINS service, first used by IBM with its LanManager product, and later used with the Microsoft Windows NT products.

```
102.54.94.97       rhino              #PRE #DOM:networking        #net group's DC
102.54.94.102      "appname  \0x14"                              #special app server
102.54.94.123      popular            #PRE                       #source server
102.54.94.117      localsrv           #PRE                       #needed for the include

#BEGIN_ALTERNATE
#INCLUDE \\localsrv\public\lmhosts
#INCLUDE \\rhino\public\lmhosts
#END_ALTERNATE
```

FIGURE 9.12
Sample LMHosts File

The LMHosts file was found on the local machine and directed the local machine to the IP address of commonly used resources. In Figure 9.12, "rhino" is the domain controller for the "networking" domain. This would be the first resource a local machine would need when it attached to the network. The machine would need to authenticate, and the user would need to log in to the domain. Other resources were listed as needed.

TEST TIP

Remember that NetBIOS name resolution can be implemented either through LMHosts files on each client node, or through WINS on the network.

In earlier days, when a (Microsoft) NetBIOS client node needed to locate a resource called Machine23, that client sent out a broadcast over the local segment asking which node had the name Machine23. If the machine existed on the local segment, it would reply with its IP address. As networks became larger and larger, with many segments, NetBIOS name resolution became a cumbersome chore. To locate resources on remote networks, every client node had to have an accurate, and probably large, LMHosts file to direct the client node to the correct IP address. The only other solution was to have Microsoft servers on either side of the router that acted as *master browse list keepers,* or to configure their LMHosts files to locate resources across the router. WINS came about because of the limitations of using broadcasts to find resources and because large LMHosts files were not really any more efficient than broadcasts.

Master browse list keeper

A node on the network that keeps track of the nodes attached to the network and their associated IP addresses. Notification by the nodes is handled by broadcast, and therefore this process is generally limited to a single-segment network.

TestTip

Remember that WINS is a Microsoft service. UNIX platforms do not recognize WINS.

WINS is both a server service and a client configuration parameter. The administrator will add the service by going to the server, accessing the server's installation options in Control Panel/Add/Remove Programs, and then choosing the Add/Remove Windows Components. The next step is to open the Networking Services and choose Windows Internet Name Service. This will allow the service to be installed. Once the service is installed, a manager is added to the Administrative Tools in the Programs menu. Figure 9.13 shows the manager for WINS in Windows 2000 Server.

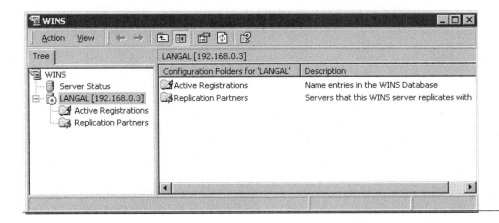

FIGURE 9.13
WINS Manager Utility in Windows 2000 Server

Now the client can be configured. The client needs the IP address of only one or more WINS servers to activate the ability of the client to use WINS instead of broadcast to locate resources. The WINS server addresses can be added to the client through DHCP scope options, or by configuring the client's Internet Protocol properties. See Figure 9.14 for manual configuration of the client.

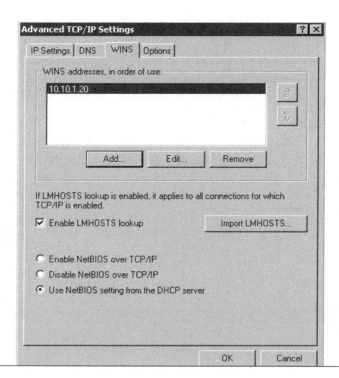

FIGURE 9.14
WINS Client Configuration

WINS is dynamic in nature. It relies on all client and server nodes registering with the WINS server. When a node that is configured to use WINS boots up to the network, it will send a message containing its NetBIOS name and IP address to the first WINS server in its list. The WINS server adds the entry to the database. Now, when a client tries to locate a resource, it will send a request directly to the WINS server, thus eliminating all of the broadcast traffic needed to locate resources prior to the WINS installation.

In a pure Microsoft network, all clients are able to register with the WINS server. When there are other clients on the network, such as UNIX machines, it is necessary to add a static entry into the WINS database so that Microsoft clients can locate the resource. The administrator must maintain these entries. If the non-Microsoft client is removed from the network permanently, the entry in the database will not be removed unless the administrator does so.

Client entries are renewed every time the client boots up to the network. This way, WINS can make sure there are no duplicate names in the enterprise. Servers must also be WINS clients to have an entry in the database. Even the WINS server itself registers in the WINS database, so that client machines can locate this most powerful resource.

In a small network environment that requires WINS, one server running the service will suffice for several hundred clients. However, when the environment includes WAN links to remote geographic locations, more than one WINS server is recommended. These servers can replicate with each other to exchange what they each know about the network. This also provides fault tolerance for WINS.

Network Address Translation/Internet Connection Sharing (NAT/ICS)

Network address translation (NAT) and *Internet connection sharing (ICS)* are two services that allow the use of private addresses within a LAN, while using one or a minimal number of public addresses at the router where the private network connects to the public network. NAT and ICS were both designed to ease the global shortage of IP addresses, to address the need for secure LANs, and to simplify administration.

Figure 9.15 shows a routed network that uses public IP addresses for all nodes. Consequently, workstations do not have any problems communicating with the outside world. With a public IP address, packets generated by host nodes inside the network will be routed to their destination address, whether the destination is inside the network or located on the public internetwork.

Internet connection sharing (ICS)

A service available in several Microsoft operating systems that allows some of the functions of network address translation. By enabling ICS, a small office or a home office can achieve Internet connectivity while still using private addressing. The ICS service is nonconfigurable and therefore its use is limited.

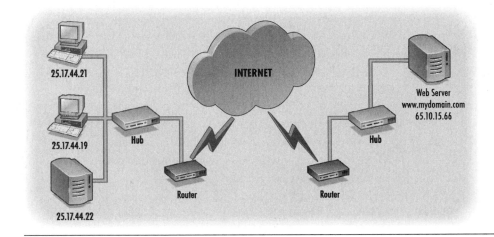

FIGURE 9.15
The Public Internetwork

Network Address Translation (NAT)

What happens when the organization decides to use the private address space for its LAN addressing? If you remember from Chapter 8, private addresses are considered any IP address from the following three ranges:

10.0.0.0 to 10.255.255.255

172.16.0.0 to 172.31.255.255

192.168.0.0 to 192.168.255.255

Internet routers do not route these addresses. Any packets having a destination address from these three ranges will be silently discarded and never reach the destination. The users on the network will have to settle for talking only to internal hosts.

That is not a viable solution for many businesses and organizations. In the last 15 years or so, businesses and educational institutions have come to rely on the resources that the Internet can provide. How do we compromise? That is, how do we maintain a private addressing scheme and still allow access to the Internet? This is where NAT and its little brother, ICS, come in.

NAT can be implemented as either a device (NAT appliance) or a software solution. With either implementation, NAT is a router at heart. Its job is to figure out how to ensure that a request sent from the private network with an unroutable source address will receive the right reply from the public side of the network (the Internet) and get it back to the device that initiated the dialog in the first place.

NAT requires that the node hosting the service have two connections: a network interface to the internal network, and a connection to an ISP. That connection may be dial-on-demand, cable modem, or even leased line. As packets are sent from the private side of the network to the public side, the packet will pass through the NAT box, be recorded in a table, and be assigned to either a public IP address (if one is available) or a unique port number. Now when a response comes back to the NAT box from an external source, NAT checks the packet against the NAT table. If an entry exists in the table, NAT will forward the packet to the private side of the network. If no mapping in the table exists, the packet is silently discarded. In this way, NAT also acts as a low-level firewall because it prevents rogue traffic from entering the private network.

As mentioned above, you can implement NAT in a variety of ways. NAT appliances are common on larger networks where large volumes of traffic will pass through the translation service. These appliances (actually specialized, router-like boxes) are fairly sophisticated and can be configured to meet the needs of even complex networks. NAT appliances may provide DHCP addressing or work in conjunction with a DHCP server. They can be configured to provide customized DNS resolution, as well.

Software NAT is becoming more common. Many of the major network operating systems include NAT services. On one hand, this implementation may not be as highly configurable as a NAT appliance. On the other hand, software NAT has the advantage of being included in a product that an organization was going to purchase anyway, so it has no extra cost. Furthermore, software NAT is easily installed and configured. Often, a software-based NAT service acts as the DHCP allocator and may be able to service only a single subnet. In larger network deployments, this would prevent its usage because it could not accommodate multiple segments.

If the NAT service provides DHCP services, then you will not need to run a DHCP server behind the NAT service on the private network. Some implementations of NAT function well in routed internal networks. The NAT interface is the default gateway for the routers. Any traffic the routers cannot send on its way will be pushed through the NAT interface, making the assumption that it must be destined for the public side of the network. Figure 9.16 shows the private address space within the private network on the left, and the public internetwork (Internet) and an available resource on the right. Note that the NAT server needs both a public and a private interface configured with the proper IP addresses.

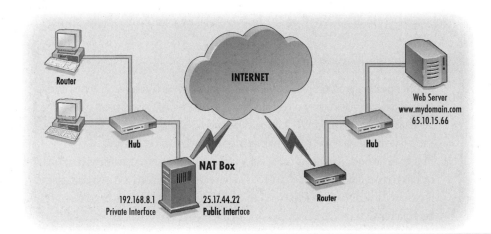

FIGURE 9.16
Use of NAT for the Private Network

Administrators can add static entries to the NAT table. If the network is hosting Web services for its organization, any port 80 (HTTP) traffic may be allowed into the network, but it will be routed only to the Web server.

This protects the network from public traffic, while still allowing the public traffic to visit the Web site of an organization.

INTERNET CONNECTION SHARING (ICS)

Internet connection sharing (ICS) is a junior NAT software product. It is available in many operating systems. ICS allows an Internet connection to be shared among a set of users without major configuration or management. It is most appropriate for small office and home office environments with fewer than 10 users. On a Microsoft Windows 2000 or XP machine where the Internet connection resides (dial-up, DSL, or cable modem connection), access the properties window for the device that is providing the connection. Under the sharing configuration, check the box for ICS. That is the configuration process. Provide a small hub, plug the other machines into the hub, make sure all machines are set to get an IP address via DHCP (including the host machine), and now the network is connected to the Internet.

Simple Network Management Protocol (SNMP)

Simple Network Management Protocol (SNMP) is an Application layer protocol that allows the exchange of information between TCP/IP devices and a management console. SNMP includes several key components, as shown in Figure 9.17.

- **SNMP Agents:** The *SNMP agents* are software modules that are installed on managed devices to allow communication between managed devices and the network management system. Agents are responsible for maintaining knowledge of the local device and formulating that knowledge into a format that SNMP and the network management system can understand.
- **Managed Devices:** A managed device is any host (workstation, server, printer, router, switch, etc.) that has an SNMP agent residing on it. The managed device collects and maintains information about the device that the agent can then use to formulate a notice that a component may have problems.
- **Network Management System:** The *SNMP network management system (NMS)* is responsible for collecting information from the agents and monitoring the state of that information.

FIGURE 9.17
Key Components of SNMP

Simple Network Management Protocol (SNMP)

A TCP/IP protocol that allows an administrator to keep track of events on the network and on individual network nodes.

SNMP agent

A small piece of software that runs on a device (computer, router, etc.) to track certain events on the device and report those events to a management console.

SNMP network management system (NMS)

The software that collects notices from SNMP agents running on devices on the managed network. The network management system is often referred to as the "management console."

Each of these components plays an important part in the management of the network. An SNMP agent is always listening to the local device. The agent uses the *management information base (MIB)* to review current readings about the parameters, or operating variables, for the device. When an agent discovers a faulty parameter on the MIB, it creates a notice called a *trap*, which it sends to the NMS. The agents also listen for advice from the NMS. The advice comes in one of two formats: either as a *get action* or a *set action*. A get is a request to the SNMP agent to locate a piece of information and send it back to the management console (or NMS). A set is the NMS request to change a parameter on the agent's device.

All SNMP agents belong to an *SNMP community*. A community is similar to a security group in that agents will talk only to a management console that belongs to their community. Community membership is considered a low-level security feature for the SNMP environment.

SNMP is an industry-standard protocol. All operating systems that use a TCP/IP stack will recognize and have provisions for SNMP within that system. Sometimes the operating system will provide an SNMP agent to install on the device, but the administrator will need to purchase a network management system to view the traps and control the devices. Some of the well-known management consoles are Hewlett-Packard OpenView and SunConnect SunNet Manager. The NMS does not have to run the same operating system as other host devices or server devices on the network. For instance, within a Microsoft Windows 2000 Active Directory network, an administrator could set up a UNIX box as the management console for the network. Depending on how sophisticated the NMS may be, the administrator can glean large amounts of information about the network and its devices in a user-friendly format, making management of that network easier.

Troubleshooting Network Services

There are many places where network services can cause communications problems for client machines. Here are some of the more common problems you may see.

DHCP TROUBLESHOOTING

- If a client node does not receive a DHCP allocated address as expected, check the following:
  - Make sure a scope has been set up on the DHCP server for that subnet.

Management information base (MIB)

A collection of facts, organized hierarchically, that contains specific information about each parameter, or managed object, on a device.

Trap

An SNMP notice about a faulty parameter on a managed device; sent by an SNMP agent to the network management service.

Get action

An SNMP management console's request to an SNMP agent to acquire further information about the agent's managed device and to forward that information to the console.

Set action

An SNMP management console's request to an SNMP agent to change information or settings on the agent's managed device.

SNMP community

A group of managed devices that report to a single management console.

- Make sure the scope is activated and capable of assigning addresses.
- Check to see that the scope has addresses available.
- If the client node is on a remote subnetwork from the DHCP server, confirm that the DHCP has a relay agent on the client subnetwork, or, alternatively, that BOOTP has been enabled on the router between the client and the DHCP server.

- If a network has excessive broadcast traffic, use a packet capture and analysis utility to determine if the problem is caused by DHCP broadcast packets. The lease time may be set too short, and therefore the client nodes may be generating excessive traffic while attempting to renew leases.
- If client machines are receiving an address from the range 192.168.0.X and the network is not using NAT, identify the machine that has enabled Internet Connection Sharing (ICS).

DNS TROUBLESHOOTING

- If a client node cannot access resources on the Internet but the node can communicate on the local network, that node may be incorrectly configured for DNS. Check the IP configuration setting for the DNS server.

WINS TROUBLESHOOTING

- If client machines on a Windows network cannot access resources, check the WINS server to make sure it is functional.
- Confirm the client configuration for a WINS server address.
- Confirm the registration of client nodes in the WINS database.

NAT TROUBLESHOOTING

- If the network is using NAT and clients cannot access resources on the Internet, make sure the client nodes are using the address of the NAT server as the DNS setting.

STUDY GUIDE

In this chapter, we looked at the services that support the use of the TCP/IP protocol stack in networked environments. You learned the characteristics of Domain Name System (DNS), Windows Internet Name Service (WINS) in Microsoft networks, Dynamic Host Configuration Protocol (DHCP), the Bootstrap Protocol (BOOTP), Network Address Translation (NAT), Internet Connection Sharing (ICS), and Simple Network Management Protocol (SNMP). Here are some key points to remember.

BOOTSTRAP PROTOCOL (BOOTP)

- The Bootstrap Protocol (BOOTP) solved the unreasonable task of making sure every workstation (or diskless workstation) had an IP address.
  - When a workstation configured to use BOOTP boots up to the network, it broadcasts its MAC address on the local segment.
  - The BOOTP server receives the broadcast packet and checks the MAC address against the BOOTPTAB file to see if an IP address has been assigned to that MAC address.
  - If an address is found, the BOOTP server sends back the IP address, subnet mask, and default gateway setting.
  - If the workstation is located on a remote segment from the BOOTP server, the router will hear the BOOTP broadcast, repackage the broadcast as an IP packet, and send it to the BOOTP server. When the server replies, the router unpackages the packet and forwards it to the workstation, which now has a valid IP address for its location on the network.

DYNAMIC HOST CONFIGURATION PROTOCOL (DHCP)

- DHCP distributes IP addresses throughout the network dynamically, reducing the amount of time, as well as the number of errors, in getting IP addresses to all workstations.
- DHCP runs as a service on most network operating system servers.

DHCP Scopes

- To configure the DHCP service, the administrator must
  - build scopes (or ranges) of IP addresses;

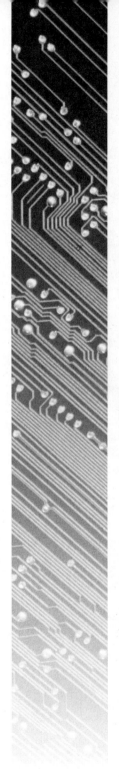

- set the scope options, such as the default gateway, the DNS server, or the WINS server address;
- create any exclusions from the scope;
- set up any reservations for the scope;
- activate the scope.
- The address sent to the client must be an address that is part of the network range for that segment. If not, the client will be unable to talk to any other nodes.
- Each IP address that is distributed by a DHCP server has a lease attached to it. The lease is the length of time the client may keep that address.
- In stable environments with desktop machines that are not moved frequently, the lease time can be set at a lengthy state, or even an indefinite state.
- In networks where machines attach and detach from the network frequently, the lease time should be set to reflect the average stay of the machines.
- The lease must be renewed for the client to keep the same address. At T1 time, or halfway through the lease, the client will attempt to renew the lease with the DHCP server. If the server is available, then the lease will be renewed. If the server is not available, the client will continue to attempt to contact the server. If no contact is made by T2 time, when 87.5 percent of the lease time has passed, then the client will repeat the DORA process in order to secure another IP address.

Acquiring an IP Address

- DHCP is also a client process that consists of four steps:
  - The client issues the DHCPDISCOVER broadcast packet to locate a DHCP server.
  - The DHCP server sends an IP address back to the client in the form of the DHCPOFFER.
  - The client sends a DHCPREQUEST packet to the DHCP server to accept the IP address.
  - The DHCP server issues a DHCPACK to let the client know the address has been allocated to that client and to send the additional scope options to the client.

DOMAIN NAME SYSTEM (DNS)

- DNS provides a host name, or friendly name, to IP address resolution.

- Originally, a file called the hosts file was used to provide host name resolution, but the tables became large and unwieldy.
- DNS is used by the Internet as well as by private networks.

The Domain Name Space

- The domain name space is divided into sections, called top-level domains. Each top-level domain represents a type of organization, such as .com for commercial entities, .mil for military entities, and .edu for educational entities.
- Below the top-level domains are the second-level domains. These represent specific organizations such as Microsoft, Comptia, Washington University, or the American Diabetes Association.
- DNS resolution responsibility is divided into zones, or portions of the DNS name space. One DNS server will be authoritative for all objects in that segment of the name space.
- When a user opens a browser and enters an address such as www.google.com in the URL locator, the client node contacts the DNS server, and the DNS server goes about finding the IP address of www.google.com.
- Any client operating system that uses the IP stack for communication will also be able to use the services of DNS resolution. UNIX relies solely on DNS, whereas Microsoft Windows clients can also use WINS to locate resources within the private network.

DNS Record Types

- When the DNS service is added to a server, the database must be populated with records for resources. Following are some of those record types:
  - A records are unique host records.
  - MX records are mail exchangers, or e-mail servers.
  - C-name records are alias names for resources.
  - NS records are the entries for name servers (DNS servers).
  - SOA records are records for the authoritative servers for specific zones.

DNS Server Roles

- Primary DNS servers own the records held in their database.
- The primary DNS server's database is the read-write copy of the database for the zone. Records can be added, deleted, or modified here.
- Secondary DNS servers hold a read-only copy of the primary server's database.

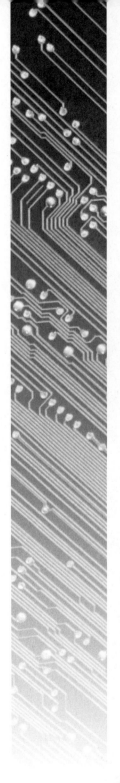

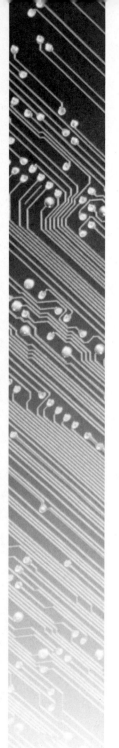

Windows Internet Name Service (WINS)

- WINS resolves the NetBIOS name of a resource to its IP address.
- WINS is a Microsoft proprietary server service.
- Microsoft Windows computers use NetBIOS to locate resources on the network rather than using DNS. The request for resolution is sent in the form of a broadcast packet. WINS servers are needed in any Microsoft network with more than one segment.
- The WINS service replaced the use of the LMHost file, which mapped NetBIOS names to IP addresses. This file had to be configured on every machine locally or the machine would be unable to locate resources on remote subnetworks, including domain controllers for authentication.
- WINS is dynamic: computers register with the WINS server when they attach to the network. They release their entry when they leave the network.
- To configure the client, add an IP address in the WINS property tab of the IP properties at the client. Now the client will register with the WINS database, and the client node will send directed requests to the WINS server when it needs a resource.
- Non-WINS clients can be added to the WINS database by creating a manual entry with the client node's name and IP address.

Network Address Translation/Internet Connection Sharing (NAT/ICS)

- NAT and ICS allow network administrators to use one of the private address spaces for the internal network, while still allowing access to Internet (public) resources.
- NAT appliances or software translate the internal private address to a public address or specified port so that the packet can be transported over the public Internet space.
- NAT requires that the hosting device, usually a server or a NAT appliance, have two connections: the network interface connection (NIC) and the access point to the public network (a dial-up connection), or some other type of connection to an ISP.
- The NAT table keeps a record of outgoing packets. The dialog is mapped within the table. When a response comes back to the NAT box, it will consult the table, identify the source machine and its IP address, and forward the packet to the private side of the NAT box.

- Administrators can add manual entries to the NAT table when it is necessary to route certain types of traffic, such as port 80 requests routed to the Web server.
- ICS is a smaller, less robust version of NAT. It also translates from a private to a public address or unique port for communications over the public internetwork.
- ICS is easy to enable on a small office or home office network. Go to the properties window of the connection device (such as a modem), click on the Sharing tab, and check the box that says "Internet Connection Sharing."
- All devices that participate in an ICS network must be configured as DHCP clients. The ICS service will allocate addresses to all client nodes.

SIMPLE NETWORK MANAGEMENT PROTOCOL (SNMP)

- SNMP has three components:
  - SNMP agents.
  - Managed devices.
  - Network management system (NMS).
- The SNMP agent is software that runs on all network devices, including computers, routers, printers, and switches. The agent is responsible for monitoring the device, and if there is a problem, for relaying that information to the NMS.
- Managed devices are any host devices where an agent has been installed.
- The NMS is responsible for collecting the information the agents send to it.
- The agent uses a management information base (MIB) to compare the current readings to the standard readings in the MIB. If there is an aberration, the agent will notify the NMS.
- The agent knows three types of commands, or utilities:
  - The get action tells the agent to find a specified piece of information about the managed device and forward it to the NMS.
  - The set action tells the agent that the NMS wants the agent to change a configuration setting.
  - A trap is the notification to the NMS when a managed device has a faulty parameter.
- All agents belong to an SNMP community. An agent will report only to an NMS that is part of the agent's community. This is considered a low-level security feature.

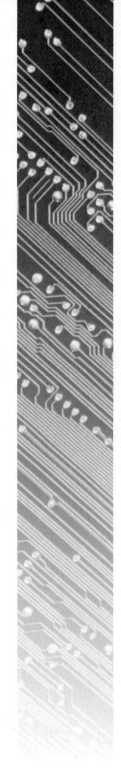

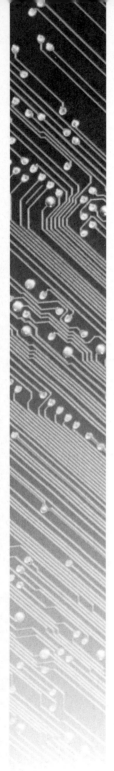

PRACTICE TEST

Try this test to check your mastery of the concepts in this chapter.

1. Which of the following do administrators use to monitor the state of the network?
   a. SNMP
   b. SMTP
   c. NAS
   d. WINS
   e. DNS

2. Which of the following resolves NetBIOS names to IP addresses?
   a. DNS
   b. WINS
   c. NDS
   d. NAS

3. An A record is used for
   a. starting the list of records.
   b. allowing a unique record to be entered into the DNS database.
   c. adding an entry for the e-mail server.
   d. creating an alias record in the database.

4. What does a UNIX workstation use to resolve host names to IP addresses?
   a. NAS
   b. DHCP
   c. DNS
   d. WINS

5. Which of the following network services allows a diskless workstation to acquire an IP address automatically?
   a. WINS
   b. DHCP
   c. DNS
   d. NAS

6. Which of the following dictates how long a client node may keep the same IP address?
   a. rent time
   b. lease time
   c. ownership time
   d. borrowing time

7. When creating DHCP scopes, you discover that some of the machines need the same address all the time because of application sharing to the network. How can you make sure these machines will receive the same address all the time, without touching each machine for static IP address configuration?
   a. Create a scope for each client machine.
   b. Create a special set of options for this set of machines.
   c. Create an exclusion in the scope.
   d. Create a reservation in the scope.

8. At T1 time in the DHCP lease, the client machine receives a DHCPNACK when it tries to renew the lease. What will happen to that client node's IP address assignment?
   a. The client node will immediately lose the address.
   b. The client node will automatically shut down.
   c. The client node will continue to attempt contact with the DHCP server to renew the lease.
   d. The client node will stop all attempts at communication with the DHCP server until T2 time.

9. There are six segments on the King Company's LAN. The administrator is running a DHCP server on the largest segment for all nodes on the network. What must be configured on the router for this situation to work?
   a. BOOTP
   b. DNS
   c. WINS
   d. SNMP

10. Which of the following allows a client node to resolve a friendly name to an IP address? (Choose two)
   a. DHCP
   b. DNS
   c. hosts file
   d. LMHost file

11. Windows Internet Name Service performs what function for an IP network?
   a. host name to IP address resolution
   b. LMHost file resolution
   c. NetBIOS to IP address resolution

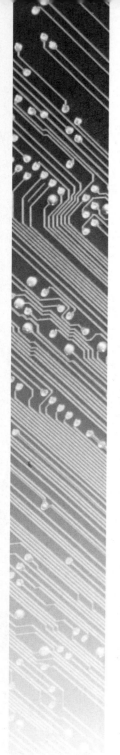

d. host file resolution

12. Identify which of the following is a fully qualified domain name (FQDN).
   a. Me.com
   b. Computer1
   c. Computer1@me .com
   d. Computer1.me.com

13. After installing SNMP agents on all devices on the network, the administrator discovers that the agents will not transmit information to the network management system (NMS). Which of the following may explain the problem?
   a. The agents have not been activated.
   b. The agents are mad at the NMS.
   c. The agents' community and the NMS's community are not the same.
   d. The administrator made mistakes when installing the agents.

14. Which of the following DNS record types indicates that the entry in the DNS database is a unique record?
   a. A records
   b. B records
   c. MX records
   d. SX records

15. To enable a Microsoft Windows client node to register with the WINS server, what step must the administrator take?
   a. Configure the client node with the right IP address and subnet mask.
   b. Configure the client node with the WINS server address.
   c. Configure the WINS server with the client node's IP address.
   d. Add a static mapping to the WINS database.

16. In every DNS zone, one DNS server is the authority for all objects in the zone. Which of the following record types indicates that the entry is the authoritative DNS server?
   a. TOA
   b. KOA
   c. QOA
   d. SOA

17. Of the services listed, which one allows the administrator to use private addresses for the internal network?
    a. APIPA
    b. DNS
    c. NAT
    d. NIC

18. Identify the three components of an SNMP-managed network. (Choose three)
    a. get action
    b. DHCP agent
    c. SNMP agent
    d. MIB
    e. NMS
    f. scope
    g. root domain
    h. managed objects
    i. managed console
    j. managed domain names

19. NAT prevents all unsolicited traffic from coming into the network.
    a. True
    b. False

20. Your network has 100 Windows NT 4.0 workstations, 100 Windows 2000 Professional workstations, 25 Windows NT 4.0 and Windows 2000 servers, and 55 UNIX workstations. Which of the following services are you required to have on your network to allow the client machines to locate resources? (Choose all that apply)
    a. SNMP
    b. DNS
    c. WINS
    d. BOOTP
    e. DHCP
    f. NAT
    g. ICS

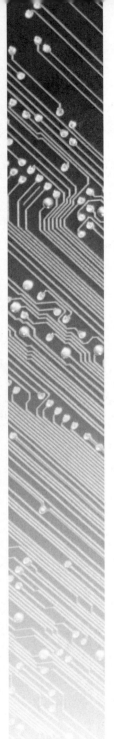

TROUBLESHOOTING

1. The Acme Company recently purchased the Johnson Company. Acme is much larger than Johnson, so the Johnson computer network was merged into the Acme network. Johnson used static host name resolution before the purchase, but Acme used DNS for name resolution. All of the Johnson servers were moved to the Acme server farm. The Johnson users can reach other servers at the server farm, but they cannot reach the servers that were moved. What should you do to correct the problem?

2. You are the technician for a network that is using TCP/IP as its transport protocol. This network has multiple subnetworks. The operating system for the servers is Windows NT 4.0. The network has a server named Jackson1 on a local subnetwork where a user resides. The user routinely connects to this server. The user gets a promotion, and moves to another area of the network. The user cannot log in to the Jackson1 server any longer. What is the problem?

CUSTOMER SERVICE

1. A network environment is made up of 250 Windows 2000 Professional machines, 50 Windows 98 machines, 15 Windows 2000 servers, and 25 UNIX workstations. The Windows users complain that they cannot access resources on the UNIX workstations. What should the administrator do to resolve this problem?

2. A user calls the help desk early on Monday morning. The user cannot connect to the Internet with a Windows XP Professional desktop. The user can log in to a server running IPX/SPX. When you have the user run the IPCONFIG utility, the IP address of this node is 169.254.0.12. What is most likely the problem?

FOR MORE INFORMATION

For links to Web sites that provide further information about the topics covered in this chapter, go to the EMC/Paradigm Internet Resource Center at www.emcp.com/College Division/Internet Resource Centers/Networking/System Administration/Web Resources: For More Information.

Public versus Private Networks

10

Network+ Examination
- **Objective 2.10:** Identify the differences between public vs. private networks.
- **Objective 3.8:** Identify the purpose, benefits, and characteristics of using a firewall.
- **Objective 3.9:** Identify the purpose, benefits, and characteristics of using a proxy.
- **Objective 3.10:** Given a scenario, predict the impact of a particular security implementation on network functionality (e.g., blocking port numbers, encryption, etc.).

ON THE JOB

Everyone who works for a business carries responsibility for the security of the assets of the business. This is especially true when talking about network resources. In the real world, you will be called on frequently to manage parts of the security plan, and you will need to "fix" the user by configuring the user's workstation correctly. Understanding the rationale for firewall and proxy services, as well as understanding the big picture of security will be helpful as you work on networks.

Boundaries between Public and Private Networks

Public network ✓

Any part of the data communications infrastructure that falls outside the boundary of the firewall for a business or organization; sometimes called the internetwork.

Private network ✓

Any portion of a data communications infrastructure that falls within a firewall for a business or organization; sometimes called the internal network.

Public networks versus *private networks:* it sounds like it would be an easy task to define the boundaries between the public side of a network and the private side of a network. Years ago, public networks were unheard of. LANs were very private, with no connectivity to the public environment at all. Many networks used protocols such as NetBEUI and IPX/SPX, thus limiting access only to private resources. Then came the explosion of the Internet and the public internetwork. Suddenly information was just a few clicks away, with vast amounts of information on any topic you could think of. So businesses began allowing their employees unlimited access to public resources via the Internet.

Soon business was busy chasing down hackers to the private network. Not only were users able to move from the private side of the network to the public side of the network, but also outsiders were able to access private resources within the network.

Every private network has assets more precious than gold—the data a business has amassed through hard work, massive research, or just plain old documentation as you go. Large databases holding customer information, product information, and company pricing structures (just to name a few examples) are all part of the asset structure of a company. This data usually cannot be replaced. Thus began the arena of the Information Technology (IT) industry that today is the fastest growing segment—security for the private network.

What constitutes the private network and public network boundaries? Look at the network diagram in Figure 10.1. Notice that the workstations and server in the lower part of the diagram sit within a boundary that, in this case, does not include the router. This part of the diagram is called the "private network." The public network is everything else—the cloud (or physical infrastructure on the public side), the Web servers, the routers that allow traffic to get to its destination. The connection to the public network designates the boundary of the private network. This usually will be a router interface. Although most routers can provide some *traffic filtering,* they do not protect the private network from clever thieves and hackers.

Traffic filtering

The action of looking at the type of data passing through a device, usually a router, and determining whether that data will be allowed to enter or leave a network boundary.

Public versus Private Networks

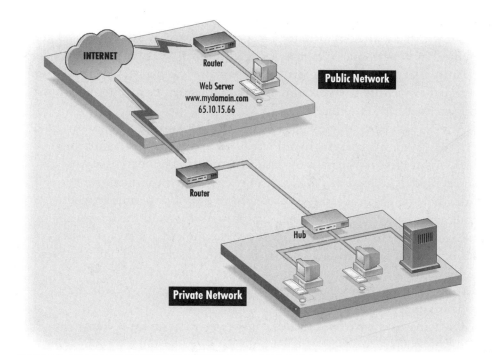

FIGURE 10.1
The Public Network and the
Private Network

This chapter will explore some of the ways administrators and security gurus can protect the private network without jeopardizing the user's access to information on the public network. This is by no means an in-depth discussion of security for the private network. Many additional options not covered here can help lock down the private network, making it less susceptible to intrusion. Both hardware and software offer solutions to security issues. The enterprise, the administrator, the type of business, and the management of the company all affect the security issues facing any network. As a team, the various stakeholders must make decisions that allow the business to function as needed, while still protecting the assets of the business.

Keep Figure 10.1 in mind as you read on in the chapter. We will revisit this diagram as we explore some of the options for securing the perimeter of the network.

Assessing Risk

Any discussion of solutions to security issues at the boundary of the network must begin with an assessment of the *risk factors* to that network.

Risk factor

Any situation, action, or object that can jeopardize the safety and integrity of the assets and resources of a business or organization.

This discussion has many stakeholders. Both technical personnel (IT managers, network administrators, security managers, and technicians) and nontechnical personnel (finance managers, human resource managers, plant security agents, and training personnel) may well be part of a security team directed to identify threats and make recommendations to eliminate those threats or at least minimize the risks.

Any networked environment faces two distinct areas of risk: internal and external. With internal risk identification, the business or organization is looking for areas of the network inside the private boundary that may be susceptible to attack from staff, unhappy employees, consultants, or unauthorized physical access to protected resources or perimeter security. Internal risks account for the majority of total threats to the network.

External threats include what most people think of as network risks—hackers getting in from the outside. To do this, hackers will typically breach a firewall or create an attack that denies service to users. Other risks can be attributed to the remote access services provided to employees of the organization.

Once the risks have been identified, the organization must clarify the value of available assets to which an unauthorized person may gain access, or the value of interrupted service to external customers. For some businesses, the cost of protection may far outweigh the value of these resources. In other circumstances, the value of the data is indeed the value of the company, and therefore, any amount of money spent to secure those resources is money well spent.

Security policy

A formalized document that identifies the risk factors for a business or organization and defines the processes, devices, and procedures to mitigate those risks.

After risks and value have been established, the security team that is assessing risks will usually begin designing a *security policy*. Each risk will be further explored, and a specific set of "fixes" will be created to protect the assets of the company. The security policy often includes elements that stretch beyond the technical. It may include enforced and tested training for new employees, identifying Web sites and types of resource access on the Internet that will not be tolerated in the workplace. It may also include recommendations for technical equipment or barriers that prevent access from the outside or restriction from the inside to the Internet. This is also where a business organization would identify the way in which remote geographical locations will communicate to carry on business.

At this stage, planning and implementation become the focus. Any needed equipment and software will be ordered and tested on the network. The configuration of the network may be changed to minimize some threats. Once the hardware and software solutions are working the way the security team expected, enforcement of the configured policies takes place.

The job is still not complete. Once all of the tools are in place to protect the network from internal and external threats, the IT staff (either network administrators or security administrators) will monitor the tools to identify any threats or attacks that take place.

Beyond all of the steps listed so far is the ongoing task of protecting the network. Continuous testing of the *security boundaries* and scheduled reassessment opportunities must be part of the overall plan. The best plan in the world will not protect a network forever. As technology changes— seemingly at the speed of light—so do the opportunities for both internal and external hackers. The security team should plan on routine re-evaluation of the network security.

In this chapter, we will look at two ways to protect the network. First, we will look at the basic firewall as a way to create a secure boundary between the internal and external networks. Second, we will explore the proxy server as a means to further control access both inside and outside the network. As a final retrospect, we will explore the effect of firewall implementations on network and Internet communications.

The Firewall

Like a castle, every successful, well-protected network has a gatekeeper at the entrance who is suspicious of everyone who comes knocking at the door. With each visitor, the gatekeeper will check his list to see if the master will grant access across the bridge to the castle. Usually the gatekeeper will make the visitor identify herself and speak the special password. Only after going through these steps will the visitor be allowed into the castle, providing she has the right to be there.

Although this description is reminiscent of a children's story, it paints the picture of the network boundary when it is protected. The gatekeeper for a network may take many forms. It may be software-based or hardware-based. In today's technology, the entity that often plays the role of gatekeeper is the *firewall.*

A firewall is defined as a system (or group of systems) that prevents unauthorized access to private network resources from Internet users. Some firewalls can also restrict traffic going out to the Internet from the private network. Typically the firewall consists of both software and hardware. In an enterprise environment, the firewall has many hardware components. The most common basic firewall is the *border router.*

Security boundary

The defined endpoint of a private network.

Firewall

A system or group of systems that prevents unauthorized access to private resources or assets from the public (Internet) infrastructure.

Border router

A routing device that is specifically configured to prevent incoming access to a private network. A border router can be configured to exchange routing information with only those routers that form the border for an autonomous system or group of associated routers.

Firewalls implement some type of *access control list (ACL)*, or policy. That is really the key to firewall security. An administrator creates the access control list. Certain types of traffic can be blocked by router port. This creates a "packet filter" at the router to prevent unwanted traffic from moving onto the network. See Figure 10.2 for an example of a port filter used as a firewall. Following are some of the types of controls established by a firewall:

- Source address
- Destination address
- Source port
- Destination port
- The TCP, IP, UDP, or ICMP protocol type
- Status of the packet as inbound or outbound from the network

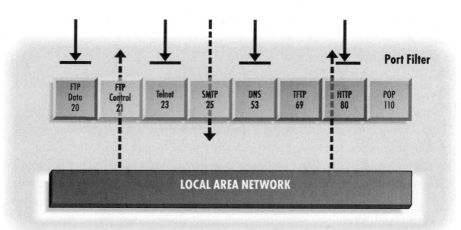

FIGURE 10.2
Inbound Port Filter

Table 10.1 pictures an example of a series of packet filters that allow only one client, 204.16.33.2, to download files from any Web server.

Rule	Direction	Source IP Address	Destination IP	Protocol	Source Port	Destination Port	Action
1	Out	204.16.33.2	External	TCP	>1024	80	Accept
2	In	External	Internal	TCP	80	>1024	Accept
3	Either	Any	Any	Any	Any	Any	Reject

TABLE 10.1
Packet Filter Table

The firewall that uses packet filtering determines an action based on network addresses and ports, not content. Therefore, this type of firewall cannot identify an attempt to breach the security of the network if the traffic complies with the access control list. Nor can the firewall identify a user who is authorized to cross the firewall. Only user authentication to the network can prevent unauthorized user invasion of the private network.

Earlier, we talked about the need to assess risk and build a business policy that protects the internal resources of a network as much as possible. That is the foundation of the access control policy. Once a business policy for risk management is in place, the controls of the access list are relatively easy to build. The enforcement of the business policy using firewall management is a hefty responsibility for any business. Typically, the network administrator handles this ongoing task.

WHAT THE FIREWALL CAN DO

Keep in mind that the general purpose of the firewall is to keep potential *hackers* out of the private network. Hackers are persistent and will continue to look for holes that allow access to interesting things behind the firewall. Often hackers will first locate an IP address where they believe an interesting computer might reside. They could get this information by doing a DNS lookup if the computer is hosting a service such as e-mail, Internet, or File Transfer Protocol (FTP). Then they will initiate a *port scan* against that system. When we discussed ports in an earlier chapter, we looked at the range of the 65,534 available ports. Ports 0 though 1023 are considered well-known ports; that is, they are universally used for the same services (for example, port 25 is for mail, port 80 is for HTTP services). A hacker merely has to run an automated scan against the computer to discover the open ports. From there, it is an easy step to access the internal resources.

To avoid a breach, your firewall will take one of two actions. A packet received from an intruder can generate an error response that says the packet was rejected if it does not match the access control list. This of course tells the intruder that a system does exist at the IP address they tried. Or the packet can be silently discarded and the intruder will assume that no computer owns that IP address—and presumably the intruder will then quit trying to invade the internal network.

On the flip side of this coin, an administrator configures a network to allow an external source appropriate access to network resources, such as Internet and e-mail services. The firewall can act as a corporate liaison to the Internet for those external users who are entitled access to specific resources. Often a company will store public information about the

Hacker

A clever programmer or computer technician who uses his or her skills to gain unauthorized access to a network's resources or assets.

Port scan ✓

A simple computer program that identifies those ports that are open to traffic from the public internetwork.

corporation, support documentation about products, bug-fixes, and so on for customers in a neutral space. The firewall allows the enterprise to build a safe area for these resources that business partners and customers can also access.

Firewalls can protect against unwarranted access by inappropriate users by closing all ports that are not critical, thus securing the network's resources. Some firewall access control lists permit only e-mail traffic (TCP port 25) inbound to the network. The only vulnerable resource then is the e-mail server itself. The network suffers no damage when the e-mail server is attacked except to have that service interrupted. Firewalls also provide a network with a single *choke point,* where security policies can be enforced and *auditing logs* can be enabled. The auditing logs give the administrator a clear view of what types of threats may be lurking just outside the network's gates, thereby providing another means to identify additional risks. Logs and summary reports may also tell the administrator the types of traffic (both inbound and outbound), the amount of traffic, and the number of illicit access attempts from the outside.

WHAT THE FIREWALL CANNOT DO

A firewall cannot protect against every possible threat. Access to network resources through a dial-in modem cannot be tracked or prevented with a firewall. Modem access to individual computers in a corporate network leaves the door wide open to unauthorized use. Remote access service (RAS) must also be guarded, and this is often outside the firewall boundary as well.

Firewalls cannot protect against internal thugs and thieves. When additional security constraints are added to the network, employees may view the new boundaries as a threat to their environment. Disgruntled employees may find a way around the constraints to sabotage the network. Or, an employee may unwittingly give away his password. Contractors and consultants are also a source of concern in many networks. Often they need extended access to resources to complete a project, and with that comes the risk that the extended access allows too much freedom within the network. Training helpdesk personnel to make sure the request for a password change is coming from a legitimate user can also protect network resources. Many a call to the helpdesk for this type of action comes from a hacker just waiting to breach the firewall. In situations like these, only well-trained technicians, not the firewall, can prevent intrusion.

Choke point

The location on a network (usually at a router) where a security policy and access control list (ACL) are enforced.

Auditing log

The recording of all defined actions by both inbound and outbound traffic.

With so many variations of destructive codes that can be embedded in e-mails, along with the loopholes in any network, a firewall cannot protect the network against viruses. Virus protection must be implemented on the network in the form of virus-checking software and employee education. By requiring virus-scanning software on all machines, the administrator can be alerted to problems before they get out of hand. If the administrator, in cooperation with the human resources department, makes employees aware that the vast majority of viruses are transmitted through floppy disks, much of the risk can be avoided.

Types of Firewalls

Two basic types of firewalls are implemented on today's networks: Network layer and Application layer.

NETWORK LAYER FIREWALLS

Network layer firewalls make their decision to allow or deny a packet based on the source address, destination address, or the port address. The router is the simplest form of a Network layer firewall because it looks at the source and destination addresses and makes decisions from that information. Although not a sophisticated form of firewall, it is fast by firewall standards and very transparent to users. As mentioned earlier, this type of firewall is often referred to as a packet-filtering firewall. Remember, a Network layer, packet-filtering firewall does not analyze traffic. It merely looks at the type of traffic (TCP, IP, HTTP, FTP, etc.) and makes a decision to allow the traffic or deny the traffic based on the rules in the access control list.

One form of Network layer firewall is the screened host firewall. In this case, all traffic passes through a single device known as a *bastion host* on its way to and from a single host device. The bastion host is outfitted with two network interface cards (NICs) to provide this service. See Figure 10.3 for the bastion host Network layer firewall.

Network layer firewall

A device that makes the decision to allow or deny a packet on the basis of the source address, destination address, or port address. It does not look at the content in the payload. Because it is using logical address information to make the decision, it takes its name from the Network layer of the OSI Model.

Bastion host

A single computer that is the only system exposed to the public infrastructure. All traffic will pass through this system and will be screened to determine if the traffic will be allowed to pass through to the private network. A bastion host is also known as a screened host firewall.

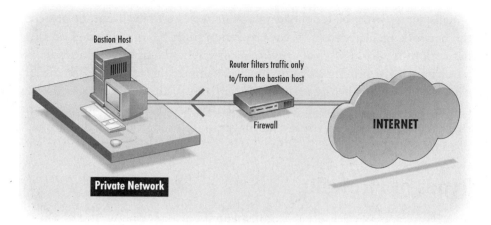

FIGURE 10.3
Screened Host Network Layer Firewall

A little later in this chapter, we will look at the demilitarized zone, another form of screening that creates a separate subnet to hold publicly used resources.

TEST TIP

For testing, be sure to understand that Network layer firewalls look only at the source and destination addresses in the packet to determine an allow or deny action, whereas Application layer firewalls can look at the payload as well as source and destination addresses.

APPLICATION LAYER FIREWALLS

An Application layer firewall involves some type of screening software that allows no traffic to pass directly between two networks. It acts as a gateway or translator between the two networks. This type of firewall usually performs extensive logging and auditing of any traffic passing through it, and it is commonly referred to as a *proxy firewall* because it acts on behalf of the internal client when establishing a connection with an external resource. Proxy or Application layer firewalls tend to decrease performance on the network because they scrutinize the incoming and outgoing traffic much more closely. See Figure 10.4 for a graphic depiction of an Application layer firewall.

Proxy firewall

A type of Application layer firewall in which a software screening program acts as a gateway, or translator, between two networks in order to protect an internal system when communicating with a system from the public side of the network.

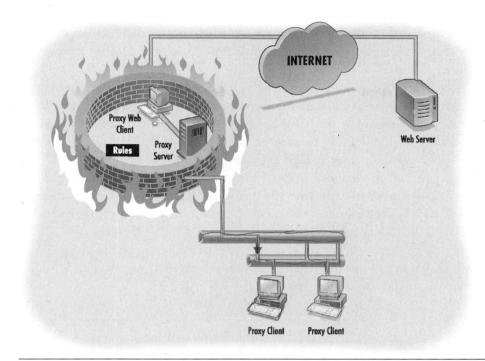

FIGURE 10.4
Application Layer (Proxy)
Firewall

Not only will the Application layer firewall look at the type of traffic, it will also analyze the packets for specific source addresses, destination ports, and content. This makes the Application layer firewall much more sophisticated (and slower).

Another type of Application layer firewall is a *dual-homed host firewall*. With a dual-homed host, two NICs are installed in the host machine. One NIC is connected to the private network, and the other NIC is connected to the public network. All traffic passes through this system to be compared against a list to determine whether the traffic will be allowed or denied to continue. This device will typically run a proxy service and will block most traffic coming through it.

Application layer firewalls often include other features to further protect the network. For instance, many proxy firewalls include Network Address Translation (NAT). By using private IP address schemes within the private network, and by providing a live address only at the door to the network, this procedure makes it more difficult for a hacker to access a known resource within the private boundary.

Some proxy firewalls also have the ability to cache Internet content, thus enhancing the performance to Internet resources. If the proxy service is part

Dual-homed host firewall

A type of Application layer firewall in which a computer or router has two NICs installed, one attached to the private network and one attached to the public network.

of a network operating system, it is often capable of filtering access to the Internet based on user account as well. It might also include a filter for the types of Internet sites the organization deems unacceptable. This type of service is known as *site blocking*.

The proxy or Application layer firewall is also application-specific. In other words, a proxy must exist for every protocol used. Robust proxy software will include a proxy for commonly used protocols, and it will often contain the code to build proxies for new protocols. Some of the commonly available proxies include HTTP, FTP, and SMTP proxies.

The proxy firewall also includes a *client-side application* that allows the desktop or laptop to work with the server proxy service. This means more work for the administrator: the client must be installed and configured prior to the user accessing an external resource. The Web browser (i.e., Internet Explorer or Netscape Navigator) must understand that an agent will act on behalf of the client when accessing external resources and receiving replies from those resources.

── TRY IT! ─────────────

If you are attached to a network and using Microsoft Internet Explorer as your browser, try this to see if your network uses a proxy to connect to the Internet.

1. Open Internet Explorer by double-clicking the desktop icon, or by starting the application by clicking Start/Programs/Internet Explorer.
2. Select Tools/Internet Options from the toolbar.
3. Click the Connections tab of the properties window.
4. Look for the button marked LAN Settings and click it once.
5. In the LAN Settings pop-up window, check the Proxy server section. If the box is checked and there is an IP address in the Address bar, you are using a proxy server to access resources on the Internet.
6. Click the Cancel button to return to the Connections tab.
7. Click the Cancel button to exit the properties window.

THE DEMILITARIZED ZONE (DMZ)

During a military conflict, a parcel of land may be set aside as a neutral area. This neutral area is known as a *demilitarized zone (DMZ)*. No military equipment or personnel may carry out the actions of conflict within this zone.

The DMZ in a network is also a neutral area. It is neither part of the internal network nor the external network (usually the Internet). This area is a subnetwork or subnetworks between two policy-enforcing hosts (routers, hardware firewalls, or Application layer firewalls).

The DMZ is the perfect place to put resources that should be available to the public but are still resources belonging to the network. For example, many network administrators create a DMZ for the organization's Web server and mail server. This allows traffic to pass back and forth to these services without risk to the internal LAN. In a large network, the DMZ may consist of several subnetworks instead of just one. See Figure 10.5 for a view of the DMZ.

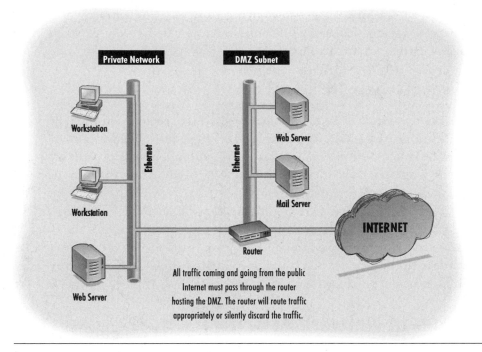

All traffic coming and going from the public Internet must pass through the router hosting the DMZ. The router will route traffic appropriately or silently discard the traffic.

FIGURE 10.5
The DMZ

THE EXTRANET

Another term you may hear from time to time is "extranet" (as opposed to intranet or Internet). The extranet is a specific part of a private network that makes use of the public infrastructure (the Internet) to share resources with business partners, suppliers, vendors, other businesses, or customers. Often very special types of resources reside in the extranet. For example, a company may provide post-installation support in the form of documents and white papers it chooses not to share with the general public. Or perhaps the extranet may store the collaborative projects shared by two or more businesses. Everyone involved in the projects must have access to the project and any resources needed to complete the project, but the general public should not have access to this information. The same is true for the services provided by one enterprise to a group of other businesses, such as an online banking program managed by one bank and used by many affiliated partners.

To protect resources, the extranet requires several key pieces. A firewall and management of the firewall server are needed. *Digital certificates* may be necessary to validate a user account for authentication into the network. The administrator may require encryption of any messages that are exchanged. Of course, the *virtual private network (VPN)* of many of today's operating systems and the public infrastructure may be required when accessing the extranet resources.

TROUBLESHOOTING FIREWALLS

If data communications are not taking place as expected, and the network has a hardware firewall, check the access control list to identify any misconfigured settings. Look for a "deny" setting that may prevent certain types of data, or data from certain locations, from passing through the firewall as expected.

In organizations that are using the Application layer firewall (proxy services), check to verify that the correct proxies are in place for the types of data that will need to pass through the proxy firewall. If a proxy did not come with the product purchased, it is often possible to write a proxy with utilities that are included with the software.

Types of Network Attacks

Several types of common network attacks occur every day.

DENIAL OF SERVICE

A *denial of service attack* is sometimes called the PING of Death. A PING packet, actually an Internet Control Message Protocol (ICMP) packet, can be sent to a host device to determine if that device is available. Four normal-sized packets are generated that attempt to contact the remote host. In a denial of service attack, one very large ICMP packet is sent to the remote device, flooding the buffer and preventing any other packets from

---

Digital certificate

A small file that records information such as an expiration date, serial number, name, public key, owner of the private key, and other critical information. This file is sent by a system acting as a certificate authority to a computer that needs to send data securely.

Virtual private network (VPN)

A connection between a source and a destination for transmitting data securely. This process uses tunneling protocols that encrypt the data during the sending process so that it cannot be read by any entity except for the destination system.

Denial of service attack

A network attack in which a rogue system sends a very large ICMP packet, or PING packet, to a destination, flooding the buffer of the destination system and preventing any other traffic from getting through. Also known as the PING of Death.

being processed. The remote host device may stop responding or reboot. This type of attack can disable a Web server or mail server in short order.

Many administrators block ICMP traffic to prevent this type of attack. The benefit is that a denial of service attack is then unlikely. The downside is that an administrator cannot test the viability of a mail or Web server from outside the network and must rely on technicians inside the network to determine if the service is available.

IP SPOOFING

With *IP spoofing*, a hacker will initiate a communication with a remote host device using an address that belongs to another entity—perhaps one that is trusted by the network. A packet-filtering firewall will not be able to determine that this is a false address and will allow the packet to pass, giving a hacker access to private network resources. Some types of firewalls can prevent this type of attack.

IP spoofing

A network attack in which a hacker uses fake credentials to communicate with a remote destination system. The credentials used will belong to another known and accepted system.

SYN FLOOD

A *SYN flood* is similar to a denial of service attack. In normal communications, the first packet in a series has the SYN flag set to on (1). This signals a new conversation. All packets that follow in the series will have the SYN flag set to off (0). In a SYN flood, however, a huge number of packets all with the SYN flag set to on (1) are sent to a remote host. Because computers will respond to a packet with the SYN flag on, the host attempts to respond to all of these SYN packets. Consequently, all other incoming packets are ignored until the SYN packets in the flood have gotten a response, thus creating a situation in which service is denied to all other communications. Some operating systems are now providing patches to help with the SYN flood attack.

SYN flood

A network attack in which a source node sends requests for TCP connections to a destination node at a rate that is faster than the destination can process the requests. The flood that results causes a denial of service.

Implementations of Network Security

Now that the terms "firewall" and "proxy" have taken on new meaning, what can this do for the private network and how will the implementation affect performance for users?

As mentioned earlier, the choice to add firewall protection into the network is really just a part of the business security plan. When choosing a firewall solution, the network administrator must look at how to implement protection while still providing a secure boundary to the network.

If an access control list (on a router with a packet-filtering firewall) is designed correctly, it will permit the common types of traffic for both outbound and inbound connections. The router (as firewall) will use a *dynamic state list* to track all sessions between hosts on the inside of the network and hosts on the outside of the firewall. The list is dynamic in that it changes as sessions are added and dropped during the normal course of communication. Only packets that are part of a recognized, active session are permitted to cross from outside the network to the inside. A host on the private network must initiate the session. If a packet comes from the public network and a current session cannot be identified for that packet, or it is not destined for a publicly available resource, the packet will be silently discarded.

When deploying the proxy firewall on a network boundary, the administrator and the team must be aware that it will cause degradation in performance. One of two philosophies is used when implementing the proxy firewall. Either access is blocked to all outside communication except for those few protocols the administrator allows, or nothing is blocked except for a few protocols (and sites, in the case of most proxy software). In either case, care must be taken to give the appropriate access while tightening up the boundary.

The proxy service is also a translator. Its job is to translate between the public and private network, keeping track of valid conversations between internal and external hosts. The private IP addresses are frequently used for the internal network addressing scheme, with one or more valid, routable addresses on the public side. Each request for communication must have an entry in the table. The proxy server spends a lot of power, time, and memory keeping track of the communication and translating internal addresses to appropriate external addresses when requests are made from the private internetwork. All that translating can slow down network performance, just as speaking in a foreign language can slow down a conversation with a friend if one of you does not speak the language and you need someone else to translate the conversation. This *latency* must be considered before implementation.

Before any firewall solution is implemented, all options for network security must be considered. Many operating systems now have built-in firewall capability. The enforcement of password policies, the use of a computer not belonging to the user, and the use of RAS and modems for access from the outside should be explored before implementation.

Finally, once the firewall or proxy is in place, that does not mean you can set it and forget it. Ongoing testing schedules must be built. Testing will give you an opportunity to check on new types of attacks and assess your network security plan.

Dynamic state list

A table that will track all sessions (or conversations) between hosts on the inside of the network and hosts on the outside of the network.

Latency

The delay, or amount of time, it takes for a data packet to get from one point to another.

Public versus Private Networks

STUDY GUIDE

In this chapter, we learned about the need to distinguish between the private network and the public network to protect the assets of an organization. Here are some key points to remember.

BOUNDARIES BETWEEN PUBLIC AND PRIVATE NETWORKS

- Among the most precious assets of a company is the data it is has amassed by doing business, and those assets must be protected.
- The boundary between the private network and the public network (Internet) is defined as the point where the LAN may access the Internet. That might be through a router or some kind of telephone device.

ASSESSING RISK

- Many people within a company have a stake in protecting the company's assets. Those stakeholders include network administrators, IT managers, security managers, technicians, financial managers, and upper management.
- Before putting any kind of network boundary protection into place, a business or organization must build a set of documents that identify two types of risk: internal and external.
- Internal risk includes any threat by those who use the private network resources: employees, contractors, and consultants.
- External risk includes any threat from people or devices that exists outside the physical boundary of the LAN. The term used to describe a threatening entity is "hacker."
- The value of the private network resources must be clarified. The value includes the cost of data loss as well as service interruption for employees and customers.
- Once the risks and value of assets have been determined, a security policy can be written to protect the network. All stakeholders in the organization must agree to enforce this policy from top down and bottom up. All employees must be subject to the same policy.
- After the policy has been written, a series of recommendations are made to enforce the policy. These may include training for new and existing employees, identification of external resources and Web sites that are unacceptable to the business, and what types of remote access the network will support (VPN using the public infrastructure, modem

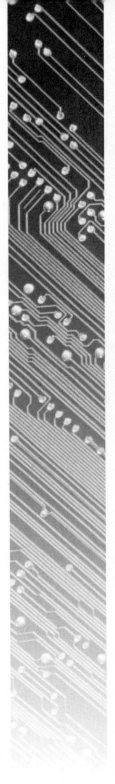

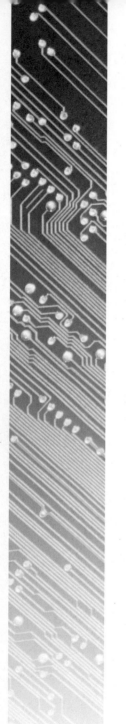

connections to a central gateway, or individual modem installations on individual workstations within the private network).

- All policies must be tested before they are implemented to ensure that employees can still do the job for the company.
- After implementing the security policy, the boundaries must be continuously monitored for attempted invasion.

THE FIREWALL

- A firewall is defined as a system (or group of systems) that prevents unauthorized access to private network resources from Internet users.
- Firewalls are often formed by a combination of hardware and software.
- All firewalls implement some kind of access control list or policy.

The most common firewall is the router.

- Routers have the ability to make decisions about whether a packet may enter the network based on
  - source and destination addresses.
  - source and destination port.
  - the TCP, IP, UDP, or ICMP protocol type.
  - the status of the packet as inbound or outbound from the network.
- This decision is known as packet filtering.
- The business security policy is the foundation of the access control list on the router.

What the Firewall Can Do

- The firewall takes one of two actions against a packet that does not comply with the access control list on a particular interface: it silently discards the packet or it generates an error message that is sent back to the source address on the packet.
- By silently discarding the packet, a would-be hacker concludes that the device he was trying to attack is not available on the network.
- When an error message is sent back to the source address, the would-be hacker is alerted to the fact that the system is indeed alive, but it does not exist at the IP address in the destination portion of the header. The hacker now will try other IP addresses to get into the network.
- Firewalls can protect the network by maintaining a list of ports that may not be accessed by inbound packets. Only those ports that are necessary for services will remain open, such as mail (port 25) or HTTP services (port 80).

Public versus Private Networks

- Firewalls are often called the "choke point" for the network because all incoming and outgoing traffic must be scrutinized in one central location.

What the Firewall Cannot Do

- A firewall cannot protect from an internally generated attack against resources.
- A firewall cannot protect against any attack that is initiated through a modem connected to an individual workstation within the private network.
- Firewalls cannot protect against social engineering attacks like password giveaway or impersonation to a helpdesk representative.
- Firewalls cannot protect against viruses. Certain types of traffic may be denied because of the access control list, but many viruses are not using extraordinary protocol types to do damage.

TYPES OF FIREWALLS

The Network Layer Firewall

- The Network layer firewall makes decisions to allow or deny packets on the basis of source and destination address and port address.
- The Network layer firewall cannot explore content within the payload of the packet.
- The screened host firewall is a single device through which all traffic passes on its way to a single host within the private network.
- The screened host firewall uses a bastion host. This machine will have two or more NICs.

Application Layer Firewalls

- Application layer firewalls use some type of software as well as hardware to screen incoming requests and packets to the network.
- An advantage to Application layer firewalls is that they often provide extensive logging and auditing of traffic as well as payload scrutiny for incoming packets. Additional services may include proxy services, NAT, and content caching.
- A proxy firewall creates a table of outgoing packets with source addresses belonging to the private network that are mapped (or assigned) to a public IP address for routing on the Internet. This type of firewall acts on behalf of the internal client.

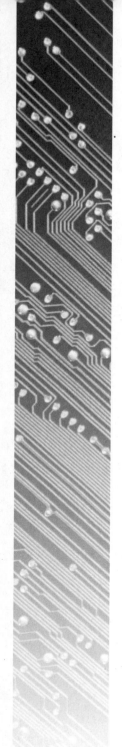

- Proxy firewalls require additional configuration at the client workstation by an administrator or technician.
- Another type of Application layer firewall is the dual-homed host. Two NICs are installed on the host machine and traffic is routed between the two NICs.
- Site-blocking firewalls have the capacity to prevent packets from using certain public resources. This may include specific IP addresses or DNS names, or sites with certain key words in the site name.
- Proxy Application layer firewalls are application-specific and require that a proxy exist for the application type. Examples include maintaining proxies for services such as HTTP, FTP, and SMPT. Most proxy services include the code to build additional proxies.

The Demilitarized Zone (DMZ)

- Many network administrators choose to create a subnetwork that is outside the boundary of the private network to contain an organization's resources. This is referred to as the demilitarized zone (DMZ).
- When using a DMZ, resources such as Web servers, FTP servers, and mail servers can be placed where they will create no harm to the private network should there be an attack to the resources.

The Extranet

- The extranet is a section of the private network that is outside the boundary of the private network but that contains resources owned by the private network.
- The extranet differs from the DMZ in that it offers shared resources to known business partners, suppliers, vendors, other businesses, or customers. Typically those services include data, storage for collaborative projects, or technical reference material.
- The extranet requires additional resources that a DMZ does not require. In addition to the routers acting as firewalls, digital certificates for authentication must be distributed to external hosts using the services. Encryption facilities may be required to protect the data during transit. VPN technology may be used to further protect messages passed between hosts.

TYPES OF NETWORK ATTACKS

- Denial of service attacks are sometimes called the PING of Death. A normal PING packet is a packet that uses ICMP to determine the viability of a host. Four return messages are generated that track the

Public versus Private Networks

response from the destination host.

- With denial of service attacks, one very large ICMP packet is sent from the source host to the destination host. This packet floods the buffer, causing any other requests to be blocked. Often the destination host will stall or reboot, causing service disruption to other requests coming into the machine.
- Many administrators block ICMP packets to prevent this attack.
- IP spoofing occurs when a hacker uses a false source address to get into a network. The source address is often one that belongs to the private network.
- A packet-filtering firewall cannot determine that this is an unwanted packet because the source address seems in order.
- Some types of firewalls can block this type of attack.
- A SYN flood looks like a denial of service attack. The first packet in a conversation between two hosts has the SYN flag set to on. This signals the request for a new conversation. In a SYN flood, huge numbers of packets will be sent to a destination host. The host will attempt to answer all incoming requests, thus preventing the machine from answering valid requests. This creates a denial of service.
- Some operating systems provide patches to prevent this type of attack.

IMPLEMENTATIONS OF NETWORK SECURITY

- The implementation of firewall technology and other security policies can have adverse as well as beneficial results.
- Access control lists, if written incorrectly, may prevent private network users from doing their jobs adequately. The lists must also be maintained for changes in the network.
- Proxy firewalls are really gateways, or translators. All gateway mechanisms impact network performance negatively. A certain amount of performance degradation should be anticipated and compensated for when using a proxy firewall.
- All firewall implementations require constant monitoring, logging, auditing, maintenance, and updating to keep performance at the best levels possible.

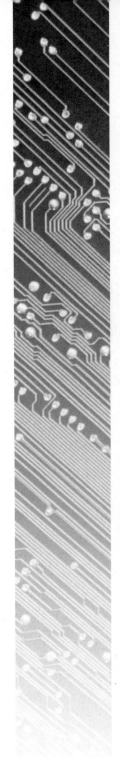

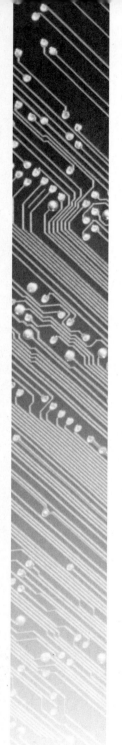

PRACTICE TEST

Try this practice test to check your mastery of the concepts in this chapter.

1. Which of the following are types of firewalls? (Choose two)
   a. packet filtering
   b. digital filtering
   c. filtering
   d. proxy service
   e. translator filtering
   f. Session layer

2. What is a firewall?
   a. a piece of software used for record keeping
   b. a system of hardware and software that blocks or permits designated traffic between networks
   c. a physical barrier to the network, usually made of concrete blocks
   d. a team of managers who make policies

3. Which of the following are characteristics of the private network? (Choose three)
   a. Host device IP addresses are exposed to the Internet.
   b. Host device IP addresses are not exposed to the Internet.
   c. Network resources are accessible from the Internet.
   d. Network resources are not accessible from the Internet.
   e. IP addresses used by host devices must be registered addresses.
   f. IP addresses used by host devices may be from the private address ranges.

4. Which kind of firewall would you use if you wanted users on the private network to be able to send and receive e-mail, but you did not want them to be able to browse any resources on the Web?
   a. packet filtering
   b. digital filtering
   c. analog filtering
   d. payload filtering

5. The purpose of a proxy server is to
   a. protect external users from the hackers inside the network.
   b. make users miserable because they cannot surf the Web.
   c. protect system data inside the network.
   d. make business partners unhappy because it takes so long to access extranet resources.

6. A firewall can read the payload of a packet to determine whether the packet should be allowed into the private network.
   a. True
   b. False

7. Which of the following are the two purposes of a firewall? (Choose two)
   a. verify the Web site is considered appropriate for the business
   b. block traffic
   c. permit traffic
   d. translate between external and internal resources

8. When determining the need for a firewall, the first step should be to
   a. assess traffic patterns on the LAN.
   b. assess the value of the private network resources.
   c. assess the risk to the network
   d. assess the users' tolerance of performance degradation.

9. When using a proxy server, which of the following services will you have available to the network? (Choose all that apply)
   a. packet filtering
   b. content caching
   c. Network Address Translation (NAT)
   d. site blocking
   e. All of the above

10. A user installs a modem in his workstation at the office because he wants to access data from home and the firewall will not permit this action. Which kind of network threat has been uncovered here?
    a. external threat
    b. hacker threat
    c. user threat
    d. internal threat

11. When a packet-filtering firewall is implemented on the network, which key element controls what types of traffic can enter and leave the private network?
    a. data value
    b. risk assessment
    c. access control list
    d. access denial list

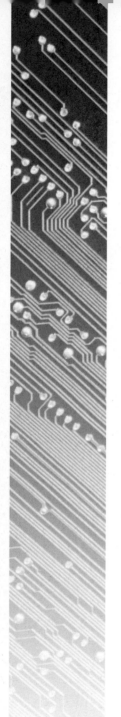

12. What key elements are used by the packet-filtering firewall to determine whether a packet may cross the threshold into the private network? (Choose all that apply)
    a. destination port
    b. TCP protocol type
    c. access control list method
    d. source address
    e. carrier type
    f. platform type
    g. inbound or outbound status of the packet

13. A firewall has the ability to prevent virus infestations on the private network.
    a. True
    b. False

14. If a firewall receives a packet that does not comply with the access control list, what will the firewall do with the packet? (Choose two)
    a. Broadcast a message to the entire LAN, letting all devices know an attack on the network is imminent.
    b. Send an error message to the source device indicating the packet did not reach its destination.
    c. Silently discard the packet.
    d. Generate a TCP packet that is placed in the router's memory.

15. Which of the following types of firewall setups uses a bastion host?
    a. screened private network
    b. screened subnetwork
    c. screened switches
    d. host

16. The extranet is the same as the screened subnetwork.
    a. True
    b. False

17. To make proxy firewalls more efficient, which of the following services is part of a proxy system? (Choose two)
    a. user password caching
    b. content caching
    c. DNS caching
    d. IP address caching

18. A large enterprise network would like to provide information services to the public internetwork, including a Web site and an FTP server for document downloads. The administrator also must protect the resources of the private network from would-be attack. Which of the following is a solution to this dilemma?
    a. the extranet
    b. the intranet
    c. the demilitarized zone
    d. the militarized zone

19. The mail server resides on a screened subnetwork. Suddenly, no mail is arriving or leaving the network. The server appears to be stalled. Which type of attack to this network resource appears to be the cause?
    a. SYN flood
    b. FIN flood
    c. denial of service
    d. hack attack
    e. IP spoofing

20. A hacker sending an extra large _____ packet creates a denial of service attack.
    a. PING
    b. TCP
    c. IP
    d. ICMP

TROUBLESHOOTING

1. The small business network that you help out with from time to time uses a cable modem router. The Internet access that is provided is permanent. The president of the company calls to tell you that suddenly the users cannot send or receive e-mail. What is the problem?

2. A company's management team is afraid of a hacker's gaining access to the private resources of the network. The administrator has installed a packet-filtering firewall to control traffic access. In building the access control list, the administrator has decided to block all incoming and outgoing traffic at port 80 and above. What would be the result of this entry in the ACL?

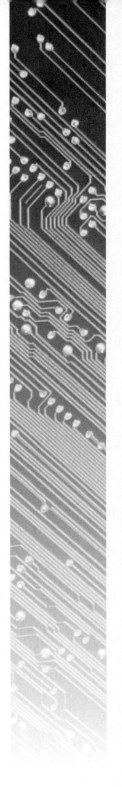

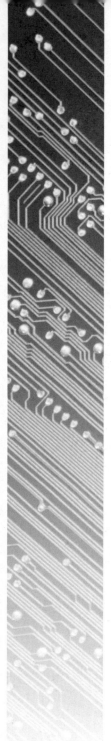

CUSTOMER SERVICE

1. A user calls to tell you that she cannot get Internet access from her desktop workstation. The IT department installed an upgraded version of the operating system and the Microsoft Office Products on her machine overnight. This was done by first wiping the machine clean and reinstalling. All other users on her subnetwork can get to external resources. Where is the problem with her machine?

2. All at once, many users contact the helpdesk technicians, each with the same story. Suddenly, no one could access Internet Web sites. The firewall router is functional. An administrator was doing some maintenance on the router just a short time ago. Where should the administrator start in troubleshooting the users' problems?

FOR MORE INFORMATION

For links to Web sites that provide further information about the topics covered in this chapter, go to the EMC/Paradigm Internet Resource Center at www.emcp.com/College Division/Internet Resource Centers/Networking/System Administration/Web Resources: For More Information.

Public versus Private Networks

WAN Technologies

Network+ Examination
- **Objective 2.11:** Identify the basic characteristics (e.g., speed, capacity, media) of the following WAN technologies:
  - Packet switching vs. circuit switching
  - ISDN
  - FDDI
  - ATM
  - Frame Relay
  - SONet/SDH
  - T1/E1
  - T3/E3
  - OCx

ON THE JOB

In today's business market, virtually every business you encounter makes use of some kind of wide area network technology. It may be as simple as connecting one office to the Internet, or as complex as connecting many international sites. As a technician, it is important that you understand the technologies used to provide these interconnections and what considerations can influence decisions to use one or the other for a particular situation.

Wide Area Network (WAN) Technologies

Wide area network (WAN)

A data communications network that spans a large geographic area and usually makes use of third-party transmission facilities or infrastructures, discretely integrating remote LANs into the structure.

Local area network (LAN)

A physical data communications infrastructure that is usually contained in a small geographic area such as an office, a floor of a building, or a whole building.

Campus area network (CAN)

A physical data communications infrastructure that is usually limited to a set of buildings in very close geographic proximity, such as buildings on a college campus.

Metropolitan area network (MAN)

A physical data communications infrastructure that involves one or more networks that work together to provide access and services in a geographic area.

To discuss the technology of *wide area networks (WANs)*, we must begin with a clear definition. A WAN is a data communications network that spans a large geographic area and usually makes use of the transmission facilities of third-party vendors. A WAN discretely integrates the *local area networks (LANs), campus area networks (CANs), metropolitan area networks (MANs),* and other WANs through the use of complex groups of equipment and services. The third-party vendors are referred to as common carriers, which include the various telephone company networks. The functions of WAN technologies are clustered in the lowest three layers of the OSI Model. See Figure 11.1 for a graphic depiction of a WAN.

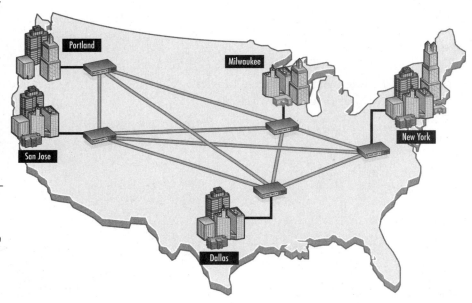

FIGURE 11.1
A Wide Area Network

A WAN may be as simple as connecting two geographically distant locations via a phone line and modem. Other technologies may be used for more complex organizations attempting to connect many locations.

A WAN provides a business with a means to connect remote geographic locations so they can share information. For example, a university may have many campus locations. One of those locations (the main campus) functions as the hub of operations, housing all of the records for students, student loan data, course curricula, and course documents. From a business perspective, the university would waste precious money if it had to duplicate all that information at every location. The additional cost of hardware and personnel to maintain the duplicate data would be prohibitive. On top of that, add the task and cost of making sure all the information is synchronized to avoid corrupt data.

The university has another alternative: it could build its own physical network, laying cable and providing the other necessary hardware to connect each location in a WAN. The WAN would offer a simpler, more cost-effective way to share all the information, especially considering that the infrastructure already exists through telephone carriers.

Switching Technologies

Two distinct types of switching technologies have evolved over the brief history of wide area networking: circuit switching and packet switching.

Circuit Switching

In data communications, a *circuit* is a path (usually a physical path) between two or more communicating entities. The pathway may include intermediate *circuit switching* stations. Often the pathway is created at the start of a conversation. That circuit is then reserved for the duration of that single conversation.

The circuit may also be pre-reserved, like a dedicated or leased line contract, awaiting data transmission.

Circuit

A pathway between two or more communicating entities.

Circuit switching

The process of moving data through a public infrastructure on a pathway reserved for the duration of that communication. The circuit may be pre-reserved or created at the start of communication.

Virtual Circuits

Some circuits are logical. That is, they represent a path between two points but are not fixed on one physical path; rather, they may include many physical paths for the data to travel. These are called *virtual circuits*. The two most common types of virtual circuits are permanent and switched.

- *Permanent virtual circuits (PVCs)* guarantee that a specified amount of bandwidth will always be available between two communication points. This eliminates the need to reserve a specific pathway in advance. PVCs are used exclusively for data transfer in situations where data transfer is fairly constant.

- *Switched virtual circuits (SVCs)* are created dynamically each time a host wants to communicate with another node. The SVC goes through three steps in its lifetime: the circuit is requested and established; data is transferred; and the circuit is terminated when the data transfer is complete. This type of virtual circuit is used in situations where data transfer is sporadic or inconsistent.

Circuit switching is a very common method used to build communication networks. It is also very familiar because it is the basis of the plain old telephone service (POTS), sometimes called the public switched telephone network (PSTN). In a circuit switched network, many users can share the same equipment and the same physical infrastructure. Each user is assured that a circuit will be available when needed. Essentially, every telephone customer gets exclusive use of two copper wires (the extension of the copper wires used by the connector and jack for your home telephone) from the source of the telephone call to the destination of the telephone call. See Figure 11.2 for telephone transmission using circuit switching.

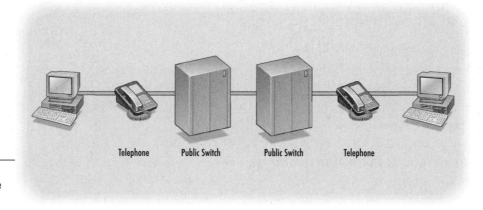

Telephone   Public Switch   Public Switch   Telephone

FIGURE 11.2
A Public Switched Telephone Network

Here is the step-by-step process to negotiate transmission in a circuit switched network:

1. The user requests the use of the circuit (the telephone number is dialed, to use the telephone analogy).
2. The destination address (or number dialed) is communicated to the local switching node.
3. A path to the destination is identified, and all intermediary switches are notified.
4. The circuit is established and is ready for use.
5. The data is sent (or the conversation takes place).
6. Once the data has been sent (or the conversation is over), a message is sent along the circuit to notify the intermediary devices that the circuit is no longer needed and can be used by another requestor.

Circuit switching does involve some time delays because it takes time to set up the circuit from source to destination. If the path is from one side of the room to another, the time needed to build the circuit is very short. But if the path is from Chicago to London, the time delay may actually be noticeable to the user. Newer equipment shortens the time delay, but not all legs of the path may have newer equipment.

PACKET SWITCHING

Packet switching is similar to the type of transmissions used on local area networks. The message from the source is broken into smaller pieces called packets. Each packet receives a header containing the source address and the destination address as well as a sequence number. The sequence number is a critical component for reassembling the packets once they have reached their destination. This is because when the packets that form the whole message are sent, there is no guarantee that every packet will take the same path from source to destination. The intervening routers make route decisions moment to moment, always choosing the most efficient path for the packet. If a router is notified that the path the last packet used has become extremely congested, the router may choose another less-congested route so that the packet will get to the destination efficiently.

The use of several routes to get a series of message packets from source to destination means that the packets will most likely arrive at different times and certainly not in the order in which they were first created. This is the reason every packet has a sequence number in the header. The packet can be reassembled in the correct order once it arrives. This also lets the

Packet Switching

The process of moving data through a public infrastructure when the path has not been predetermined at the outset of the communication. The first packet in a connection may take a different route from the second, third, and fourth packets.

destination know if a packet is missing, which would prevent the message from being correctly reassembled.

With packet switching, there is no time delay to set up a circuit. Packets are sent, usually with no guarantee of delivery (but generally all packets arrive at the destination). Routing decisions are made nanosecond by nanosecond, using the information provided by RIP (Routing Information Protocol) or OSPF (Open Shortest Path First) routing protocols, providing the most efficient path for the packets. Some time is spent identifying a path for each packet in the message, but this is usually not noticeable to the user.

WHICH SWITCHING METHOD IS BETTER?

The question of which switching method is better can be resolved only by looking at the benefits of each type.

The benefits of circuit switching include:
- a guaranteed pathway for the data;
- a guaranteed portion of the bandwidth available for transmission;
- smaller packets, because source and destination information are not needed in the header. (Only the circuit number is needed, so that intervening devices will recognize to which message the packet belongs.)

The benefits of packet switching include:
- the public infrastructure can be used for data transmission instead of incurring the expense for dedicated links between locations;
- resources such as bandwidth are used more fairly and efficiently in packet switching;
- pipelining, the ability to simultaneously use a communication link for two or more transmissions, increases the efficiency of use for the available bandwidth.

Each business or enterprise must evaluate the goals of WAN communications against the cost of the links to carry out the plan. In the following sections, we will look at many types of options available for WAN connectivity.

TEST TIP

As you move through the concepts in this chapter, be sure to remember the advantages and disadvantages of each technology, including comparable speed and availability.

WAN Technologies

Integrated Services Digital Network (ISDN)

Integrated Services Digital Network (ISDN) is the least costly form of digital communications on the market today. ISDN uses traditional telephone networks to provide a maximum bandwidth capacity of 1.544Mbps.

To understand the importance of ISDN, think about how data communications carried over common carriers originally worked. The digital data from the LAN went to a modem. At the modem, the digital data was converted to analog format and sent to the local loop. At some point in the path to the destination, the data would again be converted to digital and then back to analog at the last leg of the path. The modem on the other side of the conversation converts that analog data back to a digital format that the local network can use. ISDN eliminates all of this converting. The digital data from the network is transmitted in digital format to the destination.

ISDN uses two types of channels to carry data. The bearer channel (B channel) carries either voice or data (the payload). The data channel (D channel) is used for communication control information, such as call setup, timing, and disconnection of the call.

When purchasing ISDN services, the telephone carrier will offer two types of interfaces, which are distinguished by the amount of available bandwidth:

- *Basic rate interface (BRI)* provides 2 B channels at 64Kbps and 1 D channel at 16Kbps, for a total data transfer rate of 128Kbps.
- *Primary rate interface (PRI)* allocates 23 B channels at 64Kbps and 1 D channel at 64Kbps, for a total of 1.544Mbps bandwidth.

ISDN is a digital networking solution with all of the benefits of digital technology:

- Data capacity to service many users at the same time.
- Voice and data transmission over the same physical media at the same time, because one of the two channels of the BRI can be switched to voice if a call comes in.
- Video conferencing.
- Widespread availability.
- Cost-effective solution for small businesses and home offices.

To implement ISDN, all it takes is a call to the local telephone company. The company will schedule an installation and will usually provide the ISDN router for your home or business. Although ISDN is essentially an "on-demand" service (the ISDN router will dial when it receives a packet

---

Integrated Services Digital Network (ISDN)

A communications standard that allows digital signals to pass through existing PSTN lines.

Basic rate interface (BRI)

A telephone carrier interface that provides 2 B (bearer) channels for data transmission and 1 D (data) channel for control information transmission. Speed for BRI is 128Kbps.

Primary rate interface (PRI)

A telephone carrier interface that provides 23 B channels for data transmission and 1 D channel for control information transmission.

with a destination address outside the local network), the telephone company will charge a flat monthly fee for this service. Installation of ISDN is not restricted by distance from the local central office. As long as a local carrier with the ability to support digital transmission is available, ISDN should also be available.

One other consideration should be noted. The number of subscribers does not affect the bandwidth available for ISDN transmission. Because the same wiring carries both ISDN and telephone service, circuits and bandwidth should always be available.

Fiber Distributed Data Interface (FDDI)

Fiber Distributed Data Interface (FDDI)

A high-speed networking standard originally designed for fiber-optic cable.

Fiber Distributed Data Interface (FDDI) is a set of standards built by the International Organization for Standardization (ISO) and the American National Standards Institute (ANSI) to provide the guidelines for data transmission over fiber-optic cable. FDDI specifies a dual-ring physical configuration capable of token passing at a rate of 100Mbps.

Fiber-optic cable has extremely high capacity, so a network that is using fiber and FDDI as its protocol can service thousands of users over great distances. Fiber and FDDI is frequently used for the backbone of an enterprise network or for a WAN. The dual-ring formation of FDDI provides fault tolerance. The data transmitted in the two rings flows in opposite directions. During normal operations, one ring is considered primary and will be responsible for data transmission. The other ring remains idle. Should a fault occur with the primary ring, the second ring will close the gap at the fault and take over network operations and data flow, providing minimal downtime and little or no loss of service (see Figure 11.3).

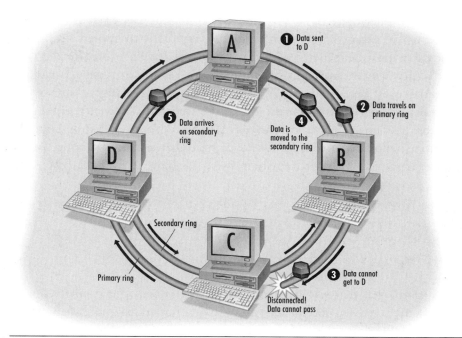

When a critical station or a cable connection fails in a FDDI network, the ring will "wrap" to counteract the failure. This means that the ring closes the "hole" to complete itself, and the ring and the network resume functioning for the users. A repair can be made to the failed station or cable segment, bringing the second fault tolerant ring back into production (see Figure 11.4).

FIGURE 11.3
Counter-Rotating FDDI Rings

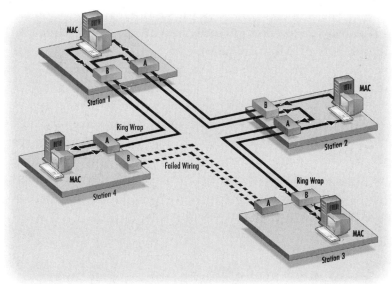

FIGURE 11.4
FDDI Network "Wrap" at Cable
or Station Failure

Although fiber-optic cable and the FDDI protocol have been around for more than 10 years, this type of network is very costly to implement. Fiber-optic cable must be installed with care by knowledgeable professionals. The light source for data transmission in fiber-optic cable is extremely hazardous to human eyes. Because the cable itself has a glass core, it is very susceptible to breakage. Any bends in the cable must be within the tolerance of the cable or the damage caused can severely diminish or prevent throughput. As mentioned above, fiber and FDDI are commonly used for backbone implementations, but they are seldom used as cabling to the desktop.

Synchronous Optical Network/Synchronous Digital Hierarchy (SONet/SDH) and Optical Carrier x (OC-x)

The technologies that support and use the global fiber-optic transmission network are so closely interrelated that they cannot and should not be separated in a conversation. Speaking of one without the other is nearly impossible. So here we look at the pieces that make the fiber-optic internetworks function.

SYNCHRONOUS OPTICAL NETWORK (SONET)

Synchronous Optical Network (SONet)

The standard for data transmission over optical media as defined by the American National Standards Institute (ANSI).

Synchronous structure

A reference to the way in which digital signals in SONet transition to indicate 1s and 0s during transmission. In a synchronous structure, the transitions always occur at exactly the same rate.

Jitter

A deviation in the pulsing of digital signals. Jitter can be thought of as a signal with the "shakes."

Synchronous Optical Network (SONet) defines the standards for optical carrier levels and synchronous transport signals for the infrastructure running over fiber-optic media. SONet has evolved as the backbone media protocol for many large enterprise networks. Speeds ranging from 51.8Mbps to 39813.1Mbps are possible.

SONet uses multiplexing to make use of every bit of available bandwidth while still getting a packet from source to destination the fastest way. This allows SONet to use low-level digital signals and a *synchronous structure.* The term "synchronous structure" refers to the transitions in the digital signals such that they occur at exactly the same rate. The phase of the signal may vary, but the variance is always within a predetermined tolerance. The causes of phase differences are *jitter* (electromagnetic wave variations caused by vibration and voltage fluctuations) and *propagation time delays* (the delay in time to get data into the transmission path).

WAN Technologies

Synchronization is achieved by using the clocking signal within a data stream. The clocking signal is really just a series of repetitive pulses, much like a second hand on a watch. The clocking signal keeps the bit rate of the transmission constant and tells where the 1s and 0s are located within the data stream.

SONet also defines the technology for transmitting many signals of differing capacities through the optical hierarchy. Here is where SONet makes use of *multiplexing.*

In Real Life

With multiplexing, the diverse signals are grouped (or aggregated) into a single signal for transmission. At the receiving end, the diverse signals are once again split into the individual bands. One example of multiplexing outside the computer world is the television signal. Many channels (or bands) are transmitted as a single signal that is separated by your television receiver so you can view CBS, NBC, ABC, the Food Network, and so forth.

SONet is a logical carrier for asynchronous transfer mode (ATM) signals because of its large capacity as well as its synchronization and multiplexing capabilities.

SYNCHRONOUS DIGITAL HIERARCHY (SDH)

The *Synchronous Digital Hierarchy (SDH)* was the result of several standards organizations defining the specific synchronization standards that would become a global set of transmission hierarchies. Transmission standards were developed in different parts of the world as separate entities. As the technology increased, countries needed one set of standards to provide the infrastructure for global communications, so the SDH became important. Globally, the infrastructure is held to the same parameters, making data flow consistent throughout the world. Because SONet falls within the parameters set by the SDH, it is sometimes considered a subset of SDH.

THE OPTICAL CARRIER (OC)

The optical carrier (OC) capacity standards are based on the synchronous transport signal (STS) used by SONet. STS has many different levels, beginning with STS-1, which defines a rate of transfer at 51.84Mbps.

Propagation time delay

The added time for a packet to get into the transmission path. Propagation time delays create latency in the delivery of the message.

Multiplexing

The action of transmitting many signals or bands of information across a carrier at the same time to form a complex signal.

Synchronous Digital Hierarchy (SDH)

The international standard for data transmission over optical media.

Therefore, an OC-1 signal transmits at 51.84Mbps. Multiples of this basic OC building block are used to define additional transmission rates. Several intermediate levels of service are defined; here are just a few to give you an idea of the enormous capacity of the optical carrier network:

- **OC-3:** Also called STS-3, this signal transmits at a line rate of 155.52Mbps.
- **OC-12:** Also referred to as STS-12, transmission rates of 622.08Mbps can be achieved.
- **OC-48:** This is STS-48, with rates of 2488.32Mbps.
- **OC-192:** At the top of the line, this STS-192 rate is 9953.28Mbps.

Asynchronous Transfer Mode (ATM)

Asynchronous transfer mode (ATM) describes a LAN/WAN transmission technology that is capable of speeds ranging from 1.54 Mbps to 622 Mbps. Using high-speed transmission media (most often fiber-optic cabling), ATM uses a switching technology to move high volumes of data, audio, and video transmissions between source and destination, lessening the internetwork strain caused by other types of WAN deployments. Although ATM can be used on the LAN, its cost usually makes it infeasible for general-purpose LAN traffic.

To provide consistent (nonlatent) transmission, ATM breaks the messages into small packages of 53 bytes each. These packages are known as *ATM cells* (see Figure 11.5). The fixed cell size reduces both the overhead for processing each package and the number of bits in the cell for error and flow control checks. As a result, transmission speeds can be much greater than with other transmission technologies. The technology is especially important to voice, audio, and video transmissions because this type of transmission carries no latency in the delivery of the message.

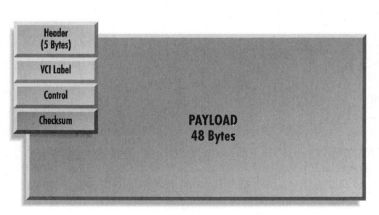

FIGURE 11.5
The 53-Byte ATM Cell

ATM uses virtual circuits (the end-to-end connections with defined end points and routes), but without bandwidth allocation assigned to the circuit. Bandwidth will be assigned on demand, as the need occurs. Because ATM also uses *classes of service,* the needs of certain types of traffic, such as multimedia, can be managed and maintained with relative ease.

ATM has the flexibility to use fiber-optic cable or copper as its transmission medium. It also can make use of the additional media protocols such as FDDI and SONet/SDH as its physical signal carrier.

TESTTIP

Understand that ATM is the only technology that uses the cell structure to control data, voice, video, and audio transmission, and that the size of the cell is 53 bytes.

Class of service

The ability of ATM to attach priorities to certain types of transmission, allowing one packet to jump ahead of another based on priority.

LAYERED TECHNOLOGY OF ATM

ATM functions in a layered format (see Table 11.1). At the Physical layer of the OSI Model, ATM provides specifications for transmission media, the signal-encoding scheme, data rates, and compatibility with other types of transmission specifications at the Physical layer (i.e., SONet).

ATM uses a second layer named after itself—the ATM layer. This layer provides services to upper layers, packet transfer capabilities, definition of the fixed cell size, and definition of the use of logical connections for transmission.

The last layer of ATM is known as the ATM Adaptation layer (AAL). The AAL changes depending on the type of service used. The AAL maps higher layer information into the cells and passes them down to the ATM layer, or collects information from the ATM cells and passes it up to higher layer technologies.

OSI Model	ATM Layers
Application	
Presentation	
Session	**ATM Adaptation Layer (AAL)**
Transport	(Convergence sublayer) (Segmentation and Reassembly sublayer)
Network	**ATM Layer**
Data Link	(Generic flow control) (Cell translation, multiplex/demultiplex)
Physical	**Transmission Convergence (TC) Sublayer** (Cell rate decoupling, header sequence generation, transmission frame adaptation, cell delineation)
	Physical Media (PM) Sublayer (Bit timing, physical medium)

TABLE 11.1
The OSI Model and the Layers of ATM

Virtual Channel Connections (VCCs) and Virtual Path Connections (VPCs)

An ATM virtual channel connection (VCC) is a virtual circuit that carries a single flow of cells, in sequence, from end to end. The VCC can be configured as a static, permanent virtual circuit (PVC) or configured as a dynamically controlled circuit called a switched virtual circuit (SVC). The SVC is the preferred choice because reconfiguration of the network is much easier. A set of VCCs can be bundled together for transmission into a virtual path connection (VPC). All VCCs that form the VPC will be transmitted from end to end across the circuit, resulting in less overhead and easier recovery should there be a major failure in the infrastructure. VPCs are often used between switches, forming a virtual trunk line between two sites.

Frame Relay

Frame relay

A packet-switching technology that transports data at a reasonable cost by allowing many frame circuits to share media through the public infrastructure.

Frame relay is a packet-switching technology designed to transport data at a reasonable cost. It does so by allowing many frame circuits to share media, betting that all the circuits will be transmitting at exactly the same time. Frame relay uses the public infrastructure, providing digital transmission at rates between 56Kbps and 1.544Kbps. Frame relay is an "always on" technology, providing instant access to remote locations.

Frame relay networks may span very large geographical distances. Because they use the infrastructure created by common carriers (sometimes called the "cloud"), frame relay networks often exist wherever there is telephone service.

To create a frame relay network, you must have a connection to your telecommunications provider. This gives the network access to the cloud. You then purchase connections, or circuits, within the cloud that will be available to your business any time they are needed. For example, the Gosh Darn Good Yarn Company has four locations: Chicago, Milwaukee, Green Bay, and Madison. To keep accurate records for inventory and sales, all locations must immediately report any increase or decrease to the inventory quantities. Permanent leased lines would be too costly. But frame relay connections for each location are a good choice (see Figure 11.6). The administrator or operations manager would contact the telecommunications company to purchase, or *provision,* six circuits creating a mesh network.

Provision

To supply with, or purchase, provisions, which may include a service or goods.

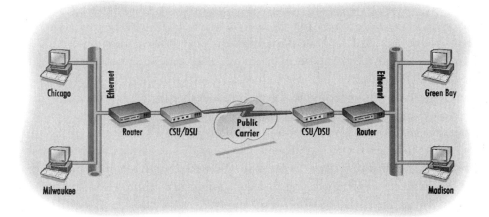

FIGURE 11.6
Frame Relay Network for Gosh Darn Good Yarn Company Locations

Your telecommunications company will offer either permanent virtual circuits (PVCs) or switched virtual circuits (SVCs). If you choose the PVC option, all connections and circuit paths will be defined at the time of provisioning. If you choose the SVC option, the path will be defined at the time of transmission. SVCs eliminate any connection setup delay, and are the most common circuit offered by telecommunications vendors.

When provisioning frame relay circuits, you will also be offered the option of a guaranteed amount of bandwidth availability. This is known as the *committed information rate (CIR)*. For example, say you believe that a 56Kbps frame relay connection between the four locations of the Gosh Darn Good Yarn Company will provide enough bandwidth to keep all information current throughout the enterprise. Your vendor will assign you a CIR of 56 Kbps. This does not mean that you will always transmit at 56Kbps. Two other levels of service come into play with the CIR: The

Committed information rate (CIR)

A unit of measure for a frame relay circuit that represents the minimum amount of bandwidth that will always be available across the purchased circuit for a frame relay network.

Committed burst rate (Bc)

The amount of additional bandwidth above the committed information rate (CIR) that may be available for a frame relay circuit.

Burst excess rate (Be)

Identifies the maximum burst bandwidth available beyond the committed information rate (CIR) for a frame relay circuit.

committed burst rate (Bc) indicates how much you may exceed the CIR transmission rate, and the *burst excess rate (Be)* indicates the maximum burst bandwidth availability.

One thing to keep in mind when provisioning frame relay and the CIR for the circuit is congestion. When the frame relay network is congested, the carrier has the option of dropping data temporarily if you exceed your CIR. In this event, a retransmit signal will be sent to the sending station to resend the data.

Frame relay is a good choice for many networks because the installation and number of components is simpler than with leased line networks. Using our example from above, to connect the four locations of the Gosh Darn Good Yarn Company using leased lines, you would need to purchase six lease lines and twelve CSU/DSUs (see Chapter 5 for review). This equipment is owned by the company and must be maintained by the company. If, however, you choose a frame relay network to connect the four locations, you would need only four leased lines and eight CSU/DSUs, and the six frame circuits to connect everyone together.

Frame relay networks are very scalable. When you add a new location, you provision one additional lease line and two CSU/DSUs.

Frame relay networks also provide redundant routes for data. Using the public carrier infrastructure, there is always an alternative path from source to destination, and frame relay can take advantage of those redundancies.

The T-Carrier Connections

T-carrier connections refer to the telecommunications links that provide remote access to network services using the telephone infrastructure to get data from source to destination. They are leased line connections billed from the local telephone system. T- connections are digital, making them a good choice for data transmission. Many businesses and enterprise networks have also turned to leasing T-connections for the newer voice technologies.

T-carrier connection, or T-connection

A telecommunications link that provides access to remote networks using the PSTN infrastructure. These are leased line connections that are always on.

T1

The unit of measure for a remote connection through a leased line over PSTN voice channels. T1 lines transmit at 1.544Mbps.

Digital signal x (DSx)

A unit of measurement for digital transmission rates over telephone voice channels.

Like other transmission methods, the T-connections use multiplexing to aggregate many channels into a single signal for transmission. This allows voice, data, video, and other signals to flow over the same infrastructure.

The typical T-connection is the *T1* leased line. This line has a total throughput of 1.544Mbps spread over 24 channels, or separate signals. The T3 leased line can transmit at 44.376Mbps. The speed of the carrier channel is actually determined by the signal level, which ANSI has defined within the OSI Model framework under the electrical signal characteristics in the Physical layer. These electrical signals are referred to as the *digital signal x (DSx)*. One data or voice channel is called a DS0. Twenty-four channels are referred to as a DS1.

Because the T-connections are leased lines, this type of access is always on. For businesses that do not need constant availability, ISDN might be a good solution. If a business wants the "always on" capability of the leased line but does not need the full available bandwidth of a T1 (1.544Mbps), the dedicated circuit of the T1 can be split. This is called a *fractional T1* (in slang, fract T1). A single channel from a T1 line runs at 64Kbps. Purchasing a fractional T1 line in increments of 64Kbps allows the business to buy for today and grow in the future by purchasing additional fractional T1 space as needed.

The T-carriers also provide the T3 connection. The T3 line is typically very expensive and is used by data-intensive businesses. This might mean using the T3 for remote site backups or data warehousing at a remote location. A T3 line equates to 28 T1 lines, or 43.376Mbps, so sometimes it is possible to purchase multiple T1s without making that leap to a T3 connection.

The European equivalent of the American T1/T3 leased line is slightly different in capacity. The European T1 line is known as the *E1* and has a bandwidth maximum of 2.048Mbps. A T3 line is known as an *E3* in Europe and provides 34.368Mbps.

T-carrier connections require some very specific hardware. Much of this hardware was discussed in Chapter 5, but we will review it briefly here so you can see how the picture fits together. The required hardware is described in Figure 11.7.

Fractional T1

A portion of a 1.544Mbps T-connection (1.544Mbps) that can be purchased in increments of 64Kbps for remote connectivity.

E1, E3

The European equivalents of the T1 and T3 carrier options. E1 transmits at 2.048Mbps and E3 transmits at 34.368Mbps.

- **Channel Service Unit/Data Service Unit (CSU/DSU):** This single device includes the two components to connect the T-connections to the customer site. The CSU is the terminator for the signal and provides error correction and line monitoring. The DSU converts the digital signal used by network devices into the digital signal sent across the cabling.
- **Multiplexer:** The multiplexer either aggregates multiple signals into a single signal for transmission, or it separates the incoming signal into separate data streams. A multiplexer can take different types of signals (voice, data) and combine them into a single, transmittable signal.
- **Network Devices:** The typical network that deploys a T1 for external connectivity is large enough to need routers, bridges, and perhaps switches within the network to manage network traffic flow.

FIGURE 11.7
Hardware Required for
T-Carrier Connections

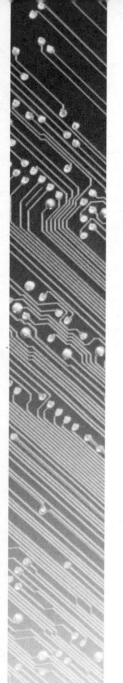

TEST TIP

Be sure to know that the multiplexer is the device that can aggregate many signals into a single transmission signal and can also separate a combined signal into its many separate signals at the destination.

STUDY GUIDE

This chapter described numerous WAN technologies available today. Here are some key points to remember.

WIDE AREA NETWORK (WAN) TECHNOLOGIES

- A wide area network (WAN) is a data communications network that spans a large geographic area and usually uses third-party vendors for transmission facilities.
- Third-party vendors are usually referred to as common carriers.
- WANs are used to interconnect remote locations of a business operation.
- The functions of WAN technologies are clustered at the three lowest layers of the OSI Model.

SWITCHING TECHNOLOGIES

Two types of switching technologies are used with WAN connections: circuit switching and packet switching.

Circuit Switching

- A circuit is a path between two or more communicating entities and usually refers to the physical path the data takes.
- Circuits may be reserved, as with a dedicated connection between two end points.

Virtual Circuits

- Logical circuits represent a path between two points and appear to indicate a physical path, but usually the data will travel over many different paths between the source and destination. This type of logical circuit is called a virtual circuit.
- One type of virtual circuit is called a permanent virtual circuit (PVC) because it guarantees that a certain amount of bandwidth will always be available when needed.
- The PVC eliminates the need to reserve a specific path in advance.
- The switched virtual circuit (SVC) is dynamically created when a request for transmission is made. When the transmission ends, the circuit is deleted. This type of circuit is good for those nodes that transmit data sporadically.
- The public telephone network (POTS, or PSTN) uses circuit switching to carry telephone calls from source to destination.
- Circuit switching involves some setup time to establish the circuit, but the time delay is usually not apparent to the user.

Packet Switching

- Packet switching is commonly used for WAN connections.
- A message is broken into smaller units called packets.
- Each packet has a header that contains the source address, the destination address, and a sequence number. The sequence number is used to reassemble the message once it reaches the destination.
- With packet switching, the pieces of the message (the packets) often take different paths from the source to the destination. Once the packets reach the destination, the message is reassembled according to the sequence numbers in the headers of the packets.
- Packet switching involves no circuit setup time. The transmission is connectionless, so there is no guarantee of delivery.
- Routers make the decisions about the path a series of packets will take.

Which Switching Method Is Better?

- Every business must evaluate the types of traffic that will be transmitted in order to determine which type of switching method is most suitable.
- Benefits of circuit switching:
  - A guaranteed pathway for the data.
  - A guaranteed portion of the bandwidth available for transmission.

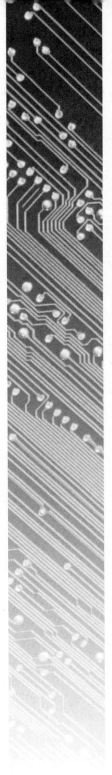

- Smaller packets because the header includes only the circuit number (not the source and destination information), so that intervening devices will recognize which message the packet belongs to.
- Benefits of packet switching:
  - The public infrastructure can be used for data transmission instead of incurring the expense for dedicated links between locations.
  - Resources such as bandwidth are used more fairly and efficiently in packet switching.
  - Pipelining, the ability to simultaneously use a communication link for two or more transmissions, increases the efficiency of use for the available bandwidth.

INTEGRATED SERVICES DIGITAL NETWORK (ISDN)

- ISDN is a cost-effective WAN connection that uses digital transmission instead of traditional telephone networks.
- ISDN uses two types of channels to carry data:
  - Bearer channels (B channels) carry the payload, which may be voice or data.
  - Data channels (D channels) carry the control information for connection setup, timing, and disconnection.
- ISDN is offered in two types of interfaces:
  - Basic rate interface (BRI) provides 2 B channels and 1 D channel, for a total transfer rate of 128Kbps.
  - Primary rate interface (PRI) allocates 23 B channels for data and 1 64Kbps D channel for control information, for a total transfer rate of 1.544Mbps.
- The benefits of ISDN include:
  - Data capacity to service many users at the same time.
  - Voice and data transmission over the same physical media at the same time, because one of the two channels of the BRI can be switched to voice if a call comes in.
  - Video conferencing.
  - Widespread availability.
  - Cost-effective solution for small businesses and home offices.
- To implement ISDN on the network, contact the local telephone service provider.

Fiber Distributed Data Interface (FDDI)

- FDDI is a set of standards developed by the ISO and ANSI that provides the guidelines for data transmission over fiber-optic cable.
- FDDI uses a dual-ring formation for token passing at a rate of 100Mbps.
- Because they transmit data through fiber-optic cable, FDDI internetworks have extremely high capacity, enabling them to service thousands of users over great distances.
- The two FDDI rings provide data flow in opposite directions.
- When a portion of the FDDI network fails (a station or a cable segment), the FDDI network can heal itself by closing the ring at the gap so that data can still be transmitted. This results in little or no network down time.
- FDDI and fiber-optic networks are usually used just for backbone deployments, because they are expensive to construct. Professionals must install fiber-optic cable to minimize damage to the cable and to the installer.

Synchronous Optical Networks/Synchronous Digital Hierarchy (SONet/SDH) and Optical Cable x (OC-x)

These three technologies have as their common ground the fiber-optic cable plant. Because of this commonality, the three cannot be easily separated when discussing the technology.

SONet

- SONet defines the standards for optical carrier levels and synchronous transport signals for the infrastructure.
- SONet uses multiplexing to use all bandwidth efficiently for the transmission of data.
- SONet uses low-level digital signals and a synchronous structure.
- "Synchronous structure" refers to the transitions of the digital signals so that they occur at exactly the same rate. This tells the media and the receiving station where the 1s and 0s are in the signal.
- A clocking signal provides the constant and even pulse to keep traffic in line.
- Asynchronous transfer mode (ATM) uses SONet because of its capacity and its ability to use multiplexing and synchronization.

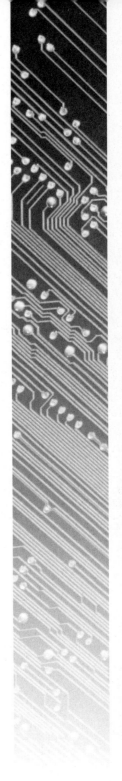

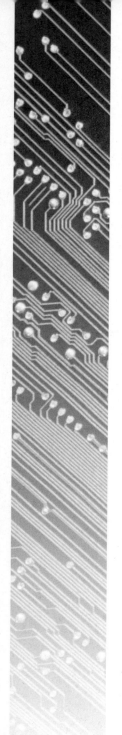

Synchronous Digital Hierarchy (SDH)

SDH was the result of several standards organizations defining a global synchronization standard for transmission. SDH unified the various existing standards for international communications.

The Optical Carrier (OC)

- The optical carrier (OC) standards are based on the synchronous transport signals (STSs) used by SONet. The STS standards have an equivalent OC standard that is expressed by a numeric indicator.
- The basic building block of OC is based on the STS-1, which has a maximum transmission speed of 51.84Mbps.
- Other examples of OC levels are:
  - OC-3: Also called STS-3, this signal transmits at a line rate of 155.52Mbps.
  - OC-12: Also referred to as STS-12, transmission rates of 622.08Mbps can be achieved.
  - OC-48: This is STS-48, with a 2488.32Mbps rate.
  - OC-192: At the top of the line, this STS-192 rate is 9953.28Mbps.

ASYNCHRONOUS TRANSFER MODE (ATM)

- Asynchronous transfer mode (ATM) is a WAN transmission technology that is capable of speeds ranging from 1.54Mbps to 622Mbps.
- ATM uses a switching technology to move high volumes of data, voice, video, and audio transmissions between end points.
- ATM is expensive, so it is seldom used for LAN transmission.
- ATM uses cells instead of packets. Each cell is 53 bytes in length. The fixed size of the cell reduces both the overhead for processing the package and the number of bits needed for error control. The reduced overhead enables ATM to function much more efficiently than other transmission methods.
- ATM uses virtual circuits between defined end points and routes, but it does not allocate bandwidth ahead of time. This allows ATM to support several classes of service and to support transmission of traffic such as multimedia files.
- ATM can be used over fiber-optic cable or some of the newer, high-capacity copper media.

Layered Technology of ATM

ATM functions with several layers:
- The Physical layer specifies transmission media, signal-encoding schemes, data rates, and compatibility.
- The ATM layer defines cell size, specifies logical connections, and provisions both access services in the upper layers and packet transfer capabilities.
- The ATM Adaptation layer (AAL) changes depending on the service being used. AAL maps higher layer information into the cells and passes them down to the ATM layer, or it assembles information from the ATM cells and passes it up to higher layer technologies.

Virtual Channel Connections (VCCs) and Virtual Path Connections (VPCs)

- A VCC is a virtual circuit that carries a sequenced, single flow of cells from end to end.
- VCCs can be statically configured permanent virtual circuits or dynamically configured switched virtual circuits.
- A set of VCCs can be bundled together to form a VPC for transmission. All VCCs that are made part of a VPC will be transmitted from end to end across the circuit as a single entity, resulting in reduced overhead and easier recovery from a failure in the route.
- A VPC acts like a virtual trunk between two sites.

FRAME RELAY

- Frame relay is a packet-switching technology that supports data transport at a reasonable cost. Frame relay uses the public infrastructure of common carriers to transmit at rates between 56Kbps and 1.544Kbps.
- Frame relay uses the "cloud" of common carriers to span large distances.
- To create a frame relay network, a connection to the provider must be established. Circuits are purchased that allow the transmission between each end of each circuit.
- Frame relay offers both PVCs and SVCs.
- Frame relay requires that a committed information rate (CIR) be established. This number is the minimum amount of bandwidth that will always be available to the circuit.
- Vendors also establish the committed burst rate (Bc), which identifies how much excess bandwidth a circuit may use.

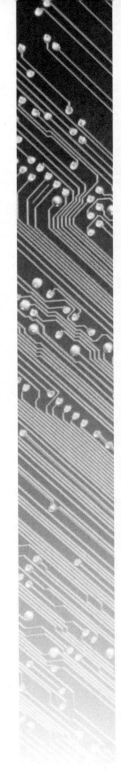

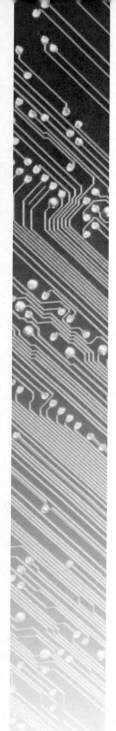

- A third rate, called the burst excess rate (Be), indicates the maximum burst transmission bandwidth available to the circuit.
- If the network is heavily congested, the vendor has the option of dropping packets if the transmission rate exceeds the CIR.
- Frame relay networks are easily scalable because they require minimal amounts of hardware and can be quickly and easily expanded to meet growing business needs.

THE T-CARRIER CONNECTION

- The T-carrier connection refers to the telecommunications links that provide remote access for business using the public telephone infrastructure as the physical media.
- T-carrier solutions are leased line solutions, billed from the local telephone company.
- T-carrier connections are digital in nature, eliminating analog to digital conversions and making them a good choice for data network interconnection.
- T-carrier connections are based on the same building block as ISDN. A T1 leased line uses 24 channels for a transmission rate of 1.544Mbps. T3 lines transmit at 44.376Mbps.
- The signal level determines the speed of the channel, which is a characteristic of the Physical layer of the OSI Model. The unit of measurement is the data signal x, or DSx. One data channel is a DS0; 24 channels are called a DS1.
- T-carrier connections are always on, making internetwork communications simple for the users.
- T-carrier lines can be purchased in increments. These increments are called fractional T1 lines. Each channel transmits at 64Kbps.
- The European equivalent of the T1 carrier is the E1, which has a capacity of 2.048Mbps. The European equivalent of the T3 line is the E3 line, transmitting at 34.368Mbps.
- T-carrier connections require the following hardware:
  o CSU/DSU
  o Multiplexer
  o Network devices

FIGURE 1.18
Star Network

WAN Technologies

PRACTICE TEST

Try this practice test to check your mastery of the concepts of this chapter.

1. Telephone service providers offer which of the following kinds of WAN connections? (Choose all that apply)
    a. ISDN
    b. OC-12
    c. T-carrier
    d. ATM

2. A multiplexer manages a single channel between source and destination.
    a. True
    b. False

3. Which of the following allows FDDI to maintain a self-healing transmission pathway?
    a. fiber-optic cabling
    b. single ring rotating counterclockwise
    c. copper cabling
    d. dual rings rotating in opposite directions

4. ATM uses which kind of technology to reduce transmission overhead and make failure recovery easier?
    a. cells
    b. packets
    c. circuits
    d. cabling

5. Which of the following two tasks is the ATM Adaptation layer (AAL) responsible for? (Choose two)
    a. feeding information to upper-layer technologies
    b. maintaining transmission speed
    c. maintaining fixed cell size
    d. feeding information to lower-layer technologies

6. ISDN is usually sold in what bandwidth?
    a. 128Kbps
    b. 64Kbps
    c. 128Mbps
    d. 64Mbps

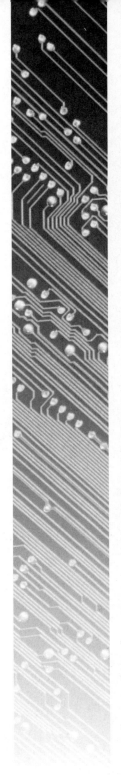

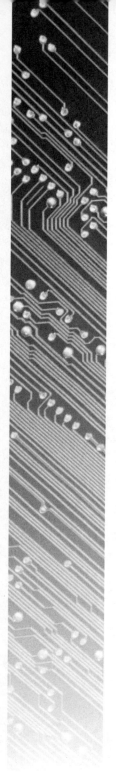

7. Which of the following WAN technologies will support the greatest speeds?
   a. ISDN
   b. ATM
   c. frame relay
   d. SONet

8. Which of the following determines the minimum amount of available bandwidth in a frame relay connection?
   a. committed burst rate
   b. maximum burst rate
   c. committed information rate
   d. committed bandwidth allocation

9. Which of the following devices allows the T-carrier connections to aggregate many channels for transmission?
   a. router
   b. switch
   c. CSU/DSU
   d. multiplexer

10. Which type of switching allows redundant path usage?
    a. circuit switching
    b. packet switching
    c. logical switching
    d. virtual switching

11. A WAN is a set of computers and servers located in one building.
    a. True
    b. False

12. At which layers of the OSI Model do most of the WAN technologies function? (Choose three)
    a. Application
    b. Presentation
    c. Session
    d. Transport
    e. Network
    f. Data Link
    g. Physical

13. What transmission speeds can ATM support?
    a. 1.544Mbps to 100Mbps
    b. 128Kbps to 1.544Mbps
    c. 64Kbps to 384Mbps
    d. 1.544Mbps to 622Mbps

14. Which of the following types of circuits is used by PSTN?
    a. virtual switched
    b. packet switched
    c. permanently switched
    d. circuit switched

15. A virtual channel connection aggregates all of the virtual path connections to form a trunk line.
    a. True
    b. False

16. Which of the following devices is needed to support frame relay connections between different geographic locations?
    a. CSU/DSU
    b. bridge
    c. router
    d. brouter

17. When provisioning ISDN for your company, if you need a large amount of bandwidth, which of the following options would you choose?
    a. BRI
    b. SVC
    c. PRI
    d. PVC

18. Which of the following WAN technologies is most suited for video conferencing?
    a. ISDN
    b. POTS/modem
    c. SONet
    d. ATM

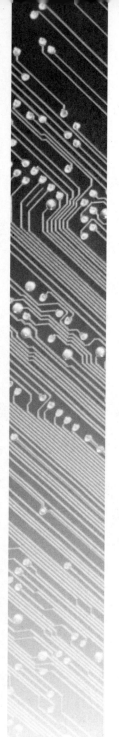

19. Which of the following is a benefit of a circuit switched WAN connection?
    a. guaranteed bandwidth availability
    b. pipelining
    c. use of the public infrastructure
    d. fair use of bandwidth

20. Which of the following identifies the ISDN channel that is responsible for transmitting control information?
    a. A channel
    b. B channel
    c. C channel
    d. D channel

21. SDH sets global standards for
    a. cabling.
    b. transmission.
    c. switching.
    d. circuits.

TROUBLESHOOTING

You are setting up WAN connections between two small remote sites. You have decided that you want analog ISDN at 128Kbps. After making numerous calls, you cannot find a vendor who can install this for you. What might be the problem?

You have purchased frame relay circuits to connect your six remote sites together. Every afternoon at about 3:00 P.M., connections from the remote sites seems unbearably slow. This is a problem because you are in charge of managing the data upload from your site to the corporate offices. Where would you start looking to solve this problem?

CUSTOMER SERVICE

You are providing network services for a customer. The customer has decided to connect his small business to the Internet but does not have a lot of money to spend each month. He has asked your advice on this matter. What solution will you recommend and why?

FOR MORE INFORMATION

For links to Web sites that provide further information about the topics covered in this chapter, go to the EMC/Paradigm Internet Resource Center at www.emcp.com/College Division/Internet Resource Centers/Networking/System Administration/Web Resources: For More Information.

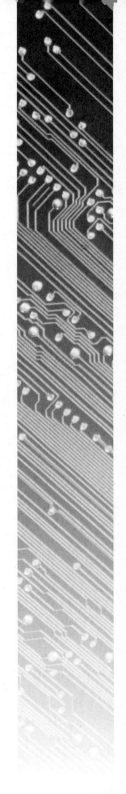

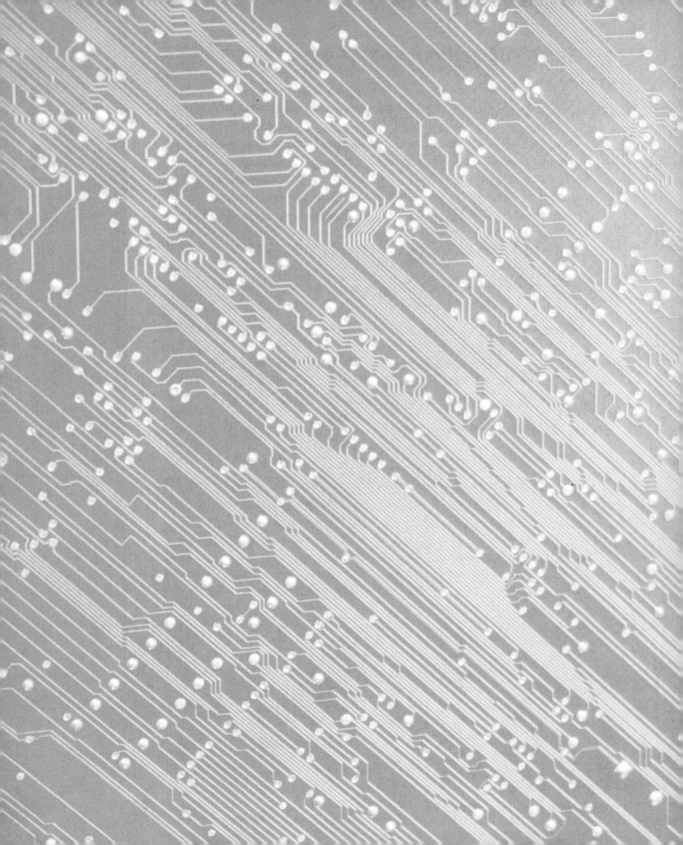

Remote Access Protocols, Services, and Troubleshooting

12

Network+ Examination
- **Objective 2.12:** Define the function of the following remote access protocols and services:
  - RAS
  - PPP
  - PPTP
  - ICA
- **Objective 3.7:** Given a remote connectivity scenario (e.g., IP, IPX, dial-up, PPPoE, authentication, physical connectivity, etc.), configure the connection.
- **Objective 4.3:** Given a troubleshooting scenario involving a remote connectivity problem (e.g., authentication failure, protocol configuration, physical connectivity), identify the cause of the problem.

ON THE JOB

Remote access is the process of connecting to a network from a remote location. For example, if you use a computer with a modem to dial up an Internet Service Provider, you have used remote access.

Remote access is a very common method of networking due to the mobile nature of both business and society. Remote access makes it convenient for employees to stay in touch with their companies or for pleasure travelers to stay connected to e-mail and the Internet. As a network technician, you will be called on to install and maintain remote access hardware and software on both clients and servers. In addition, you can expect many support calls from remote access users when they are unable to connect or access network resources. This chapter provides you with a

Remote access

The process of connecting to a network from a remote location.

thorough understanding of how each of these components works. You will also learn how to install and configure the components and how to troubleshoot problems when they occur.

TRY IT!

Use a PC with an installed modem to establish remote access with an Internet Service Provider.

1. After connecting, use the PING utility to check network connectivity with your default gateway and DNS servers.
2. View your network configuration settings.
3. Identify and view the properties of your dial-up adapter.

Understanding Remote Access *-access from anywhere*

Remote access is the process of gaining access to some type of network from a distant location. The user is not connected directly to the network through a single cable. Instead, the user connects indirectly, or on demand.

To connect to a network from a remote location, several components are necessary:

- A remote access client with a modem.
- A remote access server with one or more modems.
- A data line, typically a telephone line, that supports a connection protocol.

For example, a client computer with an installed modem dials in to a remote access server. The remote access server, which has one or more modems attached to it, will answer the request for a dial-up connection. Once the user is authenticated, she may or may not be required to log on a second time through the appropriate network client (the Client for NetWare Networks or the Microsoft Client for Microsoft Networks). Once the client is authenticated, it can access network resources, just like any other network client.

Let's look at each of these components in more detail.

Remote Access Server (RAS)

Almost all major manufacturers of network operating systems, including Microsoft and Novell, make a remote access component that can be installed on their servers. Once it is installed and configured, remote access clients have the ability to connect to the server and then access the network.

This section will focus on the installation and configuration of a Microsoft Windows 2000 *remote access server (RAS)*. The installation information below assumes that one or more modems are already connected.

RAS INSTALLATION

When you install the *Routing and Remote Access Service (RRAS)* on a Windows 2000 server, you enable support for both *multiprotocol routing* and remote access. With multiprotocol routing, manually configured routing tables enable the server to act as a static router, making routing decisions for the AppleTalk, IPX, and IP protocols. The remote access server allows the server to respond to remote client requests for connection, authentication, and access to resources.

To install RRAS on a Windows 2000 server, follow these steps:

1. Press the Start button, navigate to the Programs menu, and then to the Administrative Tools program group. In Administrative Tools, locate Routing and Remote Access. A screen similar to Figure 12.1 will appear.
2. On the Action menu, select Configure and Enable Routing and

Remote access server (RAS) ✓

A connection point that provides authentication and access services to dial-up users.

Routing and Remote Access Service (RRAS)

A service installed on a Microsoft Windows 2000 server that enables support for both multiprotocol routing and remote access.

Multiprotocol routing

Manually configured routing tables that allow a server to act as a static router to move more than one protocol between network segments.

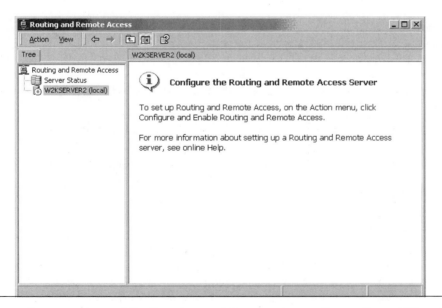

Remote Access. The Routing and Remote Access Server Setup Wizard will appear (see Figure 12.2).
3. Click the Next button. The Common Configurations dialog box

FIGURE 12.1
Routing and Remote Access Server Management Console Window

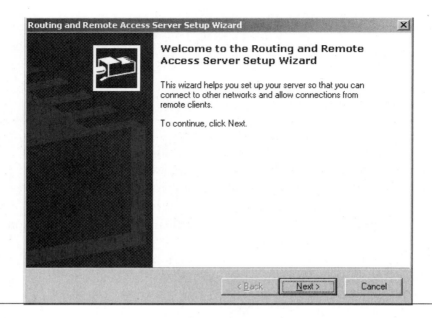

FIGURE 12.2
Routing and Remote Access
Server Setup Wizard

**Network Address
Translation (NAT)**

A service that allows a
network to use the private
addresses on the local LAN
while still maintaining a
connection for users to the
Internet.

appears (see Figure 12.3). This dialog box allows the server to provide
the following services:

- **Internet connection server** allows you to establish *Network Address Translation (NAT)* services.
- **Remote access server** allows remote clients to connect to the server through a dial-up connection.
- **Virtual private network (VPN) server** allows clients to connect to the server through the Internet.
- **Network router** configures the server to act as a multiprotocol router.
- **Manually configured server** allows you to override default server settings with specific configurations set manually at the appropriate property dialog box.

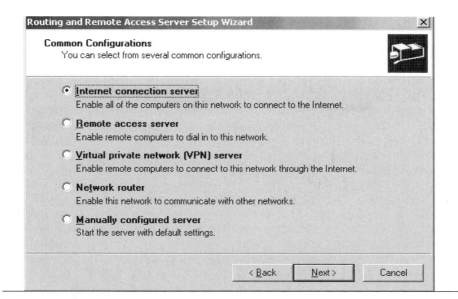

FIGURE 12.3
Common Configuration
Options

4. Select the *Remote access server* option and then click the Next button.
5. The Remote Access Server Setup dialog box will appear (see Figure 12.4), offering you the following two options:
   - **Basic remote access server** allows you to set up a server that has limited administrative control. If you choose this option, you will be prompted to exit the wizard and provided with instructions on how to continue.
   - **Advanced remote access server** allows you to configure an RRAS server that has many control and security options, to include support for policies and integration with Microsoft Active Directory.

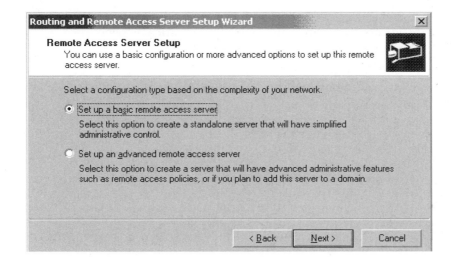

FIGURE 12.4
Remote Access Server
Setup Dialog Box

6. Select the *Set up an advanced remote access server* option and then press the Next button. The Remote Client Protocols dialog box (Figure 12.5) will appear.

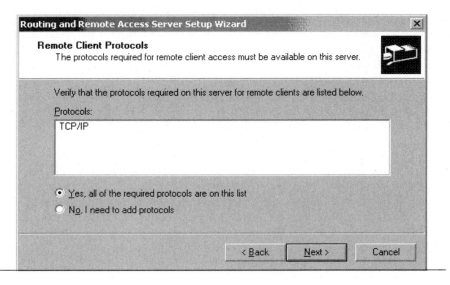

FIGURE 12.5
Remote Client Protocols
Dialog Box

7. Verify that all of the protocols you want to support at the dial-up connection are listed here. If they are not and you wish to install support for more protocols, click the option titled *No, I need to add protocols*. Once you have completed adding the required protocols, click on the option titled *Yes, all of the required protocols are on this list*. Then click the Next button.

8. If you selected the TCP/IP protocol, the IP Address Assignment dialog box (Figure 12.6) will appear. If you want to use DHCP to assign IP addressing information automatically, select the *Automatically* option. If you choose *From a specified range of addresses,* you will be presented with another dialog box that will allow you to enter the IP addressing information manually. Click the Next button.

Remote Access Protocols, Services, and Troubleshooting

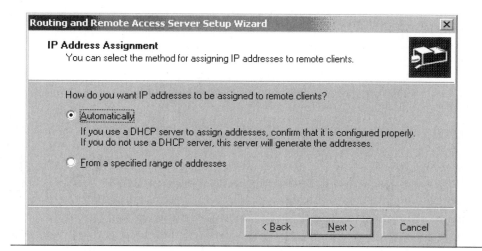

FIGURE 12.6
IP Address Assignment
Dialog Box

9. The Managing Multiple Remote Access Servers dialog box (Figure 12.7) will appear, allowing you to decide whether to use the *Remote Authentication Dial-In User Service (RADIUS)*. RADIUS adds security and accounting features to the RRAS server by monitoring clients that try to connect to the server, by authenticating client requests to access the server, and by providing enough configuration information to the client so that the client can take advantage of RRAS and network services. In addition, any transaction that occurs between client and the RADIUS server is authenticated by a shared secret. Since this shared secret is not transmitted over the network, it is not subject to being intercepted by someone monitoring the network traffic. Finally, all user passwords are encrypted as an additional layer of protection.

**Remote Authentication
Dial-In User Service
(RADIUS)**

A service that adds security
and accounting features to
the RRAS server.

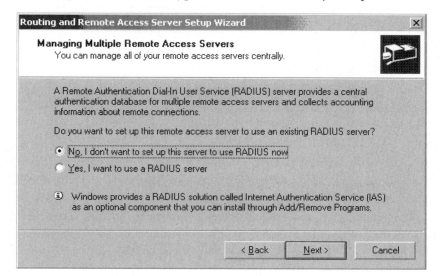

FIGURE 12.7
Managing Multiple
Remote Access Servers
Dialog Box

10. Make your selection and then click the Next button. *(Note: You may choose to install RADIUS at a later time.)* The final wizard dialog box will appear, giving you the option of reading Help items concerning RAS. Make your selection and click the Finish button. The installation is complete.

BASIC RAS INSTALLATION

As noted in Step 5 above, you may choose to use a basic RRAS installation. In this case, basic means that users can dial in to a server, but the administrator cannot control security and many of the other services that are built in to the advanced RRAS. If you select the basic installation during RRAS server installation, the wizard will terminate and take you to a help window that describes how to set up the basic configuration. To set up a basic RRAS server, follow these steps:

1. In the Control Panel, locate the *Network and Dial-up Connections* icon. Double-click the icon to open it.
2. Locate the *Make New Connection* icon and double-click it. At the first dialog box, click the Next button.
3. At the next dialog box, click the option labeled *Accept Incoming Connections*. Click Next.
4. Follow the remaining instructions in the Network Connection Wizard to complete the setup.
5. Once you have completed all of the steps, click the Finish button. Users will now be able to dial in to the RAS server.

― TRY IT! ―

Install the Routing and Remote Access Service on a Windows 2000 server.

1. Ensure a modem is installed and functioning correctly in the server.
2. Install the Routing and Remote Access Service.
3. Explore the configuration options available.

RAS CONFIGURATION

Once the advanced RRAS service has been successfully completed, you have the option of making changes to the server's configuration. Open the RAS console by pressing the Start button, navigate to the Programs menu, and then to the Administrative Tools program group. In Administrative Tools, locate Routing and Remote Access. The Console window (Figure 12.8) will appear.

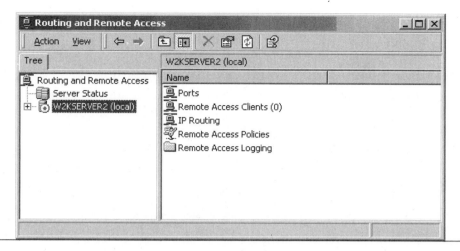

FIGURE 12.8
Routing and Remote Access
Management Console Window

To configure RRAS properties, use your right mouse button to click the server in the left-hand window pane. When the menu appears, select Properties. A dialog box will appear with five tab options from which to choose: General, Security, IP, PPP, and Event Logging.

The General Tab

Figure 12.9 depicts the General tab of the RRAS server properties dialog box. This dialog box allows you to decide whether or not the RRAS server will also function as a router or just as a remote access server. If you place a check mark in the *Router* option, a client will be able to dial up the RRAS server and, after being properly authenticated, access resources on other servers and computers on the network. If you do not check the *Router* option, the client will be able to access resources only on the RRAS server.

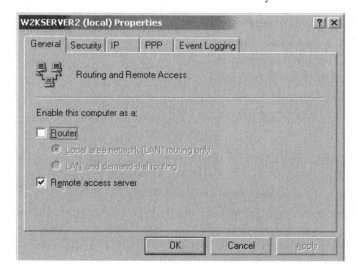

FIGURE 12.9
The General Tab in Routing
and Remote Access Server
Properties

The Security Tab

The Security dialog box (Figure 12.10) determines the type of authentication that will be required for dial-up clients. As you can see in the figure, this dialog box allows you to determine how user credentials are validated for clients dialing in to the network. Your options are standard Windows authentication and the RADIUS services discussed in the preceding section.

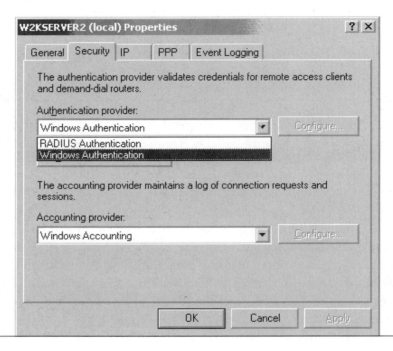

FIGURE 12.10
Security Properties Dialog Box

Extensible Authentication Protocol (EAP)

An RRAS security option for devices such as smart cards.

Microsoft Encrypted Authentication version 2 (MS-CHAP v2)

A mutual authentication process that uses one-way encrypted passwords.

You can also choose the authentication method that you want to use. Some examples follow:

- *Extensible Authentication Protocol (EAP)* is used to provide security for devices such as smart cards.
- *Microsoft Encrypted Authentication version 2 (MS-CHAP v2)* is an updated version of the Microsoft Challenge Handshake Authentication Protocol (MS-CHAP). Version 2 is a mutual authentication process that uses one-way encrypted passwords.
- *Microsoft Encrypted Authentication (MS-CHAP)* is the older Microsoft encrypted password authentication process.
- **Encrypted authentication (CHAP)** is a security service provided through the use of a hash, which is a combination of a random value and a predetermined secret.

- *Shiva Password Authentication Protocol (SPAP)* is used when connecting to Shiva servers.
- *Unencrypted password (PAP)* allows the password to be used in plain text, without encryption.

You may also choose to allow clients to connect without authentication. The exact authentication method you choose will be determined by several factors, including the type of client that is connecting and the protocols that are used. You can select more than one authentication method, since the RRAS server has the ability to negotiate the authentication type based on the client that is connecting to the server.

TESTTIP

The test does not require you to memorize authentication methods. You only need to have a passing knowledge of their purpose.

You can also choose whether to log connection requests and client sessions. Your options follow:

- **Windows Accounting:** This option will write connection requests and session information into a log file that can be identified under the Remote Access Logging tab.
- **RADIUS Accounting:** With RADIUS accounting, all connection and session traffic is logged by and stored on the RADIUS server.
- **No Accounting:** Connection and session information will not be logged.

The IP Tab

The IP properties dialog box allows you to enable IP routing, along with several other IP-based options (see Figure 12.11). These options include remote access and *demand-dial* connections. IP routing has already been defined; however, demand-dial connections require some explanation. If the modem in your server does not have a connection that is always on, you can configure a demand-dial interface using Network Address Translation (NAT).

Microsoft Encrypted Authentication (MS-CHAP)

An encrypted password authentication process.

Shiva Password Authentication Protocol (SPAP)

A security service that allows clients to dial in to Shiva servers.

Unencrypted password (PAP)

An authentication method in which passwords are passed in plain text, without encryption.

Demand-dial

Dial-up connections that are created as you need them.

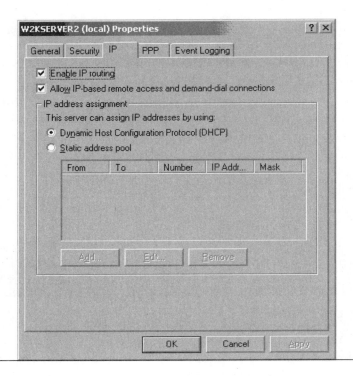

FIGURE 12.11
IP Properties Dialog Box

If you are supporting TCP/IP clients, those clients must have correct TCP/IP addressing information to communicate with both the server and other computers and servers on the network. In the IP properties dialog box, you can choose to use the Dynamic Host Configuration Protocol (DHCP). The DHCP server will then assign addresses. You can also establish a pool of IP addresses that will be handed out by the RRAS server. Clients will then be assigned an appropriate IP address and related parameters, such as subnet mask and default gateway, whenever they successfully log on to the RRAS server. Each client will use that information as long as it is connected to the RRAS server. Once the connection is terminated, that IP address is added back into the address pool.

TRY IT!

Establish a static address pool of IP addresses for your RRAS server to provide to dial-up clients.

**Point-to-Point Protocol
(PPP)**

A serial-communications protocol that allows a dial-up client to access an RRAS server.

The PPP Tab

At the PPP Properties dialog box, you can enable an RRAS server to support the *Point-to-Point Protocol (PPP)* and set several other options (see Figure 12.12). PPP is discussed in greater detail later in this chapter.

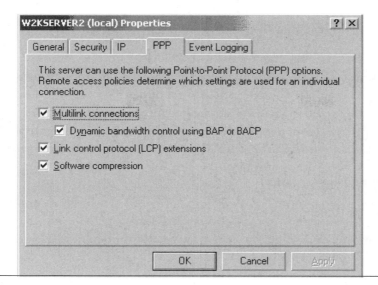

FIGURE 12.12
PPP Properties Dialog Box

One of the first options you will notice in this dialog box is *Multilink connections*. Multilink allows you to connect multiple adapters (in this case, modems) to multiple lines in order to take advantage of the bandwidth of more than one line. If you want to use multilink with a dial-up connection, the following conditions apply:

- The ISP you are dialing in to must support the synchronization of multiple modems.
- You will need to install multiple modems.
- You will need to plug a separate phone line in to each modem.

ISDN, however, is the one form of telephone connections that does not need multiple modems. This is because one ISDN modem can act as more than one device, since ISDN includes two 64-Kbps B channels. Each of these channels can be used independently of the other, essentially creating two separate physical devices. A multilink connection can be used to combine multiple ISDN B channels of a basic rate interface (BRI) connection. ISDN creates multilink connections through a process called bonding, which is the process of combining B channels through hardware support. You can use a multilink connection with any ISDN adapter; however, both the client and the server must support it.

You may also select to use *Bandwidth Allocation Protocol (BAP)* and *Bandwidth Allocation Control Protocol (BACP)* to allow for dynamic control of the multilink bandwidth. Both BAP and BACP are able to adapt to changing bandwidth conditions. BAP provides all of the parameters necessary to allow the client and server to negotiate when using multilink.

Multilink connections

Used to describe a communications line that allows you to connect multiple adapters to multiple lines in order to take advantage of the bandwidth of more than one line.

Bandwidth Allocation Protocol (BAP)

A set of rules that establishes dynamic control of a multilink bandwidth.

Bandwidth Allocation Control Protocol (BACP)

Works with BAP, functioning as a control protocol.

BAP uses a multilink connection to dynamically manage links. BACP works side-by-side with BAP as a control protocol.

Notice also that you can choose to enable *Link Control Protocol (LCP)*. BACP uses LCP to determine precedence, or who gets to transmit first, when more than one client tries to transmit a BAP request at the same time. LCP can also be used to uniquely identify a client.

The PPP Properties dialog box also allows you to select the software compression method you want to use to compress data during transmission.

Link Control Protocol (LCP)

A set of rules used in conjunction with the Bandwidth Allocation Control Protocol (BACP) to determine the order in which clients will transmit when more than one tries to send a BAP request simultaneously.

The Event Logging Tab

The Event Logging Properties dialog box (Figure 12.13) allows you to determine whether errors and warnings will be logged and, if so, how much of this information will be logged. You can also enable or disable the logging of PPP events.

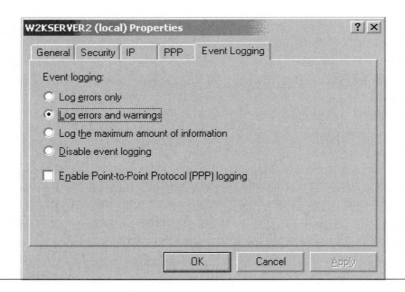

FIGURE 12.13
Event Logging Properties Dialog Box

On a Windows 2000 Professional computer, the Netsh.exe command-line utility is used to enable PPP logging. After logging is enabled, the computer will log all PPP activity to the Ppp.log file, which is located in the %SystemRoot%\Tracing folder. Like all logging, the PPP logging process requires the use of system resources, such as memory and hard disk space. To regain the use of those resources, always turn off logging when you have finished troubleshooting.

TRY IT!

Use the Netsh.exe command.

1. To view Help, at a command prompt, type **Netsh/?**
2. Enable event logging.
3. Change to the RAS context.
4. To display additional information, type **netsh show**

Remote Access Client

Enabling a client to dial in to a RAS server is a fairly straightforward proposition. From a hardware point of view, the client must have a modem installed and the modem must be connected to a phone line. Once these physical requirements are met, a dial-up connection is established using system-supplied software. For example, on a computer running the Windows 2000 Professional operating system, follow these steps:

1. Click the Start button and select Settings. From the Settings menu, select Network and Dial-up Connections. From this menu, select Make New Connection.
2. The Welcome to the Network Connection Wizard will appear. Click Next.
3. When the Network Connection Type dialog box appears (Figure 12.14), select *Dial-up to the Internet,* and then click Next.

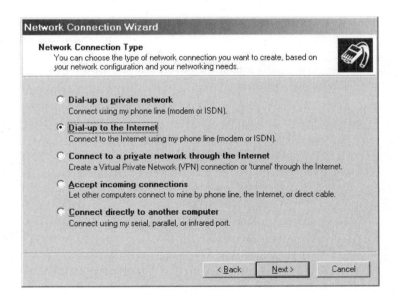

FIGURE 12.14
Selecting the Type of Connection

4. You will be asked how you would like to set up your new connection (Figure 12.15). Select *I want to set up my Internet connection manually, or I want to connect through a local area network (LAN),* and then click Next.

FIGURE 12.15
Selecting the Physical
Connection

5. At the Setting up your Internet connection dialog box (Figure 12.16), select *I connect through a phone line and a modem,* and then click Next.

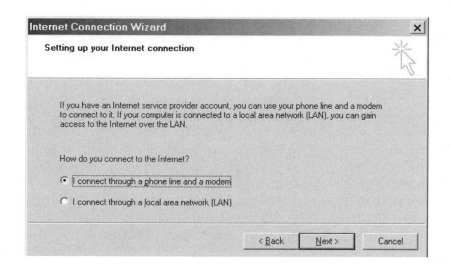

FIGURE 12.16
Connecting to the Internet

6. At the next dialog box (Figure 12.17) enter the area code and telephone number of your RRAS server.

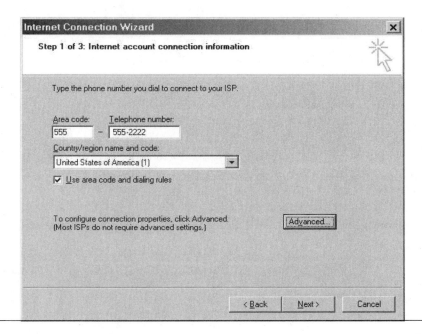

FIGURE 12.17
Entering the Area Code
and Phone Number

7. Clicking the Advanced button will allow you to enable PPP, Serial Line Internet Protocol (SLIP), or Compressed Serial Line Internet Protocol (CSLIP) as your connection protocol. You can also choose your logon procedure and assignment of IP and DNS address. Press the Next button.

8. You will be prompted to enter a user name and password to log on to the RRAS server (Figure 12.18). Enter the appropriate user name and password, and then press the Next button.

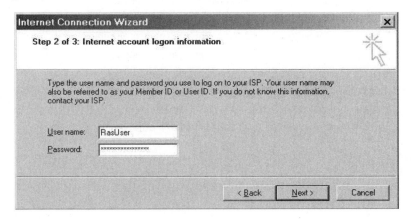

FIGURE 12.18
Entering a User Name and
Password

9. Assign a name for your connection, and then press the Next button.
10. Select *No* when prompted to establish an Internet mail account.
11. At the final dialog box, press Finish to complete the connection.
12. To use the completed account, navigate to the Network and Dial-up Connections menu. From this menu, select your new connection. A dialog box similar to Figure 12.19 will appear.

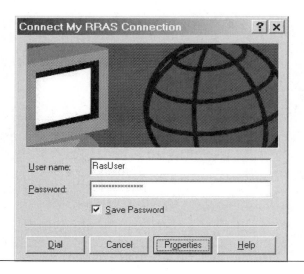

FIGURE 12.19
Connecting Using the Dial-up Connection

13. Click the Dial button to establish your connection.

Your dial-up connection has a number of properties that can be changed to help connect to an RRAS server. Examples are shown in Figure 12.20.

- **General:** Allows you to change the area code or phone number that is being dialed. When multiple connection devices are used, you can select which device to use.
- **Options:** Can be used to change dialing and redialing options.
- **Security:** Used to set security validation options, such as using an unsecure versus a secure password for logon. This selection will also allow you to identify scripts that run upon connection, and to decide whether a terminal window should appear.
- **Networking:** Displays the networking components (such as clients, protocols, and services) that are being used to make the connection to the RRAS server.
- **Sharing:** Allows you to enable and disable Internet Connection Sharing.

FIGURE 12.20
Dial-up Connection Properties

Serial Line Internet Protocol (SLIP)

For the RRAS server and client to communicate with each other, they must use a protocol. Until recently, the standard protocol has been the *Serial Line Internet Protocol (SLIP)*. SLIP is a TCP/IP-based protocol that allows the client and server to talk with each other. For example, if you use an Internet Service Provider (ISP) that you dial in to to gain access to the Internet, e-mail, etc., the ISP can provide you with a SLIP connection. The SLIP connection will then act as an intermediary, or interface, by taking your requests for a Web page and passing them on so they can be serviced. The SLIP connection will then take the Web pages from the responding server and pass them back to you.

SLIP connections are now considered an older technology with many limitations. For example, SLIP lacks the ability to negotiate IP addressing parameters at the beginning of a session (when the client initially connects to the server). Also, if any nonstandard logon procedures are used, you or the ISP may have to write a script to define those parameters. SLIP is being replaced by a newer technology, the Point-to-Point Protocol (PPP).

Serial Line Internet Protocol (SLIP)

A TCP/IP-based protocol that allows a client and server to talk with each other.

Point-to-Point Protocol (PPP)

Point-to-Point Protocol (PPP) is also a serial-communications protocol that allows a dial-up client to access an RRAS server. Once the client connects and is authenticated, requests are passed to and received from the Internet, just like with SLIP. However, this is where the similarity ends. PPP provides error-checking features that SLIP does not have, and PPP has the ability to share a data line. PPP can also handle synchronous and asynchronous communications.

PPP has the added advantage of allowing you to use more than one protocol. While SLIP can transport only TCP/IP traffic, PPP can transport TCP/IP, IPX/SPX, and even AppleTalk traffic. All of these protocols can be transported at the same time using PPP's multiprotocol transport mechanism. In practice, when you dial up a server to access the Internet, you will use only TCP/IP, since all Internet programs and utilities are TCP/IP based.

PPP also has the ability to negotiate setup and configuration parameters when the client and server make their initial connection. PPP provides additional security through the use of both Password Authentication Protocol (PAP) and Challenge *Handshake* Authentication Protocol (CHAP). Both PAP and CHAP are considered logon methods, and they are used to automate the logon procedure. Essentially, they provide a means of sending your user ID and password from the client to the server so they can be authenticated.

Handshaking

The process of the client and server agreeing on communication parameters.

TESTTIP

The PPP protocol is the newer serial-line communications protocol. Make sure that you know the benefits of PPP and the improvements it offers over SLIP.

Point-to-Point Tunneling Protocol (PPTP)

Point-to-Point Tunneling Protocol (PPTP)

A secure method of transmitting messages over the Internet. It is a frequently used encapsulation protocol that creates a "tunnel" for the data to travel safely from source to destination.

The *Point-to-Point Tunneling Protocol (PPTP)* was designed as a more secure way of transmitting messages across the Internet. PPTP is commonly used to create virtual private networks (VPNs).

We know from earlier discussions that a VPN is one or more private networks that can be accessed across the Internet. One of the biggest advantages of a VPN is convenience. For example, a salesperson who travels extensively can dial in to an ISP. Once authenticated, he can then connect across the dial-up Internet connection to a VPN connection. Once the salesperson is authenticated by the VPN, he has access to the corporate network. PPTP allows VPNs to function by providing a private tunnel that the data can pass through securely.

TESTTIP

PPTP is the protocol of choice when implementing virtual private networks.

Independent Computing Architecture (ICA) Protocol

Independent Computing Architecture (ICA)

A Presentation layer protocol that allows any Microsoft Windows client to act as a thin client.

Independent Computing Architecture (ICA) is a Presentation layer protocol that allows any Microsoft Windows client to act as a thin client. That

Remote Access Protocols, Services, and Troubleshooting

means that the client computer, even though it has a hard drive and its own processing power, connects to a central server, which actually runs the application. All keystrokes and mouse movements on the client are transmitted to the server, where they are executed. The server responds by sending screen updates back to the client computer. These screen updates are displayed in one or more windows on the client PC. All of this data is transmitted back and forth using standard networking protocols and hardware. In order to function, ICA requires three components: server software, a network protocol, and client software.

The most common implementation of ICA computing is a product made by the Citrix Company. Microsoft also makes a product named Terminal Server.

Troubleshooting RAS Problems

The important point to remember about the RAS environment is that standard networking rules apply. This means that the client computers must have some type of network adapter, in this case a modem. The client computer must be running the appropriate client software and network protocol.

TROUBLESHOOTING AUTHENTICATION FAILURE

- When an authentication failure occurs, always make sure you are typing the correct user name and password. Although user names are generally not case sensitive, passwords are, so make sure the Caps Lock key is not engaged and try again.
- If you are still unable to authenticate, check with the server administrator to make sure your account has not been locked out or changed in any way. Have the administrator reset the password and try again.
- Another area to check is the type of security and protocols that are being used. The client and the server must be able to speak the same language in order to authenticate your request to log on to the server. For example, if the server uses MS-CHAP to authenticate logon requests, the client must be able to support MS-CHAP as well.
- Make sure you have physical connectivity to the server. After clicking the Connect button on your dial-up networking dialog box, you should be able to hear the destination server answer and the handshaking process take place. Handshaking is the process of the client and server agreeing on the parameters they will use to communicate. If you do not hear any of this happening, you most likely have a physical connection problem, or you may be dialing the wrong number.

TROUBLESHOOTING PROTOCOL CONFIGURATION

Since one of the primary uses of RRAS is to enable Internet connectivity, all RRAS servers will generally use the TCP/IP protocol. Therefore, the TCP/IP protocol must be installed on the client computer. You may or may not be required to manually configure your TCP/IP addressing parameters. If you are, the standard addressing rules, such as those for address class and subnet mask, must be followed. The information must be entered correctly into the correct boxes and all settings, including those for DNS servers, must be assigned. In cases where you are required to statically, or manually assign IP addressing information, your ISP should provide you with written instructions.

Today, most ISPs will assign IP addresses to client computers dynamically. That means that when you log on to the RRAS server, the server will pass all of the addressing parameters to the client. The client must still have the TCP/IP protocol installed and it must be configured to automatically accept IP addressing.

You may also be required to configure the client software on the computer to designate if the computer belongs to a Windows domain or workgroup.

TROUBLESHOOTING PHYSICAL CONNECTIVITY

If your dial-up connection was working correctly and suddenly stopped, begin by conducting some simple checks of the modem. Although features vary from brand to brand and model to model, most modems contain one or more lights that will give you an idea whether the problem is with the modem, the telephone line, or the computer (see Figure 12.21).

- **Activity:** The activity light glows whenever information is being exchanged. It will light up when information is being passed through the device. When operating normally, the light should be flashing green. If the light is not flashing, you must determine if the failure is from the phone line, the equipment, or the computer.
- **TX and RX:** If the light is labeled TX, it stands for transmitting or transmission. If it is labeled RX, it means receiving. When operating normally, the lights should be flashing green. If the TX light is not glowing or is red, the problem most likely exists with the computer, the modem, or the physical dial-up connection between the two. If the RX light is not lit or is red, the problem is most likely with either the phone line or the modem hardware.

FIGURE 12.21
Some Status Lights Common on Most Modems

If the lights are not lit, follow these steps to check the Device Manager utility to ensure the network card is configured correctly:

1. On a computer running the Windows XP Professional operating system, press the Start button.
2. When the Start menu appears, select Control Panel. From the Control Panel, select System.
3. When the System Properties dialog box appears, select the Hardware tab. In the Hardware properties dialog box, click the Device Manager button.
4. In the Device Manager, locate the section for modems. Click it to expand it and display the individual adapters. *(Note: For these purposes, a modem and an adapter are the same.)*
5. Locate the installed modem. If the icon for the adapter is a yellow circle with an exclamation point, it indicates a problem with the adapter. If the icon is crossed out with a red *X*, then the adapter is disabled. To obtain more information about a problem device, double-click the entry for it to display its properties.
6. Check the status of the adapter to ensure it is functioning correctly. If it is not, click the Troubleshoot button to begin the troubleshooting process.
7. If the troubleshooter cannot identify and correct the problem, try physically reseating the adapter or reinstalling the driver. If neither of these works, replace the adapter with another one.

TRY IT!

Troubleshoot a modem connectivity problem.

1. Open the Device Manager, locate the modem, and view its properties.
2. View the available lights on the rear of the modem.

8. Finally, check the telephone wiring at your home or office. The easiest way to do this is to unplug the modem and plug a phone into the jack. Listen to the phone to see if a dial tone is present. If not, take the phone outside of the building to the connection box, or where the external telephone wiring connects to the building's internal phone service. Open the box and locate the RJ-11 jack. Plug the phone into that jack and listen for a dial tone. If an RJ-11 jack is not available, you will need a handset with alligator clips to conduct this test. Attach the alligator clips to the metal connectors to which the internal phone line is attached. If a tone exists, a problem exists with the

internal wiring. If you cannot hear a tone, the problem exists with the external wiring. In that case, you will need to contact the telephone company.

Many of the steps that were identified above can be used to troubleshoot a new connection as well. With a new connection, always suspect that some configuration parameter is incorrect. If checks of those parameters disclose that everything is correct, the hardware is always a good place to check. Always begin by checking the lights, since they will usually point you to where the problem is.

STUDY GUIDE

In this chapter, we discussed various subjects. Here are some key points to remember.

UNDERSTANDING REMOTE ACCESS

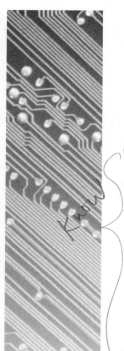

- Remote access is the process of gaining access to some type of network remotely, or from a distant location.
- To connect to a network from a remote location, several components are necessary. These components include the following:
  o A remote access client with a modem.
  o A remote access server with one or more modems.
  o A data line, typically a telephone line, that supports a connection protocol.
- Once users are authenticated, they may or may not be required to log on a second time through the appropriate network client, i.e., the Client for NetWare Networks or the Microsoft Client for Microsoft Networks.
- Once they are authenticated, users have access to network resources, just like any other network client.
- When using remote access, there are two components to consider: the remote access server and the remote access client.

REMOTE ACCESS SERVER (RAS) — Dial up or ISDN

- Almost all major manufacturers of network operating systems, such as Microsoft and Novell, make a remote access component that can be installed on their servers.
- Once remote access has been installed and configured, clients have the ability to connect to the server and then access the network.

RAS Installation

- When you install the Routing and Remote Access Service (RRAS) on a Windows 2000 server, you enable support for both multiprotocol routing and remote access.
- The multiprotocol routing component enables the server to act as a static router, making routing decisions for the AppleTalk, IPX, and IP protocols through manually configured routing tables.

RAS Configuration

- Once the advanced RRAS service has been successfully completed, you have the option of making changes to the server's configuration.

The Security Tab

- In the Security properties dialog box, you determine the type of authentication that will be provided for dial-up clients.
- You can also choose the authentication method that you want to use. Some examples are:
  - Extensible Authentication Protocol (EAP)
  - Microsoft Encrypted Authentication version 2 (MS-CHAP v2)
  - Microsoft Encrypted Authentication (MS-CHAP)
  - Encrypted authentication (CHAP)
  - Shiva Password Authentication Protocol (SPAP)
  - Unencrypted password (PAP)
- You may also choose to allow clients to connect without authentication.
- The exact authentication method you choose will be determined by the type of client that is connecting, by the protocols used, etc.

The IP Tab

- The IP properties dialog box allows you to enable IP routing, along with several other IP-based options.

The PPP Tab

- At the PPP dialog box, you can enable an RRAS server to support the Point-to-Point Protocol (PPP) and set several other options.
- Multilink allows you to connect multiple adapters to multiple lines in order to take advantage of the bandwidth of more than one line. If you want to use multilink with a dial-up connection, the following conditions apply:
  - The ISP you are dialing in to must support the synchronization of multiple modems.

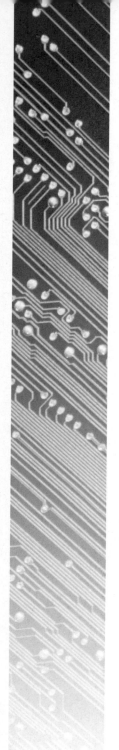

- o You will need to install multiple modems.
- o You will need to plug a separate phone line into each modem.
- ISDN is the one form of telephone connections that does not need multiple modems. This is because one ISDN adapter can act as more than one device, since ISDN includes two 64-Kbps B channels.
- Each of these channels can be used independently of the other, essentially creating two separate physical devices.
- A multilink connection can be used to combine multiple ISDN B channels of a basic rate interface (BRI) connection.
- You may also select to use Bandwidth Allocation Protocol (BAP) and Bandwidth Allocation Control Protocol (BACP) to allow for dynamic control of the multilink bandwidth.
- Both BAP and BACP are able to adapt to changing bandwidth conditions. BAP provides all of the parameters necessary to allow the client and server to negotiate when using multilink.

The Event Logging Tab

- The Event Logging dialog box allows you to determine whether to log errors and warnings and how much of this information will be logged.
- You can also enable or disable the logging of PPP events.

REMOTE ACCESS CLIENT

- From a hardware point of view, the client must have a modem installed and the modem must be connected to a phone line.
- Once these physical requirements are met, a dial-up connection is established using system-supplied software.
- Your dial-up connection has a number of properties that can be changed to help connect to an RRAS server. Examples include:
  - o General: Allows you to change the area code or phone number that is being dialed.
  - o Options: Can be used to change dialing and redialing options.
  - o Security: Used to set security validation options, such as using an unsecure versus a secure password for logon.
  - o Networking: Displays the networking components (such as clients, protocols, and services) that are being used to make the connection to the RRAS server.
  - o Sharing: Allows you to enable and disable Internet connection sharing.

Serial Line Internet Protocol (SLIP)

- For the RRAS server and client to communicate with each other, they must use a protocol.
- SLIP is a TCP/IP-based protocol that allows the client and server to talk with each other.
- SLIP connections are now an older technology with many limitations.
- SLIP is being replaced by a newer technology, the Point-to-Point Protocol (PPP).

Point-to-Point Protocol (PPP)

- Point-to-Point Protocol (PPP) is also a serial-communications protocol that allows a dial-up client to access an RRAS server.
- PPP provides error-checking features that SLIP does not have, and PPP has the ability to share a data line.
- PPP can handle synchronous and asynchronous communications.
- PPP allows you to use more than one protocol. While SLIP can transport only TCP/IP traffic, PPP can transport TCP/IP, IPX/SPX, and even AppleTalk traffic.
- All of these protocols can be transported at the same time using PPP's multiprotocol transport mechanism.
- PPP also provides additional security through the use of both Password Authentication Protocol (PAP) and Challenge Handshake Authentication Protocol (CHAP).

Point-to-Point Tunneling Protocol (PPTP)

- The Point-to-Point Tunneling Protocol (PPTP) was designed as a more secure way of transmitting messages across the Internet.
- PPTP is commonly used to create virtual private networks (VPNs).

Independent Computing Architecture (ICA) Protocol

- Independent Computing Architecture (ICA) is a Presentation layer protocol that allows any Microsoft Windows client to act as a thin client.
- As a thin client, the client computer connects to a central server, which actually runs the application.
- All keystrokes and mouse movements and strokes on the client are transmitted to the server, where they are executed.

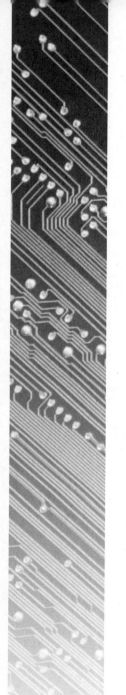

- The server responds by sending screen updates back to the client computer. These screen updates are displayed in one or more windows on the client PC.

Troubleshooting RAS Problems

- The important point to remember about the RAS environment is that standard networking rules apply.
- Client computers must have some type of network adapter, in this case a modem.
- Client computers must be running the appropriate client software and network protocol.

Troubleshooting Authentication Failure

- When an authentication failure occurs, always make sure you are typing the correct user name and password.
- Although user names are generally not case sensitive, passwords are, so make sure the Caps Lock key is not engaged and try again.
- If you are still unable to authenticate, check with the server administrator to make sure your account has not been locked out or changed in any way.
- Have the administrator reset the password and try again.
- Another area to check is the type of security and protocols that are being used.
- The client and the server must be able to speak the same language in order to authenticate your request to log on to the server.
- Make sure you have physical connectivity to the server.

Troubleshooting Protocol Configuration

- Since one of the primary uses of RRAS is to enable Internet connectivity, all RRAS servers will generally use the TCP/IP protocol.
- The TCP/IP protocol must be installed on the client computer.
- You may or may not be required to manually configure your TCP/IP addressing parameters. If you are, the standard addressing rules, including those for address class and subnet mask, must be followed.
- The information must be entered correctly into the correct boxes and all settings, including those for DNS servers, must be assigned.
- In cases where you are required to statically, or manually, assign IP addressing information, your ISP should provide you with written instructions.

- Today, most ISPs will assign IP addresses to client computers dynamically. That means that when you log on to the RRAS server, the server will pass all of the addressing parameters to the client.
- The client must still have the TCP/IP protocol installed and it must be configured to automatically accept IP addressing.
- You may also be required to configure the client software on the computer to designate if the computer belongs to a Windows domain or workgroup.

Troubleshooting Physical Connectivity

- If your dial-up connection was working correctly and suddenly stopped, begin by conducting some simple checks of the modem and phone line.
- Although features vary from brand to brand and model to model, most modems contains one or more lights that will give you an idea whether the problem is with the modem, the telephone line, or the computer.
- Some of the status lights that are common on most modems include:
  - Activity
  - TX and RX
- If the lights are not lit, check the Device Manager utility to ensure the network card is configured correctly.
- Check the status of the adapter to ensure it is functioning correctly.
- Finally, check the telephone wiring at your home or office.

PRACTICE TEST

Try this test to check your mastery of the concepts in this chapter.

1. Typically, a _____ is used to dial in to a remote access server.
   a. NIC
   b. telephone
   c. modem
   d. DSL connection

2. Once dial-up users are authenticated, they may or may not be required to log on a second time through the appropriate
   a. network client.
   b. Windows logon.
   c. terminal window.
   d. LAN connection

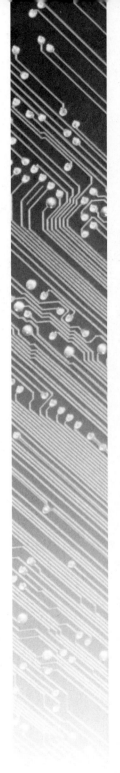

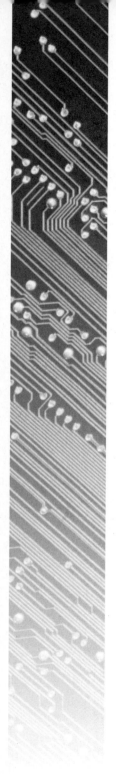

3. The multiprotocol routing component on a Windows 2000 RRAS server enables the server to act as a _____ router.
   a. dynamic
   b. static
   c. Cisco
   d. stationary

4. During installation of the Windows 2000 RRAS service, which setting allows you to establish Network Address Translation (NAT) services?
   a. Internet connection server
   b. remote access server
   c. virtual private network (VPN) server
   d. network router

5. Which of the following options are available for assigning IP addresses to clients that dial in to a Windows 2000 RRAS server? (Select two)
   a. static
   b. DHCP
   c. single address
   d. multi-address
   e. specified range

6. Which of the following services adds security and accounting features to the RRAS server by monitoring clients that try to connect to the server, by authenticating their requests allowing them access to the server, and by providing enough configuration information to the client so that the client can take advantage of RRAS and network services?
   a. routing
   b. RADIUS
   c. VPN
   d. PPTP

7. Which of the following utilities would you use to set up a basic RRAS server?
   a. Control Panel/Network Utility
   b. Control Panel/Services
   c. Control Panel/Dial-up Services
   d. Control Panel/Network and Dial-up Connections icon

8. Any transaction that occurs between client and the RADIUS server is authenticated by a
   a. password.
   b. user name.
   c. shared secret.
   d. tunnel.

9. During installation of your RRAS server, you did not enable routing. You would now like to enable routing. Which properties dialog box would allow you to do this?
   a. General
   b. Routing
   c. IP
   d. Security

10. _____ allows you to connect multiple adapters to multiple lines to take advantage of the bandwidth of more than one line.
   a. DSL
   b. Cable
   c. RRAS
   d. Multilink

11. How many modems are required to take advantage of multilink when running ISDN?
   a. one
   b. two
   c. three
   d. four

12. Which of the following are used to allow for dynamic control of the multilink bandwidth? (Select two)
   a. LCP
   b. BAP
   c. BACP
   d. PPP

13. Which of the following protocols provides error-checking features and the ability to share a data line?
   a. SLIP
   b. CSLIP
   c. PPP
   d. BAP

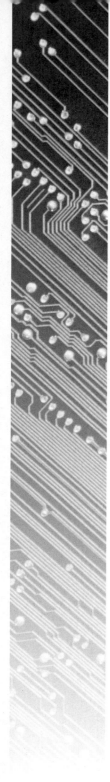

14. Which of the following protocols is commonly used when implementing virtual private networks?
    a. SLIP
    b. CSLIP
    c. PPP
    d. PPTP

15. When using ICA, where does the processing take place?
    a. thin client
    b. protocol
    c. thick client
    d. server

16. When an authentication failure occurs, which of the following is probably the first thing you should check?
    a. user name and password
    b. physical connection
    c. whether the server is on
    d. whether you are running the correct protocol

17. _____ is the process of the client and server agreeing on the parameters they will use to communicate.
    a. Authentication
    b. Logon
    c. Handshaking
    d. Negotiation

18. You are using a dial-up Internet Service Provider to access the World Wide Web and e-mail. With this information in mind, which of the following statements is true?
    a. The TCP/IP protocol does not have to be installed on the client.
    b. The TCP/IP protocol must be manually configured.
    c. The TCP/IP protocol must be installed on the client computer.
    d. The RAS server cannot dynamically assign IP addresses.

TROUBLESHOOTING

1. You have recently installed a second modem in your personal computer running the Windows 2000 Professional operating system. After attaching the telephone line and installing the necessary drivers for the second modem, you have attempted to contact your Internet Sservice Provider. You are able to contact the ISP and log in to its network; however, you are not seeing any extra bandwidth. List the items that you should check to determine where the problem lies.

2. You have had a dial-up Internet connection to an ISP for more than a year and have experienced few problems. When attempting to connect today, you were unsuccessful. While troubleshooting, you realize there is no dial tone at the modem. List some of the steps you would take to identify where the problem exists.

CUSTOMER SERVICE

1. As a manager in the MIS department, you have been asked to provide dial-up service for salespeople who travel around the United States. This dial-up service should allow the salespeople to access the corporate e-mail system and their home directories. Security is a concern, as is the ability to interact with Microsoft Active Directory. What are some of the steps you should take to set up this system?

2. In an effort to minimize administration costs, your company has directed you to implement a new technology solution aimed at moving the majority of information processing from the workstations to centrally located servers. Identify a technology that was discussed in this chapter that would fulfill your requirements.

FOR MORE INFORMATION

For links to Web sites that provide further information about the topics covered in this chapter, go to the EMC/Paradigm Internet Resource Center at www.emcp.com/College Division/Internet Resource Centers/Networking/System Administration/Web Resources: For More Information.

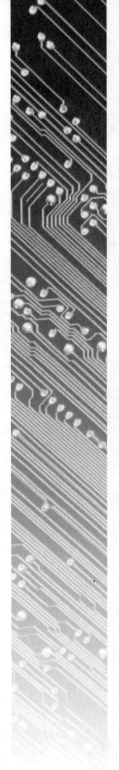

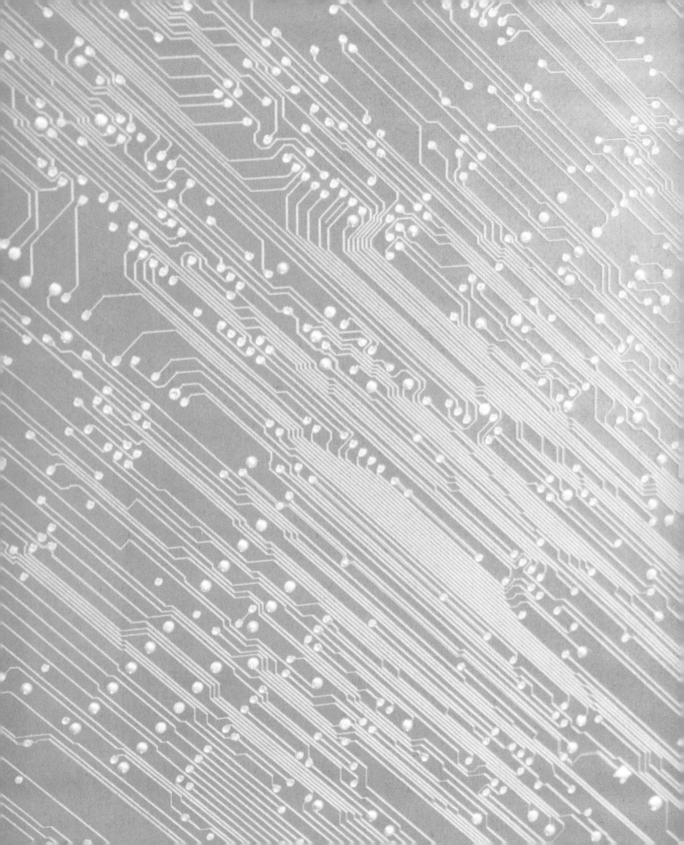

Security Protocols

Network+ Examination
- **Objective 2.13:** Identify the following security protocols and describe their purpose and function:
  - IPSec
  - L2TP
  - SSL
  - Kerberos

Security is the number one watchword with networks today. Many enterprise networks create whole departments that do nothing but write the policies for network security and manage the deployment of security policies throughout the network. As a technician, it is important that you understand the various methodologies available in the industry and be able to assess the need to use one form or another in given situations. This is also a rapidly changing segment of IT. Keeping up with new industry options is critical to staying on top of the job.

Internet Protocol Security (IPSec)

Internet Protocol Security (IPSec) is a relatively new IETF protocol designed to provide communications security across both public (Internet) and private (intranet) network infrastructures. The basis of this protocol is a framework of open standards that can ensure secure communications—preventing unauthorized individuals from viewing the contents of datagrams during transit—without being tied to any one operating system or specific devices.

Business operations have moved from the office, factory, and telephone to global communications and file exchanges through e-mail. Much of the business-to-business (B2B) and business-to-customer (B2C) communication now takes place over the Internet, a public, untrusted infrastructure. Any savvy person interested in the contents of an e-mail or file can intercept packets and read the contents of those packets, giving the hacker the opportunity to sabotage business operations or steal information about the business or its customers. To protect the privacy, authenticity, and integrity of data transmissions, an administrator can require the use of IPSec, thus protecting the data exchange.

IPSec can prevent some of the threats identified in Chapter 10. IPSec will prohibit identity spoofing, denial-of-service attacks, and *packet sniffing,* which violates the sender's privacy. If so configured, IPSec can also guarantee data integrity, thus preventing corrupt data from being used against the customer or the business.

How IPSec Works

IPSec provides the *encryption* and *authentication* mechanisms at the Network layer of the OSI Model. This means that all traffic will be subject to the policies designed for communication. IPSec can provide efficient security for all parts of the transmission. This is known as "end-to-end" security. End systems (source and destination devices) do not need to make any changes to applications to take full advantage of the security of IPSec. Figure 13.1 demonstrates how IPSec works.

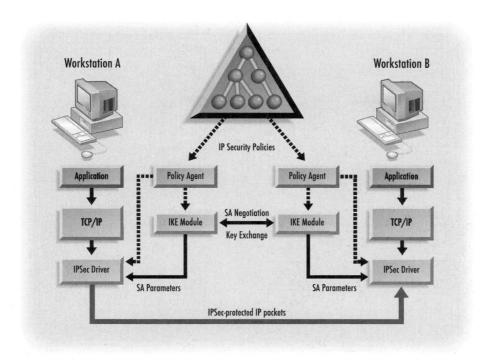

FIGURE 13.1
How IPSec Works

With IPSec, a source and destination device form a *security association* using Internet Key Exchange (IKE). A security association is a contract between two devices to use a secure transmission mechanism. Security associations are unidirectional, which means that two associations must be formed during every communication: one from A to B, and one from B to A. Figure 13.2 shows a security association in action. Figure 13.3 shows how IKE works in the process. IKE provides the mechanism through which the two devices can exchange the required key for identification and authentication. IKE is also responsible for creating the authenticated, secure tunnel between the two systems. IKE requires that both systems be able to participate in an IPSec transmission, and that they both are able to use the required type of keys. IPSec supports the key types described below.

Security association

An agreement between two devices to communicate using IPSec and certain security management functions of the IPSec framework.

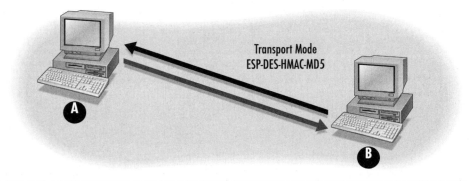

FIGURE 13.2
The Security Association

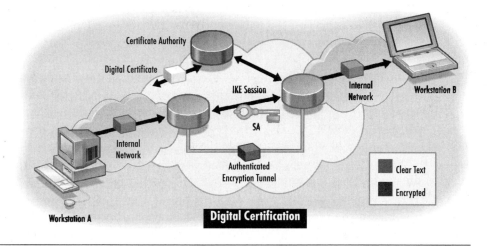

FIGURE 13.3
Internet Key Exchange in
Practice

- **Pre-shared keys:** To share a key, both the source and destination devices must have the same key installed on their system. The source system will use the pre-shared key to create a keyed hash of the data that contains the pre-shared key. When received at the destination system, that system can create the same hash using its copy of the pre-shared key. When that independent second copy of the hash is compared to the source hash, they will match, and the two devices will then know that this is an appropriate, secure communication.

Security Protocols

- **Public Key Cryptography:** *Public Key Cryptography* is often referred to as *Public Key Infrastructure (PKI)*. PKI requires that the network run a certificate server that is able to either issue certificates to entities requesting the certificates or store a set of certificates purchased from a third-party vendor. These certificates produce two types of keys: public and private. The public key is freely distributed to any entity that requests it. The private key never leaves the owner of the key. When a secure transmission is requested, the owner of the key sends the public key to the requestor. The requestor uses that key to encrypt the message and then sends it to the owner of the key pair. At the destination, the key pair owner uses the private key along with the public key to decrypt the message. Because both the public key and the private key are needed to decrypt a message, a hacker cannot sniff packets and read the contents, thus making this form of security very valuable to network administrators.

- **Digital signatures:** With *digital signatures,* the sending device "signs" the transmission digitally and sends it to the destination. The receiving party will know that the data has been received intact if the original digital signature is still intact.

  Several new packet formats are defined through the IETF IPSec standards. These packet formats give IPSec its functionality during transmission. Two examples are:

- **Authentication header (AH):** This allows IPSec to provide data integrity. In other words, the authentication header makes sure that the data is in the same state as when it was first transmitted by the source machine.

- **Encapsulating security payload (ESP):** This allows IPSec to guarantee both data integrity and confidentiality.

IPSec Modes of Operation

IPSec offers two modes of operation, making it very flexible in its deployment.

Transport Mode

In *transport mode,* only the payload (data contents) of the datagram, or packet, is encrypted. The original IP headers remain unencrypted, allowing intervening devices to know the real source and destination IP addresses of the datagram. This mode is efficient because it adds only a few bytes to the size of the packet.

Public Key Cryptography, or Public Key Infrastructure (PKI) ✓

A process in which two keys are generated, a public key and a private key, that allow data to be encrypted for transmission and decrypted only by the issuer of the public key.

Digital signature

A field in a packet that acts as the sealing signature. If the original digital signature is intact when it reaches the destination, the assumption can be made that the packet has not been tampered with en route.

Transport mode

An IPSec data transmission process in which only the payload (data contents) of a packet is encrypted.

When a message is being transmitted in transport mode, an attacker could see, for example, that the human resources manager of a company was sending a lot of packets to the legal counsel, but the attacker would not be able to see what was contained in those packets.

Because the real source and destination addresses remain intact in transport mode, other special processing functions can be implemented. For example, *Quality of Service (QoS)* prioritizes packets so that certain types can be sent before others. When used in conjunction with Resource Reservation Protocol (RSVP), QoS can allocate bandwidth to certain packets to expedite delivery.

Tunnel Mode

In *tunnel mode,* IPSec encrypts the entire IP datagram. In other words, the datagram becomes the payload for a new IP packet. This mode obscures both the payload and the source and destination addresses in the original packet.

Tunnel mode allows an intervening device such as a router to act as an IPSec proxy for the datagram. The router is actually performing the encryption process on behalf of a host from the network. The packet will be decrypted by the destination host's router and sent on to the real destination address. When deploying IPSec in tunnel mode, end systems do not have to be configured in any specific way because the end systems (source and destination) are not performing the IPSec functions.

Figure 13.4 depicts the IPSec tunnel and transport modes. Figure 13.5 depicts the IPSec process and identifies the key components in that process. Should any one of the components be absent, the communication may still take place, but the security of the transmission will be compromised.

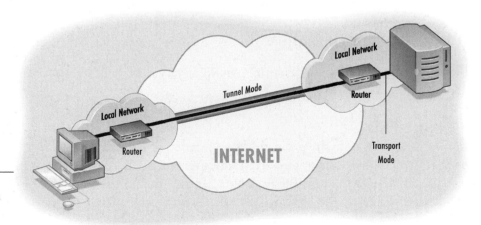

FIGURE 13.4
Tunnel and Transport Modes for IPSec

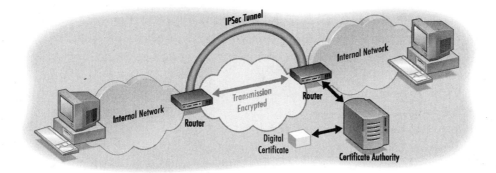

FIGURE 13.5
IPSec in Action

Virtual Private Networks (VPNs)

Within a discussion on security protocols and protection of data during transmission, it would be remiss to leave out a brief discussion of the *virtual private network (VPN)* and the function it serves in secure data transmission. Prior to the development of newer options, VPN technologies provided the most secure transmission.

A VPN offers transmission between two systems using the public infrastructure of the Internet as the medium for transmission. VPN technology extends the boundary of the private network to make use of the public infrastructure. If communications were allowed to proceed without protecting the data contained in payloads, any hacker could access and use this information, wreaking havoc on consumers and businesses. The only other alternative would be to create private dedicated networks, with each business owning all of the cables that connected it to the locations it needed to reach. Not only would this be a very costly and impractical solution to communications, but also it is unnecessary since the public infrastructure already exists.

For security, a VPN relies on some kind of tunneling protocol and some form of encapsulation. The tunneling protocol "wraps" each packet securely, thus creating a virtual tunnel through which the packets may travel. This tunnel makes the transmission impervious to sniffers and hackers who might otherwise corrupt data or steal information. The encapsulation (which is really just a new header) provides the routing information, allowing the packet to be delivered to the destination host machine. Data is usually encrypted, as well, so that even if someone were to intercept the packets, they would be unintelligible to the interceptor.

Virtual private network (VPN)

A connection between a source and a destination for transmitting data securely. This process uses tunneling protocols that encrypt the data during the sending process so that it cannot be read by any entity except for the destination system.

The most widely used method of VPN tunneling is Point-to-Point Tunneling Protocol (PPTP), an industry standard for encrypting data (see below). All modern operating systems commonly used in homes and businesses are PPTP-capable and are easily configured (in some cases, self-configuring).

VPNs offer many advantages:
- Safe transmission of data.
- Flexible, secure business networking.
- Lowered transmission costs because public media is used.
- Lowered administrative overhead because a variety of network protocols can be used and because data transmissions are secure.
- Widespread existing support for VPN structures through ISPs.

To form a VPN, both sides of the transmission must participate. Figure 13.6 shows the basic VPN structure.

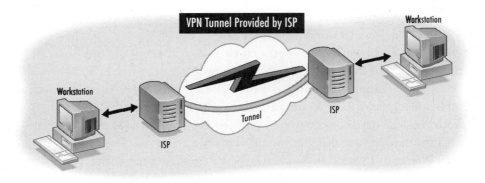

FIGURE 13.6
Virtual Private Network Using the ISP to Provide Secure Transmission

In Figure 13.6, the ISP provides the VPN connection for the packets. We could change this slightly by placing a VPN between the two computers that are transmitting. Now the responsibility for secure transmission is shifted back to the network of ownership, and the packet is protected before it reaches the Internet or an ISP (see Figure 13.7).

    Security Protocols

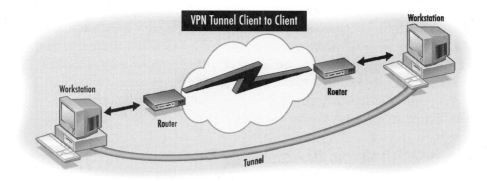

FIGURE 13.7
Using the Network VPN Server
for Secure Transmissions

Two protocols support VPN technology: Point-to-Point Tunneling Protocol (PPTP) and Layer 2 Tunneling Protocol (L2TP).

POINT-TO-POINT TUNNELING PROTOCOL (PPTP)

Point-to-Point Tunneling Protocol (PPTP) architecture is built on the Point-to-Point Protocol (PPP) used by dial-up clients for remote access connections. With PPP, all transmissions undergo connection setup negotiations, authentication requests, and error checking. PPTP takes security a step further to provide the encapsulation capability of a virtual tunnel.

PPTP supports a multiprotocol environment. That is, if your network runs TCP/IP and IPX/SPX for NetWare interoperability, users may access the network remotely using an IP connection but transmit using IPX/SPX as the communications protocol.

The PPTP encapsulation process has four steps:

1. The payload is encrypted and encapsulated with a PPP header.
2. The Data Link layer (layer 2) of the OSI Model encapsulates the PPP frame with a modified generic routing encapsulation (GRE) header.
3. The GRE-PPP payload is encapsulated with an IP header that has the source and destination addresses of the PPTP client and PPTP server.
4. The IP datagram is encapsulated with a header and trailer for layer 2 (Data Link layer) containing the technology for the Physical layer.

Microsoft Point-to-Point Encryption (MPPE) provides the encryption function in a Microsoft network. This is the standard protocol understood by more recent Microsoft operating systems. MPPE does require using either Microsoft Encrypted Authentication (MS-CHAP) or Extensible Authentication Protocol-Transport Layer Service (EAP-TLS) for authentication.

While on the topic of encryption, note that MPPE supports 40-bit, 56-bit, and 128-bit encryption. Non-Microsoft clients who use a VPN will use 40-bit encryption, so make sure to allow this lowest level. If the data will be transmitted outside of North Amierca, or if the machine itself is located outside of North America, check ahead of time to make sure that the destination country accepts 128-bit encryption, or that the machine is configured to use 40-bit or 56-bit encryption.

LAYER 2 TUNNELING PROTOCOL (L2TP)

The successor to Point-to-Point Tunneling Protocol (PPTP), Layer 2 Tunneling Protocol (L2TP) is also used to create virtual private networks for secure communications.

L2TP is actually a combination of Microsoft's Point-to-Point Tunneling Protocol and Cisco's proposed Layer 2 Forwarding (L2F) technology. L2TP encapsulates frames (layer 2 packet structures) sent over an IP network. The frames are encapsulated as UDP (User Datagram Protocol) messages. L2TP uses an L2TP Access Concentrator (LAC) and the L2TP Network Server (LNS) to complete the tunnel it creates. Figure 13.8 shows how L2TP works across an internetwork.

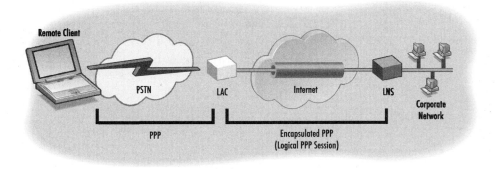

FIGURE 13.8
L2TP and the Internetwork

L2TP uses a five-step process for encapsulation. Note that if you are using encryption, you will also need to use IPSec (for further information, see the next topic).

1. The PPP payload is encapsulated with the PPP header and L2TP header.
2. The packet is then encapsulated with a UDP header containing the source and destination ports set to 1701.

3. Usually, the UDP message is encrypted and encapsulated with an IPSec encapsulating security payload (ESP) header and trailer. It will also usually include a trailer for the authentication header (AH).
4. The IPSec-encapsulated packet is again encapsulated, this time with an IP header holding the source and destination IP addresses of the VPN client and server.
5. The IP datagram is encapsulated with a header and trailer for the data link physical interface (this is dependent on the kind of transmission—Ethernet dial-up, etc.).

DEPLOYING L2TP AND IPSEC ON THE NETWORK

Often L2TP and IPSec are used together to provide secure communications. This is known as L2TP/IPSec. Microsoft promotes this combination for both Internet and intranet communications, beginning with its Windows 2000 products.

The security of the transmission is increased not only because the transmission is encapsulated and encrypted, but also because the source and destination machines must authenticate with each other, making authentication a two-step process. This is accomplished by the use of certificates installed on both systems.

When using L2TP/IPSec, IPSec provides the encryption mechanisms and L2TP creates the tunnel. The encryption methods used include 56-bit key encryption and triple DES (3Des), which uses three 56-bit keys.

When deploying L2TP/IPSec on a Microsoft network (and with physical devices that support L2TP/IPSec), keep in mind that Network Address Translation (NAT) may not be able to accept datagrams encrypted with IPSec. The real source and destination addresses are hidden, and therefore, NAT cannot translate properly, causing the NAT box to drop the IPSec packets.

Secure Sockets Layer (SSL)

Secure Sockets Layer (SSL) ✓

A protocol that provides a secure transmission over a public infrastructure whereby the client and the server can be absolutely identified. SSL is used with HTTP and FTP.

Secure Sockets Layer (SSL) is a protocol that has been designed to provide a secure connection over an insecure network, such as the Internet. The primary purpose of SSL is to provide a means whereby a client or a server can both be absolutely identified. SSL was initially developed by Netscape to transmit private information and Web pages over the Internet; however, Microsoft's Internet Explorer now also supports the protocol. Whereas IPSec can provide efficient security for all parts of the transmission, SSL provides security for only part of the transmission. SSL runs above TCP/IP and below some higher-level protocols, such as Hypertext Transfer Protocol (HTTP) and File Transfer Protocol (FTP) (see Figure 13.9).

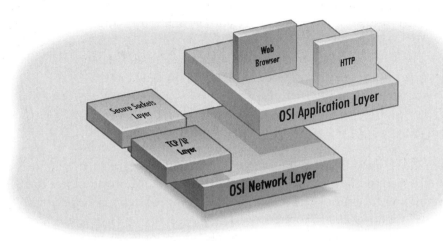

FIGURE 13.9
Secure Sockets Layer, Higher-
and Lower-Level Protocols

SSL uses a series of keys, both public and private, to encrypt the data that is transported across the secure connection. A company called RSA Security owns the public-and-private key encryption system. The RSA algorithm, or cipher, is a commonly used encryption and authentication algorithm that includes the use of a digital certificate. The public key is made available to whomever needs it, while the private key is stored in a central location and never made public. Data that is encrypted with the public key can be decrypted only with the private key.

TestTip

Know that SSL uses RSA encryption techniques. Also, ensure you are familiar with the roles that both the public and private keys play.

SSL uses TCP/IP to allow SSL-enabled servers and SSL-enabled clients to talk with each other. SSL is composed of three primary components: server authentication, client authentication, and an encrypted connection.

- **SSL server authentication:** This allows a client computer to identify the server that it is talking with. The client uses a public key to verify that the server's certificate and public ID are correct and valid, and that they have been issued by a certificate authority (CA) that is included on the client's list of trusted CAs. For example, when someone places an order for books over the Internet, he or she might want to verify the identity of the server before providing a credit card number.

- **SSL client authentication:** This is used to verify the client's identity. SSL-enabled server software checks the client's certificate and public ID to ensure they are correct and valid and that they have been issued by a CA included on the server's list of trusted CAs. A good example of this is online banking. When a user decides to check account balances or transfer funds to a debtor, the bank will confirm the user's or client's identification.

- **Encrypted SSL connection:** This ensures that all of the information transferred between the SSL-enabled client and SSL-enabled server are encrypted and decrypted during transmission Even if the data is intercepted, it will remain secure and the interceptor will not be able to read it. Furthermore, the data transmitted across the connection contains a mechanism to detect tampering, so the data can be checked to see if it was altered during transmission.

SSL Subprotocols

The SSL protocol includes two subprotocols: SSL handshake protocol and SSL record protocol.

THE SSL HANDSHAKE PROTOCOL

An SSL session begins with the SSL handshake process. During this handshake process, the server uses a public key to authenticate itself to the client. Together, the client and server create symmetric keys that will be used for the encryption, decryption, and tamper detection process that occurs during data transmission. If necessary, the handshake process will also allow the client to authenticate itself to the server. The handshake process follows these steps:

1. The client sends its SSL version number, cipher settings, randomly generated data, and any other required information to the server.
2. The server sends its SSL version number, cipher settings, randomly generated data, certificate, and any other required information to the client. Also, if the client wants to access a resource that is located on the server, and that access requires the authentication of the client, the server will request the client's certificate.
3. The client uses this information to authenticate the server. If a problem occurs and the server cannot be authenticated, a warning message is sent to the computer user and a secure connection is not

established. If the server is successfully authenticated, the client goes on to Step 4.

4. Using the data that has been passed between the client and server, the client creates the premaster secret for the session. The premaster secret is encrypted with the server's public key and then sent to the server.

5. If the server requests authentication from the client, the client signs another piece of data that is generated during the handshake process and known to both the client and server. The client sends this data, along with its certificate, to the server when it initially sends the encrypted premaster secret.

6. After the server receives all of the requested information from the client, it will attempt to authenticate the client. If the client authentication process is unsuccessful, the server terminates the session. If the client is successfully authenticated, the server decrypts the premaster secret with its own private key and then completes a series of processes to generate the master secret.

7. Once the master secret is generated, both the client and the server use the master secret to generate the session keys. Session keys are symmetric keys used to encrypt and decrypt information exchanged between the client and the server during the SSL session. The session keys also work to verify that the data has not been changed during transmission over the SSL connection.

8. The client and server each sends a message to the other informing it that all future messages from the client will be encrypted using the session key that they generated. They both then send a separate, encrypted message indicating that the handshake process is completed.

9. Once the handshake process has been completed, the SSL connection can be used to transmit data securely. Both the client and the server use the session keys to encrypt and decrypt data sent to each other and to confirm that it has not been tampered with during transmission.

THE SSL RECORD PROTOCOL

The SSL record protocol defines the message format that is used to transmit encrypted data. The record protocol uses a series of algorithms that are generated by the handshaking process to encrypt the transmitted data. For example, when users access an encrypted Web page, the Web server locates the Web page, uses the record protocol to encrypt the page, and then passes it along to the browser on the client computer. The Web browser decrypts the Web page and checks its integrity before displaying it for the user.

MAN-IN-THE-MIDDLE ATTACK

The Man in the Middle is a rogue program that intercepts all communication between the client and a server during an SSL session. The program works by intercepting the real keys that are passed back and forth during the handshake process. After intercepting the keys, the rogue program then substitutes its own keys, making it appear like the SSL-enabled server to the SSL-enabled client, and vice versa.

Once this occurs, the encrypted information that appears to be exchanged between the client and server is actually encrypted with the rogue program's public key or private key, rather than the client or server's real keys (see Figure 13.10).

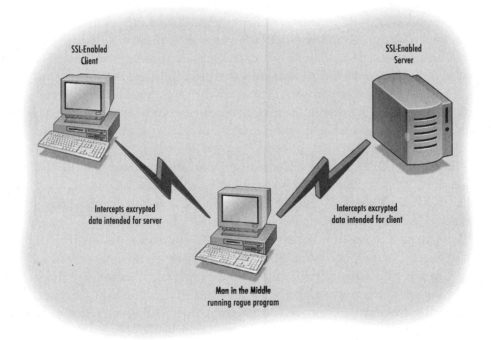

The rogue program establishes one set of session keys that it will use to communicate with the server and another set of session keys that are used to communicate with the client. In essence, it appears like the SSL-enabled server to the client and the SSL-enabled client to the server. Once it completes the handshake process, the rogue program can read and change all of the data that is transmitted between the client and server without being detected. To help combat these types of attacks, the client can be forced to check the domain name in the server certificate to ensure it matches the domain name of the server with which it is establishing the secure connection.

Kerberos

Kerberos ✓

A secure network system that uses strong encryption processes to provide authentication for users and for services that need to communicate and be validated on a network.

Principal

A user or service that routinely communicates on the network.

Kerberos is a secure network system that uses strong encryption processes that are designed to provide authentication for users and for services that need to communicate and be validated on a network. Based on the assumption that a network is never totally secure, Kerberos provides a way for these users and network services to prove their identity to gain access to other network resources. Kerberos is the default encryption and security system used with Microsoft Windows 2000 operating systems.

Kerberos works through the use of encrypted tickets and several server processes that run on one or more third-party trusted servers. Essentially, this third-party server, commonly known as the Kerberos server, is trusted by all of the *principals* on the network. The principals and the Kerberos server all share a secret password. The users then use this secret password and services to verify that messages they receive are authentic. In doing this, all of the principals on the network can communicate securely with each other.

To help you understand the Kerberos process, let's look at a real-life situation. Suppose that you wish to establish an FTP session with a server that requires a Kerberos "ticket" before it will allow you to connect and transfer data. You must then follow these steps:

1. Obtain a ticket from a Kerberos server. This is accomplished by requesting authentication from the third-party, trusted Kerberos server. This authentication server (AS) will create a session key. The session key is composed of your password and a randomly generated value based on the service you are requesting. This session key is commonly referred to as a ticket-granting ticket (TGT).

2. Once you have the TGT, it must be sent to a ticket-granting server (TGS). The TGS service and the AS service may both run on the same server, or they may be on separate servers. *(Note: Collectively, the authentication server and ticket-granting server are often referred to as the Key Distribution Center (KDC).)* The TGS verifies the ticket, time

stamps it, and returns it to the principal that submitted it. Once the ticket has been returned by the TGS, it can be submitted to the FTP server.

3. The FTP server can accept the ticket, allowing you to access the server; or the FTP server can reject the ticket, denying you access.

4. Since the ticket was time stamped by the TGS, it is valid for more than one session. Typically, a ticket will be valid for up to eight hours. During that eight-hour period, you may use and reuse the ticket for access to the FTP server. After that time, the principal must repeat the process.

See Figure 13.11 for a graphical depiction of the process.

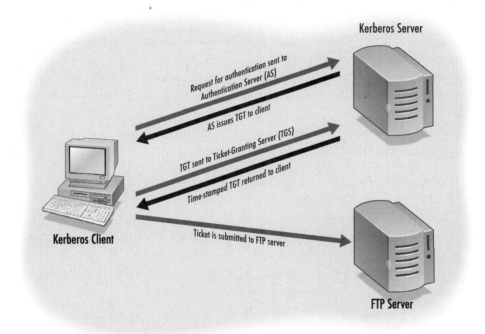

FIGURE 13.11
The Kerberos
Authentication Process

Troubleshooting Security Protocols

TROUBLESHOOTING IPSEC

IPSec problems can disguise themselves as network problems, and network problems can appear to be IPSec problems. Network problems are usually easier to identify. First, use the PING utility to verify network connectivity and throughput. If the problem is not a network issue, then try using the utilities that are part of IPSec (IPSec Monitor for Microsoft's implementation of the protocol).

TROUBLESHOOTING VPNs

When problems arise with VPN connections, two places must be verified: the VPN server and the VPN client. Here is a list of issues to check for the server and the client:

- Make sure you have the configuration for the ports on the VPN server correctly configured.
- Check the authentication settings on the VPN server. Make sure they will work with the types of clients connecting to the network.
- Verify that the IP addresses for the VPN server are correct (based on the network configuration settings).
- Make sure the client has been correctly configured by verifying the connection to the ISP and by verifying the settings for the connection to the VPN server.

TROUBLESHOOTING L2TP

- If you suspect that L2TP is not working correctly, most implementations of L2TP include debugging utilities. Use the utilities that meet the vendor's specifications.
- If you have implemented L2TP on a Windows 2000 network, remember that you cannot use NAT with it. NAT cannot translate the packet addresses and port numbers accurately because of the L2TP header that conceals the true source and destination addresses.

TROUBLESHOOTING SSL

- If a user clicks a hypertext link to a secure page and the connection fails, make sure the user's browser is capable of connecting using SSL.
- If a user is behind a proxy server, the connection will always fail because SSL will not move through proxy server.

STUDY GUIDE

In this chapter, we looked at some of the methods used to promote secure communications both over the Internet and across the intranet. Here are some key points to remember.

INTERNET PROTOCOL SECURITY (IPSEC)

- IPSec is an IETF standard designed to provide secure communications across both public and private networks.
- IPSec can deter several types of threats, including denial-of-service, identity spoofing, and packet sniffing.

HOW IPSEC WORKS

- IPSec relies on key management functions through the use of Internet Key Exchange (IKE).
- IKE provides the mechanism through which two devices (a source and a destination) can exchange the required key types for identification and authentication.
- IPSec supports the following key types:
  o Pre-shared keys are the same key installed on both the source and destination device.
  o Public Key Cryptography, also known as PKI (Public Key Infrastructure), requires a certificate to generate a key pair (public and private key).
  o Digital signatures allow a sending device to add digital code to a transmission, thus ensuring the validity of the transmission.
- Two types of headers are used with IPSec:
  o Authentication header (AH) provides data integrity.
  o Encapsulating security payload (ESP) provides data integrity and confidentiality.

IPSEC MODES OF OPERATION

Transport Mode
IPSec in transport mode encrypts the payload of the packet only. Original IP headers remain intact with correct information. Intervening devices know the real addresses of the source and destination.

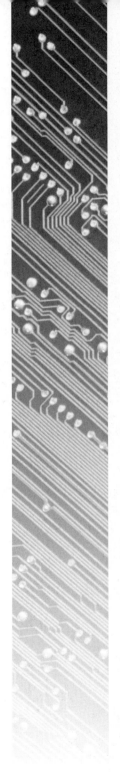

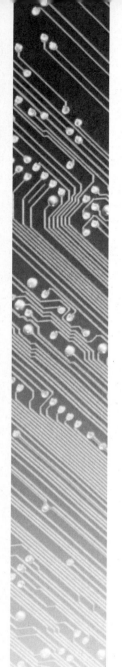

Tunnel Mode

- Tunnel mode allows the entire datagram to be encrypted.
- The real source and destination addresses are hidden, replaced by the source and destination addresses of the routers that handle the process.
- End systems do not need any configuration when deploying IPSec in tunnel mode.

VIRTUAL PRIVATE NETWORKS (VPNs)

- A VPN offers transmission between two systems using the public infrastructure as the medium for transmission, thus extending the boundary of the private network.
- VPNs rely on tunneling to create a safe transmission.
- The tunneling protocol "wraps" the packet (often just the header), creating a virtual tunnel through which the data can be transmitted.
- The encapsulation provides the needed routing information.
- VPN transmissions usually contain an encrypted payload.
- VPNs offer the following advantages:
  - Safe transmission.
  - Flexibility in the business environment.
  - Lower transmission costs.
  - Lower administrative overhead.

Point-to-Point Tunneling Protocol (PPTP)

- PPTP is built on the foundation of PPP used for remote access connections.
- Transmissions undergo connection setup negotiations, authentication, and error checking.
- PPTP supports a multiprotocol environment, using IP as the transport protocol while allowing other protocols (IPX, NetBEUI) to be used for communication on the remote network.
- On Microsoft networks, PPTP uses MPPE (Microsoft Point-to-Point Encryption) as its encryption protocol.
- PPTP supports 40-bit, 56-bit, and 128-bit encryption schemes.

Layer 2 Tunneling Protocol (L2TP)

- L2TP is a relatively new tunneling protocol, built by combining Microsoft's PPTP and Cisco's L2F protocols.
- For its encryption scheme, L2TP uses either a single 56-bit key or triple DES (three 56-bit keys).

Deploying L2TP and IPSec on the Network

- L2TP and IPSec are used together on Microsoft networks to provide secure communications over the Internet or intranet.
- When combined, L2TP provides the tunnel and IPSec provides the payload encryption necessary for security.
- To communicate using L2TP/IPSec, both the source and destination devices must understand the mechanisms and be configured to use them.

SECURE SOCKETS LAYER (SSL)

- Secure Sockets Layer (SSL) is a protocol designed to provide a secure connection over an insecure network, such as the Internet.
- SSL runs above TCP/IP and below some of the higher-level protocols such as Hypertext Transfer Protocol (HTTP) and File Transfer Protocol (FTP).
- SSL uses a series of keys, both public and private, to encrypt the data that is transported across the secure connection.
- The RSA algorithm, or cipher, is a commonly used encryption and authentication algorithm that includes the use of a digital certificate.
- The public key is made available to whomever needs it, while the private key is stored in a central location and never made public.
- Data that is encrypted with the public key can be decrypted only with the private key.

SSL Server Authentication

- SSL server authentication allows a client computer to identify the server that it is talking with.
- A client uses a public key to verify that the server's certificate and public ID are correct and valid, and that they have been issued by a certificate authority (CA) that is included on the client's list of trusted CAs.

SSL Client Authentication

- SSL client authentication is used to verify the client's identity.
- SSL-enabled server software checks the client's certificate and public ID to ensure they are correct and valid and that they have been issued by a CA included on the server's list of trusted CAs.

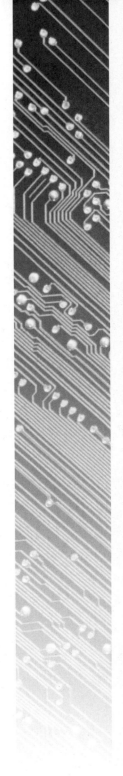

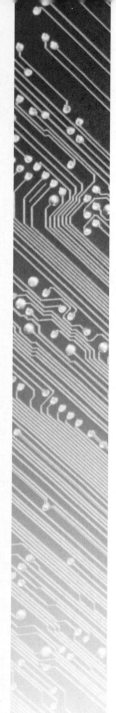

Encrypted SSL Connection

- The encrypted SSL connection ensures that all of the information transferred between the SSL-enabled client and SSL-enabled server are encrypted and decrypted during transmission.
- All of the data transmitted across the connection contains a mechanism to detect tampering, so the data can be checked to see if it was altered during transmission.

SSL SUBPROTOCOLS

- The SSL protocol includes two subprotocols, SSL handshake protocol and the SSL record protocol.

The SSL Handshake Protocol

- An SSL session begins with the SSL handshake process.
- The handshake process is an exchange of messages that the server uses to authenticate itself to the client using a public key.
- The client and the server cooperate to create symmetric keys that will be used for the encryption, decryption, and tamper detection process that occurs during data transmission.
- If necessary, the handshake process will also allow the client to authenticate itself to the server.

The SSL Record Protocol

- The SSL record protocol defines the message format that is used to transmit encrypted data.
- The record protocol uses a series of algorithms that are generated by the handshaking process to encrypt the transmitted data.

Man-in-the-Middle Attack

- The Man in the Middle is a rogue program that intercepts all communications between the client and a server during an SSL session.

KERBEROS

- Kerberos is a secure network system, using strong encryption processes that are designed to provide authentication for users and for services that need to communicate and be validated on a network.
- Kerberos provides a way for these users and network services to prove their identity to gain access to other network resources.

- Kerberos works through the use of encrypted tickets and several server processes that run on one or more third-party trusted servers.
- The principals and the Kerberos server all share a secret password.
- The secret password is used by the users and services to verify that messages they receive are authentic.
- Begin the Kerberos process by requesting authentication from a third-party, trusted Kerberos server.
- The authentication server (AS) will create a session key, commonly referred to as a ticket-granting ticket (TGT).
- The TGT is sent to a ticket-granting server (TGS).
- The TGS verifies the ticket, time stamps it, and returns it to the principal that submitted it.
- Once the TGS has returned the ticket, it can be submitted to the service you are trying to access.
- The service can accept the ticket, allowing you to access the server, or it can reject it, denying you access.
- Since the ticket was time stamped by the TGS, it is valid for more than one session.
- Kerberos is the default encryption and security system used with Microsoft Windows 2000 operating systems.

PRACTICE TEST

Try this test to check your mastery of the concepts in this chapter.

1. Which of the following has been designed to provide a secure connection over an insecure network such as the Internet?
    a. PPP
    b. Kerberos
    c. SSL
    d. ISP

2. Kerberos works through the use of _____ and several server processes that run on one or more third-party trusted servers.
    a. shared secrets
    b. encrypted tickets
    c. sessions
    d. passwords

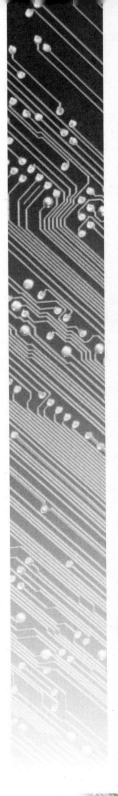

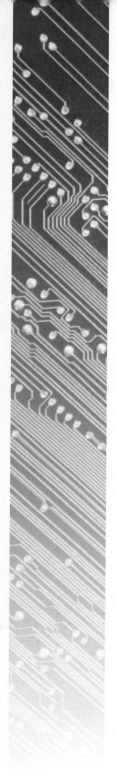

3. IPSec is which type of protocol? (Choose two)
   a. authentication
   b. encryption
   c. tunneling
   d. server

4. Digital signatures guarantee which type of delivery?
   a. intact data delivery
   b. encrypted delivery
   c. tunneled delivery
   d. in-time delivery

5. Which of the following elements will Internet Key Exchange build when used with IPSec?
   a. pre-shared keys
   b. security trailers
   c. public keys
   d. security associations

6. The _____ is a rogue program that intercepts all communications between the client and a server during an SSL session.
   a. crack
   b. Man in the Middle
   c. listening post
   d. hack

7. Which of the following is often used in conjunction with IPSec to provide end-to-end secure data transmission?
   a. SSL
   b. Kerberos
   c. L2TP
   d. transport mode

8. Which of the following IPSec modes will provide completely concealed data transmission?
   a. transport mode
   b. tunnel mode
   c. transfer mode
   d. transmission mode

9. Once you have the ticket-granting ticket, it is sent to a(n)
   a. authentication server.
   b. ticket-granting ticket.
   c. ticket-granting server.
   d. Kerberos server.

10. VPNs reserve part of the bandwidth, close it off to other transmissions, and send packets through this "tunnel" to guarantee safe delivery.
    a. True
    b. False

11. Which of the following parts of the packet will PPTP encapsulate for transmission? (Choose all that apply)
    a. RSA field
    b. header
    c. trailer
    d. payload

12. Which of the following encryption standards does L2TP use to transmit data?
    a. 40-bit encryption
    b. AH encryption
    c. triple DES
    d. 128-bit transmission

13. What is the default security system used on the Microsoft Windows 2000 operating systems?
    a. PPTP
    b. SSL
    c. L2TP
    d. Kerberos

14. Which of the following algorithms does SSL use?
    a. master key
    b. RSA
    c. session key
    d. shared secret

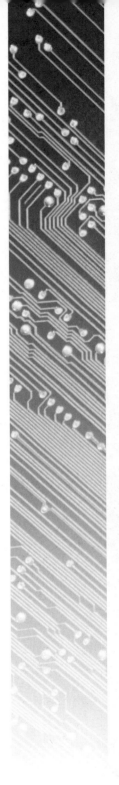

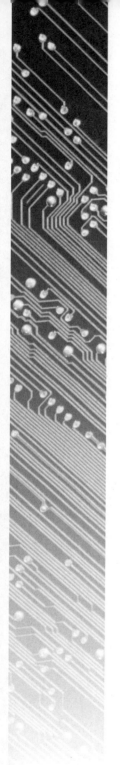

15. Which of the following encryption protocols is used with PPTP?
    a. GRE
    b. PGP
    c. MPPE
    d. MD5

16. The _____ is responsible for creating session keys.
    a. authentication server
    b. ticket-granting ticket
    c. ticket-granting server
    d. Kerberos server

17. At which layer of the OSI Model will IPSec provide encryption and authentication mechanisms?
    a. Physical
    b. Data Link
    c. Session
    d. Network

18. The handshake process is an exchange of messages that the server uses to authenticate itself to the client using a
    a. master key.
    b. session key.
    c. private key.
    d. public key.

19. When using PKI to support security on the network and for Internet-based communications, which one of the following types of keys does the owner maintain?
    a. public key
    b. master key
    c. Kerberos key
    d. private key

20. Which packet format provides security for the header and the data contained in the packet?
    a. AH
    b. ESP
    c. PPP
    d. GRE

TROUBLESHOOTING

A user complains that he cannot receive data from another client machine. The two Windows 2000 systems can PING each other and can see each other in Network Neighborhood, but transmissions fail. Your administrator has imposed security throughout the network. What could be the problem?

CUSTOMER SERVICE

You have decided to allow users to place orders with an online company using the standard Microsoft Internet Explorer Web browser. Which type of SSL authentication will most likely be used when your employees do their ordering?

FOR MORE INFORMATION

For links to Web sites that provide further information about the topics covered in this chapter, go to the EMC/Paradigm Internet Resource Center at www.emcp.com/College Division/Internet Resource Centers/Networking/System Administration/Web Resources: For More Information.

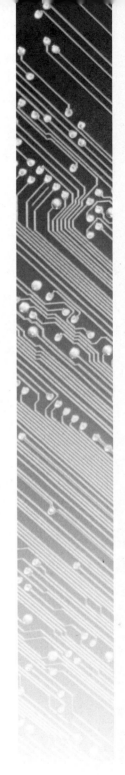

Project Lab, Part

Protocols and Standards

CHAPTER **6**

PROJECT #1: LOOKING INSIDE AN IP PACKET

1. Install the Network Monitor utility on a Windows NT 4.0 server.
2. Use Network Monitor to capture all packets entering or leaving that machine for about an hour.
3. End the capture and save it.
4. Explore the contents of some of the IP packets in the capture.
5. Identify the characteristics of the packet (elements that might be in the header, the payload, etc.).

PROJECT #2: INSTALLING THE NWLINK PROTOCOL

1. On a Windows 2000 Professional machine, open the Network and Dial-up Properties window. Right-click Local Area Connection and select *Properties*.
2. Install the NWLink protocol on the system.
3. Check the frame type configuration to make sure it is set to *Auto*.
4. Enter network number 000001.

PROJECT #3: INVESTIGATING THE NETWARE LINK STATE PROTOCOL

1. Go to the Novell Web site (www.Novell.com).
2. Research the NetWare Link State Protocol.
3. Compare the characteristics of NLSP to IPX RIP.
4. Identify which protocol is more efficient for routing, and support your argument in a written report.

PROJECT #4: USING NETBEUI

1. Set up a network of two or three computers. Make sure the computers are running a Windows operating system.
2. On each machine, remove all other protocols except NetBEUI. If it is not installed, add it now.
3. On each machine, enable sharing.
4. Share a file or folder.
5. Attempt to access that resource using only NetBEUI. What are your results?

CHAPTER 7

PROJECT #1: INSTALLING A TFTP SERVER

1. Using an Internet connection, search www.google.com for a *free* TFTP server.
2. Download the file and install the software.
3. Access the TFTP server using the IP address of the machine hosting the service.
4. Transfer files to the TFTP server.

PROJECT #2: INVESTIGATING ADDRESS RESOLUTION PROTOCOL

1. Using a machine on a Microsoft Windows network, open a Command Prompt window.
2. Type **Arp /?**
3. Use the appropriate switch to see all NetBIOS names in the ARP cache.
4. Use the PING command to locate a machine not listed in your ARP cache.
5. Type **Arp** followed by the proper switch to see if the cache has changed.
6. PING four or five machines that are not in the ARP cache.
7. Check the ARP cache again to see if the machines have been added.

PROJECT #3: USING THE REQUEST FOR COMMENTS

1. Using a connection to the Internet, go to Google (www.google.com) to locate the resource for Request for Comments.
2. Look up the RFC for the ICMP protocol.

3. Identify when the RFC was written
4. List the recommended usages of this protocol.

PROJECT #4: INVESTIGATING PORT NUMBERS

1. Using your connection to the Internet, locate the official listing of port numbers supplied by IANA.
2. Find the following information:
   a. Port number(s) for Bootstrap protocol.
   b. Port number for SU/MIT Telnet Gateway.
   c. Usage of port 108.
   d. Port number for Adobe Server 1.
   e. Usage of port 396.
   f. Usage of port 139.
   g. Port number for FTP over TLS/SSL.
   h. Port number for AppleTalk Update-Based Routing Protocol.

CHAPTER 8

PROJECT #1: INQUIRING INTO APIPA ADDRESSING

1. Using your Internet connection, search for information on the APIPA addressing used by some operating systems.
2. Identify the operating systems that use APIPA.
3. Locate information on when this option may be turned off within an operating system.

PROJECT #2: ESTABLISHING CLASSFUL ADDRESSING

1. Remove your classroom connection to the rest of the network (instructor will verify).
2. Build a network with three to five computers.
3. Make sure the TCP/IP protocol is installed on the machines.
4. Manually configure each machine with an IP address from the network 200.10.5.0, including the default subnet mask.
5. PING each machine from your machine to determine if the IP address configurations have been completed successfully.

Project #3: Establishing Subnetted Addressing

1. Remove your classroom connection to the rest of the network (instructor will verify).
2. Build a network with three to five computers.
3. Make sure the TCP/IP protocol is installed on the machines.
4. Create an IP addressing scheme using the address 210.1.10, subnet mask 255.255.255.240.
5. Configure each machine with an IP address and subnet mask from this IP addressing scheme.
6. Test the configuration by PINGing each machine on the network.

Project #4: Researching IPv6

1. Using your Internet connection, search for information on IPv6.
2. Identify at least two arenas that have implemented IPv6.
3. Identify which Microsoft operating systems are being adapted for use with IPv6.

Chapter 9

Project #1: Adding DHCP Service

1. Build a Windows 2000 server.
2. Remove your network from the LAN.
3. Configure the Windows 2000 server to dynamically assign IP addresses by adding the DHCP service to the server.
4. Configure DHCP to assign IP addresses in the range 10.1.1.0, subnet mask 255.255.255.0.
5. Activate the scope.
6. Configure client machines attached to the network to receive IP addresses dynamically.
7. Test the addresses by PINGing neighbor machines.

Project #2: Identifying Top-Level Domains

1. Open your browser. Using your connection to the Internet, locate the Web site for InterNIC.
2. At this Web site, locate the top-level domains that have been added recently.
3. Write a brief description of at least four of those new top-level domains and their specified usage.

Project #3: Configuring WINS

1. Set up a small network of four to six computers.
2. Install the Windows NT 4.0 or Windows 2000 server operating system on one of the machines.
3. Add the WINS service to the server.
4. Configure the other machines (running a Microsoft Windows operating system) to use WINS.
5. Attempt to access a resource such as a file on neighboring machines.

Project #4: Configuring NAT

1. Create a network of four to six machines.
2. Install the Windows 2000 server on one of the machines and add the NAT service (through Routing and Remote Access Service, or RRAS).
3. Configure the NAT service to distribute IP addresses.
4. Configure the rest of the machines to acquire their IP addresses dynamically.
5. PING other neighboring machines to see if NAT is working.

Chapter 10

Project #1: Identifying Network Risks

1. Using your connection to the Internet, research network risks.
2. Identify at least three common risks.
3. Research the best options to mitigate each of those risks.
4. Write a short paragraph describing each risk solution you found.

Project #2: Comparing Commonly Used Firewalls

1. Using your connection to the Internet, research PIX firewalls and NetScreen firewalls.
2. Identify the strengths and weaknesses of each brand.
3. Research cost and installation complexity.
4. Write a short paragraph defending the firewall you would choose for your network.

Project #3: Defending against Network Attacks

1. Using your connection to the Internet, research the three types of network attacks described in Chapter 10: denial of service, IP spoofing, and SYN flood attacks.
2. Research the best options for preventing these types of attacks.
3. Write a generic access control list that would prevent these types of network attacks from interfering with access to network services.

Project #4: Setting Up a Firewall

1. Disconnect your local classroom network from the main network.
2. Using a Windows 2000 server (*not* connected to the local area network), configure this server to act as a router using Routing and Remote Access Services (RRAS).
3. Using the configuration capabilities of the Windows 2000 Server RRAS, block ports and protocols that may allow hackers into your network.
4. Using the configuration capabilities of this server, block ports and protocols that may allow a network attack aimed at preventing access to resources.

Chapter 11

Project #1: Choosing ISDN Services

Form teams of two or four students in your class. Each team can complete the following steps. Each team should choose a team leader, who will assign tasks and be responsible for assembling the gathered information.
1. Using your connection to the Internet, research the companies that provide ISDN services in your area.
2. Identify the company, installation costs, support costs, and types of services offered to businesses (including BRI, PRI, and other options offered).
3. If necessary, use the telephone to complete this research. Tell the salesperson that you are a student, and would like this information for a project in your class.
4. Identify the company your team would choose to provide the ISDN service.
5. Each team leader should present to the class the information gathered during the research. Identify the reasons why you chose the provider you did.

Project #2: Choosing T-Carrier Services

1. Identify the companies that provide T-Carrier services to your area.
2. Research the purchase of these services, including the equipment you must buy or rent, the installation costs, and the monthly charges for a full T-1 line.
3. Compare the pricing and bonus services.
4. Choose one carrier and explain the choice you made in a short paragraph.

Project #3: Researching Frame Relay

1. Using your connection to the Internet, research the frame relay providers in your area.
2. Identify whether the service providers in your area are offering PVCs or SVCs.
3. Ask the provider (or locate the information on the Internet) what CIRs it offers, the Bc rate, and the Be rate.
4. Identify the cost of frame relay provisioning, and compare this to ISDN and T-1 service.

Project #4: Identifying Connection Options

Complete the following table.

Technology	Min. Speed	Max. Speed	Equipment Needed	Common Uses (Home, Business, etc.)
ISDN				
FDDI				
ATM				
Frame Relay				
SONet/SDH				
T1/E1				
T3/E3				
OCx				

## CHAPTER 12

PROJECT #1: INSTALLING A REMOTE ACCESS SERVER

1. Using the guidelines in the chapter, install the remote access service on a Windows 2000 server.
2. Begin by installing a modem in the server.
3. During the installation process, select Advanced remote access server.
4. Enable support for the TCP/IP protocol.
5. Enable and configure a static pool of IP addresses.

PROJECT #2: CONFIGURING A REMOTE ACCESS SERVER

1. Using the guidelines in the chapter, configure the remote access service that you installed in Project #1.
2. Walk through each property sheet and examine the available settings.
3. Configure Windows Accounting.
4. Enable logging of PPP events.

PROJECT #3: CONFIGURING A REMOTE ACCESS CLIENT

1. Using the guidelines in the chapter, configure a workstation as a remote access client.
2. Begin by installing a modem in the workstation.
3. Enable PPP.
4. Confirm that the appropriate networking client and protocol are installed and configured.

PROJECT #4: USING THE DEVICE MANAGER

1. Open the Device Manager and locate the modem.
2. Disable the modem and notice the change to the icon.
3. Re-enable the modem.
4. Open and view the properties for the modem.
5. Remove the modem.
6. Restart the computer and open the Device Manager. See if the modem has been reinstalled.

## CHAPTER 13

PROJECT #1: INVESTIGATING PPP

Using your connection to the Internet, answer the following questions:
1. What is PPP?
2. What hardware is needed to support PPP?
3. What software is needed to support PPP?
4. Which of the local Internet Service Providers supports PPP connections?

PROJECT #2: DIFFERENTIATING SECURITY TECHNOLOGIES

For each of the following technologies, identify at least two settings in which the technology would be an appropriate solution. Defend your answers with brief written statements.
1. IPSec
2. L2TP
3. SSL
4. Kerberos

PROJECT #3: IDENTIFYING SECURITY SETTINGS

1. Open Internet Explorer and then choose Tools/Internet Options.
2. Click the Security tab.
3. With the *Internet* option highlighted, click *Custom Level* to identify the settings for Internet Security.
4. Record the settings for:
   a. Download ActiveX controls.
   b. Download unsigned ActiveX controls.
5. In two or three sentences, indicate why you think these settings are configured as they are.

PROJECT #4: RECORDING SSL SETTINGS

1. Open Internet Explorer and then choose Tools/Internet Options.
2. Click the Advanced tab.
3. View the additional security settings for your browser.
4. Scroll down to the *Security* section. Record the SSL settings for your browser.

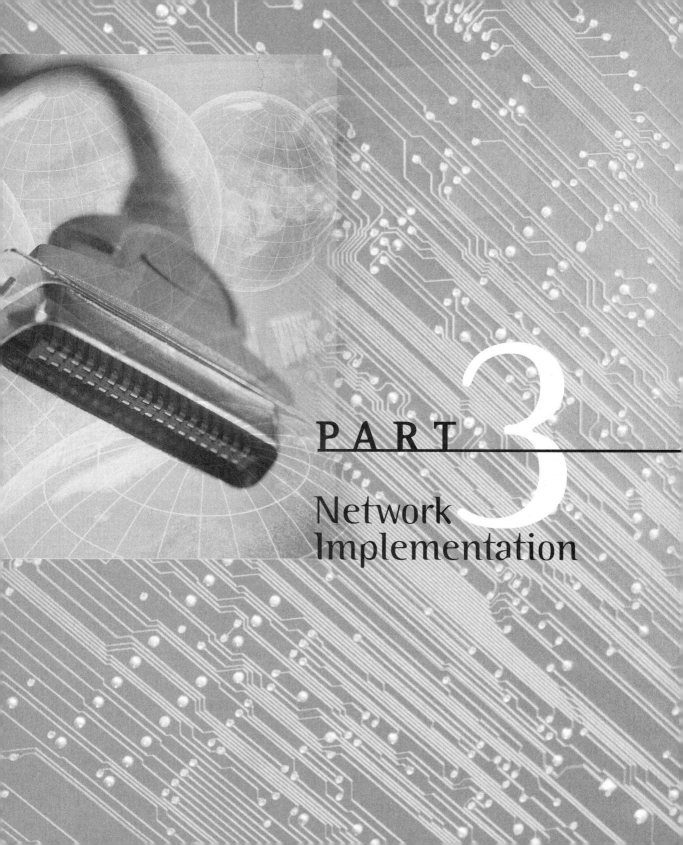

PART 3

Network Implementation

TEST OBJECTIVES IN PART 3

NETWORK+ EXAMINATION

- **Objective 3.1:** Identify the basic capabilities (i.e., client support, interoperability, authentication, file and print services, application support, and security) of the following server operating systems: UNIX/Linux; NetWare; Windows; Macintosh.

- **Objective 3.2:** Identify the basic capabilities of client workstations (i.e., client connectivity, local security mechanisms, and authentication).

- **Objective 3.4:** Identify the main characteristics of network attached storage.

- **Objective 3.5:** Identify the purpose and characteristics of fault tolerance.

- **Objective 3.6:** Identify the purpose and characteristics of disaster recovery

- **Objective 3.11:** Given a network configuration, select the appropriate NIC and network configuration settings (DHCP, DNS, WINS, protocols, NetBIOS/host name, etc.).

- **Objective 4.4:** Given specific parameters, configure a client to connect to the following servers: UNIX/Linux; NetWare; Windows; Macintosh.

- **Objective 4.8:** Given a scenario, predict the impact of modifying, adding, or removing network services (e.g., DHCP, DNS, WINS, etc.) on network resources and users.

- **Objective 4.11:** Given a network troubleshooting scenario involving a client connectivity problem (e.g., incorrect protocol/client software/authentication configuration, or insufficient rights/permissions), identify the cause of the problem.

Network Operating Systems

ON THE TEST

Network+ Examination
- **Objective 3.1:** Identify the basic capabilities (i.e., client support, interoperability, authentication, file and print services, application support, and security) of the following server operating systems:
  - UNIX/Linux
  - NetWare
  - Windows
  - Macintosh

ON THE JOB

To fully understand data communications, network technicians must understand the operating systems that allow or restrict user access to resources. Along with that understanding comes an appreciation of the reasons for carefully choosing one network operating system over another for a particular network. This chapter will take you through the features, benefits, and methods of the four major network operating systems.

UNIX/Linux

After slightly more than 30 years, *UNIX* remains one of the most widely used network operating systems in the world. Its popularity comes from the way in which the programmers at Bell Laboratories built UNIX. Here are some of the important features of UNIX:
- It supports multiple, simultaneously logged-in users.
- It organizes files hierarchically and includes demountable volumes.

UNIX

A network operating system built by Bell Laboratories that supports multiple, simultaneously logged-in users, a hierarchical file system with demountable volumes, source code portability, and the capability to start processes in the background.

- Its source codes are portable.
- It can start processes in the background.
- It enables users to build Windows systems (e.g., XWindows).

UNIX was actually the result of a research project to design an operating system that met three criteria: it had to be simple and elegant, it had to be written in a high-level language instead of assembly language, and it had to allow for the reuse of code. The research group succeeded in designing an operating system that was indeed simple and elegant, and to this day it maintains those three original criteria.

The research group built UNIX with only a small amount of code written in assembly language. The rest of the system was written in a *programming language* called C.

IN REAL LIFE

The most basic of all programming languages is machine language, which consists of a vocabulary of numbers. Next are the assembly languages, which use names rather than numbers but still are not intuitive to human beings. Then we reach the high-level languages and, above those, fourth-generation languages (4GL), which allow programmers to write code using vocabulary that nearly resembles human language. No matter which language you use to build the code, it must be either compiled or processed through a command interpreter to convert the code into machine language, which is the form the computer can understand.

The concept behind this new operating system (OS) was to define three key components that would allow the OS to remain simple and elegant, portable (to multiple types of hardware), and efficient. Those three components were the *kernel,* the *shell,* and the *applications and tools.* The kernel is the part of the operating system that is written in assembly language. The shell (actually the user interface) allows the user to send commands to the kernel. The applications and tools increase the function and efficiency of the operating system. See Figure 14.1 for the three UNIX components.

Programming language

A set of vocabulary and grammatical rules that humans use to make computers perform specific tasks; the term usually refers to high-level languages.

Kernel

The core of an operating system; provides services that allow all other subsystems within the OS to function. A kernel typically assigns processing time and priority to various programs and manages the address space contained in memory and in storage.

Shell

The interface between the operating system and the commands entered by a user.

Applications and tools

The part of an operating system that enables the computer to take steps to complete a command set or create specialized code to be executed.

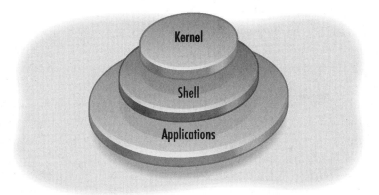

FIGURE 14.1
The Three UNIX
Components

The antitrust laws of the 1970s prohibited Bell Labs from profiting from the sale of computers and software. Instead, the company required just a small licensing fee, which entitled the user to the *source code* for the UNIX operating system. Soon the word spread, and both educational institutions and businesses were testing and expanding this new OS. Researchers at the University of California at Berkeley actively supported the early versions of UNIX and expanded the OS to include code for the TCP/IP subsystem. The UC-Berkeley versions of UNIX became known as BSD (Berkeley Software Distribution) UNIX.

About 10 years later, AT&T (Bell Labs became a part of AT&T) was broken up and the company could actively market the UNIX operating system to other manufacturers of computers. AT&T eventually sold its rights to UNIX. Those rights changed owners several times, finally landing as a commodity shared by two organizations, the Santa Cruz Operation (SCO) and The Open Group.

Today, SCO owns rights to the source code and has the right to distribute that source code as it sees fit. This allows organizations to purchase the source code and modify it to fit the organization's needs.

The Open Group owns the UNIX trademark. When a vendor purchases the source code from SCO and makes changes to it, The Open Group must test and verify the operating system before a vendor can market the new version as UNIX.

Out of this arrangement between SCO and The Open Group has come two market segments: *proprietary code* and *open source code*. The code is considered proprietary if it has been customized to run on certain platforms. Examples of proprietary UNIX systems include some familiar names: Solaris by Sun Microsystems, HP-UX by Hewlett-Packard, and AIX. Each of these flavors of UNIX runs on a particular type of computer

Source code

The original code used to write an executable program for a computer, usually a programming language that humans can understand. This code must be translated or compiled into machine language that the computer understands.

Proprietary code

A code that is owned and controlled by an organization. The code has been tested under specific situations and is usually guaranteed to work within those boundaries. Proprietary code is often sold to other companies because it is guaranteed to work.

Open source code

A source code that ships with an operating system and that can be modified to meet the needs of a business. The function of the code is not guaranteed, but it is thought to be more stable and secure than proprietary code.

and processor platform, and the code has been modified to make adjustments for the hardware.

Running proprietary UNIX offers some great advantages. The organizations that own the version of UNIX a business may choose can be held responsible for ensuring that the code will work as marketed. The seller will typically provide support for the product. The code will behave in a predictable way and be compatible with machines of the correct platform. Finally, a business may expect that the code has been optimized for the software and hardware running on the machine.

With open source UNIX, the source code ships with the operating system, and any modified versions of the code can be freely distributed. Included in this group are several well-known versions of UNIX-like operating systems. Linux is probably the most widely used. Among the Linux operating systems are Caldera, Red Hat, GNU, and Free BSD. Although open source code provides the means to build functionality into the operating system that proprietary vendors could not or would not provide, it also means that the resulting versions may not behave as expected when they are run under slightly different circumstances (slightly different hardware, for example). It also means that there is no support or accountability for the product.

For a generation that has been brought up on computers that have buttons and menus and other useful, user-friendly features, it is difficult to interpret the basic commands of the UNIX operating system. Some of those commands are listed in Figure 14.2.

- **ls:** Displays the file contents of the current directory.
- **cat file:** Displays the contents of a file.
- **who:** Shows a list of currently logged-in users.
- **grep "string" file:** Tells the system to search for the file that contains the character string listed.
- **tail file:** Tells the system to display the last 10 lines of a file.

FIGURE 14.2
Basic UNIX Commands

Network Operating Systems

By far the most frequently used command is ls. Following is just a sampling of the information this command will reveal about a file:

- Name
- Size in bytes
- Numeric identifier of the user who owns it
- Access rights for the owner, the group, and all others

SECURITY

Like other network operating systems, UNIX employs file and directory rights to allow users and groups access to resources. Amazingly, the rights and their assignments are relatively simple, especially when compared to other operating systems. To see how rights function in UNIX, first you must become familiar with the display of the file and directory rights. Below you will see the UNIX rights listing obtained by typing **ls – l** at a command prompt. ("ls – l" displays the details of all files and directories.)

```
-rwxr--r--          #  userid  group  size  data  time  file name
dwx-r-xr-x          #  userid  group  size  data  time  dir name
```

UNIX uses two sets of rights: *file and directory rights.* In the example above, the first line, the hyphen preceding the characters indicates that this is a file. In the second listing, the "d" at the beginning of the line indicates that this is a directory entry. The next nine characters in each listing are the rights for the file or directory. This set of rights is divided into three groups of three. The first three rights listed pertain to the user. The second set of three rights pertain to any rights assigned to a group (named in the "group" portion of the information). The last trio of characters indicate any other rights that may have been assigned. A hyphen in any place declares an absence of that right. The rest of the columns give information such as user ID (the login account), the group abbreviation, the size of the file or directory, the date and time it was last modified, and the name of the file or directory.

It is also important to understand what each of these rights entitles a user to do. As the rights differ somewhat between file and directory, you will see separate listings for each set of three rights in Table 14.1.

File and directory rights

The permissions that allow users to access resources on their own computer or on a remote computer (often a server).

Set of Rights	Kind of Rights	Code	Action
Directory Rights	User	Read (r)	Owner can list the files in the directory.
		Write (w)	Owner can create or delete files.
		Execute (x)	Owner can access files in the directory by name.
	Group	Read (r)	Everyone in the group may list files in the directory.
		Write (w)	Everyone in the group can create or delete files.
		Execute (x)	Everyone in the group can use the "cd" command to move into a specified directory, and they can access files in the directory by name.
	Other	Read (r)	Anybody can list files.
		Write (w)	Anybody can create or delete files.
		Execute (x)	Anybody can use the "cd" command to move into a specified directory, and they can access files in the directory by name.
File Rights	User	Read (r)	Account owner can read file.
		Write (w)	Account owner can modify or delete file.
		Execute (x)	Account owner can run files as programs.
	Group	Read (r)	Everyone in the group can read the file.
		Write (w)	Everyone in the group can modify or delete the file.
		Execute (x)	Everyone in the group can run the file as a program.
	Other	Read (r)	Anyone can read the file.
		Write (w)	Anyone can modify or delete the file.
		Execute (x)	Anyone can run the file as a program.

TABLE 14.1
UNIX Rights

Using what is outlined above, if the rights listing is

-rwer--r--

then the effective rights are read, write, and execute for the user account; read for groups; and read for everyone else.

Rights are modified in UNIX through the chmod (change a file mode) command. Only the owner of the file may change the rights settings for the file. Several symbols (or switches) may be used to complete the string when using chmod. An example of the character string you would type to change a file's rights is **chmod a+rw myfile.** This command will add the read and write rights for everyone. See Table 14.2 for the symbols for the chmod utility.

Symbol	Meaning
u	User
g	Group
o	Other
a	All
r	Read
w	Write (includes delete)
x	Execute (includes access directory)
+	Add the right
-	Remove the right

TABLE 14.2
Symbols for the chmod Utility

SAMBA

In recent years, many businesses have moved from the single-platform (just UNIX, just NetWare, just Windows) proprietary environments they once created in their IT departments to a mixed-platform universe. The integration of multiple platforms into an enterprise was generated by the benefits of each platform and the uses for each. Why not use the best product for the job? Of course, with this integration came problems. Many of the network operating systems do not innately talk to each other, and this required additional software to support interoperability.

To make UNIX talk to Windows operating systems, a common ground had to be found. Using the Common Internet File System (CIFS), introduced by Microsoft, and the reverse-engineering of the SMB (Server Message Block) protocol, a man by the name of Andrew Tridgell built the basis of *Samba* for the UNIX platform. The name Samba came from a dictionary search for words that contained the three letters S, M, and B. When the word "samba" came up, Tridgell checked it against a list of used names. Finding no other entity that used the name, Tridgell named his product Samba.

Samba, which runs on a UNIX machine, allows the UNIX platform to speak directly with the Windows platform. What this means for both administrators and users is that resources from UNIX may be seamlessly available to Windows users without additional client software installed on the local machine. CIFS and Samba also rely on the *Network Basic Input/Output System (NetBIOS)* protocol for both name resolution and browsing for resources.

Samba provides the Windows network and users with the four services of CIFS:
- File and print services
- Authentication and authorization
- Name resolution
- Service announcement (browsing)

Samba

The application that allows interoperability between UNIX and the Windows operating systems through Common Internet File System (CIFS) and Server Message Block (SMB) protocol.

Network Basic Input/Output System (NetBIOS)

An application programming interface (API), including a protocol dating back to the early IBM PC networks, that adds functions to local area networks and allows applications on different computers to communicate with each other.

To provide these services, a daemon, or UNIX application, is loaded on the UNIX server. This daemon listens for SMB requests and is able to respond because the daemon understands SMB. SMB allows an administrator to use one of two modes common to the Windows platform to give users access to a UNIX resource: share mode or user mode. With share mode, the resource carries a simple password for access. With user mode, every user must have an account and a password controlled by the environment, and permissions for each user account are assigned to the resource.

NetWare

NetWare by Novell has been available as a network operating system since the late 1980s (NetWare 2.X). Since then, Novell has continued to improve the features of NetWare to meet ever-changing demands from business. This ongoing evolution allows NetWare to provide all of the expected services of a network operating system and to offer cutting-edge technologies for service to global markets.

To understand the true nature of NetWare, it helps to understand a bit of the history of the products. NetWare started as a simple means to connect many computers for the purpose of sharing information. (Legend has it that some very smart students were building games for the early personal computers and wanted to play together. To do this, the computers had to talk to each other, and therein is the birth of NetWare.) Since then, it has become a very sophisticated, feature-packed computing environment.

NETWARE 3.12/3.2

Although a few versions of NetWare existed before 3.X, they are no longer in service. So we begin with version 3.12. The NetWare 3.12 network operating system (NOS) allowed businesses to build a network on which computers could talk to each other, but only one computer would run the NOS and would control access to the resources on the network. Data would be stored in a common area, and that common storage area (on a server) could be protected through the use of rights, also known as *trustee assignments* (or permissions).

NetWare

A network operating system developed by Novell. NetWare has many versions, including several that support directory services (X.500 standard).

Trustee assignments

NetWare's term for access permissions, or file and directory rights.

When NetWare 3.X was first introduced in the late 1980s, it was thought to be a very innovative operating system. Looking back, however, it was quite cumbersome. First of all, NetWare 3.12 and NetWare 3.2 (an enhancement that was comprised largely of year 2000 fixes) both used a proprietary communications protocol for the network—IPX/SPX (see Chapter 6, *Networking Protocols*). Although IP was used for other operating systems, NetWare required an add-on to the operating system called NetWare IP, which was also largely proprietary. Second, NetWare required that the enterprise support client licensing on each individual server. If a user required access to data on three NetWare 3.X servers, each server needed to carry a license for that client, and each server had to have an account for that user. This is known as a *server-centric* environment.

NetWare 3.X used a flat database design known as the *bindery* to maintain the user accounts that administrators build. The database consisted of three files: NETOBJ, NETPROP, and NET$VAL. NET$OBJ identified the type of object—user or group. NET$PROP identified the property set, or characteristics, of the object. NET$VAL allowed unique values to identify unique objects. For instance, an administrator could create a user account. That user account has a property called "user name," which might consist of the person's first initial and last name—"jlogan" is the unique value for the property user name for the user account object.

NetWare requires that a Novell client (actually just a piece of software) be installed on a workstation. When a user turns on her computer, the Novell client on the local machine contacts the server and checks for a user account on the server. If an account exists, the user is able to access resources (file and print) to which she has rights. If a user account is not present, or the user account does not have the proper rights, no access to the resources is allowed. This process of contacting the server, checking for a user account, and allowing the user to access network services is NetWare 3.X's authentication process.

NetWare uses special software to add functionality to the operating system. Called *NetWare Loadable Modules (NLMs),* these small programs run within the NetWare operating system. Specific types of NLMs are responsible for certain types of functions, as shown in Figure 14.3.

Server-centric

Describes a network environment that relies on an individual, very specific server to gain access to the network and its resources. For example, NetWare 3.X and earlier versions require users either to log in to a specific server or to have individual accounts on all servers that host user resources.

Bindery

In NetWare 3.X network operating systems, a flat database comprised of three files—NETOBJ, NETPROP, and NET$VAL—that hold information on the user account and its characteristics.

NetWare Loadable Module (NLM)

A program that runs within the NetWare operating system and allows certain functions within the NOS, such as support for long file names (provided by LONG.NAM).

- **.NLM:** The generic format for any added function.
- **.DSK:** The extension for any disk driver on the NetWare operating system.
- **.NAM:** Supports file names greater than eight characters in length.
- **.LAN:** Supports network interface card drivers.

FIGURE 14.3
Types of NetWare Loadable Modules

In the first versions of NetWare, client support consisted of software for DOS and Macintosh computers. When Windows 95 surfaced as the operating system of choice in businesses, additional support was added to the client, but it was still basically a DOS client. Novell also provides client software for later versions of the Windows 9.X operating systems as well as for Windows NT 4.0 Workstation and Windows 2000 Professional.

Although NetWare 3.X did support several client operating systems, it had minimal support for true interoperability with other network operating systems. UNIX print services support was an add-on product, and support for long names required an additional NLM. The true interoperability came when UNIX and Microsoft Windows added support for IPX/SPX to their environments.

NOVELL DIRECTORY SERVICES (NDS)

The NetWare 4.1 product changed the face of NetWare and Novell forever. When version 4.0 was released, Novell had sewn the seeds for a network to have *directory services*. With NetWare 4.1, Novell perfected the directory services to a fine art—especially for that time (about 1994). Novell Directory Services (NDS) took the X.500 standards for directory services and implemented them in an operating system that was no longer tied to a specific server. NetWare 4.X offered a *network-centric* environment, which meant that instead of being able to access network services only through an individual server, users could gain access through any server. It no longer mattered where a user account was created because the directory service was available to all servers on the network (or internetwork). The database that kept track of all objects, such as user account objects, printer objects, group objects, and so on, was replicated to all servers on the NDS network.

Directory services

A distributed, hierarchical database that holds all account and object information for a network and that is replicated on multiple servers on the network. Most directory services (such as those for NetWare and for Microsoft's Active Directory) are built to a standard called X.500 that is defined by a Request for Comment (RFC).

Network-centric

Describes a network operating system in which user accounts and existing objects (printers, groups, containers) can be replicated on any server that is included in the directory services database.

The NDS brought with it some concepts that can be confusing for NetWare 3.X administrators. For example, the organization of the directory service relies on logical entities called *containers*. These logical containers are like a set of nested bowls. One bowl holds another bowl, which in turn holds another bowl. Now, assume that the innermost bowl contains 12 pieces of candy. Whereas the bowls are containers, the 12 pieces of candy cannot hold anything, so they are known as *leaf objects,* or terminal objects. The NetWare containers and leaf objects are arranged in an inverted tree, much like the hierarchy of DNS.

NetWare 3.X administrators using NDS also must understand the various types of containers. The biggest container is the [ROOT]. As you might guess, its name defines its function: the [ROOT] holds the rest of the tree. Organizational containers are next in the hierarchy of units. They can hold other organizational units (OUs) and leaf objects. That means OUs can be nested, or placed, within other OUs. See Figure 14.4 for a view of the NDS tree structure.

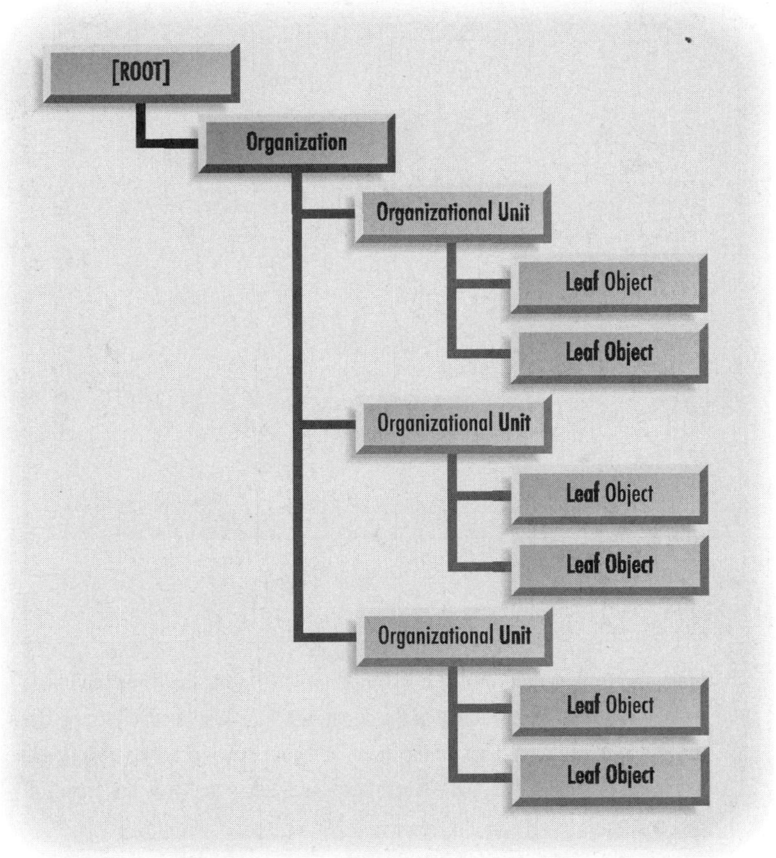

Container

In a directory service, a logical entity that contains other objects.

Leaf object

An object that cannot contain other objects.

FIGURE 14.4
The NDS Tree Structure

The NDS tree structure of NetWare 4.1 and later makes NetWare a scalable operating system. Whether your network has 2 servers and 20 users or 2,000 servers and 25,000 users, NetWare is an appropriate network operating system. It has the ability to provide the security and resource access necessary in every unique environment.

NWAdmin

An administrative tool used in NetWare 4.X and later that allows an administrator to create and manipulate objects in the Novell Directory Services (NDS).

Novell also introduced the administrative tool *NWAdmin* with the introduction of NDS. NWAdmin is a Windows-like utility (see Figure 14.5) that presents the tree and all of its objects. This utility allows manipulation and management of those objects. Here the administrator could take care of creating users, groups, and printers, assigning rights to objects and properties, as well as file and directory rights, and generally build the database as needed for the enterprise.

FIGURE 14.5
The NWAdmin Utility

In Real Life

From a workstation attached to a NetWare network, locate the NWAdmin utility. Usually you will find this utility in the public directory, Win95 subdirectory. Open the utility by double-clicking on the name. Although you will not be able to make any changes to objects in the NDS tree, expand the tree and view the organization of NDS.

All versions of NetWare also include a utility called Monitor. Monitor keeps track of what is going on with the server. This includes how many users are accessing the network, the state of memory in the server, and the state of available file space. Monitor is an NLM and must be started using the syntax "Load Monitor."

─ TRY IT! ─

If you have access to a NetWare server (version 4.1 or 4.11), go to the server and at the server command line, type **load Monitor**. This will start the Monitor utility. Take a few minutes to explore the statistics shown. Note items such as the number of logged-in users.

NDS is also a *fault tolerant network* environment, because the NDS database can be partitioned and replicated on multiple servers. Should one server fail, the database retains its integrity since other servers within the enterprise have copies of the database. Users can still log in and access network resources outside of the faulty partition.

Novell continues to support desktop operating systems by providing client software to connect to NetWare networks. These desktop operating systems include Windows 9.X, NT, and 2000. Novell has remained committed to partnering with other program developers to build applications for the NDS environment. Since 1998, Novell has included such products as Oracle, Pervasive SQL, and the Java Virtual Machine with the operating system. Almost daily, new products continue to emerge that make use of the NDS environment.

Each version of NetWare is slightly different. In the following sections we will look at features from each of the NDS versions.

NetWare 4.1

NetWare 4 was the first version of NetWare that incorporated a directory services capability. Unfortunately, the operating system had many bugs. Novell quickly released NetWare 4.02, which proved to be more stable. The industry did not truly embrace NDS until NetWare 4.1 was released. This was the first version to see widespread installations. Following are some features of NetWare 4.1:

- **NetWare Application Launcher (NAL):** Gives administrators the ability to push applications to the desktop and to remove those applications or upgrade an existing application without visiting every machine on the network.

Fault tolerant network

Describes a network that is partitioned, with directory information for each partition stored on several servers, so that when one node on the system fails, users can still log in and access resources from another partition; part of the operating system can fail without shutting down the entire system.

- **Support for thousands of connections per server:** Does not limit the number of connections per server to 250, as NetWare 3.X did.
- **A management utility with a graphical user interface:** Consolidates nearly all administrative tasks into the NWAdmin utility, making management of the network easier.

NetWare 4.11

NetWare 4.11 is often referred to as IntraNetWare because this version added some features that supported the intranets within businesses:

- **Novell Web Server:** Provides support for intranet use. Prior to this version, administrators had to purchase additional software to support internal Web delivery.
- **Support for up to 32 processors:** Innately supports symmetrical multiprocessing (SMP) within the operating system.
- **DHCP and DNS:** Adds these two support utilities along with the addition of Web server support.
- **Multiprotocol router (MPR):** Performs all of the functions of a typical router. MPR is articulated through another utility called Novell Internet Access Server.

NetWare 5.0

NetWare 5.0 brought about another major set of improvements to the product:

- **Pure IP:** Makes NetWare intranet and Internet ready without using a proprietary version of IP or an encapsulation of the IP packets. Networks that run multiple network operating systems now need only one protocol—IP—instead of IPX/SPX and IP.
- **Long file name support by default:** Allows file and directory names to be longer than the eight-character maximum previous imposed on names; NLM support is no longer required for names longer than eight characters.
- **ConsoleOne:** Administrates the NDS. A Java-based management console, this first attempt was slow, cumbersome, and somewhat limited in function, but it laid the basis for a Web management utility.
- **Network Address Translation (NAT):** This service was supported with Service Pack 1 for NetWare 5.0.
- **NetWare Distributed Print Services (NDPS):** Provides a network management scheme for print facilities, which revolutionized print services by removing cumbersome management utilities that operated from a local print server.

NetWare 5.1

The NetWare 5.1 upgrade made only a few large changes, as follows:

- **Enterprise Web Server and IBM WebSphere:** Offers Web server software.
- **NetWare Management Portal:** Added a browser-based management utility to the operating system, allowing an administrator to access administrative functions regardless of the platform on the workstation.

NetWare 6.0

NetWare 6.0 includes several innovative options for networking in the twenty-first century:

- **Native file access protocols:** Gives access to files on a NetWare server from virtually any operating system without installing local client software.
- **eDirectory:** Lays the foundation for all directory-enabled services. A stand-alone, cross-platform directory service, eDirectory is Novell's global version of NDS.
- **iPrint and iFolder:** Supports the anytime, anywhere access of a global networking system. iPrint gives users access to print services from anywhere on the Internet. iFolder gives users instant, continuous access to their data from laptops, desktops, Web browsers, or remote devices.
- **DNS/DHCP Web-based management utilities:** Adds more Web-based utilities to manage services. Represents another move closer to global directory services.
- **Per-user Licensing:** Licenses users within the enterprise. Users are no longer tied to per-server licensing.

SECURITY

Security in the world of Novell and NetWare is handled at four levels: login, rights, attribute, and file server.

Login security is the first line of defense for the network. To get inside the network and gain access to resources, the user must provide a user name and password that can be validated by the NDS. When building the password policy for the enterprise, the administrator should keep in mind that the more difficult the password, the harder it will be for a hacker to get in. Users must also be made to understand the importance of keeping passwords to themselves.

NetWare uses a set of rights, or permissions (shown in Figure 14.6), to give access to file and print resources. These rights, or a combination of these rights, can be used to secure file and directory resources. For instance, administrators will commonly assign users the rights to Read and File Scan, which allow users to see resources and to read the contents or start an application. With NetWare, users have no rights to a resource until they have been granted. This means that the file and directory resources are secure until assignments are made. One other point to keep in mind with NetWare rights is that they are inheritable. When rights are assigned to a directory, the files within that directory inherit those rights. The administrator has the option to prevent the rights from being inherited. Figure 14.7 shows the rights assignments available in NetWare for Organization1 and for user tlogan.

- **Supervisor:** Includes all other rights.
- **Write:** Gives a user the ability to open and modify files within a directory.
- **File Scan:** Allows a user to see files in a directory listing.
- **Read:** Lets a user open files in a directory and read the contents, or run an application.
- **Create:** Allows a user to create new files and new subdirectories within a directory.
- **Modify:** Allows a user to rename or change the attributes of files, directories, and subdirectories.
- **Erase:** Permits a user to delete directories and files.
- **Access Control:** Gives the user the ability to change rights assignments and to grant all rights except Supervisor to other accounts. Note that Access Control can be a dangerous right.

FIGURE 14.6
Basic NetWare Rights

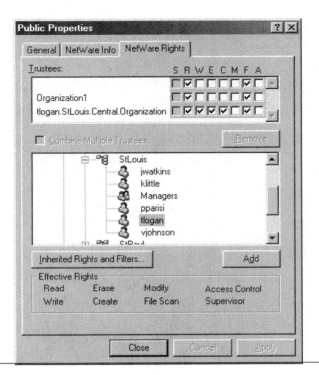

FIGURE 14.7
NetWare Rights
Assignments

Just to keep administrators on their toes, NetWare 4.1 and later also includes a set of rights to NDS objects, and of course they are different from the file and directory rights. NDS rights include both object access and property access rights.

Attribute security creates special properties on directories or files. Attributes override rights assignments. If you are familiar with the early DOS environment, you will remember that every file had a set of attributes that the administrator could turn on (make effective) or off (ignore). These attributes were **R**ead, **A**rchive needed, **S**ystem, and **H**idden. NetWare uses these and a few additional attributes to control what can and cannot be done to a file or directory. See Figure 14.8 for the attributes that can be assigned to a folder.

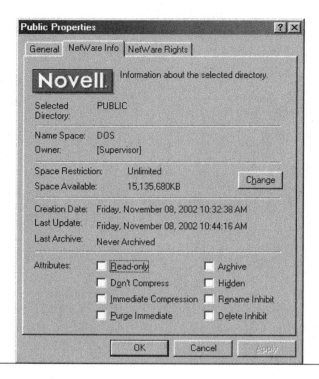

FIGURE 14.8
NetWare Attributes Assignment for the Public Directory

File server security refers to the physical environment for the servers in the organization. It is important to remember that if a server is left out in the open for general access, that server's security is compromised. Servers should be maintained in a climate-controlled, locked environment where access is permitted only to those administrators or delegate administrators that need access.

Troubleshooting NetWare Servers

- NetWare 3.X servers often run out of memory because of a memory leak. Always make sure the server has enough memory to run all of the applications. If the server has an adequate amount of memory installed and it is still running out of resources, consider three ways to solve the problem: (1) Reboot the server routinely. That may mean once a week, or it could mean once a month. (2) Watch and document memory statistics from the Monitor utility. (3) Always make sure all patches from Novell are applied to the server. Like any other manufacturer, Novell seeks to correct all problems by issuing patches for the operating system.
- If you are running NetWare 4.X and your users complain that they cannot save files to the server using the same names they use on their

workstations, check to see if the LONG.NAM NLM is loaded on the server. This gives the system the ability to handle names greater than the 8.3 naming convention of DOS.

- Keep in mind that security in NetWare is handled with the philosophy that no one has any rights until they have been granted. When a user complains that he cannot access resources, make sure the user account is in the proper groups and review the user's rights to make sure they have been granted correctly.
- The NDS, like the directory services on any NOS, is somewhat fragile. Always make changes to the database in small steps (if possible), and allow enough time for the changes to propagate.
- If a server must be offline for a period of time exceeding two or three days, remove any partitions from that server and remove the server from any replica rings within the NDS. This is an administrator's task, but the technician should also be mindful of this step.

Windows

Microsoft released the Windows 3.0 operating system in 1990. It was revolutionary because DOS users had a *graphical user interface (GUI)* that replaced the old DOS interface. Still, the operating system ran on workstations rather than a server. Computers could be attached on a network, but the only way to protect data with this early version of Windows was through share-level security. Each machine maintained its own access list for files and directories, both of which were stored locally.

The Windows platform continued to evolve at the workstation operating system level. Following the Windows 3.0 and 3.1 workstation platforms, we saw Windows 95, Windows 98, and finally Windows Millennium Edition (Windows ME). While development of the 9X platform continued, Microsoft released NT Workstation 3.1. NT 3.5 Workstation was released shortly thereafter, followed by NT 3.51 Workstation. In 1996, NT 4.0 Workstation was released as part of the new NT 4.0 Server product. The next major revolution in workstation products came in 2000 with the release of Windows 2000 Professional. Of course, the latest release of the Windows product, Windows XP Professional Edition and Windows XP Home Edition, offered not only a new user interface, but also advanced features that included enhanced security features, multimedia enhancements, and the use of wizards to allow easier setup of features provided by the operating system.

Graphical user interface (GUI)

An interface between a human and a computer that is friendly for the user to navigate. Instead of using command language to access resources, a user simply selects from an array of colorful icons that identify resources.

Through much of this time, Microsoft was also developing server products. In 1993, Microsoft introduced Windows NT 3.1. The "NT" stands for "new technology," and Microsoft lived up to that title. With this release, Windows became a true network operating system. The server product was designed to act as a dedicated server in a client-server environment. Features included scalability, power, and fault tolerance. Security was centralized, along with server management. Users now participated in a single logon environment for access to all resources on the network. This environment included a new option for handling access to files and folders—*new technology file system (NTFS)*. Now files and folders could be protected by assigning or removing permissions from locally stored data or from data stored on the network servers. NT went through a transformation in 2000 with the release of the Windows 2000 Server and Professional products, and again in 2001 with the release of Windows XP Professional and Home products.

Below we will look at the two network operating systems made famous by Microsoft: NT 4.0 and Windows 2000.

New technology file system (NTFS)

The file system developed for Windows NT, Windows 2000, and Windows XP.

NT 4.0

In 1996, Microsoft released the Windows NT 4.0 Server product as an upgrade to the earlier NT 3.5/3.51 Server product. NT 4.0 contains all of the features and benefits of earlier versions, as well as many improvements. Although NT 4.0 is no longer available off the shelf, many installations of this network operating system remain in the field and will continue to be supported by businesses and administrators, so you should understand some of its features.

NT 4.0, like any NOS worth its weight, provides features that protect the network as well as make administration and user access as easy as possible. *Centralized security* is one of those critical components. In the case of NT 4.0, access to the network is dependent on two criteria: domain membership and user account.

Centralized security

The management of security issues, such as permissions to resources and account authentication, from one central point, usually through the tools included with a network operating system.

In Real Life

A domain is a logical grouping of network objects that fall under a common set of procedures and rules. The network objects might be user accounts, printers, servers, and file resources. The common set of procedures and rules specify who can gain access to the network, what resources user accounts may use, and how access to the network is provided (local area network, remote access services, Web access).

The first server to be installed on an NT 4.0 network takes on a special role. It becomes the primary domain controller (PDC). This PDC establishes the domain and allows the administrator to set up the rules of operation. It also holds the master copy of the domain database—the only read/write copy within the domain. When the administrator creates user accounts, the Security Accounts Manager (SAM) adds each account to the SAM database. To protect the SAM database as it grows, the administrator can add additional domain controllers. These domain controllers fulfill the role known as backup domain controllers (BDCs). The BDCs maintain a read-only copy of the SAM database. The PDC exchanges database information with the BDCs on a schedule. Now if something should happen to that all-important PDC, one of the BDCs can be promoted to the role of PDC, and the network is happy once again.

NT also offers a set of administrative tools, all of which use a GUI display. This makes management easier for the administrator. Tools are added automatically, either at the time of original installation, or as additional features that are added later. If the business policy is to keep servers in a secure, climate-controlled room, then the administrative tools can be added to either a Windows NT workstation or to a Windows 9X workstation, making remote management possible.

One of the most significant features of the NT environment is the single logon for user accounts. Prior to a true client-server network operating system, users would have to authenticate with each resource they needed to do their job. This resulted in several logon actions. With NT, a user logs on once, and that logon request satisfies all resources that this is a trusted member of the domain environment.

NT 4.0 is a full 32-bit operating system. This changed how applications function with the operating system and how resources are allocated to applications. With a 32-bit operating system, applications are allocated a section of the memory space that belongs to that application only. Should the application fail, or somehow create a fault, the failed application can be shut down without risk to any other applications that might be running at the same time. With the older 16-bit environment, when multiple applications are running at the same time, all applications share the same memory space. When one of those applications fails, all other 16-bit applications will also fail. The introduction of the 32-bit operating system made the NT product more stable for the enterprise.

Microsoft has long provided tools for NetWare interoperability. This includes a client product, Client Services for NetWare (CSNW), as well as Gateway Services for NetWare (GSNW). With GSNW, NT users can access NetWare resources without the need to add client software to the local workstation. The service is maintained on the NT server. The NT server is then the only client to the NetWare server. The NT administrator will make NetWare resources available within the NT framework, and they will look just like NT resources.

Another important feature of the NT environment is Remote Access Service (RAS). RAS gives users the ability to access network resources from outside the LAN. Access may be provided using dial-up connectivity (a modem connection) or using an Internet connection. In both cases, NT secures that doorway where RAS clients come into the network to make sure only authentic users gain access.

Through service packs and option packs, Microsoft has added many more features. One of the most interesting, and one that changed internal networks, was the addition of Web services to the NT operating system. After Option Pack 4, administrators could add a stable Web server product, as well as a search facility for the Web site (Index Server), certificate services to support public key infrastructure (Certificate Server), and a content manager (Site Server Express). These added products allowed network administrators to build full-fledged intranets for their enterprise. Documents that formerly had been available only in the human resources office could now be published on the Web server and made available to all user accounts on the network.

WINDOWS 2000/ACTIVE DIRECTORY SERVICES

Active Directory Services

The Microsoft implementation of the X.500 directory-service standards.

With the release of Windows 2000 Server and Professional, Microsoft introduced a network operating system with true directory services. Known as *Active Directory Services,* it conforms to the X.500 standards for directory services but looks very different from the one built by NetWare.

To name objects within Active Directory, Microsoft made use of a system that has withstood the test of time—the Domain Name System (DNS). As you will see, all objects belong to a domain, and thus take their names from their domain membership. If you remember back to the discussion of DNS in Chapter 9, you will recall that the DNS hierarchy includes top-level domains, second-level domains, and possible third- and fourth-level domains. Windows 2000 uses the same hierarchy.

Whereas NT built a hierarchy of servers to maintain database information, Windows 2000 and Active Directory (AD) distribute copies of the AD database on all AD domain controllers, thus eliminating the single point of failure (the PDC) that was part of the NT environment. In AD, if one domain controller fails, another has the same information and can service users and network requests just as well as the failed server. This is known as a *multimaster system.* In addition to storing information about objects (users, security groups, printers), the AD database also stores information about the structure of the network, relationships between different parts of the directory, and resource availability.

Multimaster system

A system in which copies of the directory services database are stored on many servers, and each of these servers is able to make changes to the database. Changes are propagated on all servers that maintain a copy of the database.

Microsoft took some of the standard X.500 objects and put them to use with AD, just as Novell used some of the standard objects in its directory services. In Windows 2000, containers called domains establish security boundaries for AD. This means that all objects within a domain are subject to the same rules of operation. The rules are propagated as "policies" throughout the domain. The policy that provides the security boundary is the password policy for the domain.

Domains can be joined together as *trees.* A tree is a group of domains that share a contiguous name space. (That name space comes up again. This implies Domain Name Space naming.) See Figure 14.9 for a graphic depiction of the name space hierarchy.

Tree

A set of domains in Active Directory that share a contiguous name space.

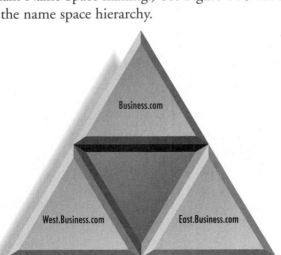

FIGURE 14.9
Domain Name Space in Active Directory

Trees can also be joined together to form *forests*. A forest is a group of trees that share the same schema. The schema refers to the format for the Active Directory database—the types of objects the database will recognize and the properties of those objects. See Figure 14.10 for a graphic depiction of a forest.

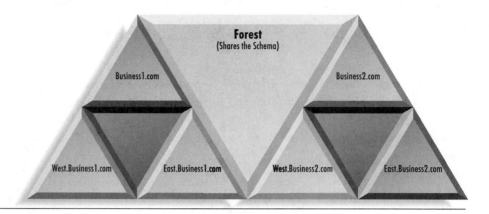

FIGURE 14.10
The Active Directory Forest

One last entity in the Active Directory that bears discussion is the *organizational unit (OU)*. In the AD, an organizational unit is a container that is used to group objects with common needs, so that policies (sets of rules) can be applied. The membership in an OU does not change an object's name. Membership simply means that the object will be subject to a specialized set of security rules. See Figure 14.11 for a graphic depiction of an organizational unit.

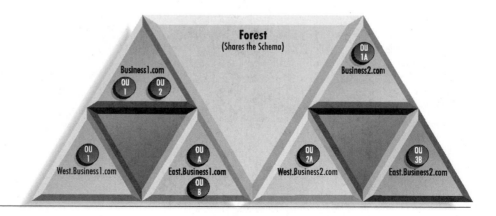

FIGURE 14.11
The Organizational Unit

Aside from the addition of Active Directory, many of the features of the old NT product were improved significantly in Windows 2000. A few of the most important features include the following:

- **Remote Installation Services (RIS):** Allows administrators to install the Windows 2000 Professional product on workstations from a central location, without visiting each machine and going through a lengthy installation process. It automates the installation process by using special connection services and answer files, thus eliminating the need to enter specific information during the installation.

- **Dynamic DNS:** In addition to supplying naming conventions, this service also locates AD resources and is thus a requirement for running Active Directory. Because this version of DNS is dynamic, it automatically registers objects with the database, thus eliminating administrator intervention.

- **Encrypting File System (EFS):** Encrypts files stored either on the local machine or on a network file server. While files still travel the network in an unencrypted state, EFS is very useful for anyone who travels with a laptop computer. Should the laptop be stolen, the files would be unintelligible to the thief.

- **Microsoft Management Console (MMC):** Allows administrators to build a console with the tools they need to manage the entire network or a specific part of the network. These customized tools can also be saved and given to a delegate administrator who might be responsible for specific tasks. Figure 14.12 displays the MMC, which is one of the prebuilt consoles in Windows 2000.

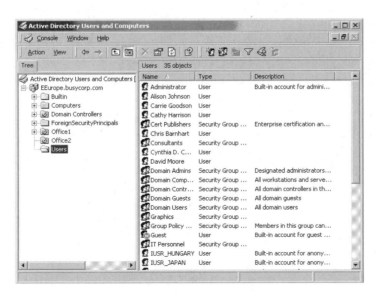

FIGURE 14.12
Active Directory Users and Microsoft Management Console in Windows 2000

- **Routing and Remote Access Service (RRAS):** Groups these two services together because they have many overlapping functions. Can also include Network Address Translation (NAT) for additional remote access protection, as well as Routing Information Protocol (RIP) or Open Shortest Path First (OSPF) for routers.

These are but a few of the many new features and enhancements to the Windows 2000 operating system. Several more features are discussed in the security section to follow.

SECURITY

The security features discussed in this section apply to the Windows 2000 Active Directory environment. Microsoft strengthened the security in Windows 2000 to meet the changing needs of business and to address some of the issues administrators raised with earlier versions. Security in Windows 2000 is handled at two levels: Group Policy settings and file and folder security.

NT 4.0 used System Policy to force a secure environment for its user and computer accounts. When a policy was applied to accounts, it made permanent changes to the registry of the machine. This was a cumbersome way of handling both security settings and environment settings. Whenever a change was required, a new System Policy would be created, and that policy would have to be applied to every machine and user account involved in the policy changes. System Policy "tattooed" the registry.

Group Policy was introduced with Windows 2000. Group Policy is quite different from System Policy in that it does not tattoo the registry. Rather, settings are applied for the session and are removed after the session. When a change in policy takes place while a user or computer is participating in a session, the policy can be refreshed on the fly and the new settings will take effect. This reduces the cost of administration because it sharply reduces the amount of work an administrator must do to make sure the policy is applied.

Group Policy is also very flexible. An administrator can build a policy and apply it at several different container levels. Policy can be applied at the local (machine) level, the domain, the organizational unit, the child organizational unit, or the *site*. See Figure 14.13 for the local policy management console.

Site

In Windows 2000, a section of the Active Directory that is represented by a physical location. A site is referred to as a set of well-connected IP subnetworks. Windows 2000 uses the site to control the AD database replication.

FIGURE 14.13
Local Policy Management
Console

If you look at Figure 14.13, you will see the option *Log on locally* is highlighted for this particular machine. This policy setting allows the administrator to identify those users who might need to access this machine while sitting in front of it, perhaps for local system management. Additional policy settings include some of the same options available in NT 4.0: shut down the machine; back up files; restore files. But some of the settings are quite different: increase (disk) quotas; profile single process; synchronize directory service data. Group Policy gives the administrator granular or very specific control over the domain controllers, servers, and workstations in the enterprise.

Windows 2000 allows the delegation of authority for those users who may be acting as an administrator for certain sets of objects within the AD. This often includes the management of Group Policy objects, as well. In very large networks, the organizational unit may be used to assemble sets of users or computers that must have certain restrictions. A domain administrator (the administrator that has access to all objects in the domain) may not have the time or inclination to deal with such small issues as password changes or policy restrictions for the organizational unit. The Delegation of Authority Wizard will help the administrator identify and assign the proper rights and permissions to a user who can take over the management of the OU.

One advanced feature of Windows 2000 is the ability to validate authentication requests from users trying to log on to the network. Authentication requests can be validated by users' certificates. The certificate is a digital object that is assigned to a user account. Certificate Services, an innate part of Windows 2000, allows certificates to be built and assigned to users. When a request for authentication is received, AD checks the certificate against what it already knows about this certificate, and either allows or prevents the user from logging on to the domain. Microsoft has built Certificate Server to be X.509 compliant. That is, it conforms to the standards required for secure certificate environments.

Wisely, Microsoft has also included a tool that allows an administrator to analyze the security settings on domain controllers, servers, and workstations. This can be used as a preventative tool to make sure all intended settings are actually being applied, or it can be used as a troubleshooting tool when a user has rights or abilities to take certain actions that they should not have, or vice versa.

In addition to a large selection of policy settings to control the actions of computers and users, files and folders must also be protected. Windows 2000, like earlier versions of the NT operating system, employs the permission settings of the NTFS file system. NTFS allows administrators to grant or deny a permission for access to files and folders. The permissions also "flow down" through the directory tree. That is, a permission applied to a folder or directory will also affect the files within the folder. The files "inherit" the permissions from the folder level.

Microsoft uses the philosophy that everyone should have access to resources unless a specific user's permissions have been removed. The access given to everyone is full control, or all permissions. This is accomplished by giving the Everyone security group full control at the root of the drive. Figure 14.14 shows the assignment of all permissions at the root of the C drive.

FIGURE 14.14
Permissions Assignment for the C Drive

Microsoft distinguishes between folder permissions and file permissions. Although quite similar, there are some differences. Folder permissions are described in Figure 14.15; file permissions are described in Figure 14.16.

- **Full Control:** Enables a user to read, execute, create, edit, delete, and traverse folders, as well as change permissions and take ownership of a folder. In addition, the user can read the permissions and read and write the folder attributes.
- **Modify:** Gives the user the ability to read, execute, create, edit, delete, and traverse folders. Additionally, the user can read the permissions and read and write the folder attributes.
- **Read and Execute:** Allows the user to read and execute the contents of folders. It also allows the user to read the permissions and the attributes.
- **List Folder Contents:** Grants the same abilities as Read and Execute.
- **Read:** Allows a user to list the folder and read its data, attributes, and permissions.
- **Write:** Enables the user to create files and write data, create folders and append data, write attributes, and read permissions.

FIGURE 14.15
Folder Permissions

- **Full Control:** Enables a user to read, execute, create, edit, delete subfolders and files, and traverse folders, as well as change permissions and take ownership of the folder. In addition, the user can read the permissions and read and write the folder attributes.
- **Modify:** Gives the user the ability to read, execute, create, edit, delete folders, and traverse folders. Additionally, the user can read the permissions and read and write the folder attributes.
- **Read and Execute:** Allows the user to read and execute the contents of folders. It also allows the user to read the permissions and the attributes.
- **Read:** Allows a user to list the folder and read the data, read the attributes, and read the permissions.
- **Write:** Enables the user to create files and write data, create folders and append data, write attributes, and read permissions.

FIGURE 14.16
File Permissions

Microsoft recommends that administrators remove the Everyone group from the permission list at the root of a drive, while making sure the administrator has full control to the root. Then, the administrator can hand out permissions as needed, eliminating the possibility of a user gaining too much access.

NTFS permissions alone control access when a user is sitting at the machine where the resource resides. However, many times, the resource is accessed across the network. To make that resource available across the network, it must be shared. The Property tab of most resources (file, folder, and printer) includes a Sharing tab that allows the administrator to make the resource network accessible. Also, a set of permissions is attached to the Share. Figure 14.17 shows the sharing option for the System folder on a Windows 2000 server. Figure 14.18 shows the share permissions for the System folder. When a resource is accessed across the network, the NTFS and the share permissions combine to give the user the rights needed to use that resource.

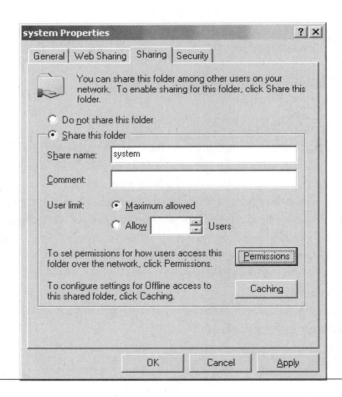

FIGURE 14.17
Sharing Tab for the System Folder on a Windows 2000 Server

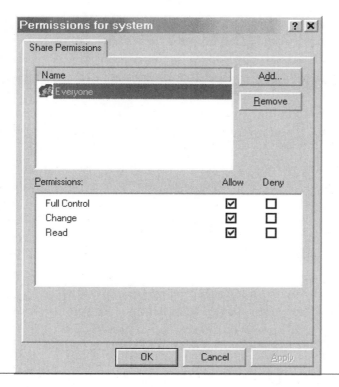

FIGURE 14.18
Share Permissions for the
System Folder on a
Windows 2000 Server

Another feature of the Windows platform is the ability to audit access to files, folders, and print resources, as well as to Active Directory objects. This is important in a security plan. It can help the administrator identify internal (or even external) hackers. When the administrator has delegated authority to a user, trusting him to be responsible for certain tasks, the administrator can check that the user is doing what he should be doing and not taking advantage of any permissions or rights he might have gained in the delegation of authority.

Troubleshooting Windows Network Operating Systems

There are many reasons why a server may not perform as expected in a network environment. When problems occur, be sure to document them so you can look for failure patterns and correct the problems.

- If the server exhibits a hang (that is, it refuses to respond to keyboard or mouse commands), try using the Task Manager to identify a service that is overusing the processor. To use Task Manager, simultaneously press the

Control, Alt, and Delete keys. This will bring up a window that allows you to choose from several options. Choose the *Task Manager* option. Select the Processes tab and look for a process that is using an unusually large amount of memory or CPU time. If that process can be ended without endangering the stability of the server, end the process and document the results. Also document the process and the source application. If you cannot locate an offending process and the server is still unresponsive, try rebooting the server.

- Once the server is functional again, watch the Task Manager statistics carefully to identify any other processes that may be causing the server to hang.
- If a 32-bit application fails on a server, the application can be shut down. Normally, this will not cause difficulty for any other applications or the operating system. It is good practice to reboot the server, if possible when no clients are attached to it, just to stabilize the system. NT 4.0 requires a periodic reboot to function correctly.
- Always test and install service packs and hot fixes from Microsoft. These often solve problems with the stability of the NOS as well as with security issues (especially true in Windows 2000 Internet Information Server).
- If a user cannot log in to the domain, check to see that the user account has not been disabled or deleted. Also check to make sure the user is entering the password and domain correctly.
- In Windows 2000, the Active Directory will occasionally display objects in the MMC for Active Directory Users and Computers using a globally unique identifier (GUID). This is a 32-character identifier that all objects in the Active Directory are assigned. When objects show in the MMC as a GUID, it usually means the AD has not been able to identify the object and does not know what to do with it. This can be a sign of database corruption, or a symptom of the failure of replication of the database between domain controllers. The administrator should be notified as soon as possible.

Macintosh

The Macintosh (or Mac) computer and operating system reaches back in history to 1983, when the Apple Lisa computer and LisaDesk operating system were first released. In 1985, release 2-10 was outfitted with MacWorks and renamed Macintosh XL. Over the years, Apple continued to release new versions of the operating system as well as new models of computers to run the Macintosh operating system. Each successive release added some functionality and more stability. Because of the GUI, the Mac became a favorite of the academic world and the creative world, including artists, graphics designers, and print shops. Today, it is still a favorite among these groups. Macintosh users are some of the most loyal users in the industry.

The Mac operating system and computers were typically not used as the basis for a network. Rather, they were used as workstations within a different type of network, such as NetWare or Windows. Both NetWare and Windows provide services within their own NOS for Macintosh computers on the network. Recently, Apple has introduced the Mac OS X Server product to support networking, as an enhancement to the OS 9 and Xserve products.

The Mac OS X product is a major rewrite from previous releases. Apple chose to create a kernel in this version that is UNIX-based, making it more stable, scalable, and powerful than previous versions. Like all earlier versions, this one is very user-friendly and Internet-friendly.

Mac supports the AppleTalk protocol suite, but it also supports TCP/IP, which is the protocol of choice today. Many common business applications, however, have not been translated into the Mac code. A few translations do exist, most notable among them being Word compatibility for the Mac. This opens the door to greater business usage. If the network is all Macintosh computers, an administrator can set up both internal and external (Internet) e-mail services and database functionality on the Mac.

The latest version of the Mac OS, version 10, supports local user account security. Many of the more susceptible services of the Mac are turned off at installation and can be turned on only by the administrative user. This prevents access through a weak portal, if one exists. Third-party vendors build code to support the Kerberos security used by the Windows 2000 product.

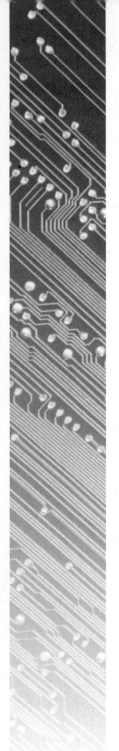

STUDY GUIDE

In this chapter we discussed four network operating systems and their features and benefits. Here are some key points to remember.

UNIX/LINUX

- UNIX is one of the oldest of the network operating systems, built nearly 30 years ago.
- The development of UNIX was based on three criteria:
    o It had to be simple and elegant.
    o It had to be written in a high-level programming language.
    o It had to allow for reuse of code.
- The original developers at Bell Labs met all three criteria.
- Because of the antitrust laws of the 1970s, Bell Labs could not profit from the sale of the computers and hardware. They allowed the source code to be distributed for a small licensing fee.
- Developers at the University of California at Berkeley enhanced the original source code and expanded the OS to include a TCP/IP subsystem. This version of UNIX became known as BSD (Berkeley Software Distribution) UNIX.
- Two organizations share the management and ownership of UNIX today. The Santa Cruz Operation (SCO) owns the rights to the source code and can distribute that source code as it sees fit. The Open Group owns the UNIX trademark and must test and verify the source code before any other entity can market a new version with the UNIX name.
- Two types of code exist: proprietary and open source.
- Proprietary code gives administrators the confidence that the version of UNIX they are using will do what the code was designed to do and that the developers of that particular version can be held accountable for the function of the operating system.
- Open source UNIX allows any organization to create UNIX-like operating systems, such as Linux and GNU. Open source UNIX offers no generalized support or accountability.
- UNIX has three basic components: the kernel, the shell, and the applications and tools.

- Many of the UNIX commands seem cryptic. Some of the more common commands are:
  - ls
  - cat file
  - who
  - grep
- When using the ls command to list files, the display will include the name, size of the file, a numeric identifier for the owner, and the access rights for users and groups.

Security

- UNIX uses file and directory rights to restrict access to resources.
- Rights are assigned to users, groups, or anyone.
- The rights employed by UNIX are:
  - read
  - write
  - execute
- To modify the rights to a file or directory, the chmod utility is executed against the file or directory, usually with one or more symbols or switches.

Samba

- Samba is the application that gives UNIX the ability to see and use NetBIOS resources and talk to Windows operating systems.
- Interoperability is provided by CIFS (Common Internet File System) and SMB (Server Message Block).
- The four services Samba provides are:
  - file and print services
  - authentication and authorization
  - name resolution
  - service announcement (browsing)
- Samba and UNIX use applications called daemons to provide these services.

NETWARE

- NetWare is a network operating system that was developed about 15 years ago.
- Many versions of NetWare are in use today.

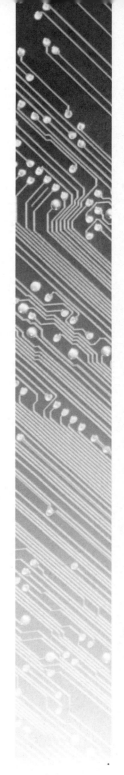

NetWare 3.12/3.2

- NetWare 3.12/3.2 is based on a bindery that maintains information about users and groups. The three files that comprise the bindery are the NETOBJ, NETPROP, and NET$VAL.
- NetWare requires software on the client machine to access the resources of the network.
- The workstation operating systems that are compatible with NetWare client software are DOS, Windows 9.X, Windows NT, Windows 2000, Windows XP, and Macintosh.
- Special pieces of software called NetWare Loadable Modules (NLMs) run on the NetWare server. Most NLMs have an extension of .NLM, but some are very specialized. The different types of NLMs are:
  - .DSK
  - .NAM
  - .LAN
  - .NLM

Novell Directory Services (NDS)

- Built by Novell in 1994, Novell Directory Services follows the X.500 standards for directory services.
- The NDS uses containers to hold other containers and leaf objects. This is the logical organization of the NDS.
- The containers that are supported by NDS are the root and the organizational unit (OU).
- To manage the objects of the NDS, the administrator will use the NWAdmin utility.
- The Monitor utility is loaded at the server. It keeps track of the number of users logged in, the remaining physical memory, and the state of the available file storage space.
- The NDS database is maintained much like the DNS database on the Internet. Copies of portions, or partitions, of the database can be stored on different servers, providing fault tolerance to the NDS.

NetWare 4.1

- The release of NetWare 4.1 included three new features:
  - NetWare Application Launcher (NAL)
  - Support for thousands of connections per server
  - The NWAdmin utility
- NetWare 4.1 was the first fully functional version of NDS.

NetWare 4.11

- NetWare 4.11 is also called IntraNetWare because it was the first version to include Web server and FTP applications, making the intranet a reality.
- DNS and DHCP services were also included in this version.

NetWare 5.0

- NetWare 5.0 was a major milestone for Novell because this version introduced Pure IP, a real, much more generic TCP/IP protocol stack for NetWare products. This made NetWare a more attractive commodity because now administrators needed to run only one protocol on the network (TCP/IP) and all clients and servers could talk to each other.
- Additional features of this version include
    - long file name support by default.
    - ConsoleOne, a Java-based management utility.
    - Network Address Translation (NAT).
    - NetWare Distributed Print Services (NDPS).

NetWare 5.1

- This version did not make major changes to the NOS or to NDS.
- One new option that was added was the NetWare Management Portal, which allows browser-based management of the NDS and resources.

NetWare 6.0

- Novell has taken NetWare 6.0 into the global market with several new features and tools.
- The eDirectory is a stand-alone, cross-platform that is the foundation for a global directory service.
- iPrint and iFolder support the anytime, anywhere user access to NetWare resources.
- DNS/DHCP now have Web-based management utilities that require only a browser interface and no longer require specific client software.

Security

- Novell uses four levels of security: login, rights, attribute, and file server.
- Login security pertains to the password policies required by the business operation.

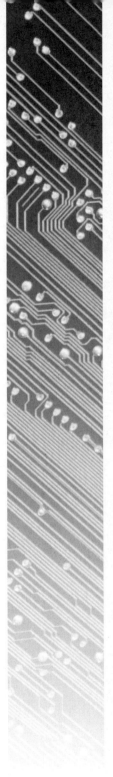

- Rights security is used to control access to files and directories. The file and directory rights include:
  - Supervisor
  - Write
  - File Scan
  - Read
  - Create
  - Modify
  - Erase
  - Access Control
- Novell uses a philosophy that says users should not have access to a resource until they are given that access.
- Rights in NetWare file systems are inherited. That is, rights will flow down the directory and file tree until they are stopped or until they have reached a terminal file.
- Attribute security supercedes any file and directory rights. Attributes are special settings that control what can be done with the file or directory.
- File server security refers to the physical safety of the file servers. Physical safety includes preventing access by unauthorized people as well as climate control.

WINDOWS

- The Windows family of operating systems dates back to 1990, when Windows 3.0 was released as a desktop operating system.
- Enhancements to the product include Windows 3.1, 3.11, Windows 95, Windows 98, Windows ME, and the development of the NT products.
- Microsoft was also developing the server products through the development cycle of the workstation products.
- Windows NT Server (version 3.1) was first released in 1993, followed closely by NT 3.5 and NT 3.51.
- In 1996, NT 4.0 was released, followed by Windows 2000 Server.

NT 4.0

- NT 4.0 stabilized the NT product.
- It enhanced the domain environment from earlier products.
- NT uses a master domain model in which one domain maintains user accounts and one server, the primary domain controller (PDC), holds the only read-write copy of the domain database.

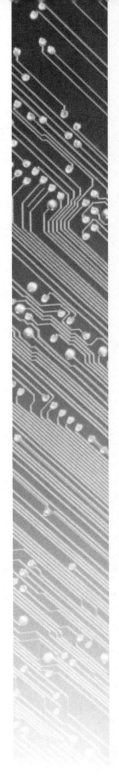

- Backup domain controllers (BDCs) store a read-only copy of the database and get updates from the PDC.
- NT 4.0 is a full 32-bit operating system.
- Applications running in 32 bits are maintained in a memory space that is separate from any other 32-bit application. If one 32-bit application fails, the others stay up and running, but the administrator can shut down just the offending application.
- Microsoft includes tools for Novell interoperability with the Client Services for NetWare (CSNW) and Gateway Services for NetWare (GSNW). GSNW, loaded at the NT 4.0 server, allows NetWare resources to be accessed as if they were part of the NT server.
- Through service packs and option packs, new features and tools are added to the NT 4.0 operating system. Option Pack 4 added a stable Web and FTP server product to NT, as well as a Web server management utility called Site Server Express and the Certificate Server product to support advanced security.

Windows 2000/Active Directory Services

- Windows 2000 and Active Directory Services conform to the X.500 standards for directory services.
- Active Directory (AD) uses the Domain Name System (DNS) to uniquely identify objects within the AD.
- AD distributes the information about objects in the database across multiple AD servers. This provides fault tolerance for the database and makes this model a multimaster system (no one server is in charge).
- The objects used by AD include the domain, the tree, the forest, and the organizational unit.
- The domain is a security boundary because the password policy affects all objects within the domain but not outside the domain. The password policy is set at the domain level and will be applied to all objects regardless of their membership to an organizational unit.
- A tree is a set of domains that share a contiguous name space.
- A forest is a set of trees that share the same schema for the database.
- Some of the new features of Windows 2000, besides Active Directory, include Remote Installation Services (RIS), Dynamic DNS to support Active Directory, Encrypting File System (EFS) to encrypt files at the storage point, the Microsoft Management Console (MMC), and Routing and Remote Access Service (RRAS).

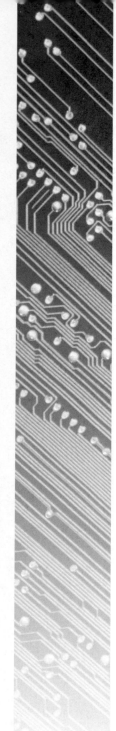

Security

- Security in Windows 2000 is managed at two levels: Group Policy settings and file and folder security.
- Group Policy can be applied at the site, the domain, or the organizational unit.
- Group Policy does not "tattoo" the registry of the machine. Rather, the settings are session-specific and can be refreshed if a policy changes during a session.
- Windows 2000 uses NTFS permissions at the folder or file level to give access to resources. The permissions available for folders include the following:
  - Full Control
  - Modify
  - Read and Execute
  - List Folder Contents
  - Read
  - Write
- File permissions include:
  - Full Control
  - Modify
  - Read and Execute
  - Read
  - Write
- NTFS permissions apply when the user is sitting at the resource (the local machine) and accessing resources.
- When users access resources across the network, share permissions are assigned and combined with the NTFS permissions for the effective permissions to the resource. Share permissions offer the following options:
  - Full Control
  - Read
  - Change
- Each NTFS and share permission has both an *Allow* and a *Deny* option.
- Auditing allows the administrator to keep track of access to resources.

MACINTOSH

- The history of the Macintosh goes back to 1983 when the Lisa computer and LisaDesk operating system were released.

- The Macintosh operating system is a very user-friendly OS that is used by artists, graphic artists, and the education community.
- The most recent version of the operating system is Mac OS X. Apple integrated a UNIX-based kernel in this recent version.
- Mac computers and the operating system function with both the AppleTalk protocol and TCP/IP, making the Mac able to coexist on a network.
- Many network operating systems include software add-ons or clients to allow Macintosh machines to communicate with and use resources from NetWare and Windows servers.
- The Mac environment does not support a classic server, but it does have server services for the sharing of resources among network users.
- Security for the Mac includes local user account security.
- Noncritical services are turned off by default with the Mac OS, thus preventing accidental weak portals into the network.

PRACTICE TEST

Try this test to check your mastery of the concepts in this chapter.

1. Which of the following services must be available when Active Directory is added to a Windows 2000 server?
   a. DHCP
   b. SMTP
   c. DNS
   d. FTP

2. Which network operating system relies on a bindery to store objects?
   a. Linux
   b. UNIX
   c. NetWare 6.0
   d. NetWare 3.12
   e. Windows NT

3. The applications that add functionality to the NetWare operating systems are called
   a. CIFS.
   b. NLMs.
   c. APIS.
   d. MODS.

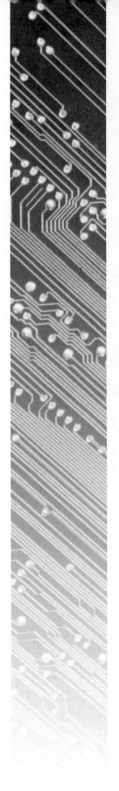

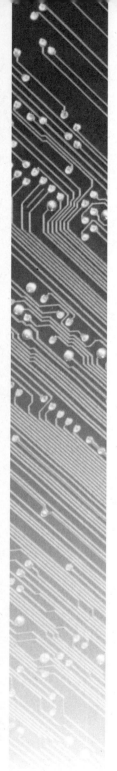

4. For a UNIX user to execute an application, which of the following rights must the user be granted?
   a. Execute to the folder.
   b. Write to the folder.
   c. Execute to the file.
   d. Read to the file.

5. Which of the following are components of the UNIX operating system? (Choose three)
   a. shell
   b. bindery
   c. database
   d. kernel
   e. applications and tools
   f. DNS
   g. partition
   h. replica

6. Which of the following events created an environment in which network compatibility was no longer an issue for the NetWare operating systems?
   a. the introduction of NDS
   b. the introduction of Pure IP
   c. the addition of DHCP and DNS services
   d. the development of the Web server product

7. Which type of NetWare Loadable Module loads the driver for the network interface card?
   a. NLM
   b. DSK
   c. SAN
   d. LAN

8. Under the NT 4.0 operating system, which of the following is the storage unit for user accounts and other important information?
   a. SAM
   b. AD
   c. domain
   d. tree

9. The NetWare operating systems after version 4.0 provide fault tolerance for the NDS database through what action?
   a. creating copies and storing those copies off site
   b. backing up one of the NetWare servers every night
   c. partitioning the database
   d. using one special server to hold NDS information

10. Which tool manages integration of NetWare resources into a Windows NT or Windows 2000 network?
    a. GSNW
    b. CSNW
    c. RSNW
    d. RIS

11. In the NDS directory, the logical presentation of the network is called the NDS
    a. hat.
    b. house.
    c. branch.
    d. tree.

12. In the Windows products, which combination below indicates the user's effective permissions to a resource?
    a. rights and NTFS permissions
    b. NTFS permissions and share permissions
    c. rights and abilities
    d. share permissions and rights

13. When deploying Active Directory Services on a network, all trees in the forest must use the same
    a. schema.
    b. naming conventions.
    c. DNS server.
    d. domain.

14. Of the following operating systems, which one is considered the most user-friendly?
    a. NetWare 5.0
    b. Windows 2000
    c. Windows NT
    d. Macintosh

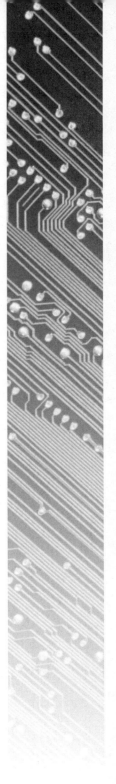

15. In NetWare, for a user to access a resource, what are the minimum rights that must be granted to the user?
    a. Supervisor
    b. Modify
    c. Read and File Scan
    d. Read, Write, Create, File Scan, and Delete

16. What is the name of the UNIX service application?
    a. software
    b. daemon
    c. grep
    d. module

17. Which version of the Windows network operating system was the first to support a true 32-bit platform?
    a. Windows 3.1
    b. Windows NT 3.5
    c. Windows NT 3.51
    d. Windows NT 4.0

18. Which of the following protocols does the Macintosh operating system support? (Choose all that apply)
    a. TCP/IP
    b. NetBEUI
    c. IPX/SPX
    d. AppleTalk
    e. OSPF
    f. DLC

19. Of the four operating systems listed, which is considered to be the best for enterprise file services and security, but not the most user-friendly?
    a. NetWare
    b. UNIX
    c. Macintosh
    d. Windows

20. Which protocol is required by NetWare 3.X?
    a. TCP/IP
    b. IPX/SPX
    c. NetBEUI
    d. NWLink

21. Which version of Windows is considered a multimaster operating system?
   a. Windows 3.0
   b. Windows 3.11
   c. Windows NT
   d. Windows 2000

22. Which application provides interoperability between UNIX and the Windows network?
   a. GSNW
   b. Samba
   c. TCP/IP services for UNIX
   d. NetBIOS

TROUBLESHOOTING

A new employee has just joined the accounting department of a local company. On the first day of work, a fellow employee is doing some training on the two applications the new employee must use. The training for the first application goes well. The new employee can access the application and all of the storage areas for data. When the new employee attempts to access the second application, which runs from the same server, he cannot use the software. Other users in the department are not experiencing any problems. What is the first step in resolving this problem?

CUSTOMER SERVICE

1. You are at a client site to do maintenance on 20 workstations on the network. The owner of the company comes to chat with you about upgrading the network. She asks which network operating system would provide a secure environment for the resources on the network, be easy to install and maintain, have a built-in GUI management console, and be compatible with numerous workstation platforms. Based on what you know about the top four operating systems, which one would you recommend and why?

2. You are the network administrator for a network that has built a mixed-platform network. Currently there are three NT 4.0 servers and six NetWare 4.11 servers. Your users' machines are all Windows 95/98. Which client software should you add to the users' machines so that all computers can access resources on all servers?

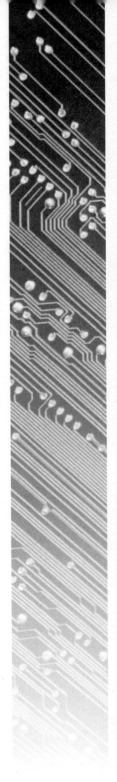

FOR MORE INFORMATION

For links to Web sites that provide further information about the topics covered in this chapter, go to the EMC/Paradigm Internet Resource Center at www.emcp.com/College Division/Internet Resource Centers/Networking/System Administration/Web Resources: For More Information.

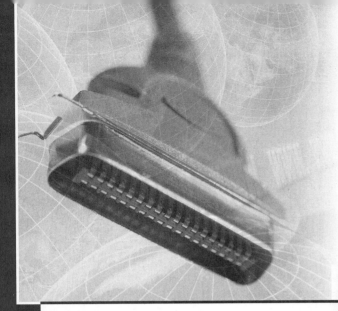

Network Integrity

15

Network+ Examination
- **Objective 3.4:** Identify the main characteristics of network attached storage.
- **Objective 3.5:** Identify the purpose and characteristics of fault tolerance.
- **Objective 3.6:** Identify the purpose and characteristics of disaster recovery.

ON THE JOB

As a network technician, you will be asked to do many of the everyday tasks that keep the network running. Most of those tasks have a direct effect on the integrity of the network. It is important that you understand the methods and options as well as the necessary tasks that keep the network running smoothly. Pay close attention to power management and backup operations; you will see these areas in the field often.

Network Integrity

The dictionary definition of the term "integrity" is as follows:
1. The state of being unimpaired; soundness.
2. The quality or condition of being whole or undivided; completeness.

If we apply this set of meanings to the network, the definition for network integrity would be *maintaining the state of the network such that all parts function as a whole in a sound and unimpaired state.* This is a broad and all-inclusive definition that covers the responsibilities of the network administrator. To completely understand this definition, it is important to look at what this means for the network administration team.

This chapter will cover the following topics under the umbrella of network integrity:

- Documentation
- Disaster planning and recovery
- Power protection
- Fault tolerance
- System backups
- Network attached storage

Documentation

The first step to network integrity is knowing the network. The network administration team should build documentation for all components that are part of the network. Standard network documentation includes several key pieces, as described in Figure 15.1.

- **LAN/WAN topology:** Where the cables, data ports, and computers reside.
- **Hardware inventory:** Serial numbers for all devices that are part of the network.
- **Software inventory:** License information and documentation.
- **Change logs:** Reports of changes, updates, and application of service packs to servers, devices, and workstations (kept with each device).
- **Server information:** How the server was built, date of purchase, vendor, and model.
- **Router and switch configurations:** What ports go to what segments; access control lists on routers.
- **User policies and profiles**: Restrictions or user configurations set at the network level.
- **Baseline documents:** Baseline measurements from all servers and other critical devices on the network.
- **Mission-critical applications and hardware:** Configuration of software that is critical to business functioning and the hardware that the software runs on.
- **Network service configuration:** DNS, DHCP, WINS, and RAS configurations.
- **Procedures:** If this happens, we take these steps to correct the problem; when we need to do this, we do it this way.

FIGURE 15.1
Key Pieces of Standard
Network Documentation

The critical nature of good documentation can best be explained by example. A company with a small network of about 350 users, two servers, and three routers fires its network administrator. The company is suspicious that perhaps the former network administrator left back doors into the network that would allow him to get in and damage critical operations. To assure the board of trustees and upper management, the company hires a consulting firm to check the documentation for the network and close any and all back doors that may still be available. In determining their bid for this job, the consultants discover the network does not have any documentation, so they revise the bid to include an hourly rate for two engineers to document the network. The consultants charge $200 per person per hour. The two engineers spend 36 hours each (72 hours total) learning the network, digging up what little information is available, investigating both servers for loopholes, and writing down all of this information.

When the job is done and the brand new binder titled "Network Documentation" is handed over, the consulting firm also hands the company a bill that could range anywhere from $15,000 to $60,000 to close the loopholes in the network, and another $14,400 to investigate the network and create the documentation. The entire documentation expense could have been avoided had the network administrator documented the network in the first place.

In addition to recording general network operations, documentation is also essential for troubleshooting. The one basic truth about networks is that they will fail at some time. In a small network environment, it may be possible to remember that two weeks ago the administrator added a new service pack to the servers. When problems begin to show up, the network administrator may realize that the problems began shortly after the service packs were added. That is a good place to start looking for the root cause of the problems that are occurring today.

In large enterprise networks with complex switching and routing configurations, thousands of users, and perhaps hundreds of servers, it is impossible to remember who did what to which element. Only through good documentation will the possible source of problems be recognized and rectified. Documentation not only can save money, but also it can assist in the quick resolution of network issues.

When our company from the example above hires a new administrator, how will that administrator learn the network unless the documentation is available and up-to-date? The immense learning curve for new personnel can be severely shortened if the network is correctly documented.

The actual ongoing documentation may be quite formal or much more casual. (See "For More Information" for this chapter on your Internet Resource Center for a Web site offering documentation forms.) If a formal approach is needed, then forms should be created to hold the types of information deemed important to network operations. Each server should have its own book to record any changes made to that server. Examples of records that could be entered include operating system upgrades, service packs, configuration changes, and service records. Simple forms for this purpose can be created in any word processing program. The key is to build the forms, make them available, and be consistent in the recording of information.

If the network is smaller and less formalized, the administrator could buy a case of small notebooks. Each server would be assigned a notebook, and each administrator and technician would be given one, as well. When a change is made to the server, an entry can be made in the book, recording the date, the change, and who made the change. Administrators and technicians would typically record visits to users' machines to resolve problems, updates to the workstations, and any other tidbits of information that may help resolve problems at a later date.

Regardless of the method of documentation, the key is to record any and all changes to devices on the network. Although the human mind is capable of great memory, in a pinch, it will be the one critical detail that will escape, preventing the fast resolution to a problem.

Disaster Planning and Recovery

The term "disaster" implies an event that causes widespread destruction and distress, or perhaps even total failure. Disasters come in all sizes and shapes, from the failure of a power supply to earthquake, flood, and fire. How the business plans for these potential events can dictate the success or failure of that business.

Therefore, the next critical piece in maintaining network integrity is planning for the worst-case scenario, also known as the disaster. Psychologists and psychiatrists often help patients face scary and unknown situations by making the patient look at the situation and decide what he or she would do if everything went wrong. This is known as worst-case scenario planning. This same process applies to the management of a network, no matter what size the network happens to be. Every networked business environment must look at how the business would survive should there be a disaster.

For some businesses, just making sure backups have integrity is enough disaster planning. For other businesses, completely redundant sites may be the answer to disaster planning. Wherever in the continuum the business operation happens to fall, the process of disaster planning is the same.

Network Integrity

THE DISASTER RECOVERY PLAN

The *disaster recovery plan* for a business is a businesswide endeavor. Key to the planning are not only the network administration team but also the members of every department, division, and management level. This may sound like an impossible chore with so many stakeholders in the game, but surely it is not. The most important part of disaster recovery planning is complete support for the plan and commitment to the expense and time necessary to build and maintain a good one. Is the plan a lot of work? Absolutely! But the value of a well-constructed disaster recovery plan is nearly indefinable. In the event of a widespread natural disaster, your plan could mean the difference between getting back to business quickly and going out of business overnight. The majority of all businesses that encounter a large disaster without a recovery plan are out of business or bankrupt within one year. Remember that the goal of the disaster recovery plan is to resume business as quickly as possible. How soon and by what means will this business be up and running again?

The method of a well-constructed disaster recovery plan at its most simplistic level includes several stages:

1. Creating the disaster recovery (DR) team. During this phase of the process, a project manager is designated, and a team of stakeholders is formed. That team often includes the network administrator(s), department representatives, top-level management representatives, supporting vendor representatives, and anyone else who has either a direct vested interest or knowledge of the business.

2. Identifying the risks that threaten the network. During this stage, all potential risks—from the power going out for a minute or two all the way to mass flooding, fire, or earthquake—are assessed as potential threats, and documented appropriately. Any perceived security risks should be included in this assessment. Once the risk factors are defined, they must be ordered according to the value of each threat. For example, a business in northern California around the San Jose area would list "earthquake" at the top or close to the top of the list. A business in Hays, Kansas, might put "earthquake" at the bottom of the list and "tornado" at the top.

3. Assessing the impact on the business. The key to this stage of the planning process is to identify how much hardship a business can withstand. To do this, answer the following questions:

- What are the critical systems and functions within this business?
- What is the financial impact of each potential disaster?
- How quickly must systems resume operations to maintain steady business?

Disaster recovery plan

A set of documents that outline procedures to follow when a network experiences a catastrophic event. This may cover anything from a momentary power failure to a major natural disaster.

Once these answers have come forth, the stakeholders have the information needed to identify how the network interacts with the functions of the business.

4. Defining needs. Once stakeholders have identified and recorded the risks and completed the business impact assessment, they need to develop a profile of recovery requirements. Begin by assessing whether the operation requirements after a disaster must look exactly like the current environment.

- Can the business tolerate some change to the operation?
- Do all functions rely on computer technology, or can some processes resume operation with paper and pen?

Next, list the resources that support critical operations identified in the business impact assessment. The hardware (including computer resources and telecommunications equipment), software, documentation, facilities, and personnel needs for basic business operations are part of this list.

Finally, estimate the cost of the recovery requirements. Continue to elicit the support of upper management throughout this stage. Without commitment of appropriate funds, the plan will not work.

5. Developing a detailed plan. At this point in the process of DR planning, the procedures definitions, vendor contracts (if needed), data recovery mechanisms, individual recovery teams, and standards are defined and documented. If the business operation requires a redundant site, then that is part of this plan. If the business requires a vendor commitment to supply a certain number of computers of a certain configuration, contracts and documentation are a part of this stage. It is critical to detail every step that is needed to bring the business back up after a major disaster. Staffing may be short due to the disaster. People may not be functioning at previous attention levels. The business may have to hire new personnel. If everything is documented in the first place, there is less chance of confusion in a crisis.

6. Testing. Exercise, or test, the DR plan to validate the decisions that have been made up to this point. Any problems in the plan will become apparent and can be rectified before a disaster strikes.

7. Maintaining the plan. The disaster recovery plan is a living document. As changes are made to the business, changes must be made to the DR plan as well. A team of stakeholders must be responsible for changes to the plan. Periodically, and any time a major change is made, the DR plan should be tested again. This keeps procedures fresh and has the added benefit of training new employees in DR processes.

The disaster recovery plan is not a project that can be completed in a couple of weeks or even a couple of months. For the enterprise network, this process may take a year or more of ongoing teamwork to get the plan to a model that works nearly without flaws. Should implementation of the plan become necessary, the time that was spent covering every detail will minimize recovery mistakes, and the business will be able to resume functioning in the shortest amount of time possible.

Mirrored Servers (Failover Clustering)

Perhaps your business runs a mission-critical application or group of applications that require a network uptime of 99.9 percent. The application software may support other businesses as well. A bank is a good example of an entity that supports other businesses—smaller banks and 24/7 businesses that process money through the larger bank. What happens when the server fails in this case? The effect of a server failure is no longer singular. Rather, several business operations are affected, and they may experience reduced revenue due to loss of business. Because of these risks, a network administrator may choose to set up a mirrored server environment, also known as failover clustering.

With mirrored servers, two servers with identical hardware and software configurations are attached to the network and to each other. Both servers record all stored data. The designated primary server services the requests from the network. The secondary server listens for a "heartbeat," or pulse, from the primary server. If the secondary server does not get a heartbeat in the designated time frame, it begins answering requests from the network. A common time setting to wait for a lapsed heartbeat is 30 to 45 seconds. This is known as the *cutover time*. The changeover from primary to secondary mirrored servers is transparent to the users.

Mirrored servers assure those who use network services that operations will continue in the face of a hardware failure on a mission-critical server.

Clustered Servers

Clustered servers are similar to mirrored servers in that both run simultaneously and both record all data sent to the primary server. However, clustered servers offer one major benefit that mirrored servers do not. With a cluster, all servers in the cluster are acting as one large server. Even though they are all recording the same data, they each have the ability to answer requests from the network and can provide true load balancing. This results in better performance for network requests.

Cutover time

The amount of time it takes to switch from a failed server to a working server.

Clustered servers

Two or more servers connected together in such a way that they act like a single server but provide fault tolerance in the event of failure of the primary server.

Clustering services often provide replication services, too. To provide disaster recovery functions, two or three servers are located off-site and used in the event of a disaster that destroys the original installation. All data is replicated to those remote servers, and they are always up and running, available to answer network requests should they be asked to do so.

Although clustering seems like a fine idea for any network, two conditions preclude many businesses from using clustered servers. First, setting up and maintaining this service is very expensive. The only way to justify the expense of clustering is to do extensive analysis of the cost of server downtime. If the cost-to-benefit ratio appeals to the keeper of the purse, server clustering may be the answer.

The second reason that a business may not choose clustered servers as a solution is the complexity of the operations. The more servers in the cluster, the more complex the management and maintenance of the cluster become.

Power Protection

One very common "disaster" for a network is the loss of power or power spikes and brownouts. These events take their toll on equipment if it is not protected through power protection devices. A surge on the power line can destroy boards inside the computer. Even a momentary drop in power can weaken components in the computers, reducing the expected lifespan of the component. This is especially true for high-end systems such as servers.

Keep in mind that all power, once it leaves the electricity production plant, becomes "dirty" in a very short distance. Current must sometimes travel many miles before it reaches its destination. During the transfer across many sets of power lines, natural and system faults can cause the power to spike or dip. Another possibility is that the location of the business might be in the middle of an aging power grid, making the electricity more susceptible to intermittent problems.

What you choose to do to protect systems from variations in power and power loss will largely depend on the nature of the systems in your network. Workstations should be connected to surge protectors. Network servers use either online uninterruptible power supplies or standby uninterruptible power supplies to protect both the hardware and the data stored on the servers. Should the network servers supply mission-critical services, such as police information systems, 911 services, or hospital services, the organization can take one step further and provide a gas-powered generator for backup power supply.

SURGE PROTECTORS

Surge protectors (see Figure 15.2) are available from discount stores, computer stores, and hardware stores. The purpose of the surge protector is to do just what its name suggests: protect computer equipment against surges or spikes in power. Generally, a surge protector will have an on/off switch and some form of circuit breaker built in. The low-end surge protectors are designed as multiple outlet strips with a single circuit breaker set to trip (turn off the strip) at a predetermined power spike. In all surge protectors, small surges or spikes are allowed to pass. Only large spikes will turn off the power strip.

FIGURE 15.2
A Surge Protector

Over time, with numerous spikes in current value, the surge protector will deteriorate in its ability to detect surges. The key is to use high-quality protectors and to replace them on a regular basis—once a year, or at least every two years. This will diminish the threat of damaging current levels getting through to sensitive computer equipment.

ONLINE UNINTERRUPTIBLE POWER SUPPLY (UPS)

The *online uninterruptible power supply (UPS)* works in a much different way from the surge protector. The purpose of the UPS is to maintain power to the computer long enough for the system to shut down gracefully and to provide clean power to the box.

The way an online UPS provides power to a computer is quite simple. The UPS is plugged into a wall outlet. The computer is plugged into the UPS. (Usually the UPS has multiple outlets, allowing other peripherals to use the UPS.) The UPS is heavy because its major component is a battery, much like the one in a car. Power comes in through the wall outlet to the UPS, is stored in the battery portion of the UPS as DC current, is converted into AC power, and is then sent to the computer. The UPS usually has system management support (often a serial port) that allows the UPS to be monitored and configured by a computer connected through the serial port.

The battery always has a capacity that is equal to the usage of the computer components multiplied by the number of minutes the battery must power the components. When figuring out how large a UPS to buy for a particular system, calculate the total number of watts your system consumes and convert the wattage to voltage amps: 1 watt (W) = 1.4 voltage amps (VAs). For example, say the sum total wattage for a computer system is 500 watts, and the system needs 5 minutes to properly shut down. The calculation is 500 W x 1.4 VA = 700 VA. You could purchase a 700 VA UPS to protect the equipment for a 5-minute window. But now say you need that server to remain available during a 45-minute outage. In that case, you would need a 3000 VA UPS to maintain power to that system for 45 minutes. See Figure 15.3 for a typical online UPS. *(Note: There are many UPS calculators on the Internet. They will allow you to make the best purchase for your systems.)*

FIGURE 15.3
An Online UPS

The UPS also cleans power that is sent to the devices connected to it. The power is equalized, and any line noise is removed.

STANDBY UPS

The *standby UPS* handles power to the computer in a slightly different way. With a standby unit, continuous power is supplied to the device(s) directly from the power source. When the UPS detects a reduction in power, it switches to battery power supply. With sensitive devices such as some servers, that small gap in time between discovery that power is no longer available and the switch to the battery may be long enough to cause a server shutdown or reboot.

Standby UPS

A UPS that switches to battery power when it detects a power failure. The switch to battery power may take several seconds, causing servers to shut down and users to lose their connections to the servers.

TESTTIP

For testing, make sure you understand the difference between an online UPS and a standby UPS.

Fault Tolerance

Fault tolerance is a system's capacity to continue functioning given a "fault," or malfunction, of one or more components in the system. Computer systems are comprised of individual components. Each has a certain life

Fault tolerance

The ability of a system to continue functioning when a malfunction or fault occurs in one or more components of the system.

expectancy, and each of those expectations varies component to component. When a fault occurs, that in turn may cause a failure of one or more systems in the network, which also may compromise the access users have to data or applications. Therefore, it is important to plan for fault tolerance in your network.

DISK FAULT TOLERANCE

A hard disk is a mechanical device that stores data within a computer. The hard drive is used constantly for read and write requests. Because it is mechanical in nature, it will fail at some point. This type of failure can bring down the production of an entire network, and cost a business many thousands of dollars in lost work time. Frequently, when the hard disk fails, the data stored there is irretrievable.

To protect against such a failure, several disk management solutions can be implemented. These solutions are often grouped into a format known as a *redundant array of inexpensive disks (RAID)*. RAID has eight levels (0 to 7), which are discussed below. Generally RAID 0, 1, and 5 are the most commonly used. RAID can be implemented as either a hardware or a software solution. The software method is controlled by the operating system, and therefore can deteriorate performance of the server. If no other solution is available that is within budget limitations, by all means use software RAID. However, the safest and most efficient implementation is hardware RAID. Check the operating system documentation to see which of the following types of RAID solutions are supported by the operating system. This section will assume that hardware RAID is the chosen solution for disk fault tolerance.

RAID Level 0

RAID level 0 uses a *disk array* in which data is written in segments across all disks in the array. A minimum of two hard disks is required to implement this form of RAID. Files are distributed for storage across all disks. See Figure 15.4 for an example.

Redundant array of inexpensive disks (RAID)

A disk subsystem installed in a server in order to store data across all disks. Often this array has a parity bit associated with the data to allow recovery in the event of failure of one disk.

Disk array

A set of two or more disks that are treated as a single storage unit.

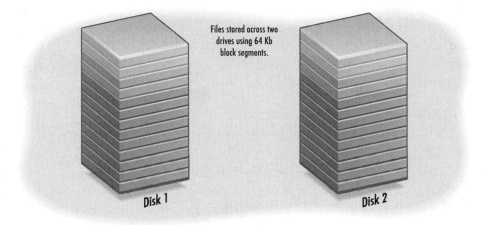

Files stored across two drives using 64 Kb block segments.

Disk 1   Disk 2

FIGURE 15.4
RAID Level 0

The administrator determines the size of the segments of a file that are written across the disks in the array. The segments are known as "stripes," or data stripes. This RAID method is often referred to as "striping without parity," because level 0 has no fault tolerance. In other words, data stored on the hard disks can be recreated only by restoring the data from backup tapes. (See the section on backups later in this chapter.) Both read and write performance is excellent because RAID level 0 has multiple read-write heads on the hard disks managing the storage and retrieval of the data.

IN REAL LIFE

"Parity" refers to a special bit that is created when data is written to a hard disk that sets up a technique to check whether the data has been lost or overwritten or otherwise damaged. The bit is added to the segment of the file to be stored. The bits are counted, and when an attempt is made to move that file (retrieval of the stored data), the bits are counted and compared to the number in the parity bit. If they match, all is well. If they do not match, the data is damaged.

RAID level 0 uses all available disk space. To calculate the storage space, add the available space on all drives in the array. As an example, if your array has three drives, each with a 10-gigabyte capacity, the available storage space is 30 gigabytes.

RAID 0 should be used only for storage of noncritical data that requires high-speed access and changes infrequently. It is a cost-efficient solution because it can be implemented not only with a hardware *RAID controller* card installed in the machine, but also often through software data storage management.

RAID controller

A special board that is installed in a computer, the purpose of which is to control the data flow to and from multiple hard disks attached by cables to the controller itself.

An important point to remember is that RAID level 0 provides no fault tolerance for the data stored in the array. The only way to successfully recover from a drive failure is to restore the data from backup tapes of the data. Backups must be checked randomly for integrity, and a strict schedule of backups must be maintained.

RAID Level 1

RAID level 1 is commonly called disk mirroring. That is, data is written simultaneously to two hard disks through one controller, creating a duplicate drive. Disk mirroring can be implemented using either a hardware RAID controller or through the software of the operating system. Level 1 provides excellent fault tolerance because a duplicate copy of the data exists on a second drive, and the potential for both drives to fail at the same time is small. See Figure 15.5 for an example.

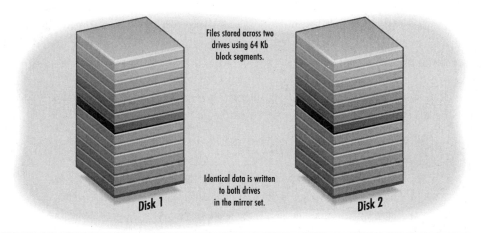

FIGURE 15.5
RAID Level 1

Another variation of RAID level 1 is commonly used where more fault tolerance is needed. In disk duplexing, two controllers are installed in the system, and each controller manages one of the hard disks. Now, either a drive or a controller can fail, and the stored data can still be retrieved from the disk.

Disk mirroring or duplexing provides fair-to-good read performance and good write performance. To work well, a disk mirror needs fast, high-end drives.

When a disk in the mirror set fails, the remaining disk just keeps on reading and writing against requests that are made. Often, the users will not know that a disk has failed. The administrator may discover the failure either by looking at the physical server (and observing that the drive lights are no longer lit on one drive), or by receiving a message sent to the administrator (if the system is set up to send alerts). Many servers today hold *hot spares,* that is, another drive is already installed in the system, and on failure of one drive, the hot spare drive will activate and begin recreating the data on the new hot spare. Many servers also allow *hot swapping.* Here, a damaged disk can be removed and a new drive put in merely by unlocking the drive from the outside of the box, pulling out the bad drive, and replacing the drive with a new one. Once a new, functional drive is detected, the data can be recreated.

RAID level 1 will always use just two disks. The available storage space is equal to the size of one of the disks, or 50 percent of the total disk space.

RAID level 1 is recommended where fault tolerance is necessary but cost is a concern. This is not a good option if extremely large amounts of data must be stored on a system. The time needed to recreate a mirror set would be extraordinary. Consequently, RAID 1 is frequently used for accounting and financial data storage and small database system servers.

RAID Level 2

RAID level 2 is known as bit-level striping with Hamming code ECC. RAID 2 provides fault tolerance in hard disks, but it is not used in modern systems because it does not use a standard method of mirroring, striping, or parity.

Another disadvantage is that this method of RAID requires many, many disks, often from 10 to 40 individual drives. This makes the RAID 2 implementation very costly and a management nightmare because the disks must be spindle-synchronized.

Actual storage space availability ranges between 71 and 82 percent of the total capacity of the drives. Read and write access performance is poor to fair with writes and fair to very good with reads.

RAID Level 3

RAID level 3 is commonly known as byte-level striping with dedicated parity. Data is striped across multiple drives at the byte level, with the number of bytes used varying in each write. One entire disk is dedicated to parity. This causes a slowdown in performance, because anytime a data set is randomly read, the bits on the parity drive must be checked constantly to guarantee integrity of the data.

This RAID method requires a special, relatively costly controller and a minimum of three disks. The available storage space will be equal to the

Hot spare

A disk that is installed in the server or disk array, but that is not used to store data until one of the online (used) disks fails.

Hot swapping

Removing a disk from the server or array when it fails and replacing it with a functioning disk without shutting down the server or array.

loss of one drive. If the array has four 20-gigabyte drives, the available storage is 60 gigabytes.

Read performance ranks in the good to very good levels, but write performance runs only poor to fair-good because of the time needed to write the parity information on the drive.

This type of fault tolerance is often used when working with large files (graphics) that require high transfer rates to and from the client machine.

RAID Level 4

This RAID method is called block-level striping with dedicated parity. Again, one drive is dedicated to the parity bit storage to manage the integrity of the stored data. Although similar to bit-level striping, RAID 4 uses blocks that are determined by the administrator. As with earlier RAID formats, the available storage space is equal to the space of all of the drives in the array minus the amount of space on one drive. Of course, at least three drives are required.

Read performance ranks good to very good, and write performance ranks poor to good.

This type of RAID array is used as a midline between RAID 3 and 5, although it is not frequently implemented.

RAID Level 5

RAID level 5 is the commonly implemented form of RAID when maximum storage space, fault tolerance, and relatively decent performance are required. It is known as striping with parity (or distributed parity). See Figure 15.6 for an example.

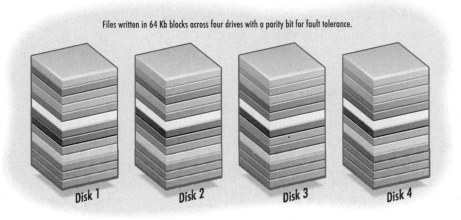

Files written in 64 Kb blocks across four drives with a parity bit for fault tolerance.

Disk 1   Disk 2   Disk 3   Disk 4

FIGURE 15.6
RAID Level 5

In RAID 5, data is written across all disks along with a parity bit for protection of the data. Where some of the earlier RAID methods dedicated an entire disk to the parity information, RAID level 5 distributes the parity information throughout the data store. This makes this method faster and more efficient.

RAID 5 can be implemented through hardware RAID controllers or through software (OS) management. At least three disks must be used for the array. All drives should be identical. Like RAID levels 2, 3, and 4, loss of one drive is easily tolerated. That failed drive may be replaced on the fly with a hot spare or by hot swapping the bad drive for a new drive.

Read performance with RAID 5 is good to very good. Write performance is only fair to good because, no matter what the method, time is required to write the parity bit. The loss of a drive during production time will slow users' access to data but will not prevent access because of failure. Should two drives fail at the same time, the drives must be replaced and the data must be restored from backup tapes.

RAID level 5 is the best of all the RAID levels because it provides good performance, fault tolerance, and relatively easy recovery from drive failure.

RAID Level 6

RAID level 6 uses block-level striping with dual-distributed parity. This might be called RAID 5 on vitamins. Where RAID 5 writes the single parity bit across the drives, RAID 6 writes *two* parity bits for each block of data written. Data stripe size can be adjusted, which may improve performance under certain conditions.

RAID 6 requires a minimum of four disks, thus increasing the ratio of cost to storage space. The equivalent of two drives in the array is used to store the parity bits.

An administrator can expect the read performance to be good to very good, and the write performance (again, due to the parity bits) is poor to fair.

RAID Level 7

RAID level 7 is a proprietary implementation of RAID that delivers exceptional read and write performance but is very expensive to implement because of its proprietary nature. It uses an asynchronous cached striping with a dedicated parity drive. Because it is not an industry standard, it bears mentioning, but you should not expect to see this method much in the field. Check with the vendor for details about the methods used to store and protect the data.

Component Fault Tolerance

When discussing fault tolerance, the first item to come to mind is disk fault tolerance. However, general component fault tolerance must also be mentioned. In high-end server systems, the system is commonly built with two power supplies and an additional network interface card (NIC). This allows the administrator to quickly recover from a failure of either of these components.

Troubleshooting RAID Arrays

- If your servers are using RAID 5 arrays for storage and users complain that access to resources has slowed to a crawl, check the drives in the array. It is likely that one of the drives has failed. Users can still access file resources because the parity bit is recreating the data, but the process is slow and processor intensive.
- If your servers are using RAID 0, your users will lose their ability to access data. The failed drive must be removed and replaced, and the data restored from tape.

Backups

Backup

A copy of all data stored on a disk (or disks), usually written to magnetic tape. A backup can also be written to CDs, hard drives, and removable disks such as Zip disks. Typically this copy of the data is stored off-site for security. It is used to recover data in the event of a disaster.

In small, medium, large, and enterprise networks, the administrator must back up all data that is critical to the operation of the business—in other words, everything. *Backups* are the most important safety net for a business and an information technology (IT) department. There are several types of backup schedules and methods that can be implemented. The one chosen will depend on the volume of data, on the rate at which the data changes per day, and on how much the administrator and business want to spend to support the backup strategy.

Backup software and media are two of the first considerations when determining a backup strategy or policy. Three options for software and media are available:

- Small- and large-capacity removable disks (floppy disks, Zip disks, swappable hard drives, Sharq drives, Iomega Jaz drives)
- Removable optical discs (CD-ROM, CD-RW, CD-R, Magneto optical discs, DVD)
- Magnetic tape (DAT, DLT, AIT)

Many utilities and software applications exist that allow the administrator to interface with the backup device graphically, to configure schedules for backups, to track media used, and to manage any tangential processes. All of the major operating systems—Microsoft NT and 2000, Novell NetWare, and UNIX/Linux—have built in some form of backup software.

TEST TIP

Learn and remember each of the backup types and when they are used.

There are three standard backup types:
- Full
- Incremental
- Differential

The backup format for a network typically uses either the full backup nightly (if the amount of data to be rendered to tape can be backed up overnight) or the full backup once a week and either an incremental or differential backup at all other times. Which strategy you choose depends on several factors:
- Amount of data to be backed up
- Speed of backup devices
- Type of restore process that is most efficient for the organization

Often, different strategies are planned for different servers, so you will need to fully understand each type of backup, detailed in the following sections.

FULL BACKUPS

A *full backup* takes all data from a server (or even a critical workstation) and commits the entire data store to a backup medium. This process can exceed the time available to perform the backup because of the large amount of data that must be written to the backup medium. This type of backup is usually done once a week on a Friday. While the backup is in process, users cannot access data and any files that are open may not be included in the backup. That is the reason for doing it only once a week.

Note that during a full backup, the *archive bit* for each file is reset to reflect that the backup picked up the file and a copy exists on the medium used for backup. The archive bit functions as a flag. When the archive bit is set to "on," it signals that the file has changed and must be backed up again. Once the bit has been reset, the flag is gone. A full backup is the only type that will commit all files to tape, regardless of whether they have

Full backup

A copy of all of the data (both changed and unchanged) on a hard drive or disk array.

Archive bit

An attribute of a file that tells backup software whether the file needs to be backed up because it has changed.

been changed since the last backup. Should a file or many files be lost and need to be restored, the technician locates the most recent backup, and restores the lost data from one tape.

The tape system and capacity of the medium must match the amount of data to be backed up. If the tape capacity is less than the amount of data, the backup will not be completed, and data restoration will be impossible. Figure 15.7 shows the amount of data backed up during each session of a full backup that is performed every night.

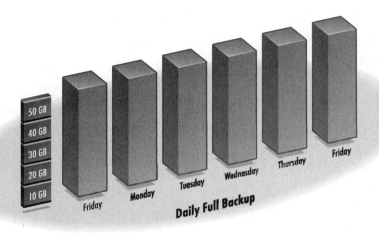

FIGURE 15.7
Full Backup Data Store

INCREMENTAL BACKUPS

Incremental backup

A copy of all data that has been changed since the last backup (whether full, incremental, or differential).

Incremental backups take less time to complete than full backups because only files that have changed since the last backup will be committed to tape. When a file is changed, the archive bit is turned on. When the incremental backup is complete, all archive bits are reset to off. That means a much smaller amount of data must be backed up. See Figure 15.8 for the incremental backup data volume.

Network Integrity

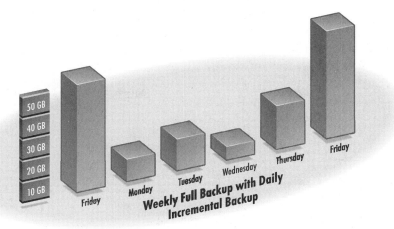

FIGURE 15.8
Incremental Backup Data
Volume

To completely restore lost data on a server when incremental backups have been performed, the last full backup plus all incremental backups since the last full backup must be available. Also, the data must be restored in chronological order. Once the process is complete, the server data store has been returned to the state it was in before the loss and immediately after the last incremental backup. This restoration process can be labor intensive if the crash occurs the day before the next full backup; it can require multiple tapes and multiple restore actions before it is complete.

TEST TIP

For the test, understand that the most difficult data restoration is the combination of the last full backup and incremental backups. All incremental backup tapes must be restored in order to provide data integrity.

DIFFERENTIAL BACKUPS

Differential backups are used in conjunction with the last full backup. With a differential backup, any file that has changed since the last full backup is committed to tape. The archive bit on a changed file is not reset during a differential backup. That means that the file will continue to be committed to tape with each differential backup and will be reset only when another full backup is completed. See Figure 15.9 for the differential backup data volume.

Differential backup

A copy of all data that has been changed since the last full backup.

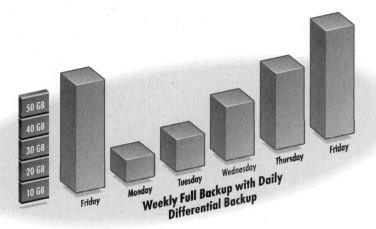

FIGURE 15.9
Differential Backup Data
Volume

Restorations from differential backups are easier than from incremental backups. The only tapes needed for restoration are the last full backup and the most recent differential backup. This is just slightly more work than restoring from a full backup; consequently, many network administrators use differential backups to ensure that data is safe.

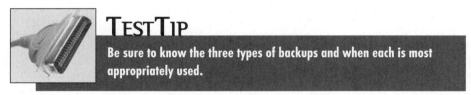

TESTTIP

Be sure to know the three types of backups and when each is most appropriately used.

OTHER CONSIDERATIONS FOR BACKUP STRATEGIES

A few other considerations are important to keep in mind when deploying a network backup strategy.

Tape Rotation

Magnetic media, such as tapes, should be rotated on a weekly, monthly, or yearly schedule to preserve the integrity of the medium itself. Every time a tape is used for a backup, it is stretched slightly, and over time it loses its ability to hold data. Setting up a rotation can lengthen the lifespan of the physical media.

A weekly tape rotation uses 7 tapes and allows the administrator to go back one week to restore data. A monthly rotation uses 31 tapes and gives the administrator a full 30 or 31 days of archived data to restore from. A yearly tape rotation, where there is a tape for each day of the year, gives the administrator the ability to go back a full 365 days when attempting to restore data to a server.

Tape Storage

Magnetic tape is subject to damage from many sources. Sun, heat, water, and humidity can render tapes unusable. Other sources of corruption include any magnet and overuse (causing stretching of the tape material).

Tapes used for backups may be stored either on-site or off-site at a third-party storage facility. To bring a business back online after a major catastrophe such as fire, flood, tornado, or earthquake, the backed-up data must be available to restore to a server. In such an event, if the tapes are stored on-site they may be destroyed in the disaster. Another consideration for tape storage is the effect that movement, sunlight, magnets, climate conditions, and coffee can have on tapes. All five of these can deteriorate the tapes to render them unusable immediately or over a period of time. Store backup media appropriately.

TROUBLESHOOTING BACKUPS

- If your backups are not completing in the time allotted to the backup process (especially full backups that usually run overnight), check the amount of data you are trying to back up. You may have exceeded the storage capacity of the tape. To resolve this, you will have to divide the amount of data to be backed up over two tape drives or purchase a larger capacity tape system.
- If you are asked to restore data from a tape and are unable to do so, check the integrity of the tape. Over time, tape stretches as it is pulled through a tape drive. The tension on the tape can make it lose its integrity. For tape preservation, remember to place tapes on a rotation schedule.

Network Attached Storage (NAS)

Network attached storage (NAS) is a relatively new but simple data storage concept. The NAS solution is nothing more than a network device with huge amounts of data storage capacity, something like a large warehouse for all of the data. The key with NAS is that it is not dependent on any specific platform (operating system). The client software component runs on all platforms, and the file systems available are common to many operating systems. While the most obvious use of NAS is for general network data

Network attached storage (NAS)

Data storage warehouse attached to the network that is not dependent on any specific operating system or platform. NAS allows a large volume of data to be stored and accessible to users.

storage, a NAS device might also handle cache and proxy storage, audio and video streaming file storage, or backup files. This makes NAS a very versatile solution for networks that must store vast amounts of data.

A NAS device uses all of its resources to manage the organization and maintenance of the files stored there. The device does not get bogged down with requests for any other services, nor does it have to compete for CPU time. The device itself is often configured to support RAID 5 fault tolerance to protect the data, and of course, the data store should also be backed up routinely.

Another benefit to using NAS as a data storage solution comes from the types of file systems supported by NAS devices. NAS devices understand standard network protocols, Network File System (NFS; used by UNIX), and Common Internet File System (CIFS; developed largely by Microsoft and using an SMB variation).

NAS is also easily scalable for a network that is growing. This allows the administrator to purchase a NAS system that is properly sized for the current network. Later, the administrator can return to the vendor and add storage capacity without buying a whole new storage system. Because the NAS device is independent of the network servers, it can be brought down for maintenance or expansion without bringing down the entire network, including all applications and user access to other resources.

STUDY GUIDE

In this chapter, we learned that maintaining network integrity means planning for the worst disasters. We also learned many small steps the technician and network administrator can take to protect the network from the effects of less damaging, but equally frustrating, failures. Here are some key points to remember.

NETWORK INTEGRITY

- Network integrity means maintaining the state of the network such that all parts function as a whole in a sound and unimpaired state.
- Include the following areas in a plan to maintain network integrity:
  o Documentation
  o Disaster planning and recovery
  o Power protection
  o Fault tolerance
  o System backups

DOCUMENTATION

- Documentation for the network includes information on the following:
  - LAN/WAN topology
  - Hardware inventory
  - Software inventory
  - Change logs
  - Server information
  - Router and switch configurations
  - User policies and profiles
  - Baseline documents
  - Mission-critical applications and hardware
  - Network service configuration
  - Procedures
- Good network documentation aids in troubleshooting problems that occur within the network, such as failed connections, failed servers, hung applications, failed WAN connects, and failed access to resources.
- Documentation can be formalized using custom forms or can be kept informally using inexpensive notebooks to record changes and repairs.

DISASTER PLANNING AND RECOVERY

- A disaster is an event that causes widespread destruction or distress, or total failure.
- Planning for the worst-case scenario allows the network administrator, in collaboration with the planning team and technicians, to anticipate the consequences of both natural and human-induced disasters.
- Disaster planning may be as simple as writing a procedure to back up all data, or as complex as contracting for completely redundant sites so that a network could sustain a disaster without loss of service.

The Disaster Recovery Plan

- A disaster recovery (DR) plan follows a set of well-defined steps:
  1. Creating the disaster recovery (DR) team
  2. Identifying the risks that threaten the network
  3. Assessing the impact on the business
  4. Defining needs
  5. Developing a detailed plan
  6. Testing
  7. Maintaining the plan

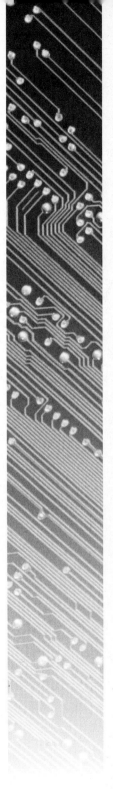

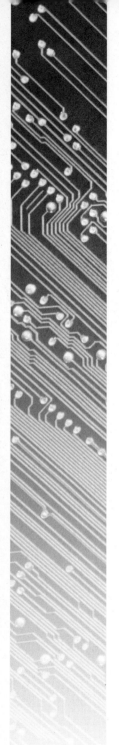

- A disaster recovery plan is a living document that may take many weeks or months to develop and implement, and this plan must be consistently updated as changes are made to the network.

Mirrored Servers (Failover Clustering)

- Mirrored servers provide 99.9 percent uptime for mission-critical applications and data.
- To build mirrored servers, both servers must be configured with identical equipment and software, and both must be attached to the network.
- The primary mirrored server answers requests from the network and issues a "heartbeat" to its twin to let the secondary mirrored server know that the primary is servicing the network.
- When the secondary server does not hear a heartbeat in a predetermined time frame, it will begin answering requests from the network. The window between failure of the primary server and cutover to the secondary is usually 30 to 45 seconds.

Clustered Servers

- Clustered servers represent two or more servers that are configured with identical applications and file structures, all attached to the network, and all answering requests from the network. All servers are acting as one very large server.
- Clustered servers can make use of replication services. Several servers may be located off-site and participate in replication to ensure that data is identical on all boxes in the event of failure within the network or disaster.
- Clustering is very expensive to implement and is a complex implementation. For this reason, small- to medium-size businesses usually do not choose this option for disaster planning and recovery.

POWER PROTECTION

- Power loss is one of the small disasters that an administrator can mitigate without undo expense or complex configurations.
- Several types of power protection can be used on the network. The choice will depend on the nature of the operations and the stability of the geographical location of the business.

Surge Protectors

- Surge protectors are designed to minimize the effects of power spikes, surges, and brownouts.
- Surge protectors do not protect equipment from "dirty power," noise on the line, or power failure.
- Over time, the circuit breaker in a surge protector loses its sensitivity to power fluctuations and can allow great variation in power to pass through to components. This weakens the components and may contribute to premature failure.
- Surge protectors on equipment should be replaced at least yearly to reduce the likelihood of component damage.

Online Uninterruptible Power Supply (UPS)

- The purpose of a UPS is to provide enough power for enough time to allow a server or other critical machine the ability to shut down gracefully.
- An online UPS provides protection for equipment by conditioning the power before it reaches the equipment.
- Inside the UPS is a battery that stores power coming from a wall outlet. That power is then sent to the equipment. All noise and fluctuation is minimized, thus making the power used by the server "clean" again and providing a power source should there be a loss of power.
- The size of the UPS depends on the wattage of the attached equipment. 1 W = 1.4 VA. To calculate the wattage of the equipment, multiply it by 1.4, and determine the length of time necessary to complete the shutdown process and any other routines that must be done while the machine is still running. Usually, a UPS will provide 15 to 20 minutes' worth of power by default. If longer times are needed, then multiply the total wattage by the total amount of time to determine the size of the UPS.

Standby UPS

- A standby UPS allows power to go directly to the equipment while charging a battery in the UPS. When a power failure occurs, the UPS detects a reduction in power and cuts over to battery power.
- Some devices, such as servers, may reboot or shut down during a short gap between loss of power and cutover to a battery backup.

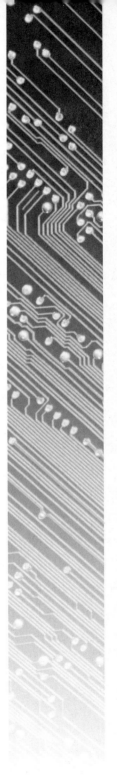

FAULT TOLERANCE

- Fault tolerance is the system's capacity to continue functioning given a "fault," or malfunction of one or more components.

Disk Fault Tolerance

- Disk fault tolerance provides the network with the ability to recover when a hard-disk storage device fails, and to prevent loss of data stored on that device.
- To protect data, one of several strategies to address disk fault tolerance can be implemented in the servers. The most common is some form of a redundant array of inexpensive disks (RAID).

RAID Level 0

- RAID level 0 is commonly called disk striping without parity.
- This form of RAID allows data to be written across multiple disks but does not provide any fault tolerance.
- Implementation of RAID 0 requires at least two hard disks.
- With RAID 0, both read and write performance will improve over single disk usage.
- RAID 0 uses all available disk space for storage.
- This form of RAID is useful for noncritical data that is routinely backed up.

RAID Level 1

- RAID level 1 is commonly referred to as disk mirroring (or disk duplexing when two controllers are used).
- With RAID 1, data is written to both disks at the same time. Should one disk fail, the other disk takes over servicing requests from the network.
- Implementation of RAID level 1 requires two disks.
- Mirroring, or duplexing, will provide good read and write access to data on the disk.
- Only 50 percent of the total disk space can be used for storage.
- This form of RAID is used where fault tolerance is needed but cost is a concern.

RAID Level 2

- RAID level 2 is known as bit-level striping with Hamming code ECC.
- This level of RAID is not used in modern systems.

RAID Level 3

- RAID level 3 uses byte-level striping with dedicated parity.
- Data is striped across multiple drives and a parity bit is written to a dedicated hard disk for recovery of lost data.
- Read performance with RAID 3 is good, but write performance is only poor to fair.
- This type of RAID is costly to implement and is not as efficient as other implementations.

RAID Level 4

- RAID level 4 uses a method called block-level striping with dedicated parity.
- The difference between RAID 3 and RAID 4 is simply that level 4 uses blocks of a size determined by the administrator and level 3 uses a stripe at the byte level.
- Read performance is good and write performance is fair.
- This type of RAID is a midline between levels 3 and 5, but it is not frequently implemented.

RAID Level 5

- RAID level 5 is commonly known as striping with parity.
- This form of RAID requires at least three disks. Data is striped across the disks, and a parity bit is written to the disk as well. This is not a dedicated parity disk system.
- Read performance is very good, while write performance is fair.
- When figuring available storage space, add the amount of disk space on all drives and subtract the amount of space on one drive.
- RAID 5 is considered to be the best choice for fault tolerance and performance.

RAID Level 6

- RAID level 6 uses block-level striping with dual-distributed parity.
- Implementation of this form of RAID requires a minimum of four disks. The equivalent of two disks is lost to parity.
- The read performance is good and the write performance is poor to fair due to the parity bits written to the drives.

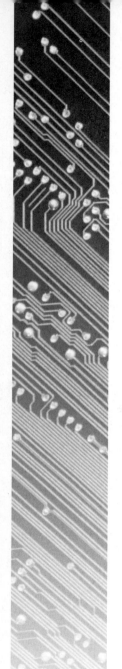

RAID Level 7

- RAID level 7 is a proprietary form that uses an asynchronous cached striping mechanism with dedicated parity storage.
- Although a defined RAID level, consult the vendor for more information.

SYSTEM BACKUPS

- When determining a backup strategy, you must first consider how you want to accomplish the backup (using what hardware) and what software you will use to complete this task.
- Some of the options for backup include:
  - small- and large-capacity removable disks.
  - optical disks.
  - magnetic tape (the most commonly used media).
- Once the media is identified, the administrator will determine a schedule of backups using one or more of the following methods:
  - Full backups
  - Incremental backups
  - Differential backups

Full Backups

- A full backup takes all data and commits it to tape.
- During a full backup, the archive bit (attribute) is reset to off to notify the backup software that the file has been saved to tape.
- Full backups done on a daily basis allow quick restoration of data because only one tape will be used to complete the restoration.

Incremental Backups

- During an incremental backup, only files that have been changed since the last backup are committed to tape. The last backup may have been a full, an incremental, or a differential backup.
- This method of backup is used in conjunction with weekly full backups.
- Incremental backups reduce the amount of time it takes to complete the backup process because of the limited selection of files that are backed up.
- When restoring, the administrator or technician must locate the last full backup and all incremental backup tapes since the last full backup.
- Incremental backups reset the archive bit to off.

Differential Backups

- A differential backup saves all files that have changed since the last full backup.
- To restore data, only the tapes from the last full backup and the last (most recent) differential backup will be used.
- This method of backing up data is used in conjunction with weekly full backups.
- A weekly full backup and daily differential backups are considered the most efficient and safest strategy for maintaining data integrity.

Other Considerations for Backup Strategies

- Tape rotation patterns are determined when the backup strategy is designed.
- Tape rotation choices include:
  - daily rotation.
  - weekly rotation.
  - monthly rotation.
  - yearly rotation.
- With each option, the administrator must consider what archive of past data must be maintained for the business, and whether the cost of maintaining a large archive of tapes outweighs the protection of the data.
- Most businesses use either a weekly rotation or a monthly rotation to manage archived data.
- Tape storage is important to consider as well.
- Magnetic tape is susceptible to damage from natural elements, including heat, sun, water, and humidity. Proper storage is necessary for disaster recovery.
- Tapes should be stored either in climate-controlled rooms that are physically protected or at an off-site storage facility. The best option for disaster recovery is to contract with a third party to maintain the tape archive at a remote location. This method allows the tapes to remain safe should there be a disaster at the location of the business. Restoration of the data can then take place at the new location should the old one be rendered unusable.

NETWORK ATTACHED STORAGE (NAS)

- NAS is a relatively new data storage concept that attaches large data storage boxes to the network but that does not require a server to manage the storage.

- NAS can use multiple file formats such as CIFS and NFS, allowing the storage facility to be independent of any one platform (operating system).
- When considering NAS, keep in mind that the NAS box is a storage facility and does not expend any resources providing any other services to the network.
- NAS boxes can be brought down for maintenance without causing a network shutdown.

PRACTICE TEST

Try this test to check your mastery of the concepts in this chapter.

1. Which of the following tape rotations gives the administrator the best archive of data?
   a. daily rotations
   b. weekly rotations
   c. monthly rotations
   d. yearly rotations

2. Which of the following options provide fault tolerance for the network? (Choose all that apply)
   a. uninterruptible power supply (UPS)
   b. redundant array of inexpensive disks (RAID)
   c. off-site tape storage
   d. tape-drive backups
   e. clustered servers

3. What is the minimum number of drives needed to build a RAID 5 array?
   a. two
   b. three
   c. four
   d. five

4. You have made sure that all data is backed up every night. Your tapes are rotated monthly. You do a quick check of each tape each morning to make sure the tapes are clean and can be used for a restoration. Where should the backup tapes be stored for disaster recovery?
   a. at your home
   b. in your car
   c. in the network administrator's office
   d. in a locked safe on-site
   e. in a locked safe off-site

Network Integrity

5. Which of the following items are parts of a comprehensive network documentation effort? (Choose three)
   a. cable diagram
   b. detailed list of users
   c. hardware and software inventory
   d. change logs
   e. employee reviews
   f. telephone numbers for top IT management staff

6. Which of the following backup types assures the administrator that all data can be restored at any given time?
   a. daily full backups
   b. daily incremental backups
   c. weekly full backups
   d. weekly differential backups

7. Surge protectors are the best defense against dirty power and spikes and surges.
   a. True
   b. False

8. To achieve disk fault tolerance with relatively quick recovery from disk loss, you would implement
   a. disk mirroring.
   b. disk duplexing.
   c. RAID 5.
   d. RAID 0.

9. Clustered servers provide high availability for mission-critical applications on the network. Which of the following is an additional benefit that comes with clustered servers?
   a. load balancing
   b. reduction in expenses
   c. lowered maintenance costs
   d. cutover time reduction

10. Which actions contribute to a good disaster recovery plan? (Choose three)
   a. a contract with a company for replacement of equipment on demand
   b. completely redundant sites
   c. tape backups of every server, every night

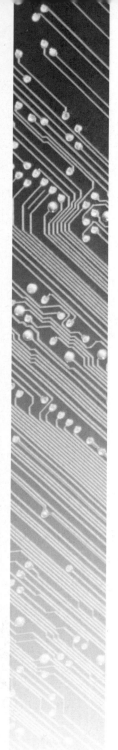

    d. storing backup tapes in a safe at work

    e. RAID 5 on all servers

    f. uninterruptible power supplies on all servers

11. Your server configuration includes two servers with identical equipment, both connected to the network. One server answers requests from the network. What type of fault tolerance does this describe?

    a. clustering

    b. RAID 1

    c. RAID 5

    d. disk mirroring

    e. failover clusters

12. Which of the following file systems will NAS recognize?

    a. CIFS

    b. AUFS

    c. NTFS

    d. NFS

13. You have installed a UPS on your server. It is configured to provide immediate power assistance in the event of a power failure. What type of UPS configuration have you implemented?

    a. standby

    b. online

    c. offline

    d. ready-type

14. Which of the following implementations of RAID provides striping with parity for data protection and recovery and efficient use of disk space?

    a. RAID 0

    b. RAID 1

    c. RAID 5

    d. RAID 6

15. You faithfully back up your server every night. Over the last week, your backups have stalled out before they complete. What is the problem with your backup?

    a. The tape drive is failing.

    b. The tapes are old.

    c. The amount of data exceeds the capacity of the tape.

    d. The configuration for the tape drive has become corrupt.

16. Which of the following backup strategies makes the best use of time and tapes and allows for relatively fast restorations?
    a. full backup weekly, incremental backup daily
    b. incremental backup daily
    c. full backup daily, differential backup weekly
    d. full backup weekly, differential backup daily

17. Which of the following RAID levels greatly improves read and write access without fault tolerance?
    a. 0
    b. 1
    c. 3
    d. 5

18. Disk mirroring and disk duplexing are considered RAID level 1. What are the differences between mirroring and duplexing? (Choose all that apply)
    a. Duplexing is a lot slower.
    b. Disk mirroring offers more protection against failure.
    c. The controller from disk 0 can fail or disk 0 can fail, while users can still access the data.
    d. Both drives can fail in duplexed disks, but users can still access data.

19. The minimum number of drives needed for RAID 5 is
    a. one.
    b. two.
    c. three.
    d. six.
    e. ten.

20. Which of the following will an incremental backup include on the tape?
    a. files changed since the last backup
    b. files changed since the last full backup
    c. files changed since the last differential backup
    d. files that have not changed since the last full backup

21. Network attached storage will work only with Microsoft file systems.
    a. True
    b. False

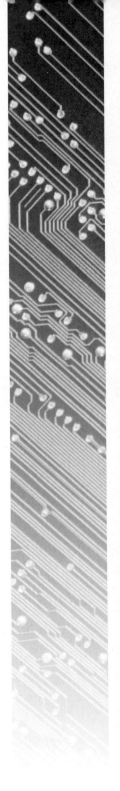

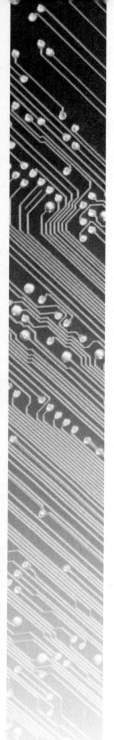

TROUBLESHOOTING

1. You are responsible for the backup plan on your network. You have decided that you want to be protected from all data loss, and you want to recover files quickly and easily. The plan you have chosen is to do a full backup every night. During the last week or so, first thing in the morning, users complain that they cannot access files. This problem disappears about 30 minutes later. What could be the problem?

2. You live in northern California. Your network administrator has asked you to outline a strategy for recovery of the physical plant after a disaster. The plan needs to address how the business can be up and running quickly after a natural disaster. Of the many options discussed in this chapter, what strategy will you employ?

CUSTOMER SERVICE

1. A user calls the help desk to tell you that he has deleted the folder containing your boss's presentation for tomorrow morning. What steps will you take to recover from this user error?

2. A worker runs an application used by six other people on the network. Data is also stored on this worker's machine. Several times in the last two months, the power has suddenly gone off. As a result, you have had to reinstall the application, and even recreate some of the data because the machine turned off abruptly. What can you do to solve the worker's problem?

FOR MORE INFORMATION

For links to Web sites that provide further information about the topics covered in this chapter, go to the EMC/Paradigm Internet Resource Center at www.emcp.com/College Division/Internet Resource Centers/Networking/System Administration/Web Resources: For More Information.

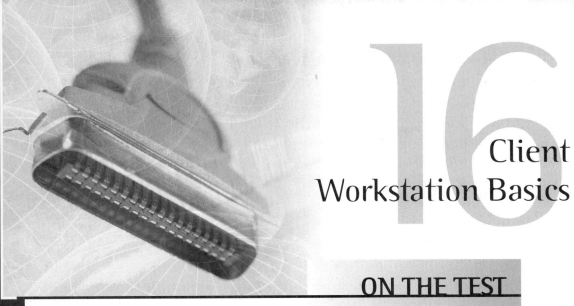

16

Client Workstation Basics

Network+ Examination
- **Objective 3.2:** Identify the basic capabilities of client workstations (i.e., client connectivity, local security mechanisms, and authentication).
- **Objective 3.11:** Given a network configuration, select the appropriate NIC and network configuration settings (DHCP, DNS, WINS, protocols, NetBIOS/host name, etc.).
- **Objective 4.4:** Given specific parameters, configure a client to connect to the following servers: UNIX/Linux; NetWare; Windows; Macintosh.
- **Objective 4.8:** Given a scenario, predict the impact of modifying, adding, or removing network services (e.g., DHCP, DNS, WINS, etc.) on network resources and users.
- **Objective 4.11:** Given a network troubleshooting scenario involving a client connectivity problem (e.g., incorrect protocol/client software/authentication configuration, or insufficient rights/permissions), identify the cause of the problem.

ON THE JOB

One of the primary jobs that a Network+ certified technician will perform is connecting client computers to a network. The tasks that are required can be placed in the two broad categories of hardware and software. The first step is to install the hardware and software necessary to connect to the network. That is the easy part. Once these components are installed, many configuration steps are required, and these steps vary from network to network, client to client. The purpose of this chapter is to provide you with the information necessary to select, install, and configure the appropriate pieces of client hardware and software in any given network configuration.

Understanding Network Client Computers

A *network client computer* can be defined simply as a computer that has the necessary hardware and software installed to allow it to connect to a network. Once that network connection is established, the client can access resources and services that are commonly available in a network environment. You will recall from Chapter 1 that the primary reason for establishing networks is to share resources, such a files, folders, and printers. Once a computer becomes a network client, it can print to shared network printers and access shared resources that are made available on the network.

Moreover, most network clients can also function as a *server*, providing shared resources to other clients on the network. For example, a network client can share folders containing files to other network clients.

Connecting clients to a network requires a combination of hardware and software. We will begin our discussion with the hardware element, the adapter.

In Real Life

Network client configuration varies from operating system to operating system; however, most Windows machines act in a very similar manner. All of the demonstrations and screen shots in this chapter focus on the Windows XP operating system.

Adapters

Adapters are the pieces of hardware that allow the cable to connect to the computer. Adapters are typically installed in a vacant slot on the system's motherboard or connected to a serial or USB port on the outside of the computer. Once the hardware is installed, a piece of software known as a device driver is installed to allow the operating system to communicate with the hardware. Following are some of the more common adapters:

- Integrated Services Digital Network (ISDN) cards
- Modems
- Network interface cards (NICs)

Selecting and Installing Network Interface Cards (NICs)

The most common type of adapter used in a networked computer is a network interface card (NIC). The NIC is a piece of hardware in the form of an expansion card that is installed inside the computer (see Figure 16.1). When selecting a NIC for your network installation, your choice will be governed by the following factors:

- The type of expansion slots available on the computer's motherboard
- The type of network (e.g., Ethernet, Token Ring, etc.)
- The type of cable media and corresponding connectors that will be used

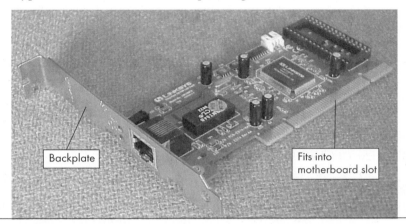

FIGURE 16.1
Network Interface Card

The quickest way to check for available expansion slot types is to remove the cover from the central processing unit (CPU). With the cover off, examine the empty expansion slots in the motherboard. The size and placement of the slots will tell you the type of expansion bus the computer is using. If you are unsure about the type of expansion slot, consult a technical reference or the motherboard reference manual to identify the type of slot the computer contains. When dealing with computers that have been manufactured in the last two to three years, you will find the *peripheral component interconnect (PCI)* slot to be the most common (see Figure 16.2).

Peripheral component interconnect (PCI)

The most common bus type found in computers manufactured after 1995.

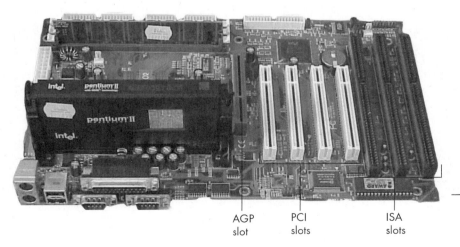

AGP slot   PCI slots   ISA slots

FIGURE 16.2
Motherboard Containing PCI Slots

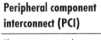

Once an appropriate NIC is installed in an open slot on the computer's motherboard, a piece of software known as a driver is installed to allow the computer to communicate with the NIC. Each operating system requires its own device driver, so make sure you select the correct one. In most cases, when the computer is powered on, it will automatically locate the newly installed NIC and prompt you to provide the location of the installation software. Once you have provided the correct software installation path, the computer will copy the necessary files and the hardware will begin to function. Occasionally, you will be required to restart the computer before you can use the new NIC.

TROUBLESHOOTING NIC INSTALLATION

In the event the computer does not detect the newly installed hardware, you can choose to install the software manually through the *Add Hardware* icon located within the Control Panel. To use this utility, follow these instructions (some of the specifics may vary, depending on your operating system):

1. Click the Start button. When the Start menu appears, select Control Panel. When the Control Panel menu appears, select Add Hardware (see Figure 16.3).
2. This will launch the Add Hardware Wizard (see Figure 16.4).

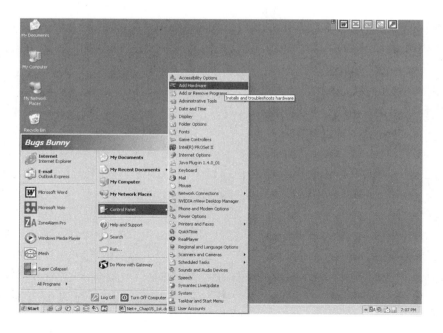

FIGURE 16.3
Control Panel/Add Hardware

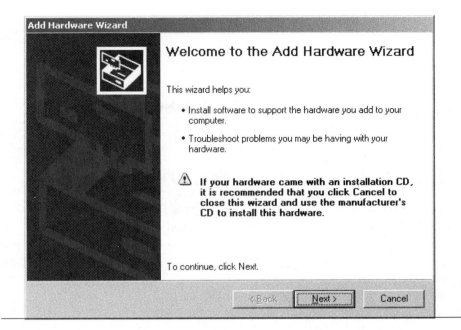

FIGURE 16.4
Add Hardware Wizard

3. Once the wizard launches, it will describe its function and prompt you to click the Next button.

4. Upon clicking Next, the wizard searches the computer for newly installed hardware. If it locates the hardware, it prompts you for the location of the installation files. Specify the path to the files; then the files will be copied and the device will be ready for use.

5. If a newly installed device is not located, the wizard prompts you for the device type: video card, network adapter, modem, etc.

6. Specify the device type. The wizard prompts you for the location of the installation files. Specify the path to the files; then the files will be copied and the device will be ready for use.

In Real Life

Most operating systems do a good job of identifying newly installed hardware. If you install a new piece of hardware and the operating system does not find it on boot-up, consider rechecking the hardware to ensure it has been installed correctly.

Ensure that the network medium (i.e., the cable) is properly attached on both ends. Typically, one end will be attached to the newly installed network interface card and the other to a wall jack.

Network Software and Properties

Network software generally falls into three broad categories: clients, protocols, and services. This software is installed on the client computer through the Network Properties dialog box. Although the appearance of the Properties dialog box varies with each operating system, a typical dialog box looks similar to Figure 16.5.

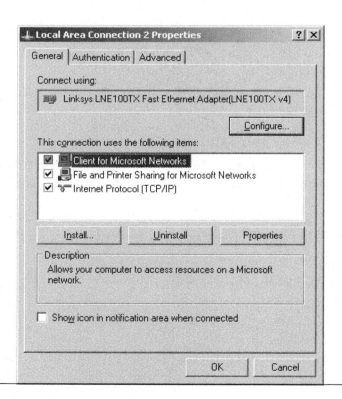

FIGURE 16.5
LAN Properties Dialog Box

To access the Network Properties dialog box, follow these steps:

1. Using the left mouse button, click the Start button. When the Start menu appears, select Control Panel. When the Control Panel menu appears, select Network Connections.

2. Another menu appears that lists all local area connections; select the appropriate connection. A Status window similar to Figure 16.6 will appear.

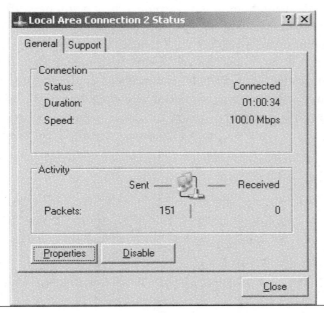

FIGURE 16.6
LAN Connection Status Window

3. Click the Properties button. The Network Properties dialog box will appear. To install new networking software, click the Install button. You will be presented with the option to install new clients, protocols, or network services (see Figure 16.7).

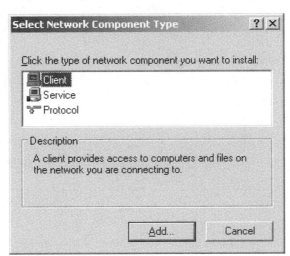

FIGURE 16.7
Choosing Network Components

Client Software

Client software is installed on a computer to allow the computer to send requests to a server or another computer on the network. Client software is often referred to as a *redirector* because it has the ability to redirect requests for resources that are not located on the local machine. For example, as shown in Figure 16.8, computers that are connected to networks often have drives that are mapped to other computers. When you open the My Computer object, you will see all mapped network and local drives. With My Computer open, if you use your mouse to double-click your local hard drive, the operating system has the ability to service your request to look at the contents of the hard drive. However, if you double-click a *mapped drive,* the computer will pass your request to view the contents of the mapped drive to the client software. That is, the client software redirects your request from the local computer to another computer on the network.

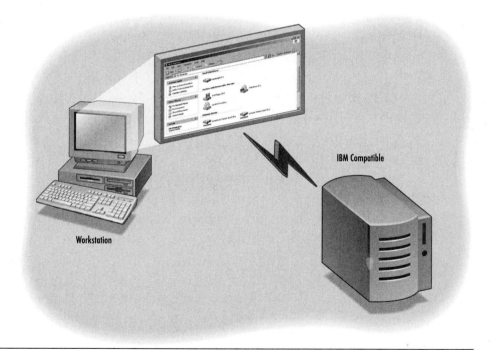

Workstation

IBM Compatible

FIGURE 16.8
A mapped drive sends a request for resources to the client software.

IN REAL LIFE

A mapped drive is a logical connection that points to information physically stored on another computer. For example, most networks allow users to maintain a home directory on a network server. The home directory allows users to store data files in a central place where they can be backed up on a regular basis. Rather than requiring the user to open the Network Neighborhood object, locate the server, and then locate the resource, a drive is mapped directly to the home directory. Once the drive is mapped, a user can open the My Computer object, locate the drive letter and double-click to open it. Users can also save data directly to the mapped drive.

The most common network client software in use today are the clients for Microsoft and Novell networks.

MICROSOFT CLIENT FOR MICROSOFT NETWORKS

A Microsoft Windows operating system automatically installs the *Microsoft Client for Microsoft Networks* on a computer whenever the OS detects that a network adapter has been installed. The Microsoft Client allows networked computers to communicate with other computers and servers on a Microsoft-based network. For example, when installing computers for use in a Windows NT or 2000 domain, or on a Windows 98 peer-to-peer network, you must install the Microsoft Client so that the computer can access the network. To install new client software, follow these steps:

1. Open the Network Properties dialog box and click the Install button.
2. When the Select Network Component Type dialog box appears, select Client and click the Add button.
3. A list of available clients will appear. Select the client you wish to install and click the OK button.
4. You will be prompted for the source installation files. Type in the path to the source files.

Once the client software is installed, it must be configured. The configuration will vary based on whether the client is part of a domain or a peer-to-peer network. *(Note: Peer-to-peer networks are commonly referred to as workgroups.)*

Microsoft Client for Microsoft Networks

Software that allows computers to communicate with each other on a Microsoft-based network.

TRY IT!

Install the Microsoft Client for Microsoft Networks.

Domain Configuration

Windows domain

A client-server network that uses Microsoft servers to control network security.

A *Windows domain* is a client-server network that uses Windows servers as domain controllers. The purpose of a domain controller is to handle security of the network, including users, groups, and resources. To configure a computer to participate in a Windows domain, follow these steps:

1. Open the Control Panel and locate the *System* icon. Double-click the icon.
2. When the System Properties dialog box appears, select the Computer Name tab.
3. At the Computer Name tab, locate and click the Network ID button.
4. The Network Identification Wizard appears (see Figure 16.9).

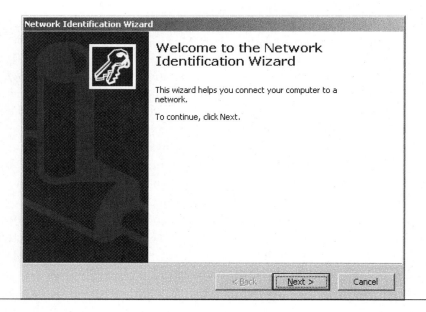

FIGURE 16.9
Network Identification Wizard

5. Click Next. The first Connecting to the Network window appears (see Figure 16.10). Select the option *This computer is part of a business network, and I use it to connect to other computers at work.* Click Next.

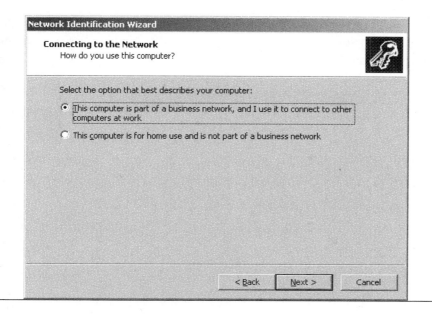

FIGURE 16.10
Connecting to the Network

6. At the next Connecting to the Network window (Figure 16.11), select *My company uses a network with a domain.* Click Next.

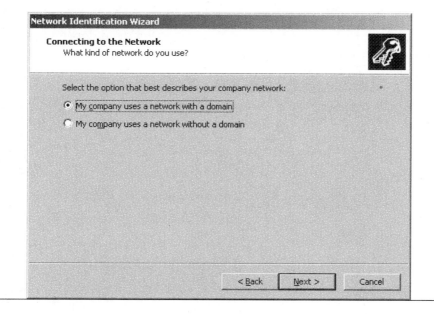

FIGURE 16.11
Connecting to the Network,
Continued

7. The Network Information window (Figure 16.12) provides the information you need to add a computer to the domain. Ensure that you have this information before proceeding. Click Next.

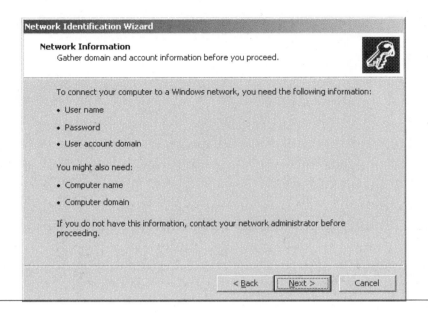

FIGURE 16.12
Network Information

8. The User Account and Domain Information dialog box appears (Figure 16.13). Enter the user name, password, and domain in the appropriate boxes. Click Next.

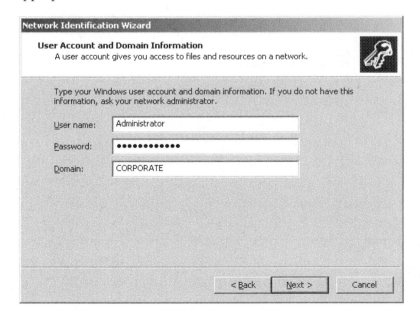

FIGURE 16.13
User Account and Domain
Information

9. The computer will attempt to contact a server operating as a domain controller and negotiate to join the domain. When the process has completed, a window will appear stating that the computer has successfully joined the domain and that you must restart the computer for the change to be effective (see Figure 16.14).

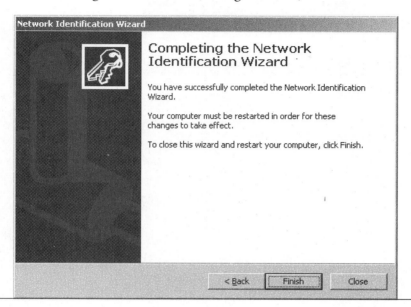

FIGURE 16.14
Completing the
Configuration

— TRY IT! —

Configure Microsoft Client for Microsoft Networks.

1. Configure the client to participate in a Microsoft Windows domain.
2. Test the client by logging in to the domain.
3. Connect to a shared resource in the domain.

Peer-to-Peer (Workgroup) Configuration

The procedures to join a peer-to-peer network, or *workgroup,* are very similar to those for joining a domain. To join or create a workgroup with Windows XP, follow these steps:

1. Open the Control Panel and locate and double-click the *System* icon.
2. When the System Properties dialog box appears, select the Computer Name tab.
3. At the Computer Name tab, locate and click the Network ID button.

Workgroup

A name commonly used for a peer-to-peer network

4. The Network Identification Wizard appears.
5. Click Next. The first Connecting to the Network window appears. Select the option *This computer is part of a business network, and I use it to connect to other computers at work.* Click Next.
6. At the next Connecting to the Network window, select *My company uses a network without a domain.* Click Next.
7. The Workgroup identification dialog box appears (see Figure 16.15).

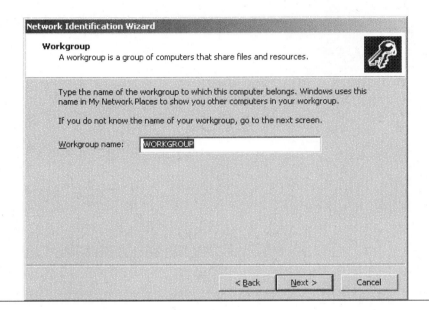

FIGURE 16.15
Workgroup Identification

8. Insert the name of your workgroup and click Next.
9. When the process has completed, a window appears stating that the computer has successfully joined the workgroup and that you must restart the computer for the change to be effective.
10. Restart the computer.

TRY IT!

Configure Microsoft Client for Microsoft Networks.

1. Configure the client to participate in a workgroup.
2. Test the client by logging in to the workgroup.
3. Map a drive to a shared resource in the workgroup.

CLIENT FOR NOVELL NETWORKS

Most Microsoft operating systems include the *Client Service for NetWare;* however, it is generally preferable to use Novell's client software. The Novell Client software allows Windows workstations to access and use all of the services available on Novell NetWare servers running Novell Directory Services and ZenWorks, which is Novell's desktop management software. The Novell Client also supports services and utilities including integrated messaging, multiprotocol support, management, security, and file and print services. Novell Client is available as a free download from the Novell Web site.

Client Service for NetWare

Microsoft software that allows networked computers to communicate with each other on a Novell-based network.

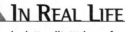

IN REAL LIFE

Always check Novell's Web site for the most recent version of its client, as well as any documents supporting the installation. Keep in mind that clients are software and occasionally a new client is needed to support a new feature or to fix a problem with an earlier version.

The client is downloaded as a self-extracting executable file. Double-click the file to begin extraction. The extraction process copies the installation files to the Temp directory on the local computer's hard drive. Once the files are extracted, locate the Setupnw.exe file, which will be located in the Temp directory. When you double-click Setupnw.exe, the client installation process will begin with a screen similar to Figure 16.16.

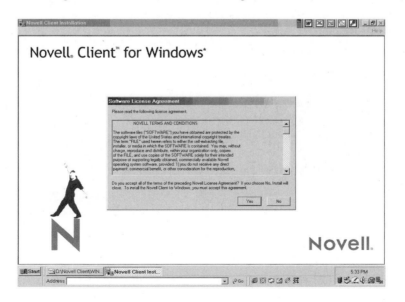

FIGURE 16.16
Novell Client Installation Screen

1. At the initial screen, click the Yes button, accepting the terms and conditions. Click Next.
2. At the installation option window, select *Typical Installation*. Click the Install button (see Figure 16.17).

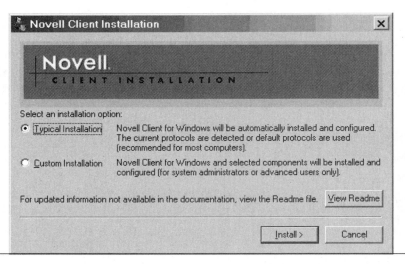

FIGURE 16.17
Installation Option Window

3. The setup process will begin copying files. When it is completed, you will be prompted to restart the computer.
4. Once the computer restarts, you will be prompted for the following information:
   - User name
   - Password
   - Novell Directory Services tree and context
   - Server name

   This information can be obtained from your network administrator.

TRY IT!

Install and configure the Novell Client software.

1. Configure the client to participate in a Novell network.
2. Test the client by logging in to the network.
3. Explore the network for available resources such as printers and folders.

Macintosh Clients

The Apple Macintosh, or "Mac" for short, can be a client to both Microsoft Windows and Novell NetWare servers. Unlike the clients detailed above, Macs do not really include client software for a specific network operating system. Instead, they have a built-in security module that allows them to communicate with the servers. Special services software is installed on the servers to allow them to support Mac clients.

UNIX Clients

A network client that wants to connect to a UNIX server usually does not log in to the UNIX server directly. Instead, it will make use of a third piece of software that allows the client to access specific resources. An example is the Network File System (NFS), which allows clients to access files directly, without logging in to the UNIX server first.

Troubleshooting Client Software Installation

Since clients are software, problems are usually caused by configuration errors that manifest themselves during network logon.

In Microsoft Networks, confirm the following information:

- The computer is a member of the domain, if required, and the domain name and computer name are spelled correctly.
- The domain name specified in the client box is correct.
- You are attempting to log on with a domain user name.
- The password matches the user name and is spelled correctly.
- Since passwords are case sensitive, make sure the Caps Lock key is not engaged.

In Novell networks, check these items:

- The client you are using is the most current.
- The client you are using is compatible with the Novell network operating system and supporting components, such as Novell Directory Services and ZenWorks.
- The correct context is specified at the client.
- The user name and password are correct.

Protocols

Protocols can be defined as the rules or procedures computers use to communicate with each other. Each protocol must be installed on the computer and, depending on the protocol, some configuration may be required. Although a computer may have several protocols installed, each computer on the network must have at least one protocol in common. The most common protocols are NetBEUI, IPX/SPX, and TCP/IP. To install a new protocol with Windows XP, follow these steps.

1. Open the Network Properties dialog box. Once opened, click the Install button.
2. When the Select Network Component Type dialog box appears, select *Protocol* and click the Add button.
3. A list of available protocols will appear. Select the protocol you wish to install and press the OK button.
4. You will be prompted for the source installation files. Type in the path to the source files.

Once the protocol is installed, it must be configured. The configuration will vary based on the protocol installed.

TEST TIP

Make sure you can differentiate among the protocols described below. Know the routing, addressing schemes, interoperability, and naming conventions for each protocol.

NETBIOS ENHANCED USER INTERFACE (NETBEUI)

The NetBIOS Enhanced User Interface (NetBEUI) is an updated version of the NetBIOS protocol that was used in earlier IBM LAN Manager networks. NetBEUI is not routable and has no configurable parameters. Once it is installed, it is ready for use.

⌐ TRY IT! ─────────

Install the NetBEUI protocol.

TEST TIP

NetBEUI is designed for speed in a small network. It is not routable and operates at both the Network and Transport layers of the OSI Model.

INTERNETWORK PACKET EXCHANGE/SEQUENCED PACKET EXCHANGE (IPX/SPX)

Internetwork Packet Exchange/Sequenced Packet Exchange (IPX/SPX) is the protocol used in Novell networks. IPX/SPX is a fully routable protocol that requires minimal configuration, a network number, and a frame type. To install IPX/SPX, follow the steps outlined earlier in this chapter for installing a new protocol. Once it is installed, open the Network Properties dialog box to set the configuration parameters.

In Windows XP, follow these steps to configure the protocol:

1. Select the IPX/SPX protocol. Click the Properties button.
2. A Properties dialog box similar to that in Figure 16.18 will appear. Two properties must be configured: the internal network number and the frame type.

FIGURE 16.18
IPX/SPX Properties

Network Numbers

The IPX protocol relies on two different types of network numbering, or addressing, schemes for network communications. These schemes are known as external and internal network numbers.

External network number

A network numbering, or addressing, scheme that identifies the external cable segment to which a workstation is connected.

- The *external network number* consists of up to eight hexadecimal digits that are used to identify the external cable segment to which the workstation is connected. External network numbers are assigned to network segments, installed protocols, or selected frame types. When working with Microsoft Windows clients, an external network number must be assigned for each frame type that is selected on the client machine. Each client machine on a segment, running the same frame type, will have the same external network number. Also, that number must be unique for each segment, meaning that no two segments can use the same external network number.

Internal network number

A network numbering, or addressing, scheme that identifies servers on the network.

- The *internal network number* is a unique hexadecimal number that is used to identify servers on the network. This number is randomly assigned to the server during the installation process, or it can be set manually. With Microsoft Windows clients, the internal network number has two purposes. First, it is used for internal routing. Second, it uniquely identifies the client computer. The internal network number is commonly referred to as a "virtual network number."

Frame Type

Frame type

Defines the format of data that will be transmitted between nodes on a network.

The version of NetWare you are running and the additional protocols implemented on the network will determine which *frame type* or types must be enabled. The frame type that you specify (see Figure 6.19) determines how the installed network adapter formats the data that will be transmitted between nodes on a network. All frame types are IEEE defined.

- **802.3:** Often referred to as 802.3 RAW. It is the default frame setting for NetWare 3.11 and earlier versions.
- **802.2:** Used by later versions of NetWare (4.X and later). It is a fully IEEE-compliant encapsulation method.
- **ETHERNET_II:** Encapsulates the packets in an IPX-compatible format, which is necessary to provide interoperability between NetWare networks and TCP/IP. This frame type was also used by DEC networks and AppleTalk Phase I (the original AppleTalk protocol) networks.
- **ETHERNET_SNAP:** Required for AppleTalk Phase II. It is a standard IEEE 802.2 frame with SNAP extensions.

FIGURE 16.19
IPX/SPX Frame Types

Check with the network administrator to determine which frame type is in use on your network. If in doubt, select Auto as the frame type. IPX/SPX is implemented in the Windows family of products as the *NWLink Protocol*.

NWLink Protocol

Microsoft's implementation of IPX/SPX for Windows products.

TEST TIP

If you have a client that has trouble connecting while using the IPX/SPX protocol, check the frame type to ensure it matches that in use on the network.

TEST TIP

If you are running multiple frame types on the same network, you must specify the types manually. Auto Detect will detect only the first type it sees.

TRY IT!

Install the IPX/SPX protocol.

1. Configure the network number.
2. Configure the frame type.

Troubleshooting the IPX/SPX Protocol

IPX/SPX is fairly easy to troubleshoot because it has only two parameters to configure: the network number and frame type.

- The network number should be obtained from the network administrator. Ensure that the number is entered correctly.
- Check the frame type to make sure the correct type is entered. If only one frame type is in use on the network, you may select the *Auto Detect* option.
- If more than one frame type is being used, you must manually select all frame types being used.

TRANSMISSION CONTROL PROTOCOL/INTERNET PROTOCOL (TCP/IP)

Transmission Control Protocol/Internet Protocol (TCP/IP) is not just one or two protocols, but a whole suite of protocols that can provide services and functions on the network. This protocol requires a special addressing scheme that is logical in nature. Where a MAC address represents the physical network interface, an IP address represents a logical location on the network or internetwork. All nodes participating in a TCP/IP network must acquire a unique IP address to access services and communicate with other nodes.

The information required to configure a computer to run TCP/IP depends upon the situation. If the computer will communicate only with computers on its own subnetwork, then the following data is required:

- IP address
- Subnet mask

If the computer will need to communicate outside of its own subnetwork, then the following information is required:

- IP address
- Subnet mask

Default gateway

The path a node uses when it wishes to communicate outside its own network. Typically a router.

- *Default gateway*

If you wish to use friendly names instead of IP addresses when communicating, you will need to add IP addresses for Windows Internet Name Service (WINS) servers or for Domain Name System (DNS) servers. These services will be detailed later in the chapter.

The IP addressing parameters can be added to the client manually or automatically. If you plan to address clients manually, this will entail going to each individual client, opening the TCP/IP Properties dialog box, and adding the appropriate information. The following steps demonstrate manual addressing with a Windows XP client.

1. Using the steps outlined earlier in the chapter, open the Network Properties dialog box. Select TCP/IP and click the Properties button. The TCP/IP Properties dialog box will appear (Figure 16.20).

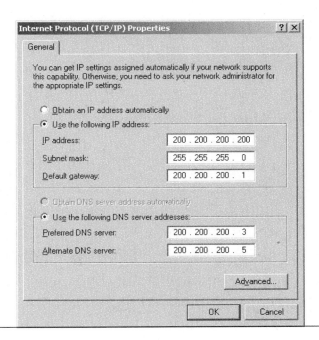

FiGURE 16.20
TCP/IP Properties Dialog Box

2. Based on your network requirements, enter the appropriate information.
3. To enter WINS data or advanced properties, click the Advanced button in the TCP/IP Properties dialog box.
4. At the Advanced TCP/IP Settings dialog box, select the IP Settings or WINS tab and enter your data (see Figure 16.21).
5. When you have finished adding information, click the OK button to exit Network properties.

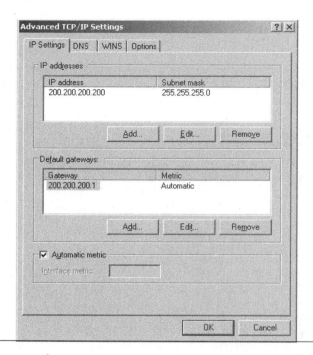

FIGURE 16.21
Advanced TCP/IP Settings
Dialog Box

An automated method of adding IP addressing information to a client involves the use of Dynamic Host Configuration Protocol (DHCP).

⎯ TRY IT! ⎯

Install TCP/IP.

1. Manually add an IP address and subnet mask.
2. Use the PING utility to test your connection with another computer on your network.
3. Add a default gateway address.
4. Use the PING utility to test your connection with a computer located on another network.

TESTTIP

TCP/IP is the default protocol for networks using either UNIX or Microsoft Windows NT, 2000, or XP. Highly routable, TCP/IP is the protocol of choice for Internet use. TCP functions at the Transport layer of the OSI Model, while IP functions at the Network layer.

Client Workstation Basics

Troubleshooting the TCP/IP Protocol

TCP/IP addressing is one of the most difficult concepts to learn in networking. Due to the complexities involved, addressing errors are common. Although TCP/IP addressing is discussed in Chapter 8, some key troubleshooting tips are appropriate here:

- Ensure the IP address of the client is correct for the subnetwork the computer is located on.
- The subnet mask must be appropriate for the IP address.
- Use the PING utility to check the protocol stack on the device.
- Use the PING utility to ensure the default gateway is functioning correctly.
- Use the PING utility to check connectivity with sites beyond the default gateway.
- Use the PING utility to ensure the DNS and WINS servers are functioning correctly.

(Note: The following sections concerning Dynamic Host Configuration Protocol, Domain Name System, and Windows Internet Name Service each consist of a server and a client component. The server side of each was covered in Chapter 9. Although this chapter contains a brief description of the server processes, it is mainly concerned with the client side operation of the services.)

DYNAMIC HOST CONFIGURATION PROTOCOL (DHCP)

Dynamic Host Configuration Protocol (DHCP) is used to dynamically, or automatically, assign Internet Protocol (IP) addresses whenever TCP/IP is being used on a network. DHCP consists of both a server and a client component. To assign TCP/IP addresses automatically, the DHCP Server Service must be installed on a server. Once the server component is installed, it develops a scope, or range of addresses that may be assigned, and other addressing parameters. The DHCP scope is then activated, which means that the server can begin handing out TCP/IP addresses. In a Windows 2000 Active Directory environment, the additional step of authorizing the DHCP server is required.

To configure a client to automatically accept addresses, the client must have the built-in ability to be a DHCP client. Most current operating systems—including all Microsoft Windows, Linux, and Apple Macintosh products—can be DHCP clients. The exact procedure for configuring the client varies slightly from product to product, but the general steps are very similar:

1. At the LAN Properties dialog box, highlight the Internet Protocol (TCP/IP) entry and click the Properties button. A dialog box similar to Figure 16.22 will appear.
2. Select the option *Obtain an IP address automatically*.
3. Click OK.
4. At the Local Area Connection Properties dialog box, click OK.
5. At the Status window, click Close.
6. Restart the computer.

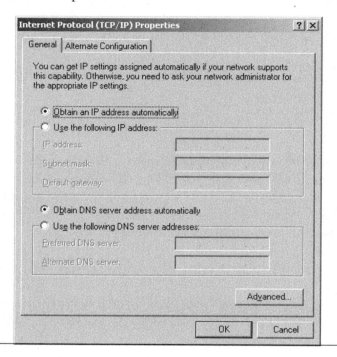

FIGURE 16.22
Internet Protocol (TCP/IP) Properties Dialog Box

Once the computer has restarted, it will attempt to obtain an IP address using the following steps:

1. When a DHCP client powers up, it sends DHCPDISCOVER packets across the network. The purpose of this broadcast is to locate DHCP servers on the network.
2. All DHCP servers that receive this broadcast will respond with a DHCPOFFER, which typically contains information such as:
   - IP address that is being offered.
   - IP address lease time.
   - subnet mask.
   - broadcast address.

- routers on subnetwork.
- domain name.
- Domain Name System address.

3. The client selects the offer it wants. Normally it selects the first DHCPOFFER received. Once the selection is made, the client responds with a DHCPREQUEST, which is again a broadcast. The reason it sends a broadcast is to alert all servers of which offer it has selected.

4. When the selected DHCP server receives the DHCPREQUEST, it replies to the client with an acknowledgement, or DHCPACK packet, which completes the DHCP transaction.

TESTTIP

An easy way to remember this process is to use the word DORA, which stands for
- Discover
- Offer
- Request
- Acknowledgement

TRY IT!

Configure your computer to use DHCP.

1. Add the IP address for one or more DHCP servers.
2. Test your configuration by using the PING utility to contact another computer.
3. Use the appropriate utility to view your TCP/IP settings.

TESTTIP

Some of the configuration parameters that DHCP may supply to a client include the following:

- IP address.
- Subnet mask.
- Default gateway address.
- Domain Name System (DNS) address.
- NetBIOS Name Service address.

Domain Name System (DNS)

Domain Name System (DNS) is used to resolve host or fully qualified domain names (FQDNs) to IP addresses. For example, suppose you open a Web browser and, in the location box, type **www.yahoo.com.** Before you can connect to that Web site, the FQDN must be resolved to the actual IP address. DNS is the service that handles the FQDN to IP address resolution. To configure a client to use DNS, the IP address of one or more DNS servers must be added to the computer's TCP/IP properties.

The exact procedure for configuring the client for DNS varies slightly from product to product, but the general steps are similar. First, locate and open the Properties dialog box for the TCP/IP protocol. When using Windows XP, follow these steps:

1. Click the Start button. When the Start menu appears, select Control Panel. When the Control Panel menu appears, select Network Connections.
2. Another menu appears that lists all local area connections. At that menu, select the appropriate local area connection.
3. Another menu appears. At that menu, select Local Area Connection. A Status window similar to Figure 16.23 will appear.

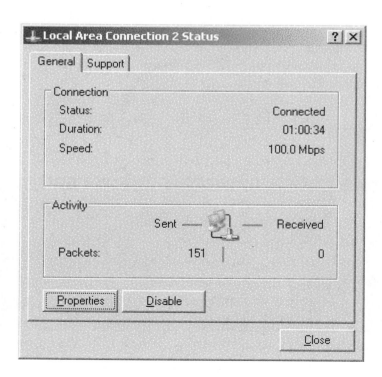

FIGURE 16.23
LAN Connection Status Window

Client Workstation Basics

4. Click the Properties button. A dialog box similar to Figure 16.24 will appear.

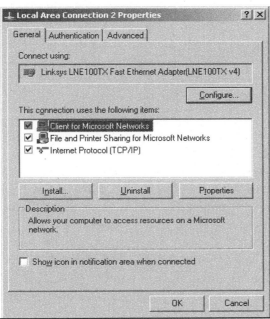

FIGURE 16.24
LAN Connection Properties
Dialog Box

5. At the LAN Connection Properties dialog box, highlight the Internet Protocol (TCP/IP) entry and click the Properties button. A dialog box similar to Figure 16.25 will appear.

FIGURE 16.25
Internet Protocol (TCP/IP)
Properties Dialog Box

6. At the bottom of the Properties dialog box, you will find the settings for DNS. Notice that you have two options. First, you can choose to obtain DNS addressing information from a DHCP server, or you can insert the addresses manually. If you choose to use DHCP, no further action is required. If you plan to assign DNS server IP addresses manually, click the option *Use the following DNS server addresses.*

7. Add an IP address for the primary DNS server. You may also choose to add the IP address of a secondary DNS server.

8. Click OK.

9. At the Local Area Connection Properties dialog box, click OK.

10. At the Status window, click Close.

You may also choose to assign advanced DNS options at the client level. Some of the options that are available include the ability to modify the resolution behavior for unqualified DNS names and to modify DNS dynamic update behavior.

To activate these advanced features, use the procedures outlined above for displaying the TCP/IP Properties dialog box. Once the properties are displayed, click the Advanced button. When the Advanced TCP/IP Settings dialog box appears, select the DNS tab. A dialog box similar to that in Figure 16.26 will appear. To modify the resolution behavior for unqualified DNS names, follow these steps:

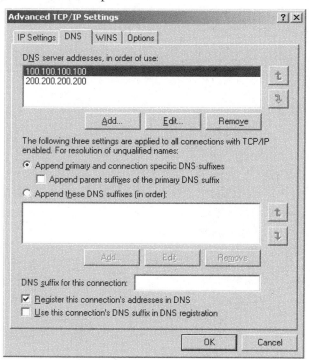

FIGURE 16.26
DNS Settings

Client Workstation Basics

1. To resolve an unqualified name by appending the primary DNS suffix and the DNS suffix of each connection, select the option *Append primary and connection specific DNS suffixes.* If you want to search the parent suffixes of the primary DNS suffix up to the second-level domain, click the check box next to *Append parent suffixes of the primary DNS suffix.*

2. To resolve an unqualified name by appending the suffixes from a list of entries that you provide, select the option *Append these DNS suffixes (in order).*

3. Click the Add button to add suffixes to the list. A dialog box similar to Figure 16.27 will appear.

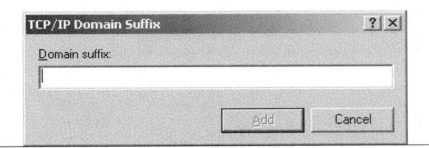

FIGURE 16.27
Adding DNS Suffixes

4. Type in the appropriate domain name along with the suffix. For example, type **Yahoo.com**.

5. Click OK. The entry will be added in the domain suffix window.

To configure a connection-specific DNS suffix, type a DNS suffix in the *DNS suffix for this connection* text box in the Advanced TCP/IP Settings dialog box.

Dynamic DNS can be used to register the IP addresses of the client computer along with the primary domain name. To enable dynamic updates, click the check box next to *Register this connection's addresses in DNS.* The domain name of the computer is the DNS suffix added to the computer name. The domain name of the computer can be viewed by opening the *System Properties* icon in the Control Panel. Once the System Properties dialog box appears, click the Computer Name tab.

To use a DNS dynamic update to register the IP addresses and the domain name of the computer, place a check mark in the box next to *Use this connection's DNS suffix in DNS registration.*

Troubleshooting Domain Name System Resolution

At the client end, you are most likely to encounter DNS problems while trying to connect to a Web site by fully qualified domain name.

- Check the physical connections of the workstation by opening the Network Neighborhood or My Network Places and browsing network resources.
- In Network properties, ensure the IP address or addresses of the DNS servers are correct.
- Use the PING utility to test connectivity to the DNS server or servers.
- Try to connect to the Web site by typing its IP address in the address block of the Web browser. If you can connect by IP address but not by fully qualified domain name, a DNS server problem is indicated. Contact the DNS server administrator.

HOST TABLE FILES

Originally, a file called the host table or HOSTS was used to list all of the resources and their IP addresses. That worked until the Web began to grow. The tables became unwieldy and the time required to parse the tables began to impact the internetwork of computers. Added to this size issue was the fact that updates to the table were difficult to get out to all of the servers needing the information, so large parts of the Web could be outdated or inaccessible.

The following is an example of a host file included with the Microsoft Windows XP Professional operating system.

```
# Copyright (c) 1993-1999 Microsoft Corp.
#
# This is a sample HOSTS file used by Microsoft TCP/IP for Windows.
#
#       102.54.94.97    rhino.acme.com        # source server
#       38.25.63.10     x.acme.com            # x client host
```

127.0.0.1   localhost
216.177.73.139 auto.search.msn.com
216.177.73.139 search.netscape.com
216.177.73.139 ieautosearch

Notice that the host file contains the mappings of IP addresses to host names. Each entry is the IP address followed by the name. Also, each entry should be kept on an individual line. The IP address and the host name should be separated by at least one space. Remember that entries in this file are case sensitive. For that reason, you will often see an IP address followed by the several variations of the host name. For example,

203.46.132.18 computer1 Computer1 COMPUTER1

Comments may be inserted on individual lines or following the machine name. They are denoted by the # symbol.

TRY IT!

Modify and test the host table file.

1. Locate and open your host table file.
2. Add the name and IP address of a neighboring computer.
3. Test your connection by connecting to the computer by host name.

TEST TIP

The host table file contains a list of host names and their corresponding IP address mappings. It is a regular text file, and it is case sensitive.

TEST TIP

UNIX computers use DNS and host table files for name resolution.

UNDERSTANDING NETWORK BASIC INPUT/OUTPUT SYSTEM (NETBIOS) NAMES

Network Basic Input/Output System (NetBIOS) is an application programming interface (API) that adds functions designed specifically for local area networks. To communicate on a NetBIOS network, each node needs to be identified by a unique name. Every client computer in a Microsoft network is assigned a name, commonly referred to as a host name. That host name is considered a NetBIOS name. A NetBIOS name must be at least 3 and no more than 16 characters in length; however, the administrator can use only 15 of those characters. The 16th character of the name is a hexadecimal value (between 00-FF) that is assigned by the operating system to indicate the resource or service type. For example, the workstation service assigns the value [00h] to the end of its computer name. Therefore, the computer named Payroll3, which runs the workstation service, would be identified as Payroll3[00h].

NetBIOS names may be resolved through broadcasts or through some other method, such as the Windows Internet Name Service or LMHosts files.

Windows Internet Name Service (WINS)

You will want to remember three very important points about *Windows Internet Name Service (WINS)*:

- First, WINS has absolutely nothing to do with the Internet.
- Second, WINS applies only to Microsoft networks.
- Finally, WINS is used to resolve NetBIOS names with IP addresses.

WINS, like DNS, consists of a server and a client component. To use WINS, it must first be installed on a Windows server and then configured on the client. This configuration consists of adding the IP addresses of one or more WINS servers. To configure the client, open the Network properties and then the Internet Protocol (TCP/IP) Properties dialog box, as explained earlier in this chapter. Then continue with these steps:

1. In the Internet Protocol (TCP/IP) Properties dialog box, click the Advanced button.
2. At the Advanced TCP/IP Settings dialog box, select the WINS tab (see Figure 16.28).

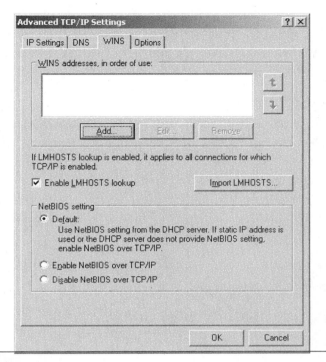

FIGURE 16.28
WINS Settings

3. At the WINS tab, click the Add button, and the dialog box for adding the address of the WINS server (Figure 16.29) will appear.

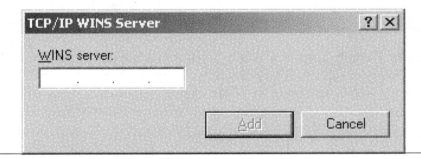

FIGURE 16.29
Adding WINS Addresses

4. Enter the IP address of the WINS server. Click the Add button.
5. Add the addresses of each WINS server by repeating steps 3 and 4 for each address.
6. When you have completed adding the addresses, select OK and exit from the Properties dialog boxes.
7. Restart the computer.

When the computer restarts, it will send a packet to each of the WINS servers you specified by IP address. The packet is used to register with the client's NetBIOS name, IP address, and service ID. That information is added to the WINS database stored on the servers. When a client attempts to communicate with another computer on a WINS-enabled network, it must first resolve the client's NetBIOS name to an IP address. For example, in Figure 16.30, the end user at computer ClientA has decided to map a drive to a shared folder named Spreadsheets on a computer named ClientW. Before ClientA can communicate with ClientW, the name "ClientW" must be resolved to the client's IP address.

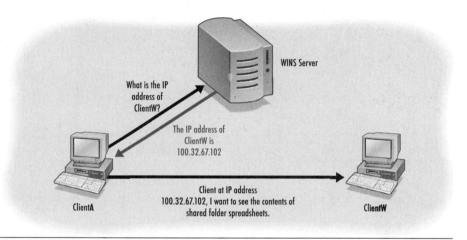

WINS Server

What is the IP address of ClientW?

The IP address of ClientW is 100.32.67.102

ClientA

Client at IP address 100.32.67.102, I want to see the contents of shared folder spreadsheets.

ClientW

FIGURE 16.30
How a WINS Server Resolves Names

In this example, the user at ClientA will open a command prompt and type **net use s: \\ClientW\Spreadsheets**. When the user presses the Enter key, a request will be sent to the WINS server that has been specified by IP address on ClientA. The WINS server will check its database for a computer named ClientW. When it finds the name, it will match it with ClientW's IP address and that information will be passed back to ClientA. ClientA can then communicate directly with ClientW.

TestTip

WINS is a dynamic database located on a Windows server, which stores and resolves NetBIOS names to IP address mappings.

LMHosts File

The LMHosts file is a text file that contains static mappings of IP addresses to computer (NetBIOS) names. Microsoft clients can use the LMHosts file to assist with NetBIOS name resolution. Think of the LMHosts file as the manual version of WINS.

Each Microsoft operating system contains a sample LMHosts file (LMHosts.sam) that can be modified as necessary and then saved as "LMHosts" without an extension. After the file has been created, save it to the %systemroot%\System32\Drivers\Etc directory. An excerpt from an LMHosts.sam file is depicted below:

```
102.54.94.97    rhino       #PRE #DOM:networking  #net group's DC
# 102.54.94.102   "appname  \0x14"                #special app server
# 102.54.94.123   popular       #PRE        #source server
# 102.54.94.117   localsrv      #PRE        #needed for the include
```

When working with LMHosts, each entry should be kept on an individual line. The IP address is placed in the first column, followed by the corresponding computer name. The address and the computer name are separated by at least one space or tab. The # character is used to denote the start of a comment or a keyword. The keywords shown in Figure 16.31 can be used in the LMHosts file.

- **#PRE:** Causes the entry to be preloaded into the name cache. By default, entries are not pre-loaded but are parsed only after dynamic name resolution fails.
- **#DOM:<domain>:** Associates the entry with the domain specified by <domain>. This affects how the browser and logon services behave in TCP/IP environments.
- **#INCLUDE <filename>:** Forces the RFC NetBIOS (NBT) software to seek the specified <filename> and parse it as if it were stored on the local machine. This allows a centralized LMHosts file to be maintained on a server.
- **#BEGIN_ALTERNATE and #END_ALTERNATE:** Allow multiple #INCLUDE statements to be grouped together.
- **\0xnn (nonprinting character support):** Specifies a hexadecimal value for a nonprinting character, which can be embedded in mappings by first surrounding the NetBIOS name in quotations and then using the \0xnn notation.

FIGURE 16.31
Keywords or Extensions Used in LMHosts File

— TRY IT! —

Modify and test the LMHosts file.

1. Locate and open your sample LMHosts file.
2. Save the file to the correct directory.
3. Add the name and IP address of a neighboring computer.
4. Test your connection by connecting to the computer by host name.

TESTTIP

Remember that NetBIOS name resolution can be implemented either through LMHosts files on each client or through WINS on the network.

Services

Network services provide functionality to the client computer. In English, that means that a network service allows a client to do things on a network that it otherwise could not do. Some typical examples of network services are described in Figure 16.32.

- **File and Print Sharing for Microsoft Networks:** Allows client computers to act as servers, sharing their resources with other computers on a Microsoft network.
- **File and Print Sharing for Novell Networks:** Allows client computers to act as servers, sharing their resources with other computers on a Novell network.
- **Remote Registry Service:** Allows a network administrator to connect to the registry of another computer on the network.
- **QoS(Quality of Service) Packet Scheduler:** Makes adjustments in data transfer when a computer operating over a slow network link, such as a modem, is communicating with a computer using a fast data link, such as 100Base-T. This adjustment allows for better data communications.
- **Service Advertising Protocol (SAP):** Maintains a list of NetWare servers and services used on the network.

FIGURE 16.32
Some Typical Network
Services

To install network services, follow these steps:
1. Access the Network Properties dialog box and click the Install button.
2. When the Select Network Component Type dialog box appears, select the Service entry. A dialog box similar to Figure 16.33 will appear.

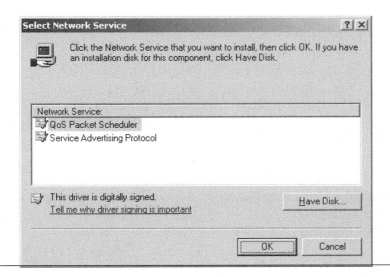

FIGURE 16.33
Network Services

3. Make your selection and press the OK button.
4. You will be prompted for the source installation files. Type in the path to the source files.

Understanding Security

In the computer world, the term "security" is so broad that experts could fill a whole book and still not cover the entire topic. In a network environment, some type of security or control is built into almost every function. In the context of this chapter, we will address security as it applies to clients and their access to local and network resources.

LOCAL SECURITY

Local security

Security that affects only the computer you are sitting at.

In computer networks, when you hear the word "local" think of the computer that you are sitting in front of. Therefore, when you hear the term *local security*, think of security that affects only the computer you are working at. Local security starts with the logon process, typically a user name and password. It includes groups, or roles, and file system security.

Logon and Role/Group Security

Each operating system has different logon security requirements. For example, with a computer running the Windows 98 operating system, you are not required to log on before using the computer. If a logon box does appear, you can generally hit the Escape key and bypass the logon box. However, if the computer is running Windows NT Workstation or Windows 2000/XP Professional, you must provide a user name and password to log on to that machine. Also, the user account that you use to log on to the computer exists only on that computer, because the account was created at that computer.

In Windows XP, follow these steps to create a new user account:

1. Click the Start button. On the Start menu, locate the Control Panel. When the Control Panel menu appears, click User Accounts. A screen similar to Figure 16.34 will appear.

2. Choose *Create a new account* from the three options this dialog box offers *(Change an account, Create a new account,* or *Change the way users log on or off)*.

3. At the next dialog box, type in a name for the user and click the Next button.

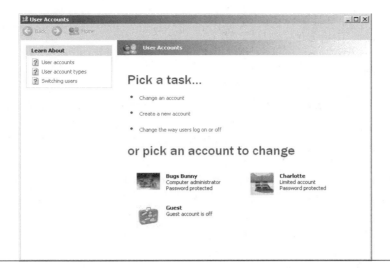

FIGURE 16.34
User Accounts Opening
Screen

4. At the Pick an Account Type dialog box, pick a *role* for the user from the following options:
   - *Administrator*—offers full user rights to the computer. That is, administrators can make all changes, create and manage all user accounts, and install new software.
   - *Limited*—offers restricted user rights. Limited users can make changes to their own account and data files, but they cannot install some types of programs. Also, they have very limited system management abilities.
5. After selecting a role, click the Create Account button. The new user account will appear. To make changes to this account, simply click it and you will be presented with a list of options, depicted in Figure 16.35.

Role

On a Windows XP workstation, the amount of control a user has—specified as either *administrator or limited*—over a computer and its resources.

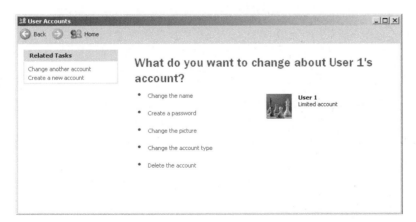

FIGURE 16.35
User Accounts Properties
Dialog box

TRY IT!

Create a new user and role assignment.

1. Create a new user account.

2. Assign the role of administrator to the user account.

Group

On a Windows NT or 2000 Professional network, a container used to organize users by the rights and permissions they have been granted.

Windows NT workstations and Windows 2000 Professional operating systems do not use roles; instead, they use groups. *Groups* are containers used to organize users by the rights and permissions they have been granted. In Windows 2000 Professional, follow these steps:

1. Press the Start button. On the Start menu, locate the Control Panel.

2. On the Control Panel menu, select Users and Groups. A dialog box will appear, similar to Figure 16.36.

FIGURE 16.36
Properties for Windows 2000 Professional Users and Passwords

3. At the Users and Passwords dialog box, select the Advanced tab. In the Advanced User Management section, click the Advanced button. A Local Users and Groups Microsoft Management Console (MMC) snap-in appears (see Figure 16.37).

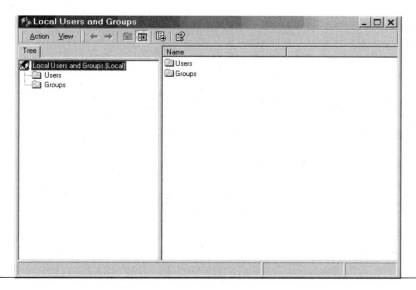

FIGURE 16.37
Windows 2000
Professional Local Users
and Groups MMC Snap-In

4. In the left pane, double-click the Groups folder. The groups will appear in the right pane. Double-click on a group to view its members.

5. To add new members, click the Add button. You will be given a list of available users to add to the group.

6. Select the appropriate users and click the OK button.

TRY IT!

Create a new local user, a new group, and add the user to the group.

1. Create a new user account.
2. Create a new group.
3. Add the user to the new group.

Remember that local accounts exist only on the workstation that they were created on. A user cannot now walk to another machine and log on to it using this account. Also, this account cannot be used to log on to a network.

File System Security

Some file systems, such as the new technology file system (NTFS), allow you to set permissions on files and folders. For example, if two users share a single computer, each user could have a private folder for storing data files. Even though the folders are located on the same hard drive, permissions can be set to keep users from seeing the contents of someone else's folder. For example, suppose two users named John and Jane share a single computer. On the hard drive of the computer, each has created a personal folder. While Jane is logged on to the machine, she has full access to the contents of her folder. However, she has been blocked from opening John's folder and viewing the contents. Likewise, when John is logged on, he can view and modify the contents of his folder but not Jane's.

— TRY IT! —

Create a new local user and assign her a role.

1. Locate a computer that uses the NTFS file system.
2. In Windows Explorer, create a new folder.
3. Assign permissions to that new folder.

NETWORK SECURITY

Network security

The security measures and procedures designed for all the resources on the network.

Network security is very similar to local security in several aspects. For example, when logging on to a network, the user must supply a user name and password. Also, groups or roles control the rights of users. The major differences are that the user accounts and groups are created at a server and not on the local computer. Therefore, when you log on, you must use a user name and password that was created at a server. Figure 16.38 depicts a login box for a Novell network. Since the account for User5 in this example was created on a Novell server, the user is logging on to the network.

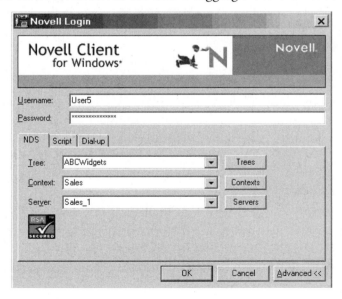

FIGURE 16.38
Novell NetWare Login Box

TROUBLESHOOTING SECURITY

Troubleshooting Logon Security

One of the most common network problems you will encounter is a user's inability to log on to the network. When a user reports this type of problem to you, try these steps.

- Ensure that you are using the correct user name and password.
- Remember that passwords are case sensitive.
- For Microsoft networks, check the client to ensure that you are attempting to log on to the correct domain.
- For Novell networks, ensure that your tree and context are correct.

Troubleshooting Role/Group Security

Roles determine the rights available to a user; always be sure you have selected the proper role for the user. Users are typically assigned permissions to resources by groups. If a user appears to be in the correct group but still cannot access a resource, check the following:

- Make sure the user is not in more than one group with conflicting permissions.
- Normally, a setting of "No Access" overrides all other permissions. Make sure the user, or the group he is in, is not blocked from the resource.
- Ensure that the user is logging on to the network and not the local workstation.

Troubleshooting File System Security

File system security problems manifest themselves by prohibiting user access to one or more files or folders. Check these items when troubleshooting denied access problems that you believe are caused by security settings at the file system level:

- File system security can conflict with security set at the share level. If you believe this is occurring, check permissions at both levels.
- When using both file and share permissions, the most restrictive permission applies.

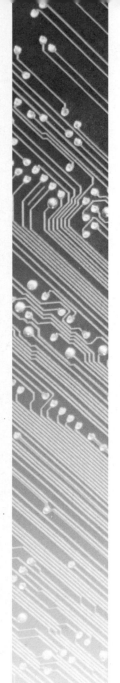

STUDY GUIDE

In this chapter, we discussed various hardware and software components that are required to connect a client computer to a network. We also provided instructions for configuring each of those components. Here are some key points to remember.

UNDERSTANDING NETWORK CLIENT COMPUTERS

- A network client computer can be defined simply as a computer that has the necessary hardware and software installed to allow it to connect to a network.
- Most network clients can also function as a server, which serves, or provides a service to, the other clients on the network.

ADAPTERS

- An adapter is the piece of hardware that allows a cable to connect to a computer.
- Once the adapter is installed, a piece of software known as a device driver is installed to allow the operating system to communicate with the adapter.
- Some of the more common adapters:
  - Integrated Services Digital Network (ISDN) cards
  - modems
  - network interface cards (NICs)

Selecting and Installing Network Interface Cards (NICs)

- The most common type of adapter used in a networked computer is a network interface card (NIC).
- The NIC is a piece of hardware in the form of an expansion card that is installed inside the computer.
- The type of expansion slots that are available on a computer's motherboard will determine the NIC needed for the network installation.

Troubleshooting NIC Installation

If the computer does not detect the newly installed hardware, you can choose to install the software manually through the *Add Hardware* icon located on the Control Panel.

Network Software and Properties

- Network software generally falls into three broad categories: clients, protocols, and services.
- Software is installed on the client computer through the Network Properties dialog box.

Client Software

- Client software is installed on a computer to allow the computer to send requests to a server or another computer on the network.
- Client software, or just client, is often referred to as a redirector because it has the ability to redirect requests for resources that are not located on the local machine.
- The most common network clients in use today are those for Microsoft and Novell networks.

Microsoft Client for Microsoft Networks

- The Microsoft Client for Microsoft Networks is installed automatically in Microsoft Windows operating systems whenever a network adapter installation is detected.
- The Microsoft client allows networked computers to communicate with other computers and servers on a Microsoft network.

Domain Configuration
- A Windows domain is a client-server network that uses Windows servers as domain controllers.
- The purpose of a domain controller is to handle security of the network, including users, groups, and resources.

Peer-to-Peer (Workgroup) Configuration
- The procedures to join a workgroup are very similar to those for joining a domain.

Client for Novell Networks

- Most Microsoft operating systems include a client for Novell NetWare networks; however, it is generally preferable to use Novell Client software.

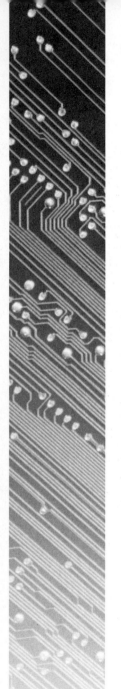

- The Novell Client software allows Windows workstations to access and use all of the services available on Novell NetWare servers running Novell Directory Services and ZenWorks.

TROUBLESHOOTING CLIENT INSTALLATION

- Since clients are software, problems are usually caused by configuration errors that manifest themselves during network logon.
- On Microsoft networks, confirm the following information:
  - The computer is a member of the domain if required and the domain name and computer name are spelled correctly.
  - The domain name specified in the client box is correct.
  - You are attempting to log on with a domain user name.
  - The password matches the user name and is spelled correctly.
  - Since passwords are case sensitive, ensure the Caps Lock key is not engaged.
- In Novell networks, check these items:
  - The client you are using is the most current.
  - The client you are using is compatible with the Novell network operating system and supporting components, such as Novell Directory Services and ZenWorks.
  - The correct context is specified at the client.
  - The user name and password are correct.

PROTOCOLS

- Protocols can be defined as the rules, or procedures, computers use to communicate with each other.
- Each protocol must be installed on the computer and, depending on the protocol, some configuration may be required.
- Although a computer may have several protocols installed, each computer on the network must have at least one protocol in common.
- The most common protocols are NetBEUI, IPX/SPX, and TCP/IP.

NetBios Enhanced User Interface (NetBEUI)

- The NetBios Enhanced User Interface (NetBEUI) extends the NetBIOS protocol that was found on earlier IBM LAN Manager networks.
- NetBEUI is not routable and has no configurable parameters.
- Once NetBEUI is installed, it is ready for use.

INTERNETWORK PACKET EXCHANGE/SEQUENCED PACKET EXCHANGE (IPX/SPX)

- The Internet Packet Exchange/Sequenced Packet Exchange (IPX/SPX) is the protocol used on Novell networks.
- IPX/SPX is a fully routable protocol that requires minimal configuration. Follow the steps outlined earlier in the chapter to install the protocol.

Network Numbers

- The IPX protocol relies on two different types of network numbering, or addressing, schemes for network communications.
- These schemes are known as internal and external network numbers.
- The external network number consists of up to eight hexadecimal digits that are used to identify the external cable segment that the workstation is connected to.
- External network numbers are assigned to network segments, installed protocols, or selected frame types.
- When working with Microsoft Windows clients, an external network number must be assigned for each frame type that is selected on the client machine.
- The internal network number is a unique hexadecimal number that is used to identify servers on the network.
- This number is either randomly assigned to the server during the installation process or set manually.
- With Microsoft Windows clients, the internal network number has two purposes:
  - Internal routing
  - Uniquely identifying the client computer

Frame Type

- The version of NetWare you are running and the additional protocols implemented on the network will determine which frame types must be enabled. All frame types are IEEE-defined.
  - **802.3:** This frame type is often referred to as 802.3 RAW. It is the default frame type setting for NetWare 3.11 and earlier versions.
  - **802.2:** Later versions of NetWare (4.X and later) use this frame type. It is a fully IEEE-compliant encapsulation method.
  - **ETHERNET_II:** When providing interoperability with NetWare networks and TCP/IP, the packets must be encapsulated in an IPX-compatible format. This frame type was also used by DEC networks

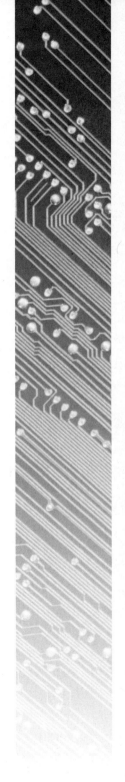

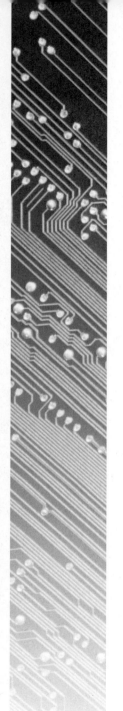

and AppleTalk Phase I (the original AppleTalk protocol) networks.

- **ETHERNET_SNAP:** AppleTalk Phase II requires this frame type. It is a standard IEEE 802.2 frame with SNAP extensions.
- IPX/SPX is implemented in the Windows family of products as the NWLink Protocol.

Troubleshooting IPX/SPX

- IPX/SPX is fairly easy to troubleshoot because it has only two parameters to configure: the network number and frame type.
- The network number should be obtained from the network administrator. Ensure that the number is entered correctly.
- Check the frame type to make sure the correct type is entered. If only one frame type is in use on the network, select the *Auto Detect* option.
- If more than one frame type is being used, you must manually select both frame types.

TRANSMISSION CONTROL PROTOCOL/INTERNET PROTOCOL (TCP/IP)

- TCP/IP is not just one or two protocols, but a whole suite of protocols that can provide services and functions on the network.
- Where a MAC address represents the physical network interface, an IP address represents a logical location on the network or internetwork.
- All nodes participating in a TCP/IP network must acquire a unique IP address to access services and communicate with other nodes.
- The information required to configure a computer to run the TCP/IP protocol depends upon the situation. If the computer will communicate only with computers on its own subnet, the following data is required:
  - IP address
  - Subnet mask
- If the computer will need to communicate outside of its own subnet, the following information is required:
  - IP address
  - Subnet mask
  - Default gateway
- If you wish to use friendly names instead of IP addresses when communicating, you will need to add IP addresses for WINS or DNS servers.

- IP addressing parameters can be added to the client manually or automatically.

Troubleshooting the TCP/IP Protocol

- TCP/IP addressing is one of the most difficult concepts to learn in networking. Due to the complexities involved, addressing errors are common.
  - Ensure the IP address of the client is correct for the subnetwork the computer is located on.
  - The subnet mask must be appropriate for the IP address.
  - Use the PING utility to check the protocol stack on the device.
  - Use the PING utility to ensure the default gateway is functioning correctly.
  - Use the PING utility to check connectivity with sites beyond the default gateway.
  - Use the PING utility to ensure the DNS and WINS servers are functioning correctly.

DYNAMIC HOST CONFIGURATION PROTOCOL (DHCP)

- Dynamic Host Configuration Protocol (DHCP) is used to dynamically, or automatically, assign IP addresses whenever TCP/IP protocol is being used on a network.
- DHCP consists of both a server and a client component. To assign TCP/IP addresses automatically, the DHCP Server Service must be installed on a server.
- Once the server component is installed, it develops a scope, or range of addresses that may be assigned, and other addressing parameters.
- To configure a client to automatically accept addresses, the client must have the built-in ability to be a DHCP client.
- Once the computer has restarted, it will attempt to obtain an IP address using the following steps:
  1. When a DHCP client powers up, it sends DHCPDISCOVER packets across the network
  2. All DHCP servers that receive this broadcast will respond with a DHCPOFFER, which typically contains the following information:
     - IP address that is being offered
     - IP address lease time
     - Subnet mask
     - Broadcast address

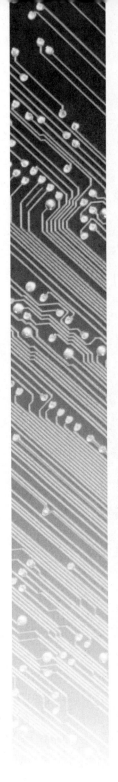

- o Routers on the subnetwork
- o Domain name
- o Domain Name System (DNS) address
3. The client selects the offer it wants. Normally it selects the first DHCPOFFER received.
4. When the selected DHCP server receives the DHCPREQUEST, it responds to the client with an acknowledgement, or DHCPACK packet, which completes the DHCP transaction.

DOMAIN NAME SYSTEM (DNS)

- The Domain Name System (DNS) is used to resolve host or fully qualified domain names (FQDNs) to IP addresses.
- To configure a client to use DNS, the IP address of one or more DNS servers must be added to the computer's TCP/IP properties.

Troubleshooting Domain Name System Resolution

- At the client end, you are most likely to encounter DNS problems while trying to connect to a Web site by fully qualified domain name.
  - o Check the physical connections of the workstation by opening the Network Neighborhood or My Network Places and browsing network resources.
  - o In Network properties, ensure the IP address or addresses of the DNS servers are correct.
  - o Use the PING utility to test connectivity to the DNS server or servers.
  - o Try to connect to the Web site by typing its IP address in the address block of the Web browser. If you can connect by IP address but not by fully qualified domain name, a DNS server problem is indicated. Contact the administrator of the DNS server.

HOST TABLE FILES

- Originally, a file called the host table was used to list all network resources' IP addresses.
- The host file contains the mappings of IP addresses to host names.
- Each entry is made up of the IP address followed by the name.

Understanding Network Basic Input/Output System (NetBIOS) Names

- NetBIOS is an acronym for Network Basic Input/Output System.
- NetBIOS is an application programming interface (API) that adds functions designed specifically for local area networks.
- To communicate on a NetBIOS network, each node needs to be identified by a unique name.
- Every client computer on a Microsoft network is assigned a name, commonly referred to as a host name. That host name is considered a NetBIOS name.
- That name must contain 16 or fewer characters, and it may be letters or numbers.
- NetBIOS names may be resolved through broadcasts or through some other method, such as WINS or LMHosts files.

Windows Internet Name Service (WINS)

- There are three very important points about the Windows Internet Name Service (WINS):
  - First, WINS has absolutely nothing to do with the Internet.
  - Second, WINS applies only to Microsoft networks.
  - Finally, WINS is used to resolve NetBIOS names to IP addresses.
- WINS, like DNS, consists of a server and a client component. To use WINS, it must be installed on a Windows server.

LMHosts File

- The LMHosts file is a text file that contains static mappings of IP addresses to computer (NetBIOS) names.
- The LMHosts file can be used by Microsoft clients to assist with NetBIOS name resolution.
- Think of the LMHosts file as the manual version of WINS.
- Each Microsoft operating system contains a sample LMHosts file (LMHosts.sam) that can be modified as necessary and then saved as "LMHosts" without an extension.
- After the file has been created, save it to the %systemroot%\System32\Drivers\Etc directory.
- The following keywords or extensions can be used in the LMHosts file:
  - #PRE
  - #DOM:<domain>
  - #INCLUDE <filename>

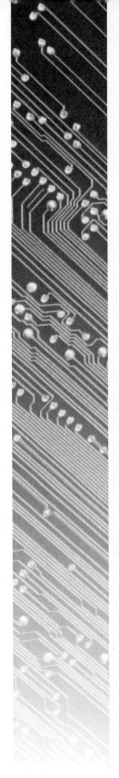

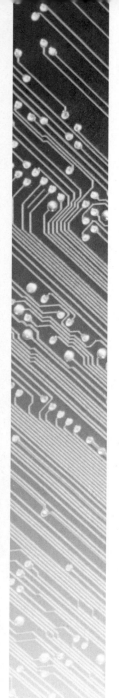

- o #BEGIN_ALTERNATE and #END_ALTERNATE
- o \0xnn (nonprinting character support)

SERVICES

- Network services provide functionality to the client computer.
- Some typical examples of network services:
  - o File and Print Sharing for Microsoft Networks
  - o File and Print Sharing for Novell Networks
  - o Remote Registry Service
  - o QoS Packet Scheduler
  - o Service Advertising Protocol (SAP)

UNDERSTANDING SECURITY

- In a network environment, some type of security or control is built in to almost every function.

LOCAL SECURITY

- On computer networks, when you hear the word "local" think of the computer that you are sitting in front of.
- When you hear the term "local security," think of security that affects only the computer you are working at.
- Local security starts with the logon process, typically a user name and password.
- It includes groups or roles, and file system security.

Logon and Role/Group Security

- Each operating system has different logon security requirements.
- The user account that you use to log on to the computer exists only on that computer because the account was created at that computer.

File System Security

- Some file systems, such as the new technology file system (NTFS), allow you to set permissions on files and folders.

NETWORK SECURITY

- Network security is very similar to local security in several aspects. For example, when logging on to a network, the user must supply a user name and password.
- For both types of security, users can be controlled by groups or roles.
- The major difference with network security is that the user accounts and groups are created at a server and not on the local computer.
- When you log on, you must use a user name and password that was created at a server.

TROUBLESHOOTING SECURITY

Troubleshooting Logon Security

- Ensure you are using the correct user name and password.
- Remember that passwords are case sensitive.
- For Microsoft networks, check the client to ensure that you are attempting to log on to the correct domain.
- For Novell networks, ensure that your tree and context are correct.

Troubleshooting Role/Group Security

- Roles determine the rights available to a user. When using roles, always ensure that you have selected the proper role for the user. Users are typically assigned permissions to resources by groups. If a user appears to be in the correct group but still cannot access a resource, check the following:
  - Make sure the user is not in more than one group with conflicting permissions.
  - Normally, a setting of "No Access" overrides all other permissions. Make sure the user, or the group he is in, is not blocked from the resource.
  - Ensure that the user is logging on to the network and not the local workstation.

Troubleshooting File System Security

- File system security can conflict with security set at the share level. If you believe this is occurring, check permissions at both levels.
- When using both file and share permissions, the most restrictive permission applies.

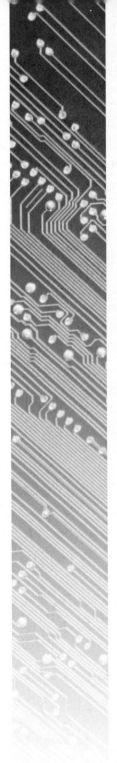

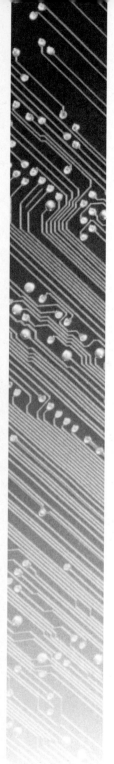

PRACTICE TEST

Try this test to check your mastery of the concepts in this chapter.

1. _____ are the pieces of hardware that allow a cable to connect to the computer.
   a. Protocols
   b. Clients
   c. Adapters
   d. Services

2. When selecting a network interface card for you computer, which of the following items will govern your choice?
   a. brand of computer
   b. operating system
   c. available expansion slots
   d. brand of motherboard

3. Once a network adapter has been installed, what else must be installed for the adapter to function?
   a. protocol
   b. driver
   c. client
   d. network cable

4. After a network interface card was installed, the computer was restarted. Upon startup, the operating system failed to find the NIC. Which utility would you use to manually install the necessary software for the NIC?
   a. Device Manager
   b. Control Panel, Add Hardware
   c. Control Panel, Add/Remove Programs
   d. Control Panel, Controllers

5. Which of the following items is commonly referred to as a redirector?
   a. protocol
   b. driver
   c. client
   d. adapter

6. A logical connection from your client computer and a shared folder on another computer on the network is commonly referred to as a(n)
   a. logical drive.
   b. physical drive.
   c. external drive.
   d. mapped drive.

7. Where on the computer would you go to install the Microsoft Client for Microsoft Networks?
   a. Network properties
   b. Control Panel, Add Hardware
   c. Control Panel, Add/Remove Programs
   d. Device Manager

8. What types of computers are used to control security in a Microsoft domain?
   a. Novell servers
   b. domain controllers
   c. UNIX servers
   d. member servers

9. Which client should be installed on a client computer when supporting NetWare networks?
   a. Microsoft client
   b. Novell client
   c. UNIX client
   d. Apple client

10. Where on the computer would you go to install network protocols?
    a. Network properties
    b. Control Panel, Add Hardware
    c. Control Panel, Add/Remove Programs
    d. Device Manager

11. What frame type would you select for a client computer that will connect to a Novell 4.11 server?
    a. 802.2
    b. 802.3
    c. Ethernet_II
    d. Ethernet_SNAP

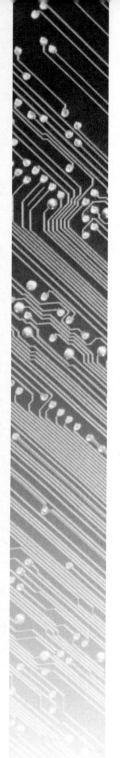

12. Which of the following utilities is used to automatically assign Internet Protocol addresses to clients?
    a. WINS
    b. DNS
    c. DHCP
    d. Computer Management

13. Which of the following utilities would you select if you wanted to resolve names commonly found on the Internet?
    a. WINS
    b. DNS
    c. DHCP
    d. Computer Management

14. Which of the following protocols has no configurable protocols?
    a. NetBEUI
    b. NetBIOS
    c. TCP/IP
    d. IPX/SPX

15. Which of the following pieces of addressing information is required for computers that use TCP/IP and that will communicate only with other computers on their own subnetwork? (Select all that apply)
    a. IP address
    b. subnet mask
    c. default gateway
    d. WINS server address

16. What action must be taken at a Windows NT server running DHCP before it can begin handing out IP addressing information?
    a. The scope must be authorized.
    b. The scope must be activated.
    c. The scope must be replicated.
    d. No action is required

17. What are the four steps, in order, that a client takes to receive IP addressing information from a DHCP server?
    a. discover, offer, request, acknowledge
    b. request, offer, discover, acknowledge
    c. discover, authorize, request, acknowledge
    d. acknowledge, offer, request, discover

18. Which of the following services allows client computers to act as servers, sharing their resources with other computers on a network?
    a. Remote Registry Service
    b. QoS Packet Scheduler
    c. Service Advertising Protocol (SAP)
    d. File and Print Sharing for Microsoft Networks

19. You have recently created a new user account on a Windows XP workstation to allow a user to install a new software suite. A user has phoned the help desk to report that he cannot log on to the network with this account. What is the most likely problem?
    a. The user account is a network account.
    b. The user account is a local account.
    c. The user account is locked out.
    d. The user account has been deleted.

20. In which of the following situations are users required to enter a user name and password during logon?
    a. when logging on to a local client only
    b. when logging on to a networked client only
    c. when logging on to a local and a network client
    d. None of the above

TROUBLESHOOTING

1. You have just completed installing a new network adapter in a client workstation on your client-server network. After installation, you attached a twisted pair cable with an RJ-45 connector to the NIC. Once the hardware installation was completed, the computer was turned on and allowed to boot. During the boot process, the operating system failed to locate the new network adapter. What steps must you take to install the driver for this adapter?

2. Your company has recently allowed users to access the Internet from their client workstations. As a result, you have begun installing TCP/IP and manually configuring the associated parameters on all of the client computers. Several of your users who have computers that have been configured have complained that they still cannot connect to the Internet. Initial troubleshooting steps indicate that you can open the Network Neighborhood and see other computers on your network. What is the most likely problem?

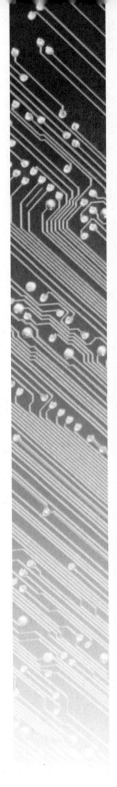

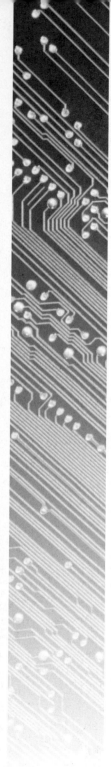

CUSTOMER SERVICE

1. You are the network administrator for a network consisting of Microsoft Windows 2000 servers and Microsoft Windows 98 client computers. The network uses TCP/IP and is divided into six subnetworks. You want to ensure that network users can connect to shared folders that are physically located on network servers and that they can connect to servers on the Internet by host name. Describe the solutions that are necessary to meet these requirements.

2. Your company, which uses a Microsoft network, has recently purchased a smaller company that uses Novell NetWare version 3.11 servers. Although you plan to migrate from those servers to Windows 2000 servers in the near future, you must continue to support the Novell servers until new software becomes available. What is required for clients on the Microsoft network to connect to the Novell server?

FOR MORE INFORMATION

For links to Web sites that provide further information about the topics covered in this chapter, go to the EMC/Paradigm Internet Resource Center at www.emcp.com/College Division/Internet Resource Centers/Networking/System Administration/Web Resources: For More Information.

Project Lab, Part 3
Network Implementation

## CHAPTER 14

PROJECT #1: IDENTIFYING OPERATING SYSTEMS

Identify the characteristics of each of the operating systems listed in the left column by matching it with the appropriate description in the right column.

_____1. UNIX   A. Active Directory Services
_____2. NetWare 5.X   B. Bindery
_____3. Windows NT 4.0   C. Highly configurable open source code
_____4. NetWare 3.12   D. Native TCP/IP
_____5. Windows 2000   E. Uses the flat domain system

PROJECT #2: UNDERSTANDING CIFS

Using your connection to the Internet, answer the following questions about CIFS.

1. What is the name of the component of CIFS that allows printing, file management, and file manipulation? _____

2. What are four platforms supported by CIFS that are not mentioned in Chapter 14?

   _____

3. What does the MRXSMB.SYS do?

   _____

4. What types of users does CIFS support?

   _____

PROJECT #3: ASSIGNING NETWARE RIGHTS

A user calls the help desk because she cannot access a file that is located on the server. This file is stored in a different department's folder. What rights (trustee assignments) must the user have in order to create a file, edit the file, and eventually delete the file? Write a paragraph describing the procedures she must follow in order to secure assignment of those rights.

PROJECT #4: OBTAINING WINDOWS NT/WINDOWS 2000 PERMISSIONS

A user is caught snooping in the financial records of your company. How did the user get the permissions to see these files? There are two ways the user may have received those permissions. Write a few paragraphs describing the steps the user would have to follow in each of the two methods of obtaining the permissions.

CHAPTER 15

PROJECT #1: PROVIDING NETWORK DOCUMENTATION

1. Document your local area network or a segment of that network. Contact your local network administrator to act as an advisor.
2. Include in your report the following information:
   a. LAN/WAN topology: where the cables, data ports, and computers reside.
   b. Hardware inventory: serial numbers for all devices that are part of the network.
   c. Router and switch configurations: what ports go to what segments; access control lists on routers.
   d. Mission-critical applications and hardware: configuration of software that is critical to business function and the hardware it runs on.
   e. Network service configuration: DNS, DHCP, WINS, and RAS configurations.

PROJECT #2: BUILDING A DISASTER PLAN

Build a disaster recovery plan for the network or segment you documented in Project #1. Include in this plan your best ideas on how to keep the network running in the event of a disaster. Ask the local network administrator to act as an advisor. Include in your plan the following:
1. Risks to the network.
2. Business impact assessment.
3. Definition of needs.
4. Detailed plan of action.

Project #3: Defining Chapter Terms

Based on what you have learned in Chapter 15, complete the following matching items. Identify the concept or parameters of the items in the left column by matching them with items in the right column.

___1. RAID 5   A. Large platform-independent storage system

___2. NAS   B. All data that has changed since the last full backup

___3. Online UPS   C. Computers that are identical in hardware and data

___4. RAID 1   D. All data

___5. Incremental backup   E. Power supply that comes online when outage is detected

___6. Standby UPS   F. Data storage across multiple disks (not fault tolerant)

___7. Mirrored servers   G. Data storage across three or more disks (fault tolerant)

___8. Differential backup   H. Data storage across two disks (fault tolerant)

___9. RAID 0   I. Power supply that is available immediately on failure

___10. Full backup   J. All data that has changed since the last backup

Project #4: Drawing a RAID 5 Array

On a separate sheet of paper, draw a six-disk RAID 5 array. Show in the drawing how data and parity bits will be distributed.

Chapter 16

Project #1: Installing a Network Interface Card

1. Select a network interface card for your computer.
2. Document or discuss the factors that you used in selecting the network card.
3. Install the network interface card in a workstation.
4. Install the driver.
5. Install the appropriate protocol, client, and service to support a Microsoft network environment.

6. Install the appropriate protocol, client, and service to support a Novell network environment.

Project #2: Configuring Network Clients

1. Once the appropriate client has been installed, configure it to log on to a Microsoft Windows domain.
2. Once the appropriate client has been installed, configure it to operate in a Windows peer-to-peer network.
3. Once the appropriate client has been installed, configure it to log on to a Novell directory services tree. Configure the following:
   - tree
   - context
   - server

Project #3: Configuring Network Protocols

1. Install the TCP/IP protocol.
   - Configure the client to use DHCP.
   - Configure the client to use TCP/IP on a single subnet.
   - Configure TCP/IP to use TCP/IP in a routed network.
   - Configure TCP/IP to use both WINS and DNS.
2. Configure IPX/SPX.
   - Set the network number.
   - Select the appropriate frame type.

Project #4: Mapping Network Drives

1. Map a network drive to a shared resource in a peer-to-peer network.
2. Map a network drive to a shared resource in a Windows network.
3. Map a network drive to a resource in a Novell network.

Project #5: Installing and Configuring a Dynamic Host Configuration Protocol Server

1. Install the DHCP server service on a Windows or Novell server.
2. Once installed, configure the service, to include:
   a. a range of IP addresses.
   b. subnet mask.
   c. default gateway.
   d. DNS/WINS server address.
   e. lease time (T1/T2 times).

Project #6: Installing and Configuring a Windows Internet Name Service Server

1. Install the WINS service on a Windows server.
2. Restart the server.
3. Configure a client for the WINS server.
4. Restart the client.
5. Monitor the WINS server for name resolution statistics.

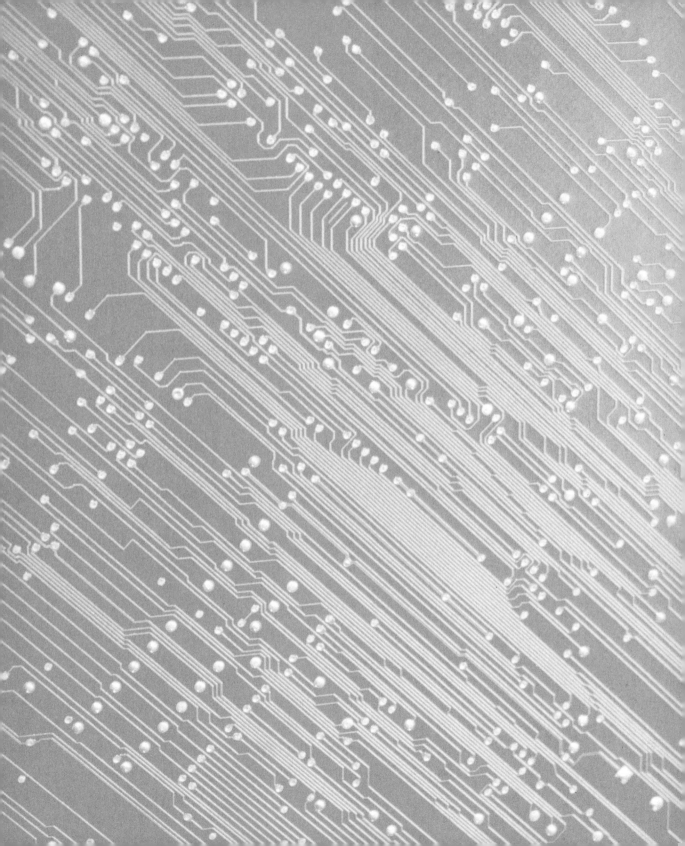

PART 4

Network Support
and Troubleshooting

TEST OBJECTIVES IN PART 4

NETWORK+ EXAMINATION

- **Objective 4.1:** Given a troubleshooting scenario, select the appropriate TCP/IP utility from among the following: Tracert; PING; ARP; Netstat; Nbtstat; IPCONFIG/IFCONFIG; Winipcfg; Nslookup.

- **Objective 4.2:** Given a troubleshooting scenario involving a small office/home office network failure (e.g., xDSL, cable, home satellite, wireless, POTS), identify the cause of the failure.

- **Objective 4.5:** Given a wiring task, select the appropriate tool (e.g.,wire crimper, media tester/certifier, punch-down tool, tone generator, optical tester, etc.).

- **Objective 4.6:** Given a network scenario, interpret visual indicators (e.g., link lights, collision lights, etc.) to determine the nature of the problem.

- **Objective 4.7:** Given output from a domestic utility (e.g., tracert, PING, IPCONFIG, etc.), identify the utility and interpret the output.

- **Objective 4.9:** Given a network problem scenario, select an appropriate course of action based on a general troubleshooting strategy. This strategy includes the following steps:1. Establish the symptoms. 2. Identify the affected area. 3. Establish what has changed. 4. Select the most probable cause. 5. Implement a solution. 6. Test the result. 7. Recognize the potential effects of the solution. 8. Document the solution.

Using a Structured Troubleshooting Strategy

17

Network+ Examination

- **Objective 4.9:** Given a network problem scenario, select an appropriate course of action based on a general troubleshooting strategy. This strategy includes the following steps:
  1. Establish the symptoms.
  2. Identify the affected area.
  3. Establish what has changed.
  4. Select the most probable cause.
  5. Implement a solution.
  6. Test the result.
  7. Recognize the potential effects of the solution.
  8. Document the solution.

ON THE JOB

Troubleshooting is a tough job. To be effective, a technician must have a good understanding of all of the elements involved in a business environment: personal computer hardware and software, networking, database connectivity, and common business applications. Beyond that, an effective troubleshooter must possess a lot of patience, a large dose of common sense, and a structured approach. Although patience and common sense are both beyond the scope of this book, this chapter will provide you with the information necessary to establish a structured approach to problem solving.

Understanding Troubleshooting

Troubleshooting is more than just fixing problems. It is the process of taking a large, complex problem, and, through the use of various techniques, excluding all potential causes until only the actual cause remains. Once the cause is identified, it can then be fixed. Good troubleshooting skills require a commonsense, structured approach. The hit-and-miss mentality that many technicians practice results in misdiagnosed problems, in wasted time and materials, and in extended downtime for the affected user.

Establish the Symptoms

A typical call to the help desk sounds something like this:

Caller: "My computer doesn't work."
Help Desk: "What do you mean your computer doesn't work?"
Caller: "Just what I said, it doesn't work."
Help Desk: "Could you be a little more specific?"

And so it goes until the person on the help desk has walked through a laundry list of questions designed to narrow down the problem.

At this stage of the process you are primarily working with symptoms of the problem. For example, when someone reports an inability to log on to the network, she is reporting a symptom. The actual problem may be that the Caps Lock key is engaged, which causes the password she is typing to be incorrect. As a result of typing the password incorrectly, the user's account has been locked and must be unlocked by an administrator before the user can attempt to log on to the network again. Most symptoms manifest themselves as a failure of some type. It is this failure that will be reported to you. Separating the symptoms from the actual problem is more of an art than a science.

Failures may or may not be accompanied by one or more error messages. For example, if a user repeatedly receives a message stating, "Logon authentication incorrect. Please check your user name and password," you can be fairly certain what the problem is. However, if a user hits the power button on the CPU and nothing happens, the problem is less apparent.

Your primary job at this point is to take the steps necessary to identify the symptoms. This is typically done by asking questions of the user. These questions may be open-ended or closed-ended.

OPEN-ENDED QUESTIONS

Open-ended questions are designed to elicit additional information. The plan here is to engage in a dialog with the user by asking her to describe the problem. For example, you might ask, "What do you observe when the problem happens?" The user will provide a narrative account of what is happening or not happening with the computer. Open-ended questions are very useful early in the process, when a user first reports a failure to you. Examples of open-ended questions include:

- What did you observe when the problem happened?
- What were you doing when the error occurred?

CLOSED-ENDED QUESTIONS

With *closed-ended questions*, you are looking for a specific answer. Many times the answer will be yes or no, or a selection of one or more options. For example, you might ask, "Is the green light showing on the front of the monitor?" Or, "What happens when you type your password and press the Enter key?" With closed-ended questions, you are not looking for elaboration. Instead, you want a specific information. Examples of closed-ended questions are:

- Is there an error message?
- What does the error message say?
- Is your computer plugged into the wall?
- Is anyone else having this problem?
- Have any recent changes been made to the computer?

THE BASIC QUESTIONS

Always remember to answer the essential questions: who, what, when, where, why, and how. Here are a few examples:

- Who
  - Who reported the problem?
  - Who found the actual problem?
  - Whom does the problem affect?
- What
  - What are the symptoms of this particular problem?
  - What type of device is having the problem?
  - What was the user doing when she first noticed the problem?

- When
  - When was the problem first noticed?
  - When did the problem actually start?
- Where
  - Where is the affected device?
  - Where was the device when the problem occurred? (Used primarily with laptop computers.)
- Why
  - Why was this problem noticed?
  - Why is this problem occurring?
- How
  - How did this problem occur?
  - Can you make this problem reoccur? If so, how?

There is simply no substitute for a thorough understanding of the systems you are supporting. Unfortunately, there are few real "computer experts" these days because, frankly, there is just too much to know. Most information technology (IT) people tend to specialize in a single area, such as programming, networking, databases, and so on. Because of the complexity of business systems, it is almost impossible for one person to know everything about every computer subject. However, that should not be used as an excuse to limit your knowledge of the system. Even if your primary responsibility is database administration, you still need to understand enough about networking to figure out why a user cannot connect to the database management system. Likewise, you will be hard pressed to be an effective hardware maintenance person if you do not understand the basics of networking. You will never be an effective troubleshooter unless you have an understanding of how all of the systems in your enterprise work together.

Is There a Problem?

One of the questions you must always answer is, "Does the problem really exist or is the system simply operating the way it is intended?" For example, your network may make use of a firewall product that limits which Web pages users can view on the World Wide Web. If a user is trying to access a blocked Web page, the user may report it as a system problem. Likewise, you may have a policy in effect dictating that if a password is typed incorrectly three times, then the user account is locked. If a user has the Caps Lock key activated and then types a password incorrectly three times, the result is that the account will be locked. In this case, the actual problem exists between the seat and the keyboard, not with the technology. That problem must be resolved or it will continue to occur. In most cases, businesses will offer some type of user training. That training can range from formal, instructor-led training in a classroom setting to some simple verbal or written instructions provided by the IT staff. You should be prepared to provide that training as the opportunity presents itself.

Identify the Affected Area

This section is concerned with the *scope* of the problem. A common question to ask at this point is, "How widespread is the problem?" Is the problem limited to a single user, group, computer, server, or subnetwork, or does it involve an entire network? This question is generally fairly easy to answer. If one user calls the help desk to report a problem, you can usually deduce that it affects only one user or computer. On the other hand, if your phones start ringing with calls from multiple users reporting the same problem, you can be fairly certain that the problem is more widespread.

Scope

Defines the magnitude of a problem.

By identifying the affected area, you can determine how you will focus your troubleshooting efforts. For example, if only one user is unable to log on to the network, you can be fairly certain that the problem exists with either the user account or the computer the person is using. On the other hand, if 20 users call to complain that they cannot log on to the network, your focus will change to the server providing network security, the network cabling, the network hardware, and so on.

Establish What Has Changed

A good question to ask is, "Has anything changed recently?" For example, has any new software been installed on the computer? Has the computer been upgraded to a new operating system, or has a new service pack recently been applied? If so, what was the upgrade and when was it performed?

Many times, users will not be able to tell you what the actual upgrade or repair was, only that one has been performed. A dialog with other areas of the IT department will help you determine what software upgrades or repairs have been made to user workstations.

Another good question to ask is, "Have other users with recent upgrades reported similar problems?" This question relates back to the scope of the problem. For example, if a service pack has recently been applied to 20 workstations and all of them start experiencing problems, you can probably draw the conclusion that the service pack installation is to blame. On the other hand, if a service pack was applied to 20 workstations and only one of them is having a problem, you may want to exclude the service pack as the sole cause of the problem.

In Real Life

When applying service packs or installing new software or hardware components, always test the installation first on one or two computers. That way, if the implementation creates problems, you can recognize and repair the problems before they affect the production environment.

Always keep in mind that the user may have made changes on her own but has decided not to tell you about them. For example, a budding computer expert may have picked up a registry-editing tip from a local computer magazine. Instead of trying out this new trick on her own computer at home, she chose to try it on the computer she uses at work. Once the change is made, it affects the computer to the point that it will not start. Understandably, the user may not tell you she made this change. Problems of this type may be identified through talking with coworkers of the budding computer expert. You should always ask users if they made any changes to the computer, although they may not be honest with you.

Could You Do This Before?

Determine if an employee has been able to perform the task in question in the past. For example, an employee might contact the help desk to report that he cannot print to a specialty color printer. Through your initial investigation, you determine that only a few key employees have access to the printer, and that the complaining employee is not one of those key employees. In this case, it is not a failure of the system, but actually a success in that access to this printer is being controlled as it is supposed to be.

On the other hand, if the employee could print to the printer at one time but now cannot, is it a result of a policy change? That is, has your company decided to limit access to the printer and as a result, this particular employee was specifically removed from the access list? If not, is the printer or the employee's workstation experiencing a problem?

Many times, a user will have certain expectations of a computer system based on home use or past job experiences. For example, a previous employer may have allowed everyone in the company full access to the Internet. When the employee joined your company, he expected the same type of access. If your company mandates that only a select few workers will have Internet access, the new employee may take that as a failure of the system. Most of the time, problems of this type can be resolved through user training or some type of new employee orientation.

RECREATE THE PROBLEM

See if you can recreate the problem. This is especially helpful when a user is not able to adequately describe the circumstances to you, or if the problem occurs at random intervals. Recreating the problem is also a good way to determine if the problem rests with the user and can be resolved with some on-the-spot training, or if indeed a problem exists with the system. Note, however, that in some cases it may not be desirable to recreate the problem, particularly if it may cause data to be lost.

Select the Most Probable Cause

Once you have asked a sufficient number of questions, you should have a fairly good idea *where* the problem is, although you may not be able to describe *what* the problem is. The issue here is that you rarely have only one possible answer to the problem. For example, if several users report they can no longer access the Internet, asking questions will still leave you with several possible options. For example:

- Is the WAN connection to the Internet down?
- Is there a problem with the router?
- Is the DNS server operating correctly?
- Is the DHCP server operating?
- Is a network switch malfunctioning?

At this point, you will start using some more techniques. For example, you may need to make a trip to the users' computers, if possible, and run some diagnostics or utilities to eliminate some of the possibilities.

Always keep an open mind and avoid jumping to conclusions when it comes to troubleshooting. Many techs will formulate a solution to a problem before they have all of the information necessary to make an informed decision. Ensure that you have all of the facts and completely understand all of the symptoms before attempting a solution.

WHAT CAN YOU ELIMINATE?

In the Internet problem described above, in which several users report they can no longer access the Internet, you could begin by testing the functionality of the DHCP server by using the IP configuration utility at the workstation. If the workstation is correctly configured with all of the required IP parameters, you can rule out problems with the DHCP server. You can also PING the client to rule out problems with the protocol stack at the client level.

To test your router and WAN connection, PING your default gateway. If the PING is successful, PING a host on the other side of the gateway. If you can PING a remote host, you know that both the router and the WAN link are functioning correctly.

Finally, PING a fully qualified domain name, such as www.yahoo.com. If you cannot successfully PING the domain name, try to PING the IP address of this Web server. If you can PING the IP address but not the domain name, you know there are problems with DNS.

By testing one possibility at a time—TCP/IP, DHCP, router, and DNS—you have systematically eliminated one problem after another, until only the actual problem remains. In this case, the users who called to report that the Internet is down are only partly correct. While the connection to the Internet is functional, it does not work the way it is supposed to. That is, the user cannot open a Web browser, type a host name in the location box, and connect to the Internet. Through the use of the process of elimination and basic troubleshooting utilities, you have been able to quickly identify *where* the problem exists. Now you must determine *what* the problem is. In other words, you know the problem rests with DNS, you just do not know what the problem is with DNS.

TROUBLESHOOTING TOOLS

Always use all of the troubleshooting tools that are available to you. For example, most computers provide either some type of event viewing utility or log files with which to view system problems. These files log, or document, everything that happens at the server. Looking through these log files might direct you to the problem, or at least identify for you the area where the problem is occurring.

Using a Structured Troubleshooting Strategy

Event Viewer

Figure 17.1 depicts the *Event Viewer* utility from a computer running the Windows XP operating system. *(Note: The Event Viewer utility is similar in Windows NT, Windows 2000, and Windows XP.)* To access the Event Viewer in Windows XP, follow these steps:

1. Press the Start button.
2. Select the Control Panel.
3. In the Control Panel, locate and double-click the *Administrative Tools* icon.
4. When the Administrative Tools program group appears, select Event Viewer.

Event Viewer

A utility that maintains log files about programs, security, and system events that occur on a computer.

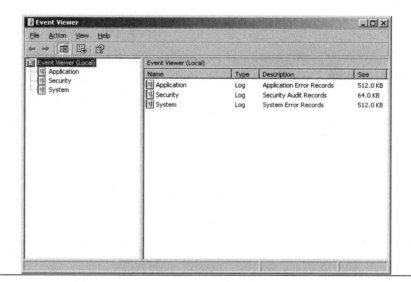

FIGURE 17.1
Windows XP Event Viewer

The Windows Event Viewer contains three logs: Application, Security, and System (see Figure 17.2). To view the entries in the log, simply click the Application, Security, or System logs in the left pane. The appropriate log entries will appear in the right pane. In Figure 17.3, the System log was selected. Notice the various entries.

- **Application log:** Contains events that are caused by applications or programs. For example, if Microsoft SQL Server is installed on a server and an error occurs, that event will be logged here.
- **Security log:** Records events that relate directly to system security, such as valid and invalid logon attempts. Also, you can use the security log to keep track of file auditing. Generally, you must be a system administrator to view the security log.
- **System log:** Contains events that are reported by system components. For example, if a driver or service fails to load during system startup, that failure is recorded in the system log. The operating system specifies the event types that are logged.

FIGURE 17.2
Logs Contained in the Windows
Event Viewer

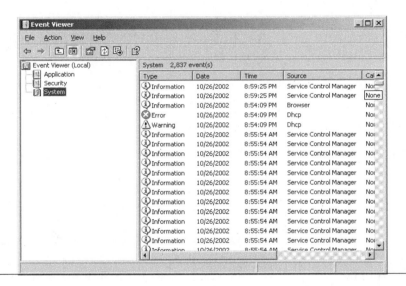

FIGURE 17.3
System Log Entries

The log indicates three different types of entries: Information, Warning, and Error (see Figure 17.4). To view additional information for a specific event, double-click the entry in the right pane. For example, Figure 17.5 depicts detailed information for the DHCP Warning message shown in Figure 17.3.

Using a Structured Troubleshooting Strategy

- **Information:** Describes a successful operation. For example, when an application, driver, or service loads successfully, an Information event will be logged.
- **Warning:** Indicates events that may signal possible future problems. For example, if a system begins to get low on disk space, it will issue a Warning.
- **Error:** Indicates a significant problem, which may result in a loss of data or function. For example, if a device driver fails to load during system startup, an Error will be logged.

FIGURE 17.4
Types of Log Entries

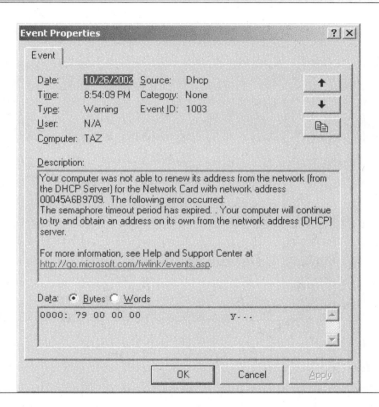

FIGURE 17.5
Expanded Information for
the DHCP Warning
Message

This Warning message states:

Your computer was not able to renew its address from the network (from the DHCP Server) for the Network Card with network address 00045A6B9709. The following error occurred: The semaphore timeout period has expired. Your computer will continue to try and obtain an address on its own from the network address (DHCP) server.

For more information, see Help and Support Center at http://go.microsoft.com/fwlink/events.asp.

If a user reported problems connecting to the Internet, a review of this log entry would plainly reveal the cause: the computer could not obtain an IP address; therefore, it is unable to connect because it does not have the required Internet Protocol addressing information. Although this could indicate a problem with either the local workstation or the DHCP server, it provides you with a good place to begin your troubleshooting efforts.

If you have trouble understanding the message, click the provided hyperlink for more information (see Figure 17.6).

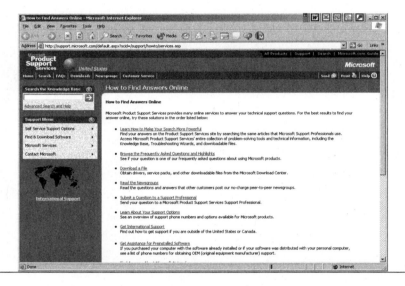

FIGURE 17.6
Online Help

Log Files

Log file

A simple text file that is used to monitor a particular process or event.

Most *log files* are simple text files that can be viewed through a text editor such as Notepad. These log files normally monitor one particular item or process and report on the successes and failures of that item or process. For example, Figure 17.7 depicts the file devicetable.log. This log file monitors and reports dynamic drive detection.

Using a Structured Troubleshooting Strategy

```
devicetable.log - Notepad
File  Edit  Format  View  Help
[DINAMIC DRIVE DETECTION]
{"HL-DT-ST DVD-ROM GDR8160B,HL-DT-ST,003242E0,cdrom.drv,DriveNum=4094,0014,"}
{ drive detected as: Reader,m_dwDeviceType = 5}
{ Capabilites: Flag1(0x83), Flag2(0x800a00), Flag3(0xa), WriteCDRSpeed(0x0), WriteCDRWSpeed(0x0)}
Write CDR Speed:
Write CDRW Speed:
Device Type : CDROM
Device Bus Type: ATAPI
It Supports DAO: N
It supports SAO: N
It supports CDText Read: N
It supports CDText Write: N
It supports BUFE: N
It supports BUFE on real write only: N
It supports DDCD Read: N
It supports DDCD-R Write: N
It supports DDCD-R Write and Test: N
It supports DDCD-RW Write: N
It supports Raw Read: N
It supports Raw Write: N

[DINAMIC DRIVE DETECTION]
{"HL-DT-ST DVD-ROM GDR8160B,HL-DT-ST,003242E0,cdrom.drv,DriveNum=4094,0014,"}
{ drive detected as: Reader,m_dwDeviceType = 5}
{ Capabilites: Flag1(0x83), Flag2(0x800a00), Flag3(0xa), WriteCDRSpeed(0x0), WriteCDRWSpeed(0x0)}
Write CDR Speed:
Write CDRW Speed:
Device Type : CDROM
Device Bus Type: ATAPI
It Supports DAO: N
It supports SAO: N
It supports CDText Read: N
It supports CDText Write: N
It supports BUFE: N
It supports BUFE on real write only: N
It supports DDCD Read: N
It supports DDCD-R Write: N
It supports DDCD-R Write and Test: N
It supports DDCD-RW Write: N
It supports Raw Read: N
It supports Raw Write: N

[DINAMIC DRIVE DETECTION]
{"HL-DT-ST DVD-ROM GDR8160B,HL-DT-ST,003242F0,cdrom.drv,DriveNum=4094,0014,"}
{ drive detected as: Reader,m_dwDeviceType = 5}
{ Capabilites: Flag1(0x83), Flag2(0x800a00), Flag3(0xa), WriteCDRSpeed(0x0), WriteCDRWSpeed(0x0)}
Write CDR Speed:
Write CDRW Speed:
Device Type : CDROM
Device Bus Type: ATAPI
It Supports DAO: N
It supports SAO: N
It supports CDText Read: N
```

FIGURE 17.7
Device Table Log File

Note that this log contains entries that indicate only successful detections. If you were having trouble with dynamic drive detection, this log file would be a logical place to begin your troubleshooting efforts.

Each operating system contains a number of log files. The easiest way to locate them is to use the search utility for your particular computer.

FORMULATE A SOLUTION

Once you have a good idea of where the problem is, you can begin formulating a plan of attack to fix it. This plan should be based on your knowledge of the way the system is supposed to operate, as well as on any ancillary factors that affect the operation of that particular object. In this case, not only do you need a thorough understanding of how DNS works, but you will also need a solid understanding of the network and the protocols in use, since each of these items plays a part in the overall operation of DNS.

Always consider consulting a technical reference when troubleshooting. Most major manufacturers of computer hardware and software have a Web site loaded with support information for their products. Figure 17.8 shows the Microsoft Knowledge Base. It is fully searchable by operating system and issue.

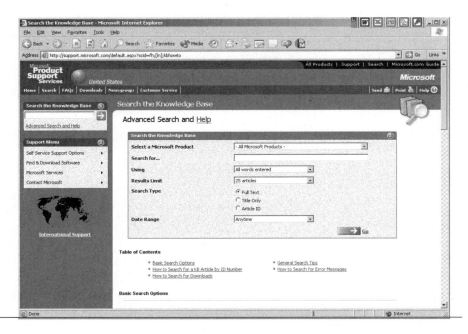

FIGURE 17.8
The Microsoft Knowledge Base

Many times, the manufacturer has already identified the problem and can provide the information or software necessary to fix it. Based on your knowledge of the system and your understanding of the problem, you will start to develop one or more solutions.

Implement a Solution

This section offers some basic but very important advice. First, always try not to make the problem worse. If you do not understand the problem or are not familiar with the technology, talk with someone who knows the technology and can help you.

ONE STEP AT A TIME

Implement only one solution at a time. There are two reasons for this. First, if you do three things and the problem is corrected, you do not know which of these actions fixed the problem. Conversely, if your actions made the problem worse, you do not know which one of the actions made the problem worse; therefore, you have to undo all three actions.

At this point you should have a number of ideas about what it will take to fix the problem. In our DNS example, these solutions will range from restarting the server to reinstalling the DNS server service and rebuilding the DNS database. So which step should you take first?

Always start with the easiest solution. The easiest solution will be the one that is logical, practical, and does not break anything else. In this case, you may want to begin your troubleshooting efforts by simply restarting the server that runs DNS. This solution is quick, requires minimal effort, and causes no damage to the original configuration. If that does not resolve the problem, move to the next logical step.

Each step should build on the previous step. For example, if restarting the server does not correct the problem, what is the next most logical step to try that is not destructive? Continue working through these steps until you have resolved the problem.

CONSIDER THE USER

While you are working to resolve the problem, do not forget about the person who is actually experiencing the problem—the user. In many cases, while you are working to resolve the problem, the user is left in a holding pattern. If the user is required to do research on the Internet and cannot connect to the Internet, he is not able to do his job. Likewise, if the power supply in a user's computer fails and you must order a new power supply, the user will not have her computer for whatever length of time it takes to order, receive, and install the new power supply. In this case, you will probably want to provide the user with another computer to use until hers is repaired and placed back into service. This action may not be possible in all situations. For example, if a router dies and you must get a replacement, you cannot really do anything to fix the problem temporarily. However, when possible, always try to accommodate the user to the extent possible.

In all cases, keep the user informed on your progress. If you believe that it will take two hours to fix the problem, be sure you communicate that information to the user. Also, be realistic with your time estimates. If you try to fudge the time required, it will reflect badly on you as a technician and the IT department as a whole.

Test the Result

Testing the result means simply asking: "Did it work?" Restart the DNS server. Then have the user launch the Web browser, type a fully qualified domain name in the location box, and press the Enter button. If a Web page pops up, the problem is fixed. If the user still cannot connect to the

Internet, move to plan B. Once you have made the changes detailed in plan B, have the user try to connect again. Continue to try each step that you identified as a possible solution and then test it. Keep in mind that you should implement only one potential solution at a time. After you implement that one solution, try it to see if it works. If not, try another possible solution and then test it.

Recognize the Potential Effects of the Solution

Will the "fix" that you developed "unfix" something else? Occasionally, you will repair one problem only to cause another. For example, several manufacturers supply client software for workstations that access servers running their network operating systems. It is not uncommon to install new client software or a service pack to fix a known problem. Many times, this new software will fix the original problem but create a new problem with another component of the workstation. This is especially prevalent when working with several companies that make competing products.

Some side effects are not as obvious. For example, assume that you have a large number of users who work on laptop computers. These computers are assigned IP addresses through DHCP and have a lease period of 365 days. Since the laptop computers tend to be mobile, they receive an IP address and then keep it for one year, even though they may never use it again. To combat this problem, you have decided to change the lease period to one day. Although this fixes the problem of laptop computers monopolizing IP addresses, it creates another problem. Specifically, now each computer must negotiate for an IP address every day. Not only that, but every 12 hours (T1 time) the computer must contact the DHCP server to renegotiate IP addressing parameters. This extra work causes additional network traffic, which translates into network slowdowns at certain times of the day. In other words, you fixed the original problem but created an unrelated problem in the process.

The best way to head off these problems is to consider all of the factors involved and to conduct extensive research prior to implementing a new software solution. Independent discussion groups and good technical references are a great place to start. In most cases, real users or administrators of a product moderate these discussion groups. Since these folks have no vested interest in the product, they tend to be more honest about the problems that they have experienced with different manufacturers' software. A good technical reference will inform you of how all network components work together. Occasionally, you will have to step back and consider issues that are not initially obvious, such as bandwidth, performance, network services, and so on. There is simply no substitute for a thorough understanding of networking and how each component of a network integrates with other components.

Document the Solution

Once the problem is fixed, write down what you did. Most problems recur at some time. Once a problem has been successfully resolved, document the problem and the solution in a format that is available to others. The documentation can be stored in some type of formal, structured facility or in a simple loose-leaf notebook. Many companies use a knowledge base to document their troubleshooting efforts.

KNOWLEDGE BASE

A *knowledge base* is generally a computerized system that allows you to log reported problems along with the steps a technician took to repair them. A knowledge base can range from the very simple to the elaborate. For example, the simplest type of knowledge base does not have to be logged on a computer; rather, it might be a series of folders or binders containing technical notes that are compiled and maintained by technicians. After they respond to and fix a problem, they make notes and store them in the binders so that other technicians can refer to them if they run into a problem.

   A knowledge base can also be a very sophisticated database that can be queried by keyword or asked a question in the form of a text string. A good example of a sophisticated system would be some help-desk management software. With this software, user calls for assistance are automatically logged into the database. This logging includes information such as user name, department, brand and type of computer, serial number and model of computer, and a concise description of the problem. Upon receipt of a problem, a ticket is generated, along with a ticket or call number, which is then assigned to a technician. Once the problem is repaired, the technician opens the ticket in the computer and adds information such as how the problem was fixed and how long it took. The ticket will also reflect whether new hardware or software was required to fix the problem. This information is then stored in the database management system. Once it is stored, another technician can run a series of queries (questions) for similar

Knowledge base

A computerized log of reported computer problems and the steps a technician took to repair them.

problems. For example, if a technician is assigned a help-desk ticket about a sound card that is not working, he can search the knowledge base for information about previous problems and solutions for fixing sound card problems.

This information will keep the tech from repeating all of the troubleshooting steps that have been performed on a previous trouble ticket. In essence, it saves a lot of time and also serves as a very good training tool.

FREQUENTLY ASKED QUESTIONS (FAQs)

Another simple knowledge base might consist of one or more Web pages made up largely of text that users or technicians can browse for *frequently asked questions (FAQs)*. To access the FAQ page, users open a Web browser, type the URL of the Web server, and the page is presented for their use.

FAQs are commonly used to describe how to fix common problems or how to perform routine tasks. For example, your Web site may contain an FAQ that instructs users how to change their passwords. Another might describe how to reset a printer and print server in the case of a printer failure. FAQs are especially useful when a company employs a number of fairly "computer-literate" end users. Since these end users have some degree of comfort with a computer, they should be able to fix minor problems that occur from time to time. Likewise, FAQs can be useful when using newly trained technicians to fix problems. These technicians can use the FAQ page to learn to fix recurring problems, such as unlocking a user account or creating a new user account.

TEST TIP

When presented with a scenario, be able to determine which steps have been accomplished and what the next step should be in the troubleshooting process. CompTIA provides the following guidelines to follow when troubleshooting network problems:

1. Establish the symptoms.
2. Identify the affected area.
3. Establish what has changed.
4. Select the most probable cause.
5. Implement a solution.
6. Test the result.
7. Recognize the potential effects of the solution.
8. Document the solution.

Frequently asked questions (FAQs)

A series of questions about common concerns; in troubleshooting, created to describe how to fix common problems and perform routine tasks.

Using a Structured Troubleshooting Strategy

STUDY GUIDE

In this chapter, we discussed various troubleshooting strategies. Here are some key points to remember.

- To be effective, a technician must have a good understanding of all of the elements involved in a business environment: personal computer hardware and software, networking, database connectivity, and common business applications.

UNDERSTANDING TROUBLESHOOTING

- Troubleshooting is the process of taking a large, complex problem, and through the use of various techniques, excluding all potential causes until only the actual cause remains.
- Once the actual cause is identified, it can then be fixed.
- Good troubleshooting skills require common sense and a structured approach.

ESTABLISH THE SYMPTOMS

- At this stage of the process, you are working primarily with symptoms of the actual problem.
- Most symptoms manifest themselves as a failure of some type.
- Failures may or may not be accompanied by one or more error messages.

Open-Ended Questions

- Open-ended questions are designed to elicit additional information. The plan here is to engage in a dialog with the user.
- Examples of open-ended questions:
  - What did you observe when the problem happened?
  - What were you doing when the error occurred?

Closed-Ended Questions

- With closed-ended questions, you are looking for a specific answer. Many times the answer will be yes or no, or a selection of one or more options.
- Examples of closed-ended questions:
  - Is there an error message?
  - What does the error message say?
  - Is your computer plugged into the wall?
  - Is anyone else having this problem?
  - Have any recent changes been made to the computer?

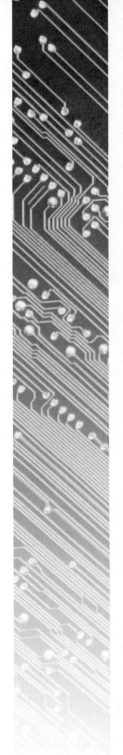

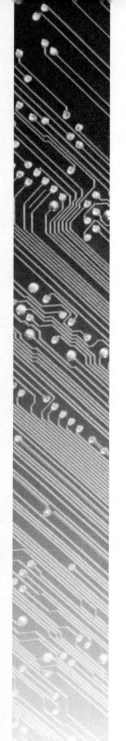

The Basic Questions

Always remember to answer the essential questions: who, what, when, where, why, and how. Here are a few examples:

- Who
    - Who reported the problem?
    - Who found the actual problem?
    - Whom does the problem affect?
- What
    - What are the symptoms of this particular problem?
    - What type of device is having the problem?
    - What was the user doing when she first noticed the problem?
- When
    - When was the problem first noticed?
    - When did the problem actually start?
- Where
    - Where is the affected device?
    - Where was the device when the problem occurred? (Used primarily with laptop computers.)
- Why
    - Why was this problem noticed?
    - Why is this problem occurring?
- How
    - How did this problem occur?
    - Can you make this problem reoccur? If so, how?

Is There a Problem?

- One of the questions you must always answer is, "Does the problem really exist, or is the system simply operating the way it is intended?"

IDENTIFY THE AFFECTED AREA

- A common question to ask at this point is, "How widespread is the problem?" That is, is the problem limited to a single user, group, computer, server, subnet, or an entire network?
- If one user calls the help desk to report a problem, you can usually deduce that it affects only one user or computer.
- If your phones start ringing off the hook with multiple users reporting the same problem, you can be fairly certain that the problem is widespread.
- The importance here is how you will focus your troubleshooting efforts.

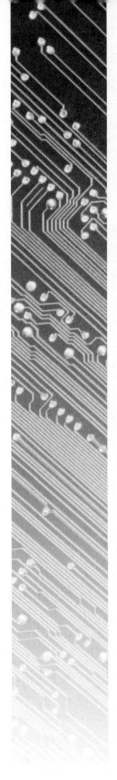

ESTABLISH WHAT HAS CHANGED

- A good question to ask is, "Has anything changed recently?" For example, has any new software been installed on the computer?
- A dialog with other areas of the IT department will help you determine what software upgrades or repairs have been made to user workstations.
- Always keep in mind that the user may have made changes on her own but has decided not to tell you about them.

Could You Do This Before?

- Determine if an employee has been able to perform a task in the past.
- Many times, a user will have certain expectations of a computer system based on home use or past job experiences.

Recreate the Problem

- See if you can recreate the problem. This is especially helpful when the user has not adequately described the circumstances to you, or when the problem occurs at random intervals.
- Recreating the problem is a good way to determine if the problem rests with the user or the system.
- Note that in some cases it may not be desirable to recreate the problem, particularly if it may cause data to be lost.

SELECT THE MOST PROBABLE CAUSE

- Once you have asked a sufficient number of questions, you should have a fairly good idea *where* the problem is, although you still may not be able to describe *what* the problem is.
- You rarely have only one possible answer to the problem.
- At this point, you will start using some more techniques. For example, you may need to make a trip to the users' computers, if possible, and run some diagnostics or utilities to eliminate some of the possibilities.
- Always keep an open mind and avoid jumping to conclusions when it comes to troubleshooting.

What Can You Eliminate?

- By testing one possibility at a time—for example, TCP/IP, DHCP, router, and DNS—you have systematically eliminated one problem after another, until only the actual problem remains.

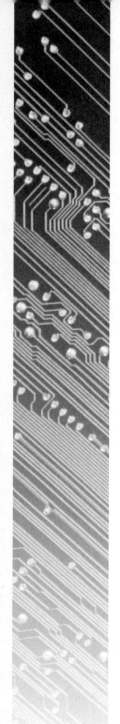

- Through the process of elimination and basic troubleshooting utilities, you have been able to quickly identify where the problem exists.
- Now you must determine what the problem is. You know the problem rests with DNS, you just do not know what the problem is with DNS.

Troubleshooting Tools

- Always use all of the troubleshooting tools that are available to you.
- Most computers provide utility or log files with which to view system problems. These files log, or document, everything that happens at the server.
- Looking through these log files might direct you to the problem, or at least identify the area where the problem is occurring.

Event Viewer

- The Windows Event Viewer contains three logs: Application, Security, and System.
- The Application log contains events that are caused by applications or programs.
- The Security log records events that relate directly to system security, such as valid and invalid logon attempts.
- The System log contains events that are reported by system components.
- Each type of log indicates three different types of entries: Information, Warning, and Error.
  - Information: Describes a successful operation. For example, when an application, driver, or service loads successfully, an Information event will be logged.
  - Warning: An event that may be an indicator of a possible future problem. For example, if a system begins to get low on disk space, it will issue a Warning.
  - Error: Indicates a significant problem. This problem may result in a loss of data or function. For example, if a device driver fails to load during system startup, an Error will be logged.
- To view additional information for a specific event, double-click the entry in the right pane.

Log Files

- Most log files are simple text files that can be viewed through a text editor such as Notepad.

- These log files normally monitor one particular item or process and report on the successes and failures of that item or process.
- Each operating system contains a number of log files. The easiest way to locate them is to use the search utility for your particular computer.

Formulate a Solution

- Once you have a good idea where the problem is, you can begin formulating a plan of attack to fix it.
- This plan should be based on your knowledge of the way the system is supposed to operate, as well as on any ancillary factors that affect the operation of that particular object.
- Always consider consulting a technical reference when troubleshooting.
- Most major manufacturers of computer hardware and software have a Web site loaded with support information for their products.
- Many times, the manufacturer has already identified the problem and can provide the information or software necessary to fix it.
- Based on your knowledge of the system and your understanding of the problem, you will start to develop one or more solutions.

IMPLEMENT A SOLUTION

- Always try not to make the problem worse.

One Step at a Time

- Implement only one solution at a time. There are two reasons for this:
  - First, if you do three things and the problem is corrected, you do not know which of these actions fixed the problem.
  - Conversely, if your actions made the problem worse, you do not know which one of the actions made the problem worse; therefore, you have to undo all three actions.
- Each step should build on the previous step. For example, if restarting the server does not correct the problem, what is the next most logical step to try that is not destructive? Continue working through these steps until you have resolved the problem.

Consider the User

- While you are working to resolve the problem, do not forget about the person who is actually experiencing the problem—the user.
- When possible, always try to accommodate the user to the extent possible.

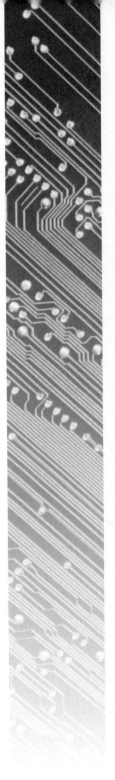

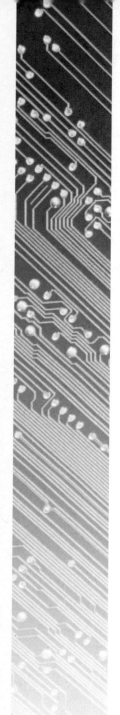

- In all cases, keep the user informed on your progress. If you believe that it will take two hours to fix the problem, be sure you communicate that information to the user.
- Be realistic with your time estimates. If you try to fudge the time required, it will reflect badly on you as a technician and the IT department as a whole.

Test the Result

- Testing the result means simply, did it work?
- Keep in mind that you should implement only one potential solution at a time.
- After you implement that one solution, try it to see if it works. If not, try another possible solution and then test it.

Recognize the Potential Effects of the Solution

- Will the "fix" that you developed "unfix" something else? Occasionally, you will repair one problem only to cause another. This is especially prevalent when working with several companies that make competing products.
- Some side effects are not obvious.
- The best way to head off side effects is to consider all of the factors involved and to conduct extensive research prior to implementing a new software solution.
- Independent discussion groups and good technical references are a great place to start.
- When working with discussion groups, in most cases, real users or administrators of a product moderate these groups. Since these folks have no vested interest in the product, they tend to be more honest about the problems that they have experienced with different manufacturers' software.
- A good technical reference will inform you of how all network components work together.

Document the Solution

- Once the problem is fixed, write down the solution. Most problems recur at some time.
- Once a problem has been successfully resolved, document the problem and the solution in a format that is available to others.

Using a Structured Troubleshooting Strategy

- The documentation can be stored in some type of formal, structured facility or in a simple loose-leaf notebook.
- Many companies use a knowledge base to document their troubleshooting efforts.

Knowledge Base

- A knowledge base is generally a computerized system that logs reported problems along with the steps a technician took to repair them.
- A knowledge base can range from the very simple to the elaborate.
- The simplest type of knowledge base does not have to be logged on a computer; rather, it might be a series of folders or binders containing technical notes that are compiled and maintained by technicians.
- A knowledge base can be a very sophisticated database that can be queried by keyword or asked a question in the form of a text string.

Frequently Asked Questions (FAQs)

- Another simple knowledge base might consist of one or more Web pages made up largely of text that users or technicians can browse for frequently asked questions (FAQs).

PRACTICE TEST

Try this test to check your mastery of the concepts in this chapter.

1. When someone reports an inability to log on to the network, he is reporting a(n) _____ of the actual problem.
   a. solution
   b. answer
   c. symptom
   d. part

2. Asking a question that will give you a specific response is an example of a(n) _____ question.
   a. open-ended
   b. closed-ended
   c. abrupt
   d. declarative

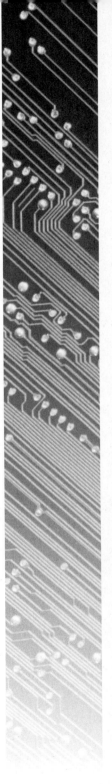

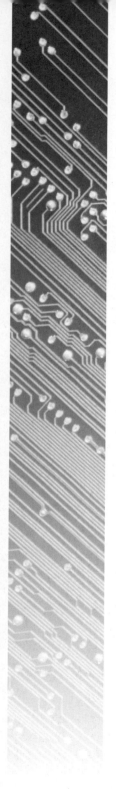

3. "What were you doing when the error occurred?" is an example of a(n) _____ question.
   a. open-ended
   b. closed-ended
   c. abrupt
   d. explorative

4. When you ask the question "How widespread is the problem?" you are attempting to determine the _____ of the problem.
   a. solution
   b. source
   c. scope
   d. nature

5. Twenty users have called to complain that they cannot log on to the network. On which of the following options should you focus?
   a. the users' passwords
   b. the groups to which the users belong
   c. current system password policies
   d. the network switch that connects this group of users to the network

6. The IT staff recently applied a hot fix to ten workstations. Users on five of those workstations now report that they can no longer connect to shared network printers. Of the choices listed below, which is the most logical culprit?
   a. the workstations' operating system
   b. the printers
   c. the hot fix
   d. the print servers

7. A user has contacted the help desk concerning a computer problem; however, the user is not able to adequately describe the circumstances to you. What would be a good way to deal with this situation?
   a. Tell the user to call back with more information.
   b. Try to recreate the problem yourself.
   c. Have the user contact a coworker and have the coworker call back with a description of the problem.
   d. Log the call and respond to it when you get time.

Using a Structured Troubleshooting Strategy

8. A new employee has reported that he is not able to access the Internet. Your company has a policy that only select members of the senior staff can have Internet access. The caller is a mid-level manager. Based on your knowledge of this situation, which of the following statements best describes this situation?
   a. The system is working the way it was designed.
   b. The system is experiencing a failure.
   c. The user is making a mistake when typing in the Uniform Resource Locator.
   d. The HR department should have given the new user Internet access.

9. When reviewing log files in the Windows Event Viewer, which log usually requires administrator rights to view its contents?
   a. System
   b. Security
   c. Application
   d. Intrusion

10. Which of the following log files would probably contain information about networking parameters?
    a. Faxsetup.log
    b. TCPIP.log
    c. System.log
    d. Q105738.txt

11. While looking through the Event Viewer on a Windows NT 4.0 server, you noticed several information entries regarding the DHCP server. What action should you take?
    a. Restart the DHCP server.
    b. Rebuild the DHCP database.
    c. Restart the DNS server.
    d. Take no action.

12. You would like to establish a method whereby users of your network can look up and resolve minor technical issues. Which of the following best fits your criteria?
    a. full-featured knowledge base
    b. knowledge base consisting of technical manuals in a binder that is stored in the IT department
    c. a hyperlink on the company intranet to a section for frequently asked questions
    d. a binder stored in the IT department that contains technical manuals in a section labeled "frequently asked questions"

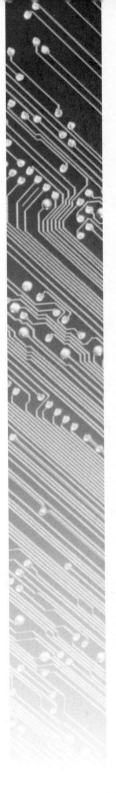

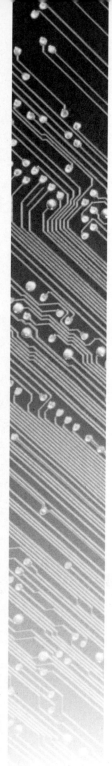

TROUBLESHOOTING

1. A user has reported to you she is not able to access a folder of Excel spreadsheets that are stored on a network server. List several questions that you would ask, along with steps you would take to help troubleshoot this problem.

2. A hardware technician has reported to you that he has just installed a new Ethernet network card in a computer. Once it was installed, an unshielded twisted pair cable with an RJ-45 connector was connected to the network card. Upon restarting the computer, a driver was installed. After all of this work, the computer is apparently not seeing the network, as neither he nor the user can log on to the network. List at least five steps that the technician can take to troubleshoot the problem.

CUSTOMER SERVICE

1. You have been referred a trouble ticket stating that a user cannot connect to a database system that you administer. You have checked the database server and database user account and have determined the problem does not lie there. You have deduced that the problem is due to a network failure and have referred it to another technician. The technician refers it back to you, stating that it is still your problem, especially since he does not understand database systems. Where do you draw the line, and who is responsible?

2. Every morning a user contacts you to report that he cannot log on to the network. The user goes on to report that on the first logon attempt at his Windows 2000 Professional workstation, he receives a message that his account is locked. Your network uses a system policy that states accounts will be locked after three unsuccessful logon attempts. You have watched the user log on and note that he is doing it correctly. You suspect that someone is attempting to log on to the computer at night. Where could you obtain more information about these possible unauthorized logon attempts?

Using a Structured Troubleshooting Strategy

FOR MORE INFORMATION

For links to Web sites that provide further information about the topics covered in this chapter, go to the EMC/Paradigm Internet Resource Center at www.emcp.com/College Division/Internet Resource Centers/Networking/System Administration/Web Resources: For More Information.

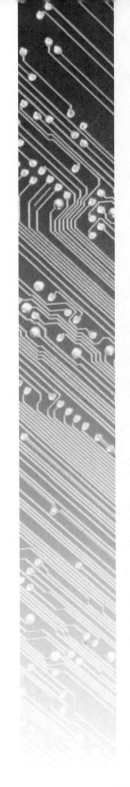

18

Network
Troubleshooting
Tools

ON THE TEST

Network+ Examination
- **Objective 4.5:** Given a wiring task, select the appropriate tool (e.g., wire crimper, media tester/certifier, punch-down tool, tone generator, optical tester, etc.).
- **Objective 4.6:** Given a network scenario, interpret visual indicators (e.g., link lights, collision lights, etc.) to determine the nature of the problem.

ON THE JOB

Technicians in all walks of life need a good set of tools. This is especially true when working in a network environment where problems are bound to occur. This chapter identifies some of the basic, generic tools that should be a part of every computer person's toolkit. It also describes tools that are peculiar to networking and discusses when the use of those tools is appropriate.

General Tools

Every technician requires a set of tools to perform all of the tasks he will encounter while troubleshooting network problems. This set of tools can range from a screwdriver and pair of pliers to a fully stocked toolkit containing specialized diagnostic equipment. Figure 18.1 shows a basic technician's toolkit.

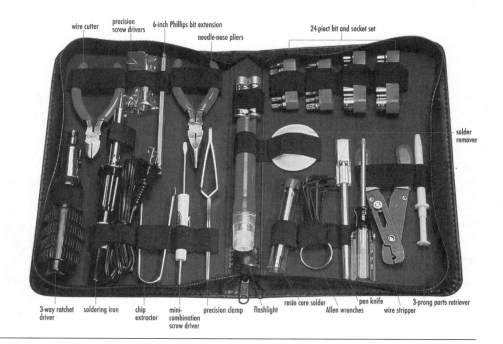

FIGURE 18.1
Basic PC Technician's Toolkit

At a minimum, a basic toolkit should include the following items:

- Soldering gun, de-solder pump, and roll of solder.
- Wire cutters and strippers.
- Needle-nose pliers.
- Crescent wrench.
- Integrated chip (IC) inserter and extractor.
- Tweezers and reverse-action tweezers.
- Flat blade screwdrivers in assorted sizes.
- Phillips blade screwdrivers in assorted sizes.
- Nut drivers.
- Spare parts tube.
- Electrostatic discharge (ESD) wrist strap.

Technicians who perform the majority of their troubleshooting tasks in the field, or away from an office, should consider some additional tools:

- Wire crimper, scissors, and cutting pliers.
- A set of hex keys.
- Combination wrench set.
- Large set of screwdrivers.
- Metal tweezers.
- Three-prong holder.

Network Troubleshooting Tools

- Portable vise.
- Utility knife.
- Drill and brush.
- Mini-vacuum.
- Flashlight.

In addition, try to maintain a supply of spare parts. Although most companies will balk at maintaining an extensive parts supply due to the cost involved, most will allow you to store commonly used items. For example, these items should be readily available to you:

- Network interface cards (NICs).
- Hubs, switches, bridges, etc.
- Routers.
- Patch cables.
- Network cables.
- Copies of software, to include the following:
  - Drivers for the network interface cards.
  - Network clients.
  - Operating system CDs.

Along with the basic tools listed above, each technician should have available some specialized tools suited to the tasks each technician performs.

TEST TIP

When presented with a troubleshooting scenario, be sure you know which tool to use in that particular situation.

Specialty Tools

Specialty tools are those that are used in special or peculiar circumstances. When working with networks, many tools are peculiar to only that environment, and probably will not be used anywhere else. Although these tools may not be used on a day-to-day basis, no other tool can substitute for them when they are needed.

Specialty tool

A tool designed specifically for a particular circumstance.

WIRE CRIMPER

Wire crimpers are used to attach terminals, or connectors, onto pieces of wire (see Figure 18.2). The head of the crimper contains indentations known as cavities. Once the terminator is slipped over the wire, the jaws of

Wire crimper

A tool used to attach terminals, or connectors, onto pieces of wire.

the crimper are opened and the terminator is slipped into the appropriate cavity. When the handles are squeezed shut, the terminator is mashed onto the wire.

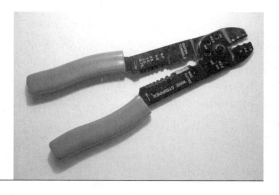

FIGURE 18.2
Wire Crimper

Correct cavity selection is critical and is based on wire size. For example, for most crimpers, if the wire is 22-16 *American Wire Gauge (AWG),* you would place the wire and terminator in the front cavity. If it is 16-14 AWG, you would place the wire and terminator into the middle cavity. If it is 12-10 AWG, you would place the wire and terminator into the rear cavity. The cavities on most standard wire crimpers are color coded to correspond to wire size markings.

American Wire Gauge (AWG)

A U.S. standard used to measure the diameter of nonferrous wire.

In Real Life

American Wire Gauge (AWG) is a U.S. standard used to measure the diameter of nonferrous wire—primarily copper and aluminum, although other materials may also be used. Standard types of wire are electrical wires used in homes and the wire used with telephones. The wire used for electricity in homes is number 12 or 14 AWG. The wire used to connect telephones is usually 22, 24, or 26. The higher the gauge, the smaller the diameter.

In addition to attaching terminators to standard AWG wire, crimpers are commonly used to connect coaxial cable with BNC connectors. The cavities on coaxial crimpers are shaped in such a way that the actual crimp is made in a hexagonal configuration. This makes for a much more secure connection. With coaxial crimpers, the front cavity is used to connect coaxial cable to RG-59 cable. The middle cavity is used for RG-5, 6, 21, 143, 212, 222, and 304 cables. The rear cavity is used to connect RG-8, 9, 11, 149, and 213 cables.

Crimpers are also used to attach RJ-11 and RJ-45 connectors to twisted pair cable, although they operate a little differently from those described above. RJ crimpers are useful when creating your own cables because they allow you to make cables of nonstandard lengths. That is, when you purchase commercially made cables, they are generally cut to set lengths, such as 25, 50, and 100 feet. Using an RJ crimper, some wire, and a few connectors, you will be able to make whatever length cable you need.

The RJ crimper works by crimping and mashing the gold teeth in the RJ connector onto the individual wires that have been inserted into the connector (see Figure 18.3).

Most of these tools also have the ability to cut wire or to strip the plastic jacket from the individual wires. This is especially useful if you have a cable that has been improperly wired and you need to cut off a connector and add a new one.

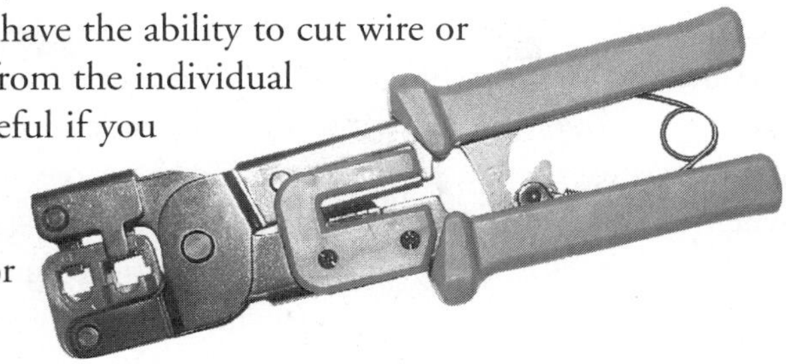

As with most tools, crimpers come in many grades, or levels of quality. Spending a little more money for a good quality metal tool can save you the hassle of having to replace a cheaper one that breaks after one or two uses.

FIGURE 18.3
RJ Crimper

⎯ TRY IT! ⎯

Use a pair of crimpers to attach a connector to a cable.

MEDIA TESTER

Network cables are a never-ending source of problems. Cables that are improperly strung or that have improperly installed connectors may result in a multitude of transmission problems. *Media testers,* also commonly referred to as cable testers, are used to isolate these types of problems so they can be corrected. A cable tester is a required item for any technician who will be called on to troubleshoot network problems.

Media testers are used to test cable media, or in plain language, network and telephone cables (see Figure 18.4). Most cable testers can be used to test both twisted pair and coaxial cable. Media testers can test and confirm the actual wiring configuration for twisted pair cable to include whether or not the RJ-45 connectors are attached correctly. With coaxial cable, the physical cable and termination can be tested.

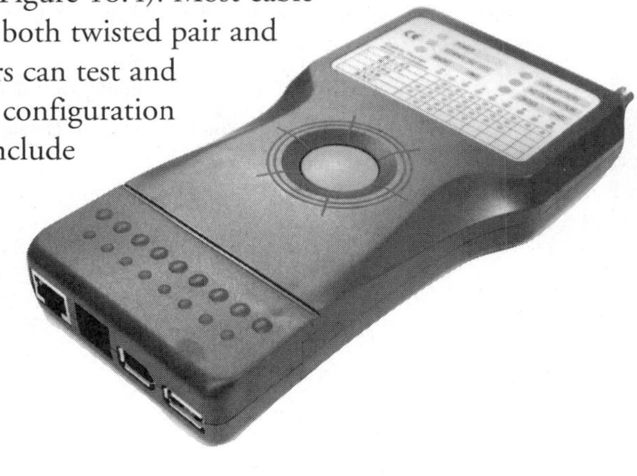

Media tester

A tool used to test for problems and confirm wiring configuration and termination in network and telephone cables; also called a cable tester.

FIGURE 18.4
Media Tester

Continuity

Agreement, or harmony, between parts, in this case between the type of cable and the electrical standards identified by the manufacturer.

Crosstalk

A type of electromagnetic interference caused by the bleeding of an electrical signal from one wire to another housed within the same sheath.

Electrical noise

A type of electromagnetic interference on one electrical device that emanates from another, completely separate electrical device.

Attenuation

The degradation, or fading, of an electrical signal that occurs as the signal travels down a length of cable.

Capacitance

A measure of the charge in the electrostatic field of a passive electronic component called a capacitor. Used to determine if the cable is kinked or if it has been stretched.

Cable tracing

Traces the path a cable takes through a wall or ceiling.

Although testers vary from model to model, normally a media tester includes either one or two parts. One-part testers have two jacks built in to the tester. Plug both ends of the cable into the jacks and follow the manufacturer's instructions. One-part testers are useful for short cables, such as patch cables. For two-part testers, you will have the actual tester and a remote terminator. Plug one end of the cable into the media tester. Plug the other end of the cable into the remote terminator and follow the manufacturer's instructions for testing the cable. Two-part testers are useful when dealing with long cable runs.

Media testers work by sending an electrical signal down the length of the cable. Once the signal reaches the other end, the quality and strength of the signal is evaluated. Media testers can also detect faults in the cabling such as open or unconnected wires, shorts, miswiring, and crossed cable pairs.

Most common cable testers can be used to perform the tests described in Figure 18.5. Some media testers include advanced features, which allow you to conduct the tests described in Figure 18.6.

- *Continuity:* Determines whether a cable meets the electrical standards identified by the manufacturer.
- *Crosstalk:* Determines whether crosstalk is occurring on the cable. Crosstalk is noise that comes from adjacent wire pairs. Twisted pair cable uses the twisted wires to help reduce the amount of crosstalk that occurs between wires that are located near each other.
- *Electrical noise:* Tracks the source of electrical noise, which can be caused by a number of sources, including electrical cables and fluorescent lights. Since this noise may occur sporadically, line noise tests may need to be conducted over a period of time to obtain accurate readings.
- *Attenuation:* Determines the amount of signal loss on a piece of cable.
- *Capacitance:* Tells you if the cable is kinked or stretched, based on the measurement of picofarads (pF) per foot.
- *Cable tracing:* Traces the path a cable takes through a wall or ceiling by using a tone generator to send a signal through the cable. While the tone is traveling through the cable, you can listen through the wall or ceiling for the tone.

FIGURE 18.5
Tests Commonly Performed with a Cable Tester

- **Device type:** Identifies the device type attached to the cable, such as hub, workstation, printer, etc.
- **LAN speedometer:** Verifies the speed of the data link, such as 10 or 100 Mbps.
- **Cable type simulator:** Indicates the type of patch cable required (i.e., straight through or crossover cable).
- **Network monitor:** Indicates that data is being transmitted and provides the transmission speed.
- **Tone probe and tone generator:** Trace the location of installed cables.
- **Cable-pair tester:** Verifies how wires are paired with each other and identifies whether the cables are wired straight through or in a crossover configuration.
- **Cable termination tester:** Determines whether a device is attached to the end of a cable.

FIGURE 18.6
Tests Performed by Media
Tester with Advanced Features

When purchasing a cable tester, be sure you pick one that meets the requirements of the cable type you are testing.

TRY IT!

Use a media tester to check a piece of cable.

TIME DOMAIN REFLECTOMETER (TDR)

The *Time Domain Reflectometer (TDR)* is a type of cable tester used to determine if a cable is broken or has a short. A TDR works by sending a signal to the end of a cable, or to the flaw point, and then measuring the length of time it takes for the signal to bounce back. If a cable is broken or has a short, the signal bounces back at a different speed (measured in amplitudes), depending on the location of the defect. To calculate the distance to a fault in the cable, TDRs use the following principle:

**Time Domain
Reflectometer (TDR)**

A type of cable tester used to determine if the cable is broken or has a short.

$$\text{Distance} = \text{Rate of propagation} \times \text{Time}$$

TDRs are made for testing both copper and fiber-optic cables.
- **Copper cable:** The TDR sends an electrical signal down a length of cable and then records the amount of time it takes for the signal to reflect back.
- **Fiber-optic cable:** An Optical Time Domain Reflectometer (OTDR) uses reflected light to identify items such as the length of the fiber-optic cable, the location of cable breaks, and the effects of attenuation. OTDRs perform one type of optical testing, which is discussed in more detail below.

TRY IT!

Use a TDR to test a defective cable.

OPTICAL TESTER

Like copper cables, fiber-optic cables can also experience problems or failures. In the past, once the cable was cut to length, the ends had to be polished and then the connectors glued on. The installer had to be extremely careful while making cables or they would not work well, or at all. Another important consideration for fiber-optic cable is the bend radius; if a cable is bent too sharply it will break. Once the cable breaks, the break must be located and spliced.

Optical testers are used to test fiber-optic cabling systems by detecting reflected light. By attaching probes to the optical fibers, items such as the output power of signal fibers and attenuation can be measured. Optical testers are commonly used to evaluate connector joints and splices in the cabling system and to locate faults.

Most testers use a laser or light-emitting diode (LED) light source, which transmits light down the length of the cable. The testers commonly include an optical power meter that is used to show the strength of the reflected light (see Figure 18.7). Some high-end test systems have an internal memory, which allows test data to be stored. These testers may also have the ability to connect to a personal computer and download test data in a format that can be analyzed and either stored or printed.

Optical tester

A tool used to test fiber-optic cabling systems by detecting reflected light.

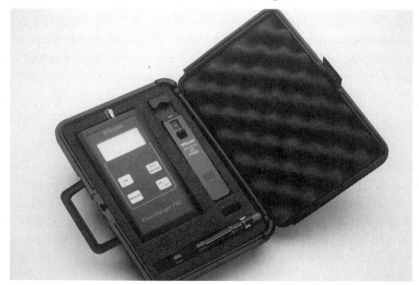

FIGURE 18.7
Optical Tester

PUNCH-DOWN TOOL

Punch-down tools are used to attach telephone and data wires to punch-down blocks and to the rear side of patch panels. The actual tool (see Figure 18.8) is a hand-held device containing both a plunger and cutter assembly.

Punch-down tool

A tool used to attach telephone and data wires to punch-down blocks and to the rear side of patch panels.

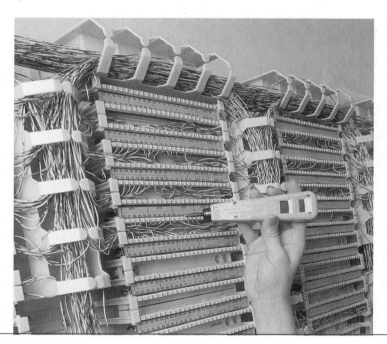

FIGURE 18.8
Punch-Down Toool in Use at
Telephone Punch-Down Block

To use this tool, place a single wire across a clip on the punch-down block or patch panel. Place the punch-down tool over the wire and push down. The plunger forces the wire into the clip on the punch-down block, locking it into place. The cutter then trims the end of the wire, keeping the connection clean.

Good quality punch-down tools have adjustments that can be made using wheels embedded in the handle. Typically, you can adjust the impact level and the height, to accommodate different types of connectors.

TRY IT!

Use a punch-down tool to connect wires to a punch-down block or patch panel.

TONE GENERATOR

Tone generator

A tool used to trace problems in both voice and data lines.

Tone generators are used to trace problems in both voice and data lines. To use a tone generator to trace a voice or telephone problem, plug the RJ-11 connector from the tone generator into a modular telephone jack. If working at the punch-down block, use alligator clamps to connect the generator directly to the connectors or wires (see Figure 18.9). Finally, turn on the tone generator to begin transmitting a signal down the length of the wire. At the next junction of the wire, a tone probe is used to detect the tone. For example, if you are experiencing telephone problems and suspect a piece of the telephone line, begin by plugging the tone generator into the RJ-11 wall jack and turn on the tone generator. At the first termination point, usually a punch-down block, attach the tone probe to the appropriate connectors. If the tone from the tone generator is detected, that particular line is working correctly. At the punch-down block, use alligator clips to attach the generator to the appropriate connectors. Turn on the tone generator. At the next termination point, use the tone probe to try to detect the tone. Continue this process until the tone is lost. This will indicate the wire segment where the problem lies.

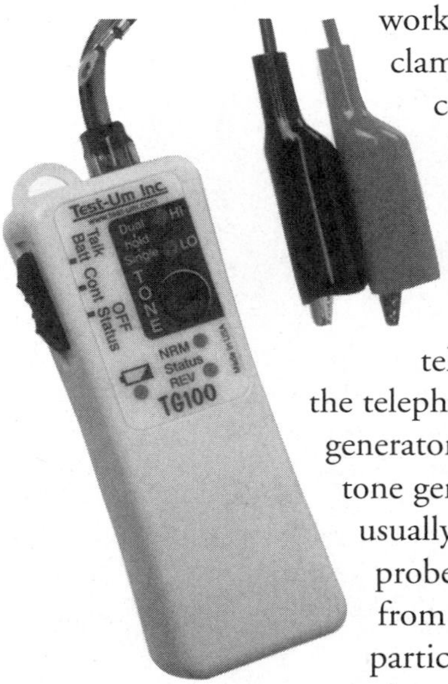

FIGURE 18.9
Tone Generator

If you plan to use the tone generator to trace data problems, plug the RJ-45 connector from the tone generator into the wall jack, switch, or hub, and follow the directions outlined above for voice testing.

TRY IT!

Use a tone generator to trace a network cable.

LOOPBACK PLUG

A loopback plug is used to ensure that electrical signals are being sent out of a network interface card. To make a loopback plug, a single piece of twisted pair cable and an RJ-45 connector are required. On the RJ-45 connector, using the twisted pair cable, connect pin 1 to pin 3 and pin 2 to pin 6. When the plug is completed, insert it into the back of the network interface card.

Loopback plugs operate in a manner similar to the PING utility. You may recall that when using PING, the workstation sends out a packet to another device and waits for a response. A loopback plug does essentially the same thing; however, the signal travels from the network interface card, through the short section of wire connected to the loopback plug, and then back into the network interface card. This test verifies that the network interface card is sending data.

Loopback plugs can also be used to test network devices, such as routers and CSU/DSUs; however, the pin configuration is different for those devices.

TEST TIP

You should know that, to make a loopback plug, you would use twisted pair cable to connect pin 1 to pin 3 and pin 2 to pin 6 on the RJ-45 connector.

TRY IT!

1. Obtain an RJ-45 connector and a short piece of twisted pair cable.
2. Attach the wires to the connector as noted above.
3. Use the PING command to test the new loopback plug.

Visual Indicators

Many devices have built-in lights that are designed to show you when a connection has been made and when data collisions occur. Some of the more common pieces of hardware that contain these types of lights are network interface cards, hubs, switches, bridges, and routers.

LINK LIGHTS

Link light

A light built into a piece of hardware to demonstrate link connectivity at the Physical layer of the OSI Model.

Link lights are designed to demonstrate link connectivity at the Physical layer of the OSI Model. In simpler terms, that means that a link light will appear lit when a physical connection is made between two network devices. For example, if a twisted pair cable is plugged into a network interface card on one end and a hub on the other end, both devices should have a single glowing light (see Figure 18.10). This light indicates that both devices are connected to each other.

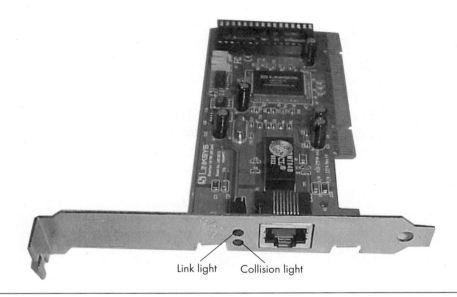

Link light   Collision light

FIGURE 18.10
Link Light and Collision Light on a Network Interface Card

To check link connectivity, look for a solid green light that is lit on the network interface card. This glowing light indicates that link connectivity is established. If the link light is not glowing, a problem with the physical connection is indicated.

TROUBLESHOOTING A LINK PROBLEM

If you are troubleshooting a network problem and you believe that connectivity may be the problem, always check to see if the link light is lit. If not, check these items:

- Try to reseat the connection by unplugging the connection and plugging it back in. For example, when working with twisted pair cables and RJ-45 connectors, unplug the connector from the rear of the network interface card. While it is unplugged, check for loose connections or damaged pins. If the connection looks good, reconnect it.

- Unplug the cable from the other end—that is, the wall jack, hub, switch, etc.—and reconnect it. Inspect the cable and connector as outlined above. If the cable or connectors look questionable, replace the cable.
- Restart the computer. Restarting will initialize the NIC, which may re-establish the connection.
- At the hub or switch, check the corresponding link light. If it is not lit, plug the cable into another port. If link connectivity is established, you will know that the port on the hub was defective.
- Check to make sure the hub or switch has power.
- If you are using a managed switch, check to see if someone has made changes to the switch configuration, or if a port has been disabled.
- While at the hub, check the cable and connector just like you did at the workstation. Replace the cable if you have any questions about its dependability.
- Use a cable tester to verify that all of the patch cables and network cable runs are operating correctly.
- If a new patch cable has been installed, check to make sure it is not a crossover cable.

Collision Lights

Collision lights are used to detect collisions on an Ethernet network. Whenever a device transmits data and a collision occurs, this light (see Figure 18.10) will glow. Although collisions are normal in an Ethernet environment, they should not occur on a regular basis. Therefore, if the collision light glows continuously, a problem may exist with a device on the network segment. For example, a malfunctioning network interface card may cause a broadcast storm. A broadcast storm occurs when an incorrect packet is broadcast on a network causing all of the network hosts to respond to it all at once. Since the broadcast is erroneous, the answers to the broadcast are also erroneous, which causes the process to begin repeating itself over and over, thereby creating a large amount of network traffic. Anytime the network experiences a dramatic decrease in bandwidth, caused by a dramatic increase in network traffic, many collisions will occur, which adds to the network traffic. If this situation is not rectified, a network meltdown will soon occur. The best way to correct the problem is to replace the offending piece of hardware.

Collision light

A light built into devices that transmit data in order to detect collisions on an Ethernet network.

TRY IT!

View the link and collision lights on the rear of an operating network interface card.

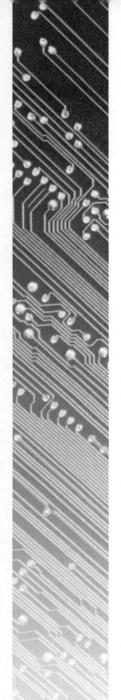

STUDY GUIDE

In this chapter, we discussed network troubleshooting tools. Here are some key points to remember.

GENERAL TOOLS

- Every technician requires a set of tools to perform the tasks associated with troubleshooting network problems.
- A set of tools can range from a screwdriver and pair of pliers to a fully stocked toolkit containing specialized diagnostic equipment.
- Technicians who perform the majority of their troubleshooting tasks in the field, or away from an office, should consider some additional tools.
- Maintain a supply of spare parts.

SPECIALTY TOOLS

- Specialty tools are those that are used in special or peculiar circumstances.

Wire Crimper

- Wire crimpers are used to attach terminals or connectors onto pieces of wire.
- The head of the crimper contains indentations known as cavities. Once the terminator is slipped over the wire, the jaws of the crimper are opened and the terminator is slipped into the appropriate cavity. When the handles are squeezed shut, the terminator is mashed onto the wire.
- Correct cavity selection is critical and is based on wire size.
- The cavities on most standard wire crimpers are color coded to correspond to wire size markings.
- Crimpers are commonly used to connect coaxial cable with BNC connectors.
- The cavities on coaxial crimpers are shaped in such a way that the actual crimp is made in a hexagonal configuration. This makes for a much more secure connection.

MEDIA TESTER

- Media testers are used to test cable media, or, in plain language, network and telephone cables.

- Most cable testers can be used to test both twisted pair and coaxial cable. Media testers can test and confirm the actual wiring configuration for twisted pair cable, including whether the RJ-45 connectors are attached correctly.
- With coaxial cable, the physical cable and termination can be tested.
- Media testers work by sending an electrical signal down the length of the cable. Once the signal reaches the other end, or a flaw point, the quality and strength of the signal is evaluated.
- Most common cable testers can be used to perform the following tests:
  - Continuity: Determines whether a cable meets the electrical standards identified by the manufacturer.
  - Crosstalk: Crosstalk is noise that comes from adjacent wire pairs. Twisted pair cable uses the twisted wires to help reduce the amount of crosstalk that occurs between wires that are located near each other.
  - Electrical noise: Tracks the source of electrical noise, including electrical cables and fluorescent lights. Since this noise may occur sporadically, line noise tests may need to be conducted over a period of time to obtain accurate readings.
  - Attenuation: Determines the amount of signal loss on a piece of cable.
  - Capacitance: Tells you if the cable is kinked or has been stretched, based on the measurement of picofarads (pF) per foot.
  - Cable tracing: Tracks the path a cable takes through a wall or ceiling by using a tone generator to send a signal through the cable. While the tone is traveling through the cable, you can listen through the wall or ceiling for the tone.
- When purchasing a cable tester, be sure to pick one that meets the requirements of the cable type you are testing.

TIME DOMAIN REFLECTOMETER (TDR)

- Time Domain Reflectometers (TDRs) are a type of cable tester.
- TDRs are used to determine if the cable is broken or has a short.
- A TDR works by sending a signal to the end of a cable and then measuring the length of time it takes for the signal bounce back. If a cable is broken or has a short, the signal bounces back at a different speed (measured in amplitudes), depending on the location of the defect.
- TDRs are made for testing both copper and fiber-optic cables.
  - Copper cables: The TDR sends an electrical signal down a length of cable and then records the amount of time it takes for the signal to reflect back.

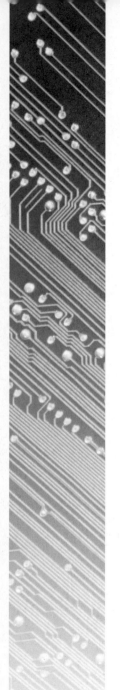

○ Fiber-optic cables: Optical Time Domain Reflectometers (OTDRs) use reflected light to identify items such as the length of the fiber-optic cable, the location of cable breaks, and the affects of attenuation.

OPTICAL TESTER

- Optical testers are used to test fiber-optic cabling systems by detecting reflected light.
- By attaching probes to the optical fibers, items such as attenuation and the output power of signal fibers can be measured.
- Optical testers are commonly used to evaluate connector joints and splices in the cabling system and to locate faults.

PUNCH-DOWN TOOL

- Punch-down tools are used to attach telephone and data wires to punch-down blocks and patch panels.
- The actual tool is a hand-held device containing a plunger and cutter assembly.

TONE GENERATOR

- Tone generators are used to trace problems in phone lines.
- To use a tone generator, plug the RJ-11 connector from the tone generator into a modular telephone jack. If working at the punch-down block, use alligator clamps to connect the generator directly to the connectors or wires.
- Turn on the tone generator to begin transmitting a signal down the length of the wire.
- At the next junction of the wire, a tone probe is used to detect the tone.

LOOPBACK PLUG

- A loopback plug is used to ensure that electrical signals are being sent out of a network interface card.
- To make a loopback plug, a single piece of twisted pair cable and an RJ-45 connector are required.
- On the connector, connect pin 1 to pin 3 and pin 2 to pin 6.

VISUAL INDICATORS

- Many devices have built-in lights that are designed to show you when a connection has been made and when data collisions occur.
- Some of the more common pieces of hardware that contain these types of lights are network interface cards, hubs, switches, bridges, and routers.

Link Lights

- Link lights are designed to demonstrate link connectivity at the Physical layer of the OSI Model. In simpler terms, that means that a link exists between two network devices.
- Link light status will vary from device to device.

Troubleshooting a Link Problem

- If you are troubleshooting a network problem and you believe that connectivity may be the problem, always check to see if the link light is lit. If not, check these items:
  - Try to reseat the connection by unplugging the connection and plugging it back in.
  - Unplug the cable from the other end—that is, the wall jack, hub, switch, etc.—and reconnect it. Inspect the cable and connector as outlined above. If the cable or connectors look questionable, replace the cable.
  - Restart the computer. Restarting should initialize the NIC, which may re-establish the connection.
  - At the hub or switch, check the corresponding link light. If it is not lit, plug the cable into another port. If link connectivity is established, you will know the port on the hub was defective.
  - Check to make sure the hub or switch has power.
  - If you are using a managed switch, check to see if someone has made changes to the switch configuration, or if a port has been disabled.
  - While at the hub, check the cable and connector just like you did at the workstation. Replace the cable if you have any questions about its dependability.
  - Use a cable tester to verify that all of the patch cables and network cable runs are operating correctly.
  - If a new patch cable has been installed, check to make sure it is not a crossover cable.

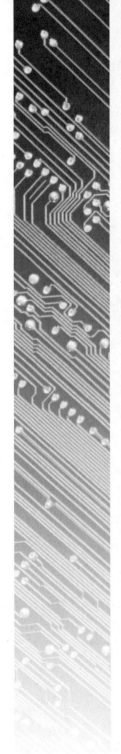

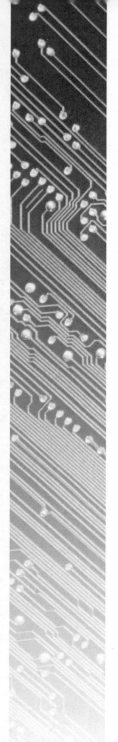

Collision Lights

- Collision lights are used to detect collisions on an Ethernet network.
- Whenever a device transmits data and a collision occurs, this light will glow.

PRACTICE TEST

Try this test to check your mastery of the concepts in this chapter.

1. Which of the following items should be included in a spare parts inventory? (Select all that apply)
   a. NICs
   b. patch cables
   c. fiber-optic cable tester
   d. router

2. Which of the following tools would you use to attach a BNC connector to a piece of coaxial cable?
   a. crimper
   b. hexagonal key set
   c. metal tweezers
   d. punch-down tool

3. Which of the following gauges of AWG wire has the smallest diameter?
   a. 12
   b. 14
   c. 22
   d. 24

4. You suspect that a 50-foot run of shielded twisted pair wire is defective. Which of the following tools would you use to confirm or refute your suspicion?
   a. optical tester
   b. RJ crimper
   c. media tester
   d. link light

5. Using a cable tester, which of the following tests would you run to determine if a cable meets the electrical standards identified by the manufacturer?
   a. crosstalk
   b. continuity
   c. capacitance
   d. attenuation

6. Using a cable tester, which of the following tests would you run to determine if a cable has been kinked or stretched?
   a. crosstalk
   b. continuity
   c. capacitance
   d. attenuation

7. Which of the following items sends an electrical signal down a length of cable and then records the amount of time it takes for the signal to reflect back?
   a. Time Domain Reflectometer
   b. cable tracing
   c. optical tester
   d. cable tracer

8. Which of the following items would you use to determine if a piece of copper cable has a short?
   a. Time Domain Reflectometer
   b. optical tester
   c. cable tracer
   d. collision light

9. Which of the following devices would be used to evaluate splices in the cabling system?
   a. Time Domain Reflectometer
   b. cable tracing
   c. optical tester
   d. cable tracer

10. You have been asked to attach a series of network cable runs to the back of a patch panel. Which of the following tools would you use to make these connections?
    a. RJ crimper
    b. crimping tool

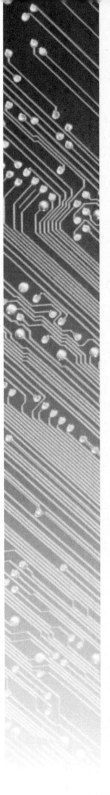

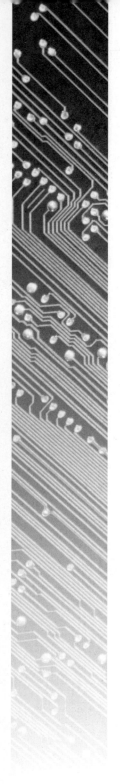

  c. punch-down tool
  d. media tester

11. Which of the following devices iss used in conjunction with a tone generator to trace problems in voice and data lines?
  a. tone box
  b. tone handset
  c. tone receiver
  d. tone probe

12. A network hub has several lights on the front. Which of the following describes the use of those lights? (Select two)
  a. link connectivity
  b. error control
  c. data collisions
  d. data transfer

TROUBLESHOOTING

1. A network user has contacted you to report that he is unable to log on to the network. During troubleshooting you discover that the link light on the network interface card is not lit. Describe several steps that you would take to correct this problem.
2. You have recently purchased some new network twisted pair cables from a third-party vendor. At the workstations where these cables are in use, employees have complained about slow network speeds and other problems. Describe the tool and procedures you would use to test these cables.

CUSTOMER SERVICE

1. As chief of the customer service branch, you have been asked to procure some basic tools for your help-desk technicians. Describe some of the common tools that these toolkits should contain.
2. Several of your technicians have reported a serious slowdown in network response. Their initial troubleshooting efforts have been unproductive, so the problem has been passed on to you. While working on the problem, you have noticed that the collision light on various computers stays on almost constantly. A check of network traffic with a network monitor has disclosed an extraordinary amount

of traffic on the network. What does this information suggest and how would you correct it?

FOR MORE INFORMATION

For links to Web sites that provide further information about the topics covered in this chapter, go to the EMC/Paradigm Internet Resource Center at www.emcp.com/College Division/Internet Resource Centers/Networking/System Administration/Web Resources: For More Information.

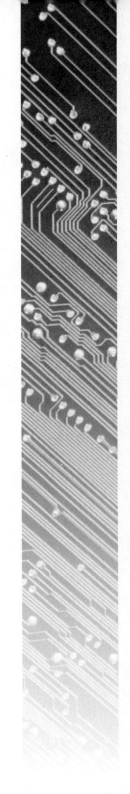

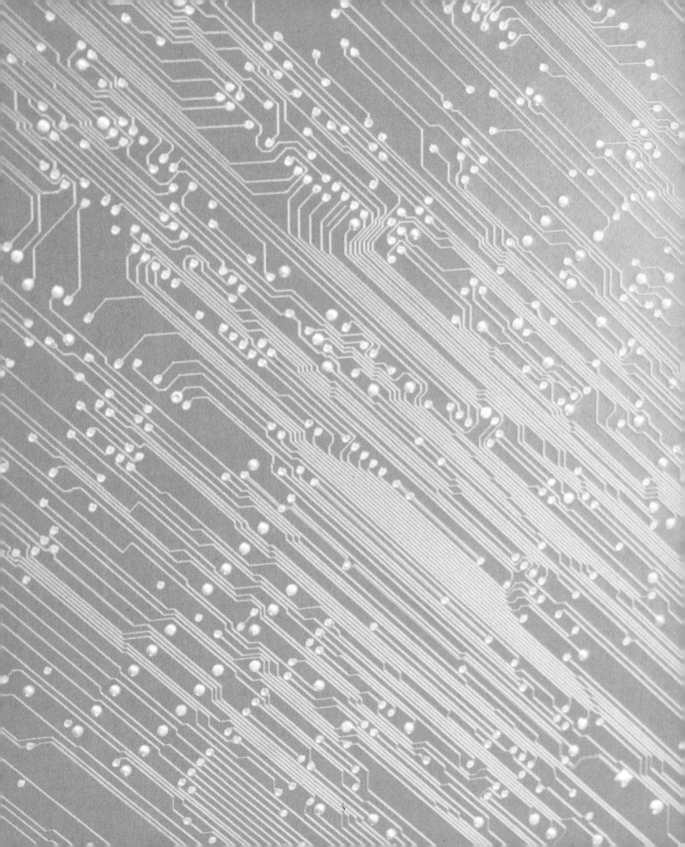

Troubleshooting Network Problems Using TCP/IP Utilities

19

ON THE TEST

Network+ Examination

- **Objective 4.1:** Given a troubleshooting scenario, select the appropriate TCP/IP utility from among the following:
  - Tracert
  - PING
  - ARP
  - Netstat
  - Nbtstat
  - IPCONFIG/IFCONFIG
  - Winipcfg
  - Nslookup
- **Objective 4.7:** Given output from a domestic utlity (e.g., tracert, PING, IPCONFIG, etc.), identify the utility and interpret the output.

ON THE JOB

Although it is known for being unfriendly to users, TCP/IP is also the protocol most often used on modern networks. Therefore, not only do you need to understand how to install and configure TCP/IP, but also you must understand the tools available to troubleshoot the problems that are bound to occur. Fortunately, the TCP/IP suite contains many tools, both command-line and graphic, to help you troubleshoot problems as they surface. The purpose of this chapter is to acquaint you with the specific capabilities of these utilities, the many options that are available with each, and the situations in which you would most likely use them.

Traceroute (Tracert)

Traceroute (tracert)

A TCP/IP command-line diagnostic utility that is used to determine the route a packet uses to get to a destination.

Internet Control Message Protocol (ICMP)

A TCP/IP protocol that is used for message control and error reporting.

Traceroute (tracert) is a command-line diagnostic utility that is used to determine the route a packet uses to get to a destination. Tracert determines the route by sending *Internet Control Message Protocol (ICMP)* packets to the destination that you specify, either by IP address or DNS name. Each of these ICMP packets contains a Time-to-Live (TTL) value, which specifies how many hops a packet can travel. When the packet reaches a router, the router decrements the packet's TTL by at least one hop and then forwards the packet to the next device. If the TTL on a packet reaches zero before the packet reaches its destination, the receiving router will send an ICMP "time exceeded" message back to the originating computer.

Tracert sends the first ICMP packet with a TTL of one. When the first router receives the packet, it decrements the TTL value by one, to zero, and then sends a message back to the originating computer. The sending computer will then send an ICMP packet with a TTL value of two. This way, the packet will go to the first router, which decrements the TTL value to one and then forwards the packet to the next router in the path. When the next router receives the packet, it decrements the TTL value to zero and then generates a message to the sending computer. This process continues until the destination host is reached or the maximum TTL value has been reached. An example tracert session is depicted in Figure 19.1.

```
C:\WINNT\System32\cmd.exe                                    _|_|X|

C:\>tracert www.emcp.com

Tracing route to emcp.com [216.245.180.91]
over a maximum of 30 hops:

  1      6 ms      7 ms      7 ms   10.200.128.1
  2     11 ms      6 ms      7 ms   68.112.13.1
  3     36 ms      9 ms     13 ms   68.112.12.254
  4     15 ms     17 ms     22 ms   sl-gw11-kc-2-0.sprintlink.net [160.81.45.97]
  5     17 ms     18 ms     50 ms   sl-bb20-kc-14-1.sprintlink.net [144.232.23.61]
  6     17 ms     16 ms     18 ms   sl-gw9-kc-8-0.sprintlink.net [144.232.23.50]
  7     28 ms     29 ms     29 ms   sl-agili-1-0-0.sprintlink.net [144.232.215.134]

  8     29 ms     28 ms     32 ms   ag-si-s2-r2-vlan909.agiliti.net [216.245.174.51]

  9     29 ms     31 ms     47 ms   ahcnokfw006-vlan4.agiliti.net [216.245.166.138]

 10     35 ms     30 ms     28 ms   216.245.180.91

Trace complete.

C:\>_
```

FIGURE 19.1
Sample Tracert Session

In this particular example, notice the number of hops required to reach the destination, the time it took to reach the destination, and the identity of the routers that were contacted enroute.

USING TRACERT FOR TROUBLESHOOTING

Use tracert to determine where packet traffic is being stopped. Tracert can tell you if any routers are offline or are having configuration problems. It can also indicate that an incorrect IP address is being used or that a specific network does not exist. Tracert can also pinpoint bottlenecks in the network. For example, if you suspect that the connection provided to you by a certain Internet Service Provider is slow, run tracert to determine how many hops your data takes before it leaves the ISP.

─ TRY IT! ─

Use the tracert utility to trace packet traffic from your computer to another host.

1. Trace your traffic using an IP address.
2. Trace your packet traffic to a fully qualified domain name such as www.google.com.

TRACERT OPTION SWITCHES

Tracert has a number of options that are available by adding switches after the tracert command. By typing **tracert/?** at the command line, you can view the options shown in Figure 19.2.

- **Usage:** tracert [-d] [-h maximum_hops] [-j host-list] [-w timeout] target_name
- **-d:** Do not resolve IP addresses to host names.
- **-h maximum_hops:** Specifies the maximum number of hops to use while searching for the target host.
- **-j host-list:** Hosts may be separated by intermediate routers, also referred to as loose-source routing.
- **-w timeout:** The length of time in milliseconds that the sending host should wait for each reply.

FIGURE 19.2
Tracert Option Switches

PING

PING

A utility that tests whether TCP/IP is functioning correctly on a host computer and that checks connectivity between devices.

The *PING* utility is used to test whether TCP/IP protocol is functioning correctly on a host computer and to check connectivity between devices. Like tracert, PING uses the Internet Control Message Protocol (ICMP) echo function to send a packet through the network to another host. If there is a good connection between the hosts, a good return packet will be received.

PING can also report the number of router hops between the two computers and the amount of time it takes for a packet to make the complete trip. You can PING a host by DNS name or IP address. An example of a PING session is depicted in Figure 19.3.

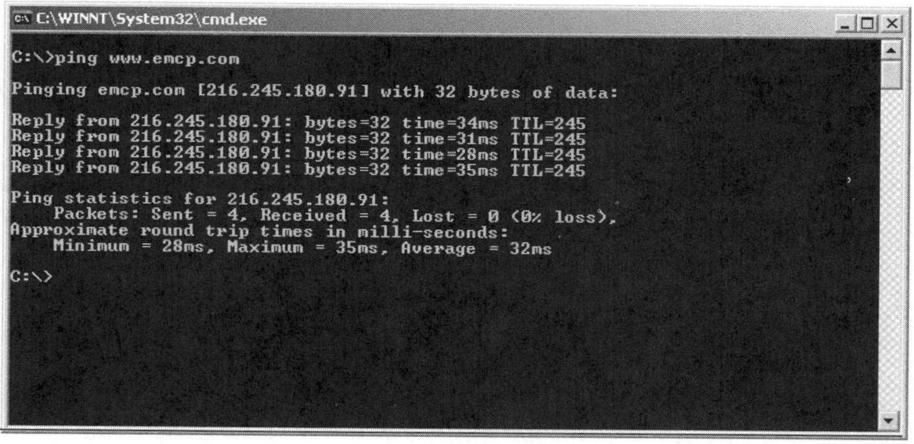

FIGURE 19.3
Sample PING Session

USING PING FOR TROUBLESHOOTING

PING can be used to test a local host or a connection to another host. When using PING to test network connectivity, always begin with the local computer, that is, the computer you are currently using. You can use either the machine's IP address or the local loopback address of 127.0.0.1. Once you determine that the local machine's IP address is functioning correctly, PING the default gateway. This will determine whether you have connectivity across your side of the network. Once you can successfully PING the default gateway, PING a host on the far side of the router—for example, you may choose to PING a host on another network segment within your own company or a popular Web site. By following a logical pattern and working away from the machine, you can easily locate the source of a network connectivity problem.

PING can also be used to test name resolution services. For example, if you can PING your favorite Web site by IP address but not by DNS name, the results indicate that the host is available across the network but that a problem exists with name resolution services.

PING OPTION SWITCHES

PING has a number of options that are available by adding switches to the PING command. By typing **ping/?** at the command line, you can view the options shown in Figure 19.4.

- **Usage:** ping [-t] [-a] [-n count] [-l size] [-f] [-i TTL] [-v TOS] [-r count] [-s count] [[-j host-list] | [-k host-list]] [-w timeout] target_name
- **-t:** PING the specified host until manually stopped.
  - ○ To see statistics and then continue - Ctrl-Break.
  - ○ To stop completely - Ctrl-C.
- **-a:** Resolve IP addresses to host names.
- **-n count:** Number of ICMP echo requests to send.
- **-l size:** Specifies the size of the Send buffer.
- **-f:** Sets the Don't Fragment flag in a packet.
- **-i TTL:** Specifies the Time to Live.
- **-v TOS:** Specifies the type of service.
- **-r count:** Records the route for count hops.
- **-s count:** Specifies a time stamp for count hops.
- **-j host-list:** Hosts may be separated by intermediate routers, also referred to as loose-source routing.
- **-k host-list:** Limit source route to specified host list.
- **-w timeout:** Specifies timeout value in milliseconds to wait for each reply.

FIGURE 19.4
PING Option Switches

Address Resolution Protocol (ARP)/Reverse Address Resolution Protocol (RARP)

Address Resolution Protocol (ARP) is a service protocol that is part of the TCP/IP suite of protocols. ARP queries the network segment by broadcasting an IP address. The response to this broadcast is the MAC address of the node holding the destination IP address. The node will respond if it is attached to the network and listening for broadcasts.

Reverse Address Resolution Protocol (RARP) is a utility protocol that allows the mapping of a MAC address (Data Link layer physical address) to an IP address (Network layer logical address).

To understand how ARP works, follow this example. Suppose Computer25, with an IP address of 200.200.200.25, wants to communicate with Computer50, which is located on the same network, with the IP address 200.200.200.50. Computer25 would follow these steps:

1. The source computer (Computer25) begins by checking its ARP cache to see if it already contains the destination computer's (Computer50's) MAC address.
2. If it does not, Computer25 will send a broadcast across the network. Included in this broadcast is the destination computer's IP address.
3. All computers on the network will see the broadcast and cross-reference the destination IP address with entries in their ARP cache.
4. If they do not have that address stored in their cache, they will discard the message.
5. If a computer receiving the broadcast finds the IP address in its cache, that computer will add the IP and MAC addresses of the sending computer (Computer25) to its ARP cache and then send a reply back to the sending computer. The reply will contain the MAC address of Computer50.

6. Computer25 will add the MAC address of Computer50 to its own ARP cache. Once the address is added, Computer25 can communicate with Computer50.

For a graphical depiction of the process, see Figure 19.5.

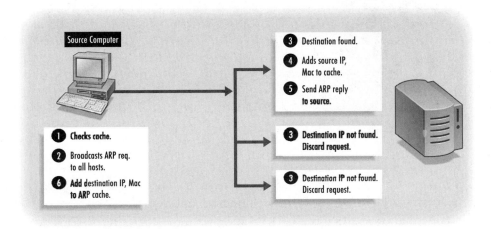

FIGURE 19.5
The ARP Process

When a computer wants to communicate with a computer on another network, the source computer uses the logical IP address to send a packet across the networks from router to router. When the packet gets to the router closest to the actual destination node, the router must ask the local segment to identify specifically which node is using that particular IP address. The ARP request is then broadcast over the local segment. The node holding the destination IP address replies to the broadcast by sending its MAC address to the router interface. Then the router can put the MAC address in the header of the packet and send the packet on its way to the destination.

Most operating systems allow the local node to cache ARP responses for a period of time. Figure 19.6 displays the contents of the local ARP cache.

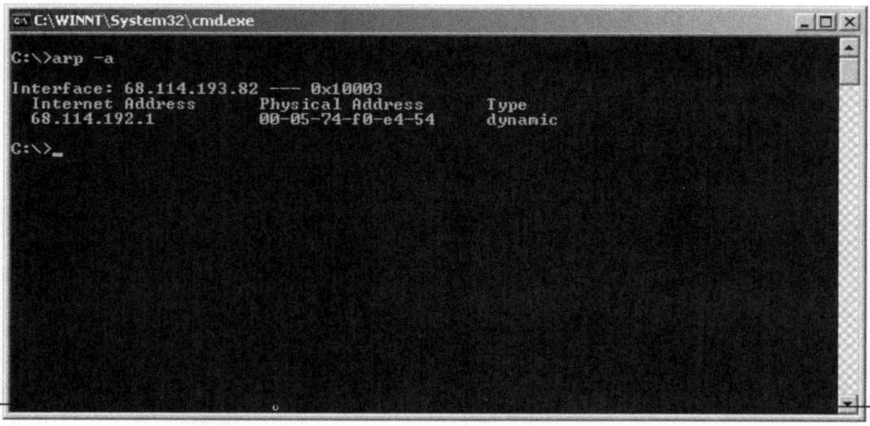

FIGURE 19.6
Contents of an ARP Cache

Reverse Address Resolution Protocol (RARP) does just the opposite. When a node's MAC address is known but its IP address is not, a RARP broadcast will be issued to the local segment requesting the IP address from the node that owns the specific MAC address. Some operating systems do not recognize RARP. Also, RARP is not run directly from the command line on most operating systems.

USING ARP FOR TROUBLESHOOTING

ARP is very useful in situations where more than one host machine has the same IP address. In this case, begin by using the PING utility to PING the IP address in question. You should receive a message that the echo-request message timed out. From a command prompt, display the ARP cache using the ARP -a command. The ARP cache will display a mapping of the IP and physical address of the problem machine.

ARP OPTION SWITCHES

ARP has a number of options that are available by adding switches to the ARP command. By typing **ARP/?** at the command line, you can view the options described in Figure 19.7.

- **Usage:** Displays and modifies the IP-to-physical address translation tables used by the Address Resolution Protocol (ARP).

   ARP -s inet_addr eth_addr [if_addr]
   ARP -d inet_addr [if_addr]
   ARP -a [inet_addr] [-N if_addr]

- **-a:** Displays ARP entries currently in the cache.

- **-g:** Same as -a.

- **inet_addr:** Specifies an Internet (IP) address.

- **-N if_addr:** Displays the ARP entries for the network interface specified by if_addr.

- **-d:** Deletes the host specified by inet_addr. You may use the * wildcard to delete all hosts.

- **-s:** Adds the host and associated Internet address to the ARP cache. The entry is permanent. To add an entry to the ARP cache, type the following line at a command prompt:

   C:>ARP -s   203.67.32.16   07-BF-00-F2-12-16

- **eth_addr:** Specifies the physical address of an Ethernet adapter.

- **if_addr:** Specifies the Internet address of the interface whose address translation table should be modified.

FIGURE 19.7
ARP Option Switches

— TRY IT! —

Use the ARP utility.

1. Display the ARP cache on your computer.
2. PING several other computers on your network.
3. View your ARP cache again.
4. Add a host and associated Internet address to the ARP cache.

Netstat

Netstat is used to display protocol statistics and current TCP/IP network connections. Netstat can also be used to view all of the TCP/IP connections in use by a host, whether they are inbound or outbound. When used with the -a switch, netstat will also display the port type, TCP or UDP, where the connection is being made on the local machine, the IP address of the connecting machine, and the current state of the connection. For an example, refer to Figure 19.8.

Netstat

A TCP/IP utility that displays protocol statistics and current TCP/IP network connections.

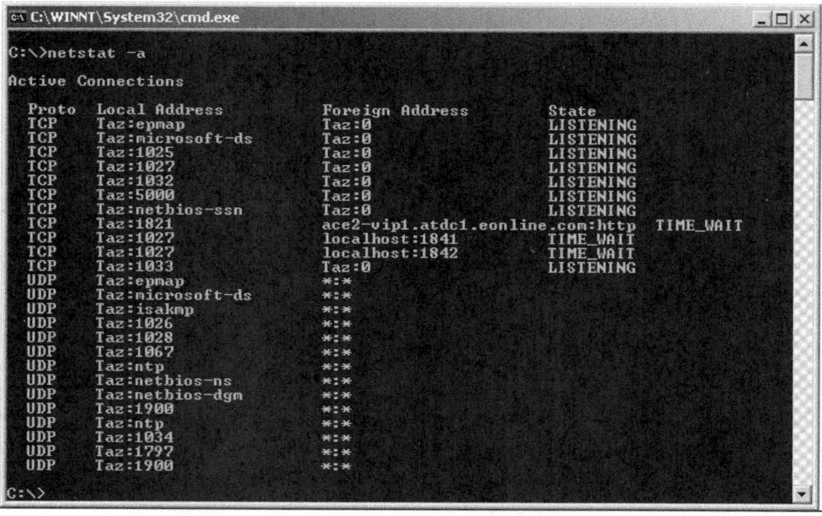

FIGURE 19.8
A Netstat Example

USING NETSTAT FOR TROUBLESHOOTING

Netstat can be extremely useful when troubleshooting network problems that you believe are protocol related. For example, if users report that they cannot transfer files from the corporate FTP server, try typing **netstat -a** at the server. The results screen will disclose whether the port for the FTP service is active. If it is not, you may need to either restart the FTP service or the server.

You may also use the netstat -r command to show the routing table that is maintained on the local machine (see Figure 19.9). Careful analysis of the routing table will disclose how network traffic is being routed when it leaves the local machine. This data could then be used to pinpoint network configuration errors.

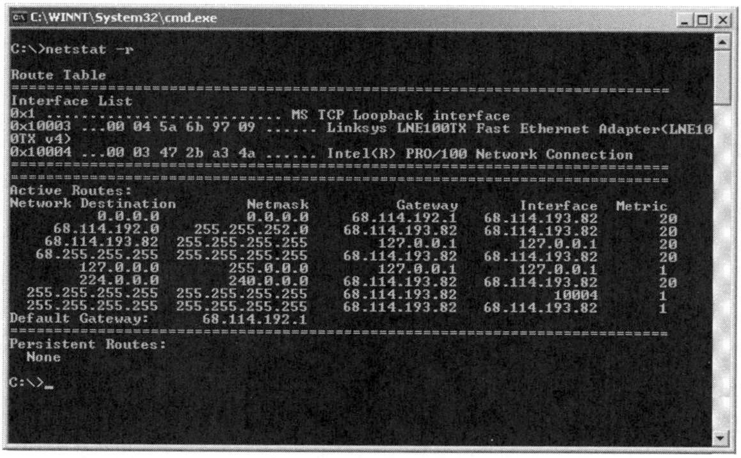

FIGURE 19.9
Sample Netstat Routing Table

Troubleshooting Network Problems Using TCP/IP Utilities

NETSTAT OPTION SWITCHES

Netstat has a number of options that are available by adding switches to the Netstat command. By typing **netstat/?** at the command line, you can view the options described in Figure 19.10.

- **Usage:** NETSTAT [-a] [-e] [-n] [-o] [-s] [-p proto] [-r] [interval]
- **-a:** Displays all connections and listening ports.
- **-e:** Displays Ethernet statistics. This may be combined with the -s option.
- **-n:** Displays addresses and port numbers in numerical form.
- **-o:** Displays the owning process ID associated with each connection.
- **-p proto:** Shows connections for the protocol specified by proto. Proto may be TCP, UDP, TCPv6, or UDPv6. If used with the -s option to display per-protocol statistics, proto may be IP, IPv6, ICMP, ICMPv6, TCP, TCPv6, UDP, or UDPv6.
- **-r:** Displays the routing table.
- **-s:** Displays per-protocol statistics. By default, statistics are shown for IP, IPv6, ICMP, ICMPv6, TCP, TCPv6, UDP, and UDPv6. The -p option may be used to specify a subset of the default.
- **Interval:** Redisplays selected statistics, pausing interval seconds between each display. Press Ctrl + C to stop redisplaying statistics. If omitted, netstat will print the current configuration information once.

FIGURE 19.10
Netstat Option Switches

TRY IT!

Use the netstat utility.
1. Display several ports for a server running FTP or Web services.
2. Show connections for a specified protocol.
3. Display the routing table of a computer or server.

Nbtstat

Nbtstat is used to display protocol statistics and current TCP/IP connections using NetBIOS over TCP/IP (NBT). It will also display current information stored in the NetBIOS cache. Since almost all Microsoft networks use NetBIOS, nbtstat can be used in a variety of troubleshooting situations.

Nbtstat

A TCP/IP utility that displays protocol statistics and current TCP/IP connections using NetBIOS over TCP/IP (NBT).

Using Nbtstat for Troubleshooting

With the -r switch, nbtstat can be used to determine if a Windows Internet Name Service (WINS) server is functioning correctly. After running the command, if all of the NetBIOS names on the network are being resolved by broadcasts, you will know that the WINS server is not functioning correctly and probably needs attention (see Figure 19.11).

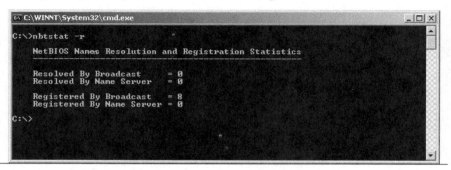

FIGURE 19.11
Using Nbtstat to Check Name Resolution Queries

Nbtstat Option Switches

Nbtstat has a number of options that are available by adding switches to the nbtstat command. By typing **nbtstat/?** at the command line, you can view the options described in Figure 19.12.

- **Usage:** NBTSTAT [[-a RemoteName] [-A IP address] [-c] [-n] [-r] [-R] [-RR] [-s] [-S] [interval]]
- **-a (Adapter status):** Lists a remote machine's name table. The machine name must be provided.
- **-A (Adapter status):** Lists a remote machine's name table. The machine's IP address must be supplied.
- **-c (cache):** Lists the contents of NBT's cache by machine names and IP addresses.
- **-n (names):** Lists local NetBIOS names.
- **-r (resolved):** Provides a list of names resolved by broadcast and WINS.
- **-R (Reload):** Empties and reloads the remote cache name table.
- **-S (Sessions):** Lists the sessions table by destination IP addresses.
- **-s (sessions):** Lists the sessions table and converts the destination IP addresses to the computer's NetBIOS names.
- **-RR (ReleaseRefresh):** Sends name release packets to WINS and then begins a refresh.
- **RemoteName:** Name of the remote host machine.
- **IP address:** Displays the IP address.
- **Interval:** Displays statistics, pausing at set intervals between each display. Press Ctrl+C to stop displaying statistics.

FIGURE 19.12
Nbstat Option Switches

━ **TRY IT!** ━━━━━━━━━━━━━━━

Use the nbtstat utility.

1. Display the name table of a remote computer or server.
2. Show the contents of your computer's NBT cache.
3. Obtain a list of names resolved by a WINS server.
4. Display the IP address of a remote machine.
5. Empty and reload the remote cache name table.

IP Configuration (IPCONFIG)

The *IPCONFIG (IP Configuration)* utility displays current IP configuration parameters for a host computer running certain types of Windows operating systems, such as Windows 98, Windows NT, Windows 2000, and Windows XP. Typing **IPCONFIG** at the command line will return details similar to those shown in Figure 19.13.

```
C:\IPCONFIG
Windows IP Configuration
Ethernet adapter Local Area Connection 2:

        Connection-specific DNS Suffix  . : kc.mo.ok.charter.net
        IP Address. . . . . . . . . . . . : 68.114.193.82
        Subnet Mask . . . . . . . . . . . : 255.255.252.0
        Default Gateway . . . . . . . . . : 68.114.192.1


Ethernet adapter Local Area Connection:
Media State . . . . . . . . . . . : Media disconnected
```

Running IPCONFIG with the /all switch will return complete IP configuration information, similar to that shown in Figure 19.14.

IPCONFIG (IP Configuration)

A TCP/IP utility that displays current IP configuration parameters for a host computer running certain types of Windows operating systems.

FIGURE 19.13
Configuration Details

```
C:\IPCONFIG /all
Windows IP Configuration

        Host Name . . . . . . . . . . . : Computer1
        Primary DNS Suffix  . . . . . . . :
        Node Type . . . . . . . . . . . . : Hybrid
        IP Routing Enabled. . . . . . . . : No
        WINS Proxy Enabled. . . . . . . . : No

Ethernet adapter Local Area Connection 2:
        Connection-specific DNS Suffix  . : stl.mo.nr.charter.net
        Description . . . . . . . . . . . : Linksys LNE100TX Fast Ethernet
                                            Adapter
        Physical Address. . . . . . . . . : 00-04-5A-6B-97-09
        Dhcp Enabled. . . . . . . . . . . : Yes
        Autoconfiguration Enabled . . . . : Yes
        IP Address. . . . . . . . . . . : 103.114.193.82
        Subnet Mask . . . . . . . . . . . : 255.255.252.0
        Default Gateway . . . . . . . . . : 103.114.192.1
        DHCP Server . . . . . . . . . . . : 103.112.12.37
        DNS Servers . . . . . . . . . . . : 103.112.12.36
                                            103.112.12.37
        Primary WINS Server . . . . . . . : 127.0.0.1
        Lease Obtained. . . . . . . . . . : Monday, October 14, 2002
                                            8:40:27 AM
        Lease Expires . . . . . . . . . . : Monday, October 21, 2002
                                            8:40:27 PM

Ethernet adapter Local Area Connection:

        Media State . . . . . . . . . . . : Media disconnected
        Description . . . . . . . . . . . : Intel(R) PRO/100 Network
Connection
        Physical Address. . . . . . . . . : 00-03-47-2B-A3-4A
```

USING IPCONFIG FOR TROUBLESHOOTING

Since the IPCONFIG utility shows all IP addressing information for a particular host, it is a great way to make sure that a host is configured correctly. For example, you can quickly check that you are using the correct subnet mask for the IP address you have chosen, or you can ensure that the default gateway for your subnet is correctly identified.

TESTTIP

IPCONFIG is used on host computers running Microsoft Windows 98, Windows NT, Windows 2000, and Windows XP.

IPCONFIG OPTION SWITCHES

IPCONFIG has a number of options that are available by adding switches to the IPCONFIG command. By typing **IPCONFIG/?** at the command line, you can view the options described in Figure 19.15.

- **Usage:** ipconfig [/? | /all | /renew [adapter] | /release [adapter] |
   /flushdns | /displaydns | /registerdns |
   /showclassid adapter |
   /setclassid adapter [classid]]
- "Adapter" is the Connection name. (Wildcard characters * and ? are allowed.)
- **/?:** Displays help.
- **/all:** Displays all IP configuration parameters.
- **/release:** When using DHCP, this switch releases the IP address for the adapter that you specify.
- **/renew:** When using DHCP, this switch renews the IP address for the adapter that you specify.
- **/flushdns:** Purges all the information located in the DNS resolver cache.
- **/registerdns:** Refreshes all DHCP lease information and re-registers DNS names.
- **/displaydns:** Displays the contents of the DNS resolver cache.
- **/showclassid:** Displays all the DHCP class IDs for the network adapter.
- **/setclassid:** Modifies the class ID for DHCP.

FIGURE 19.15
IPCONFIG Option Switches

By default, IPCONFIG will display only the IP address, subnet mask, and default gateway for each adapter that has the TCP/IP protocol bound to it. If no adapter name is specified when using the release and renew parameters, then the IP address leases for all adapters that have the TCP/IP protocol bound to them will be released or renewed.

WINIPCFG

WINIPCFG

A TCP/IP graphical utility displaying IP configuration information on Microsoft Windows 95 and 98 operating systems.

The *WINIPCFG* command is very similar to IPCONFIG, except WINPCFG returns a dialog box containing IP configuration information similar to that shown in Figure 19.16. To view additional information, click the More Info button and you will see a dialog box similar to that shown in Figure 19.17. You can then click buttons to release or renew DHCP-assigned IP addressing information. WINIPCFG is the IP configuration utility found on computers running the Windows 95 and 98 operating systems.

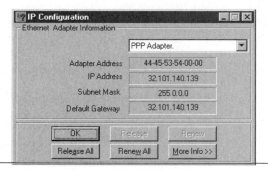

FIGURE 19.16
Typical WINIPCFG
Configuration Information

FIGURE 19.17
WINIPCFG Dialog Box after
Clicking the More Info Button

TEST TIP

WINIPCFG is used on host computers running Microsoft Windows 95 and Windows 98.

— TRY IT! —

Use WINIPCFG.

1. Display the basic IP address settings for your computer.
2. Display all IP addressing information for your computer.
3. Release DHCP assigned addressing parameters.
4. Renew IP addressing information from a DHCP server.

IFCONFIG

The *IFCONFIG* utility configures kernel-resident network interfaces in a UNIX environment. Running IFCONFIG without any switches will display the settings for all currently active network interfaces.

While IFCONFIG contains many option switches, only those most commonly used are listed in Figure 19.18.

- **interface:** Specifies the name of the active interface (usually the name of the network driver), followed by a number.
- **Up:** Activates the designated interface.
- **Down:** Shuts down an interface.
- **[-]ARP:** Allows you to enable or disable the ARP protocol on a specified interface.
- **[-]promisc:** Used to enable or disable promiscuous mode on an interface.
- **netmask addr:** Sets the IP network mask for the designated interface.
- **add addr/prefixlen:** Adds an IPv6 address to an interface.
- **del addr/prefixlen:** Deletes an IPv6 address from an interface.

FIGURE 19.18
IFCONFIG Option Switches

Nslookup

Nslookup is a program that allows you to directly query a DNS server by host name or IP address. For example, in Figure 19.19 the fully qualified domain name emcp.com was queried using nslookup. In this example, the DNS server that was specified on the computer running nslookup was not authoritative for the zone in which emcp.com is located. Therefore, it returned a nonauthoritative answer containing the name and the IP address.

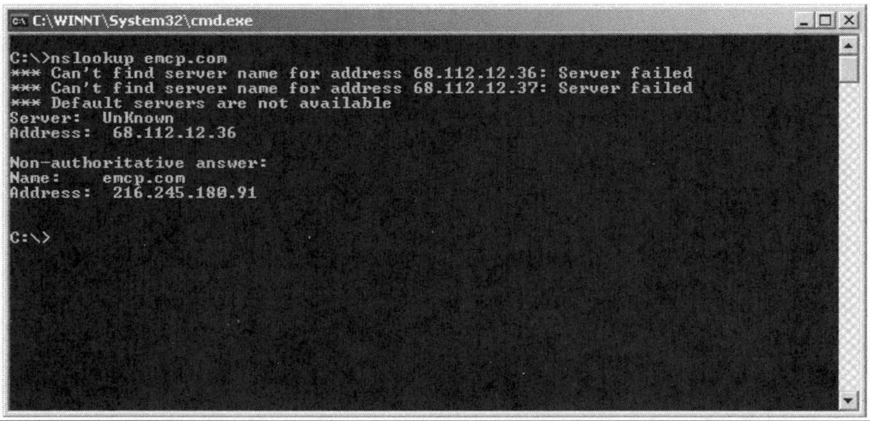

FIGURE 19.19
Using Nslookup by Host Name

Nslookup can also be used to locate a host name when the IP address is known. In the example in Figure 19.20, the IP address 64.58.79.230 was queried using nslookup. This query returned the host name of the Web server for Yahoo.com.

FIGURE 19.20
Using Nslookup by IP Address

NSLOOKUP MODES OF OPERATION

Interactive mode

A TCP/IP method that allows users to query name servers for information about various hosts and domains.

Nslookup operates in two different modes—interactive and noninteractive.

- *Interactive mode* allows the user to query name servers for information about various hosts and domains. This mode also allows you to specify additional parameters when using nslookup. Below, you will see the results of entering nslookup in interactive mode. Interactive mode is

Troubleshooting Network Problems Using TCP/IP Utilities

entered automatically when no arguments are given. You will know you are using interactive mode by looking at the command prompt. In this example it has changed from C:\> to >.

- C:\>nslookup
  *** Can't find server name for address 68.112.12.36: Server failed
  *** Can't find server name for address 68.112.12.37: Server failed
  *** Default servers are not available
  Default Server: UnKnown
  Address: 68.112.12.36

  >

  At the > prompt, you may type the extra commands shown in Figure 19.21.
- *Noninteractive (command-line) mode* is used to return just the name or other requested information for a host or domain. When using noninteractive mode, you supply the name or Internet address of the host as an argument. For example, in Figure 19.19, nslookup is followed by the host name. Once nslookup completes the query, it returns the user to a command prompt.

Noninteractive (command-line) mode

A TCP/IP method that returns just the name or other requested information for a host or domain.

NSLOOKUP OPTION SWITCHES

Nslookup has a number of options that are available in interactive mode. To view these options, type **help** at the interactive mode prompt. Some of the more common commands are listed in Figure 19.21.

- **>help:**
  Commands (identifiers are shown in uppercase, [] means optional):
- **NAME:** Prints information about the host/domain NAME using the default server.
- **NAME1 NAME2:** Same as the NAME command, but using NAME2 as the server.
- **set OPTION:** Used to set an option.
- **all:** Displays print options for the current server and host.
- **[no]debug:** Prints debugging information.
- **[no]d2:** Prints comprehensive debugging information.
- **[no]defname:** Appends the domain name to each query.
- **[no]recurse:** Asks for a recursive answer to each query.
- **[no]search:** Uses the domain search list.
- **[no]vc:** Specifies to always use a virtual circuit.
- **domain=NAME:** Used to set a default domain name.
- **root=NAME:** Used to set the root server.

FIGURE 19.21
Some Nslookup Option Switches in Interactive Mode

continued

- **retry=X:** Sets the number of retries to X.
- **timeout=X:** Sets the initial timeout interval to X seconds.
- **Type=X:** Sets the record query type (ex. A,ANY,CNAME,MX,NS,PTR,SOA,SRV).
- **class=X:** Sets the query class (ex. IN (Internet), ANY).
- **finger [USER]:** Uses the finger command to identify the user at the default host.
- **root:** Sets the current default server to the root.
- **ls [opt] DOMAIN [>FILE] – :** Lists addresses in DOMAIN (optional: redirects the output to FILE).
- **-a:** Lists canonical names and aliases.
- **-d:** Lists all records.
- **exit:** Exits the program.

FIGURE 19.21
continued

⌐ TRY IT! ⌐

Use nslookup to query a DNS server.

1. Select interactive mode.
2. Display help.
3. List addresses in the domain.
4. List all records of the NDS server.
5. Use finger to identify the default user at a host.

STUDY GUIDE

In this chapter, we discussed various utilities that can be used to troubleshoot TCP/IP-related problems. Here are some key points to remember.

TRACEROUTE (TRACERT)

- Traceroute (tracert) is a command-line diagnostic utility that determines the route a packet takes to get to a destination.
- Tracert determines the route by sending Internet Control Message Protocol (ICMP) packets to the destination that you specify, either by IP address or DNS name.

USING TRACERT FOR TROUBLESHOOTING

- Use tracert to determine where packet traffic is being stopped.
- Tracert can show whether any routers are offline or are having configuration problems.
- Tracert can indicate that an incorrect IP address is being used or that a specific network does not exist.
- Tracert can pinpoint bottlenecks on the network.

PING

- The PING utility tests whether the TCP/IP protocol is functioning correctly on a host computer and checks connectivity between devices.
- Like tracert, PING uses the Internet Control Message Protocol (ICMP) echo function to send a packet through the network to another host. If a good connection is established between the hosts, a good return packet will be received.
- PING can also report the number of router hops between the two computers and the amount of time it takes for a packet to make the complete trip.
- Using PING, you can try to connect to a host by DNS name or IP address.

USING PING FOR TROUBLESHOOTING

- PING can be used to test a local host or a connection to another host.

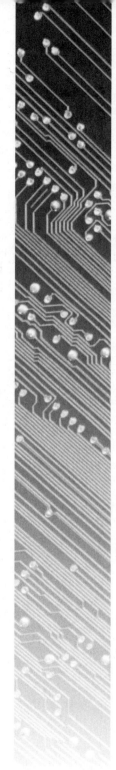

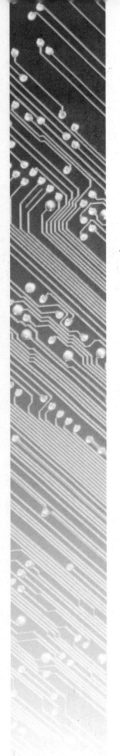

- Always begin by PINGing the local computer, that is, the computer you are currently using. You can PING the IP address or the local loopback address of 127.0.0.1.
- Once you determine that the local machine's IP address is functioning correctly, PING your default gateway. This will determine whether you have connectivity across your side of the network.
- Once you can successfully PING the default gateway, PING a host on the far side of the router. For example, you may choose a host on another network segment within your own company or a popular Web site.
- PING can also be used to test name resolution services.

ADDRESS RESOLUTION PROTOCOL (ARP)/REVERSE ADDRESS RESOLUTION PROTOCOL (RARP)

- Address Resolution Protocol (ARP) is used to resolve an IP address to the MAC (physical) address of a machine.
- Reverse Address Resolution Protocol (RARP) does just the opposite, resolving a MAC address to an IP address.
- To understand how ARP works, suppose Computer25, with an IP address of 200.200.200.25, wants to communicate with Computer50, which is located on the same network, with the IP address 200.200.200.50. Computer25 will follow these steps:
  - The source computer (Computer25) begins by checking its ARP cache to see if it already contains the destination computer's (Computer50's) MAC address.
  - If it does not, Computer25 will send a broadcast across the network. Included in this broadcast is the destination computer's IP address.
  - All computers on the network will see the broadcast and cross-reference the destination IP address with entries in their ARP cache.
  - If they do not have that address stored in their cache, they will discard the message.
  - If a computer receiving the broadcast finds the IP address in its cache, that computer will add the IP and MAC addresses of the sending computer (Computer25) to its ARP cache and then send a reply back to the sending computer. The reply will contain the MAC address of Computer50.
  - Computer25 will add the MAC address of Computer50 to its own ARP cache. Once the address is added, Computer25 can communicate with Computer50.

Using ARP for Troubleshooting

- ARP is very useful in situations where more than one host machine has the same IP address.

Netstat

- Netstat is used to display protocol statistics and current TCP/IP network connections.
- Netstat can also be used to view all of the TCP/IP connections used by a host, whether they are inbound or outbound.

Using Netstat for Troubleshooting

- Netstat can be extremely useful when troubleshooting network problems that you believe are protocol related. For example, if users report that they cannot transfer files from the corporate FTP server, at the server, type **netstat -a.** The results will disclose whether the port for the FTP service is active. If it is not, you may need to either restart the FTP service or the server.
- The netstat -r command shows the routing table that is maintained on the local machine.
- Careful analysis of the routing table will disclose how network traffic is being routed when it leaves the local machine. This data could then be used to pinpoint network configuration errors.

Nbtstat

- Nbtstat is used to display protocol statistics and current TCP/IP connections using NBT (NetBIOS over TCP/IP).
- It will also display current information stored in the NetBIOS cache. Since almost all Microsoft networks use NetBIOS, nbtstat can troubleshoot a variety of situations.

Using Nbtstat for Troubleshooting

- With the -r switch, nbtstat can be used to determine if a Windows Internet Name Service (WINS) server is functioning correctly.

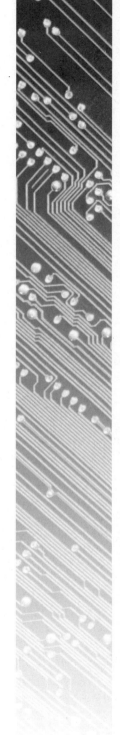

IP Configuration (IPCONFIG)

- The IP Configuration (IPCONFIG) utility is used to display current IP configuration parameters for a host computer running certain types of Windows operating systems, such as Windows 98, Windows NT, Windows 2000, and Windows XP.

Using IPCONFIG for Troubleshooting

- Since the IPCONFIG utility shows all IP addressing information for a particular host, it is a great way to make sure that a host is configured correctly.

WINIPCFG

- WINIPCFG returns a graphical box containing IP configuration information.
- You can then click buttons opting either to release or renew DHCP-assigned IP addressing information.
- WINIPCFG is the IP configuration utility found on computers running the Windows 95 and 98 operating systems.

IFCONFIG

- The IFCONFIG utility configures kernel-resident network interfaces in a UNIX environment.
- Running IFCONFIG without any switches will display the settings for all currently active network interfaces.

Nslookup

- Nslookup is a program that queries a DNS server by host name or IP address.

Nslookup Modes of Operation

- Interactive mode allows the user to query name servers for information about various hosts and domains.
- Interactive mode allows you to specify additional parameters when using nslookup.

- Interactive mode is entered automatically when no arguments are given.
- You will know you are using interactive mode by looking at the command prompt.
- Noninteractive (command-line) mode returns just the name or other requested information for a host or domain.
- With noninteractive mode, you supply the name or Internet address of the host as an argument.

PRACTICE TEST

Try this test to check your mastery of the concepts in this chapter.

1. Which of the following utilities would you use to follow the path your data takes from one host to another?
   a. PING
   b. netstat
   c. nbtstat
   d. tracert

2. You would like to PING a workstation continually until it is manually interrupted. Which of the following commands would you type at the command prompt?
   a. PING -r
   b. PING -s
   c. PING -t
   d. PING -w

3. What type of packet does tracert use?
   a. ICMP
   b. POP
   c. UDP
   d. TCP/IP

4. PING can be used to contact which of the following objects?
   a. MAC address
   b. DNS name
   c. IP address
   d. WINS name

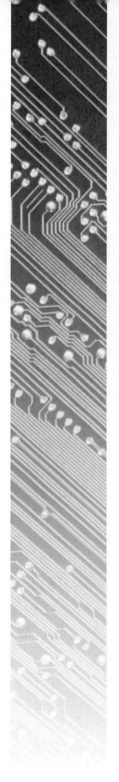

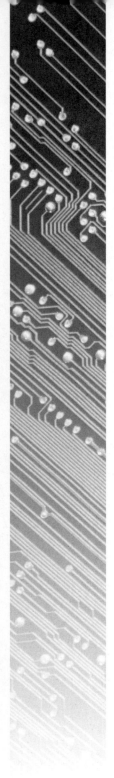

5. Several users have reported problems connecting to Web pages on the Internet. During troubleshooting, you find that you can PING Web sites by IP address but not by name. Which of the following is the most likely problem?
   a. The WINS server is not functioning correctly.
   b. The DNS server is not working correctly.
   c. The DHCP server is not working correctly.
   d. The Web server needs to be rebooted.

6. Which of the following troubleshooting commands is not run from the command line?
   a. PING
   b. tracert
   c. ARP
   d. RARP

7. Which of the following commands is useful in identifying machines with duplicate IP addresses?
   a. PING
   b. ARP
   c. RARP
   d. netstat

8. One of your technicians installed a network interface card in a workstation but cannot now remember which workstation. You have the MAC address of the network interface card and could locate the machine if you knew the IP address. Which of the following utilities would be useful to you in this situation?
   a. RARP
   b. ARP
   c. PING
   d. nbtstat

9. Which of the following commands would you type to display current entries in the ARP cache?
   a. ARP -c
   b. RARP -c
   c. ARP -a
   d. RARP -a

10. You are troubleshooting an IP connectivity problem and would like to PING the protocol stack on a workstation. Which of the following commands could you type at a command prompt to PING the local machine?
    a. PING 127.0.0.0
    b. PING 127.1.0.0
    c. PING 127.0.1.0
    d. PING 127.0.0.1

11. Several users have reported problems retrieving their e-mail from the corporate e-mail server. While troubleshooting the problem, you find that you can PING the server but are unable to access the e-mail service. Which of the following utilities would help you determine if the e-mail service is running?
    a. netstat -b
    b. netstat -a
    c. nbtstat -a
    d. nbtstat -b

12. Which of the following commands can be used to view the routing table on the local machine?
    a. netstat -r
    b. PING -r
    c. tracert -r
    d. nbtstat -r

13. Which of the following commands provides a list of names resolved by broadcast and WINS?
    a. netstat -r
    b. PING -r
    c. tracert -r
    d. nbtstat -r

14. What command would you type at a command prompt to view the TCP/IP configuration on a computer running the Windows 95 operating system?
    a. IPCONFIG
    b. IFCONFIG
    c. IPHELP
    d. WINIPCFG

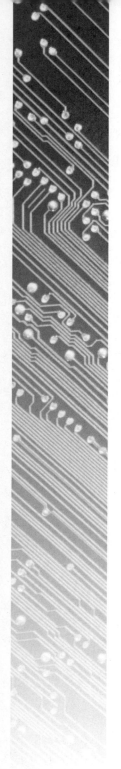

15. Which of the following commands would you type at the command prompt on a computer running the Windows XP operating system in order to see the IP address of your DHCP server?
    a. IPCONFIG
    b. IPCONFIG/DHCP
    c. IPCONFIG/all

16. Which of the following commands can be used to activate a network interface on a machine running the UNIX operating system?
    a. IFCONFIG
    b. IFCONFIG/all
    c. IFCONFIG/act
    d. IFCONFIG/Up

17. You are running nslookup on a machine with the Windows XP Professional operating system. How can you tell which mode you are running in?
    a. The command prompt changes.
    b. The background screen turns blue.
    c. You are prompted for a user name.
    d. You are prompted for a password.

18. You would like to run several commands with a series of switches using nslookup. Which mode should you use?
    a. online
    b. command-line
    c. interactive
    d. noninteractive

19. Which of the following switches, when used with nslookup, will list all addresses in a specified domain?
    a. Dir
    b. Ls
    c. Dom
    d. Show

20. Which command-line switch can be used with most utilities to display help topics and syntax?
    a. /Help
    b. F3
    c. F1
    d. /?

TROUBLESHOOTING

1. Over the past week, a network user has reported several problems connecting to other computers, Web sites, and the company mail server. Based on these reports, you suspect a problem with the user's TCP/IP connectivity. Explain the steps that you would follow to troubleshoot this possible connectivity problem.

2. You suspect that one of the WINS servers on your local area network is not responding to name queries. Identify the tool that would be used to test your theory and describe the steps that would be required.

CUSTOMER SERVICE

1. You have spent several days tracing and identifying network problems using the tracert utility. After you report your findings, your manager has asked you to brief your coworkers on the tracert process. How would you explain the processes that tracert uses to identify the path data takes?

2. You have been asked to obtain information from your corporate DNS server. Specifically, your manager has asked you to obtain one list of all hosts and another list containing each host with an alias. Also, the domain name must be appended to each query. You may also be required to specify timeout periods during your queries. Identify the utility you would use and describe the specific steps that would be required to accomplish this task.

FOR MORE INFORMATION

For links to Web sites that provide further information about the topics covered in this chapter, go to the EMC/Paradigm Internet Resource Center at www.emcp.com/College Division/Internet Resource Centers/Networking/System Administration/Web Resources: For More Information.

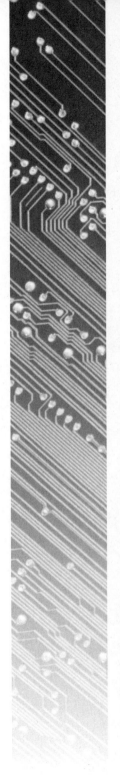

Troubleshooting Small Office/Home Office Network Failures

ON THE TEST

Network+ Examination
- **Objective 4.2:** Given a troubleshooting scenario involving a small office/home office network failure (e.g., xDSL, cable, home satellite, wireless, POTS), identify the cause of the failure.

ON THE JOB

Many of the technologies discussed in this chapter are new or different from those you have worked with in the past. Keep in mind, however, that we are still talking about networking, and many of the troubleshooting skills you have learned up to this point still apply. For example, almost all of these technologies use a cable of some sort. A standard media tester can be used to test these cables and other Physical layer components. DSL, cable, and satellite networking generally use network interface cards. Therefore, hardware and software troubleshooting steps for NICs still apply. Keep the structured troubleshooting strategy in mind. Always begin by determining the scope of the problem, even when working on a small network.

Small Office/Home Office (SOHO) Environments

Small office/home office, or *SOHO,* as it is more commonly known, is a term that has been coined in the past few years and was spawned largely by network users who were telecommuting, or working out of their homes. In

SOHO

An acronym for small office/home office.

the SOHO environment, many users connect to some type of network remotely. That is, they are not connected directly to the network. Instead, they connect indirectly, or on demand. For example, a user might have a modem dial into a remote access server (see Figure 20.1). Once authenticated, the user may or may not be required to log on a second time through the appropriate network client, that is, the Client for NetWare Networks or the Microsoft Client for Microsoft Networks. Once users are authenticated, they have access to network resources, just like any other network client.

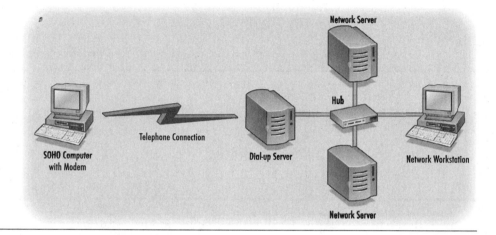

FIGURE 20.1
SOHO Workstation Using a Dial-Up Connection to a Remote Access Server

In a small office environment, users may have a small peer-to-peer or client-server network setup. They may or may not need access to anything outside of their own network other than the Internet. Users of a small office network commonly access the Internet through a shared connection, such as a DSL line using Internet Connection Sharing (ICS) (see Figure 20.2). ICS is a service available in several Microsoft operating systems that allows some of the functions of Network Address Translation. By enabling ICS, a small office or a home office can achieve Internet connectivity while still using private addressing. The ICS service is nonconfigurable and therefore its use is limited.

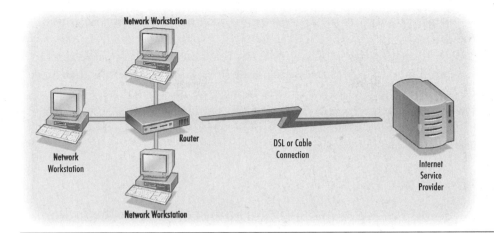

FIGURE 20.2
Small Office Network
Connecting to the Internet
via Internet Service
Provider

Standard networking rules apply to the SOHO environment. This means that the client computers must have some type of network adapter (commonly a network interface card or modem), and the adapter must be attached to the appropriate client, which in turn is running the appropriate protocol. Therefore, when you start troubleshooting connectivity problems, most of the basic network troubleshooting rules still apply.

To troubleshoot beyond the client workstation, network media, and network hardware, you will need an understanding of the various technologies used to make the outside connection, including DSL, cable, satellite, and so on. Each section in this chapter begins with a discussion of a particular technology. After that, specific troubleshooting methods for that technology will be discussed.

TestTip

Understand the benefits and drawbacks of each technology. For example, to use DSL you must be within a certain distance from the central telephone office. Distance is not a limitation with cable connections.

Digital Subscriber Line (DSL)

Digital Subscriber Line (DSL) is a broadband technology that makes use of unused frequencies on normal telephone lines to transmit data at varying speeds, depending on the type of DSL being used. Often, you will see DSL

Digital Subscriber Line (DSL)

A device that uses higher POTS frequencies than a traditional modem to provide faster data transfer speeds.

services referred to as xDSL. The "x" denotes the various types of DSL, such as ADSL, VDSL, SDSL, and so on. Each of these is defined later in this chapter.

One of the primary benefits of DSL is that voice and data traffic can be sent simultaneously over the same phone line. Another benefit is that users do not have to dial in to an ISP before they can use the service. DSL is always on; therefore, a connection is always available while working on a client workstation. There are two primary types of DSL service—asymmetric and symmetric.

Asymmetric DSL

Residential DSL uses a type of DSL called *asymmetric DSL (ADSL)*, which uses its own phone line to send and receive data traffic. The connection is asymmetric because the data sent from your computer—called uploading, or *upstream*, data—travels at a different speed from the data sent to your computer—called downloading, or *downstream*, data. For home users, ADSL is normally optimized for faster downloading than uploading. Several different types of ADSL are available, as shown in Figure 20.3.

- **Full-rate:** Offers speeds up to 6 Mbps. Voice and data are sent simultaneously over an existing telephone line. Full rate is the most common type of ADSL, used by both businesses and residential customers.
- **G.lite:** Targeted specifically for home Internet users. G.lite supports speeds up to 1.5 Mbps downstream and up to 500 Kbps upstream.
- **Rate-adaptive (RADSL):** A nonstandard version of ADSL.
- **Very-high-bit-rate (VDSL):** Supports data transfer speeds up to 26 Mbps over short distances, usually not more than 50 meters. These connections are normally short *loops*, such as neighborhood telephone cabinets that are connected to a central office using fiber-optic cable. VDSL can also be configured to transfer data symmetrically. In some markets, VDSL is being tested for videoconferencing.

Asymmetric DSL (ADSL)

A DSL connection in which data sent from a computer travels at a different speed from data sent to a computer.

Upstream

Sending, or uploading; used to describe data being sent from a computer.

Downstream

Receiving, or downloading; used to describe data being sent to a computer.

Loop

In communications, a telephone line that runs between a building and the local telephone-switching center; also called a local loop.

FIGURE 20.3
Types of ADSL

TestTip

Full-rate ADSL is the type of DSL most commonly used by business and residential customers.

In Real Life

The loop is the twisted pair telephone line that runs between your house and the local telephone-switching center. Since this telephone service uses twisted pair cable, imagine one phone line running to your house and one traveling back to the local switching center, acting as a big loop of wire. Hence, the name local loop.

Symmetric DSL

Symmetric DSL usually requires its own dedicated phone line and allows uploads and downloads to travel at the same speed. Since symmetric DSL uses a dedicated phone line, it is ideal for Web sites that host videoconferencing. Several different types of symmetric DSL are available, as shown in Figure 20.4.

Symmetric DSL

A DSL line that usually requires its own dedicated telephone line and that allows uploads and downloads to travel at the same speed.

- **Symmetric DSL (SDSL):** A proprietary version of DSL that supports data transfer speeds from 128 Kbps to 2.32 Mbps. SDSL is a generic term for a number of supplier-specific implementations that use a single copper wire pair to support variable transfer rates of symmetric service.
- **Symmetric high-bit-rate DSL (SHDSL):** An industry standard that achieves 20 percent longer line reach than older versions of symmetric DSL. SHDSL supports data transfer speeds ranging from 192 Kbps to 2.3 Mbps and with less crosstalk between cable pairs. One pair of wires may be used for short loops, while two wire pairs may be used for longer loops. SHDSL is designed specifically for data transfers that need fast uploading speeds. For that reason, SHDSL is aimed primarily at business customers.
- **High-data-rate DSL (HDSL):** Service that supports speeds up to 2.3 Mbps. HDSL is available at both 1.5 and 2.3 Mbps and uses one, two, or three pairs of twisted copper wire. The newer generation of HDSL is HDSL2, which requires only one wire pair.
- **2nd generation HDSL (HDSL2):** Provides a speed of 1.5 Mbps and supports voice, data, and video using either asynchronous transfer mode (ATM) or frame relay over a single copper wire pair. HDSL2 does not provide voice telephone service on the same wire pair, but it requires only one wire pair to support data transfer.
- **Integrated Services Digital Network DSL (IDSL):** Supports data transfer rates up to 144 Kbps using standard telephone lines. IDSL has the ability to deliver services through a digital loop carrier (DLC), which is a device often placed in newer telephone cabinets. The DLC is designed to simplify the distribution of cable and wiring for the phone company. ADSL and its G.lite variation are implemented directly into these DLCs. IDSL differs from Integrated Services Digital Network (ISDN) in that it is always on. IDSL can use the same terminal adapter, or modem, that is used for ISDN.

FIGURE 20.4
Types of Symmetric DSL

Keep in mind that DSL is not available in all areas because of distance limitations. To obtain DSL service, you must be within a specific distance from the central telephone office. Furthermore, these distances will determine the speed of your data connection. Table 20.1 provides a quick reference for DSL services and maximum distances.

DSL Type	Distance (in feet)	Maximum Data Speed
IDSL	18,000	0.160 Mbps
SDSL	12,000	0.784 Mbps
HDSL	12,000	1.544 Mbps
ADSL	18,000	9.0 Mbps
VDSL	4,500	52.80 Mbps

TABLE 20.1
DSL Speeds and Maximum Distances

TRY IT!

Contact the local phone company to inquire about DSL availability and rate plans.

CONNECTING TO DSL

After obtaining the necessary service from your provider, you will need to establish the physical connection. The connection from a personal computer to DSL is fairly straightforward. First, you will need to install a network interface card in the computer. After the card is installed, start the computer and install the appropriate driver when prompted. Following the directions from your DSL provider, you will also need to install and configure a client and the necessary protocols, normally a Microsoft Client for Microsoft Networks and TCP/IP.

An Ethernet cable will then be connected from the back of the network interface card into a DSL modem or router. A standard telephone cable is connected at the modem or router on one end and into a standard telephone wall jack on the other, completing the connection.

TRY IT!

Connect and configure a computer for Internet access using DSL.

TROUBLESHOOTING AN ESTABLISHED DSL CONNECTION

If your DSL connection was working correctly and then suddenly stopped, begin by conducting some simple checks of the DSL modem or router. Although features vary from brand to brand and model to model, most

DSL hardware contains an array of lights that will give you an idea whether the problem is with the DSL line, the equipment, or the computer. Some of the status lights that are common on most DSL hardware are described in Figure 20.5.

- **Power:** Indicates whether the device is on or off. Try to recycle the power on the device. In most cases you can simply unplug the power cable, wait a few seconds, and plug it back in.
- **Sync, Ready, or DSL:** Indicates whether your device is able to detect a DSL-conditioned phone line. A red or flashing red light indicates a problem with the phone line, which would probably need to be resolved by the phone company.
- **Activity:** Glows whenever information is being exchanged. It will light up when information is being passed through the device. When operating normally, the light should be flashing green. If the light is not flashing, you must determine if the failure is from the phone line, the equipment, or the computer.
- **TX and RX:** If the light is labeled TX, it stands for transmitting or transmission. If it is labeled RX, it means receiving. When operating normally, the lights should be flashing green. If the TX light is not glowing or is red, the problem most likely exists with the computer, the DSL hardware, or the Ethernet connection between the two. If the RX light is not lit or is red, the problem is most likely with either the phone line or the DSL hardware.
- **Ethernet:** Indicates that the DSL hardware detects an Ethernet connection with your computer. If the light is red or is not lit, check the cable that makes the connection with your network interface card. Also, check to ensure the network card is properly installed and configured.

FIGURE 20.5
Common Status Lights on DSL Hardware

When checking the status of the network interface card, begin by checking the link and collision lights. If they are operating correctly, check, and replace if necessary, the Ethernet cable between the network card and the DSL modem or router. If the lights are not lit, follow these steps to check the Device Manager utility to ensure that the network interface card is configured correctly:

1. On a computer running the Windows XP Professional operating system, click the Start button.
2. When the Start menu appears, select Control Panel. From the Control Panel, select System.
3. When the System Properties dialog box appears, click the Hardware tab. On the Hardware tab, click the Device Manager button. A dialog box similar to Figure 20.6 should appear.

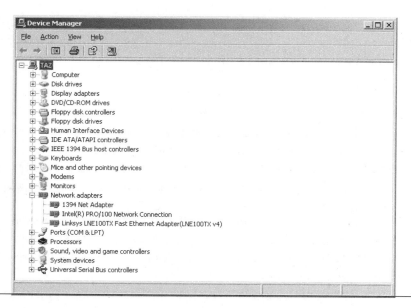

FIGURE 20.6
Windows XP Professional
Device Manager

4. In the Device Manager, locate the section for network adapters. Click it to expand it and display the individual network adapters.

5. Locate the installed network adapter. If the icon for the adapter is a yellow circle with an exclamation point, this indicates a problem with the adapter. If the icon has a red "X" on it, that indicates the adapter is disabled. To obtain more information about a problem device, double-click it. A properties dialog box similar to that in Figure 20.7 will appear.

FIGURE 20.7
Network Adapter Properties

Troubleshooting Small Office/Home Office Network Failures

6. Check the status of the adapter to ensure that it is functioning correctly. If it is not, click the Troubleshoot button to begin the troubleshooting process.

If the troubleshooter cannot identify and correct the problem, try physically reseating the adapter or reinstalling the driver. If neither of these works, replace the adapter.

Finally, check the telephone wiring at your home or office. The easiest way to do this is to unplug the DSL adapter and plug a phone into the jack. Pick up the receiver and listen for a dial tone. If you do not hear the tone, take the phone outside of the building to the connection box, or wherever the external telephone wiring connects to the building's internal phone service. Open the box and locate the RJ-11 jack. Plug the phone into that jack and listen for a dial tone. If an RJ-11 jack is not available, you will need a handset with alligator clips to conduct the next test. Attach the alligator clips to the metal connectors to which the internal phone line is attached. If a tone exists, a problem exists with the internal wiring. If you still cannot hear a tone, the problem is with the external wiring. In that case you will need to contact the telephone company.

TROUBLESHOOTING A NEW DSL CONNECTION

Many of the steps that were identified above can be used to troubleshoot a new connection. With a new connection, always suspect that some configuration parameter is incorrect. If checks of those parameters disclose that everything is correct, the DSL hardware is always a good place to check. Begin by checking the lights, since they often point you to where the problem lies. Also, always make sure the phone company has accomplished the work that is necessary or all of your troubleshooting efforts will be for nothing.

Cable

A cable connection works with the cable television service that runs into your home. The service is provided by your local cable television provider and, like DSL, may or may not be available in all areas.

The installation of cable service is fairly straightforward. First, the incoming television cable is cut and connected to one side of a *splitter* (see Figure 20.8). Normally, it will be connected to a port marked "In."

Splitter

A small hardware device that converts one incoming television cable line into multiple outgoing lines.

The end of the cable going to the television will be connected to an "Out" port, which restores the original connection. Next, a new piece of cable will be connected to another "Out" port. The other end of the new cable will be connected to a cable modem (see Figure 20.9). Make sure that no devices are placed between the cable splitter and the cable modem. The signal from the cable modem is very strong; if a television is connected in the path between the modem and the splitter, the signal to the television would be disturbed. Finally, the cable modem will be connected to a network interface card in a computer.

FIGURE 20.8
Cable Splitter

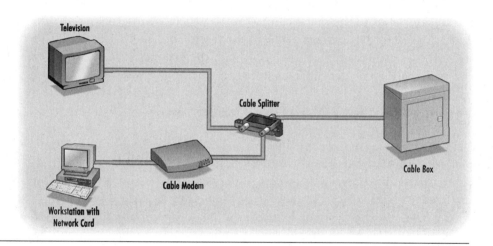

FIGURE 20.9
Typical Cable Modem Setup

A cable modem is different from a standard modem, although it still modulates and demodulates signals. Cable modems perform more functions than a standard phone line modem, including routing and tuning of the signal. An Ethernet cable attaches the cable modem to a network interface card that is installed inside the workstation.

A benefit of cable service is that users do not have to dial in to an ISP before they can use the service. Cable is always on; therefore, a connection is always available while working on a client workstation.

Cable modem speeds vary by service and direction of data traffic. Upstream data travels from your computer to another destination. Downstream data is transmitted to your computer. Currently, cable modem speeds for downstream traffic typically top out at about 1.5 Mbps, with actual performance in the range of 1.0 to 1.5 Mbps. Upstream speeds generally top out between 128 and 256 Kbps. The upstream and downstream speeds for your implementation will vary based on the package that you purchase. Most cable providers offer several different packages with different speeds. As the speed increases, the price of the package goes up. You may also be required to pay an installation fee or purchase equipment, such as the cable modem or a network interface card. An Internet search of cable service providers can disclose a range of available plans. Some typical offerings are depicted in Table 20.2.

Plan	Downstream Speed	Upstream Speed	Monthly Price
Plan 1	256 Kbps	128 Kbps	$34.95
Plan 2	768 Kbps	128 Kbps	$42.95
Plan 3	1.5 Mbps	128 Kbps	$59.95

TABLE 20.2
Typical Cable Service Plans

TRY IT!

Contact your local cable company to inquire about cable availability and rate plans.

One advantage of cable over DSL is that cable is not subject to the distance limitations of DSL. The distance capability for cable is virtually unlimited.

IN REAL LIFE

Debate continues about which is better, cable or DSL. In truth, "best" is defined by what is available at your location and which is the most reliable. While cable has a higher overall bandwidth, the connection is shared with other cable users in your neighborhood, so your actual performance may be lower than advertised, or it may fluctuate depending on time of day. Although cable can provide better throughput, DSL generally supplies a more constant data stream and *latency* is lower.

Latency

The delay, or amount of time, it takes for a data packet to get from one point to another.

TRY IT!

Connect and configure a computer for Internet access using cable.

TROUBLESHOOTING AN ESTABLISHED CABLE CONNECTION

If your cable connection was working correctly and suddenly stopped, begin by conducting some simple checks of the cable modem. Although features vary from brand to brand and model to model, most cable modems include an array of lights that will give you an idea whether the problem is with the cable line, the equipment, or the computer. Some of the status lights that are common on most cable hardware are described in Figure 20.10.

- **Power:** Indicates whether the cable modem is on or off. Try to recycle the power on the device. In most cases you can simply unplug the power cable, wait a few seconds, and plug it back in.
- **Cable (may also be labeled Status or Error):** Indicates whether the modem has a good connection to the service provider.
- **Data, Active, Activity, or Cable Activity:** Indicates whether the modem is receiving information from the computer. When operating normally, the light should be flashing green. If the light is not flashing, you must determine if the failure is from the cable line, the equipment, or the computer.
- **RD (Receive) and TD (Transmit):** If the light is labeled TD, it stands for transmitting or transmission. If it is labeled RD, it means receiving. When operating normally, the lights should be flashing green. If the TD light is not glowing or is red, the problem most likely exists with the computer, the cable hardware, or the Ethernet connection between the two. If the RD light is not lit or is red, the problem is most likely with either the cable line or the hardware.
- **Test:** Indicates when a self-test is being performed. If the light remains lit, the cable modem has failed the self-test. If a modem fails the test, try recycling the power to reset the modem. If the problem still is not fixed, trying replacing the modem.

FIGURE 20.10
Common Status Lights on Cable Hardware

When checking the status of the network interface card, begin by checking the link and collision lights. If they are operating correctly, check (and replace if necessary) the Ethernet cable between the network interface card and the modem. If the lights still are not lit, follow the steps that were outlined in the DSL troubleshooting section for checking the Device Manager utility to ensure that the network interface card is configured correctly.

Finally, check the cable wiring at your home or office. Unfortunately, this is not as simple as checking a telephone line. While you might try plugging another device into the line, realistically, all you can test is the wiring inside your home or office building. Always make sure that all connections are secure. If none of your cable devices work, suspect the external line. If only one of several devices is experiencing a problem, either use a cable tester to check the cable on the nonworking device or just replace the cable with a cable that you know is working. If the cables are good and the problem still exists, try replacing the splitter, although these items seldom fail. If all of the internal components appear to be working, you will need to contact the cable company.

TROUBLESHOOTING A NEW CABLE CONNECTION

Many of the steps that were identified above can be used to troubleshoot a new connection. With a new connection always suspect that some configuration parameter is incorrect. If checks of those parameters disclose that everything is correct, the cable hardware is always a good place to check. Begin by checking the lights on the network interface card and modem, since they will likely point you to where the problem lies. Also, always make sure the cable company has completed the work that is necessary, or all of your troubleshooting efforts will be for nothing.

Home Satellite

Satellite communication systems send and receive signals between Earth-based stations and geosynchronous space satellites (see Figure 20.11).

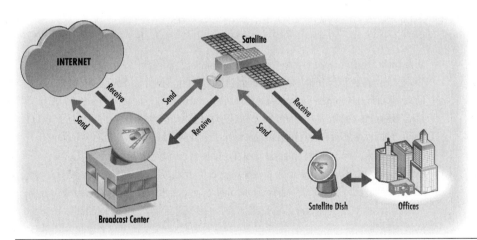

Satellite communication system

A system that sends and receives signals between Earth-based stations and geosynchronous space satellites, then transmits them to home- or office-based receiving satellite dishes.

FIGURE 20.11
Satellite Networking

Broadcast center

An Earth-based station that transmits high-powered, high-frequency signals to a satellite.

Uplink

Signals sent from Earth to a satellite.

Broadcast centers, also known as Earth centers, are used to transmit high-powered, high-frequency signals to the satellite. The signals are referred to as *uplink*. The satellite then transmits that information back to Earth, to satellite dishes that are within the coverage area of the satellite. These signals are referred to as *downlink*. Home users and businesses own many of these receiving satellite dishes. The data from the satellite is then patched into an existing network, allowing computers to communicate. This operation works in reverse whenever data is transmitted from the satellite

Downlink

Signals sent from a satellite to Earth.

Footprint

In satellite communications, the area reached by signals from a particular satellite.

dish to the Internet or to another network. Satellite technology offers some advantages for computer networks:

- It is always on. You do not need to dial in to a service provider to obtain access.
- Satellites allow users to be mobile. As long as a user moves within the *footprint,* or coverage area, of the satellite, the user has a connection to the network and can continue to surf the Internet, send e-mail, and so on.

Satellite technology also has some disadvantages:

- **Latency:** A delay in data transmission occurs when a satellite communicates back and forth between Earth-based systems, such as the broadcast center and a home satellite dish. This delay is due to the distance that the data must travel between the satellite and Earth-based systems.
- **Noise:** The strength of a signal sent by a satellite begins to weaken as it travels. Since these signals travel a long way, you end up with a low signal-to-noise ratio. In essence, this means you have less signal strength and more noise.
- **Bandwidth:** The radio frequency spectrum is fairly narrow, meaning that the amount of bandwidth available is limited.

Figure 20.12 describes several varieties of satellites.

Low-Earth-orbit (LEO) satellite

A satellite that is located closest to Earth, about 900 miles away from the surface.

Medium-Earth-orbit (MEO) satellite

A satellite that travels above Earth in the 5,000- to 8,000-mile range.

Geosynchronous-Earth-orbit (GEO) satellite

A satellite that operates in a stationary orbit 22,300 miles above Earth.

- **Low-Earth Orbit:** *Low-Earth-orbit (LEO) satellites* are located closest to Earth, between 500 and 1,000 miles away from Earth's surface. Because they are so close, they have a small footprint; however, their close proximity equates to a fast response time for sending and receiving data.
- **Medium-Earth Orbit:** *Medium-Earth-orbit (MEO) satellites* travel above Earth in the 5,000- to 8,000-mile range. Since they have a higher orbit than LEOs, they have a broader footprint. As distance away from Earth increases, so does the delay in data travel.
- **Geosynchronous-Earth Orbit:** *Geosynchronous-Earth-orbit (GEO) satellites* operate in stationary orbits that are 22,300 miles above Earth. They cover a very large area with a large footprint, but they suffer from significant delays (about half a second) in transferring data traffic back and forth to Earth.

FIGURE 20.12
Varieties of Satellites

The standard home setup consists of a small (approximately two by three feet) satellite dish, also called an antenna, mounted on or near your home. The dish must have an unobstructed view of the sky. The dish is connected to a satellite modem using coaxial cable. The modem may be either internal or external. If the modem is internal, it is installed directly into an open slot in the computer, and the cable is connected directly to the back of it. If the modem is external, it is connected to the computer through an Ethernet cable, which in turn is connected to a network interface card or a USB cable.

Home satellite systems typically provide download speeds in the range of 150 to 500 Kbps, and upload speeds of 128 Kbps. Note that some systems are "receive only" systems, which require a telephone line and a modem to transmit data. This means you must either keep your existing dial-up ISP account or get a new account, which will add to the cost.

TRY IT!

Contact your local satellite provider to determine availability and rate plans for satellite Internet access.

TROUBLESHOOTING A SATELLITE CONNECTION

Several things can go wrong with a satellite system. If it is not installed correctly, the Earth-based satellite receiver will not be able to locate a signal. Or, if it can locate a signal, you may not be able to make adjustments to items such as *azimuth, elevation, pointing angle,* and *antenna polarization.* The correct adjustments ensure maximum signal strength and accuracy. If the system was previously working correctly and you have noticed a marked drop in bandwidth, or no bandwidth at all, you will need to recheck these settings.

IN REAL LIFE

When adjusting an azimuth, the measurements start from the north, going east, then south, and then west. For example, an object in the east has an azimuth of 90°, while an object in the southwest would have an azimuth of 225°. The azimuth of celestial objects changes with time (objects appearing to rise in the east and set in the west). If you know the altitude and the azimuth of an object, such as a satellite, then you will know where to look for an object in the sky.

TRY IT!

Connect and configure a computer for Internet access using satellite service.

If you decide to install or troubleshoot satellite equipment yourself, most systems include video and written instructions on where to locate the antenna, how to set it up, how to make adjustments, and so on. You may also choose to have the antenna professionally installed.

Azimuth

A measurement used to specify the location of a celestial object.

Elevation

The height to which something is elevated above a point of reference, normally Earth's surface, or the horizon.

Pointing angle

An angle determined by the latitude and longitude point of an Earth-based station and the longitude of the satellite. Sometimes called elevation.

Antenna polarization

The physical alignment of antennas.

Since the connection between the antenna and computer is coaxial cable, check the connections to make sure they are tight and that the connectors have not separated from the wire. If they have, you will need to use a pair of wire crimpers to cut off the old BNC connector and attach a new one. You may also consider checking the cable with a media tester.

If you are sure that the antenna is adjusted to the correct parameters and the cable is working properly, the next step in the chain is the satellite modem. Most modems have a set of lights on the front, just like cable modems, to give you an idea if everything is working correctly. Check the lights to ensure that the unit is on and that the data uplink and downlink connections are active. Try cycling the power by turning off the modem, waiting a few minutes, and turning it back on. If that fails to fix the problem, check the Ethernet cable running to the network interface card. Then check the network interface card using the procedures that were outlined earlier in this chapter.

Keep in mind that rain and snow will affect the performance of a satellite system, just as they do with satellite-based television.

TEST TIP

Rain and snow will affect the performance of a satellite system, just as they do with satellite-based television.

Wireless

Wireless networking was described in depth in Chapter 3. To refresh your memory, here is a quick review of that information.

In a typical wireless local area network (WLAN) configuration, a device that both transmits and receives—commonly referred to as an access point—connects to the wired network from a fixed location using a standard Ethernet cable. The access point receives, buffers, and transmits data between wireless components, for example, between a laptop computer with a wireless network adapter installed and a network. An access point can support a small group of users and generally has a range up to several hundred feet. The access point can be installed anywhere provided there is good radio coverage. This type of wireless network operates in infrastructure mode.

When a device with a wireless adapter is turned on, it scans the wireless frequencies either for a wireless access point (AP) or for other wireless devices operating in ad hoc mode. If the device is operating in infrastructure mode, the device selects the wireless AP with which to connect. Once the connection is made, the wireless device switches to the channel assigned by the AP and negotiates the use of a port. This is known as establishing an association.

If a problem such as low signal strength prevents a wireless device from connecting with a particular AP, the wireless device scans for other wireless APs. If another AP is located, the wireless device switches to the channel of that AP and negotiates the use of a port. This process is called reassociation.

Another form of wireless communication is known as ad hoc mode, or peer-to-peer mode. In ad hoc mode, wireless clients communicate directly with each other, without the use of a wireless AP. An example would be two personal digital assistants (PDAs) that transfer information directly from one to the other.

TROUBLESHOOTING A WIRELESS CONNECTION

Many technicians become overwhelmed when working with new technologies, such as wireless networks. One of the easiest ways to overcome this feeling is to remember that, for the most part, a wireless network performs just like a wired network.

To begin troubleshooting any problem, always perform a communications test. One of the easiest ways to do this is to use the PING utility to test the hardware. Begin with your local computer to ensure that it is working correctly. Next, PING the AP's IP address. If the AP does not respond to the PING, suspect a malfunctioning AP. Try cycling the power on the AP to reset it. Wait a few minutes and then try PINGing the AP again. If the PING utility fails to establish a connection with either the local computer or the AP, check the following AP configurations:

- Verify that the *service set identifier (SSID)* is correct. Each wireless network has its own SSID. If it is incorrect, the computer will ignore the AP and search for an AP with the specified SSID.
- Check to see if the *wired equivalent privacy (WEP) encryption* is configured correctly for the network interface card and the AP you are using. Each network interface card and AP requires you to specify the WEP encryption key differently.
- Test the signal strength. Most manufacturers of wireless equipment have some mechanism for this, usually a software utility that is designed to measure signal strength.
- Change channels on the AP and the wireless client to see if signal strength improves. Keep in mind that a wireless telephone or microwave

Service set identifier (SSID)

An identifier that acts as a password in the header of a packet used on a wireless LAN.

Wired equivalent privacy (WEP) encryption

A security protocol that is used on wireless LANs.

oven may interfere with wireless clients. Try unplugging the wireless telephone and turning off the microwave to see if the situation improves.

Plain Old Telephone System (POTS)

The plain old telephone system (POTS), also referred to as the public switched telephone network (PSTN), is the standard phone system that you use to place phone calls or to connect to an ISP using a modem.

POTS began as an analog circuit-switching system operated by humans and later evolved into a system of electromechanical switches. The system is now almost completely digital, except for the "final mile," in which the connection is made to a subscriber. The signal that enters and leaves your telephone is analog. That analog signal is transmitted over a twisted pair cable. Once the signal reaches the telephone company, it is digitized, providing a 64-Kbps data stream. Several of these data streams are usually combined to create a wider stream, or more bandwidth. When the telephone in your residence receives a call, the digital signal is converted back to analog and delivered to the phone.

TROUBLESHOOTING POTS

When your local telephone stops working, follow the same steps noted earlier for troubleshooting a new DSL connection. Begin by checking the telephone wiring at your home or office. The easiest way to do this is listen to a connected phone to see if a dial tone is present. If not, take the phone outside of the building to the connection box, or to wherever the external telephone wiring connects to the building's internal phone service. Open the box and locate the RJ-11 jack. Plug the phone into that jack and listen for a dial tone. If an RJ-11 jack is not available, you will need a handset with alligator clips to conduct the next test. Attach the alligator clips to the metal connectors to which the internal phone line is attached. If a tone exists, a problem exists with the internal wiring. If you still cannot hear a tone, the problem exists with the external wiring. In that case you will need to contact the telephone company.

TROUBLESHOOTING MODEMS CONNECTED TO POTS

Since standard modems rely on POTS to communicate, some troubleshooting information is logical at this point. Always check the telephone wiring as described above. If you can rule out the wiring as a cause of your problem, then check the Device Manager utility to ensure that the modem is configured correctly. Follow these steps:

1. On a computer running the Windows XP Professional operating system, click the Start button.

2. When the Start menu appears, select Control Panel. From the Control Panel, select System.

3. When the System Properties dialog box appears, select the Hardware tab. On the Hardware tab click the Device Manager button. A dialog box similar to Figure 20.13 should appear.

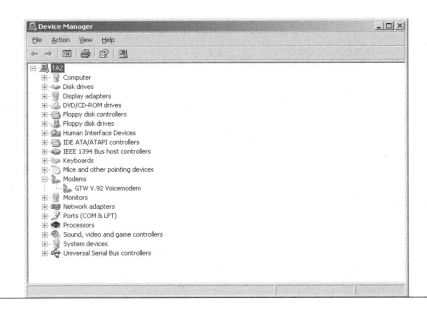

FIGURE 20.13
Windows XP Professional Device Manager

4. In the Device Manager, locate the section for modems. Click it to expand it and display the individual modems.

5. Locate the installed modem. If the icon for the modem is a yellow circle with an exclamation point, this indicates a problem with the modem. If the icon has a red "X" on it, that indicates the modem is disabled. To obtain more information about a problem device, double-click it. A properties dialog box similar to that in Figure 20.14 will appear.

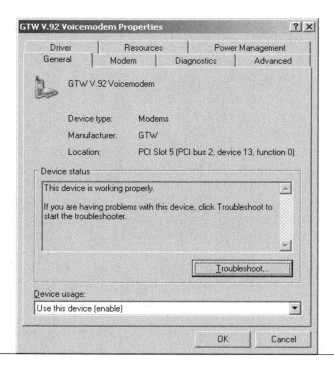

FIGURE 20.14
Modem Properties

6. Check the status of the modem to ensure it is functioning correctly. If it is not, press the Troubleshoot button to begin the troubleshooting process.

If the troubleshooter cannot identify and correct the problem, try physically reseating the modem or reinstalling the driver. If neither of these works, replace the modem.

You may also try issuing commands to the modem. Most modems have a standard set of commands that can be issued through a terminal window. To try these commands, follow these instructions:

1. Click the Start button. When the Start menu appears, select Programs. When the Programs menu appears, select Accessories.
2. From the Accessories menu, select Communications and then HyperTerminal.
3. When the HyperTerminal window appears, assign a name for your connection and click OK.
4. The Connect To dialog box appears (see Figure 20.15). Select the COM port that your modem is using. (If you are not sure which COM port to select, open the Device Manager and check the modem's properties.) Click OK.

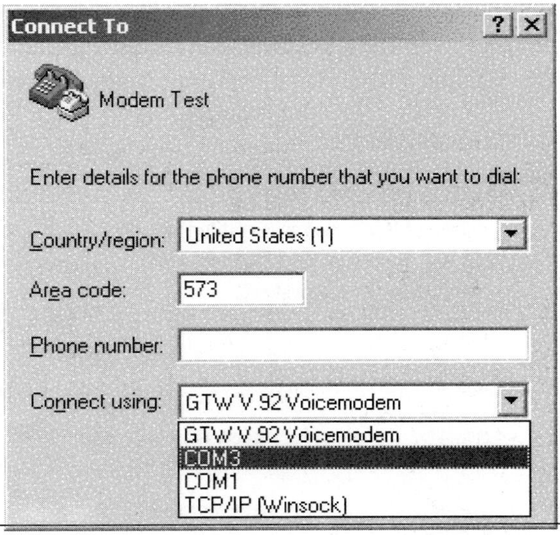

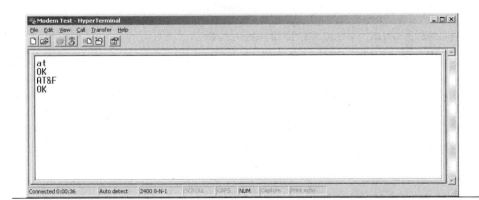

FIGURE 20.15
Selecting Your Modem's
COM Port

5. When the settings for the COM port appear, accept the defaults by clicking OK.
6. The HyperTerminal connection window will appear (see Figure 20.16). Type the appropriate commands, pressing the Enter key to send the commands.

FIGURE 20.16
Using the HyperTerminal
Utility to Communicate
with a Modem

The manual that accompanied your modem should contain a list of all of the commands that your modem understands. This is important, because different manufacturers use different modem commands, or initialization strings.

The commands in Table 20.3 are standard for most modems. Note that they are not case sensitive. Also, you can type more than one command at a time to form a string.

Command	Result
AT&F	Resets the modem to the default factory settings.
AT&F1	Resets the modem to the secondary default factory settings.
L0	Sets the modem speaker to the lowest volume.
L1	Sets the modem speaker to a low volume.
L2	Sets the modem speaker to a high volume.
L3	Sets the modem speaker to the highest volume.
M0	Turns off the modem speaker completely.
M1	Turns on the modem speaker.
S11=x	Sets the dialing speed of the modem, with X being any number between 50 and 255 (lower is faster).
W2	Allows Windows to report your true connection speed.
X2	Checks for a dial tone before dialing.
X3	Does not check for a dial tone before dialing.

TABLE 20.3
Standard Modem Commands

TRY IT!

Control your modem with AT commands.

1. Reset the modem to factory settings.
2. Adjust the modem speaker volume to high.
3. Instruct the modem to check for a dial tone before dialing.

Typically, a modem will begin responding to new commands the next time it is used. Occasionally, you will have to restart the computer for the change to take effect.

If a modem does not support an issued command, it will report an error. A typical error is error 630, which means, "The modem is not responding."

This error may also occur if the modem is damaged and will not respond to any commands. If that happens, replace the modem with one that is known to work and try it again.

Most Windows operating systems give you the ability to log the steps that your modem takes when trying to establish a connection. This logging usually must be enabled. To enable logging, follow these steps:

1. Open the Control Panel by clicking the Start button, selecting Settings, and then selecting Control Panel.

2. Once the Control Panel is open, locate and double-click Phone and Modem Options.
3. On the Modems tab, select the modem you wish to log.
4. Click Properties. In the Properties dialog box, click the Diagnostics tab.
5. In Logging, select the *Append to Log* check box if you are working on a computer running Windows 2000 Professional or *Record a Log* if you are working on a computer running Windows 2000 Server.
6. The modem log file can be located in %systemroot%\ModemLog_Model.txt. *(Note: Systemroot is usually C:\Winnt\System32\. Model is the name of the modem as it appears in the list of installed modems on the Modems tab of Phone and Modem Options.)* A typical modem log file is depicted in Figure 20.17. Viewing this log file may point to errors experienced by your phone line or modem.

FIGURE 20.17
A Typical Modem Log

STUDY GUIDE

In this chapter, we discussed troubleshooting network failures in small offices and home offices. Here are some key points to remember.

SMALL OFFICE/HOME OFFICE (SOHO) ENVIRONMENTS

- In the SOHO environment, many users connect to some type of network remotely. That is, they are not connected directly to the network. Instead, they connect indirectly, or on demand.
- For example, a user might use a modem to dial in to a remote access server.
- Once authenticated, the user may or may not be required to log on a second time through the appropriate network client—either Novell Client for NetWare Networks or Microsoft Client for Microsoft Networks.
- Once authenticated, a user has access to network resources, just like any other network client.
- In a small office environment, the user may have a network setup that is either peer-to-peer or client-server. The user may or may not need access to anything outside this network, other than the Internet.
- Users of a small office network commonly access the Internet through a shared connection, such as a DSL using Internet Connection Sharing.

DIGITAL SUBSCRIBER LINE (DSL)

- Digital Subscriber Line (DSL) is a broadband technology that makes use of unused frequencies on normal telephone lines to transmit data at varying speeds, depending on the type of DSL being used.
- One of the primary benefits of DSL is that voice and data traffic can be sent simultaneously over the same telephone line.
- DSL is always on; therefore, a connection is always available while working on a client workstation.
- There are two primary types of DSL service—asymmetric and symmetric.

Asymmetric DSL

- Residential DSL uses a type of DSL called asymmetric DSL or ADSL, which uses its own telephone line to send and receive data traffic.
- The connection is asymmetric because the data sent from your computer—called uploading, or upstream, data—travels at a different

speed from the data sent to your computer—called downloading, or downstream, data.

- For home users, ADSL is normally set up for faster downloading than uploading. Several different types of ADSL are available:
  - Full-rate ADSL offers speeds up to 6 Mbps. Voice and data are sent simultaneously over an existing telephone line. Full rate is the most common type of ADSL used by businesses and residential customers.
  - G.lite targets home Internet users and supports speeds up to 1.5 Mbps downstream and up to 500 Kbps upstream.
  - Rate-adaptive (RADSL) is a nonstandard version of ADSL.
  - Very-high-bit-rate (VDSL) supports data transfer speeds up to 26 Mbps over short distances, usually not more than 50 meters.

Symmetric DSL

- Symmetric DSL usually requires its own dedicated telephone line and allows uploads and downloads to travel at the same speed. Several different types of symmetric DSL are available.
- Symmetric DSL (SDSL) is a proprietary version of DSL that supports data transfer speeds from 128 Kbps to 2.32 Mbps. SDSL is a generic term for a number of supplier-specific implementations that use a single copper wire pair to support variable transfer rates of symmetric service.
- Symmetric high-bit-rate DSL (SHDSL) is an industry standard that achieves 20 percent longer line reach than older versions of symmetric DSL.
  - SHDSL supports data transfer speeds ranging from 192 Kbps to 2.3 Mbps with less crosstalk between cable pairs.
  - One pair of wires may be used for short loops, while two wire pairs may be used for longer loops.
  - SHDSL is designed specifically for data transfers that need fast upload speeds. For that reason, SHDSL is aimed primarily at business customers.
- High-data-rate DSL (HDSL) is available at both 1.5 and 2.3 Mbps and uses one, two, or three pairs of twisted copper wire.
- 2nd generation HDSL (HDSL2) transfers data at 1.5 Mbps and supports voice, data, and video using either asynchronous transfer mode (ATM) or frame relay over a single copper wire pair.
  - HDSL2 does not provide voice telephone service on the same wire pair.
  - HSDL2 requires only one wire pair to support data transfer.

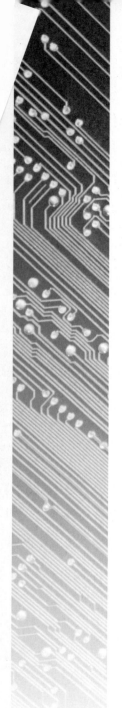

- Integrated Services Digital Network DSL (IDSL) supports data transfer rates up to 144 Kbps using standard telephone lines.
  - IDSL has the ability to deliver services through a digital loop carrier (DLC), which is a device often placed in newer neighborhood telephone cabinets.
  - The DLC is designed to simplify the distribution of cable and wiring for the telephone company.
  - ADSL and its G.lite variation are implemented directly into these DLCs.
- DSL will not be available in all areas due to distance limitations. That is, in order to obtain DSL service, you must be within a specific distance from the central telephone office

Connecting to DSL

- After obtaining the necessary service from your provider, you will need to establish the physical connection.
- First, install a network interface card in the computer. After the card is installed, start the computer and install the appropriate driver when prompted.
- Following the directions from your DSL provider, install and configure a client and the necessary protocols—usually Microsoft Client for Microsoft Networks and TCP/IP.
- Next, connect an Ethernet cable from the back of the network interface card to the DSL modem or router.
- Complete the connection by plugging a standard telephone cable into the modem or router on one end and into a standard telephone wall jack on the other.

Troubleshooting an Established DSL Connection

- If your DSL connection was working correctly and suddenly stopped, begin by conducting some simple checks of the DSL modem or router.
- Most DSL hardware contains an array of lights that will give you an idea whether the problem is with the DSL line, the equipment, or the computer.
- When checking the status of the network interface card, begin by checking the link and collision lights.
- If they are operating correctly, check (and replace if necessary) the Ethernet cable between the network interface card and the DSL modem or router.
- If the lights are not lit, check the Device Manager utility to ensure that the network interface card is configured correctly.

- Check the status of the adapter to ensure that it is functioning correctly. If it is not, click the Troubleshoot button to begin the troubleshooting process.
- Finally, check the telephone wiring at your home or office.

Troubleshooting a New DSL Connection

- Many of the steps that were identified above can be used to troubleshoot a new connection.
- With a new connection, always suspect that some configuration parameter is incorrect.
- If checks of those parameters disclose that everything is correct, check the DSL hardware. Begin with the lights, since they will likely point you to where the problem lies.
- Always make sure the telephone company has accomplished the work that is necessary, or all of your troubleshooting efforts will be for nothing.

CABLE

- A cable connection works with the cable television service that runs to your home.
- The service is provided by your local cable television provider and, like DSL, may not be available in all areas.
- Installing cable service is fairly straightforward. First, the incoming television cable is cut and connected to one side of a splitter.
- Next, a new piece of cable will be connected to an outgoing port.
- The other end of the new cable will be connected to a cable modem.
- Make sure that no devices are placed between the cable splitter and the cable modem. The signal from the cable modem is very strong; if a television is connected in the path between the modem and the splitter, the signal to the television would be disturbed.
- A cable modem is a different from a standard modem, although it still modulates and demodulates signals.
- Cable modems perform more functions than a standard phone line modem, including routing and tuning of the signal.
- An Ethernet cable attaches the cable modem to a network interface card that is installed inside the workstation.
- Cable is always on; therefore, a connection is always available while working on a client workstation.
- Cable modem speeds vary by service and direction of data traffic.

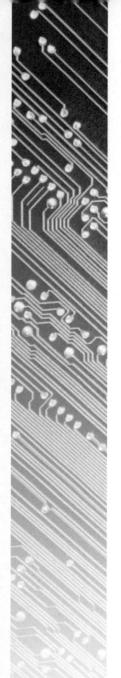

- o Upstream data travels from your computer to another destination.
- o Downstream data travels to your computer.
- Cable modem speeds for downstream traffic typically top out at about 1.5 Mbps, with actual performance in the range of 1 to 1.5 Mbps.
- Upstream speeds generally top out at 256 Kbps.
- One advantage that cable has over DSL is that cable is not subject to the distance limitations of DSL. The distance limit for cable is virtually unlimited.

Troubleshooting an Established Cable Connection

- If your cable connection was working correctly and suddenly stopped, begin by conducting some simple checks of the cable modem.
- Although features vary between brands and between models, most cable modems include an array of lights that will give you an idea whether the problem is with the cable line, the equipment, or the computer.
- When checking the status of the network interface card, begin by checking the link and collision lights.
  - o If they are operating correctly, check (and replace if necessary) the Ethernet cable between the network interface card and the modem.
  - o If the lights are not lit, follow the steps that were outlined in the DSL section to check the Device Manager utility to ensure that the network interface card is configured correctly.
- Finally, check the cable wiring inside your home or office building.
  - o Make sure that all connections are secure.
  - o If none of your cable devices work, suspect the external line.
  - o If only one of several devices is experiencing a problem, use a cable tester to check the cable on the nonworking device, or just replace the cable with one that is known to work.
  - o If the cables are good, try replacing the splitter, although these items seldom fail.
  - o If all of the internal components appear to be working, you will need to contact the cable company.

Troubleshooting a New Cable Connection

- With a new connection, always suspect that some configuration parameter is incorrect.
- If checks of those parameters disclose that everything is correct, try the cable hardware.
- Begin by checking the lights on the network interface card and modem, since they will likely point you to where the problem lies.

Troubleshooting Small Office/Home Office Network Failures

- Always make sure that the cable company has accomplished the work that is necessary, or all of your troubleshooting efforts will be for nothing.

HOME SATELLITE

- Satellite communication systems send and receive signals between Earth-based stations and geosynchronous space satellites.
- Broadcast centers, also known as Earth centers, transmit high-powered, high-frequency signals to the satellite. These signals are referred to as uplink.
- The satellite then transmits that information back to Earth, to satellite dishes that are within the coverage area of the satellite. These signals are referred to as downlink.
- The data from the satellite is then patched into an existing network, allowing computers to communicate.
- This operation works in reverse whenever data is transmitted from the satellite dish to the Internet or to another network.
- Advantages of satellite technology:
  ○ It is always on.
  ○ Satellites allow users to be mobile.
- Disadvantages of satellite technology:
  ○ Latency—the delay in data transmission that occurs when the satellite communicates back and forth between Earth-based systems, such as a broadcast center and a home satellite dish. This delay is due to the distance between the satellite and Earth.
  ○ Noise—a low signal-to-noise ratio results as signals travel; the farther away, the weaker the signal and the greater the noise.
  ○ Bandwidth—because the radio frequency spectrum is fairly narrow, the amount of bandwidth available is limited.
- Low-Earth-orbit (LEO) satellites are located closest to Earth, about 900 miles above the surface.
- The close proximity of LEOs gives them a small footprint.
- The close proximity of LEOs enables a fast response time when sending and receiving data.
- Medium-Earth-orbit (MEO) satellites travel above Earth in the 5,000-to-8,000-mile range.
- With a higher orbit than LEOs, MEOs have a broader footprint.
- Because they are farther away than LEOs, MEOs have a greater delay in data travel.

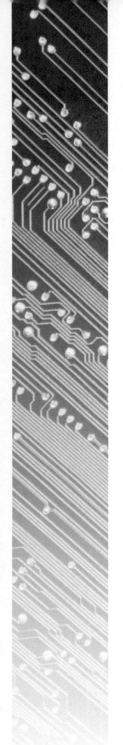

- Geosynchronous-Earth-orbit (GEO) satellites operate in high stationary orbits 22,300 miles above Earth.
- GEOs cover a very large footprint, but they suffer from significant delays (about half a second) in transferring data traffic back and forth to Earth.
- The standard home satellite setup consists of a small (two by three feet) satellite dish—also called an antenna—that is mounted on or near your home.
- The dish must have a clear, unobstructed view of the sky.
- The dish is connected to either an internal or external satellite modem using coaxial cable.
- Internal modems are installed directly into an open slot in the computer, and the cable is connected directly to the back of the computer.
- External modems are connected through an Ethernet cable to a network interface card or a USB cable.
- Home satellite systems typically download data at 150 to 500 Kbps and upload data at 128 Kbps.
- Some systems are "receive only," which require a telephone line and a modem to transmit data. This means you must either keep your existing dial-up ISP account or get a new account, which will add to the cost.

Troubleshooting a Satellite Connection

- Make sure the satellite connection is correctly installed, with the Earth-based satellite receiver set to the proper parameters. If you can locate a signal, the system has been set up properly.
- Once the signal is located, you must be able to make adjustments to items such as azimuth, elevation, pointing angle, and antenna polarization. The correct adjustments ensure maximum signal-strength accuracy.
- If the system was previously installed and working correctly, and you have noticed a marked drop in bandwidth, or no bandwidth at all, you will need to recheck the settings for azimuth, elevation, pointing angle, and antenna polarization.
- Since coaxial cable is used to connect the antenna to the computer, check to make sure that the connections are tight and that the connectors have not separated from the wire.
- If you are sure that the antenna is adjusted to the correct parameters and the cable is working properly, the next step in the chain is the satellite modem.
  - Most modems have a set of lights on the front, just like cable modems, to give you an idea if everything is working correctly.

- Then check the network interface card using the procedures that were outlined earlier in this chapter.
- Rain and snow will affect the performance of a satellite system, just as they do with satellite television.

WIRELESS

- A typical wireless local area network (WLAN) uses a device that both transmits and receives, commonly referred to as an access point. The access point connects to the wired network from a fixed location using a standard Ethernet cable.
- The access point receives, buffers, and transmits data between wireless components, such as a laptop computer with a wireless network adapter installed and the wired network.
- An access point can support a small group of users and generally has a range up to several hundred feet.
- The access point can be installed anywhere that has good radio coverage.
- This type of wireless network operates in infrastructure mode.

Troubleshooting a Wireless Connection

- Always perform a communications test using the PING utility.
  - Begin by PINGing your local computer to ensure that it is working correctly. Next, PING the AP's IP address.
  - If the AP does not respond, suspect a malfunctioning AP.
  - Try cycling the power on the AP to reset it.
- Wait a few minutes and then try PINGing the AP again. If it still fails to respond, check the configuration of the AP:
  - Verify that the service set identifier (SSID) is correct. Each wireless network has its own SSID. If it is incorrect, the computer will ignore the AP and search for an AP with the specified SSID.
  - Check to see if the wired equivalent privacy (WEP) encryption is configured correctly for the network interface card and the AP you are using. Each network card and AP requires you to specify the WEP encryption key differently.
  - Test the signal strength. Most manufacturers of wireless equipment have some mechanism, usually a software utility, that is designed to measure signal strength.
- Change channels on the AP and the wireless client to see if signal strength improves.

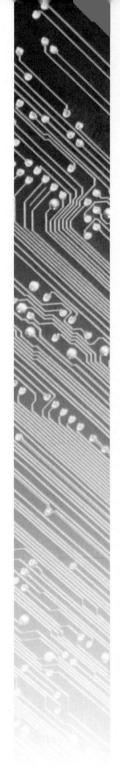

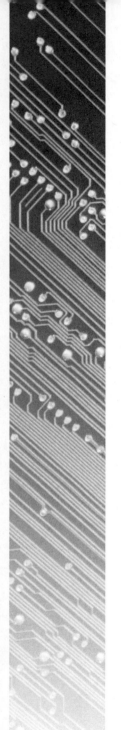

- Keep in mind that a wireless phone or microwave oven may interfere with wireless clients. Try unplugging the wireless phone and turning off the microwave to see if the situation improves.

PLAIN OLD TELEPHONE SYSTEM (POTS)

- The plain old telephone system (POTS), also referred to as the public switched telephone network (PSTN), is the standard phone system that you use to place phone calls or connect to an ISP using a modem.
- The signal that enters and leaves your phone is analog. That analog signal is transmitted over a twisted pair cable. Once the signal reaches the telephone company, it is digitized, providing a data stream of 64 Kbps.

Troubleshooting POTS

- When your local telephone stops working, begin by checking the telephone wiring at your home or office.

Troubleshooting Modems Connected to POTS

- Always check the telephone wiring.
- If you can rule out the wiring as a cause of your problem, check the modem.
- You may also try issuing commands to the modem.
- Most modems have a standard set of commands that can be issued through a terminal window.
- Typically, a modem will begin responding to new commands the next time it is used. Occasionally, you will have to restart the computer for the change to take effect.
- If a modem does not support an issued command, it will report an error.
- Most Windows operating systems give you the ability to log the steps that your modem takes when trying to establish a connection.

PRACTICE TEST

Try this test to check your mastery of the concepts in this chapter.

1. Which of the following media types does DSL use to transmit data?
   a. cable service
   b. telephone line
   c. satellite
   d. wireless

2. What is the purpose of ICS software?
   a. It allows users to share an Internet connection.
   b. It is client software.
   c. It does away with the need for a protocol.
   d. It is the client software for satellite networks.

3. What type of DSL service do most home users require?
   a. ADSL
   b. SDSL
   c. HDSL
   d. SHDSL

4. What is the maximum distance limitation of ADSL?
   a. 12,000 feet
   b. 14,000 feet
   c. 16,000 feet
   d. 18,000 feet

5. Which of the following implementations of DSL has the fastest data transfer speeds over short distances?
   a. SDSL
   b. HDSL
   c. ADSL
   d. VDSL

6. Which of the following terms properly defines latency?
   a. signal strength
   b. bandwidth
   c. delay
   d. noise

7. You have recently installed the hardware necessary for a new cable connection. After completing all of the connections, you attempt to use the cable connection and find that it does not work. While troubleshooting the problem, you open the Device Manager utility and discover a red "X" on the icon for the newly installed network interface card. What does this indicate?
   a. The modem is not installed.
   b. The modem is working correctly.
   c. The modem is disabled.
   d. The modem is in the wrong slot on the motherboard.

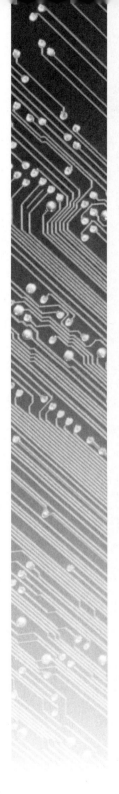

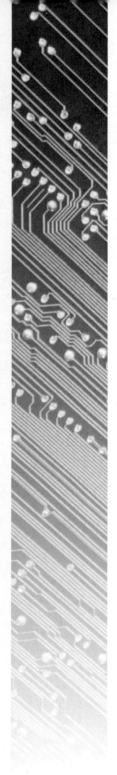

8. In a cable modem installation, to what does the cable connect inside a residence?
   a. the cable modem
   b. a cable splitter
   c. the network interface card
   d. a wall jack

9. Cable modem speeds for downstream traffic typically top out at about _____, with actual performance in the range of
   a. 1.5 Mbps; 1 to 1.5 Mbps.
   b. 1.5 Kbps; 1 to 1.5 Kbps.
   c. 2.5 Mbps; 2.5 to 3 Mbps.
   d. 2.5 Kbps; 2.5 to 3 Kbps.

10. What is one advantage that cable has over DSL?
    a. Cable has shorter distance limitations than DSL.
    b. Cable has longer distance limitations than DSL.
    c. Cable is always on.
    d. Only cable uses a network interface card.

11. What does the cable light on a cable modem indicate?
    a. whether the modem is on or off
    b. whether the Ethernet cable is working
    c. whether the network interface card is transmitting data
    d. whether the modem has a good connection to the service provider

12. You notice that the test light on your cable modem is always on. What does this indicate?
    a. The modem is working correctly.
    b. The modem is conducting a self-test.
    c. The modem failed the self-test and should be checked.
    d. The modem is transmitting data.

13. _____ are used to transmit high-powered, high-frequency signals to the satellite.
    a. Broadcast centers
    b. Small satellite dishes
    c. Telephone centers
    d. Television centers

14. What types of satellites are used for data networks?
    a. LEOs
    b. GEOs
    c. MEOs
    d. XEOs

15. Which of the following is a disadvantage of using satellite technology for networking? (Select all that apply)
    a. bandwidth
    b. latency
    c. mobility
    d. noise

16. Home satellite systems typically provide download speeds in the range of _____, and upload speeds of
    a. 150 to 500 Kbps; 256 Kbps.
    b. 150 to 500 Kbps; 128 Kbps.
    c. 750 to 1,000 Mbps; 256 Mbps.
    d. 750 to 1,000 Kbps; 128 Kbps.

17. When troubleshooting a connectivity problem on a wireless network, what is one of the first steps you should take?
    a. Reset the AP.
    b. Unplug the wireless network interface card and plug it back in.
    c. Run a connectivity test.
    d. Connect the device with Ethernet cable.

18. You are troubleshooting a connectivity problem with a laptop containing a wireless network interface card. While conducting some tests, you notice that the computer appears to be ignoring the AP and searching for a different AP. What is the most likely problem?
    a. The SSID is incorrect.
    b. The WEP is incorrect.
    c. The DHCP server is not working.
    d. The DNS server settings are incorrect.

19. While troubleshooting a problem with your phone line, you open the telephone box on the exterior of your house and plug in a phone. Once the phone is plugged in, you test for a dial tone and find none. Where does the problem probably exist?
    a. in the internal house wiring
    b. in the external telephone company wiring

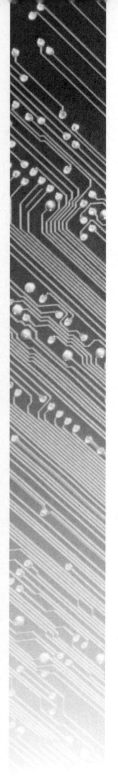

c. in the telephone

d. in the cable box

20. You have made some changes to your modem and it has stopped working. What command could you send the modem to reset it back to factory settings?

a. AT&F1

b. AT&L0

c. AT&F

d. AT&M

TROUBLESHOOTING

1. A person who telecommutes to work via DSL called the help desk to report that he cannot connect to the corporate network. The user informs you that he has only one phone line connected to his house and he is currently using it. Where would you begin your troubleshooting efforts?

2. You work the help desk for a cable television firm that has just started installing cable Internet service. A customer who has recently been connected to the cable Internet service has called to complain that ever since the service was installed, her television reception is unreliable when the computer is on. Based on this conversation, what could you deduce as the most likely problem?

CUSTOMER SERVICE

1. You have decided to contract for cable service in your home. You have also decided to install the service yourself. Describe the steps it will take to implement this technology in your home.

2. You and several of your neighbors have contracted with a local service firm to install satellite Internet access. The service has never delivered the promised bandwidth, and calls to the company with complaints have yielded no results. As a result, you have decided to troubleshoot the problem yourself. What are some logical steps you should take to try to resolve the problems?

FOR MORE INFORMATION

For links to Web sites that provide further information about the topics covered in this chapter, go to the EMC/Paradigm Internet Resource Center at www.emcp.com/College Division/Internet Resource Centers/Networking/System Administration/Web Resources: For More Information.

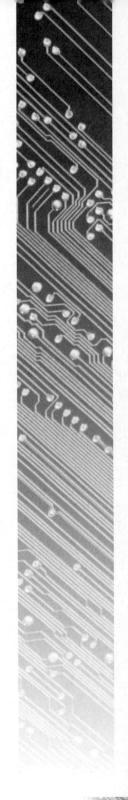

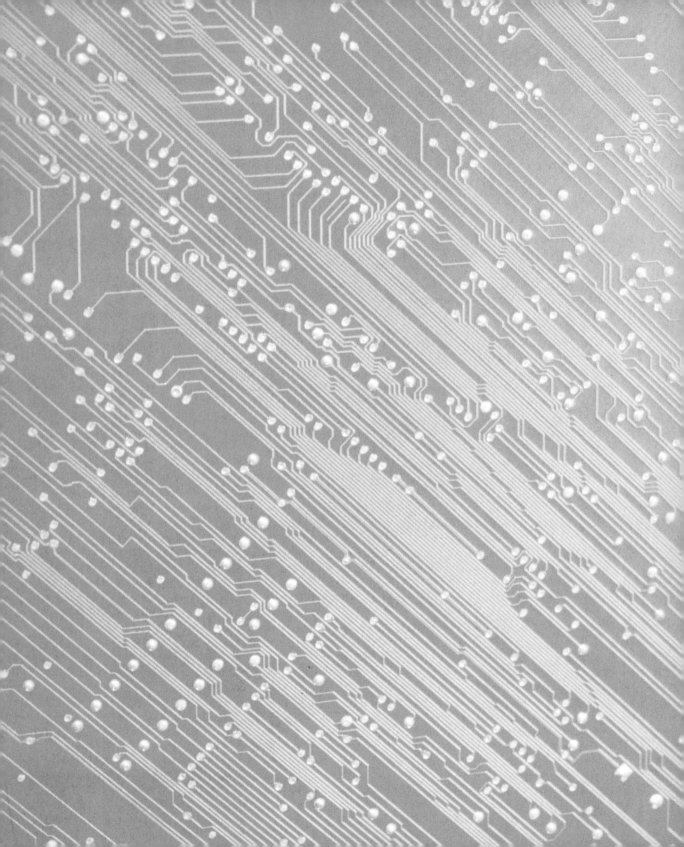

Project Lab, Part
Network Support and Troubleshooting

4

CHAPTER 17

PROJECT #1: ASKING OPEN- AND CLOSED-ENDED QUESTIONS

A user has phoned the help desk to report that his computer "will not work."
1. Develop five open-ended questions designed to help you understand the problem.
2. Develop five closed-ended questions designed to help you understand the problem.
3. For each of the six basic areas, write one question designed to help you understand the problem.

PROJECT #2: LEARNING TO RESOLVE PROBLEMS QUICKLY

Divide the class into pairs and follow these procedures:
1. One person in the pair will brainstorm and develop a common computer problem.
2. The second person can ask 10 questions (5 open-ended and 5 closed-ended) in an attempt to identify the problem.
3. The two people trade roles and repeat steps 1 and 2.

PROJECT #3: USING THE WINDOWS EVENT VIEWER

1. On a Windows-based computer, open the Event Viewer.
2. View the System, Application, and Security logs.
3. Double-click an event to view the details.
4. Clear the Event Viewer.
5. Display the properties for one or more logs.
6. Change the maximum log size to 256 KB.

PROJECT #4: WORKING WITH LOG FILES

1. Search the hard disk of your computer for log files. *(Hint: search for *.log.)*
2. Open to view several of the log files that are found.
3. Pay particular attention to how many and the nature of log files that are available on your computer.

CHAPTER 18

PROJECT #1: WORKING WITH TOOLKITS

1. Identify and document the tools that are found in a technician's toolkit.
2. Identify and document the tools that are found in a field technician's toolkit.
3. Identify and document the spare parts that should be found in a spare parts locker.

PROJECT #2: USING WIRE CRIMPERS

1. Using a pair of wire crimpers, attach an RJ-45 connector to a piece of twisted pair wire.
2. Using a pair of wire crimpers, attach a BNC connector to a piece of coaxial cable.
3. Use a pair of wire strippers to strip the plastic jacket from the individual wires of a twisted pair cable.

PROJECT #3: USING A MEDIA TESTER

1. Use a media tester to test a twisted pair cable and its connectors.
2. Use a media tester to test a coaxial cable and its connectors.
3. Use an optical media tester to test a fiber-optic cable and its connectors.
4. Use a Time Domain Reflectometer to determine if the cable is broken or has a short.
5. Document your results.

PROJECT #4: USING A TONE GENERATOR

1. Use a tone generator to trace a voice line.
2. Use a tone generator to trace a data line.
3. Document your results.

CHAPTER 19

PROJECT #1: USING TRACERT

1. Use tracert to trace a connection to a Web site or network host.
2. Instruct tracert to not resolve IP addresses to host names.
3. Specify the maximum number of hops to use while searching for the target host.
4. Specify a timeout value.
5. Document the steps you took in each procedure.

PROJECT #2: USING PING

1. Use PING to see if the TCP/IP protocol is functioning correctly on a host computer and to check connectivity between devices.
2. PING the specified host until manually stopped.
3. Tell PING to resolve IP addresses to host names.
4. Specify the number of ICMP echo requests to send.
5. Specify the size of the Send buffer.
6. Specify the Time to Live as 128.
7. Document the steps you took in each procedure.

PROJECT #3: USING ARP

1. Use ARP to display the address resolution protocol cache.
2. Use ARP to specify an Internet address.
3. Use ARP to display an ARP entry by a specific network interface.
4. Use ARP to delete an entry from ARP cache.
5. Add an entry manually to the ARP cache.
6. Document the steps you took in each procedure.

PROJECT #4: USING NETSTAT

1. Use netstat to view all of the TCP/IP connections in use on a computer.
2. Display Ethernet statistics.
3. Display addresses and port numbers in numerical form.
4. Display the owning process ID associated with each connection.
5. Show connections for the protocol specified by protocol.
6. Display the routing table.
7. Document the steps you took in each procedure.

PROJECT #5: USING NBTSTAT

1. Use nbtstat to determine if a Windows Internet Name Service (WINS) server is functioning correctly.
2. List the contents of NBT's cache by machine names and IP address.
3. List local NetBIOS names.
4. Obtain a list of names resolved by broadcast and WINS.
5. Empty and reload the remote cache name table.
6. List the sessions table by destination IP addresses.
7. Document the steps you took in each procedure.

PROJECT #6: USING IPCONFIG AND WINIPCFG

1. Display current IP configuration parameters for a host computer.
2. Release a DHCP-assigned TCP/IP address.
3. Request a new DHCP-assigned IP address.
4. Document the steps you took in each procedure.

PROJECT #7: USING NSLOOKUP

1. Use nslookup to directly query a DNS server by host name.
2. Use nslookup to directly query a DNS server by IP address.
3. Print information about the host/domain NAME using the default server.
4. Display a list of common commands available in nslookup.
5. Print debugging information.
6. Print comprehensive debugging information.
7. Document the steps you took in each procedure.

## CHAPTER 20

PROJECT #1: INVESTIGATING DSL

1. Contact a local DSL provider and obtain information about the following items:
   a. Services provided
   b. Upload speeds
   c. Download speeds
   d. Monthly cost
   e. DSL type offered for home and business users
   f. Availability
   g. Distance limitations
2. Report to the class on your findings.

PROJECT #2: INVESTIGATING CABLE

1. Contact a local cable provider and obtain information about the following items:
   a. Services provided
   b. Upload speeds
   c. Download speeds
   d. Monthly cost
   e. Availability
2. Report to the class on your findings.

PROJECT #3: INVESTIGATING SATELLITE

1. Contact a local satellite provider and obtain information about the following items:
   a. Services provided
   b. Upload speeds
   c. Download speeds
   d. Monthly cost
   e. Availability
   f. Assistance in setup and configuration
2. Report to the class on your findings.

Project #4: Establishing a Wireless Network Using Infrastructure Mode

1. Obtain a wireless access point (AP).
   a. Connect the AP to a wired network.
   b. Configure the AP.
2. Install a wireless network card in a laptop computer.
   a. Install the driver.
   b. Configure the card for wireless network access.
   c. Connect to the network.

Project #5: Establishing a Wireless Network Using Ad Hoc Mode

1. Obtain two ad hoc devices (PDAs).
2. Transfer data from one device to the other.

Project #6: Troubleshooting a Modem Using AT Commands

1. Use HyperTerminal to communicate directly with a modem.
2. Reset the modem to the default factory settings.
3. Reset the modem to the secondary default factory settings.
4. Set the modem speaker to the lowest volume.
5. Instruct Windows to report your true connection speed.
6. Instruct the modem to check for a dial tone before it starts dialing.

GLOSSARY

100Base-FX A type of network that uses fiber-optic cabling to transfer data at 100Mbps, while maintaining the existing Ethernet standards.

100Base-T4 A category of Fast Ethernet that can attain data transfer speeds up to 100Mbps over Cat3 cable. 100Base-T4 uses four pairs of wiring.

100Base-TX A category of Fast Ethernet that requires Cat5 UTP cable.

10Base-2 A network that uses thin coaxial cable (Thinnet) and BNC connectors.

10Base-5 A network that uses thick coaxial cable (Thicknet).

802.11 The IEEE standard that addresses the actions that must take place at the Physical layer and Media Access Control sublayer for communications on a WLAN.

802.5 The IEEE standard that identifies the access protocols, cabling, and interfaces for Token Ring LANs.

Access control list (ACL) A table that is entered on a router that identifies those users or devices that are allowed to send and receive packets from the public infrastructure. An ACL can be written to include and exclude certain IP addresses or domain names.

Access point A device on a wireless LAN that receives, buffers, and transmits data between wireless components.

Active Directory Services The Microsoft implementation of the X.500 directory-service standards.

Active hub A hub that is able to amplify or regenerate a data signal.

Active monitor A station on a ring network that monitors network activities, such as the timing of a circulating token, to prevent network failures.

Active topology A topology in which each node is involved in the passing process and maintains the ability to regenerate the token.

Ad hoc mode A form of wireless communication in which wireless clients communicate directly with each other via radio waves, without going through a wireless access point (AP).

Adapter A piece of hardware that allows a cable to be connected to a computer.

Address Resolution Protocol (ARP) A service protocol, part of the TCP/IP suite of protocols, that queries the network segment by broadcasting an IP address. The response is the MAC address of the node holding the destination IP address.

American wire gauge (AWG) A U.S. standard used to measure the diameter of nonferrous wire.

ANDING A logical function that looks for the presence or absence of a match between two numbers that have been converted into binary notation. The results can be either 0 or 1, but the sum is 1 only when both of the numbers are 1.

Antenna polarization The physical alignment of antennas.

AppleTalk A protocol that services Macintosh computers. The protocol was designed for peer-to-peer networks (small networks without a server), but it has been enhanced over time and is now capable of routing between networks.

Application layer The layer of the OSI Model that provides services to applications running on computers on the network.

Applications and tools The part of an operating system that enables the computer to take steps to complete a command set or create specialized code to be executed.

Archive bit An attribute of a file that tells backup software whether the file needs to be backed up because it has changed.

ARPA (Advanced Research Projects Agency) domain The DNS domain that provides the reverse lookup capabilities of DNS by listing key domains by their IP address first and friendly name second.

ARPANET (Advanced Research Projects Agency Network) The name given to the finished program developed by DARPA. ARPANET became the basis of the Internet as we know it today.

ASCII (American Standard Code for Information Interchange) A code that represents alphanumeric characters as numbers (which will eventually be resolved into a series of bits in the on/off state). The code also contains representations for certain functions that were necessary when it was first developed.

Asymmetric DSL (ADSL) A DSL connection in which data sent from a computer travels at a different speeds from data sent to a computer.

Asynchronous Signals between a sender and a receiver occur based on different clocks without a reference to unify them.

Asynchronous transfer mode (ATM) A transmission technology that transmits at relatively high speeds (usually over fiber-optic cable) by using a switching technology to move high volumes of data, voice, audio, and video.

ATM cell A 53-byte package used for transmission over an ATM network.

Attachment Unit Interface (AUI) A 15-pin connector that is used as an interface between a computer's network interface card and an Ethernet cable.

Attenuation The degradation, or fading, of an electrical signal that occurs as the signal travels down a length of cable.

Audit log The recording of all defined actions by both inbound and outbound traffic.

Authentication The verification (by a network operating system) of the identity of users, clients, data, etc., to determine whether they will be allowed access to a network.

Authoritative DNS server The DNS server that has the original record in its table for a requested resource. A DNS server is authoritative for all resources contained within its part of the domain name space. Other DNS servers may have a cached listing for the resource, but those servers are not the authority for the resource.

Auto reconfiguration A part of the beaconing process in which devices located within the failure domain automatically perform diagnostics in an attempt to reconfigure the network around the failed area.

Auto-detect A function whereby the computer will find a setting (or piece of hardware) without intervention from a user or administrator.

Automatic Private IP Addressing (APIPA) A function that self-assigns an IP address when a DHCP client cannot obtain an IP address any other way.

Auto-sensing The ability of an adapter to automatically detect 10Mbps or 100Mbps data transmission speeds.

Azimuth A measurement used to specify the location of a celestial object.

Backup A copy of all data stored on a disk (or disks), usually written to magnetic tape. A backup can also be written to CDs, hard drives, and removable disks such as Zip disks. Typically this copy of the data is stored off-site for security. It is used to recover data in the event of a disaster.

Bandwidth Allocation Control Protocol (BACP) Works with BAP, functioning as a control protocol.

Bandwidth Allocation Protocol (BAP) A set of rules that establishes dynamic control of a multilink bandwidth.

Baseband transmission A digital communications signal in which only one signal may be present on the wire at a time. Data networks generally use baseband communications.

Basic rate interface (BRI) A telephone carrier interface that provides two B (bearer) channels for data transmission and one D (data) channel for control information transmission. Speed for BRI is 128Kbps.

Bastion host A single computer that is the only system exposed to the public infrastructure. All traffic will pass through this system and will be screened to determine if the traffic will be allowed to pass through to the private network. A bastion host is also known as a screened host firewall.

Bayonet nut connector, or BNC connector A two-pin connector commonly used on Thinnet coaxial cable.

Beaconing The process of establishing a fault domain when a hardware error occurs on a token passing network.

Binary (base-two) number system A numbering scheme that has only two numbers: 0 and 1.

Bindery In NetWare 3.X network operating systems, a flat database comprised of three files—NETOBJ, NETPROP, and NET$VAL—that hold information on the user account and its characteristics.

Bit Short for **bi**nary digi**t**; the smallest unit of information that can be processed by a computer. A bit has two states: either on (1) or off (0). A collection of 8 bits assembled into a larger unit of information is known as a byte.

BOOTP (Bootstrap Protocol) An addressing protocol that assigns IP addresses to workstations and that initiates the operating system in that process.

Border router A routing device that is specifically configured to prevent incoming access to a private network. A border router can be configured to exchange routing information with only those routers that form the border for an autonomous system or group of associated routers.

Bridge A networking device that is used to connect dissimilar networks together.

Broadband transmission A digital communications signal in which multiple signals can be transmitted on the cable at the same time. An example is cable TV.

Broadcast A message sent to all nodes on a network segment. Broadcasts are not transmitted by routers; therefore, their usefulness is limited to the local segment.

Broadcast center An Earth-based station that transmits high-powered, high-frequency signals to a satellite.

Broadcast-based process A process in which all requests are created in a broadcast format. This works well for single-segment networks, but because broadcast messages do not go through routers, LANs need additional services to be able to distribute IP addresses dynamically through broadcasts.

Burst excess rate (Be) Identifies the maximum burst bandwidth available beyond the committed information rate (CIR) for a frame relay circuit.

Bus topology A physical arrangement of nodes on a network in which several lengths of cable connect the nodes directly to each other.

Byte A unit of data that is 8 bits in length. Bytes are used to refer to units of data because they express the size of the data unit more efficiently than bits.

Cable modem A high-speed networking technology that uses the same coaxial cable that powers cable television.

Cable tracing Traces the path a cable takes through a wall or ceiling.

Campus area network (CAN) A physical data communications infrastructure that is usually limited to a set of buildings in very close geographic proximity, such as buildings on a college campus.

Capacitance A measure of the charge in the electromagnetic field of a passive electronic component called a capacitor. Used to determine if the cable is kinked or if it has been stratched.

Carrier Sense Multiple Access with Collision Avoidance (CSMA/CA) A media access method with rules concerning how nodes communicate while sharing a common cabling system. In this case, transmission collisions are avoided completely rather than being detected and later resending the data.

Carrier Sense Multiple Access with Collision Detection (CSMA/CD) A network access method with rules concerning how Ethernet stations communicate while sharing a common cabling system. When a collision is detected, the transmission is halted and the data is resent later.

Centralized security The management of security issues, such as permissions to resources and account authentication, from one central point, usually through the tools included with a network operating system.

Channel Service Unit (CSU) A piece of equipment containing an interface that is used to terminate a data line.

Checksum A count of the number of bits in a transmission that can be compared with the Checksum field in the packet. If the numbers agree, the packet has arrived safely. If the numbers disagree, the packet must be retransmitted.

Choke point The location on a network (usually at a router) where a security policy and access control list (ACL) are enforced.

Circuit A pathway between two or more communicating entities.

Circuit switching The process of moving data through a public infrastructure on a pathway reserved for the duration of that communication. The circuit may be pre-reserved or created at the start of communication.

Cladding Something that covers or overlays; in the case of fiber-optic cabling, a glass layer that acts as a mirror, reflecting light back into the core of the glass fiber.

Class of service The ability of ATM to attach priorities to certain types of transmission, allowing one packet to jump ahead of another based on priority.

Classful addressing The conventional pattern used in IP addressing in which the address class determines how many of the opening bits in the address represent the network number.

Client A computer that has the necessary hardware and software installed to enable it to connect to a network.

Client Service for NetWare Microsoft software that allows networked computers to communicate with each other on a Novell-based network.

Client software A computer program that allows a computer to send requests to a server or another computer on the network.

Client-server configuration An arrangement in which one or more computers are designated as servers to centrally control security for all other computers, called clients, on the network.

Client-side application The software that must be installed on all client computers (users' workstations) in order to make use of the proxy service installed on the private network.

Client-side process A software function that a workstation uses to accomplish a task. Examples include using the operating system capabilities to share documents with other network users, or acquiring an IP address through a number of conversations with the DHCP server.

Closed-ended question A question, usually about a concrete detail, that is designed to elicit a specific answer.

Clustered servers Two or more servers connected together in such a way that they act like a single server but provide fault tolerance in the event of failure of the primary server.

Coaxial cable A type of cable that has two conductors, a center copper core that is shrouded by insulating Teflon or plastic foam, and a foil wrap or a braided metal shield that covers the insulating plastic foam.

Collision light A light built into devices that transmit data in order to detect collisions on an Ethernet network.

Committed burst rate (Bc) The amount of additional bandwidth above the committed information rate (CIR) that may be available for a frame relay circuit.

Committed information rate (CIR) A unit of measure for a frame relay circuit that represents the minimum amount of bandwidth that will always be available across the purchased circuit for a frame relay network.

Concentrator A device that functions like a hub to combine transmissions from a cluster of nodes. Concentrators are used in fiber-optic networks.

Connectionless mode A method used by the LLC to communicate upward to the Network layer of the OSI Model by simply sending out packets of information, with no follow-up to monitor the flow of information. Connectionless communication tends to be fast.

Connection-Oriented mode A method used by the LLC to communicate upward to the Network layer of the OSI Model. When the receiving node sends a message, the sending node acknowledges receipt of the information, which enables the LLC to check for transmission errors. Connection-oriented communications are slower than connectionless communications.

Container In a directory service, a logical entity that contains other objects.

Continuity Agreement, or harmony, between parts, in this case between the type of cable and the electrical standards identified by the manufacturer.

Convergence The time it takes for all routers to update their routing tables.

Crossover cable A cable in which the pin-out connections have been changed on one end of the cable. Typically used when connecting network hardware, such as hubs, together.

Crosstalk A type of electromagnetic interference caused by the bleeding of an electrical signal from one wire to another housed within the same sheath.

Cutover time The amount of time it takes to switch from a failed server to a working server.

Cyclical redundancy checking (CRC) A process used with connection-oriented mode in which the LLC checks network data for errors between sending and receiving nodes and retransmits data when it loses integrity.

Daemon An application that runs on a node for the purpose of handling specific service requests made of the local operating system.

Data frames Units in which the Data Link layer breaks down data into bits for transmission across a physical medium, such as copper wire.

Data Link layer The layer of the OSI Model that is responsible for media access and physical addresses on the network.

Data Service Unit (DSU) A piece of networking hardware that converts a LAN digital data frame for use on a WAN, and vice versa.

DEC-Intel-Xerox (DIX) A 15-pin connector that uses a pin-out configuration slightly different from the AUI connector.

Default gateway The path a node uses when it wishes to communicate outside its own network. Typically a router.

Defense Advanced Research Projects Agency (DARPA) A Department of Defense (DOD) research group that originated the TCP/IP suite of protocols.

Demand-dial Dial-up connections that are created as you need them.

Demilitarized zone (DMZ) A neutral subnetwork between two routers that is screened from public access and yet not part of the internal network. The DMZ often hosts Web servers, mail servers, and FTP servers.

Denial of service attack A network attack in which a rogue system sends a very large ICMP packet, or PING packet, to a destination, flooding the buffer of the destination system and preventing any other traffic from getting through. Also known as the PING of Death.

Destination address An address that identifies the receiver of the message in the header of the datagram.

Deterministic Used to describe a topology in which stations access the network in a predetermined sequence.

DHCP exclusion An option that allows an administrator to remove one or more addresses within a scope from the pool of automatically assignable addresses.

DHCP lease A designated length of time that the client node may use an IP address.

DHCP reservation An address assignment to a client node that will remain constant for that node instead of changing each time the node boots up to the network. Servers, printers, and other devices must remain at a constant address so that users and services can reach them. The reservation eliminates the need to manually add addresses to the configuration for each machine.

DHCP scope A range of IP addresses that can be assigned to a specific segment of nodes on the network. Any DHCP-configured node on a given segment will receive an IP address that allows it to talk with other nodes on that segment.

Differential backup A copy of all data that has been changed since the last full backup.

Digital certificate A small file that records information such as an expiration date, serial number, name, public key, owner of the private key, and other critical information. This file is sent by a system acting as a certificate authority to a computer that needs to send data securely.

Digital signal x (DSx) A unit of measurement for digital transmission rates over telephone voice channels.

Digital signature A field in a packet that acts as the sealing signature. If the original digital signature is intact when it reaches the destination, the assumption can be made that the packet has not been tampered with en route.

Digital Subscriber Line (DSL) A device that uses higher POTS frequencies than a traditional model to provide faster data transfer speeds.

Digital Subscriber Line (DSL) modem A modulation technique that allows data transmission over higher POTS frequencies for faster transfer speeds.

Direct current (DC) An electric current that flows in one direction only.

Directory services A distributed, hierarchical database that holds all account and object information for a network and that is replicated on multiple servers on the network. Most directory services (such as those for NetWare and for Microsoft's Active Directory) are built to a standard called X.500 that is defined by a Request for Comment (RFC).

Disaster recovery plan A set of documents that outline procedures to follow when a network experiences a catastrophic event. This may cover anything from a momentary power failure to a major natural disaster.

Disk array A set of two or more disks that are treated as a single storage unit.

Diskless workstation A desktop computer that does not contain a disk or hard drive.

Distance vector An algorithm used by routers to periodically broadcast the entire contents of their routing tables.

DNS record type A designation attached to an entry in the DNS database that identifies its use.

For example, an MX record identifies a node as an e-mail server (or mail exchanger).

Domain name space The inverted, hierarchical tree structure of the Domain Name System. Domain name space can also be used in reference to a specific part of the name space.

Domain Name System (DNS) A service protocol that translates the node's "friendly" name to an IP address that can be used by nodes and devices to identify an exact location for the machine or service.

DORA process The conversation between a client node and the DHCP server in which the node receives an IP address dynamically.

Downlink Signals sent from a satellite to Earth.

Downstream Receiving, or downloading; used to describe data being sent to a computer.

Dual-homed host firewall A type of Application layer firewall in which a computer or router has two NICs installed, one attached to the private network and one attached to the public network.

Duplex fiber A type of fiber-optic cable with two strands of fiber bound together in separate jackets.

Duplexing The transmission of data on a network.

Dynamic Host Configuration Protocol (DHCP) A TCP/IP protocol that allows administrators to distribute IP addresses to nodes on the network automatically and to manage that distribution process centrally.

Dynamic state list A table that will track all sessions (or conversations) between hosts on the inside of the network and hosts on the outside of the network.

Dynamic table A routing table that is built automatically by the router.

E1, E3 The European equivalents of the T1 and T3 carrier options. E1 transmits at 2.048Mbps and E3 transmits at 34.368Mbps.

Electrical noise A type of electromagnetic interference on one electrical device that emanates from another, completely separate electrical device.

Electromagnetic interference (EMI) Interference on one electrical device that emanates from another electrical device, either between wires within the same plastic sheath (crosstalk) or between two completely separate devices.

Elevation The height to which something is elevated above a point of reference, normally Earth's surface, or horizon.

Encapsulation A process in which upper-layer protocol information is packaged into a frame.

Encoding scheme A means of building a signal for transmission, developed to take advantage of the available bandwidth and efficiently move data across a network or internetwork.

Encryption The conversion of data in a packet into code to prevent unauthorized viewing of the data. Encryption standards include several algorithms, including 40-bit, 56-bit, and 128-bit schemes.

Ethernet, or 802.3 The IEEE standard for the CSMA/CD network access method, which enables multiple nodes to share a common cabling system. Developed jointly by Digital, Intel, and Xerox, Ethernet is sometimes called DIX.

Event Viewer A utility that maintains log files about programs, security, and system events that occur on a computer.

Extensible Authentication Protocol (EAP) An RRAS security option for devices such as smart cards.

External network number A network numbering, or addressing, scheme that identifies the external cable segment to which a workstation is connected.

Fast Ethernet A form of Ethernet networking that can obtain data transfer speeds up to 100Mbps; also referred to as 100Base-T.

Fault domain An area on a token passing network that has been isolated in an attempt to recover from a hardware error.

Fault tolerance The ability of a system to continue functioning when a malfunction or fault occurs in one or more components of the system.

Fault tolerant network Describes a network that is partitioned, with directory information for each partition stored on several servers, so that when one node on the system fails, users can still log in and access resources from another partition; part of the operating system can fail without shutting down the entire system.

Fiber Distributed Data Interface (FDDI) A high-speed networking standard originally designed for fiber-optic cable.

Fiber-optic cabling A cable that uses light-conducting glass fibers as its core.

File and directory rights The permissions that allow users to access resources on their own computer or on a remote computer (often a server).

File Transfer Protocol (FTP) A protocol that allows the transfer of files between nodes regardless of the operating system or computer platform.

Firewall A system or group of systems that prevents unauthorized access to private resources or assets from the public (Internet) infrastructure.

Footprint In satellite communications, the area reached by signals from a particular satellite.

Forest A collection of trees in Active Directory that share the same schema (or structure) of the AD database.

Fractional T1 A portion of a 1.544Mbps T-connection (1.544Mbps) that can be purchased in increments of 64Kbps for remote connectivity.

Frame relay A packet-switching technology that transports data at a reasonable cost by allowing many frame circuits to share media through the public infrastructure.

Frame type Defines the format of data that will be transmitted between nodes on a network.

Frequently asked questions (FAQs) A series of questions about common concerns; in troubleshooting, created to describe how to fix common problems and perform routine tasks.

Full backup A copy of all of the data (both changed and unchanged) on a hard drive or disk array.

Full duplex The transmission of data in two directions simultaneously. Network devices can both transmit and receive at the same time.

Fully qualified domain name (FQDN) The complete name of a node that defines its exact location within the DNS hierarchy.

Gateway Hardware or software, or both, that is used to translate data or protocols from one network to another.

Geosynchronous-Earth-orbit (GEO) satellite A satellite that operates in a stationary orbit 22,300 miles above Earth.

Get action An SNMP management console's request to an SNMP agent to acquire further information about the agent's managed device and to forward that information to the console.

Gigabit Ethernet A transmission technology that is based on Ethernet standards providing a data transfer rate of 1 billion bits per second.

Graphical user interface (GUI) An interface between a human and a computer that is friendly for the user to navigate. Instead of using command language to access resources, a user simply selects from an array of colorful icons that identify resources.

Group On a Windows NT or 2000 Professional network, a container used to organize users by the rights and permissions they have been granted.

Hacker A clever programmer or computer technician who uses his or her skills to gain unauthorized access to a network's resources or assets.

Half duplex The transmission of data in just one direction at a time. For example, a computer can either send or receive traffic; it cannot do both at once.

Handshaking The process of the client and server agreeing on communication parameters.

Header A section of a datagram, or packet, that precedes the payload, or data unit, of the packet. The header contains vital information—such as the source address, destination address, and port number—that allows the packet to travel from the source to the destination.

Hexadecimal number A number that relies on a base-16 numbering system, which uses 16 base units including 0. The 16 corresponds to 10 in the decimal system. Hexadecimal numbers are expressed using a combination of the characters A–F and the numbers 0–9.

Host number The portion of an IP address that refers to a unique node on the network.

Host table An ASCII file that contains a listing of network resources (client nodes, servers, printers) by host name (friendly name) and associated IP address. Host tables are used to locate resources on the network.

Hot spare A disk that is installed in the server or disk array, but that is not used to store data until one of the online (used) disks fails.

Hot swapping Removing a disk from the server or array when it fails and replacing it with a functioning disk without shutting down the server or array.

Hub A piece of networking hardware used to connect computers and printers to each other in a star topology.

Hypertext Transfer Protocol (HTTP) A generic, stateless protocol that allows the transfer of files (including text, graphics, and video) to a computer using rules that the browser software can understand.

Hypertext Transfer Protocol over Secure Sockets Layer (HTTPS) An extension of HTTP that is used to protect the transfer of sensitive or confidential data from a browser to a Web resource or vice versa. The authenticity of users and computers is validated with certificates, or keys, to ensure security.

IFCONFIG A TCP/IP utility that configures kernel-resident network interfaces in a UNIX environment.

Incremental backup A copy of all data that has been changed since the last backup (whether full, incremental, or differential).

Independent Computing Architecture (ICA) A Presentation layer protocol that allows any Microsoft Windows client to act as a thin client.

Infrastructure mode A form of wireless communication that enables the wireless components on a LAN to connect via an access point to the wired network.

Infrastructure, or multipoint networking A method used by wireless devices to connect to a fixed network through a wireless bridge that serves as an AP.

Integrated Services Digital Network (ISDN) A communications standard that allows digital signals to pass through existing PSTN lines.

Interactive mode A TCP/IP method that allows users to query name servers for information about various hosts and domains.

Internal network number A network numbering, or addressing, scheme that identifies servers on the network.

International Organization for Standardization (ISO) A global organization formed to create unified, worldwide standards for the transmission of data communications on computer networks.

Internet connection sharing (ICS) A service available in several Microsoft operating systems that allows some of the functions of network address translation. By enabling ICS, a small

office or a home office can achieve Internet connectivity while still using private addressing. The ICS service is nonconfigurable and therefore its use is limited.

Internet Control Message Protocol (ICMP) A TCP/IP protocol that is used for message control and error reporting.

Internet Message Access Protocol (IMAP) A client-server e-mail protocol that allows a user to access her or his mailbox from any computer. IMAP will store all messages on the server for access to the mailbox from any computer.

Internet Protocol (IP) A connectionless protocol, or set of rules, that is responsible for the transport of datagrams across a network.

Internet Protocol Security (IPSec) A security protocol that supports authentication, encryption of data, and compression of data during transmission. It is expected to become the standard for communication over networks and internetworks to protect the privacy and security of message transmission.

Internetwork Packet Exchange (IPX) A connectionless, Network layer protocol that is responsible for the transport of datagrams across a network or internetwork.

Internetwork Two or more networks connected by a device, usually a router, capable of recognizing multiple network segments.

Interoperability The ability of an operating system to talk to operating systems from other vendors.

IP spoofing A network attack in which a hacker uses fake credentials to communicate with a remote destination system. The credentials used will belong to another known and accepted system.

IPCONFIG (IP Configuration) A TCP/IP utility that displays current IP configuration parameters for a host computer running certain types of Windows operating systems.

IPX socket A network-addressable service access point that binds an application process to a unique identifier for that process. Sockets are created using function calls or APIs (Application Programming Interfaces) in the software. A socket is considered an endpoint in a connection. Servers use sockets to distinguish one request for service from another.

IPX/SPX (Internetwork Packet Exchange/Sequenced Packet Exchange) A Novell proprietary protocol suite that uses the Network and Transport layers of the OSI Model to transport and deliver data across a network or internetwork.

Jitter A deviation in the pulsing of digital signals. Jitter can be thought of as a signal with the "shakes."

Kerberos A secure network system that uses strong encryption processes to provide authentication for users and for services that need to communicate and be validated on a network.

Kernel The core of an operating system; provides services that allow all other subsystems within the OS to function. A kernel typically assigns processing time and priority to various programs and manages the address space contained in memory and in storage.

Knowledge base A computerized log of reported computer problems and the steps a technician took to repair them.

Latency The delay, or amount of time, it takes for a data packet to get from one point to another.

Layer 3 switch A switch that operates at the Network layer (layer 3) of the OSI Model rather than at the Data Link layer; incorporates features of both switches and routers.

Leaf object An object that cannot contain other objects.

Least significant bit The rightmost bit in an IP address when represented in binary format. The least significant bit is sometimes referred to as the "low order bit."

Link Control Protocol (LCP) A set of rules used in conjunction with the Bandwidth Allocation Control Protocol (BACP) to determine the order in which clients will transmit when more than one tries to send a BAP request simultaneously.

Link light A light built into a piece of hardware to demonstrate link connectivity at the Physical layer of the OSI Model.

Link state An algorithm that uses multicast instead of broadcasts to send updates.

LMHosts file A method of resolving NetBIOS names to their IP addresses. This implementation preceded the dynamic WINS service, first used by IBM with its LanManager product, and later used with the Microsoft Windows NT products.

Local area network (LAN) A physical data communications infrastructure that is usually contained in a small geographic area such as an office, a floor of a building, or a whole building.

Local bridge A networking device used when there is a direct connection between LAN segments.

Local security Security that affects only the computer you are sitting at.

Log file A simple text file that is used to monitor a particular process or event.

Logical addressing A way of uniquely identifying a node on a network with a temporary identifier.

Logical Link Control (LLC) A sublayer of the Data Link layer of the OSI Model; defines the way network communications take place.

Logical topology The method or path data uses to travel across a network from node to node.

Loop In communications, a telephone line that runs between a building and the local telephone-switching center; also called a local loop.

Loopback address A special IP address used to test a computer's installation of the TCP/IP protocol.

Low-Earth-orbit (LEO) satellite A satellite that is located closest to Earth, about 900 miles away from the surface.

Managed, or intelligent, hub A hub that is able to configure and monitor individual ports.

Management information base (MIB) A collection of facts, organized hierarchically, that contains specific information about each parameter, or managed object, on a device.

Mapped drive A logical connection, represented by a drive letter, to a shared network resource.

Master browse list keeper A node on the network that keeps track of the nodes attached to the network and their associated IP addresses. Notification by the nodes is handled by broadcast, and therefore this process is generally limited to a single-segment network.

Media access control (MAC) A sublayer of the Data Link layer of the OSI Model; responsible for physical addresses on the network.

Media tester A tool used to test for problems and confirm wiring configuration and termination in network and telephone cables; also called a cable tester.

Media The physical cable through which the data travels.

Medium-Earth-orbit (MEO) satellite A satellite that travels above Earth in the 5,000- to 8,000-mile range.

Mesh topology A physical arrangement of nodes on a network in which every node has a path, or connection, with every other node on the network.

Metropolitan area network (MAN) A physical data communications infrastructure that involves one or more networks that work together to provide access and services in a geographic area.

Microsoft Client for Microsoft Networks Software program that allows computers to communicate with each other on a Microsoft-based network.

Microsoft Encrypted Authentication (MS-CHAP) An encrypted password authentication process.

Microsoft Encrypted Authentication version 2 (MS-CHAP v2): A mutual authentication process that uses one-way encrypted passwords.

Modem Hardware that converts computer data into a form that can be transmitted and received over cable media.

Most significant bit The leftmost bit in an IP address when represented in binary format. The bit's placement may be leftmost in the entire address, or leftmost in the octet to which it belongs. The most significant bit is sometimes referred to as the "high order bit."

Multicast Sending updates to a specific group of routers.

Multilink connections Used to describe a communications line that allows you to connect multiple adapters to multiple lines in order to take advantage of the bandwidth of more than one line.

Multimaster system A system in which copies of the directory services database are stored on many servers, and each of these servers is able to make changes to the database. Changes are propagated on all servers that maintain a copy of the database.

Multimode fiber A type of fiber-optic cabling with a relatively large core, usually 62.5 microns in diameter, that can handle many rays of light at once, making it ideal for voice and data applications.

Multiplexing The action of transmitting many signals or bands of information across a carrier at the same time to form a complex signal.

Multiprotocol routing Manually configured routing tables that allow a server to act as a static router to move more than one protocol between network segments.

Name Binding Protocol (NBP) An AppleTalk protocol that provides friendly names and name resolution for nodes on an AppleTalk network.

Nbstat A TCP/IP utility that displays protocol statistics and current TCP/IP connections using NetBIOS over TCP/IP (NBT).

NetBEUI (NetBIOS Enhanced User Interface) A fast, efficient, nonconfigurable, nonroutable protocol used by single-segment networks, usually peer-to-peer.

NetBIOS (Network Basic Input/Output System) A protocol dating back to the early IBM PC networks that allows applications on different computers to communicate with each other.

NetBIOS Name Service (NBNS) The generic TCP/IP implementation of the Windows Internet Name Service; allows location of resources by associating a NetBIOS name to an IP address. NBNS functions in a very similar way to DNS.

Netstat A TCP/IP utility that displays protocol statistics and current TCP/IP network connections.

NetWare A network operating system developed by Novell. NetWare has many versions, including several that support directory services (X.500 standard).

NetWare Link State Protocol (NLSP) A routing protocol that provides the efficient exchange of routing table information between routers on an IPX network; addresses the limitations of RIP for IPX, which was designed for small independent networks.

NetWare Loadable Module (NLM) A program that runs within the NetWare operating system and allows certain functions within the NOS, such as support for long file names (provided by LONG.NAM).

Network access method A set of communication rules that allows multiple devices on a network to share cabling without corrupting data during transmission.

Network Address Translation (NAT) A service that allows a network to use the private addresses on the local LAN while still maintaining a connection for users to the Internet.

Network attached storage (NAS) Data storage warehouse attached to the network that is not dependent on any specific operating system or platform. NAS allows a large volume of data to be sorted and accessible to users.

Network Basic Input Output System (NetBIOS) An application programming interface (API), including a protocol dating back to the early IBM PC networks, that adds functions to local area networks and allows applications on different computers to communicate with each other.

Network client computer A computer that has the necessary hardware and software installed to enable it to connect to a network and access resources that other users have made available on that network.

Network interface card (NIC) Hardware in the form of an expansion card that is installed inside the computer to allow the computer to connect to the network.

Network layer firewall A device that makes the decision to allow or deny a packet on the basis of the source address, destination address, or port address. It does not look at the content in the payload. Because it is using logical address information to make the decision, it takes its name from the Network layer of the OSI Model.

Network layer The layer of the OSI Model that manages logical addressing of nodes and routing of packets through the internetwork.

Network number The part of an IP address that all hosts on an IP network segment share; defines a unique segment of computers on a LAN or internetwork.

Network security The security measures and procedures designed for all the resources on the network.

Network services Provision of functions above and beyond those provided by desktop operating systems.

Network Time Protocol (NTP) A protocol that provides network computers with the ability to synchronize their clocks with each other.

Network-centric Describes a network operating system in which user accounts and existing objects (printers, groups, containers) can be replicated on any server that is included in the directory services database.

Networking Connecting two computers to communicate, or share information, with each other.

New technology file system (NTFS) The file system developed for Windows NT, Windows 2000, and Windows XP.

Node or host Any device that is connected to communicate on a computer network. The device can be a computer, printer, server, switch, hub, etc.

Noninteractive (command-line) mode A TCP/IP method that returns just the name or other requested information for a host or domain.

Nslookup A TCP/IP program that queries a DNS server by host name or IP address.

NWAdmin An administrative tool used in NetWare 4.X and later that allows an administrator to create and manipulate objects in the Novell Directory Services (NDS).

NWLink Protocol Microsoft's implementation of IPX/SPX for Windows products.

Octet In IP addressing, a group of 8 bits.

Ohm A measurement of the resistance to an electrical current. One ohm is equal to the current of one ampere, which will flow when the voltage of one volt is applied.

Online uninterruptible power supply (UPS) A UPS that stores power and directly supplies power to all connected devices. This type of UPS will provide continuous power for a period of time even when the power source is lost, preventing server shutdown and loss of connections.

Open Shortest Path First (OSPF) A link state protocol used by routers, designed to address some of the limitations imposed by Routing Information Protocol.

Open source code A source code that ships with an operating system and that can be modified to meet the needs of a business. The function of the code is not guaranteed, but it is thought to be more stable and secure than proprietary code.

Open Systems Interconnection (OSI) Model A standardized, layered framework for data communications that allows devices and protocols from different vendors to be used harmoniously on a network or internetwork.

Open-ended question A broad question that is designed to elicit information beyond a simple yes or no answer.

Optical tester A tool used to test fiber-optic cabling systems by detecting reflected light.

Organizational unit (OU) A logical container in Active Directory that is used to group objects.

Packet One segment of a message that has been prepared for network transmission and that contains the address of both sender and receiver. Also contains a sequence number used for reassembling all segments of the message once the message has been received.

Packet sniffing The unauthorized action of removing packets from a transmission infrastructure and reading their contents.

Packet switching The process of moving data through a public infrastructure when the path has not been predetermined at the outset of the communication. The first packet in a connection may take a different route from the second, third, and fourth packets.

Passive hub A hub that does not amplify, clean up, or change the data signal.

Peer-to-peer network A network in which each computer is an equal member.

Peripheral component interconnect (PCI) The most common bus type found in computers manufactured after 1995.

Permanent virtual circuit (PVC) A specified amount of bandwidth that is always available between two communication end points.

Physical (MAC) address The 48-bit address on the NIC that serves as the network address for the device. When displayed, it appears as 12 digits, grouped into pairs, separated by dashes; for example: 00-04-5A-6C-98-06.

Physical layer The layer of the OSI Model that defines the physical aspects of a network: network interface cards, cable, and connectors.

Physical topology The location and arrangement of all cable, devices, servers, workstations, and any other components of a network.

PING A utility that tests whether TCP/IP is functioning correctly on a host computer and that checks connectivity between devices.

Plenum-grade cable Cable that is resistant to fire and does not emit poisonous gasses when burned.

Plug and Play compatibility A function first developed by Microsoft for the Windows 95 platform that enables an operating system to recognize a new device placed in a computer.

Pointing angle An angle determined by the latitude and longitude point of an Earth-based station and the longitude of the satellite. Sometimes called elevation.

Point-to-Point Protocol (PPP) A serial-communications protocol that allows a dial up client to access an RRAS server.

Point-to-Point Tunneling Protocol (PPTP) A secure method of transmitting messages over the Internet. It is a frequently used encapsulation protocol that creates a "tunnel" for the data to travel safely from source to destination.

Port number A number that designates the identity of a process to which packets, or a message, will be forwarded. The port number is part of both the TCP and UDP header formats.

Port scan A simple computer program that identifies those ports that are open to traffic from the public internetwork.

Port, or service access point The software process, or service, on a destination device through which data is received.

Post Office Protocol v.3 (POP3) A client-server e-mail protocol that allows mail messages to be stored until the account holder chooses to read those messages.

POTS An acronym for "plain old telephone service."

Presentation layer The layer of the OSI Model that makes sure that the data format can be understood between the sending and receiving nodes. This layer also manages encryption and compression.

Primary DNS server The DNS server that owns the records for that part of the DNS name space. Records can be changed on a primary DNS server.

Primary rate interface (PRI) A telephone carrier interface that provides 23 B channels for data transmission and 1 D channel for control information transmission.

Principal A user or service that routinely communicates on the network.

Private network Any portion of a data communications infrastructure that falls within a firewall for business or organization; sometimes called the internal network.

Programming language A set of vocabulary and grammatical rules that humans use to make computers perform specific tasks; the term usually refers to high-level languages.

Project 802 A set of standards created by the Institute of Electrical and Electronics Engineers (IEEE) that establishes requirements for hardware that interacts with the Physical and Data Link layers of the Open Systems Interconnection (OSI) Model.

Propagation time delay The added time for a packet to get into the transmission path. Propagation time delays create latency in the delivery of the message.

Proprietary code A code that is owned and controlled by an organization. The code has been tested under specific situations and is usually guaranteed to work within those boundaries. Proprietary code is often sold to other companies because it is guaranteed to work.

Proprietary Relating to or characteristic of a product or methodology that is owned exclusively by a single company, which takes a special interest in safeguarding internal knowledge and information about that product or methodology from others, especially competitors.

Protocol A set of rules used by computers to communicate with other devices.

Protocol Data Unit (PDU) A packet of data units that is sent between peer layers in a specific protocol. A PDU carries protocol control information and sometimes user data of the layer. Each layer of the OSI Model has a specific PDU associated with it. For example, at the Physical layer, the PDU is known as a PPDU (Physical Protocol Data Unit).

Provision To supply with, or purchase, provisions, which may include a service or goods.

Proxy firewall A type of Application layer firewall in which a software screening program acts as a gateway, or translator, between two networks in order to protect an internal system when communicating with a system from the public side of the network.

Proxy service Specialized software that allows network address translation to take place, plus caching of Internet resources, blocking certain public IP addresses, and granting access permis-

sions to access the Internet. As the term "proxy" implies, proxy service acts on behalf of an internal client machine.

PSTN An acronym for "public switched telephone network."

Public carrier A telephone line leased from a telephone company.

Public domain A product that is not owned by any one concern, person, or group, but is available for use by the general population without fee. Often public domain products are governed and managed by an agency or committee.

Public Key Cryptography, or Public Key Infrastructure (PKI) A process in which two keys are generated, a public key and a private key, that allow data to be encrypted for transmission and decrypted only by the issuer of the public key.

Public network Any part of the data communications infrastructure that falls outside the boundary of the firewall for a business or organization; sometimes called the internetwork.

Punch-down tool A tool used to attach telephone and data wires to punch-down blocks and to the rear side of patch panels.

Quality of Service (QoS) An IPSec function offered in transport mode that attempts to guarantee the transmission rate and error rate of packets transmitted across Internet media.

RAID controller A special board that is installed in a computer, the purpose of which is to control the data flow to and from multiple hard disks attached by cables to the controller itself.

Redirector Another term for client software.

Redundant array of inexpensive disks (RAID) A disk subsystem installed in a server in order to store data across all disks. Often this array has a parity bit associated with the data to allow recovery in the event of failure of one disk.

Remote access server (RAS) A connection point that provides authentication and access services to dial-up users.

Remote access The process of connecting to a network from a remote location.

Remote Authentication Dial-In User Service (RADIUS) A service that adds security and accounting features to the RRAS server.

Remote bridge A networking device that is used over WAN connections.

Remote procedure call A request (or call) made by a local machine, or an application running on that machine, for a procedure from a remote server. The remote server then sends the requested information to the local machine.

Resolver A node that has requested that a DNS server resolve, or convert, a resource's user-friendly name into its IP address.

Reverse Address Resolution Protocol (RARP) A utility protocol that allows the mapping of a MAC address (Data Link layer physical address) to an IP address (Network layer logical address).

Ring topology A physical arrangement of nodes on a network in which the cable connects each computer to the next, so that the cable forms a continuous loop, or ring.

Risk factor Any situation, action, or object that can jeopardize the safety and integrity of the assets and resources of a business or organization.

RJ-45 connector An eight-pin modular plug that connects into ports on network interface cards, patch panels, switches, etc.

Role On a Windows XT workstation, the amount of control a user has—specified as either *administrator* or *limited*—over a computer and its resources.

Router A device used to connect either multiple LAN segments together to form a WAN, or large networks together to form an internetwork.

Routing and Remote Access Service (RRAS) A service installed on a Microsoft Windows 2000 server that enables support for both multiprotocol routing and remote access.

Routing Information Protocol (RIP) A distance vector protocol with a specific set of rules and behaviors employed by a router for the purpose of moving datagrams from the source node to the destination node across an internetwork. The two most commonly used forms of RIP are employed by IP networks (RIP for IP) and IPX networks (RIP for IPX).

Routing protocol A set of rules that allows a router to make decisions about how a datagram will move from the source node to the destination node. The routing protocol often provides services such as exchanging network information with its neighbors.

Routing table A file used by the router to make routing decisions.

S/T interface The interface used by an ISDN adapter when transmitting data over short distances.

Samba The application that allows interoperability between UNIX and the Windows operating systems through Common Internet File System (CIFS) and Server Message Block (SMB) protocol.

Satellite communication system A system that sends and receives signals between Earth-based stations and geosynchronous space satellites, then transmits them to home- or office-based receiving satellite dishes.

Scope Defines the magnitude of a problem.

Scope options Optional settings that may be sent to a node on a segment when the node requests an IP address. Examples of scope options include the default gateway setting, the DNS server address, and the domain name for the node.

Secondary DNS server A server that holds a read-only copy of the DNS database owned by a primary DNS server. The secondary server can respond to local requests for DNS resolution, but it cannot change records.

Secure Sockets Layer (SSL) A protocol that provides a secure transmission over a public infrastructure whereby the client and the server can be absolutely identified. SSL is used with HTTP and FTP.

Security association An agreement between two devices to communicate using IPSec and certain security management functions of the IPSec framework.

Security boundary The defined endpoint of a private network.

Security policy A formalized document that identifies the risk factors for a business or organization and defines the processes, devices, and procedures to mitigate those risks.

Sequenced Packet Exchange (SPX) A connection-oriented protocol that provides services such as error-checking to the IPX protocol.

Serial Line Internet Protocol (SLIP) A TCP/IP-based protocol that allows a client and server to talk with each other.

Server A computer that serves, or provides a service or resource to, other clients on a network.

Server service A special piece of software that runs on a network server to add some kind of capability to the server or to the network. Examples of server services that can be added to server operating systems include Remote Access Service (RAS) and Domain Name Service (DNS).

Server-centric Describes a network environment that relies on an individual, very specific server to gain access to the network and its resources. For example, NetWare 3.X and earlier versions require users either to log in to a specific server or to have individual accounts on all servers that host user resources.

Service set identifier (SSID) An identifier that acts as a password in the header of a packet used on a wireless LAN.

Session layer The layer of the OSI Model that defines the session between two nodes, including the setup, maintenance, and closure of the conversation. This layer also manages "friendly" names for nodes on the network using NetBIOS.

Set action An SNMP management console's request to an SNMP agent to change information or settings on the agent's managed device.

Share-level security A security system in which one or more passwords are assigned to a shared resource.

Sharing Making a resource on one computer available to users on other computers.

Shell The interface between the operating system and the commands entered by a user.

Shielded twisted pair (STP) cable A twisted pair cable with a foil or braided-metal shield encasing the pairs of wires to draw electromagnetic interference away from the inside of the wire pairs.

Shiva Password Authentication Protocol (SPAP) A security service that allows clients to dial in to Shiva servers.

Signal An electric current that carries data from one place to another; often used generically to indicate anything that is sent or received across a cable plant.

Signal bounce A phenomenon that occurs when a piece of coaxial cable loses a terminator, causing network traffic to move from end to end on the wire and interrupting the communications taking place on the wire.

Simple Mail Transfer Protocol (SMTP) An upper-layer TCP/IP protocol used to send and receive e-mail messages. SMTP is usually used in conjunction with POP3 or Internet Message Access Protocol (IMAP) because SMTP does not have the ability to queue messages.

Simple Network Management Protocol (SNMP) A TCP/IP protocol that allows an administrator to keep track of events on the network and on individual network nodes.

Simplex fiber A type of fiber-optic cable containing a single strand of fiber.

Single-mode fiber A type of fiber-optic cabling that contains a single, tiny strand of fiber-optic glass, usually 7.1 or 8.5 microns in diameter. Typically used in telephone applications, cable television, or as a backbone.

Site blocking The action taken by a proxy firewall to deny access from a private network to certain defined locations on the public network (Internet).

Site In Windows 2000, a section of the Active Directory that is represented by a physical location. A site is referred to as a set of well-connected IP subnetworks. Windows 2000 uses the site to control the AD database replication.

Slash notation A shorthand way of indicating the subnet mask for an IP address. In slash notation, the IP address 200.20.1.1 with subnet mask 255.255.255.0 would instead be written 200.20.1.0/24, indicating that 24 bits are used in the network portion of the IP address.

Sneaker-netting Copying files onto external or removable media, such as a floppy or Zip disk, and passing the disk from one computer to another.

SNMP agent A small piece of software that runs on a device (computer, router, etc.) to track certain events on the device and report those events to a management console.

SNMP community A group of managed devices that report to a single management console.

SNMP network management system (NMS) The software that collects notices from SNMP agents running on devices on the managed network. The network management system is often referred to as the "management console."

SOHO An acronym for small office/home office.

Source address An address that identifies the sender of the message in the header of the datagram.

Source code The original code used to write an executable program for a computer, usually a programming language that humans can understand. This code must be translated or compiled into machine language that the computer understands.

Source-route bridge A bridge that uses broadcasts to locate all available routes. Found on Token Ring networks.

Source-route transparent bridge A bridge that combines aspects of both source-route and translational bridges. Enables communications on mixed Ethernet and Token Ring networks.

Specialty tool A tool designed specifically for a particular circumstance.

Splitter A small hardware device that converts one incoming television cable line into multiple outgoing lines.

Square (SC) connector A square-shaped connector with a locking mechanism that is crimped or latched onto fiber-optic cabling.

Standards Specifications that ensure that products will function at the level promised by the manufacturer and will work with other vendors' products.

Standby UPS A UPS that switches to battery power when it detects a power failure. The switch to battery power may take several seconds, causing servers to shut down and users to lose their connections to the servers.

Star topology A physical arrangement of nodes on a network in which each node uses its own cable to connect to a central device, typically a switch or a hub.

Static table A routing table that is built manually by an administrator.

Straight tip (ST) connector A round, keyed, bayonet-style connector that functions much the same as a BNC connector and that is attached to coaxial cable.

Subnet mask A series of bits in an IP address that identifies for host machines which bits in the address are network number bits and which are host number bits.

Subnetting The action of using available host bits in an IP address to create additional network identifiers, or subnets. This is often done to segment an IP network, or it is used because the segments are small and cannot use an entire class network address efficiently.

Surge protector A device used to protect computers and other electrical devices from transient power fluctuations that can cause damage to those devices.

Switch A networking device that learns the physical address of connected devices and routes traffic accordingly.

Switched virtual circuit (SVC) A circuit created on demand and then deleted when a communication between two end points has finished. SVCs have no permanent allotment of bandwidth.

Symmetric DSL A DSL line that usually requires its own dedicated telephone line and that allows uploads and downloads to travel at the same speed.

SYN flood A network attack in which a source node sends requests for TCP connections to a destination node at a rate that is faster than the destination can process the requests. The flood that results causes a denial of service.

Synchronous Digital Hierarchy (SDH) The international standard for data transmission over optical media.

Synchronous Optical Network (SONet) The standard for data transmission over optical media as defined by the American National Standards Institute (ANSI).

Synchronous structure A reference to the way in which digital signals in SONet transition to indicate 1s and 0s during transmission. In a synchronous structure, the transitions always occur at exactly the same rate.

Synchronous When two entities are in a synchronous state, they are coordinated in a time field.

T1 The unit of measure for a remote connection through a leased line over PSTN voice channels. T1 lines transmit at 1.544Mbps.

T1 time The time at which a client node will attempt to renew its IP address lease. This occurs when 50 percent of the lease time has been used.

T2 time The time at which a client node will begin the DORA process to request a new IP address. This happens if the lease has not been renewed by the point at which 87.5 percent of the lease time has been used.

T-carrier connection, or T-connection A telecommunications link that provides access to remote networks using the PSTN infrastructure. These are leased line connections that are always on.

TCP/IP (Transmission Control Protocol/Internet Protocol) A set of protocols, or rules, that enables the transmission of datagrams across a network and that provides additional services to those datagrams, such as guaranteed delivery, node addressing, and application services.

Telnet An upper-layer TCP/IP protocol that allows access to a remote device (typically routers and computers).

Terminal adapter The interface between the ISDN line and the computer.

Time Domain Reflectometer (TDR) A type of cable tester used to determine if the cable is broken or has a short.

Token passing A method used on a ring network to transmit data from node to node in a packet, called a token.

Token Ring A network that is set up with a ring topology and that uses packets called tokens to transmit data from node to node.

Tone generator A tool used to trace problems in both voice and data lines.

Top-level domain A domain that falls immediately under the {root} domain in the domain name space hierarchy.

Topology From a Greek word that means "locality" or "layout"; the physical layout of a computer network.

Traceroute (tracert) A TCP/IP command-line diagnostic utility that is used to determine the route a packet uses to get to a destination.

Tracert (traceroute) A TCP/IP command-line diagnostic utility that is used to determine the route a packet uses to get to a destination.

Traditional modem A device that allows a computer to connect to a network over a dial-up telephone line.

Traffic filtering The action of looking at the type of data passing through a device, usually a router, and determining whether that data will be allowed to enter or leave a network boundary.

Translational bridge A bridge that connects dissimilar networks, such as Ethernet and Token Ring.

Transmission Control Protocol (TCP) A connection-oriented protocol, or set of rules, that is responsible for the guaranteed delivery of datagrams across a network.

Transparent bridge A bridge that can automatically identify all of the devices connected to the network segment.

Transport layer The layer of the OSI Model that provides reliable and guaranteed delivery of data packets through the network or internetwork.

Transport mode An IPSec data transmission process in which only the payload (data contents) of a packet is encrypted.

Trap A SNMP notice about a faulty parameter on a managed device; sent by an SNMP agent to the network management service.

Tree A set of domains in Active Directory that share contiguous name space.

Trivial File Transfer Protocol (TFTP) A file transfer protocol that uses UDP for transport and that (unlike FTP) provides no additional services, such as authentication.

Trunk, or backbone The main wire that connects all of the nodes on the network.

Trustee assignments NetWare's term for access permissions, or file and directory rights.

Tunnel mode An IPSec transmission process in which an entire IP datagram is encrypted, completely disguising the original packet.

Twisted pair cable A cable with at least two pairs of insulated copper wires that are twisted together and housed in a plastic sheath.

U interface The interface used by an ISDN adapter when transmitting data signals over long distances.

Unencrypted password (PAP) An authentication method in which passwords are passed in plain text, without encryption.

UNIX A network operating system built by Bell Laboratories that supports multiple, simultaneously logged-in users, a hierarchical file system with demountable volumes, source code portability, and the capability to start processes in the background.

Unshielded twisted pair (UTP) cable A cable with two or four pairs of insulated copper wires twisted together and housed in a plastic sheath, each individual wire insulated by a color-coded protective cover. Does not contain additional shielding for the twisted pairs, so it is more susceptible than STP to electromagnetic interference.

Uplink Signals sent from Earth to a satellite.

Upstream Sending, or uploading; used to describe data being sent from a computer.

User Datagram Protocol (UDP) A communications protocol that closely resembles IP in its transport abilities; however, like TCP, it provides two services to make delivery more reliable than IP: a checksum and port numbering. UDP does not guarantee delivery.

User-level security A security system in which access to network resources is assigned to the individual user or group, not to the object being accessed.

Virtual circuit A logical definition of a path between two nodes. The physical path does not have to remain the same for each packet that is sent to the destination.

Virtual local area network (VLAN) A collection of network devices that are grouped into a logical network, without regard to physical location.

Virtual private network (VPN) A connection between a source and a destination for transmitting data securely. This process uses tunneling protocols that encrypt the data during the sending process so that it cannot be read by any entity except for the destination system.

Virtual private network (VPN) A connection between a source and a destination for transmitting data securely. This process uses tunneling protocols that encrypt the data during the sending process so that it cannot be read by any entity except for the destination system.

Voltage The potential difference in charge between two entities in an electrical field. The greater the voltage, the greater the electrical current.

Wide area network (WAN) A data communications network that spans a large geographic area and usually makes use of third-party transmission facilities or infrastructures, discretely integrating remote LANs into the structure.

Wide area network (WAN) A data communications network that spans a large geographic area and usually makes use of third-party transmission facilities or infrastructures, discretely integrating remote LANs into the structure.

Windows domain A client-server network that uses Microsoft servers to control network security.

Windows Internet Name Service (WINS) A Microsoft proprietary service that allows client nodes to resolve NetBIOS names to IP addresses.

Windows Internet Name Service (WINS) A Microsoft proprietary service that allows client nodes to resolve NetBIOS names with IP addresses.

WINIPCFG A TCP/IP graphical utility displaying IP configuration information on Microsoft Windows 95 and 98 operating systems.

Wire crimper A tool used to attach terminals, or connectors, onto pieces of wire.

Wired equivalent privacy (WEP) encryption A security protocol that is used on wireless LANs.

Wireless topology A physical arrangement of nodes within a certain distance that will allow them to communicate with other nodes or access points on the network using either radio frequency (RF) or infrared (IR) frequencies, or channels.

Workgroup A name commonly used for a peer-to-peer network.

Zone A section of the DNS name space.

INDEX